The Religious History of Munda and Oraon Tribes

The Religious History of Munda and Oraon Tribes

Dr Diwakar Minz

Translated from Hindi to English
by
Mrs Lakshmi Singh (Retd. I.A.S.)

KALPAZ

First Published, 2017

Published by

Kalpaz Publications
C-30, Satyawati Nagar,
Delhi – 110052
E-mail: kalpaz@hotmail.com
Ph.: 9212142040

Printed at: G. Print Process, Delhi

Cataloging in Publication Data—DK
Courtesy: D.K. Agencies (P) Ltd. <docinfo@dkagencies.com>

Minz, Diwakar, author.
The religious history of the Mundas and Oraons Tribes / Dr Diwakar Minz.
pages cm
Includes bibliographical references.
ISBN 9789353246235 (PB)

1. Munda (Indic people)—Religion. 2. Oraon (Indic people)—Religion. 3. Chota Nāgpur (India)—Religious life and customs. I. Title.

DS432.M8M56 2016 DDC 305.8954054127 23

Dedicated to my adored father

Late Siri Goinda Minz,

B.Sc., L.L.B., I. A. S.

(Born 28.02.1923, Died 24.07.1992)

Whose intellectual life began with receiving merit scholarship for outstanding success in Matriculation examination and whose multi-faceted brilliant personality enabled him to become the first tribal officer in the unreserved category of the Bihar Civil Service. He was further promoted to I. A. S. and did the tribals proud by becoming vice-chanceller of Ranchi University Ranchi and Special Secretary to Bihar government. He was like a bright star of hope, inspiration and guidance to the neglected and listless tribal brethren. His internal desire had been to see my decade-long efforts of writing the religious history of tribal life fructify as a book but whose desire I could not fulfil during his life-time. This book is dedicated to the sacred memory of my adored father who will always be remembered and who is the source of continuous inspiration.

— **Dr Diwakar Minz**

Contents

Foreword 11
Preface 13
Acknowledgement 17
Mundari Words and their Explanation 19
Kudukh Words and their Explanation 25
Glossary of Abbreviations 31

Chapter - 1
Introduction 33
• Pertaining to Munda Tribe • Pertaining to Oraon Tribe • Source • First Chapter: Preface • Second Chapter: Historical Introduction of Munda and Oraon Tribes • Third Chapter: Munda Religion, Sarna Religion • Fourth Chapter: Sarna Religion: Oraon Religion • Fifth Chapter: Conclusion.

Chapter - 2
Historical Introduction of Munda and Oraon Tribes 45
• Sir Herbert Risley's Theory • The Opinion of Dr J. H. Hutton • Negrito • Proto Australoid • Mongoloid • Mediterranean • Western Brachycephales • Nordic • Munda Tribe : Origin and Development • The Proof of Language • Anthropological Proof • Prehistoric Proof • Traditional Proof • Fixing of Time Period • Migration to Chhotanagpur • Oraon Tribe Kurukh and Oraon Words – their Origin • Place of Origin and Migration to Chhotanagpur • The Main Principle Regarding Place of Origin • Dravidian Versus Tamil • Mongolian Principle • The Central Asia Theory • The Semetic Theory • Mesopotamian Theory • The Theory about Egypt • The Mediterranean Theory • Language Proof • Traditional Evidence • The Flight from Rohtasgarh • One other Influence • The Intermingling of the Mundas and Oraons • The Munda Tribe of Chhotanagpur • The Mukhiya (head) and Pahan (Priest) in Village Organisation • The Oraon Tribe of Chhotanagpur • The Priest (pahan) and Mukhiya (head) in the Village Organisation • The Emergence of Raja Phanimukut Rai and the Protection of Munda/Oraon Culture from the Invasions of the Mughals • Traditional Village Arrangements and their Cultural Heritage.

Chapter - 3
Munda Religion: Sarna Religion 111
• Munda Religion : Sarna Religion • Modern Times and Munda Religion • The Deities of Mundas • Singbonga • The Divine Form of Singbonga in Religious Stories • The Birth of Man and Expansion of Race • The Expansion

of Race • The First Plough • Division of Time • Rain of Fire • Asur Avdan • Singbonga's Intelligence Personified Wife • Nage Aera • Banita Bonga • Occult Practices • Occult Practices : An Anti Religious System • Occult Practices and Initiation of Witches • Magic Spells • The Relationship between Witches and Bongas • The First Witch of Creation – Singbonga's Wife • Devra: A Parallel Religious Institution Against Sorcery • Mahadev and Parvati: In Black Magic and Parallel Religious Institution • Other Activities based on Superstitions: Hembul roa • The Sight of the Evil Eye • Aadaat : The Evil Eye of praise • Soso-tapa • Parv (festivals) • The Re-appointment of Dhangars • Fagu • Ba or Sarhul • Hone-ba • Batauli • Karam • Dasai • Kolom Singbonga • Jome – Nava • Ind Festival • Sohrai • Soso-Bonga • Kili or Gotra and Totem • Twenty one Parha : Twenty one Kili • Chief Kilis and their Emergence • Tuti Kili • Bodra Kili • Soy Kili • Horo or Kachchap Kili • Nag Kili • Another story • The Transformation of Kili • Change in Kili • Kili and Parha • Totem • Sanskar or Purification Ceremonies • Chedey Uri • Kudi-lel • "Da-Adgu" • Bala • Signs • Lagon- tol or Idi • Sanketik Vivah • Mandola-dul • Kalsa galang • Cho • Uli Adandi • Daprom or Mangrapi • Da-hirchi and Chumman • Sasang-goso • Da-au • Dul-da • Sinduri-rakab or Sindoori tika • Samdhi-Bhet : Milan • Kata anung • Chumavan • Baba-hatukam • Jimma • The Rituals Conducted in the Groom's Home after Marriage • Shav-sanskar or Dah Sanskar • Raya • Umbul-ader • Jung-Topa • Roa.

Chapter - 4

Oraon Religion: Sarna Religion 235

• Sarna Religion : Kurukh Religion • Pahan and his Assistant • Assistant • The Selection of Pahan and Assistant • Selection of Assistant • The Gods of the Oraons • Dharmes • The Forefathers (gods) or Pach Baler • Chala Pachcho • Paat naad or Hill King • Dadha-Desauli • Mahadaniya • Mahadev • Devi Mai • Chappar Budhiya • Chandi Pahar • Badanda Peeper • Vanshakti Garha-dhora-chatur-Seeman • Toosa Burha • Classified Gods-goddesses and Naad • Chandi • Selection of Chandi-pahan : Pestle Movement Procedure • Worship • Achhrayal/Achhrain • Joda • Khunt Naad • Badanda Pachcho • Chingri Naad • Goensali Naad • Surjahi Worship • Magic and Spells • Witch • Witch-Initiation • Witches-work Procedure • Mati • The Desired Goddess of Mati : Kali Mai (mother) • Treatment by Matis • Finding out the Naad • "Bahi-Pakarna" • The Handing over of Naad to Darha Naad • Bhagat or Sokha • Getting the position of Bhagat or Sokha • Mahadev-Kuri and Worship of God • The Social Life of the Bhagat • The cure and treatment of disease • Gotra and Totem • Gotra and Totem • Totem: Division and Change • The Religious Side of Totem • Festivals • Phagu • Sarhul/Khaddi/Khekhel Benja • Declaration of Sarhul festival and Preparations • Dari-chhitna • Nega-Amm • The Collecting of Cocks, Fishes and Crabs for Worship • The Religious Bath of Sarhul • Song • Water Sport • Isoom sindri or the Marriage of Pahan-Pahnain • Invocation of Pach-Balar • Distribution of Blessed Rice • Chalam Gucha or going to the Sarna Place in a Procession • The Preparation for the Worship • The Offering of Sacrifice • Kakro Sarjana or the Frying of Crabs • The Welcoming of the Pahan by the Pahanain • Cheprai Murga • Ona Mokhna • The Feast of the Women • Dhangar Pahan or Mutri – Chandi's Pahan • Poomp Kherna or Phul Khusi • The Handing over of the Batari (water pot) • The Seating in the Winnowing Fan • Hariari Festival • Kadlota • Karam Festival • The Growing of Jawa Flowers • The Cutting of Karam Branch • Planting of the Karam Branches • Synopsis of a

Prevalent Legend • Brief Summary of the Second Popular Story • Karam Darshan 52 (philosophy) • Jitiya Festival • Sohrai • Kharra Puja (worship) or Kharihani • Sanskar • Fifth Day or Purification Ritual • Joda-Kamna • Paisari • Naming Ceremony or "Name Pinjna" • Joodo-Eda or Tying of Hair • Jokh Edpa or Entry into Dhumkuriya • Marriage Ceremony • Decision Regarding Signs and Bad Signs • Muhi-Era • Lagan Bandhi • Koha–pahi • Poomp-Mejhna • Milanee • Koha-pahi • Preparations for the Wedding • Gurkhi-nikharna • Isung Sindri • Khiri Tengna • Sabha Sindri • Mandi ona • Welcoming of the Bride in the Groom's House • Death Ceremony • Ache Makha or Chhai Bhitarna • The Ritual of Chai Bhitarna • Formal Burial • The Rule and Method of Death Ceremony • The First Day • Second Day • Third Day • Utur Khila • Hochole-poomp pesa • Harbodi or Immersing of Bones in Water • Fourth Day • Fifth Day.

Chapter - 5

Conclusion 357

• Munda religion • Rain of Fire and Singbonga • The Appearance of Sarna Religion • The Development of Sanskar (ceremonies) and Festivals • The Development of Necromancy, Witch and Devra etc. Institutions • Oraon/kudukh • Comparative Historical Survey of Sarna Religion of the Mundas and Oraons • Singbonga versus Dharmes • Other Gods • Festivals • The Main Festivals of Mundas • The Main Festivals of Oraons • Ceremonies • The Main Ceremonies of Mundas • The Main Ceremonies of Oraons • Gotra or Kili.

Annexures 383

Bibliography 403

Index 409

Foreword

In India, the State of Jharkhand along with the forest areas of the surrounding Gondwana Plateau is the centre of dense population of tribals. Among these tribes, the Munda and Oraon tribes are not only important in view of their number but also for their cultural and religious heritage. Most of the tribes have Munda and Oraon roots, while their religious beliefs and customs, too, are accordingly based on them.

Some scholars have tried to study their religious beliefs and customs but till date no effort has been made to reveal the historical aspect of these religions. In this book, the place of origin of Munda and Oraon tribes has been traced, and those routes have been considered through which these tribes reached Chhotanagpur. Those influences have also been kept in mind which affected and helped in developing the practical and philosophical structure of their religion during the period of their migration. Since the writer is a tribal and has lived in proximity of tribal religion and society, he has brought together through a decade of intense labor those facts which give reasonable basis to the history of tribal religion.

Prior to this, some Christian missionaries studied the Munda and Oraon religions as also their development. They have stated that their religions are monotheistic and based on ghosts and spirits. The author has opposed this view. He has presented a sequential study of the development of godliness of tribal gods. He has thrown light on tribal religious philosophy inherent in the development of different religious institutions which can be glimpsed in the religions of so called civilized communities of the world. The author believes that the way the world has conceptualized Nature or visible natural incidents to be the material basis of the appearance and development of gods of ancient tribes, similarly the Munda and Oraon tribal gods can be traced to Nature. In some European and Indian religions the way the idea of one Supreme God alongwith sectoral gods has developed, in the same way sectoral gods can be found in Munda and Oraon religions. Since tribal religions do not have written texts, those studying them have had full license to interpret them in their own ways. If the various aspects of these religions are studied in their historical perspective, then it will be found that the religions of Munda and Oraon tribes are more or less on the same level as those of renowned outstanding multitheistic religions and this will uproot all the wrong notions spread about these religions till date. This book presented with historical facts is very useful for those who have an interest in tribal religions.

— **Dr Rameshwar Oraon, I.P.S.**
Chairman, Ntional Commission
of Scheduled Tribe,
New Delhi, India.

Preface

The main aim of this book is to present the religions of the Munda and Oraon tribes in their historical perspective. Earlier, some anthropological and sociological work has been done on these religions, and related books have also been published. From the point of view of authorship, these publications can be divided into three categories. One category is of the Christian missionary padres who studied the Munda and Oraon religions and customs in order to fulfil the need to first know the religion of those races who they wanted to convert.[1] The second category of writers comprised high officials of the East India Company Government. Although their study and writings were objective and free from prejudice, yet they had to remember that they were government officers hence their compositions had to depict a positive picture of the government. There were, however, only a few who shed light on the life and religions of the Mundas and Oraons but their studies were not much different from those of the Christian missionaries. The third category is of Indian sociologists and anthropologists who were limited to the racial qualities and social aspects of their religions, but they too publicised and spread the viewpoints of the earlier missionary writers regarding the tribal religions so that the Mundas and Oraons would form a low opinion of their own religion. The extensive propaganda adopted by the missionaries regarding tribal religions deeply affected a very large sector of the Mundas and Oraons who started feeling that their religions were inferior and lower than other religions. The spread of wrong notions regarding tribal religions affected most writers and intellectuals due to which their way of thinking could not be free of missionary tradition. All writers and their books more or less tread the path shown by the missionaries. Thus, an erroneous picture of the tribals emerged in the country and the world. Nobody tried to look into the past image of tribal religions the background of which would have enabled a proper and justifiable assessment of Munda and Oraon religions in their present form. Resultantly, due to lack of harmony among themselves, several social and political crises had to be faced by the government.

The sole intention of presenting the Munda and Oraon religions in their historical context is to do away with the wrong notions propagated about them so that their real forms can be revealed. In most of the so-called civilised communities of the world, their gods have their material bases in some natural elements, incident or splendid vision. Munda and Oraon religions are no exception to this. In these religions, too, Singbonga and Dharmes have become God alongwith the spirits of the widows of the Asurs who have become area deities. Their identification or definition originated from the name of a particular area and developed accordingly, as also their deification and related strength. The emergence of the godliness of these deities, their material form, are a part of special areas of nature which have given them their definition, name and identity, but the analysts have defined them as the unappeased souls of the Asur widows which has created an unjustified and wrong notion that Singbonga who lives in the sky and whose material form is the sun, became God, and the deities related to natural goods and phenomena of this earth became ghosts who acquired the habit of sending afflictions to Mundas and Oraons and to receive offerings from them.

The gods in their anger send afflictions and after appeasement take the diseases back- is a belief in most religions. Varun, the king of the gods of the Rigveda, visited his displeasure on Harishchandra of the Ikshwaku clan in the form of the disease dropsy, and after appeasement freed him from it. Similar situations can be traced to other Aryan religions of India. There is probably no religion in the world to the gods of which no offering is made and they do not show displeasure at their neglect. The finding of the missionaries that the Munda and Oraon religions are monotheistic and the rest are ghosts, negates the importance of the regional gods. In this context, the greatness of the goddess Nage Era of the Munda religion and the goddess Chala Pachcho of the Oraons can be seen because by protecting the brother-sister duo they saved the race from extinction. Thus, Nage Era and Chala Pachcho are the mother goddesses of their races. Such conduct will be termed benevolent, and such laudable work cannot be attributed to ghosts and spirits. Therefore to conclude that these religions have only one God, that is Singbonga or Dharmes, and Munda and Oraon religions are monotheistic is not justifiable.

The prevalent customs and various developed religious institutions of Munda and Oraon religions confirm the aforementioned belief. It is true that maximum work on these religions has been done by Christian missionaries and the significance of their contribution cannot be denied, but it is also true that whatever picture they painted of these religions was superficial and prejudiced. Due to this, many mistaken ideas regarding Munda and Oraon religions spread among the tribals. If we assess the present form of the religions of these races against the background of the appearance and development of their various institutions and deities, we will find that the Munda and Oraon religions have independent form, and in addition to Singbonga and Dharmes, there are some area deities who have been accepted by Munda and Oraon societies. There is another speciality of the Munda and Oraon religions in which Singbonga and Dharmes reincarnate themselves as "Khasra Balak" to destroy sin and sinners. The belief in re-incarnation is another special feature of these two religions.

— Dr Diwakar Minz

Acknowledgement

The effort to provide historical evidence in support of and to prove the hypothesis of this book had been sown as a seed which sprouted in childhood itself. The nearness of my venerable father and the religious discussions amongst his friends had impressed upon my juvenile mind the thought that our religion was not being projected correctly. Since the Mundas and Oraons do not have any religious books, the writers wrote about them through their own view-points. Hence, two questions present a challenge to me–one pertaining to religion and doing away with wrong ideas, and the other of preparing a religious book of the race. The result of the first challenge is in front of you, the readers. As regards the question of preparing a religious book of the race, this appears to be very complicated and difficult to perform although as a student of matriculation I had thought that the Vedas are a collection of hymns based on hearing hence in my religion the traditionally passed on beliefs could be collected and edited in book form which would later on become evidence. But it is not just that what I had thought in my childhood. At present I am silent because the effort would be very arduous and laborious.

Full credit goes to my late father, Siri Goinda Minz, who has been a great source of inspiration, motivation in dignity, my family atmosphere for enabling me to consolidate my thoughts and guiding my opinions in the present direction. I am obliged to Research Supervisor Dr Harishankar Pandey, a renowned historian as also a theologian, who has given a direction to the identity of tribals. I am obliged to my friends, colleagues, and especially to those illiterate rural tribals who not only gave shelter to me in their villages but took great pains to throw light on every aspect. I am also very much thankful to Mrs Lakshmi Singh, Retd. I.A.S. and former Chief Secretary of Jharkhand, Flat No. 6/B, Shanti Appartments, Shradhanand Road, Ranchi-1. Mob. 9431392274 who has translated the Hindi version into English. I am grateful to Kalpaz Publications, New Delhi, for publication of my book.

— **Dr Diwakar Minz**

Mundari Words and their Explanation

Word	Explanation
Ading	: A place in Mundari homes where "rowa" is established. Six-seven days after some-body's death, the religious rite of "umbul-ader" is performed, in which the "umbul" is brought to the "ading" and established. Umbul= rowa=soul of the dead person.
Adoba sootam	: freshly spun pure cotton thread which is used in religions rites. As per traditional religious belief, fresh thread is thought to be alive on which the god/soul climbs up and leaves for the sky through the other end.
Asur	: a primitive tribe engaged in smelting of iron which, as per legend of the Mundas, used to rule Chhotanagpur before the Mundas.
Asulo	: oblation or offering or food dedicated to please the deities.
Omedanda	: that place where, after coming from Rohtasgarh, the Mundas divided into two groups. One group went to Santal Pargana where they came to be called "Santal." The other group of Mundas reached Ranchi via Lohardagga.
Ikasi Pidi Te	: Eightyone uplands and eighty three plains.
Tirasi Badi te	: God King Singbonga arrived after having disappeared with the help of the twelve learnings. The mention of this place in Asur legends indictates that prior to entering Chhotanagpur, during their migration period the Mundas had stayed there for some time. This place was located somewhere in North India.
Umbul	: shadow. After death, a human being's soul comes out of his body. This soul is his shadow.
Kili	: clan.

Kompat : pure Munda.

Khorposh : villages or States given to the king's kith and kin for maintenance.

Khunt : sub-clan or local branch of a clan.

Gara : heavenly punishment.

Giti-ora : dormitory of young boys and girls: a type of social, disciplined institution.

Gomke : lord, master.

Chati-jowar : purification rite performed at the birth of a child. This is often done on the eighth day after birth. It is after this function that the child is admitted as a member of the family.

Charpangu : a kind of powder used in the making of hadiya.

Chatu : carrying a water-filled pot meaning, thereby, girls who can carry water-filled pitchers, that is, young women.

Chowra-Bhowra : names of the two dogs which had driven away the horse breaking human images. The horse denotes wicked deeds hence is thought to be a symbol of sin.

Jee : that which resides in a human being and keeps him alive.

Jenome-jugre : eternally.

Jame-sakam : meal on a leaf-plate, meaning fixed life-period. After the meal is over, the body like the leaf-plate becomes meaningless. The meal, that is life period, is fixed.

Dinda : unmarried young men and women who are virgins.

Tapan-ili : rice wine used in sacred religious functions for oblations to the deities or at the time of sacrifice, worship, etc. This is prepared four to five days earlier by the wife of the pahan (priest). It is fermented in a pitcher or pot which is absolutely new and does not have black or any other spot on it. The pahan's wife fetches water from a nearby well or brook after midnight to pour on the fermented rice wine. Water taken after midnight is supposed to be untouched hence clean and pure.

: Till the sacred rice wine is prepared, the pahan's wife observes religious fast and purity. Ili=hadiya=rice wine.

Dantari : the human being whom Singbonga for the first time enlightened with the knowledge and learning of "deora" Thus, Dantari was the first disciple of Singbonga. Dantari is also called the "preceptor of the creation" or "preceptor of fruitfulness". He was a great scholar of medical science. The similarity in the words Dantari and Dhanwantari is to be noted.

Deous Otiosus : the god who becomes indifferent to and detached from human beings and the world.

Deora : a priest who performs religious functions, recites mantras or prayers, and who sings religious hymns. He also works as a diviner or witch doctor, and has knowledge of indigenous system of medicine and occult practices.

Dokha-bing : Mentioned in traditional tales the legendary snake, the sighting of which means that death is near.

Nang-nangate : from time immemorial.

Naguri dishum : the western area of Khunti comprising of Doesa, Sisai, Palkote and Basiya. In this area, the Munda inhabitants have been influenced by Sadan or indigenous non-tribal culture. The dead bodies of Mundas of this area are placed with their heads toward the north and feet toward the south which is opposite to that of Hansda custom.

Nage Era : (1) a goddess who shoulders the responsibility of protecting the villagers and lives in shallow ponds.

(2) after the Asur men were burnt to ashes, their women became deities. The period thereafter marks the end of the Asur-period and the beginning of a new period called "Nage Era." During this period the pregnant widows left behind gave birth to Asur offsprings which became the reason for the continuity of their existence and their development. (see Annexure Soso Bonga).

Pitu sing : a plant, the root of which is used to make hadiya or rice wine.

Banda Pungu : a leaf cup for drinking hadiya, a corner of which is folded. That is why it is called "tail-less." In any function when the main speaker folds the leaf plate, then the assembled people start drinking the hadiya.

Batauli : as per popular belief, every village is the habitat of a great god or mahaburu, a desauli god or god of the village limits, and a chandore ikir god or god of a grove situated beside a pond. They are regarded as the lords and protectors of that area. The villagers organise a function to please them in which special food is offered to them. This function is called batauli.

Ba-jayar (Ba-jaier) : That sal tree which has been dedicated to "lutkum hadam" and "lutkum budhiya" on which these original ancestors supposedly live. As per order of Singbonga, there must be a sal tree in the middle of a cluster of villages. This tree will either be a lone tree or else together with some more trees, will form a "Sarna". In this Sarna grove, the sal tree will be the tallest and most sacred, and even its small twig lying on the ground can be removed only by the pahan or priest, not by anybody else. Even the pahan has to keep these lutkums happy for this work for which he has to sacrifice cocks. All sal trees, despite being sacred, cannot be "ba-jaier" meaning thereby that despite being sacred cannot be home to Munda aja-aji lutkum.

Ba or baha : the festival celebrated at the beginning of the year when sarjome (sal) tree is at its flowering best. There is no particular date fixed for this festival. Every village can fix the date of this festival as per convenience, but this date has to fall in the middle of February and March when nature is blooming all around with new leaves and buds.

Buru : the Almighty God as per Hoffman, Singbonga cannot be the original god of the Mundas-Buru was probably the original God. Singbonga probably originated with the passage of time.

(J. B. Hoffman, Christian padre, had studied Munda religion, and had prepared the comprehensive "Encyclopaedia Mundarika." This is his own thinking).

Bonga : deity / spirit

Bonga (note: see annexure Asur. As per Sosobonga, the widows of the Asurs caught hold of Singbonga who had been flying skyward. They clung to him and demanded work for themselves. Singbonga shrugged them off after having told them their work. Wherever they fell, they became bonga or deity of that place. Now these spirits are not believed to be female souls or ghosts, although while praying to them the suffix "na" is added. This suffix is added in Mundari language when talking to women. The Christian writers have propagated that bongas are ghosts and have concluded that Munda religion is monotheistic whereas the Mundas worship the bongas perceiving them to be deities. When Singbonga is thought to be the Supreme God, then the other bongas are deities, not spirits or ghosts).

Singbonga : the Supreme, Almighty God, the king of the gods, Bhagwan. As per Menas Odiya, Singbonga had been seen by only four persons- the original ancestors (tota hadam and tota burha) and the lutkums (old man-old woman duo).

Ikir bonga : the deity living in deep waters.

Nage bonga : the god of the valley.

Marang buru-bonga : the god residing on the high peak of a mountain.

Desauli bonga : the god who lives on the boundary of the village which he protects.

Chondore-ikir-bonga : the god who lives in a grove close to a pond.

Chandi-bonga : the god who lives in a circular rock or rounded stone and protects and helps during hunting.

Marang Kanda : religious rite pertaining to re-admittance of an ostracized member of the race.

Majhiyas : Privileged land of the landlord.

Mage : this is a sacred festival. This is the last of the chain of festivals wherein the account books of contract between the tenant and the landlord or servant and master pertaining to the closing year are closed and fresh ones are opened. This festival is observed in the month of December in the Hasda area and in the month of January in the Naguri area.

Manki : the head of a stretch or some villages.

Mua-masanko : destructive ghost.

Rowa : soul. After the death of a person, the soul becomes free of the body but the longing for the body still remains. The soul hovers above the body till it reaches the graveyard. A spun thread connecting the dead body is taken out of the grave into the open air above so that the soul can climb up. A few days later the soul is taken as the umbul or shadow of the body. The animals do not have "rowa". The rowa is indestructible.

Rajhas : the land on regular rent meant for settlement, available to the king.

Lipi-susri : the loyal chatak bird which had been sent by Singbonga to instruct and persuade the Asurs. As per Munda

		convention, in the beginning all birds had been white, but due to getting burnt by the ashes of the furnaces of the Asurs, they became black, brown and of various other colours.
Lutkum (Budha and Budhi)	:	the Munda couple known as "Aja-Aji" who used to live on the limits of the village of the Asurs, and who were served by Singbonga as the boy with the itch. The Mundas accept this couple as their first ancestors. The couple had seen the appearance of Singbonga.
Sarna	:	sacred grove. During the clearing of the forest for agricultural purposes and habitation, one part used to be left alone and protected. Ever since, this part is accepted as holy and adorable, and no tree is cut from this portion. The beginning of Sarna-religion is connected to this feeling and emotion of aboriginal life. This conduct, philosophy and faith or belief in totality is called Sarna religion.
Sasan	:	graveyard where the bones of the dead of a particular clan are buried or interred beneath a stone after observance of religious rites. The concerned village has a right and the ancestral home has influence over the graveyard.
Sosotapa	:	the performance of religious rites or revenge requital against evil-eye and destructive worship (ritual conducted for the destruction of enemies).
Seben leltan	:	He who can see and hear everything, that is, Singbonga.
Sirmareni	:	highest.
Hadam	:	creator of the universe/original ancestor or burha.
Hasda	:	the eastern part of Khunti comprising of the Munda areas falling in the police station jurisdictions of Murhu and Khunti. As per tradition followed in this region, dead bodies are positioned with their head towards the south and feet toward the north. Just opposite to them, the dead bodies of Naguri dishum are positioned with the head toward the north and feet toward the south, thus reflecting Hindu influence.
Hirchi-gidi	:	to purify with the sprinkling of water. This holy water is prepared with the leaven of rice wine, turmeric water, and drops of blood taken out of the leg of a white cock. This water is considered so holy that by merely touching it a person becomes free of blemish or sin.
Horo	:	Munda (man).

Kudukh Words and their Explanation

Word	Explanation
Akhra	: an expansive circular place in the middle of the village which is used for organising community dances, singing, village assembly or religious rites.
Agiya	: in some places, called agua also. He has a dominant role in arranging marriages/match making. The sides of the groom and bride have separate match makers. From the groom's side, some people under the leadership of the agiya go to the bride's place to fix the marriage but if en route some omen takes place, then the group goes back and this effort of match making is cancelled. The agiya thinks that any bad omen indicates the disapproval of Dharmes hence efforts are started again to find out another bride. In the same way, at the indication of any bad omen, the agiya from the bride's side may cancel the match. If there is no bad omen, then the marriage takes place under the supervision of the agiya.
Ojha	: just like the bhagat, the ojha treats to cure diseases and maladies. His position is in between mati and bhagat.
Ula	: means inner corner of the home. Here the soul of the dead person is temporarily established prior to surrender of his bones.
Kaman	: it is also called mourning, and now many Oraons under the influence of Hindus name it as the ten-day ceremony performed after the death of a member of the family. On the tenth day of this ceremony, all the male members of the family tonsure their heads and undergo purification bath. On this day the soul of the dead person, prior to being united with his ancestors, is temporarily established in the ula.

Karam : an important festival. During this festival, the karam tree is worshipped and a branch of the tree is brought home and planted. On this day, the Oraons pray to Dharmes for happiness and good times. Prayers are also offered for agricultural prosperity and for getting good grooms for the unmarried girls and that they are blessed with children.

Kurukh : Oraon and Oraon language is recognised by this name.

Kundi : the word has come from water tank. That watery place where the pulkhi stone is kept and be neath which the bones of the dead are buried. One clan has one kundi fixed in its name.

Koha-benja : the great marriage. The religious rituals and festivities observed at the time of funeral rites. This is an important part of the funeral rites whereby the soul of the dead person unites with the family of his ancestors.

Khaddi : the festival of Sarhul. This is celebrated in March-April when the sal trees are in full bloom, laden with flowers. This festival is of utmost importance to the agrarian Oraon life because on this day Chala Pachcho Devi or Sarna goddess gets married to Dharmes, or the Earth goddess gets married to the sun which increases the fertility of the earth. In a practical way, symbolically, the marriage of the priest's wife with the priest or pahan is celebrated.

Gotor or gotra : the development of gotra (clan) took place in Chhotanagpur. Marriage within the same gotra is prohibited. The gotra is considered in many religious rituals and rites. In order to identify gotra, each gotra is connected to a totem.

Chandi : worshipped especially by bachelor youths and the priest. She is the goddess of hunting who not only helps for a good hunt but also protects the hunter from animals during the hunt. Her habitat is the hill at the edge of the village or an open space known as "Chandi tanr."

Chala-Pachcho : Sarna old woman or Sarna goddess. Chala Pachcho had developed in Oraon religion prior to their entry into Chhotanagpur. She is supposed to be the goddess of agriculture. The Sarna place where Mundas, for the protection of their village, had identified to be the place of "hatu bongako," was adopted in Oraon religion to be the place for establishing Chala-Pachcho or Sarna Devi.

Joda Kamna : this rite is performed at first child-birth. As per Oraon belief, after the marriage of a girl, she brings spirits and "nads" from her family and village to her in-laws' home. The father of the girl or any elderly person from her side participates in this rite and through worship gets rid of the influence of the ancestors and the village spirits.

Danda Katta : This rite is also called "danda rengna" or "bhelwa fadi." This worship is conducted in nearly all important occasions to ward off destructive evil influences. This is a very common religious rite prevailing amidst the Oraon and Munda tribes. The worship is conducted prior to any auspicious activity. During the invocation of Dharmes, a white cock is sacrificed or an egg is offered to him. A symbolical picture or image is prepared for this worship by using a mixture of coal dust, flour and red mud taken from the hearth.

Dharmes : The Almighty of the Oraons. The Creator, the Supreme Father and the Supreme God of the Oraons. Prior to coming to Chhotanagpur, the Oraons accepted the Sun as their only God and they accordingly worshipped the Sun. The appearance and development of Dharmes has been equivalent to Parmeshwar, the Supreme God of the Hindus, in Chhotanagpur. Although this thought process has developed from the Sun, the Oraons invoke the Sun as "Suraj Bhagwan" and accept Dharmes as Bhagwan or Supreme God. Whenever white cocks are offered, in most religious functions, Dharmes is invoked.

Najar gujar : "Najar-gujar" is like "bai-bhak." The Oraons think them to be the reason for their troubles and bad days. In order to destroy their evil influence, prayers are offered to Dharmes, and worship of "danda katta" or "bhelwa fadi" is conducted.

Nad : The soul of the dead which is nearly always called "ghost" by the Christian and other researchers. As per Oraon religion, nad are of two kinds- one, who has undergone a natural death, and the other who has undergone an unnatural death. After natural death, the nad or the soul gets a place among his ancestors. After unnatural death, the soul remains unsatisfied and in order to take revenge, gets satisfaction in killing the instigated persons or torturing them. After completing the lotted age in this torturous-dilemma, the soul of the dead person attains salvation.

Name Pijna : The naming ceremony. The mother sits with her baby in front of a tureen filled with water. A grain of rice is placed in the water in the name of the baby. Thereafter, taking the names of the ancestors, rice grains are placed one by one in the water. Whichever rice grain touches and settles beside the rice grain in the name of the baby, the name of the ancestor of that grain of rice then becomes the name of the baby. Normally the nickname of the baby originates from the day of its birth, namely, somra, somri, mangra, mangri, etc.

Naig : The priest representing the whole community. For family or personal welfare, worship and offering of sacrifice is done by the head of the family, but for the welfare of the whole village and the community, the naig performs the worship and religious ceremonies. The naig commands a respectful position in the village.

Pach Balar : The family of the ancestors. After natural death, the soul of the dead is united with the ancestors following the ceremony of Koha-benja or "had-bodi". This is how he becomes a member of Pach-balar. As per Oraon religion, Pach-balar inhabits "patal lok" or the under-world. Just like the earth, the Pach-balar of patal lok reside amongst their own clans.

Pat raja : The deity or nad established on the hill bordering the village. As per Oraon belief, Pat-Raja moves about astride a small pony. He perambulates the village and protects it from any impending disease or disaster. The Oraons worship him on time and offer cocks in sacrifice.

Pulkhi : A piece of stone kept erect in a water tank. While conducting the rite of "had bodi" the bones of the dead are buried beneath it. The Oraon women clean the pulkhi stone, wash it with water, and apply marks on it of a paste of vermillion and oil. Every gotra has its own pulkhi stone beneath which the bones of the dead belonging to that gotra are buried. As per Oraon belief, in this way the soul of the dead is united with "pach-balar," that is, the family of his ancestors.

Bai-bhak : Curse or words of destruction uttered by mouth. As per Oraon superstition, such curses have the backing of evil spirits, hence to ward them off, the worship of "danda-katta" or "bhelwa-fadi" is conducted.

Bidi-Belas : Prior to entry into Chhotanagpur, the highest God of the Oraons, that is the Sun. But the Sun did not command that reverence which the Hindus gave to Bhagwan and which in Chhotanagpur Dharmes also commanded.

Benja : Marriage. This word denotes not only marriage but also all religious ceremonies connected with it.

Bhagat : Just like the matis, the bhagats nullify the evil effects of blackmagic. They are skilled in thus making the afflicted patients disease-free, but their capability is not considered to be the result of any training- it is the result of the grace of Mahadeo that they acquire this skill. Their dietary habits and conduct are pious.

Bhaiya-bahin : The first couple of man and woman through which the Oraon offspring and race developed and increased.

Bhuifoot-Mahadeo : An ordinary yet sensitive Oraon dreams that Mahadeo is beneath a particular place or He is coming out of that particular ground. He is visited with this dream that he should worship Him. So that Oraon spreads this message after which the Shivalinga stone is obtained from that place. This Shivalinga is called "Bhuifoot Mahadeo."

Mahadeo-manda : That place where bhagat, ojha, mati conduct the worship of Mahadeo. A trident is planted on this spot. In some places flags are also hung. Manda means mandap which means a canopy raised for ceremonial purposes.

Mati : Mati is also called deora. He is skilled in curing patients afflicted with diseases and illnesses sent by witches and black-magic practitioners, and also other influences. This skill is passed on by the teacher to his disciple. The matis worship Mahadeo. Sometimes they invoke souls and in order to fulfil the selfish ends of their clients, they send diseases and afflictions as also destructive forces to others.

Sarna-soop=

Chala-keter : As per Oraon religion, it is that winnowing fan in which Sarna Devi sits and, along with the winnowing fan she keeps moving. It is with the help of this winnowing fan that the pahan is selected.

Sarna-kuti or Chala Kutti : A separate room in the house of the pahan where the Sarna-soop is kept. A peg is planted in such a manner that the winnowing fan hung on it does not move even when a strong wind blows. If the soop shakes, then Sarna Devi in anger might visit the Oraons with some epidemic. This is a very sacred spot where the pahan or somebody with the permission of the pahan can enter.

Sira-sita : as per traditional religious lore and description, that swampy place where, at the time of the rain of fire, the ancestors of the Oraons were found protected in the form of brother-sister. They were utilised by Dharmes to generate Oraon race.

Had-bodi : funeral rites, which as per Oraon religion are defined as "mahan vivah" or great marriage, include a special ceremony of "asthhi samarpan" or surrender of bones. As per this ceremony, the bones of the dead person are surrendered in the water tank of the gotra or clan with the prayer that his soul may go to the nether world and unite there with his ancestors. Since bones are surrendered in the water tank, the Sadans or indigenous non-tribals came to call the ceremony "had bodi." Thus, "had bodi" is not "koha benja" in the way that the padres and other writers have defined- it is just one of the important rites of the ceremony of "Koha benja."

Glossary of Abbreviations

A.I.	= Ancient India (R. C. Majumdar)
A.R.	= Archaeological Report (Cunningham)
C.I.	= Caste in India (J. H. Hutton)
E.B.	= Ethnology of Bengal (E. Dalton)
E.B. (M)	= Encyclopedia Mundarica (J. B. Hoffmann)
J.A.S.B.	= Journal of Asiatic Society of Bengal
J.B.O.R.S.	= Journal of Bihar and Orissa Research Society
J.R.A.S.	= Journal of Royal Asiatic Society
M.C.	= The Mundas and their country (S. C. Roy)
O.C.	= The Oraons of Chhotanagpur (S. C. Roy)
O.R.C.	= Oraon Religion and Customs (S. C. Roy)
R.S.M.T.	= The Religious system of the Munda tribe
Pu	= Puran
Brah	= Brahman
Bha. San. Ka	= Bharatiya Sanskriti avam Kala
M. Bha.	= Mahabharat
Mu. Kan.	= The Mundas and their Country
Mu. Lo.	= Munda Lok Kathhayen

Chapter - 1

Introduction

In India, the forested areas of Gondwana Plateau situated in the southern portion of Jharkhand State are home to a dense population of tribals. This region is 300 to 1200 metres above sea-level and situated within 22° to 25° latitude (north) and spread between 85° to 87-45° longitude. This area falls within Chhotanagpur Division encompassing five main districts of Ranchi (including Gumla and Lohardaga), Palamau, Hazaribagh, Dhanbad and Singhbhum. The north-eastern extension of this plateau has a dense population of Santhal tribe which shares a common ancestor with the Munda tribe. This region is called Santhal Pargana and from administrative view-point it used to be a part of Bhagalpur Division, but with the creation of Jharkhand State it has become a part of this State and is called Santhal Pargana Division.[1]

In Jharkhand State, the population of tribals is 28 per cent of the whole population (as per census of 1991),[2] and the number of tribes is thirty three. Among these tribes, the Munda and Oraon tribes are more developed and better placed not only population-wise, but also economically, educationally, socially, culturally and even religion-wise. Hence, their position in Chhotanagpur is considered to be prominent.

For the past three to four decades, the importance of Jharkhand in the map of India has been increasing. Although the Government of India and other State Governments have been continuously trying to uplift the living standards of the tribals and to bring them to the national mainstream, yet the tribals still have the mind-set that they are being exploited and are apprehensive about losing their identity. Their apprehension is not without reason. The identity of Mundas and Oraons, their remarkable culture, their special religion, are clearly to be seen in their traditional life-styles which also offer systematic knowledge of their religious history. Hindu, Muslim, Sikh, Christian- nearly all religions have their sacred religious texts, but the Munda and Oraon tribes have no religious text. It is a matter of anxiety therefore that there has been no effort in this direction till date.

The Christian missionaries have started some work on the religions of the Munda and Oraon tribes and their history, but historical objectivity has not been completely followed in these works. For the first time in the year 1866, the article written by Col. E.T. Dalton titled, "The Kols of Chhotanagpur" and published in the journal of the Asiatic Society of Bengal was an official attempt to throw light on the life of the Mundas. In 1871, a compilation of Mundari psalms was published by A. Nautrat. In 1903, the book, "The Religion and Custom of Oraon" written by Rev. Father P. Dehan was published, and two years later in 1905 "Kurukh folk-lore" written by Rev. F. Han was published which is a praiseworthy collection of religious legends of the Oraon tribe, their religious customs and conventions, and folk-songs based on festivals. In order to compile this vast collection, Father Han had to put in ten years (1890-1900) of hard labour and patience. In this direction, the collection of 1200 poems, between 1930-34 by B. Dharamdas Lakra, of the Lohardaga and Gumla areas and titled, "Leel Kho- R'a' khey-khel" throws some light on the form and history of Oraon religion.

Father J. Hoffmann has done maximum work on Munda religion and beliefs and their traditions, "Encyclopaedia Mundarica" (1930-79), in addition to Mundari Grammar and Mundari dictionary, is the only book which covers extensively and in depth Munda religion and philosophy and throws light on them. Father P. Ponnet's, "Munda Ethics" (1978) and father A. Vaughan Exam's book, "The Religious System of the Munda tribe" published in 1982 from Agustine are noteworthy books on Munda religion and their traditional history.

In the past decades, some work regarding Oraon religion and customs have been published. Among these, Rekha O. Dhan's book, "These are my tribesmen-Oraon" published in 1967, Rev. Edmund Campion's book, "My Oraon Culture" published in 1980, Boniface Tirkey's, "Oraon Symbols" published in 1980 and "Smiling Oraon" published in 1989 are noteworthy.

Amongst Indian scholars, S. C. Roy's books, "Mundas and their Country" published in 1912, "The Oraon of Chhotanagpur" published in 1915 and several research works published in the journal "Man of India" regarding tribal religious life are materials of historical importance. But uptil now, no attempt has been made which would have presented a systematic and sequential historical study of the religions of the Munda and Oraon tribes. In the past decades of growing importance of these tribes, this study has become even more necessary and useful.

The study of religious history of prominent Munda and Oraon tribes has been conducted with the following five phases in mind:

Pertaining to Munda tribe

First phase:	Position of tribe and religion during the migratory process from place of origin to Rohtasgarh (in the form of background)	From primeval time to sixth century BC

Second Phase :	Entry in Chhotanagpur, the fall of the Asurs and the coming into being of Sarna religion.	Munda religion =Sarna religion (sixth century BC to fourth century BC)
Third Phase :	(a) (i) The appearance of Bongas in Sarna religion and their importance. (ii) The classification of gods and bongas in Sarna religion. (b) The increase in the number of Bongas in Sarna religion. (c) The opposite religious current, the expansion of the influence of magic and occult practices. (d) The development of parallel religious institution of Deora, Ojha, and Sokha in Sarna religion.	
Fourth Phase :	The influence of Kabir Panthis (followers of Kabir sect) and Vaishnav religious followers (devotees of God Vishnu) on Sarna religion.	(16th to 18th Century A.D.)
Fifth Phase :	The awakening of reformist tendencies in Sarna religion and the reformist movement.	(19th century to 1947)

Pertaining to Oraon tribe

First Phase :	Position of tribe and religion during the migratory process from to fourth place of origin to Shahabad and Rohtasgarh (in the form of background).	(from primeval time century B.C.)
Second Phase:	Entry into Chhotanagpur and welcome by Mundas and economic, social change due to contact	(Gradually from fourth century B.C.)
Third Phase: (a)	Cultural, religious exchanges between Mundas and Oraons and their racial intermingling.	(.......till 16th Century
(b)	Religious transition period : Kurukh religion = Sarna religion.	
(c)	The importance and classification of Chala Pachcho and other regional gods/ goddesses in Sarna religion.	

(d) (I) The gradual extension of influence in Sarna religion of opposite religious trends of nad and magic and occult practices.

(II) The development of parallel religious institution of Ojha, Mati, Bhagat and Sokhas in Sarna religion.

(e) The worship of Hindu gods-goddesses, Mahadev, Bhuiphoot Mahadeo, Devi Mai, Durga, Kali and the prevalence of Manda i.e. mandap (Pavillion) and kuti (Shrine).

Fourth Phase :	The influence in Sarna religion of various religious communities, Kabir panthis, Vaishnav devotees etc.	(16th to 18th Century)
Fifth Phase :	Reformist and positive tendencies in Sarna religion and the Neha and Tana Bhagat movement.	(from 19th Century to 1947)

Source

The Mundas and Oraon tribes have no religious books or literature of their own. In the epics and Puranas (ancient books of Hindu mythology) of Indian literature, slight light is thrown on the social and religious life of these tribes in various references here and there. Their racial qualities and characteristics pertaining to language have been the bases of efforts to trace out those places and races with whom they had affinity and on the basis of whose religious life, through comparative analyses, the religious history of Munda and Oraon Tribes has been tried to be linked. Knowledge about the habitation and life-style of the Asurs in Chhotanagpur prior to the coming of the Mundas is derived from various stone implements, utensils and copper ornaments obtained from the region as also the finds in 1867 near the Boodhadih hill of Tamar and in 1915-20 in the articles unearthed through excavation of remains of Majhgaon in Chainpur. Similarly, study of the graveyards of the Mundas, the pulkhi-stones of the Oraons, and the articles buried along with the bodies and bones illuminate the life after death philosophy pertaining to humans, the importance of ancestors, clan-custom, etc, various religious facts of these tribes. But maximum historical material can be derived from the religious stories, legends, songs and invocations of these tribes which stand protected in the traditional word of mouth process. S. C. Roy has termed them to be semi-historical material.

At this stage, it is necessary to ponder about the skill of history writing and historical material. The Munda and Oraon religious stories, mythology, traditional customs, various invocations and songs, which are protected through memorisation among the ancient Mundas and Oraons and the pahans, form the main material source of religious history. The history of religion is the history of the thinking and philosophy of a particular race which becomes customary through the tradition of various customs and religious duties. This encompasses the entirety and is not individual neither based nor related to incidents. In the structuring of human history, imagination has played a clear role. Prior to this, the wise and learned chroniclers have in history arranged the ideals of various races based on imagination and this imagination has been their ancient myths. Ancient myths mean such thoughts and ideals which emerged from the visible evidence of the tribes and spread all over through public voice. These thoughts or ideals remained unwritten through many generations of the past and verbally through word of mouth were handed over to the later generations. When they were collected and presented in an orderly manner, they came to be called history. They become the truth of history and connect the past with the present, and construct history's unbroken tradition.

The origin of the earth, origin of flora and fauna, the birth of man and extension of races, the division of time, the first ploughing, rain of fire, the legends of Asurs, the origin of bongas and nads, etc., various religious verses which by word of mouth remain protected in the memorisation process of the tribes through the eras, are important for being valuable material of religious history. It is through these that knowledge regarding various rituals of the Munda and Oraon tribes, festivals, worshipping-rites, importance of the ancestors, influence of the deities and their rise and fall in the hierarchical order, etc. can be gained. The learning obtained by the historians from listening to their stories and hymns and by observing the various religious rules and regulations of the tribes is confirmed in the comparative study of the religious rituals, thinking and philosophy of the other breakaway tribes through the help of which, interpolated and non-historical material can be separated. In addition, the archaeological remains of the described geographical places and incidents act as evidence to help in the confirmation of the hypothesis.

Although the religion of the Chhotanagpur Munda and Oraon tribes has an extended influence over their judicial system and right to property, yet basically the study of their religious history has been limited to their refinement, religious rituals, ancestors, festivals, the appearance of deities and their development, the coming into existence of bongas and naads, opposite religious system of magic and occult along with the development of various parallel religious institutions to cancel their evil influence namely deora, mati, bhagat, ojha, sokha etc., and Hindu gods and goddesses, the use of their mantras or prayers, and the reformist positive tendencies and various movements.

The whole work is contained in the following chapters:

First chapter	= Preface
Second chapter	= Historical Introduction of Munda and Oraon Tribes
Third chapter	= Munda Religion : Sarna Religion
Fourth chapter	= Oraon Religion : Sarna Religion
Fifth chapter	= Conclusion

First chapter: Preface

In this chapter, the importance of the subject and impressive work done uptil now on Munda and Oraon religions has been estimated. During the search for source material, in addition to archaeological material, enough help has been obtained from "sasandiris" and pieces of stone erected in "pulkhis" but most material has been gathered from the traditional stories, prayers related to various religious rituals, songs related to festivals, etc. which till today is the lore handed down for years from generation to generation about stories of the past.

Second chapter: Historical Introduction of Munda and Oraon Tribes

This chapter is divided into two parts. In the first and second parts the migration of the Munda tribe and Oraon tribe respectively from their place of origin to Chhotanagpur has been considered and those problems have been specifically analysed which are controversial and related to the religious life of these tribes. In the traditional tales, the place of origin of the Munda tribe has been accepted as district Azamgarh of Uttar Pradesh but from historical point of view it has not been proved to be correct. As per linguistic, racial and archaeological evidence available, the place of origin of the Munda tribe which is also called "Kol" can be identified to be the "Jawan" region of Southwest China from where migration to India could have been possible through two routes: (a) the southeast route as per William Schmidt and colleagues via Indo-China, Vietnam, Malaya, Burma, Assam and (b) the northern route as per Hodgeson, Hutton, etc from southern China to Mongolia, via Tibet through the Himalayan passes to western India, from western India via Kurukshetra, the Ganga-Yamuna plains to Rohtasgarh and from there in sixth century B.C. entry into their "Otey Disum" Chhotanagpur, defeating the Asurs living there from before, and their permanently settling down there forming the background of the development of Sarna religion.

The Oraon tribe of Dravidian (?) roots- their ancestral place and in India their migration to Chhotanagpur, the two main concepts of which have been analysed. The authropologists, on racial basis, have accepted the Dravidians to be the outcome of the merger of the Aegean (Proto-Australoid) race of the Mediterranian Sea and Armenide races of Asia Minor, and on this ground accepted that the Dravidians came from the Mediterranian region via the Arabian Sea to northwest India. As per the theory of M. L. Tirkey, the Oraon tribe had reached Shahabad-Rohtasgarh after crossing the Ganga-Yamuna plains from northwest India, whereas E. Dalton, Dehan, and S. C. Roy have theorised that the Oraon came from the Deccan to Konkan, from there to Gujarat where they followed the bank of the Narmada river and went eastward, crossed the Vindhya Range and reached Shahabad of Bihar.

In the course of tracing the ancestral place of the Dravidians, this probability has been examined that the ancestors of the Oraons originated either from south India or they are connected to South India, to an age, the thick dark layer of which has not yet been penetrated by history.

The objective of tracing the ancestral place and fixing the route adopted by the Munda and Oraon tribes to reach Chhotanagpur is to prepare the background of the various cultural and religious influences they faced during the centuries of migration.

The Munda tribe, also called Kol, had taken the side of the Kauravas in the Kurukshetra war, and during the course of reaching Rohtasgarh from the west had, due to the influence of the Aryans, subdivided into various sub-tribes. Similarly the Oraons were also influenced due to the proximity of the Aryans. By the time they reached Chhotanagpur, the Oraon tribe was in a more sophisticated and developed condition than the Mundas.

The appearance and development of Sarna religion of the Mundas and Oraons have taken place in the forest limits of Chhotanagpur but despite the name being the same, the philosophy and structure as well as development of various religious institutions of both religions are different. These differences are due to the religious conduct acquired earlier and assimilated which have influenced the present circumstances.

Third chapter: Munda Religion, Sarna Religion

In a comparative study of Munda religion prior to the war with the Asurs and post-Munda victory over the Asurs, the appearance of the Bongas and the expansion of their influence can be called an important historical episode. Prior to entry into Chhotanagpur, the ruling deity of the Mundas was the Sun who during the course of time came to be worshipped as Hadam and Singbonga. Rev. Father Hoffemanne believes that prior to coming to Chhotanagpur, the Munda tribe during their migratory period, had been influenced by some community which believed in the "Sun-cult." In this context it has been seen that in the primary stages of the religions of most of the world's tribes, the importance of the Sun has been the most. The Munda tribe is no exception to it.

The Sarna religion of the Mundas appeared with the beginning of their entry into Chhotanagpur. During the clearing of the forests, on the border of the village, a portion of the forest would be left as a limit which would be called "Sarna sthal" and in which it was presumed that "hatu-bongako" used to live. "Hatu-bongako" shouldered the responsibility of protecting the village. In due course of time, Sarna-burhi or Sarna Devi came into being. Sarna-burhi is the goddess for the protection of the village and its agricultural prosperity.

The Munda religious lore speaks of the great flood and the origin of the earth, constellations, the creation of flora and fauna, the birth of human beings and the expansion of the races, the first plough, division of time and increase of sinful conduct, and the destruction of the human race due to rain of fire, etc. These descriptions throw light on their religious condition prior to their entry into Chhotanagpur. With their advent into Chhotanagpur the Mundas faced the Asurs living there from before and after the defeat of the Asurs, under the orders of Singbonga, the Sarna religion accepted the Asur widows as "bonga." Over the years, the Munda tribe became afflicted with the growing number of Bongas and evil influence of occult practices. In an effort to connect occult practices with religion, Singbonga's consort Parvati was given the designation of First Witch and the "Saat Parbatiya" cult was propagated. In order to cancel the evil influence of occult practices, the institutions of deora, Ojha, sokha came to be defined as Hinduism influenced parallel religious current within the Sarna religion. The development of kili or gotra and their connected totems form a historical aspect of Sarna religion. In Sutiambey, in order to maintain the sanctity of marriage and purity of lineage, arrangement was made for starting "Ikkis Parha : Ikkis Kili" with the approval of Chairmen of twenty one parganas (a pargana comprises of several villages). Kili or gotra or clan has been the chief consideration in all rites and ceremonies from birth to death.

In Munda religion, festivals have been planned throughout the year by balancing the seasons and agricultural operations. Some scholars have tried to trace the influence of Hindu festivals on Munda festivals but after analysing most of the festivals it has been found that it is the contribution of Munda religion itself.

Fourth chapter: Sarna Religion: Oraon Religion

The Oraon tribe of pre-Dravidian origin spent its earlier years in the forest limits of the Deccan plateau. The description and mention of incidents in the Balmiki Ramayan regarding the Oraon tribe being friend of Dasrathi Ram confirm the various traditional religious tales and descriptions prevalent among the Oraons. "Surya" (the Sun), that is "Bidi Belas" being the Almighty God of the Oraons, developed into "Dharmes" in the religion of the Oraons during their stay in Chhotanagpur. In the early phase of this development, Dharmes was Surya, but in the process the virtues of the Sun were absorbed to evolve a deity equivalent to the Hindu Bhagwan. Later, the difference between Dharmes and Dasrathi Ram became narrowed down. There are many religious stories wherein it has been mentioned that Mother Sita was the wife of Dharmes, and Haluman (Hanuman) was his nephew. The contact with Aryans resulted in the Oraons being socially superior to the Mundas in their dietary habits and life-style. The Mundas learnt about agriculture from the Oraons.

After being defeated in Rohtasgarh, the Oraons had reached Chhotanagpur in about the same condition as the Munda tribe. Due to pressure of the Oraons, the Munda tribe left their home and hearth as well as the cleared land and fled towards the east and south east. Naturally, the homesteads, Sarna place and other areas connected with the religion and deities of the Mundas came to be under the jurisdiction of the Oraons. Since the Oraons did not want to be victimised by the Munda gods and goddesses, they utilised the services of Munda priests for their worship and that is how the Sarna places and religious arrangement regarding the regional gods and goddesses as per Munda practice were saved from being destroyed. In the course of time, the gods-godesses and spirits or nads of the Oraons developed in these places of worship or areas as per their belief. The appearance of Chala-Pachcho as well as pahar or pat raja, darha desauli, Chaturseeman etc. can be thought to be a later development parallel to Munda religion.

In order to repel/cancel the destructive and evil influences of occult practices and ghosts, a parallel institution of mati, ojha, sokha and bhagat came up in Oraon religion which invoked the powers of Mahadeo, Bhuiphoot-Mahadeo, Chandi, Kali, Durga and Devi mai. More importance came to be given to use of cereals, fruits, flowers and milk over animal sacrifice in their mode of worship. The followers of Bhuiphoot-Mahadeo were total vegetarians and observed religious rules and fastings. In the meantime, the influence of Kabir Panthis (followers of Saint Kabir) and Vaishnav religion imparted a refined direction to Oraon religion which is supposed to be the background of the development of Tana Bhagats.

Oraon religion believes in connection or contact even after death. Consequent to the destruction of the body and end of the mortal, his indestructible and immortal soul roams on earth and the nether world. The soul is defined as a bodyless person. After death, despite being bodyless, the deceased person meets his children and close relatives and thinks about their well-being. As per religious philosophy of the Oraons, the nether world which is just below the earth has the same arrangement as this world. After death, the soul of the Oraon meets and merges with his ancestors. The gotra or clan is taken into consideration during funeral rites. Oraon life is attached to religious rites and observances from birth to death.

Oraon festivals occur throughout the year as per the cycle of seasons. To what extent Hindu religion has influenced these festivals has been estimated. The Oraons are cheerful, simple, patient, laborious and large-hearted by nature, whereas the Mundas are more rebellious and fundamentalist. Resultantly, reforms and development have taken place in Oraon religion more speedily.

Fifth chapter: Conclusion

In this chapter, while briefly touching the important subjects of the previous four chapters, thought has been given to those reformist movements which have been able to give a positive direction to the Munda and Oraon tribes. The religion of the Mundas which prior to entry into Chhotanagpur had believed the Sun to be the Supreme God, thereafter started believing in ghosts-spirits and magical invisible powers subsequent to the defeat of the Asurs at their hands. In Chhotanagpur, two types of Bongas developed. One type of Bonga was welfare-oriented and sanctified by religion whereas the other type of Bongas was torturous. The torturous Bongas were thought to be outside the Munda religion and were not worshipped by the pahans or priests. The Oraons came after the Mundas had settled down in Chhotanagpur and there was enough intermingling of culture, religion and race between the two tribes. As a result of this inter-mingling, the Oraons who had been superior to the Mundas from the point of view of society and religion due to the influence of the Aryan contact became of the same level as the Mundas. The Tana Bhagats believe that the original religion of the Oraons is Kurukh, and the concept of ghosts-spirits and evil souls has been imported from Munda religion.

In the fifteenth century, after coming into contact with Chaitanya Mahaprabhu, most of the Mundas of Panchpargana became Vaishnav in religious observance with the awakening of faith in them. The Kabir panthis also influenced the dietary habits and life style of the Mundas. Some Mundas even adopted the Kabir Panth. The Birsa movement had accommodated the virtues of the Christian and Vaishnav faiths. The movement had succeeded to a certain extent in keeping the Mundas away from meat and wine. On the return of Durjansal to Chhotanagpur in the sixteenth century, Mundas of some areas started competing with one another to reach the social level of the Hindus. The Hindu influence could be seen in their procedures of worship, various rituals and festivals so much so that they named themselves and their clans/ gotras based on those of Hindus. After an interval of centuries, the sandi clan of Mundas of Panchpargana came to be known as of Sandilya gotra. The temples established by believers of different religions in the area also influenced the religious thinking of the Mundas. Due to coming in contact with open society, there has been development of upward, positive tendencies in the deities, rules of rituals, festivals, worshipping procedures, etc. of the Mundas.

Compared to the Mundas, the Oraons are racially more simple in nature, humble, large-hearted and accept any influence after slight objection. After entering Chhotanagpur, the Oraons had easily accepted the Sarna places and other religious places established from before by the Mundas as well as their religious customs. The difference was that the Oraons set up their own gods and goddesses in those places where the Mundas had earlier placed their own deities. In the Sarna place where Chandi Bonga of the Mundas had been established, there "Chala Pachcho" goddess of the Oraons was established. Similarly, certain religious beliefs of the Oraons prevalent in the pre-Chhotanagpur period got refined after coming to Chhotanagpur. The highest of the gods "Biri Belas" who used to be worshipped by the Oraons in the form of Surya the Sun, became known as Dharmes after entry into Chhotanagpur. Although this development is the development of Surya the Sun, yet parallel worship of Surya and Dharmes went on. Surya or Sooraj Bhagwan (Sungod) was not destroyed but remained in his place and Dharmes emerging from him began to show the signs of Dashrathi Ram and this is how gradually Dharmes came to be worshipped as Supreme God, superior to Surya.

The contact with Mundas and Hindus is reflected in various aspects of Oraon religion, namely, gods, worship rituals, culture, festivals etc. Amongst Oraons, Bhuiphoot Mahadeo, Devi mai and Devikuti, as well as tradition of bhagats undoubtedly are the result of Hindu influence. Ghosts and spirits, magic and spells are thought to be the contribution of Mundas. This whole development took place in phases.

In the early decades of the nineteenth century, the Kabir Panthis (or followers of Kabir) came to Madhya Pradesh in Raipur and Bilaspur districts. They also came to Simdega, Gumla, Ghagra, etc. and initiated reformist movement among the tribals of the western sector. They used the "chowka" or kitchen method to turn the tribals into kabirpanthis, influenced them to abstain from meat eating and imbibing liquor, and directed them to worship the one and only Supreme God. They were successful in giving a new direction to Oraon religion through "bhagat" movements, lessening the rampant influence of magic and spells in the lives of the Oraons and bringing about overall improvement through logical arguments in the various aspects of Oraon religion.

In this chapter, a concise comparative study of religions of Oraons and Mundas has been done. This study is based on historical background. The sanctifying movement of the Arya Samajis as well as "Sanskrit Bihar" and Bal Yogeshwar's Divine Light mission have also been briefly reviewed. Thus, the religious background prior to entering Chhotanagpur, and phasewise study of the various stages of different aspects of the religions of Oraon and Munda tribes in Chhotanagpur have been presented.

(B) Important places of Hindu worship in the area:

Another important source of Hindu influence upon the tribals of Chhotanagpur has been the innumerable ancient temples in the area. These temples may be divided into five classes :

(a) Those temples wherein idols of gods and goddesses have been placed but the temples have become famous for their architecture.

These temples from historical and architectural point of view or influenced by Shiv-Shakti sect, are as per temple architecture of Orissa or temples of Vaishnava sect. The prominent among them being:–

Shiv-Shakti-Surya Sect temples	Panch Pargana (in Ranchi)	Burhadih, Haradih, Bamla, Palna, Panadih
Temple of Mahamaya	Ghagra (Ranchi) Majhgaon (Ranchi) Palamu	in Hapamuni in Tanginath Betaar
Vaishnav Temple	Ranchi Palamu	Deosa nagar, Jagarnathpur, Boreya, Korambey. Nagarutari and in the fort of the Cheros.

(b) Those temples whose remnants remain, or Shivaling or else idols of other gods and goddesses remain. The ruins of temples found in the valleys of Kanchi and Karkari rivers appear to be of fourteenth to fifteenth century AD. They prove the influence of architecture of Bhubaneshwar. The temples mostly in Ranchi are found in the below mentioned places :

(i) Ram rekha, Anjan, Nagfeni, Devki, Palkote

(ii) Rajrappa (Hazaribagh).

(c) **Sati Places** – Where somebody had become a sati (i.e. entered the funeral pyre of her dead husband), and with the passage of time the place came to be worshipped as sati-sthan or place of sati, namely, Palkote (Ranchi), Soley (Palamu), Jharia and Beesa (Dhanbad), Serengdag (Hazaribagh).

(d) Monastery or places associated with old saints where the tribals frequently heard sermons, namely, Katua (Ranchi), Kherapahar (Palamu), Kutulah and Bitul khurd (Hazaribagh).

(e) Those places which earlier had been associated with Buddhists but which, with the passage of time came under the authority of Hindus, namely, Guhiyapal (Singhbhum), Urvtruria (Dhanbad), Seraj Kund, Jamuna, and Bhaduli (Hazaribagh).

Period of Construction: Most of the temples were built from the Pal era to fifteenth century A.D., but some have definitely been built even prior to the Buddhist period.

Chapter - 2

Historical Introduction of Munda and Oraon Tribes

The place of origin of tribals residing in India and their path of entry into India are not well known due to lack of literary and proven archaeological sources, but study of their physique and language comparisons help to arrive at conclusions regarding the same. Anthropologists believe that although bodily construction may undergo change due to intermingling of communities, yet certain fundamental specialities remain based upon which the original ancestry may be traced or the branches of those sub-clans may be found out to which the community had been linked. Although language related proof may be acceptable to identify the ancestry of tribals yet this cannot be accepted within the scientific historical mode. It is not necessary that the tribals speaking one original language will be from one lineage. But it is certain that wherever any tribal language is spoken in the world, the people of that place must have been in touch with that tribe. Schimdt has tried to find out the path through which tribes have entered India, based on language because the similar language spoken in different parts of the world indicates that the concerned tribe must have been connected to that place. Although Schmidt's methodology is primarily based on philology, his language linked conclusions have not stood up to the test of new explorations of philologists.

The place of origin, migration path and culture of India's pre-historic races as well as some special important notions and philosophies related to their characteristics can be thus considered.

Sir Herbert Risley's Theory

Anthropologists have from time to time expressed their opinion regarding the racial problems of India's population. Amongst these thinkers Herbert

Risley's thinking has been respected and accepted for most part of the period. Risley has divided the races in India in seven categories:

(a)	Dravid	(Dravidian)
(b)	Turk-Irani	(Turko Iranian)
(c)	Indian Arya	(Indo-Aryan)
(d)	Scytho Dravid	(Scytho-Dravidian)
(e)	Arya-Dravid	(Aryo-Dravidian)
(f)	Mongoliya	(Mongoloid)
(g)	Mongoliya-Dravid	(Mongolo-Dravidian).

As per classification of Sir Herbert Risley, the influence of the Dravid race can be seen in most of the racial-groups. According to Risley, the Dravidian type of races are chiefly to be found in south India. The height of Dravidians is shorter than the normal, complexion is very dark nearly black, the head is long and the hair is thick and at times curly. The noses of Dravidians are broad and depressed in the middle but not so much depressed as to make the face appear flat.

The Indo-Aryan group of races are mainly to be found in Kashmir, Punjab and Rajputana. They are tall in height, complexion is fair, the pupils of their eyes are black, they have thick hair on their body and face, their heads are long and their noses are prominently sharp but not very long.

The Turko-Iranian races of Indians are mostly found in the western side of the Indus river comprising of Baluchistan, Punjab and Sindh on the western side of River Indus and the British colonial north-west Frontier Province areas. Turko-Aryans are taller than normal, fair, and their heads are broad. Their faces and bodies are hairy, eyes are mostly black but sometimes brown and noses are long and sharp.

Scytho-Dravid races can be found mostly in Eastern Sindh, Gujarat and Maharashtra. Their physical construction is slightly different from that of the Turko-Iranian race. Their height is comparatively less, their heads are longer, noses short but peaked, breadth being lesser. According to Risley, the Aryo-Dravidian race is found in Easter Punjab, Uttar Pradesh and Bihar States. Their heads are long but have a tendency of gradually becoming shorter, complexion changes from wheatish to dark, noses average and broad, both, compared to Indo-Aryan races, broad. Similarly, their height is normal and some are below average.

The Mongoloid races in India are mostly to be found in Assam, the South eastern terai region of the Himalayas and the British colonial Burma. Their heads are broad, complexion brown yellow, hair on their faces is negligible, height much below average, noses are broad and faces are slightly flat. Their eyes are normally small and blinking. Similarly, Mongolo-Dravidian race of Indians is mostly found in Bengal and Odisha States. Their heads are broad, complexion dark, height short or average, thick hair on face and head, noses are average but not pointed-broad yet not flat.

The Opinion of Dr J. H. Hutton

The basis of Sir Herbert Risley's opinion is apparently that Dravidians were the first settlers of India. But he has been unable to produce any factual proof regarding the same. Actually, prior to Dravidians, a particular race inhabited India which is referred to by historians as pre-Dravidian. Due to new information, the old theories become weak because of lack of logical reasoning. The one-sided opinion of Risley gives way to the considerations of Dr J. H. Hutton which are more logically based. Dr J. H. Hutton has studied in his own way the migrating pre-historic races of India. Based on his studies, Hutton in the year 1933 parted ways from Risley to present his own conclusion according to which the races that came to India can be classified into eight groups. According to Hutton these groups are : (1) Negrito (2) Proto Australoid (3) Ancient Mediterraneans (4) Cultured and civilised Mediterranean (5) Armenoid (6) Alpines (7) Vedic Aryans or Nordic and (8) Mongoloid.

Hutton's classification is not based only on anthropology – it relates also to language similarity, civilisation and culture. Although scholars of today are not ready to accept that language and cultural similarities are the reasons for connecting one race with another race, yet such similarities cannot be ignored also.

Actually it is difficult to split a race into groups based on the similarities of language and culture as also certain physical indications. It is nearly impossible to separately classify various races because for thousands of years there has been an inter-mingling of blood and closeness of language and influence of culture. Yet anthropologist Ichstadt (mpbozmak) had on the basis of anthropological study of physique and culture concluded in 1933 that the Indian races can be classified into three main groups : (1) Europid (2) Negrid (3) Mongoloid. Thereafter Ichstadt has followed it up with 18 sub-races being categorised. The tribes residing in the forests of India have been classified by Ichstadt as Godid and Molid sub-races. Although Ichstadt's classification as compared to those of Risley and Hutton is more modern, but the anthropologists of India have interpreted the racial groups in their own way.

The anthropologists of India have made a deep study of the tribes living in India and they have found out that the people of India can be connected to six original lineages. Although these tribes have for hundreds of years faced geographical and environmental hazards as also intermingling with other races resulting in losing much of their racial qualities yet finer study may be able to find out about their original lineage. The origin of Mundas and Oraon tribes and their path of entry into India have been traced out on this basis.

Anthropologist Dr B. S. Guha, on the basis of most modern available evidence has found the tribes of India to be connected to six human lineages of the world. He has concluded that in South India, intermingling of races has been more than in central India. The six human races are as follows:-

(a) Negrito = negro features
(b) Proto-Australoid = primary Southern form
(c) Mongoloid = Mongolian features
(d) Mediterranean = Mediterranean
(e) Brachycephale = having rounded forehead
(f) Nordic = northwestern.

Out of these, Negrito, Proto Australoid and Mongoloid races are concerned with primitive races which have come to India from the northwest, northeast or Tibet. Of these, the oldest is Negrito race which came from Africa in pre-historic times through the coastal areas of Arabia and Iran and through the sea route to India. These people were of the Pre-Stone Age.

Negrito

The Negrito race is supposed to be the oldest race among the inhabitants of India. Dark complexion, curly hair on the head, flat nose, thick lips are the identifiable features of Negritos. These people were from the Pre-Stone Age period, ignorant of dairying/animal husbandry and agriculture. They used to hunt and gather tubers and roots for food. They had come from Africa via coastal areas of Arabia and Iran, reached the northwestern part of India through the sea route and settled there. Some clans of this race have settled in Andaman group of islands. Some traces of this race may still be found in the people of Cochin and Travancore and Paniyan, Irula, Kasamba and Kadir of the South, and Nagas of Assam. From India, this race went to Malay peninsula, New Guinea, and far off former Melanesia group of islands through land and water routes.

Proto Australoid

After the Negritos, the second race to come to India was Proto Australoid. People of this race were black in colour, had flat noses, and long heads. This race gradually spread throughout India. This race, too, had come during pre-historic times via the Mediterranean Sea. They belong to the Philistine Proto Australoid lineage. Austric or Agneya was the ancient branch of this race. The descendants of this primitive tribe are the Kols, Bhils, Mundas etc. of India. Whatever implements of language and culture they had brought with them got developed and refined in India. They were the people who had laid the foundation of subsequent Stone Age civilisation in India. They spread their primitive culture in various directions of life and took them afar.

After the coming of the Austric race, when the Mongoloid and Aryan races started pressurising them then many of their branches moved out to the

South Eastern countries and groups of islands. It is apparent from the language structure and culture that the hunters reaching Sri Lanka and Australia are primitive tribes of the Austric race which had come to India very early and settled there. Prior to leaving for the southern countries, the Austric race in India had got over its primitiveness and had developed its own language and culture.

Mongoloid

This race has two main sub-divisions: the inhabitants of hills of Assam, Chittagong, Burma, and border of Indo-China form one subdivision, while the second is of the inhabitants of Sikkim and Bhutan who had settled there after coming from Tibet, being Tibetan-Mongoloid. Most of them accept/speak khmer and within this fold Naga, Garo, Kuki, Mikir, Dafla, Anor and Khasi tribes are counted as Mongoloid.

Mediterranean

An important race which came to India during ancient times is Dravidian. The Aegean (Proto Australoid) race of Mediterranean, and Armenide race of West Asia Minor merged with each other to form the Dravidian race, and this race entered India through the North Western portion and spread throughout the country. Although at this time speakers of Dravidian languages are mostly to be found in south India, yet there was a time when Dravidians held sway over Punjab, Sindh to Gujarat, Maharashtra, Assam, Bengal, nearly the entire country. The present Brahui language in the form of Dravidian language is still spoken in Baluchistan.

Western Brachycephales

The sub-groups of Alpine, Dinaric and Armenide races, the physical structure of who is nearly the same, come within Western Brachycephales. According to most scholars, they had come to India from Central Asia. Their features can be seen specially in the inhabitants of Bengal, Orissa and Gujarat. They are scattered even in the Deccan Plateau of India.

Nordic

In the current population of India, enough mingling of these races has happened due to which these sub-races have more or less lost their racial purity. As to the question of their language, Austric, Tibetan-Chinese, Dravidian and Aryan languages are in vogue. The spoken language of the first and fifth race has become extinct. Therefore the fact which comes up is that it is not necessary that races speaking the same language have emerged from a specific human lineage or the different branches of the original lineage divided into various sub-races use the same language. Still, the unity of language or their similarity does prove the unity of sub-races or else their close-connections. In the same way, the difference in language proves the difference of races.

When anthropologists had accepted the basis of identifying races only through human structure then it was helpful to explain the coming and spreading of all races from India to Australia and Madagascar to Philippines, and now they have all been drowned in the ocean. But later on when comparison was made with the fineness of Dravidian and Austric languages and the contradiction which emerged apparently made the imagination of Lemuri Island meaningless. Although previous scholars based on this imagination had accepted the Austric races of India to be a branch of the Dravidian line but actually Father Schmidt demolished this erroneous notion when he began the idea of family of Austric language and found the Dravidian language family to be separate. The Munda tribe comes within the fold of Austric Language and Australoid race while the Oraon tribe has emerged from the Dravidian race and their language is also of Dravidian origin. Thus, the lineage and source of language of Munda and Oraon tribes living side by side in Chhotanagpur are absolutely different. Mundas and Oraons are totally different tribes and their origin and development have taken place in different circumstances, therefore their study in separate sub-chapters is desirable.

Munda Tribe : Origin and Development

Munda is a sub-race of the family of Proto-Australoid. Mundari is a sub-language of Munda language of the Austric family. Munda languages mean that group of Indian Agneya language which together with the languages used by Agneya line of Santhal, Munda, Ho, Khariya, Birhor and many similar tribes have given rise to this language. According to survey conducted by George Grierson, India at that time had a total population of Agneyas of more than two crores out of which Munda speaking people counted for about forty lakhs and within them Mundari speaking populatin was of six and a half lakhs. Bihar had maximum population of six and a half lakhs of Mundari speaking people out of which a big portion stays in Chhotanagpur.

The coming of Mundas to Chhotanagpur and their previous history is shrouded in layers of darkness which have not been fully removed till date by any scholar. As per the fact finding mode of history, such material sources are totally unavailable which would reveal the place of origin of Mundas, their journey to India, their pre-historic living in India and basis of study of their subsequent development of life-style. This primitive tribe has its own language, its physical features, behaviour, folk-songs, folk tales and strengths, but apart from them they do not have any literature or source based upon which history of this tribe could possibly be written. Anthropologists have tried to search out the human ancestry of the Mundas based on their physical features. Efforts have been made to find out that race of which Mundas are a sub-race and who have faced the geographical and environmental hazards. They have tried to trace their ancestry through their language which is Mundari and which is spoken in various parts of the world. Scholars have tried to find out their place of origin through their folk tales and folk songs, their coming into existence and the history of their development as well as finding out archaeological remnants to serve as evidence and proof. The scholars are of the opinion that in the absence of any literature, folk tales and folk songs are unwritten literature and they may fulfil the responsibility of trying to find out the social, political and religious history of any race.

The Proof of Language

The Munda tribe of Chhotanagpur is a sub-race of that vast family which is called "Kol" and whose language Grierson termed as "kolerian." Fredrick Miller has called these languages Munda language. Munda is a well-known race and Austric/ Agneya language is protected to the maximum in its pristine form in Munda languages. Munda word is more respectable than the word "kolerian" and it is cultured too, therefore, Indian scholars have given precedence to the word Munda, and today it is fully in vogue. The languages which are counted in Munda language are : Kherwari, Santali, Mundari, Bhumij, Birhor, Kora, Ho, Turi, Asuri, Agari, Birjiya, Korwa, Korku, Khariya, Juang, Sawar and Godab.

Munda language is counted as one of the languages of Austric (Agneya) group's Austro-Asiatic class. In the Austro-Asiatic language family, the following languages have been comparatively defined and placed:

Language		Place
(a) Munda Community	:	Central and Eastern India
(b) Khasi	:	Northeast India, entered till the borders of Burma
(c) Nicobari	:	Nicobar group of islands
(d) Palong and Wa	:	Burmese tribes
(e) Khmer or Cambodian	:	Indo-China
(f) Cham	:	Vietnam
(g) Sakai	:	Malaya.

Schmidt had compared the above mentioned languages of the family of Austro-Asiatic with the languages spoken in many islands of the south-east and had found connecting sources which proved philologically the complete oneness of these two language groups. Schmidt accordingly established the vast "Austric" language family. The languages spoken in the south-east were named "Austronashiari" which was divided into five families by scholars:

Language family		Region and Regional Language
(1) Malayan or Indonesian	:	Malayan Language in Malaya and Sumatra, Java (three-fourths speak Yav Island Language and the rest speak

		"Suthian"= Daika in Borneo, Tanglong in Philipines, Formasi in Formosa, Malagasi in Madagascar; apart from these, language of Bali island, Maduri, Sunda, Visaya etc. are the other languages spoken in this area."
(2) Malaysian	:	Languages of black island group.
(3) Polynesian	:	Languages of Bahu Island Group: Samoa, Tonga, Toyamotu, Hawaii (Hawaii group of islands), and Maori, the main language of tribes settled in New Zealand. These languages are very close to Indonesian or Malayan family.
(4) Papuan	:	Spoken in Malaya and New Guinea group of islands in the midst of Polynesia.
(5) Australian	:	Languages spoken among the indigenous people in various areas of Australia-Dippil, Turukul, Odi-Odi, Kinki and Kamli-Rove.

Some scholars have questioned the theorising of W. Schmidt and his presentation of the vast area of Austric language family whereas others have praised his intensive and laborious effort. Although the vastness of the work does have the possibility of errors and wrong conclusions, yet no alternative language study has been made based upon which Schmidt's efforts can be assessed. Schmidt has separated Munda language from Dravidian language and has joined it with the Austro-Asiatic language family which not only presents the picture of the spread of Mundas in India but indicates also the route which the Mundas had taken to come to India.

Schmidt had connected Munda languages to Khmer language and especially to Mon and Khasi languages on the basis of linguistic facts. Schmidt had through various comparisons proved similarity among these languages through their pronunciation, syntax, grammar and vocabulary. In these languages Schmidt had found usage of 345 words of Mundari language. He also found through the study of their grammar that first person plural was being used independently as well as jointly in all these languages. The prepositional genitive was being used in the same way and the possessive suffix was also the same kind in all these languages. As regards pronunciation, Schmidt had found phonetical similarity in the pronunciation of their words. The application of suffix to root words and adding a nasal tone to make the words more emphatic are the simple characteristic of these languages.[1]

Other philologists have agreed with W. Schmidt in accepting that there is a close connection between Mon-Khmer and Munda languages based on various proofs. B. H. Hodgson and Sten Konow have not only supported the theories of Schmidt but also expressed approval of his naming these languages. They have also accepted Schmidt's grasp of a new language family. Renowned linguist T. Burrow and S. K. Chatterji have accepted the correctness of Schmidt's classification of Munda and Mon-Khmer language, but T. Burrow has also quipped that there are lots of proofs that Munda and Mon-Khmer languages are of the same family but Schmidt has not utilised them fully in his book.[2]

Famous linguist W. Von Hevesy has not only criticised the theorisings and conclusions of Schmidt but has also rejected them as being incorrect.[3] Hevesy has not accepted the connections between Munda and Mon-Khmer-languages. According to him, Munda languages are connected to Fino-Ugriyan group of languages. Hevesy has clarified that all the characteristics of Fino-Ugriyan language are surprisingly similar to Munda languages. Syntax, pronunciation, phonetics and grammar are similar. Hevesy had found out more than 1100 word-groups which were commonly used in Fino-Ugriyan and Munda languages. While remarking upon the structural non-conformity between the Mon-Khmer and Munda languages, Hevesy commented that apparently Schmidt had not paid attention to the structural difference between these two languages. Also he could not identify the suffixes and prefixes. If he had paid attention to the suffixes and prefixes of words then according to Hevesy, the common words identified by Schmidt would come down to 100 from 345.[4]

If Schmidt's theory is accepted to be correct, then it may be imagined that Mon-Khmer and Munda languages entered India through Burma. Hewitt has said that Mundas entered India through the north east.[5] Due to criticism of Schmidt's theory by Hevesy, it has come under a cloud of suspicion and it cannot therefore, be believable or unrepudiable. Hevesy, himself, however has not been successful in establishing the accuracy of his own theories, just like his preceding philologists who had been working on the semi-imaginative basis that Munda race had come from central Asia to India via the northern route. But Hevesy was certainly successful upto a certain point in disproving the theorisings of Schmidt. Schmidt has not only been criticised by Hevesy but also by T. A. Sebeok who said that the theory regarding Austro-Asiatic language family was constructed on unclear and weak bases. He laid stress on the requirement of solid bases to prove that Munda, Khasi and Mon-Khmer languages were of one family. Sebeok has alleged that the bases on which Schmidt did not include Japanese language (because of different position of genitive) in the Austric group, ignoring those same bases he had included Munda language in Austro-Asiatic language group.[6] If the parameters of Schmidt had been the same then Munda language would not have been of the Asiatic language family.

Linguist B. H. Hodgson has seriously worked on Indo-Tibetan languages. As per his conclusions, there are such tribes speaking Tibetan-Burmese language which can be found in between India and Tibet as well as in areas of Nepal and Himachal Pradesh whose language syntax, grammar and many words are akin to Munda languages. Hodgson has identified these similarities with Munda language among the hilly Kinnauri, Kanashi, Runckus, Runglai, Manchati, Bunan, Timan, Choudangli, Wyangsi, Dheemal, Dhamiya, Vayu, Jindar, Yakka, Khambu Limbu dialects.[7] Sten Konow who is a known scholar of Indo-Tibetan language has drawn attention to four important specialities of these hilly dialects which are found in equal measure in the Munda language:

(1) Wijacial counting method.

(2) The nature of singular dual and plural pronouns in joint or individual form.

(3) Transforming proper pronouns to verbs by adding suffixes.

(4) Merging the object with the verb

Accordingly Hodgson and Sten Konow have tried to prove that Munda or the connected tribes once lived in the Himalayan region. Especially, the dialect spoken in Kanwar, its grammar is absolutely similar to Mundari.

The above mentioned philologists by establishing the link of Munda language to the language spoken in Himachal Pradesh emphasise that the Munda tribe entered India through the routes of Nepal and Himachal Pradesh. Even now the ancestors of Khmer language speakers and Fino-Ugriyan language speakers are settled in South China. It is clear from these facts that Mundas did not enter India through the routes of Burma and Assam, instead they came to India via the route connecting India with Tibet. From Tibet the Mundas moved southward and came to Nepal and Himachal Pradesh whereas the Khasi tribe had entered India much earlier and had settled among those hills which are now known by this tribe's name. Since Mundas do not have the nature to stay at one place and engage in agriculture, and since they like to roam freely among the hills and forests, they moved down from Himachal Pradesh and Nepal to the Gangetic valley below.

Although the Chero tribe lived in the Gangetic valley and was well known as powerful Munda tribe, it forgot its language and culture due to the influence of Aryan language and culture. Similarly, the Bhuiya race which is a sub-race of the Munda race, has forgotten Munda language and culture due to either pressure, or voluntarily or else due to the development process. But the racial characteristics found in Mundas can still be found among the Chero and Bhuiya tribes. Thus, Cheros and Bhuiya tribes which are fully Mundas prove this fact that Mundas lived in the Gangetic plain and with the passage of time moved on to the south or southeast.

Schmidt, who advocates that the Mundas had entered India through the south-eastern route, was well-aware that some sub-races of Mundas lived in the Gangetic plain. Schmidt does not agree with the fact that Mundas came to the Gangetic plain from Himachal Pradesh or Nepal or Tibet route. Instead, opposite to this, he says that Munda tribe came to the Gangetic plain via the southeast and later on spread out. According to Schmidt, the Mundas living in the Gangetic plain are more progressive and developed than those roaming Mundas who had come from the east.

Schmidt had impressed the philologists so deeply that apart from accepting his theory about the Munda tribe having entered India through the south-east route, they did not evaluate any other route seriously. In recent times some scholars have found out not only the similarity between Munda language and the Indo-Tibetan languages but also found sameness in pure Tibetan language and Munda language.[1] Due to this, the belief that the Mundas came from Tibet to Himachal Pradesh and Nepal via the Himalayas gets strengthened.

It is not necessary that the number of Mundas entering India had been large. They came gradually over the centuries from Tibet, Himachal Pradesh and Nepal in small groups and kept on settling and in this way their numbers increased. After the recent studies, the number of those who advocate that Mundas have entered India through the Himalayan route, has increased remarkably. E. Dalton, H. B. Hodgson and J. H. Hutton found the arguments of Schmidt to be insufficient, but accepted the Himalayan route as backed by proof. Hutton has proved that along with Indo-Tibetan language Mon-Khmer languages are also connected with Munda language, and based on this, he has presented the theory of Mundas having entered India through two routes. According to Hutton, since in India two languages belonging to the Austric family are spoken, therefore there is a possibility that the Munda tribe entered India through two routes. This tribe moved from Central Asia and entered India through the western end of the Himalayas while some of them moved through the eastern edge of the Himalayas to enter India. In the first instance, the tribe spoke kolerian or Munda language, and in the second instance they spoke Mon-Khmer language which is limited to the Assam sector.[8]

The Proto-Australoid class of features can be clearly seen in the physical build of the Indian tribes, especially among the Kol or Munda and Mon-Khemer tribes which have resulted due to gradual intermingling with Negrito and Mongoloid races. Mundari language, which is a language of the Austro-Asiatic family, is spoken in one way or the other in the east of central India and south of Himalayas and Kashmir and in the eastern part of Nepal. According to Dr Sten Konnow, there once had been a time when Kols ruled over the entire north and south India. War with the Aryans and in the course of time due to coming into contact and intermingling, many words of common usage crept into Munda language from the language of the Aryans. Some scholars believe it to be also the influence of Austric language. Some Mundari words which found place in Aryan language are as follows:- names of birds, names of some trees, names of some parts of the human body as well as ordinary instruments. The word "shalmali" meaning cotton silk, "bal" meaning hair, "kambal" etc. are words of Mundari origin. "Karkpas"= "Kapas" (cotton), "tambul" = "paan" (betel leaf) are Mundari words inducted by the Aryans.

According to Professor Prylouski, sea-shells (Kowris) were used as coins in the coastal regions of India and China. This area comes within that of the Austro-Asiatic language family. The Sanskrit word "gandak" or "ganda" meaning four kowris, has been taken from the Austric language. Similarly, the meaning of "paan" in Bengali language is one anna or eighty kowris. The word "paan" is of Mundari language.

Thus, a comparative study of languages brings forth the conclusion that Munda tribe came from their place of origin to India from the estern side via two routes-one through Burma and Assam, and the second from Tibet through Himalayan routes to Himachal Pradesh. In the beginning, the southern route fixed by Schmidt had been accepted by most scholars but in recent studies the theory of Schmidt was not found to be convincing. This is the reason that scholars, basing their opinion on language, have accepted on evidentiary value that Mundas came to India not from the southern route but from Tibet through the routes of western part of Himalayas and Nepal. The finding of anthropologists that Mundas had inter-mingled with Mongolians confirms further about their entry through the Tibetan route.

Anthropological Proof

William Schmidt with the help of anthropologist E. Von Henleden and in support of his language based theory, tried to establish similarities of Munda, Khasi and South East other Mon-Khmer language speakers in their body build or hereditary racial characteristics and found out several racial resemblances.[9] Whatever racial similarities Schmidt had found out, he himself was not reassured. He knew that these small resemblances could not be the basis of strongly asserting racial connections as they were quite far from each other and not free from the blemishes of mingling. But due to this effort, Schmidt certainly came out with the conclusion that these races, although they were encircled by Mongols and Aryans, did not imbibe their racial elements. The aim of Schmidt was to prove that the Mundas came from the south-east. Since Mongols live north of Tibet or in the bordering area, Mongolian influence over the Mundas would prove their stay in Tibetan area and in this way their entry into India through the northeast would have been connected and then Schmidt's conclusions on his language based theory would stand refuted. Even then Schmidt and Akstedt have accepted the truth that in the physical build of the Mundas there are some Mongolian elements.

H. H. Risley and P. O. Boding, who have worked on the influence of Mongolians over Santhals, have rebuted the aforementioned conclusions of Schmidt and have clearly proved the presence of Mongolian racial signs among the Mundas. J. H. Hutton, on the basis of his study, has written that where the physical build is concerned, pre-Dravidian and proto-Australoid elements can be found to have been incorporated in these tribes.[10]

But the presence of Mongolian racial elements among the Mundas does not prove that the Munda tribe came to India through the eastern route of Assam-Burma. It has already been mentioned above that Mongols live in the northern border areas of Tibet, therefore, the opinion that the Mundas came through the Himalayan route via Himachal Pradesh and Nepal to India seems to be correct, especially where the possibility of intermingling with Mongols and the incorporation of their physical characteristics in the Mundas is concerned. Thus, when Mongolian characteristics are found among Mundas then there is a great possibility that the Munda tribe remained in the proximity of Mongols for a long time. Over a period of time, gradually, in small groups, they moved southward and reached Himachal Pradesh and Nepal from where the movement to the Indo-Gangetic plain seemed easy. Hewitt also argued in favour of the north-east route.[11]

G. T. Bowles while comparing the physical build of the Khasi and Mon-Khmer language speakers (who are spread over the hills of Assam and in Burma) with the Mundas, has concluded that the similar elements to prove their similarity are minimal and weak. In this way Bowles indirectly rejects the ideas that Mundas entered India through Burma and Assam route.[12] The available ideas can not be said to be proven evidence. There was a time when most scholars accepted the theory of Schmidt as correct and the South Eastern route for the Mundas to enter India was unanimously accepted. But over a period of time, the study of Tibetan Indian languages and with the finding of Mongolian racial characteristics among the Mundas as also language related study gave rise to theories that the Mundas came from South China to Tibet and again from Tibet (1) some spread through Nepal to the Gangetic plain and the hills of Assam, and (2) others moved from Tibet through the Himalayan route to Himachal Pradesh and again from there to the northwest of India and the Gangetic plain and spread.

Pre-historic Proof

Historians use the remains of pre-historic humans, their bones and skeletons and the various implements made by them in order to find about the evolution of the human race. On the bases of these skeletal remains and various implements, scholars have found out the roots of various races as also the pre-historic and proto-historic conditions of various countries. After comparative study of the evidential proofs of the human race lying scattered in various countries, scholars have come to the conclusion, through their help, about the portion of the earth from where human kind has spread Even in India based on the archaeological diggings from time to time and the materials obtained, many doubtful and incomplete facts have been resolved with their help, and enthusiasm has been ignited due to new querries coming up and new questions being asked.

In India, numerous stone implements of prehistoric and proto-historic importance have been found in Uttar Pradesh, Madhya Pradesh, Andhra Pradesh, Gujarat and Sindh. From this point of view, the archaeological remains and material found in Brahm-giri place of Mysore have special importance. This material has been identified as that of old stone-age which is much older than the Indus valley civilisation. The axes and implements which have been recovered from Indus and Tauhan rivers (Punjab) have historical value. These facts have been the basis on which efforts have been made to know the primitive conditions of India's pre-historic culture. About 50 (fifty) skeletal remains and other implements obtained from the Indus border, their study and analysis by scholars have made them conclude that Harappa and Mohenjodaro's extensive area is the mixture of cultural elements of ancient-Australian, Mediterranean and Armenian (Alwine) etc. different races. Most scholars have accepted that Mundas tribe came from the ancient Australian race-family, which is based on various proofs. The fact that Mundas lived in Indus valley is proved from the various axes and other implements as also skeletal remains of Munda races found in this place.

About half a century ago from now, R. Von Heen Geldern during his study of prehistoric facts of south-east Asia, found that the type of mason's tool for cutting and setting bricks used by Austro-Asiatic family, the same was used in Indo-China (Burma) and north-east and central India which have been the places of stay of Mundas. In this way, Heen Geldern concluded that since this tool has been recovered from those places which have been the area of Munda majority (Munda language belonging to the Austro-Asiatic language family), hence the entry of Mundas into India has been through this chain, which means, the Mundas came to India through the south-east. Geldern further says that since these Austro-Asiatic language speakers came to India much earlier than the Aryans, and the special type of mason's tool which appears to have been made prior to movement to south-east Asia, this fact proves that the Hindasians of Austronasions migrated to Hindasia at about 2000 BC. Geldern, like Schmidt, thinks that the nature of the make of the mason's tool and on the basis of language, Mon-khmer and Mundas are of the same origin. But A. H. Dani has repudiated the above mentioned conclusions. According to Dani, latest studies and archaeological finds do not prove the implements described by Heen Geldern to be connected to so called Austro-Asiatics. As per Dani, there is no sign in these implements and the situation in which they have been found in India, to prove that they had come in usage in 1500 B. C. or prior to the coming of the Aryans to India. Actually, neo-stone age culture had been prevalent in those mountainous areas centuries after Christ. Dani believes that the cut, chiseled, smooth and square implements and particularly those facetted stone adzes dug up in Indo-China and countries of the Mundas, these were offerings to the dead which were buried in the burial ground. They were just reproductions of those axes which were used in religious rituals. Dani has observed that the cut and chiseled stones, adzes, and those square implements which have been mentioned by Geldern, required special technique for making them. Square cut stones, smooth, and their corners are completely right angular which cannot be routinely rubbed into shape. In order to produce such fine implements, saws etc. must have been used as per some technique adopted or else they must have been copies of metallic implements. In this way Dani has concluded that the stone cut adzes of Indo-China and areas having greater Munda population are copies of copper axes which were used ritualistically during burials. According to Dani, these axes apparently existed in South China during 1300-1000 B.C. hence they came to India undoubtedly much later.[13]

Thus, the efforts of Heen-Geldern to prove that the Mundas had cultural affinity with people speaking Monkhmer language and the Munda tribe came to India through Burma and Assam, the facts on which these are based, they seem to be very weak and not above suspicion. Although Geldern's conclusions are similar to that of Schmidt, yet we have seen that the claim of Mundas reaching India from the north-east border and the Tibetan and Mongolian influence gets strengthened. The advent of Mundas into India in several groups from north-east Indo-Nepal and north-west India through the Himachal Pradesh route seems apparent. J. N. Hutton in his book has mentioned that on the basis that in India two dialects of the Austric language family are spoken, Mundas having entered India through two possible routes has been indicated. The Kols (Munda) speaking various Mundari languages,[14] came from the northeast Himalayan route. Since in India anthropometrical study of Mundas have thrown up certain Mongol racial characteristics in their build, hence based on language and archaeological findings, this thought that before coming to India Mundas lived in the Tibet-Mongol border, seems to be proven.

Traditional Proof

The ancient traditions of Mundas steeped in their religious verses, conduct, folk tales and folk songs throw light in their own way on their origin and development. Although tales more or less with some change are present in the whole of Munda society, their subject matter or provability of their narratives are not completely without doubt. They are also not supported by historical or archaeological evidences or else very thinly supported. The influence of Vedas and Puranas can be seen in their subject matters. The tales described in the Puranas, although they emerge in a new form after having gone through the churning of Munda religion and environment, yet their central point remains the same as in the Purana tales. In Hindu and Munda religions, the hypothesis regarding the coming of man in creation and the earth is nearly the same. In Munda religious verses, the story of final annihilation of the world is based on the story of Manu. In this story too, it is Manu who safely releases the fish swimming in the pot of water into the river and this fish at the time of the great annihilation rescues the boat of Manu with care and in this way, Manu sires Munda, Rora, Nanak and Sodto respectively, and the earth sees the advent of mankind again.[15]

Stories regarding the great flood and thereafter the creation of vegetation and creatures on this earth are also prevalent in the traditional lore of other places. Trigunayat's compilation of folk tales shows God and Lakshmi and in the tale quoted by S. C. Roy the Sungod Singbonga is shown as being anxious for creation. The earth or "otey dishum" – the way the turtle, scorpion, earthworm are used in the tales for its creation, it indicates the Hindu incorporations and their development minded thoughts wherein fish, tortoise wild boar and lion-man incarnations have been mentioned.

The Almighty Singbonga created many small and big birds as well as a particular bird called "Hur" which laid an egg. The first man and woman were born out of this egg. They became youths but were unaware of sexual relations. Singbonga taught the man and woman, who came to be called Tota Burhi and Tota Haram (naked woman-man ancestor), how to make rice wine (illie) after drinking which they became intoxicated. They gave birth to three sons- Munda, Nanak and Rora respectively. This incident happened in Azamgarh (a district of Uttar Pradesh).[16] After the death of their parents, the sons started moving about in the hills and forests of that land which thereby recorded the first footfalls of human beings. Which means, that only their parents had been the first human beings as well as the first woman and man to be born on this earth before them.

In this way, the study of the traditional folk tales and songs of Mundas reveal the fact that their verses and songs acknowledge India to be their place of origin. Their songs do not mention ever that the Mundas were born outside India, developed, and like gypsies lived a wandering life till they reached India. In their earlier and primary folk tales and songs, there is confirmation of many historical and ancient battles and incidents, but there is no mention of any incident happening outside India which could form the basis of trying to find out their outside connections. In the tales compiled by M. Topno, Lutkum Haram has been mentioned who was supposed to be the first ancestor of the Mundas and whose place of origin was some-where in central Asia. This tale has also been quoted by S. C. Roy.[17] According to this story, Lutkum Haram was the first ancestor of Horoko (Mundas). Lutkum's son was Hembo, Hembo's son was Kus, and Kus's son was Morih. Morih alongwith his animals and birds, entered northeast India from his place of birth Central Asia through the Tibetan route and went respectively to Bihar, Bundelkhand, Jabbalpur, Hoshangabad to Narmada shores, which means spread throughout north India. Morih's lineage included Korku, Marki, Santhal, Ho or Larka, Bhumij, Konko, Korva, Pinji and other similar tribes who were called Munda tribe.

They established a powerful kingdom and constructed forts, castles and ridges. They fought a great war in northwest India with the Aryans. Although after being defeated they kept on fleeing to the east and south, yet the Hindu epics and texts as also the Puranas record praise of their fighting acumen. These tribes had always made their presence felt in the history of India.

It has already been clarified that traditional folk-tales can reflect historical facts only in a very limited way but the birth of the first ancestor Lutkum of the Mundas in Central Asia and the descendants coming to India from the northeast through Tibet-Nepal is as per the conclusions of Hodgson, etc. based on language and anthropometry. We have seen that most historians, based on various evidences, have said that the ancestors of Mundas were born outside India in foreign lands. If all their opinions are presented in a concise manner, then some scholars believe that this tribe came from Madagascar, Lumuria (Prachhanna) island via Iran, Arab coast to India, while some others think that they came to India from the southeast route, but most of them opine that south China is their place of origin and from there these tribes came to Tibet-Mongolia border area, stayed there for some time after which in small groups they entered India via (a) Nepal and (b) Himachal Pradesh. Although this conclusion has been drawn based on the anthropological evidences and comparative study of language families, yet some Indian scholars argue that most of those tribes which speak Mundari, have come from the same roots and are the descendants of a common father. Their ancestors developed in the Aravalli-Vindhya hill ranges which had extended earlier to Kaimur mountain range and Sarguja and also till Chhotanagpur. This was because the implements and other archaeological finds are of stone-age era and this confirms the argument because in the hills of Manbhum and Chaibasa of Chhotanagpur, human beings dwelt in the stone-age. With the increase in the population in the forests and hills these people started setting down in the plains of northern Ganga wherefrom archaeological materials and the caves provide proof of the habitation of Munda tribe.

The advent of the Aryans and their impressive spread over the northwest resulted in the fleeing of the non-Aryans towards the east and southerly direction. Till the era of the epics, the empire of the Aryans had spread more or less over the whole of India. Indra Prastha of the Kauravas, Kanyakubj of the Panchals, the area between the Rang and Gandak rivers of the Koshals, and the area from Gandak on the west to Kushi in the east of the Vaidehas was the extent of the Aryan empire. Under these circumstances, for safety sake and their protection, the Mundas had to go east and southeast where the forests and hills gave stability to their lives. In the traditional lores wherein Azamgarh has been mentioned, where Singbonga started His Creation and the Hurbird's egg brought forth the first naked man-woman (Tota Haram and Tota Burhi) from whom the Mundas came, they maintain that landmark from where the Mundas started their historical journey to Chhotanagpur.

Apparently, it seems that the archaeological finds from Azamgarh and nearby areas of Ghazipur and Mirzapur confirm this fact that in this region, the Munda tribe had its influence. About 35 kilometers east of Azamgarh in Ghosi Pargana, there is a huge ruin of mud which as per local beliefs, it had once been the fort of the Asuras. We know that Asur is a common name used for indicating the Kols.

Fixing of Time Period

It is difficult to say when the tribe called by the name of Kol or Munda, migrated to India and spread all over, but there is evidence to prove that prior to coming of the Aryans and the creation of the Vedas, for thousands of years this tribe had held sway over the northwest of India. In the Mahabharat, it has been accepted that Asurs were born earlier than the Devtas (gods) and they were called elder brother of the Devtas.[18] In the Taiteriya Upanishad, it has been accepted that Asurs inhabited the earth and spread all over prior to the Aryans.[19] Although some European historians and philologists say that the Vedas were created in 1000 B.C. (Max Muller), in 1600 B.C. (Dunker), in 2400-2000 B.C. (B.C. Haag), yet latest proofs have prompted Prof. Jacobi to State that the Rigveda was created earlier than 4000 B.C. Now Count Bournesjema has studied those Bactrian manuscripts found in Kashmir which had been taken away to England by William Jones and which has been called Dabistan and which has a list of Mahabadrain kings who were Hindus.[20]

These kings ruled till 5600 B.C. therefore the Vedas must have been created prior to 6000 year B.C. Winternits is of the opinion that the Vedas were created not in the period 1200-500 B.C. but in the period 3000-800 B.C.[21] Definitely the Aryans must have been at the pinnacle of their civilisation at that time.[22] Famous philosopher and historian Alex Delmar in this context based upon believable evidence has proved that ancient Egypt, Syria, Greece and Italy were influenced by and indebted to Indian civilisation.[23] In this way, Aryan civilisation has been proved to be more ancient than Egypt, Syria and Greece. Under these circumstances, it will have to be accepted that Aryans entered India through the northwest much earlier than 19-20 centuries before Christ and in this context the time of the entry of Mundas into India can be fixed. The entry of Mundas in India through the Tibetan route via two routes of Himachal Pradesh and Nepal to Assam have been accepted,[24] in north-east India the Khasi and other tribes came to Assam in small groups through Tibet-Nepal route and settled there first and the area thereafter has been named after them.

Migration to Chhotanagpur

Schmidt, who opines that Mundas came to India from the south-east route, has stated that the Munda tribe spread from the east respectively to the north west and reached the Ganga Indus plain. Archaeological evidence has been obtained that vitually the Mundas came to India and settled in the northwest earlier than the Aryans entry into India.[25] Therefore Schmidt, who advocated that Mundas came to India from the south-east route, had to accept the fact about Mundas going to the north-west otherwise his own hypothesis regarding the south-east route would have been contradictory. Howsoever it be, Schmidt and the believers of his school accept this fact which Hodgson and Konnow, etc. scholars had presented. The difference is that Hodgson and Konnow acknowledge that Mundas had settled in India hundreds of years earlier than the Aryans and that the Mundas fled from the northwest to the southeast direction. On the contrary, Schmidt and his colleagues believe that Mundas came to India from the east, went to the northwest and thereafter fled to the southeast. But Schmidt is not able to provide any solid proof as to under what circumstances the Munda tribe spread to the northwest from the southeast. In fact, Schmidt's basic belief that Munda tribe entered India through the south-east is the unholy fruition of complete Dravidian linkage and surrender.

The two burial mounds which have been found in western India as mentioned by Regojin, out of them, one has been proved to be of pre-Aryan days while the other wherein iron and copper implements and utensils etc. have been found has been accepted by historians to belong to the period after Aryans came to India. Thus, the Munda tribe inhabited northwest India before the Aryans came, even when the Aryans came, and sometime even after the Aryans came. Thereafter the Munda tribe roamed in Punjab and from there to south-east Uttar Pradesh. There were two main reasons for the roaming of Mundas: first, attacked by enemies and after defeat fleeing the place, and second their racial behaviour of liking to live amid forests and hills, and clearing the forests for purpose of cultivation, and while cultivating changing their places. In the first instance, fleeing from northwest India to southeast direction and spreading due to various reasons as also their nature that they cannot remain in one place and do cultivation, but in the second instance which was of the era of Vedas and epics and the wars as a result that they came to be defeated all along, so they went to southeast in search of a more protected area and went on fleeing. Under these circumstances, the Munda tribes came to Azamgarh and settled there in security. The mounds built by them in the areas nearby to Azamgarh, that is, Ghosi, Ghazipur etc. still retain their memory. It seems that by the time Ram of the Ikshwaku clan started ruling, the Mundas had left Azamgarh because from local tradition it is known that at that time the Rajbhars inhabited that place and there is no mention of Shavars and Asurs[27] which are the other common names of Mundas. If according to Professor Hiren 26 Ram was of the 37th generation of the Ikshwaku clan or as per Sir William Jones' calculation Ram was of the 47th generation, then Ram's rule occurred in the year 2000 B.C. approximately.[28] Which means that the Mundas fled from Azamgarh about 3000 years B.C.

As per Munda usage, the Mundas came to the present day Banda district from Azamgarh and settled in some parts. They also spread to the hills of Kaimur, and thereafter to a wider area which in the ancient times was called Pulind country. In the Mahabharat,[29] the word Pulind is used to describe barbaric jungle races who were found in the deserts of Sindh and in the mountain ranges and forests of central India and which spread till the banks of the river Narmada.

In this way, the word Pulind in the Mahabharat denotes the Mundas. In Sanskrit literature Pulind and Shavar words have been used commonly for the Kols or Mundas.[30] In this way, Pulind country as it is used in Sanskrit literature to describe the place of habitation of Pulinds or Mundas confirms the places described in the Munda folk tales. In addition, such type of stones have been dug up in various places which resemble the "sasan" or burial stone used even now in Munda religion and custom.[31] About 75 km. away from Agra in the south-western bank of the Banganga many cut and polished, small and big pieces of stone have been found. Some of them are circular like those which the Munda tribals used for panchayats etc.[32] Munda tribe in those times used to be known as Kol. The aforementioned archaeological evidences apart, mention must be made of that famous village, about 15 km. south-west of Agra, which was known by the name of Koler and which was situated on the left bank of the Yamuna river from where now the Yamuna has since shifted. From the investigative report of Atkinson it is known that the original inhabitants of this whole area was that race which used to be called Koler.[33] It is not unnatural to conclude that the then koler were the descendants of the ancient Kols. The finding of the aforementioned stone pieces proves the conclusiveness and accuracy of this conclusion.

It is difficult to say for how many years the Munda tribe lived in this area, but the Mahabharat mentions that in the war between the Kauravs and Pandavas, the Mundas sided with the Kauravas in the Kurukshetra war. Sanjay has described the marshalling of the Kaurav army in the battlefield. In his description he has said that Munda alongwith Karushas, Winkajas and Keshiwrittas are in the left wing of the army array,[34] and their leader is Brihadbal. Two facts emerge out of this description, first that during the Kurukshetra war of Mahabharat, the Munda people lived in the nearby forest and mountainous areas, and second, that this race was famous as a brave martial race. Satyaki has compared the Mundas with demons who had been killed by Indra, and like Indra Satyaki proclaims proudly in the battle field that he will kill the Mundas.[35] Clearly, a brave warrior like Satyaki acknowledged the bravery and military prowess of the Mundas. Additionally, the Mundas opting to fight on the side of the Kauravas proves this fact that they opposed the Pandavas especially Krishna who had slain many giants and who had allegedly tried to destroy the primitive races.

Satyaki's Statement of "demonlike Mundas" brings another fact to the fore that in the "Parabhav" era of Treta Yug, although Mundas were not called demons, yet in wars they were given the adjective of demon. The meaning thereby is that though in bravery the Mundas equalled demons, yet they were not so cruel as the demons. At the time of entry into India the primitive races also known as Mundas were wandering tribes. By the time Treta Yug and the interregnum period before Kalyug came, the Mundas got distributed in many groups or sub-tribes and this division went on while they settled in various mountains, caves and forests. The habitation place, geographical environment, and circumstances of life, their contradictions influenced the life style of the Mundas and accordingly different kinds of culture developed. Till the time of the Vedic era, although Kol, Bhil, Musahar were addressed separately which came to be described in the story of King Wane,[36] but springing from the same root their racial separateness is not proved. While studying this, it was found that Pulind, Shavar, Kol, in their extensive meaning are the common names of several tribes. In the Katha Sarit Sagar of Somdev, (written in sixth century A.D.) which is based on epic stories of merit and praise, the words Pulind and Shavar have been used freely to denote Bhil king Vindhya Ketu. It becomes clear from this that they are sub-tribes of Kol (Munda). According to Atkinson's study, there are many tribes residing in the northwest States and hills of Vindhyas who call themselves of "Wane lineage" and Bhils are also among them.[37] In the same way, in the "Chronicle of Unnao," the Bhar and Chero tribes have more or less been accepted as one race and the Cheros have been described as a branch of the Kols.

It is necessary to clarify that the Munda tribe living in Chhotanagpur whose study is desirable has for thousands of years been divided and subdivided resulting in the present form. Distressed by the invasion of the Aryans, some Munda or Kol races kept on fleeing to the mountains and forests for safety. As and when the Aryans spread from north-west India to central and eastern India, the tribes accordingly created routes for their safety. Many tribes among the Mundas gradually forgot their language, culture and religion due to the pressure and influence of the Aryans. They became Hindus and declared themselves to be connected to Rajput lineage, so much so that these races started wearing the sacred thread. Chero and Kharwar races come in this category and although the basic racial qualities of the Mundas can be found in them, they declared themselves to be Hindus. In this way, the Mundas having reached Chotanagpur after much roaming and facing blows and counter-blows of change over hundreds of years pertaining to their language, culture and religion gradually expanded with some change into Santhal, Ho, Korwa, Khariya, Asur, Birhor, Bhumij and Munda tribes which can also be seen now. Therefore, it is difficult to find Mundas in the form of brave and fighting race as described in the Mahabharat, although in Chhotanagpur the Mundas are self-respectful, fearless and inclined to fight for their lawful rights.

After being defeated in the battlefield of Kurukshetra, the Mundas went to the northeast of India and via Panchal reached Kaushal and from there to Gorakhpur. Two ancient remnants on the Gorakhpur-Pipraich road, 6 km. and 12 km. respectively from Gorakhpur, prove that the Mundas had lived there once upon a time. They are the remains of Betalgarh and Maula Kol.[38] The Mundas went from Gorakhpur to Baliya and thereafter crossed the River Gandak to enter the Mithila region of north Bihar. There are the remains of an ancient fort in the northern part of river Ganga, exactly north of the Karamnasa River which is connected with the Mundas. The presence of Mundas in Bhagalpur is proved by the "Chai-Champa" of Champapuri which is mentioned in the folk tales of the Santhals. The village called Kolwarang or Kahalgaon east of Bhagalpur indicates the habitation of Kols. It is said that Rishi Durvasha had his hut here. About 25 kms. away from Gaya is Koch village in which remnants of two mounds built by Kol rajas have been found[39] and which proves that the Kols gradually were shrinking nearer to Chhotanagpur. There is a big village called Kabur south of Koch where a huge fort was built of mud. The ruins of this fort can still be seen there surrounding which, on all four sides, are big mounds which are a part of Munda culture. In the historical description of Gaya district these have been described as being built by Kol Rajas.[40] According to Munda tradition, the name of Rajgarh has been mentioned which is actually Rajgiri capital of Magadh country. When Fa Hien visited this place in fourth century AD, he had found an extensive garland of five mountain ranges around this city which was convenient for the habitation of the Mundas but he had found the city to be deserted. In the description of Huen Tsang, the mention of Asur cave in Yastivan and Peepal Cave behind the assembly of Jarasandh, there are evidences that the Kol tribe used to stay in those places.

District Shahabad is the storehouse of many such ancient implements which prove that area to have been the kingdom of Chero kings and the habitation of Cheros. Going east of Gaya, the Cheros, who thought themselves to be the best among the Mundas, not only proclaimed their right over this area but also embraced Hindu religion and built temples out of which three famous ones are : (1) Dev Chandi temple of Benaras. (2) Temple of Dev Munda at Mooga, (3) Temple of Dev Warsad at Markandeya.[41] Gradually, from time to time, they separated from their own race and entered into matrimony with the higher castes of Hindus and cut off connection with those Kols or Mundas who were snobbish and arrogant and who were still following the ancient tradition of worship of ghosts and spirits and who were not willing to tolerate the insulting behaviour of one part of their race i.e. the Cheros. Therefore, it appears that when living in Karush country (Shahabad) became intolerably painful, the Mundas went towards the River Sone and their eyes fell on Rohtasgarh whose natural surroundings were positive from the point of view of safety and which has always given shelter to tortured races.

Rohtasgarh, known in Munda tradition as Ruidasgarh, could however not become the permanent home of the Mundas. It is difficult to say as to how many days the Mundas could stay in the protected hills and forests of Rohtasgarh. In Munda and Santhal folk lore there is mention of attack by another tribe called Kharwar whose chief Madho Das had requested for the hand of a Munda maiden for his son but which had not been accepted by the Mundas. Enraged, the Kharwar chief Madho Das attacked the Mundas at night to avenge the insult, and having been defeated due to unpreparedness, the Mundas fled to the hills of Binji (Vindhya).

The Kharwars confirm the incident that during their migration from Khairagarh to the south they had to face Kol, Chero and Asur as well as Agoriya tribes whom they defeated and thereafter established their suzerainty and domain over the Kaimur hills. The defeated Kol race, including Korva, Asur and Birjiya, followed the bank of the Koel river and reached Palamau and western portion of Ranchi and fanned out in the area. The Koel river emanates from the plateau of mid-Ranchi and crosses Palamau, thereafter meeting the Sone River near Rohtas. The second group from Rohtasgarh comprised of Munda and Santhal tribes. They crossed the Sone river and followed the route in the south-eastern direction which becomes the boundary line between Palamau and Ranchi district as well as Hazaribagh district, and reached Omdanda. This was the first stoppage of the Mundas during the course of their living in Chhotanagpur. After having lived together for sometime, the Santhals and Mundas went different ways. The Santhals left Chhotanagpur, crossed the Damodar river and reached Shikharbhum (Hazaribagh). After staying temporarily in Shikharbhum for some days, they followed the course of the Damodar river and entered Manbhum and Santhal Pargana, whereas the Mundas upon entering Ranchi found that prior to them the Asurs had established themselves and were smelting iron. The Mundas fought with the Asurs, and the defeated Asurs fled to the western part of Ranchi where they settled down. In this way, after thousands of years of roaming, the Mundas found that place in the thick forests of Chhotanagpur which had every convenience and was safe from the invasions of outsiders.

Oraon Tribe Kurukh and Oraon Words – their Origin

The tribe having the most populous presence in the western part of Chhotanagpur plateau calls itself Kurukh but to the public at large and in government parlance this tribe is called Oraon. The word Kurukh has originated from the mythological king Karash who is said to have established Karush country from Rewa to Magadh of Bihar.[42] In this country, Shahabad was the central point.[43] According to E. A. Gait, the word kurukh is a root word of ancient Dravid language the meaning of which is "man/human being" and this word has been sourced to Karakh king whom the Oraons accept as their originator the same way Manu is supposed to have originated "manav/humankind,"[44] Some scholars are of the opinion that the main occupation of the Oraon tribe was agriculture, therefore they were agriculturists= cultivation and agriculture related tools and knowledge were more developed in them. Accordingly, the name Kurukh for the Oraon tribe is relevant in numerous ways. The first relevance is in the context of their traditional history which spells out that they were inhabitants of Kurukh country due to which they came to be called Karush or Kurukh. The second relevance is related to their traditional progenitor king Karush in the same way that manav (man) came from Manu. Similarly, Kurukh (man) came from Karash. The third relevance is related to their profession being cultivation. Some scholars think that their Hindu neighbours started calling them *krishak* (farmer) which later on changed its pronunciation. The "sha" became "kha" and "Ra" became "da" due to nasal tone of the Oraons, as a result of which the word finally became Kurukh.

Rev. Dr F. Hun in his introduction to "Kurukh Grammar" has equated kurukh word with "Horo" of the Mundas whose meaning is man/human being.[45] Dr Hun finds the word a derivative of Dravid Scythian origin word "Kuruk". Dalton has held that kurukh word is a degeneration of "Konkan." As per his information, the original place of habitation of this tribe was Konkan.[46] Dr Grierson has said that Kurukh is a degenerative of Dravid word "karug." The meaning of karug is kite and this bird is the totem of one of the lineages of the Oraons. According to Dr Grierson, it is due to this totem that the Oraon tribe gradually came to be identified by the name of kurukh. Professor Braj Behari Kumar in his Kurukh dictionary has straightaway said that the meaning of Kurukh is Oraon.[48] In India, persons speaking Kurukh language is 1,14,084[49] in number. Those speaking the Kurukh language can be found apart from Bihar, in Madhya Pradesh, West Bengal, Odisha, and some in Assam and Tripura. As per Professor Kumar, the other names of Kurukh language is Dhangri, kisani, kisan-Kurukh, etc.

In the Hindi language, the word *dhangar* is used to denote nearly every primitive race. Actually, the Oraons and other tribal people are industrious and they have achieved a lot of fame for being labourers. Due to their capacity for doing labour, the outsiders started addressing them as dhangar.[50] Since the Hindus firstly came in contact with the Oraons as hardworking labourers, therefore at the initial stage the Oraons came to be called as dhangars. With the passage of time, they came to be known as dhangars, the mention of which Grierson [51] has made in his survey and Professor Kumar in his Kurukh Kosh. Just like "dhangri," Kurukh language in some areas especially in Orissa is known as "kisani" language because in that area the Oraon tribe is chiefly connected to agriculture. In east of Ranchi, i.e. Manbhum border, the resident Oraons are adept in raising mud walls, dykes and mud dividers in fields, and as per this profession they are known as "modi." Since their number is large, hence modi race has been given the status of sub-race of Oraons. The Oraons found in Tripura, Assam, West Bengal and Darbhanga etc. places are primarily labour class and have settled there in search of livelihood. They have taken their language, their religion, their culture alongwith them and by any means have maintained connection with the Oraons of Chhotanagpur.

The name of Oraon is more prevalent compared to Kurukh. According to Dalton, Hindus gave the name of Oraon to this tribe because of their of not staying long at one place. Since they stayed at one place for sometime and thereafter were seen in another place they were described as flying or "udan" or "uran," hence this tribe came to be called Uraon tribe.[52] S. C. Roy gives another reason for the degenerative word "Oraon." According to him, some important Oraons told him that this name was given by Hindus to show them in a bad light. Hindus had thought that they were the descendants of Ravan hence began calling them "Ravanpoot." With the passage of time, the word "poot" got dropped, and the word of address "oh" got dropped, and the word of address "oh" got joined to "Ravan" hence "Oh Ravan" which later on became Oraon.[53] In this way, the name of Oraon was given by Hindus and outsiders to the Kurukh tribe which was more derogatory in nature than praiseworthy. Members of this tribe rarely address themselves as Oraon. In the word Kurukh, they find a respectable history of their own, hence they give preference to being addressed as Kurukh compared to Oraon. The name of Oraon by now is universally prevalent and in government work, the name Oraon is used to denote them. Some Oraons have indicated a lore in their religious tradition to give a respectable justification of the name Oraon. According to them, a muni (meditating holy man) was deeply meditating in the forest. Day and night for months together he remained in meditation without food and water on the same seat, as a result of which termites built mud mound to cover his body and on that mound creepers began growing. Time passed. One day a wood cutter thought the whole mound to be the stem of a tree full of roots. He hit the mound with his axe and tried to take off the mud. He was extremely astonished to find a living man in front of him. The man got up in great anger due to which the thorn of a creeper which had already stung his chest went deeper inside and broke, resulting in bleeding from his chest. The muni did not find it proper to let his blood drop to the ground, hence he took a leaf of korkota, made it into a cone and collected the blood in it. He thereafter kept the leaf cone in the nearby shade and started going for his morning ablutions. Right at that time a brother and a sister sprang up from the blood and stopping the muni prayed to him, asking him the source for their livelihood. The muni replied, "Cut the forest and start cultivation, your store house will be full of grains. If any needy person comes, then give him alms freely." In this way the brother and sister duo, originating from the muni's chest-blood, became the progenitors of the Oraons who had got the command to take up cultivation as a means of livelihood. Since they had come from the breast or "ur" of the muni, they were called Oraon. In the initial days these people were called thakur and they put on the sacred thread but due to their degenerative food and drinking habits they became degenerated. From this traditional tale, two facts are clearly revealed that the Oraons have come from a holy man and their main profession was cultivation, at first this race used to be respected as thakur but over a period of time they degenerated due to degenerative food habits.

Place of Origin and Migration to Chhotanagpur

The scholars are of different opinions regarding the place of origin of Oraons. It has become clear that they are of pre-Dravidian origin and their early life had been spent in the southern part of India. But it is difficult to trace from which part of the country or outside the country they came to south India or whether they originated in the forests and hills and caves of south India. From traditional and religious stories, it appears that they originated from south India. In their lores, apart from Mecca-Medina, there is no mention of any foreign place. But how they are connected to Mecca-Medina or there has been an interpolation in the story with the passage of time, or whether this race came from the Mediterranean sea via Arabian coastal areas through Mecca-Medina to India, these questions are shrouded in mystery and cannot be answered due to the extinction of any solution in the darkness of times gone by. There is no historical evidence available which would guide in the search of place of origin of their ancestors. The anthropologists are of the opinion that in India no kind of man has evolved from any apeman. Man has come to India from outside. But R. K. Choudhary is of the opinion that in certain caves of Madhya Pradesh, the remnants of ancient humans indicate that in South India, about 40 thousand years ago from now, homo sapiens (humans) used to live and their living habits were akin to those of stone-age humans.[54] In South India, ancient stone-age tools/weapons have been recovered from several places.

R. C. Majumdar has stated that several implements of the ice age and study of the stone layers of the valleys of the Shivalik hills show that in India man first appeared in South India in the last Phase of the first Ice Age, [55] and from here in the second Ice-age (five lakh years ago) in the earlier years they went to north India in the Punjab, Jammu, Jhelum and Indus rivers and settled in between them. Their special characteristics were living in caves, living on wild animals and fruits and for hunting, to use stones or weapons made of stone. But were they the ancestors of the Dravidians? There is no source/ evidence to prove that these so-called homo-sapiens or early man whom historians have found to be the first humans in South India had any Dravidian racial distinctions. In the southern part of Prayag is Meja tehsil from where the archaeological finds tell us of the Pleistocene age.[56]

There, evidence of the development of man from pre-stone age to neo-stone Age have been found. This evidence sheds light on stone age civilisation.

In ancient stone age man was fully dependent on nature for his means of livelihood, whereas in the neo-stone Age man took the help of nature to sow seeds and started growing crops. Whatever was the shortcoming in this age was made up in the metal age and man began to be seen in the development of his civilisation. The use of metals was not uniform in various parts of India. As per available evidence, in north India after the Copper age came the Iron age whereas in south India the Iron age straight away succeeded the Stone age. As per Wheeler, after about a hundred years from the time of Alexander, the Iron age culture had already encroached upon the ancient mainly Stone-age people of the mountainous valley of the south. From Nagpur to Wraine Ganga, the whole of south India is full of red and black implements and utensils. In the first centuries before Christ, the civilisation of Dravidian language speaking people had become-developed in the south. In northwest India, from the archaeological finds of 1920 and in later years, the Indus valley civilisation was unearthed which has been named by archaeologists to be Dravidian civilisation.

Archaeologists Sri Madho Swarup Vats and Sri Dayaram Sahni in 1920 dug up the city of Harappa. This city at that time was situated in Multan district of western India. Thereafter, in the year 1922 another archaeologist Dr Rakhal Das Banerji dug up the second city called Mohanjodaro which was about 600 kms. away from Harappa. About 120 km. away from here in the south-west was Chanduharo which was dug up on the direction of Ernest Melay in 1925. From these three places about 50 human skeletons were dug up whose scientific examination was done by Colonel Seaton and Dr B. S. Guha. They concluded that three of the skeletal remains from Mohenjodaro were of Proto-Australoid origin, some were of Mongolian origin, but most of them had racial characteristics of Mediterranean sea area. The Mediterranean area race has connections with the Dravidians.[57] Works of Dr D. N. Majumdar, Sir Eriel Stone, H. Hargreaves, Pigot, Wheeler, Amlanand Ghosh and Brajwasi Lal are mentionable as main investigator archaeologists, anthropologists and historians of this civilisation.[58] According to R. C. Majumdar, such few skeletal remains cannot form basis of this area's civilisation to be Dravidian origin civilisation as has been criticised by some scholars, but most scholars accept that Indus Valley Civilisation was progenited by the Mediterranean race of Dravidians.[59]

According to Tully, Sumer and Sindhu (India) civilisations have come from the same source. Seeing the similarity between the Sumer and Indus valley civilisations, Garden Childe has stated that there was racial connection between the progenitors of both civilisations. Dr B. S. Guha agrees with the opinion of Garden Childe. As per Hall, Sumer and Dravidian races were one race. He believed that the Dravidian races went from India to Sumer and settled there. The opinions of Hall and the aforementioned scholars have been confirmed by philologists who have studied the Brahui language of

Baluchistan. Brahui language is very close to the Kurukh language spoken by the Oraons. Just like Kurukh language, the root language of Brahui is Kannada language which is a prominent branch of Dravidian languages.[60] The Brahui language spoken in Brahui area of Baluchistan is nearly the same as Kurukh and shows the presence and influence of Dravidians in Baluchistan, although anthropologically there is no connection/ similarity between Dravidians and Brahuis. Thus, the similarity between Sumerian and Indus valley civilisations as also the similarities between Kurukh and Brahui languages give forth strong evidence to the historians that Oraons came from the Mediterranean areas and help them in tracing their route and entry to India.

According to the study made by Thurston, the Dravidians residing in south India have racial characteristics of wide nose, long head, black thick hair (at times curly but not woolly curly) and short height which approximately indicate negrito racial characteristics. In the Andaman Islands group, the tribals have woolly hair which is a negrito racial characteristic yet in south India the Dravidians living there do not have this negrito racial characteristic.[61] As per study done by anthropologists of human skeletons, some characteristics of the race can be known, but study of the complete body will show characteristics of other races due to inter-mingling. On the western coast of south India, the residing Dravidians have heads whose construction is flat and small which indicates influence of Mongolian race. The excavations of Mohenjodaro and Harappa and the skeletons recovered from there have already made known that although Indus Valley civilisation was Dravidian civilisation, yet Austroloids and Mongols have their contribution also. Marital connections naturally pass on racial qualities. Due to the influence of Mongols on the Dravidians of northwest coast, some historians have said that Mongols came from the northwest Himalayan route to the sea and following the sea coast the Mongols reached south India on the western coast and they came for trade, too, thereafter intermingling with the Dravidians. In the same way, intermingling among Mundas and Oraons and the same type of geographical and environmental influence gradually did away with their original racial features and the succeeding generation had the same type of racial characteristics. Resultantly, it was difficult under normal viewpoint to make any distinction between these tribes. This is the reason why Dr Grierson in his study of these tribes later on concluded that Oraons are a type of Munda race. But A. C. Hayden, S. S. Sarkar and P. S. Basu who are modern anthropologists have after detailed analysis from scientific point of view clearly given proof that these two, Munda and Oraon tribes, have different racial features and their lineage is absolutely different from each other.

The Main Principle Regarding Place of Origin

Researches regarding the place of origin of Dravidians has given forth some new facts and principles in the last fifty years due to which there are question marks over the old beliefs. Ever since the philologists have come to know that the Brahui language of Baluchistan is a language of the Dravidian family, the hypothesis regarding place of origin of the Dravidians got extended. The main prevalent principles of place of origin of the Dravidians are as follows:

Dravidian versus Tamil

Bishop Caldwell has firstly tried to clarify the identity of south Indians through the Dravidian and Tamil words. Bishop Caldwell was the first person to call South Indians by the name of Dravidians.[62] Prior to this, they used to be known as Tamils. Tamil designation should have been only for Tamil language speakers, but this words fame and pervasiveness included all the southern languages and their speakers, namely, Telegu, Kannada, Malayalam etc. and that is how all these languages came within the fold of Tamil and the whole of South India came to be called Tamil Pradesh (State). Caldwell limited Tamil in its actual domain, and gave the name of Dravidian to south Indians which was accepted by all.

The basis for Caldwell to reveal the term Dravidian were the Sanskrit books which had identified this area to be Dravidian, although in the Sanskrit books the word Dravidian is used only for south Indian Brahmins, not for non-Brahmins. For example, "Panch dravida" word was used. Shankaracharya has called Gyan Sambandh (connected to knowledge) which means "Gyanwan" (a knowledgeable person) which means Brahmin who has been called "Dravidasisu". In Mumbai, there are many south Indian working people who are called Dravidian the actual meaning being Dravidian Brahmin. In this way the word Dravidian became fundamental to describe Dravidian Brahmins with the Sanskrit writers. With the passage of time, according to Caldwell, the name of Dravidian not only was used for non-Brahmins but also for geographically limited South India which within its limits came to be called as Dravidian. Although Tamil and Dravidian words seem separate from each other, but in origin they are very close to each other and nearly of the same meaning.

Mongolian Principle

Kanaksa Bhai Pillai is the originator of this principle. According to him, the place of origin of Dravidians is Mongolia. They came to India via Tibet and Nepal and settled all over in the whole of Bengal. Then again from Bengal they departed for the south. Since their departure for the south was from Tamralipti port, hence on reaching south India and Lanka, they came to be called Tamil. Those who have been named as yaksh in Sanskrit literature, they were Dravidians. The hypotheses regarding arts, architecture and vanity of women are about the same amongst the inhabitants of Nepal and Malabar. According to Kanaksa Bhai, the race which migrated for the first time to south India was called Marar and later on was called "Kosar". Their language was Vijit and Vijayi which meant a mixture of Naga and Dravidian languages, traces of which can still be found in the Malayalam language and which used to be spoken by ancient Dravidians. Malayalam language is very much akin to Manchu and the old languages of north Asia.

But Kanaksa Bhai Pillai's Mongolian theory has been bitterly criticised. Sir Herbert Rislay has declared the Mongolian theory as unbelievable because the complexion of Dravidians is dark and in their physical construction their head is elongated whereas in the Mongolian race their complexion is yellow and their head and forehead is wide. On this basis it is not logical to state that the Dravidians have originated from across the Himalayas from the Mongolians. Philologists say that in their view, the Tamil of Tamralipti, Mrajmar of Maras and Kushan of Kosar do not fit in the linguistic mode, and to connect Dravidians to yakshas is sheer fancy. The similarity of architecture and some Dravidian customs occurring in Malaya and Nepal may be due to one reason, one incident or due to the influence when the Dravidian Empire spread throughout north India and Nepal had also come within its sphere. The knowledge of Kanaksa Pillai regarding the Kushan and Maurya Kings seems to be incomplete on the basis of which his conclusion can merely be said to be a guess. In this way the Mongolian theory of migration of Dravidians as envisaged by Kanaksa Bhai Pillai is not proved to be logical.

The Central Asia Theory

Bishop Caldwell's mooted theory of Central Asia is fundamentally dependent on similarity of language and is fully one sided. Caldwell has taken two main races of Central Asia "Scythian" and "Turani" and has compared their language to Dravidian language and has found out many similarities. Actually Phoenician, Turkish, Tungstian, Scythian belong to same language group and several of their grammatical rules are also nearly the same. Caldwell finds similarity in Scythian- Indo European- Dravidian languages also and in order to prove his theory, he presents the translation of "Wehistan Tablets."

In this book, portions of Scythian, idioms and social dictums are like those of Dravidians. Caldwell has mentioned nine similarities of language-related grammar and in this way has tried to establish a connection between Dravidian and Scythian languages. Although he admits that there are shortcomings in establishing similarity between these two languages, but their similarities outweigh these shortcomings. He is of the opinion that Dravidian language has not only been influenced by the Scythian language group, but also by other Indo Aryan-languages, but the Scythian influence has been the maximum, hence Caldwell thinks that Dravidian language belongs to the Scythian language group.

Caldwell also takes the basis of Brahui language of Baluchistan to determine the migration route of the Dravidians from Central Asia. The Brahui dialect is very much akin to the Kannada language of the Dravidian group. Now how did the Kannada language of the south reach the far-off northwestern part ? Caldwell gives the argument that while migrating to India from Central Asia, the Dravidians must have stopped over in Brahui sector of Baluchistan and entered India through the northwest route. The Brahui people also shifted with this migratory group and settled in the south where gradually they developed Kannada language.

Caldwell's aforementioned opinion except for language, ignores the other sides like, for example, the side of the anthropologists. The Brahui people are fair-complexioned with long pointed noses and of more than average height whereas the Dravidians are just the opposite because they are dark complexioned, have short height and have wide flaring noses. Thus, racially, there is no similarity between the Brahuis and the Dravidians. Apparently, the Brahui dialect influenced Dravidians during their stay there which was a result of their staying nearby to them.

Philologically as well as racially, both studies do not help the theory of Central Asia or Scythian Turanian theory either. The construction of the head of the Dravidian (dalicocephalic), somewhat depressed cheekbones, black and thick hair, black shiny eyes, complexion being dark, slightly lighter than the 28th colour of "bourse" are clearly the physical features of Dravidians which can never be of Mongolian origin. As regards literature and civilisation, Dravidian literature is a rich literature and they are higher on the ladder of civilisation, whereas in the language of Turanians there is no expression of emotions. In the ladder of civilisation, falling in the lower rungs, this race has got 20 similar words for the word "murder" in their language but they do not have any word to denote sympathy and love. Really, such a race as the Turanians cannot be the ancestors of Dravidians.

The Semetic Theory

According to the Semetic theory, the origin of the Dravidians is thought to be in Arabia, Egypt and Asia Minor. The basis for this theory is the development of an institution called "marumakkantyam." In this institution there is a provision for worship of the female. This kind of custom is prevalent in Arabia, Egypt and ancient Greece. According to the advocates of the Semetic theory, this kind of special provision can develop only amidst those who live side by side in one place hence the place of origin of the Dravidians is among the Semitic family group.

The critics of this theory opine that the only basis of "Marumakkantayam" cannot be a solid proof of the conclusion. The Dravidians are nearer to the Aryans than the Semetic family group, especially on the basis of physical features and characteristics. The Dravidian language is also nearer to the Aryan language. Female worship and matriarchal family structure is universal- it is not a pledge of only the Semetic group.

Mesopotamian Theory

Col. Holdich is the advocate of this theory. According to Holdich, Dravidians originated from Mesopotamia. From there they followed the Makran coastal route to India. Some of them settled down on the coastal route for centuries. They built their homes there and buried the bones of their dead in earthenware utensils. Some of them went and settled in the bordering area which is behind the Kirtahar Hills. Over here the Brahuis, who were of Turkish-Mongolian race, attacked the Dravidians and defeated them. They forced them to vacate the place and flee. Within this period, the intermingling of the Brahuis with the Dravidians resulted in the Brahuis keeping the Dravidian language with themselves but the other qualities of the Dravidians they could not imbibe. The Dravidians entered India through the western route. The Brahuis were of Mongol race.

The theorists have tried to prove that the Dravidians originally resided on that route on the basis of the similarity of Brahui language or that they were connected to the Baluchi area, but this evidence which is elastic, cannot be accepted to be conclusive proof.

The Theory about Egypt

The advocate of this theory is Bruce-Foot who has done praiseworthy excavation work in south India. He has found that when the Dravidians were passing through the neo-stone age, Egypt was in the copper age and with the help of copper axes it had defeated the neighbouring kingdoms. Bruce-Foot is of the opinion that prior to invention of copper axes, one group of Egyptians broke away and went east. This group entered India from the north-western side and went to south India where they settled there and came to be known as Dravidians. The ancient Egyptians are of Dravidian race. They definitely do not appear to be of Mongol race and neither were they of that brown race the mention of which Professor Elliott Smith makes in his book "Ancient Egyptian."

Professor Smith is of the opinion that ancient Egypt gave the sun-culture to the world. According to him, wherever the Egyptian sailors went, they took along with them their own culture. In this way, in India as well as in many coastal countries as also America, the elements of their culture can be found. Professor Perry also endorses the opinions of Elliott Smith. As per Perry, the ancient cultures of Sumer and Eelam have their roots in Egyptian culture. Professor Elliott is of the opinion that this culture spread in between 300-800 B.C. whereas according to Perry, this happened 2600 years B.C.

Although the antiquity of Egyptian culture and its influence over other countries cannot be denied, but to accept that the spread of this culture took place 800 years before Christ cannot be taken as logical by any historian because the time given is too near. F. G. Richard while commenting on the aforementioned theory has said that it was just not possible for some Egyptian sailors to spread Egyptian culture in the coastal areas of the world. According to F. G. Richard, this is an universal development process that when the culture of any race develops, then many elements hidden or apparent become active in this process. This is a highly complicated procedure. Therefore, just to think on the basis of one element that the place of origin of the Dravidians is ancient Egypt is not logical.

The Mediterranean Theory

According to this theory, the place of origin of the Dravidian race was the Mediterranean Sea area. According to anthropologists, the Dravidian race sprang from the merging of the Aegean or Proto-Australoid of the Mediterranean sea area, and the Armenide races of West Asia minor. According to J. F. Richards, there are innumerable similarities between the Indian Dravidians and the Mediterranean inhabitants. These Dravidians left the Mediterranean area and gradually moving through the coastal routes of the western countries, came to Baluchistan and Afghanistan and thereafter through the northwest opening they entered India. In the opinion of Dr Slatter, one branch of the Mediterranean sea race came to India via Mesopotamia and Baluchistan. At this time, they enriched the Dravidian race and culture. This was at a time when Sumerian civilisation had not come into existence. From western India they spread through out India and they ruled most parts of India for a pretty long time. Herbert Rislay thinks that the Dravidians are the most ancient race of India. According to him the races that entered India, namely, Aryans, Mongols, Turks, Scythians etc. merged with the Dravidians, and became responsible for the birth of Aryan-Dravidian, Mongol-Dravidian, Turk-Dravidian, Scythian-Dravidian etc. races in the population who have Dravidian origins and mixed racial features.

If the conclusion of the anthropologists are accepted that the Dravidians came from the Mediterrenean sea via Mesopotamia, Baluchistan to India, then undoubtedly the question arises that at that time whether human beings had been there in India and if so, then what kind. Who were the inhabitants of India prior to the Dravidians ? Had they developed within the land of India or they had come from outside and settled there ?

Actually, the search for the roots of Dravidians is a very complicated question. History scholars have spent enough time to find out the roots of Dravidians and their place of origin. Detailed analyses of the various artifacts recovered from several excavations have not been able to find out the place of origin of the Dravidians. The result has not been very meaningful nor useful. Anthropological, archaeological and linguistic proofs as also their plentifulness has made the problem more complicated, as a result of which no factual conclusion has emerged regarding the place of origin of the Dravidians.

The antiquity of a race is based on Dravidian civilisation and culture, so much so that Vedic culture has also been influenced by Dravidians. The custom of having temples and worship in temples was prevalent among the Dravidians whereas in Vedic religion there was no mention of temples. The temples used to be called "Kotil." Shiva and Shakti used to be worshipped. Uma and Shiva were Dravidian deities. Ling worhip is a contribution of the Dravidians. The institution of "totem" had already been developed by the Dravidian society. They had agricultural knowledge, and they used several metals namely tin, zinc and other metals. Worshipping with flowers is a procedure of Dravidian culture. According to Professor Mark Collins, the Sanskrit word "Puja" has its root in the word "pu" which means "Pushp" or flower. The Vedas emphasised on sacrificial fire and sacrifice. The Dravidians contributed the custom of using flowers in worship.

In reality, the Munda and Oraon tribes have been inter-marrying and have blood connections, and due to living in the same geographical environment and also due to other reasons, racial, linguistic and cultural intermingling have been going on for centuries hence their roots have nearly been erased due to the result of blows and counter-blows. Viewed routinely, there appears to be no difference between them. Hence to find out about their root ancestry and place of origin, the human measurement / factor, philology, implements and other tools brought to use or available archaeological finds and those traditional religious stories and heroic tales are considered which throw light on the roots and place of origin of these tribes. Their proof lies in the archaeological evidences. After studying comparatively, whatever conclusions have emerged is sufficient, scientific and objective.

Language Proof

Taking the basis of human factor while searching for the ancestry of the Oraon tribes, it has been found that this tribe is a part of the Dravidians who have mainly lived in south India. According to most anthropologists, the Dravidian race came to India from the Mediterranean Sea, and developed due to the merging of the Aegean (Proto-Australoid) of Mediterranean and Armenide tribes of West Asia minor.

As regards the question of Indus valley civilisation, the scholars are of the same opinion that this civilisation was Dravidian civilisation but when and through which route such progressive civilised Dravidians came to north-west India is still a matter of contention. Some scholars think that they came from the Mediterranean Sea via Arabian coastal route through Baluchistan to north-west India. With the passage of time, after being defeated by the Aryans, some were made slaves and some in search of security fled to the hills and thick forests and taking their cover went to south India where they settled down. Sri A. H. Keen [63] has vociferously emphasised on this route basing his argument on the Brahui language spoken in Brahui sector of Baluchistan which is a branch of Dravidian language. But contrary to this, E. A. Gate has clarified that the Mundari language spoken in Chhotanagpur is connected to a vast language family which is called Austric and which is spoken in south-east Asia and lies spread to the north of the Himalayas i.e. Tibet.[64] It is in this way that it has been possible to fix the route which the Mundas had taken for entering India. But Dravidian language which is central to south India is spoken in limited areas and the philologists have not been successful upto now in finding any connection of the Dravidian language with any other language. Resultantly, from the point of view of language, the place of origin of Dravidian language speakers is in all probability South India and from here they migrated to north-west India and Baluchistan. The theorizing of E. A. Gate is in accordance with the aforementioned fact. As per Sir Gate, when nearly the whole of north India was under the influence of Munda language speakers, at that time the Dravidians held sway over south India and influenced Maharashtra and Sindh sector and they spread to Baluchistan.[65]

The special feature of Dravidian language is that it is not connected to any foreign or tribal language and it has a completely independent language status. This is the reason why philologists opine that Dravidians originally belong to south India and from here they migrated to different places. The philologists have accepted that Kurukh (Chhotanagpur), Malto, Kui, Khond, Gondo (north India) and Brahui (Baluchistan) languages have a connection with Tamil or Dravidian language of south India. Bishop Caldwell based on his study has bracketed these languages with the Dravidian language family. Tamil, Malayalam, Kannada, Telegu, and some less spoken dialects namely, Koragu, Tulu, Toda and Kota, all come within Tamil language. Recently, in the census report the Dravidian language family has been presented in this manner:–

The three main groups of Dravidian language family : (A) Andhra language group (B) Middle language group (C) Dravidian language group

I	Telegu	Central sector, Barar, and Hyderabad State	I	Tamil
II	Kandh (Kui)	(languages spoken in the eastern portion)	II	Kannada
III	Kolami		III	Malayalam
			IV	Tulu and other few languages which are spoken outside south India of whom mainly Kurukh (Chhotanagpur) and Brahui (Baluchistan) languages.

On analysing the debate which has arisen from the usefulness of language based proofs (regarding the Mundas) we have already considered in detail that it is not necessary that tribes belonging to one language family should have come from the same roots. Outside south India, the Kurukh language speakers of Chhotanagpur i.e. the Oraons, and in north India the speakers of

Malto, Kui-Khond, and Goddi as also the speakers of Brahui language of Baluchistan do not appear to be of one lineage, especially the Brahui speakers of Baluchistan do not have any racial characteristics of Dravidians. They are fair complexioned, tall, and their facial features namely, nose marks them out to be of Iranian or Aryan descent. Whosoever they are, they are definitely not of Dravidian origin although their language belongs to the Dravidian language family.

In this way, from the point of view of language, outside India, the Dravidians and their civilisation established their existence in Baluchistan and some of it in Sumer. In the religious stories of the Oraons, their connection with Mecca and Medina has been shown. But there is no clinching evidence to connect the Dravidians with any foreign roots. Thurston,[66] based on certain theories, has tried to connect the Dravidians on the basis of language and race to other races outside India, but he has not been able to come up with any satisfactory proof and conclusion as to which foreign race the Dravidians had their roots, and how and when they came to India and that they actually were not the original inhabitants of south India.

Certain historians, on the basis of various archaeological evidences have tried to prove that in the first phase of the second Ice Age, man came into existence in south India.[67] R. K. Choudhary has stated that forty thousand years earlier from now homo sapiens started living in south India. From this statement, the opinion gets strengthened that the original inhabitants came from somewhere in the dark ages and settled down. From the language point of view, too, the Dravidian does not seem to be connected to any other language family. But the anthropologists, basing their argument on human related study, have tried to connect the Dravidians to the Proto-Australoids of the Mediterranean and the Armenides of Asia Minor, and as per their conclusions, they came via the Arabian sea-coast to north-west India and again after being defeated by the Aryans, they became successful in getting protection from the forests and mountains of south India. The connection of Oraons with these Dravidians or any other race which came to India prior to the Dravidians may be considered.

Traditional Evidence

We have discussed the authenticity of traditional evidence. Any religious story, heroic tales or conventions and customs of any race which may be the historical heritage cannot fully remain as it was originally. Still, studying these traditional customs and conventions, some light is definitely thrown on the origin and development of any race. In the context of the origin of the name Oraon we have seen how a muni (holy man) was disturbed in his meditation and the brother and sister who came out of the blood of his chest began to be called the progenitors of the Oraons. We know that in order to protect their children, animals and agriculture, the Oraons organise a religious function called "danda-katta," During this function, the story of the origin of the Oraons is related. It relates how Dharmes sent rain of fire and dispatched his nephew Haluman (Hanuman) to alert all the earth dwellers by beat of drum (nagara), but Haluman was busy in eating and due to rain of fire, the whole creation was destroyed. In the cave of the crab, a brother and sister were hiding.[68] They were the only survivors of the whole Creation and they became the first ancestors of human beings. At the order of Dharmes, they sought their livelihood in cultivation. Dharmes divided the day into two parts- day and night.

The birth of human race through this brother and sister duo and there after their development is also prevalent among the Munda tribe. Before they entered Chhotanagpur, the Asurs had been inhabiting this area. They used to smelt iron ore to take out the iron in it. Their furnaces used to burn day and night. They were laborious. Apparently, Asur and Lohar were two names of the same race, but the name Asur became more prevalent. Like other places in India, Chhotanagpur saw the Stone age succeeded by the copper age and thereafter by the Iron age. Stone age implements have been recovered from various places of the Chhotanagpur plateau, especially from the south-east sector which if they do not belong to the earlier Stone age, then they definitely belong to the neo-stone age.[69] In Burhadih village within the jurisdiction of Tamar Police station, Professor Valentine Bal while excavating the base of a hillock in 1867 had found implements which from the archaeological point of view were useful stone crafted tools.[70] Sri S. C. Roy and Rai Saheb Chunni Lala's findings prove this fact that in Chhotanagpur remnants of all ages have been found.[71] But most of the Stone age implements and materials have been obtained from those places which were far away from the influence of Asurs. They were without doubt historical proof of the inhabitants who used to live in Chhotanagpur much earlier than the Asurs.[72]

Sri S. C. Roy has gathered many archaeological remains from the area of the Asurs, and has on their basis tried to prove that the civilisation of that time in Chhotanagpur was for the most part of that same age as that of the Indus valley civilisation.[73] There is no doubt that most of the remnants obtained from both places have an astonishing similarity. In the beginning of the twentieth century, the copper tools and jewellery, iron goods, pitchers, plates found from this place, the copper axes, copper grains etc. from Basiya were studied by the Archaeological Survey of India and the conclusion was that these materials were made in the transition period of the Neostone Age and the Copper age. The Asurs were skilful artisans of copper and bronze and took recourse to copper currency.[74] They used to bury their dead along with food and pitcher of water. In Chhotanagpur, some historians are of the viewpoint that the age of the Asurs stretched till the Kushan period because some coins of Kushan area have been recovered from the habitation period of the Asurs.

It is a common precept that the Asurs in Chhotanagpur had passed through neo-stone-copper and iron period civilisation.

The tales of defeating the Asurs as described in the traditional lore of the Oraons is undoubtedly a copy of the Mundas. The Mundas had entered Chhotanagpur before the Oraons, and the Munda tribe had overpowered the Asurs. Some parts of Chhotanagpur had been under the power of the remaining Asurs when the Oraons came to Chhotanagpur and they defeated these Asurs. In this way the Asurs fled Ranchi to the jungles of the north-west for safety.

In the religious functions organised to do away with misfortunes, the tale of origin of the Oraons describes Dharmes as Grandfather Ram, Sita as his wife, and the Oraons call Hanuman as their uncle. There are many other tales from which it is known that the Oraon tribe considers Ram (son of Dasrath) to be Dharmes, and there is no difference between Sita and Parvati. But based on these tales it cannot be said that the ancestor of the non-Aryan Oraons was Aryan Ram, nonetheless Ram and Sita, or considering Dharmes and Parwati as grandparents, were actually a way of paying obeisance and respect. Hanuman was the ancestor of the Oraons, and some scholars after comparing the appearance of the Oraons, their nature, their clan and totems as also the different mentions in the Ramayan have concluded that in Tretayug this tribe residing in the forests of southern India was a part of that army with whose help Dasrathi Ram won victory over Ravana. In Balmiki Ramayan, the poet has described these monkeys as cloud-coloured,[75] having big teeth,[76] drunk with liquor[77] and dancing to the beats of the mridang (a kind of drum), in utter happiness.[78] These features are common to the Chhotanagpur Oraons and other Dravidian tribes. Filled with happiness after imbibing hadiya, dancing and singing freely to the beats of the mridang-although these characteristics are found in other tribes as well, but the ecstasy found in the Oraon tribe is not to be found elsewhere. They have had a special place. In Sanskrit literature the respectful language and address used for these monkeys have not been used for any other non-Aryan tribe. In Sanskrit literature, horrible descriptions have been given for other non-Aryan races. They have always been denoted as giants, demons, ghosts and robbers. But, opposite to them, these monkeys in the Ramayana have been addressed with love and affection.

It is but natural that if any human being is addressed as "monkey" or "bear" he will take it as an insult. The meaning of such an address is to insult the human being. But in Ram's army what type of "monkeys" and "bears" were there who have been honoured by the poet, the readers of Ramayan and the common public can visualise. Ram himself has said that they are his friends and brothers. The sense of kinship behind these words of Ram are apparent in addressing them as monkeys and bears. Without doubt, by using the words "monkeys" and "bears," the whole tribe has been given respect and affection. In the Kishkindha Kand (chapter) of Balmiki Ramayan, there has been mention where it has been said that the monkey soldiers felt respectable to be called monkeys.[79] In many portions, it has been said that they have good appearance, that is, they are beautiful to look at. Their appearance gives joy and happiness and have brightness of features. Therefore in all these contexts the question arises as to why they were called monkeys.

Apparently this pre-Dravidian primitive race living in mountainous caves and who were a part of Ram's army, had the totem of monkey. Even now the Oraon tribe residing in Chhotanagpur have monkey as a clanname, for example, hanuman clan, ordinary monkey ("gari") clan, etc. which means that the various clans of their ancestors, through whom their lineage runs, point to this. The Oraons think it a sin to kill monkeys, to injure them or to tame them. Oraons of all clans think it a taboo to eat the flesh of monkeys although they eat the flesh of other small or big animals. Thus, based on these points, one can conclude that the monkey totem had been running among their ancestors hundreds of years ago and based on this totem Ram's army was called the monkey army and there were different commanders of the different parts of this army.

The religion of the Oraons and the various beliefs regarding them in society and tradition are very much similar to the monkey army of the period of the Ramayan and the societal beliefs about them at that time, although the Oraon tribe is now at the pinnacle of its civilisation and just like other civilised societies it was patriarchal, the signs of which can still be seen in south India. Roaming around forests and caves this tribe in Ramayan times used to live off tubers, fruits and flowers; they had no knowledge of cultivation or animal husbandry, nor was the institution of marriage well developed. As a result, the offsprings were known by their mother's name. The tales of birth of almost all monkey chiefs point to the matriarchal system of society. The birth of Sugreev and Bali was from the womb of that woman-monkey who was created from a tear droplet of Grandfather Brahma which fell on this earth. At first it was born as a bear monkey but after coming out of the waters of the pond it became a woman monkey. This woman-monkey at first became pregnant by Indra and thereafter by the Sun and one by one gave birth to Sugreev and Bali. In the same way Hanuman, the hero and commander of the monkey army was born of Anjana who had become pregnant by Pavan, the wind-god. The army commander Dadhimukh had similarly been born due to Chandra, the moon god. The monkey Neel was also born the same way through Agni, the firegod.[80] It is said that normally all monkeys had been born of their mothers' wombs who had been made pregnant by gods and spirits.[81] In their primitive condition, the ancestors of the Oraons used to roam around the mountains and caves of the south, in the forests, nearly naked, subsisting on tubers and roots, fruits and flowers. The matriarchal system in the Oraon society during the Ramayan times was prevalent for quite some time.

Another tradition among the Oraon society confirms that the ancestors of present day Oraons used to be a part of Ram's army during the Ramayan times. We are aware that in present day Oraon society, witches, female spirits or female demons have a powerful hold, and taking the help of incantations and spells they are propitiated so that the oncoming problems and difficulties may be warded off. In Oraon society, witch or "O ache" and her power is described in such a manner that it is said that she can catch the shadow of any person or creature and can capture him or it. There is mention of a demoness called Angarika who used to eat human beings by catching their shadows. The prevalent notion at that time in the monkey society that by catching his shadow a person can be caught is current even now in the form of "chha-een" in society.

In this way, the ancestors of Oraons during their primitive stage lived nearly naked in the forests and caves. As per the Ramayan, the leader of the monkeys Sugreev used to live in the mountains and caves of Kishkindha. According to antiquaries, this place is situated about 30 km. north of Bellary nagar on the northern shore of the Tungabhadra River.[82] Several sub-races of these monkeys were spread over different places within their forest bounds.[83] They were spread out till the Vindhya mountain range on the north. Be it known that Ramchandra's first meeting with Sugreev, the leader of the monkeys, took place on Malay mountain. Later on we will see[84] that the Malay race which fled from Rohtasgarh did not go to Chhotanagpur but followed the Ganga River's bank and went north to the hills of Rajmahal and started living there. They were probably that part of the Oraons who used to stay on Malay mountain under the leadership and kingship of Sugreev.

The Oraon tribe living in the forest limits were a part of the Dravidian race which was in its primitive condition. These Oraons did not know about agriculture and animal husbandry. They used to live on tubers and roots, fruits and flowers. They used to confront their enemies with sticks and stones. Their offsprings were born and brought up in matriarchal tradition. But after coming in contact with the Aryans and as a result of participating in their various activities, they observed the Aryan society, learnt about animal husbandry and agriculture and understood the importance of patriarchal type of society. Thereafter, gradually they emerged from their primitive condition and started entering the fields of agriculture and animal husbandry. Due either to population pressure or any other reason, they left the areas of Tungabhadra and Narmada and slowly started moving northwards. In this way, after roaming and halting at places fit for animal husbandry and agriculture, they gradually crossed the Vindhya mountain ranges and came to the valley of the River Sone. Here they fully occupied themselves in agricultural work and due to labour and strength they became small or big landlords. Under the leadership of their king Karash, they lived peacefully and reached great heights of civilisation.

The kingdom of Karash or Karakh which used to be called the country of Karush, stretched from Rewa in Madhya Pradesh to Magadh. According to

Dr B. C. Law, as has been written in Page 48 of the Shahabad gazetteer, the Karush people used to live in four places. These were : (1) Rewa upto the limits of Mirzapur (2) Shahabad [86] (3) Pundra country (North Bengal)[87] and (4) The hills of Vindhya i. e. "Vindhya Prishta niwaseena."[88] One group went from Rewa-Mirzapur towards Malwa, and the rest came to Shahabad via Mirzapur. Again, from Shahabad they went and settled in Palamau, Singbhum and Midnapur (North Bengal) and again from there they spread in the hills of the Vindhyas. According to the gazetteer, the offsprings of these Karushes were later on called Rajbhar, and being the children of Karush, in Sanskrit and the Mahabharat they were called Karush.

Those conclusions of Dr B. C. Law which have been quoted in the Shahabad gazetteer and in which it has been said that the Rajbhars and Cheros were the first inhabitants of Shahabad and nearby areas are based on certain erroneous conclusions. Sri S. C. Roy has said that the word "Karush" has two meanings- one in the form of a noun and the other in the form of an adjective. In the form of a noun, Karush or Karukh or Kudukh have been used for the Oraon tribe because the credit of establishing the Karush country goes to king Karush. Over a period of time through centuries, whichever race came there was called Karush and Cheros were also called Karush. It has been mentioned in the Mahabharat that in the fields of Kurukshetra, the Karushes took part in the fighting. The war of Kurukshetra took place in the Dwapar Yuga and the Oraon tribe whose study is desired, this tribe had started becoming civilised by the end of the Treta Yuga and these Oraons had established Kurush country. After that, the people who defeated them and took over the governance of that area, they also came to be called Karush in the epics. Chiefly, those tribes were Chero and Bhar[89] and there is a possibility that those tribes had also participated in the war of Kurukshtra, not the Oraon tribe.

It is logical that the builders of Kurush country were the first inhabitants of that country. Since the builder of Karush country was king Karush and due to him the Oraon tribe is also known as Kudukh, hence the first inhabitants of Karush country were the Oraons. Over a period of time the Cheros conquered Kurush country (mainly Shahabad). As a result, the vanquished Oraons and the ancestors of the Malers took shelter in Rohtas.[90] Rohtas was under the rule of the Kharwars also, who like the Cheros, had tribal characteristics of the Mundas but they called themselves Suryavanshis and accepted Raja Harishchandra's son Rohtas to be their ancestor.

The Flight from Rohtasgarh

Rohtasgarh is approximately 450 metres (1490 ft.) above the sea-level, and is situated amid the dense forests of Kaimur mountain range. It has always been a secure haven for defeated races. The land of this place, agriculturally speaking, is not fertile. The sources of irrigation are very limited. Resultantly, the inhabitants of this place during ancient times used to depend on animal husbandry and a little bit of cultivation. But in those days when only animals like horses were used for transport or else people went on foot, then the high hills, thick forests, deep valleys used to become like impregnable armour taking the help of which the tribes living in the area could follow their means of livelihood without any tension. The Oraons had raised a 1500 feet high stone wall and within this boundary they used to live in peace. It was difficult for enemies to cross this barrier.

The traditional lore prevalent among the Oraons regarding their defeat in Rohtas and flight therefrom speaks of how they were defeated through the deception of the "Mlechhas" and "Hakims." Since the Hakims were unable to break through the barrier of the high security wall despite best efforts, they worked upon the greed of a milk-maid and won her over to their side. Since the milk-maid used to supply milk to the Oraon king, she could enter and come out of the fortress without being checked, so she knew about the mystery of the secure Oraons within the ramparts of the fortress. Having come to know of the facts, the enemies had entered the fortress and had successfully defeated the Oraons. As per the suggestion given by the milkmaid, the "masters" had decided to enter the fortress and start the battle on the day of the celebration of Sarhul. That day all the Oraons used to lie around in a drunken state. The enemies had waited for the festival of Sarhul and at the appropriate time, with the help of the milkmaid, they had entered the fortress. The Oraons had not offered any resistance, but it is said that the Oraon women had donned men's clothes and faced the enemy with great bravery although they could not stand their ground for a long time. The Oraon king and his subjects had been successful in running away through a secret tunnel. It is said that the enemy had tried to find out that secret tunnel in the light of big flaming torches but were unable to do so.

The Oraon women donning soldiers' clothes and battling the "Mlechchas" in order to protect their race is a unique incident in the history of India. It is commemorated in the form of "Jani Shikar."[91] In the traditional lore of the Oraons, it has been mentioned that there had been a battle with the "Mlechchas" (Persons of outcaste race) who through stratagem had taken the advantage of the festival of Sarhul to defeat them because on that day the Oraon men remain in a drunken state. At present it is a common belief that those Mlechchas were Mughals who had spread their kingdom in Delhi and Bihar at that time. This is a historical misunderstanding which even now can be found in the various articles/essays in Kudukh and write-ups during Sarhul in many publications/ magazines. This is encouraging bad blood against the Mughals (Muslims) in society. The famous English historian Risley had encouraged this mistake. He had not analysed the facts in a historical perspective nor in depth but had declared the Mlechchas as Mughals.[92] Some well educated people of Oraon society of that time had accepted Risley's finding as historical truth and through them this erroneous thinking seeped into the minds of the simple tribals.

There is an interval of centuries between the incident of Rohtasgarh and the entry of the Mughals into India. From "Nagvanshavali" (a book of verse) pertaining to the Nagvanshi kings of Chhotanagpur, it is clearly seen that in the crowning ceremony of Phanimukut Rai, the first king of this lineage, the Oraons had participated. As per this book, the crowning ceremony and elevation to the throne took place in 121 Samvat i. e. 64 A.D., S.C. Roy has also confirmed this date.[93] As per the Ranchi gazetteer, the crowning of Phanimukut Rai took place in the sixth century[94] and as per John Reed it took place in the tenth century.[95] The book "Ancient Geography" by Ptolemy was written in the second century. The presence of Oraons in Chhotanagpur is proved from this book. According to the description of Ptolemy, "Kokkongai" is a large plateau lying to the east of Ganga. As per the understanding and language of Ptolemy, kokkongai appears to be a corrupted form of Karukh word. "Gai" or "Gahi" word is a suffix of the Oraon language which conjoins a name to mean or denote a special place. In this way kokkon-gai means kokkon land. Again, kokkon-gahi-kurukkar-gahi-karukh-gahi meaning the land of the Karukhs classifies the meaning. Thus, today's Chhotanagur was the country of the Kurukhs in Ptolemy's geographical book of the second century.[96]

It is clear that till the second century, the importance and influence of the Oraons in Chhotanagpur had become established. Hence, the whole area was described as Kokkongai. Suppose if the Oraons took three to four centuries to subjugate the Mundas residing in Chhotanagpur from before and to consolidate their influence, then the flight of the Oraons from Rohtasgarh to Chhotanagpur must have been in fourth century B.C. or earlier. Thus, the ceremony marking the coming to the throne of Phanimukut Rai (64 AD) and Ptolemy's geographical description prove that the Oraon people had left Rohtasgarh after their defeat at the hands of the Mlechchas, centuries earlier to the advent of Christ.

From the history of Rohtasgarh it is clear that in this land, Kharwar, Kudukh or Oraon, Bhar, Rajput, Chero and Savars had their kingdom. It is a different subject to chronologically record their sovereignty but from the evidence dating back to Emperor Asoka (271-231 B.C.), it is clear that during the time of Asoka, the Savars had defeated the Cheros and established their sovereignty over Shahabad.[97] Magadh Kingdom had only in name included the Savars within it and had given protection to it. From this description it is proved that the Savars had established their kingdom in Shahabad in the third century B.C. Prior to the Savars, the Cheros had established their sovereignty twice in Shahabad, three Rajput brothers had their rights, and earlier to them Bhar, Kharwar and Oraons (not in that order) had their supremacy. Obviously as per counting of these dates, the defeat of the Oraons at Rohtasgarh and their flight from there could not have taken place after the fourth century B.C.

The aforementioned proofs clarify that the erroneous idea spread by Risley that the Oraons were defeated by the Mlechchas i.e. the Mughals, is proved wrong on the touchstone of time. The Mughals had first entered Bihar in 1193 A.D. during the time of Bakhtiar Khilji, and the capture of Rohtasgarh by Muslims in 1359 B.C. could not happen. In these circumstances, the question does not arise that the Oraons fought the Muslims in Rohtasgarh and got defeated by them.

Actually, in Oraon folk lore, "mlechcha" word has been taken through Sanskrit literature by neighbouring Hindus. "Mlechcha" that is "malichcha" (Sanskrit word used in slightly changed form in the vernacular) means that race or person who does not follow religion and its rituals correctly and in whose eating and living habits there is repugnance and dirtiness. The word "Mlechcha" was prevalent in India before the Mughals came, and often it would be used for primitive tribes who used to live at the bottom rung of civilisation. Chero, Kharwar, Bhar, Kol, etc. were included in this category. Compared to others, the Oraon tribe was near to Hindu civilisation and received more affection from the Aryans. Although the major groups of Kharwar and Chero who had settled down in the Sindh-Gangetic plain had comparatively become more Hinduised and consecutively had declared themselves "suryavanshi" (of the lineage of the sun) and "nagvanshi" (of the lineage of the serpent) respectively, yet the Hindus even then thought them to be mlechchas. It is apparent from the study of Dr Buchanan and his conclusions that the Cheros who at one time had established the might of their kingdom in the Gangetic plain, had slid to the lowest rung of impure and uncivilised life by the time they came to Shahabad.

Although the rich ones among them used to call themselves Rajputs and wore the sacred thread, the people who were poor and powerless and whose population was much more were living at a primitive level of civilisation. The Hindu Brahmins used to say that the Cheros were similarly "Mlechcha" and primitive as the Kharwars who used to call themselves "suryavanshi" (of the lineage of the sun). Thus, there is full probability that the word "mlechcha" used by the Oraons had meant the Cheros who at one time had been the rulers of that area and who had driven away the Oraons after defeating them in Rohtasgarh. The rule of the Cheros in Shahabad had been in two phases. As per calculation, it appears that they had vanquished the Oraons at Rohtasgarh and captured it in the first phase. As per local Oraon social workers and religious priests, the Oraons used to call their enemies by the name of Turukh because Turukh is the anti of Kurukh. It seems that the word "Turuk" or "Turk" is used by the Hindus to denote Mughals, resultantly the word "Mlechcha" which fundamentally came to mean Mughals over a period of time, that word was appropriated as a parallel to Turukh by the Oraons. This meaning is a later on interpolation. Originally the word "mlechcha" meant Chero.

In this connection, S. C. Roy has expressed the probability that the Oraons had fled to Chhotanagpur from Rohtasgarh twice. In the first instance they had been defeated by the Hindus and in the second instance they had been defeated by the Mughals. There was a long time gap between the two flights. In support of his argument, S. C. Roy has argued that the language and culture of the Oraons settled in the western portion of Chhotanagpur are very different from the language and culture of the Oraons settled in the eastern part of Chhotanagpur.[99] This difference has occurred due to lack of contact and communication for a long time between the Oraons of both areas. But S. C. Roy has not classified as to when and under what circumstances the Mughals defeated the rest of the Oraons. Again, if a part of the Oraons went away from Rohtasgarh after their defeat, then did the remaining Oraons reestablish their kingdom in Rohtasgarh ? If the Oraons had not been able to re-establish their kingdom, then where is the question of their defeat and banishment from Rohtasgarh. Hence the flowing and breathtaking exercise done by Risley or S. C. Roy with the word mlechcha to anyhow connect it with the Mughals, is not factually correct. It is possible that the rest of the Oraons had gradually in small groups left Rohtasgarh and after a long interval had reached Chhotanagpur but there is no historical evidence that after getting defeated by the Mughals (Mlechchas) they fled to Chhotanagpur in search of a safe haven and settled there. Again, the incident of Jani Shikar which has been given the form of a festival, is an incident of fourth century B.C. and the traditional folklore of the Oraons has conjoined it to the Hindus, meaning thereby that they were defeated by some Hindus (Mlechchas). In the traditional folklore, Hindus have also been called "Mlechchas." Who were those Hindus who used to be called Mlechchas?[100] Actually they were Cheros whom the Aryan Hindus, used to call "mlechcha" although the Cheros used to call themselves Hindu and the primitive tribes, keeping in mind their semi-Aryan appearance, also called them Hindus. The study of Dr Buchanan throws light on this fact.[101]

The aforementioned evidences clearly spell out that in the middle of fourth-fifth century B.C. the Oraon tribe held sway over Rohtasgarh. Their traditional folklore says that during the night of Sarhul when they were all in a drunken state, the Chero people invaded them and defeated them. In two different folklores the race which defeated the Oraons has been called "mlechcha" and "hakim." The Cheros had been partly Aryanised hence they themselves and the other primitive tribes used to call them Hindu. But the Hindus used to call the Cheros and the Kharwars "Mlechcha." Hence, in the census and other official documents, namely the Shahabad gazetteer, the race which defeated the Oraons has been called Hindu. But they became "Mlechcha" or "malik" in Hindu folklore. These mlechchas are not Muslims because the incident happened before the time of Asoka's rule when there was no trace of Muslims in India.

At this place, it is necessary to consider one probability raised by Sri S. C. Roy. He has expressed the probability that the word "Mlechcha" mentioned in the various folklores denoting the defeaters of the Oraons were actually Muslims. According to Sri Roy, centuries later, another group of Oraons after having been defeated by the Mughals in Rohtasgarh came to Chhotanagpur[102] and this group went and settled in the western part. In order to prove his idea Sri Roy has argued that the social, cultural and linguistic fabric of the Oraons settled in the eastern part is different from that of those Oraons settled in the western part.

According to Sri Roy, this difference proves that the Oraons came to Chhotanagpur in two dis-similar situations with different cultures. This probability expressed by S. C. Roy is, however, not justified by historical facts. The question of Oraons being defeated by Mughals does not arise because after the first flight from Rohtasgarh, although some Oraons had remained in Shahabad they had remained only as subjects and they could not become the rulers once again. Hence no situation could arise of their being defeated by the Mughal ruler or army. From the study done by Hunter it is known that some Oraons had stayed back in Shahabad and some had left Shahabad in small groups and come to Chhotanagpur and since the western part of Chotanagpur came first, they settled there.[103]

The historian L. S. S. O' Malley has mentioned about the Maler tribe in Santhal Pargana gazetteer; this tribe lives in the northern part of Rajmahal. As per O' Malley, the Greek historian Megasthenes, who had come to the court of Emperor Chandragupta in Patliputra in 302 B.C., has mentioned the Malli tribe in his book "Indica." O' Malley has identified Malli with the Maler tribe. The Malers of Santhal Parganas and the Oraons of Chhotanagpur are in a way uterine brothers because till their stay in Rohtasgarh, their ancestors were the same. After coming out of Rohtasgarh, they divided into two branches. One branch which was smaller, settled down in Rajmahal in the name of Maler. The other branch settled down in Chhotanagpur in the name of Oraon. Based on the book written by Megasthenes, O' Malley dates the settling down of the Malers in Rajmahal to fourth century B.C. or even earlier. This truth can be accepted for the Oraons also. The culture and social condition of the Oraons who came later were different from the Oraons who had come earlier because they had been in contact for a long period with races which had become socially developed from the Aryans; the Oraons who had come earlier to Chhotanagpur had to remain close to the Mundas who had been in a nearly primitive stage. Hence, some differences are to be found among the Oraons living in the western part and eastern part of Chhotanagpur. But using this basis to show that the Oraons coming in the second phase had been defeated by the Mughals and to connect the word "mlechcha" with the Mughals is not supported by any historical incident. Thus, the probability expressed by S. C. Roy does not have any factual basis.

Actually, the historical flight of the Oraons from Rohtasgarh took place approximately in the fourth century B.C. when they were defeated by Cheros. The ancestors of the defeated Oraons had been divided into two groups. One group which is recognised as Maley passed along the banks of the river Ganga and went and settled in Gaya and the hills of Rajmahal. The other group passed along the banks of the river Sone past the North Koel river to enter Palamau from the south-east and settled in Chhotanagpur.

One Other Influence

The famous historian O' Malley has recorded in the Santhal Parganas gazetteer that the Maler tribe, settled in the northern part of Rajmahal, came to Santhal Parganas in the fourth century. In this context Sri Malley has given an extract from the book "Indica" written by the Greek historian Megasthenes in which Megasthenes in his book has mentioned about a tribe called Malli which is none other than the Maler tribe settled in the northern part of Rajmahal.

Megasthenes had presented himself in the court of Emperor Chandragupta in Patliputra in the year 302 B.C. His book Indica was written during this time. Megasthenes has described Malli that is Maler in his book. The meaning thereby is that at least a century before Megasthenes came to India, the Maler tribe had settled in Rajmahal. Hence, the Maler tribe had completely settled down in Rajmahal in the fourth century B.C. or even earlier.

The Intermingling of the Mundas and Oraons

Prior to presenting a clear picture of the religious background of the Munda and Oraon tribes, it is essential to give a brief description of the social and cultural intermingling with each other of these tribes. After having fled Rohtasgarh, the Mundas had at first entered the forested areas of Chhotanagpur and after having cut down the jungles they prepared habitable land as also some land fit for agriculture. The Oraons were culturally superior to the Mundas because their living and dietary habits were comparably better than the Mundas. This is the reason why from the very time the Oraons entered Chhotanagpur, they were superior in all manner than the Munda landlords who had been staying there from before. The Oraons were not only meritorious, they had better weapons, better agricultural implements and household goods and they outweighed the Mundas in every way.

Most of the reseachers and scholars who have studied the relationship with each other among the Munda and Oraon tribes have termed this relationship cordial and friendly. They are of the opinion that when the Oraons entered Chhotanagpur from the western passage, the Mundas gave them shelter and food and that is how the newcomers were welcomed. S. C. Roy, commenting on the Munda-Oraon relations, has said in his book that although the Oraons were at a higher standard of civilisation compared to the Mundas yet they accepted the food given by the Mundas despite the fact that till that time the food was considered sub-standard.[104] S. C. Roy has further said that coming in contact with the Mundas and being cut off from civilised societies, the Oraon people gradually slipped to the lower rungs of civilisation.[105] In nearly the same way N. Kumar has mentioned in the Ranchi gazetteer (1970) that there is no traditional proof of any warfare between the Munda and Oraon races- on the other hand, the Mundas had given the Oraons their khuntkatti land for agriculture and space amongst themselves for settling down. According to N. Kumar, the Mundas had given these favours on condition that the Oraons would have to eat meat and they would discard their sacred thread. Throwing light on the cordial relationship between the Mundas and the Oraons, S. C. Roy has argued that the villages where they stayed, their names are Mundari and the presence of the graveyards of the Mundas clarifies that in those places the population of Mundas was in good strength. Sri Roy has further said that in nearly every Oraon village, in which Oraons were more in number, the Oraons had kept back at least one or two Munda families with them so that they would worship the bongas (spirits) of the village and keep them peaceful. In this way, the Oraons had exhibited an attitude of compromise with the Mundas.[107] Since Sri S. C. Roy is accepted as an authoritative writer on the tribal life of Chhotanagpur and his influence weighs heavily in this area on the anthropologists,[108] it is necessary to seriously consider the facts presented by him.

The conclusions drawn by Sri S. C. Roy and N. Kumar can be placed in their basic form in the following manner:

(1) The Mundas came to Chhotanagpur before the Oraons and after clearing the jungle they started living there and prepared cultivable land.

(2) The Oraons came to Chhotanagpur much after the Mundas.

(3) The Oraons were more civilised than the Mundas and their weapons, agricultural implements and household goods were much better than those of the Mundas.

(4) Upon entry into Chhotanagpur, there was no war between the Mundas and Oraons- rather; the Mundas gave shelter and food to the Oraons.

(5) In the eyes of the Oraons, the food was below standard yet they accepted the food given by the Mundas and in this way they slid down from their level of civilisation. (According to N. Kumar, the Mundas had offered shelter and food to the Oraons on condition that they would eat meat and discard their sacred thread. The Oraons had accepted this condition.[109] Why the condition was kept and what was the compulsion of the Oraons to accept it has not been written).

In western Chhotanagpur where the population of the Oraons is thick, most

(a) Villages have Mundari name.

(b) Oraon villages having graveyards, the number of Munda skeletons found in them prove that earlier there had been a dense population of Mundas.

(c) Oraons in order to pacify the bongas, had asked one or two Munda families to settle in every village.

S. C. Roy has presented facts as evidences which spell out that in the places where earlier the Mundas used to stay, the Oraons have populated that western part of Chhotanagpur and the Mundas have left that area (possibly fled the area) and settled in the south-east. But it does not prove that the Mundas voluntarily out of cordiality gave their agricultural land and settlements to the Oraons and went away from the west to the south-eastern direction, or that the Oraons had banished the Mundas from that area and in this way had taken possession over the land. Since there was no war, the scholars take this as a moral victory.

N. Kumar's comment that there is no proof (neither historical nor traditional) upon the basis of which it may be concluded that the Oraons entered Chhotanagpur and after waging a war with the Mundas they subjugated them and took possession of the land of that area which had at first belonged to the Mundas. But S. C. Roy and N. Kumar accept that the present Oraons have established their right in that very area over which the Mundas had predominance at first. Another opinion which they have is that the Mundas voluntarily and due to friendship left their agricultural fields and hearth and home for the Oraons.

About the fourth century B.C. when the Oraons had entered Chhotanagpur, both tribes had been a little above the primitive standard where civilisation and culture were concerned. Instead of existing on hunting and roots and tubers, they had taken to animal husbandry and agriculture. But fighting wars was their life's destiny. Empowered and better races taking advantage of superior means used to defeat the other races. In this way, the defeated races would flee their places over which the conquering race would establish its sovereignty. Definitely every one of the vanquished race would not flee but would accept subjugation and remain in their place. Under these circumstances it seems completely unnatural that when the Oraons fled from Rohtasgarh in search of a safe haven and thereafter entered Chhotanagpur from the western passage and faced the Mundas, the Mundas out of friendliness offered them shelter and gave up their lands, hearth and home to them and went and settled in south-east Chhotanagpur.

There must have been a test of strength between the Oraons and Mundas. Today the races sitting on the hierarchy of civilisation will not hand over their landed property to any incoming new race and thereby become homeless, so can it be expected that about 2500 years ago from now, the tribes supposedly on the lower rungs of civilisation would have voluntarily given up their lands and homes to the newcomer Oraons and would have gone away in search of fresh shelter toward the southeast direction ?

Roy and Kumar also accept that the Oraons were more developed than the Mundas. Their knowledge about agriculture was more, hence, from every viewpoint the Oraons were more empowered than the Mundas. Thus, N. Kumar's statement that the Mundas had offered conditional shelter to the Oraons, that is, that they would have to eat meat and discard their sacred thread, does not seem logical. Condition is set in those circumstances when the other party being weak is compelled to accept it. Even if the statement of N. Kumar is accepted, then how can cordiality and friendship be weighed on the scales of condition ? There is thus an indication that the Oraons became the slaves of the Mundas or else became slave like and they were compelled to accept the terms set by the Mundas and they slid to the lower rungs of civilisation. In this way, from any viewpoint, the opinion of S. C. Roy and N. Kumar that the Mundas gave shelter to the Oraons and for them they left the northwest part where earlier they had been the landlords, and without any war or power struggle they voluntarily went in search of new shelter towards the south-east part does not at all sound logical.

Sri S. C. Roy is accepted as the basic researcher of tribal life of Chhotanagpur, and before him no Indian scholar has described the life of the tribes living in the forests of Chhotanagpur. Hence, the writers and researchers coming after him are following his path and singing the same tunes in their language which tunes S. C. Roy has sung about the Munda-Oraon relations. If the various comments of Sri S. C. Roy given at various places are diligently collected and placed together, then they will themselves go against the opinion of S. C. Roy regarding Munda-Oraon relations. In his book "The Mundas and their country" S. C. Roy at on place has commented that at times a supposition is created that the Oraons had been invited by the king of the Mundas to subjugate the Mundas and this fact does not seem impossible.[111] According to S. C. Roy, due to the pressure of Oraon population from northwest Ranchi, 2100 Mundas left their homes under the leadership of Risa Munda and came to Murma Sthan in south-east Ranchi and settled there. Why did the Mundas have to leave their homes due to pressure of population ? It was natural that if the population of a tribe increased, that tribe would clear the forest and make some space for itself. If the Munda-Oraon ties were cordial then why had the Mundas to leave their ancestral homes under the pressure of the Oraons ? The supporter of Munda-Oraon relations has no answer to this question.

Improvement in Munda-Oraon relations apparently started one to two centuries earlier than the elevation to the throne of Nagvanshi king Phani Mukut Rai (year 64 A. D.). At that time marriage relations as also influence over each other's cultural and religious functions started taking place. This inter-mingling among the Mundas and Oraons kept happening for quite some time, but the population extension among the two tribes and density in special areas resulted in mostly localised inter-mingling. We have already seen that due to close contact with the Aryans, the Oraons had more leaning towards Hindu religion and precepts whereas the Mundas were gradually moving towards civilisation from their primitive state. As a result, the Oraons thought themselves to be superior than the Mundas. The Oraons had brought the word "king" with them which over a period of time changed the word "manki" into "parha raja". Despite Munda-Oraon relations being outwardly cordial, inwardly although they may not have been sour yet they always tried to show each other in an inferior light.

The Oraons had helped the Mundas to elect Phani Mukut Rai as king. After a lapse of time when the Mundas started to establish their authority over Phani Mukut Rai (of non-Munda origin) then the Oraons spread a tale in their society. According to the tale, Phani Mukut Rai was of Oraon origin[112] and his paternal grandfather Lakhan Bhagat was a resident of Sutiyambey[113]. The rest of the story remained the same that his parents died when he was born and the boy got the shade of security of the hood of a serpent and he was brought up in the house of an Oraon. This tale spread in depth in the Oraon society. Society does not go by historical proofs. For this the traditional tales are more influential. But this story is indicative of that trend among the Oraons which kept up a competitive condition with the Mundas. Although in various agitations of farmers the Mundas and Oraons were together, and, as per the British, the Mundas were more aged and had more fighting spirit than the Oraons, yet the cultural and religious intercurrent of the Mundas and Oraons, despite the unity and intermingling, were flowing in different directions. They had not only sub-racial difference, from the viewpoint of religion the Oraons had better standards than the Mundas and their leaning toward Hindu religion was more.

In Indian history, the year 1757 proved to be a landmark for British rule. After the death of Ali Vardi Khan on 10 April 1756, the authority of the Mughals in eastern India finished forever. A new era starts in India with the victory of the British in 1757 A D in the battle of Plassey. The victory in Buxar (October 1764) further consolidated this era, and eastern India came under complete control of the British.[114]

On 12 August 1765 A.D. Shah Alam handed over the Diwani (revenue collection, police, judicial and military powers) of Bengal, Bihar and Orissa to the East India Company. In this way the road to establish their own rule over India got widened for the British. Along with Bihar the area of Chhotanagpur also came to be included under the authority of the British. First of all, captain Jac of Camac entered with his armed force in Chhotanagpur in 1769 A.D.[115] In order to deal with the quarrels of the local chieftains, to help them to suppress revolts and to collect revenue from them, the British forces began to be kept without any hindrance in the various cantonments of Chhotanagpur and the British military officer began to give directions on administrative and other matters to the kings. With the advent of the British, not only the political and economic life of Chhotanagpur became affected but it also affected the social and cultural life. These changes deeply influenced the religious life of the two main tribes i.e. the Mundas and the Oraons.

With the coming of the British, the Christian missionaries got a golden opportunity to spread Christianity in Chhotanagpur which was a tribal majority area. The Gossner Evangelic Luther Mission (G. E. L.) was the first to start the drive for spread of Christianity. In 1844, Berlin's Weston John-Evangelist sent four missionaries. Despite preliminary difficulties, the conversion of poor tribals to Christianity picked up quite a lot of speed. In this direction, as compared to other missions, the role of "Sarvada" Catholic mission became very influential. Compared to Oraons, the magic of the missionaries was more successful on the Mundas.

The population of Mundas is more dense in the south-east portion of Ranchi and within the border area of Singhbhum. The influence of Kabir Panthis (followers of Kabir) has also fallen on them. There was a time when the Kabir Panthis used to command great respect in society and there would be one Kabir Panthi in every Munda family.[116] Brajram of Chaulibasa and the religious songs of Sohrai, their prayers written in Panch Pargania language were very much prevalent and in use in this area. The weaver class called swansi or tanti who used to live amid the Mundas had partially, if not fully, bent the religious thinking of the Mundas towards Kabir Panth. Compared to the Mundas, the access of the Kabir Panthis to the Oraons was much more. Among these tribals, Kabir's advice was limited to certain beliefs, namely, fasting, religious vows, cleanliness and purity in diet and these were stressed upon. The Kabir Panthis did not believe in the caste system of the Mundas. The main target of the Panthis was kindness to creatures, good behaviour, service to mankind and a society without any differentiation.

In the beginning of the medieval age, Hindu religion, especially worship of the Sun and Devi (goddess) influenced the Mundas and the Oraons. It is known from the Sri Chaitanyacharitamrit that while going from Neelanchal to Mathura, Chaitanya Mahaprabhu had passed through Jharkhand, as a result of which many tribals coming under his influence became followers of Vaishnav religion. There are many poetical creations available in Mundari, Sadani, and Panch Pargania languages related to the characters of Ram and Krishna. Hindu religion has been the most successful in giving direction to the religious beliefs of the Mundas and Oraons. The Mundas have adopted the Hindu God Siva as "Mahadeo Bonga" and Parvati as "Chandi Bonga." There are clear signs of the influence of Munda and Oraon festivals. The intermingling of Mundas and some non-Munda classes has come to such a pass that the living styles of both have become alike. Marriage, name giving ceremony and other religious functions, household implements, clothes and bedding, house, naming of homes etc.- in all of these can be seen signs of an easy merger. All these influences have resulted due to contact.

In order to study the religious history of the Munda and Oraon tribes, it is essential to have a brief introduction of those backgrounds which have been helpful in developing and bringing to order the religious systems of their present lives. We have seen that compared to the Oraons, the Munda tribe was far behind from religious and social viewpoint. Prior to their entry into Chhotanagpur, from the descriptions available of Mundas and Oraons in the epics and the Puranas, it is clear that the Mundas were called "monsters" and "demons" by the Aryans where as at one time the Oraon tribe had got the affection of the Aryans. The hero of the Aryans Dasrathi Ram, had embraced them and called them "friends." The dietary habits, habitation and living style of the Mundas as compared to that of the Oraons was low. The Oraons were chiefly connected to agriculture and their dietary habits, habitation and living style were closer to Hindus. This is the reason why, according to the scholars analysing the folk-lore of the Mundas, the Oraons living in the company of the Mundas and accepting their food, slid down the steps of civilisation at that time,[117] because the eatables of the Mundas were low in standard and their company was lowly.

The Munda Tribe of Chhotanagpur

Our area of study is the Munda tribe of Chhotanagpur. From the time the Mundas entered India till Rohtasgarh, during this period of wandering the Munda tribe gave rise to several sub-tribes and went on settling in different areas. The other races, mainly the Aryan race, influenced their language and culture, and some of them got included by the Aryans and some became fully changed. This process continued during the flight of the Mundas from Rohtasgarh and even after entry into Chotanagpur. The Munda tribe broke into sub-tribes called Santhal, Ho, Larka etc. and they mainly settled in Santhal Parganas and Singhbhum. Although one finds similarity in their religious philosophy, there are enough differences in the practical form of their religion. Actually these differences have arisen due to the various ways of development of these sub-tribes and their circumstances.

We have seen that Rohtasgarh, too, could not provide security to the Mundas for many days. One night when they were peacefully asleep, the Kharwar chieftain Madho Das[118] attacked them. The defeated Mundas crossed the River Sone and, moving towards the south-east direction, they reached Omdanda which is near the meeting point of Palamau, Hazaribagh and Ranchi. From here, one group of Mundas separated, crossed the river Damodar and gradually went and settled in Santhal Parganas. They came to be recognised as "Santhals." In this way the Santhals and Mundas had a common ancestry.

From Omdanda, the Mundas crossed Lohardagga's "Sahar Ghatiya"[119] pass and reached Ranchi, and after clearing the forests of the western part of Ranchi, they started living there. The traditional lores of Mundas mention the Asuras who were iron-smelters. These Asuras used to melt the iron mixed mud and extract the iron from it to make many necessary implements. The Mundas attacked them and defeated them and thereafter banished them.[120] Thereupon the Mundas became the sole master of the whole region.[121] Seldom would any enemy try to enter this area protected by high hills, dense forests and deep valleys. Pasture and arable land were enclosed by scenic beauty. The high water-falls and the echo of the rippling sound of hill-streams invigorated the freely roaming Mundas who subsisted on roots and tubers, fruits and flowers within the forest limits; the Mundas had at last found a place of their liking where they could permanently live a secure and peaceful life.

The Mukhiya (head) and Pahan (Priest) in Village Organisation

By now the Munda tribe had emerged from their primitive condition and taken to animal husbandry and cultivation. Although they were not expert in agriculture, yet cultivation appeared to them to be easier and beneficial for a living. The Mundas prepared arable land after clearing the forests and also prepared places to live which were called "hatu". The meaning of "hatu" is village or house. The land and area prepared after cutting the forest by any Munda family was called "Khutkatti hatu" meaning the village of original inhabitant. The total property on the land and beneath it coming within the limits of khutkatti hatu was held to be under the authority and right of the concerned family. In this way many original families had cleared the forest and made their "khutkatti hatu" the limits of which were fixed. The boundaries of khutkatti hatu were fixed by lighting fires on the corners of the four directions and the lines joining these corners were fixed. No hatu would encroach these limits because they accepted these limits to be pure and indestructible. They believed that these boundary lines were protected by "seema-bongako" meaning the gods of the village boundaries. Khutkatti hatu used to be the personal property of a clan. In this way the feeling of private property gradually developed among the Mundas. The inhabitants staying in one khutkatti hatu were divided into three classes:

(1) Members of the original family whose number increased with every generation.

(2) The son-in-law married to a girl of the village who had left his own village to settle down with his in-laws.

(3) The iron-monger, weaver, bhogta who were necessary to fulfil the needs of the village and who had accepted the headship of the Mundas and who used to eke out their existence on the land given to them by the Mundas. Such persons were called "aeta haturenko." They were not the owners of the land given to them-the land was given to them

for maintenance in lieu of services given. This land could be taken away from them. Later on these "aeta haturenko" came to be called "Praja horoko." The word "Praja horoko" clearly echoes that in the village set up at that time these people were the subjects on the lower social rungs.

The condition of the sons-in-law who used to come from outside to settle in the village was also lowly compared to the members of the original family. They were also "aeta haturenko" meaning thereby that they had come from a different village. It used to be the accepted norm that only members of the original family would have rights over the total property of a "khutkatti hatu." but since sons-in-law were special people and with their sorrow and happiness the sorrow and happiness of the original family were also connected, over a period of time the right over the land given to them was transferred to them. But a function used to be arranged to mark the event. In that function the people of the village used to assemble and the whole society would freely accept that the sons-in-law be given the ownership of that land which had earlier been given just for their upkeep. In this way the "aeta haturenko" of this category would have "praja horoko." Their social standing was of middle level. They did not have to do the work of "praja horoko" which the iron mongers, weavers, shepherds etc used to do. They were given land in order to settle them in the village, whereas the land given to the "praja horoko" had been in lieu of wages for their labour. Actually the word "Praja" was a lowly noun used to denote the "praja horoko" in order to separate them from economic and social viewpoint. In this way, the seeds of class distinction had been sown in the nascent stage of the village of the then Munda society which were based on functions.[122]

The chief of the village used to be the eldest son of the original family of the village. He used to be the chief not only from the social viewpoint but also from the religious viewpoint. In the solution of social problems, his decision used to be final, and in the religious sector his analysis and its validity was above all. The power of today's "pahan," (priest) were placed in him. Due to being head of the village he came to be known as "Munda." It is said that the name "Munda" was given to him by the Hindus, the meaning of which is top or head connoting "the best among all." In this way the word "Munda," which used to denote the village headman gradually came to be the common name of the whole tribe. In the preliminary days of development, the qualities of social head and religious priest used to be present in the village "Munda." But his economic or land related condition used to be similar to other villagers. Like the others he also used to cultivate, and at times he would take the help and labour of others, in his fields in lieu of which, wherever possible, he would labour for others. Actually speaking, the Munda used to be a common person like the others. He did not have any special facility. For the solution of some dispute or in cases of attacks by other villagers, or to attack another village, the "Munda" would take the reins of control as the chief or leader of the village. It is said that for protection from attacks or in circumstances of attack on others, the women and men would become soldiers and work in a soldierly spirit, and the looted goods would be divided equally. Despite being the head and priest, the Munda used to be an ordinary villager like the rest.[123]

From every point of view, the Munda used to be the head of the village. If required, he would consult senior and experienced people of the village for solving any complicated issue. Till date he was carrying on the duties of Munda and priest, but due to excessive workload, a decline had begun in his work. He discussed the matter with the villagers and decided to select a priest for carrying out religious tasks. A particular selection process was adopted in which the selection of the priest had the approval of Singbonga. The Pahan (priest) used to be the link between the Mundas and Singbonga. It was the work of the Pahan to satisfy Singbonga and the other bongas. The various religious duties and functions of the village would be done under his auspices.

In the village, the Pahan was next to the Munda in importance. The Pahan and Assistant Pahan would be selected. The meaning of selection was Singbonga's desire for which there is a process called "lota-chalan." Once the Pahan was selected he would remain Pahan till his death. It was only after his death that a new Pahan would be selected. Gradually, just like the "Munda" the post of Pahan became hereditary. The Pahan is a respected representative of the village. The "Munda" or "Pahan" perform social or religious work with complete devotion. They do not get any economic benefit for this, although on some special occasions the villagers gift paddy or fine rice or some other goods to the Pahan.

From the viewpoint of racial and religious transition the praja-horoko of the village had a special importance. The religious and social condition of the original family and the sons-in-law settled in the village was completely different from the various sub-races coming within "praja horoko." These sub-races had a soft attitude towards their religion. The influence of various religions and sects would easily overtake the praja horoko. They were mainly of Hindu religion. Since their problem was not religious but economic, they were not fundamentalist in religion. Additionally, since the regional Munda or all the Munda families of the village were the benefactors or masters of the praja horoko, the religiosity of the Mundas and their activities, superstitions, occult practices, and the reasons connected with various diseases and their cure and treatment-methods which these sub-races saw and experienced in their daily lives, etc. had their direct influence on them. Hence their condition appeared to be just like the Mundas. The sub-races coming within the prajahoroko had come to the khutkatti hatu from different areas with different cultures. If these sub-races had been influenced by the cultural and religious activities of the Mundas, then they too had influenced the Mundas. The society outside the world of the Mundas had kept on influencing and changing the social, religious and judicial arrangements of the Mundas. In some areas, Mundas had heavily opposed any change in their traditional arrangements. They were conservative Mundas.

The differences of opinion between the conservative Mundas and the general Mundas could not be resolved, hence the conservative group gradually moved to the south-east and south of Ranchi and settled there. This group had organised itself into one class and instead of calling themselves "Munda" (name given by the Hindus) they preferred to be called "Ho" which they thought was more traditional. The sub-race of Mundas called 'Ho' went and settled in an area of Singhbhum. This area came to be called "Kolhan." Another class called "Larka" surfaced among the Hos. The larkas were also conservative, valiant and lovers of freedom. They had played a praiseworthy role in the 'Ho' and 'Kol' revolt. Just like the Santhals, 'Ho' and 'Larka' do not come within the purview of our study. But those Mundas of Chhotanagpur come who are recognised by the name of 'Munda' in the population census and also in government work, and many foreign writers have addressed them by the name of "Sarna Munda." Their religion is known by the name of "Sarna religion."

The Oraon Tribe of Chhotanagpur

We have already seen that the tribe called Oraon from south India to across the Narmada river, came to Rohtasgarh, and within this wandering, it came out of its primitive State to become expert in animal husbandry and agriculture but nearness to the Aryans influenced the tribe's dietary and living habits which accordingly acquired a high standard. Most Oraons who found it more respectable to be called 'Kurukh' had started wearing the sacred thread like the Hindus and thought meat-eating or other sub-standard food to be repugnant hence had started discarding them.

Upon entering Chhotanagpur from Rohtasgarh, the Oraons had to face the Mundas who had mainly spread in the northwestern part of Chhotanagpur. With the entry of the new tribe Kurukh in Chhotanagpur and confrontation with the Mundas, the Mundas had to leave their hearth and home and landed property and had to move over to the south-east of Ranchi.

Some questions about this have been raised which are as follows :

(1) Did the Mundas welcome the Oraons ?

(2) Did they give them support or was it conditional ?

(3) (Narendra Kumar, Ranchi Gazetteer) They gave support on condition that they stopped wearing the sacred thread and that they accepted and ate the meat given to them ?

(4) Due to increase in the population of the Oraons, the Mundas left their homes and country and went and settled in the central and south-east parts of the plateau or

(5) Due to defeat at the hands of the Oraons, they had to flee to the south-eastern direction ?

There has been detailed discussion on this. But it is apparent that with the passage of time, a lot of closeness was to be seen in Munda-Oraon relations and both races worked together for the development of economic and political life of Chhotanagpur. Although the religious ideals and philosophy of the Mundas were very different from those of the Kurukh, yet their social and religious activities had a good influence on each other's religious beliefs, tenets and way of life. Actually their life style and religion were influenced to some extent with the coming into contact with Hindus.

The Priest (pahan) and Mukhiya (head) in the Village Organisation

With the increase in population, the number of Oraon (Kurukh) villages started increasing. In every village there used to be a mukhiya (head) who was called mahto. The mukhiya used to be the authority to look after administrative and judicial arrangements as also the religious functions. In this way he combined the authority of five jurors and priest within himself. The post of mukhiya was hereditary and the rule of primogeniture was followed. As per requirement, meaning thereby that if the mukhiya had no son or the son was abnormal, diseased, had bad habits or was underserving, then the selection of mukhiya was conducted according to the desires of supernatural powers. Meaning thereby that after selection he was declared mukhiya. The Kurukhs believed that "Dharmes" had created that person to become the mukhiya of the village. In this way, the mukhiya of the village used to be incharge of the village arrangements and religious activities. During various occasions he used to represent the village and the people of the village always used to back and help him as a source of strength.

Over a period of time, some villages came together and formed a union. This was called "parha." There used to be seven to twenty one twenty two villages in one parha. Out of the mukhiyas of the villages included in the parha, one was recognised as the chief of the parha. The parha chief or pramukh used to be addressed as "parha raja" (king) and he used to be given respect accordingly. In the parha union, in addition to the raja, there used to be an executive committee whose members were the mukhiyas of the villages of that union. All the functions of the union were divided among the executive committee and in this way every member mukhiya was given the responsibility of one department. The arrangements in a parha sangha (union), in which all the villages used to be represented, were democratic and the disputes were resolved through majority decision according to prevailing rules and customs. In this way, the decisions would also be righteous.

The limits of authority of the parha were confined to the area of the union. The parha-panch used to solve the disputes of the villages included in the union. They used to look after all activities related to tribal benefit and development. Religious places, religious duties and property and marriage related as well as other traditional religious activities- whatever decision was taken by the parha assembly was considered final and a model for other problems coming in the future. Similar problems of the future were disposed of accordingly. There was nothing in writing anywhere. The ownership of land or agricultural field used to be transferred in the presence of the mukhiya of the village by the owner-transferor picking up a fistful of mud and, calling upon Dharmes as witness, transferring it to the person who was the transferee. Land transferred in this manner, at the end of the time period, would return to the previous owner or his heir, and land transferred permanently would be used in the form of ancestral property. In this manner, the customs coming from before would work as law which would be protected by parha raja and other members of the union who were bound by the customary rules. The condition of parha raja or the members was actually not like that of an authority but like that of ordinary Kurukhs who used to shoulder the responsibility of serving the village and the union. Although their duties were social, their source of strength was religious due to which they could carry out their duties successfully, and without any legal pressure the Kurukhs of the area obeyed them.

The Emergence of Raja Phanimukut Rai and the Protection of Munda/Oraon Culture from the Invasions of the Mughals

The mukhiya used to carry out the responsibilities of judicial and administrative arrangements of the village, and the priest used to control and manage the religious ceremonies and activities. Before the emergence of kingship in tribal society of Chhotanagpur, the chief of the village alone used to combine the religious and judicial responsibilities within himself but with the passage of time the purohits or priests came into existence who thereafter became the religious head. Since as per circumstances, the pressure and influence of religion over politics and politics over religion keep on falling, the main tribes of Chhotanagpur (Munda and Oraon) had started claiming their rights over Phanimukut Rai, the first elected king of Chhotanagpur. Since Phani Mukut Rai had been reared in a Munda family, hence, even though he was not of Munda origin, the claim of the Mundas over him was accepted to be more. Dalton has accepted Phanimukut Rai to be of Munda origin.[132] But in the traditional lore of the Oraons, Phanimukut Rai has been claimed to be of Kurukh origin, a matter which we have already discussed before. Granard has[133] tried to prove Phanimukut Rai to be of Chero family, while Risley[134] states that Phanimukut Rai was from some Rajput family of Dravidian origin. Whatever it may be, kingship had started with Phanimukut Rai in Chhotanagpur and later on the heirs Phanimukut Rai had taken pride in establishing relationship with Hindu princely families and started keeping Brahmin State priests in their court. Those kings had nearly become Hinduised and no apparent signs of Munda and Oraon tribes could be seen in their descendants or their connections. They called their Hindu relatives and many powerful Hindus and settled them in Chhotanagpur by giving them land. In this manner, the population of Hindus coming from outside Chhotanagpur became so large that their way of living, marriage practices, and dietary habits very deeply influenced the tribals living nearby.

Traditional Village Arrangements and their Cultural Heritage

In Indian history, during the Hindu and Mughal periods, the traditional village arrangements and cultural traditions of the Munda and Oraon tribes were completely protected, and no outside invasion had tried to dis-arrange the same. Their parha assembly custom, their religious activities were completely protected due to the dense forests and high hills. Their culture was handed down generation to generation without any hindrance. The Mughals had at times encroached upon this area but their interest lay only in collecting revenue from this area. They had not interfered with the State affairs or tribal judicial or religious arrangements. Although in the other parts of the country the Mughals had attacked in the name of religion and plundered the areas, forcibly converted people into Islam religion, their evil eye had not fallen upon the forest dwellers of Chhotanagpur, and their parha union arrangement, their traditional culture continued as before till the advent of the British in Chhotanagpur.

This means that till the Mughal period of Indian History, the Munda and Oraon land strip lived self-respecting lives within parha self governance. The British period was a period of struggle for the tribes of Chhotanagpur.

References

1. Dr B. S. Guha, Race Elements in Indian Population (p. 09).
2. 1991 Population Census.
3. R. C. Nigam – Language Handbook of Mother Tongues in Census (New Delhi-1972) p. LI.
4. S. K. Chatterji – Language and Literature of Modern India (Calcutta 1963) pp. 13-14.
5. Shiv Shekhar Mishra – Bharatiya Sanskriti me Aryetarangsh, p. 32.
6. W. Schmidt, Die mon-Khmer Voelkar ain Bindeglied Zwischen Volkern Zentral Asiens and Austral nesiens (Braunchewing) 1906, p. 36.
7. T. Burrow, The Sanskrits Language, p. 377.
8. W. Von Hevesy, Finisch-ugrisches aus Indien (vinna) p. 13-16.
9. *Ibid*, p. 345.
10. Hewitt in Journal of Royal Asiatic Society 1889.
11. T. A. Sebeok, An Examination of the Astro Asiatic Language family in Language, Vol.18, pp. 206-207.
12. F. H. Hodgson, Essays Relating to Indian subjects.

13. Sten konow, "It seems therefore necessary to assume that Mundas or Tribes related to them have once been settled in the Himalayas where traces of their language can still be observed in grammatical features of the dialects spoken in Kanwar." "on some facts connected with the Tibeto-Burman Dialect spoken in Kanawar" an article published in Z.G.M.G. (Leipzig) 1905, Vol.59, p. 117.
14. R. C. Nigam, Language Handbook of Mother Tongues in Census, p. 33.
15. J. H. Hutton, Caste in India (2nd. Edition, Mumbai, 1951) p. 04.
16. W. Schmidt, Die Mon-Khmer Voelkar, in Bindeglied Zwischen Zentral Asiens and Astronesiens pp. 60-62. Schmidt found racial conformities as (1) a dolichocephalic to Mesocephalic skull, (2) nonslanting eyes (3) eyes round, wide open without epicanthic fold (4) noses bridgeless and broad at nostril (5) skin dark colour (6) more or less wavy hair and (7) short or at the most middle statures.
17. P. O. Bodding : "Mongolian Race marks amongst the Santhals" (An article in the Journal of Royal Asiatic Society of Bengal, Vol. 73-Kolkata) p. 26.
18. J. H. Hutton – Caste in India, p. 04.
19. Hewitt, Journal of the Royal Asiatic Society 1988 and 1989.
20. G. T. Bowies, "Linguistic and Racial Aspects of the Munda Problem" Published in "Studies in Anthropology of Oceania and Asia" (Cambridge, 1943).
21. R. Von Heine Geldern, Pre-historic Research in Netherlands Indies (New York, 1945) p. 198.
22. A. H. Dani, Pre-History and Proto-History of Eastern India (cal.1960), p. 225.
23. J. H. Hutton, Caste in India, p. 4.
24. See Annexure: Manoba Kobe: Dobra Jonome "Manuda Hone Koa nutum Marang ni: Mundas, Majhlani Roda, Eta: ni:nanka Lita ni:Sodto Puthhi Jaikena-" Collected from the area.
25. Jagdish Trigunayat- Munda Lok Kathayein (Welfare Department, Bihar Government, Patna 1968) Kathha Bhag p. 15.

    Here, due to the closeness of Lakshmi, the meaning of Bhagwan is Vishnu and the whole scene gives the feeling of "Ksheer Sagar" or the ocean of milk.
26. S. C. Roy- Mundas and their Country, p. 328.

    In the referred story the names of the sons have been mentioned as Roda, Nanka and Tenha, but in another collection of stories of Trigunayat, the creation of four brothers and sister has been stated, the names of who are Munda, Roda, Nanka, and Sodto. These brothers and sisters were able to get married and raise offsprings. (Munda Lok Kathhayein, p. 45)- in the excerpt presented by S. C. Roy, there is no mention of raising of offsprings.
27. S. C. Roy- Mundas and their Country, p. 10.
28. Atkinson's Statistical Account, XIII, p. 131.
29. Mahabharat, Shanti Parva, 84.
30. Taiteriya Upanishad 6/2.
31. Count Bjornstijema : Theory of the Hindus, p. 134.
32. Winternitz, "..... Date....... Falls in the third rather than in the second millennium Christ." Vol. I, p. 258.

33. H. B. Sarda: Hindu Superiority, p. 8.
34. Hon. Alex. Del Mar, "Indian Ancestry of the Western World" article published in Indian Review, April, 1908.
35. R. C. Nigam, Languages Handbook of Mother Tongues in Census, p. 33.
36. Z. A. Ragozin, Vedic India (Ragozin commenting on two distinct classes of sepulchral mounds found in northern India writes, "The former, we may very well infer belong to the period when the Mundas and their conquerors lived in northern India before the Aryans entered the country and pushed them to the south," p. 287).
37. Calcutta Review- Vol. LXIX, p. 350.
38. Hiren, Historical Researches, Vol.II, p. 207.
39. Sir William Jones, On the Chronology of the Hindus, an article published in Asiatic Researches, Vol. II.
40. Mahabharat, Bhishma Parva. 343.
41. Aitreya Brahman 7/18.
42. Cunningham Arch. Report Vol.VI, p. 195.
43. Cunningham Arch. Report Vol.VI, p. 17.
44. Atkinson's Statistical Account of the North West Province, Vol.VIII, Part-I, p. 153.
45. Mahabharat, Drone Parva 117/23.
46. Mahabharat, Bhishma Parva 117/23-25 (Munda netan hanipyami danavaniv wagava).
47. Bhagwat Purana, Khand 4/ chapter 15 (Prathmo mushantar dwitiyo Kollamev cha tritiyo bhill sankhyatmity ete cha udrihrita).
48. Atkinson's Settlement Account, Vol. V, p. 342.
49. Atkinson's Settlement Account, Vol.V, p. 757.
    Cunningham's Archaeological Report Vol.XIII, p. 61.
50. T. F. Peppe, Asiatic Societies Journal (Bengal Branch) Part-I, p. 119.
51. W. Peppe Esq. in the Asiatic Society's Journal, Calcutta Vol. XXXV Part-I, p. 53.
52. Cunningham's Archaeological Report, Vol. XVI, pp. 59-60.
53. E. F. Pargeeter JRAS (1914) p. 271.
54. Shahabad Gazetteer, p. 47.
55. S. C. Roy, The Oraons of Chhotanagpur, p. 10 (footnote).
56. Rev. F. Hahn, Kurukh Grammar (Introduction).
57. Dalton's Ethnology, p. 245.
58. Dr Grierson, Grierson's Linguistic Survey, Vol. IV, p. 406.
59. Professor Braj Behari, Kurukh Kosh (Nagaland Bhasha Parishad, Kohima).
60. Based on Population census of 1971.
61. Walter Hamilton (i) A Geographical, Statistical and Historical Description of Hindustan (London, John Murwag 1820) Vol.I, p. 288 (ii) East India Gazetteer (London 1828) pp. 415 and 416 Col. Dalton (iii) Ethnology of Bengal (1872), p. 245.

62. Grierson, Linguistic Survey, Part IV, p. 245.
63. Col. Dalton, Ethnology, p. 245.
64. S. C. Roy, The Oraons of Chhotanagpur, p. 15.
65. R. K. Chaudhary- Prachin Bharat Ka Rajnaitik evam Sanskritik Itihas, p. 27.
66. R. C. Majumdar- "......That" "Early man" in India originated in south India, and migrated towards Punjab at the close of the first Ice Age"- Ancient India, p. 13.
67. R. K. Chaudhary- Prachin Bharat Ka Rajnaitik evam Sanskritic Itihas, p. 27.
68. Vachaspati Gerola- "The Aegean (Proto Australoid) of the Mediterranean Sea and West Asia Minor's Armenide races merged with each other and gave birth to the Dravidian race- Bha. san. K. p. 104.
69. Vachaspati Gerola- Bharatiya Sanskriti our Kala, p. 107.
70. R. C. Majumdar- "The most widely accepted view is that the authors of Sindhu Valley Civilisation were Dravidians i.e. of the Mediterranean type....", Ancient India, p. 28.
71. (i) Vachaspati, Bharatiya Sanskriti aur Kala, p. 105.
    (ii) E. R. Gait, Mundas and their Country (S. C. Roy), Intro. XVI.
    (iii) R. C. Majumdar, Ancient India, p. 18.
72. Thurston, Caste and Tribes of South India (App. I)
73. V. D. Mahajan, Ancient India, p. 44.
74. A. H. Keane in Mundas and their Country, Introduction, p. XIV.
75. The subject related to proof of language in the context of migration of the Mundas has already been discussed in detail.
76. E. A. Gait, Introduction (Mundas and their Country) p. Xvi.
77. Bishop Caldwell, Dravidian Grammar, p. 4FF.
78. Thurston, Caste and Tribes of Southern India (Madras 1909) Introduction xix-xxxvi.
79. R. C. Majumdar, Ancient India, p. 13 (already discussed).
80. Annexure, "Agnivarsha" .... Bhaiya bahi nin-nura sira-sita.
81. J.B.O.R.S. Vol. II (1916), p. 65.
82. Proceeding of Asiatic Society of Bengal 1870.
83. Note on Ruins of Majhagaon (Chainpur) in JBORS Vol. I (1915), pp. 117-124.
84. J.B.O.R.S. Vol. II (1911) p. 62.
85. Man in India, Vol. XVII, pp. 220-221.
86. Ranchi Gazetteer, p. 39.
87. Balmiki Ramayan, Kishkindha Kand, 37/5, 17/1.
88. Balmiki Ramayan, Kishkindha Kand, 22/24, 26, 4.
89. Balmiki Ramayan, Kishkindha Kand, 33/38, 37/45.
90. Balmiki Ramayan, Kishkindha Kand, 37/27.
91. Balmiki Ramayan, Kishkindha Kand, 26/6, 15/2.
92. Balmiki Ramayan, Aranya Kand, 63/11.

93. Balmiki Ramayan, Aranya Kand, 50/19-20.
94. Balmiki Ramayan, Lanka Kand, 30/22 -24.
95. Balmiki Ramayan, Kishkindha Kand, 37/19.
96. JASB XIV, 519.
97. Balmiki Ramayan, Kish Kindha Kand, 5.
98. After defeat at Rohtasgarh when the Oraons started to flee in search of shelter elsewhere, then they got divided into two groups. One group went along the banks of the Sone River, came to Palamau lying on the south-east of the North Koel River and thereafter reached Chhotanagpur and came to be called "Oraon." The other group following the bank of the River Ganga went north and settled on the hills of Rajmahal. This group of the Oraons is called "Maley."
99. Panini 4/6–178.
100. Ramayan Bal Kand 28/18 – 23.
101. Bhagwat Purana, 10/66.
102. Vayu Purana, 459, Matsya-114 : 54, Markandeya Puran 57.53-5.
103. Colonel Dalton, as quoted in Shahabad Gazetteer, p. 154.

     Historians connect the relationship of Chero and Bhar tribes with the Mundas. Those Mundas who were in close contact with the Aryans in the Indo- Gangetic plain had become so exceedingly changed due to the influence of the language, culture and religion of the Aryans that there remained no signs of identification of being Mundas except certain physical and racial characteristics. They used to connect themselves with the higher class of the Aryans, especially the Kshatriyas. The Kharwars thought themselves to be Suryavanshis (of the lineage of the Sun). (Shahabad Gazetteer, p. 867).
104. S. C. Roy, "But the word Karush used in the Mahabharat is the adjectival form of Karush and simply means people from Karush country."- The Oraons of Chhotanagpur, p. 23 (Footnote).
105. *Ibid* : "when..... Kolarian tribes of the Chero became predominant in Karus-des the ancestors of the Maler and Oraons appear to have taken shelter on the Rohtas Plateau." p. 23.
106. "Jani Shikar" prevalent among the tribals of Chhotanagpur is now organised in the form of a festival in which the women dressed in men's wear and armed with bows and arrows come out of the village in a group and symbolically display that their female ancestors had donned soldiers' dress to fight the "mlechchas" for the protection of their race.
107. Risley: Tribes and Castes of Bengal, Calcutta, 1891, Vol. II, p. 139.
108. S. C. Roy, "Mundas and their Country," p. 77.
109. Dr. Buchanan, "Eastern India," Vol. I, p. 494.
110. S. C. Roy, The Oraons of Chhotanagpur, p. 26.
111. "The traditions of the Oraons relate that they held the fort of Rohtasgarh till ousted by Hindus"- Bengal, Bihar, Orissa, Census Report 1911, Part - I, p. 402.
112. Dr. Buchanan, "The Cheros once lord of the Gangetic provinces..... that they live exactly in the same manner as Rajputs.......But the Brahmins allege

that the Cheros live as impure as highland Kharwar" – Eastern India, Vol. I, p. 494.

113. S. C. Roy, "A probable explanation for the mention of Hindus in one tradition, of the Mohammedans in another tradition, as having expelled the Oraons from the Rohtas plateau appears to be that two different waves of Oraons in migration into Chhotanagpur took place, one at a long interval after the other"- The Oraons of Chhotanagpur, p. 26.
114. W. W. Hunter's observation quoted in Shahabad Gazetteer, p. 146.
115. L. S. S. O'Mailey, Santhal Pargana Gazetteer, second Indian Reprint 1999, New Delhi, pp. 23-24.
116. S. C. Roy- Oraons of Chhotanagpur, p. 27.
117. *Ibid.*
118. Ranchi Gazetteer, p. 138.
119. S. C. Roy, "Oraons acted in a conciliatory spirit"- Oraons of Chhotanagpur, p. 27.
120. P. Das Sharma, The Passing scene, Introduction, p. 02.
121. S. C. Roy, "It is sometimes supposed that the Oraons came to Chhotanagpur having been invited by the then Raja of Chhotanagpur to help in suppressing the Mundas..... This account does not appear to be quite unlikely." – Mundas and their Country, p. 69 (footnote).
122. Herbert Risley describes Nagbansis of Chhotanagpur "as a subtribe of pseudo-Rajputs, probably of Dravidian descent "- Tribe and Caste, Vol.II, p. 121.
123. S. C. Roy, "Mundas and their Country," p. 68 (footnote).
124. Shahabad Gazetteer..... "Major Munro laid the foundations of a momentous change and made the British the masters of Eastern India," p. 79.
125. Ranchi Gazetteer, p. 44.
126. Kumar Suresh Singh- Birsa Munda evam unka Andolan, p. 13.
127. S. C. Roy- The Oraons of Chhotanagpur, p. 27.
128. "In the traditional tales of Mundas, the reason for the attack has been said to be that Kharwar chief Madhodas, upon seeing the helplessness of his son in love, requested for the hand of a Munda maiden for marrying his son, but the Mundas rejected the same. The Kharwars took this "rejection" as an insult and in order to take revenge they attacked the Mundas at night when they were fast asleep and defeated them. The traditional tales of the Santhals and Kharwars also confirm this incident. (Be it known that the Santhals and Mundas had the same ancestors in Rohtasgarh). According to the tradition of the Kharwars, they had fled from Khairagarh to the south and had reached the hills of Kaimur where they confronted the Kols (Munda), Cheros and Asurs whom they defeated and took command of the Kaimur hills. The hills of Kaimur mean Rohtasgarh." See : "Primitive Races of Shahabad" Published in Calcutta Review, Vol. LXX, pp. 349 and 356.
129. Ranchi Gazetteer (1970) p. 41.
130. S. C. Roy, "Mundas and their Country," p. 60.
131. *Ibid.*

132. B. K. Roy Burmon : Obviously the seeds of ethnic differentiation were shown through functional differentiation even during this period" – Ethnic relations in Chhotanagpur (an article published in the book" The Passing Scene" Ed. P. "Das Sharma" p. 163).
133. S. C. Roy, "His (Munda's) position has been aptly described as that of a "Primus Inter Pares"- a chief among equals,"- Mundas and their Country, p. 65.
134. Dalton's Ethnology, pp. 162 and 168.
135. Rev. F. Grignard, Anthropos, Vol. IV.
136. Herbert Risley, Tribes and Castes, Vol. II, p. 121.

Chapter - 3

Munda Religion: Sarna Religion

The definition and analysis of "dharma" has been done with extreme fineness, and extensively by the Indian scholars. According to them, right from the Vedic era, Aryan and non-Aryan cultures have developed themselves in the field of religion. Churning and investigating the bottomless depths of life and the world, they have perceived the form of religion to be human religion through which, in this world and the next world, the progress of virtue, purpose, desire and salvation, that is final beatitude, these four objects of man's creation and existence may be obtained, and this is religion. Which means that, that which takes everybody equally towards progress and guides towards welfare that is religion. In this way, religion is rectitude; it is discipline, through which the whole of human life and this universe are controlled. The expression of religion takes place in the conduct, thought, faith or emotion of man. Religious expression is more clearly seen in the life styles of the Munda and Oraon tribes. Although the Hinduised "thought" of "salvation" and "next world" has not developed in Munda life, yet all their activities are controlled and directed by their religious beliefs, so much so that religion plays an important role in the conduct of their panchayat and judicial arrangements.

Munda Religion : Sarna Religion

Munda religion is known as "Sarna religion." This religion is in existence since the time of the ancestors of the Mundas. It is connected to the "original Mundas." Original Munda is the tribe belonging to the root or original lineage from which other branches have separated, expanded and in a new environment have adopted such language, culture and religion which are different from Sarna religion and Munda culture. After entry into Chhotanagpur, that Munda tribe, which cleared the forests for agriculture and settlement, and which confined itself to Ranchi and nearby areas, and also followed the Sarna religion of its ancestors, is the original Munda tribe, from the religious point of view. We do not at all mean those Mundas who have converted to other religions

(Christian) because not only their religion but their dress, food habits, worship, festivals, all are changed and imported; they have strayed from the path of Sarna religion of their ancestors. The Mundas who are connected to the Sarna religion of the ancestors are also known as "Sarna Munda."

The religion of the Mundas came to be called and known as "Sarna religion" after their entry into Chhotanagpur. Before their entry into Chotanagpur, knowledge regarding the form of religion of the Mundas, could be gathered from the various implements found at various places pertaining to the coming of this tribe to India and its migration to Chhotanagpur; it could also be made clear from the available descriptions in Sanskrit literature as also from their folk lore/songs about the places concerned with their creation and the birth of their race and its expansion. They had belief in paranormal force, they were worshippers of nature, they believed in the formlessness of God, they were influenced by occult practices and they were self-respecting about their religion and race. After settling down in Chhotanagpur, their religious flow maintained nearly the same pace although time, place and circumstances tried to enclose the aforementioned Munda religion in a local structure which gave rise to "Sarna religion" from the original Munda religion. Since it is believed that Mundas came to Chhotanagpur in sixth century B.C., hence Sarna religion also came up in about the same time.

After coming to Chhotanagpur, the Munda family cut down or burnt the forest and prepared land for settlement and cultivation, and the area thus cleared came to be called "khutkutti hatu" over which the lordship of the Munda family came to be accepted. At the edge of the village a small part of the forest was bounded in such a manner that all the trees and plants coming within its fold were accepted as holy and pure and the village people came to believe that "hatu bongako" (village god) resides on the trees of the enclosure, and day and night he looks after the protection and well-being of the village. In order to keep the "hatu bongako" pleased, the villagers not only offered prayers and worship but also offered gifts and sacrifices. The whole place is considered to be holy and pure, and the place is called "Sarna."[1] The trees of "Sarna" are not cut down because otherwise the "hatu bongako" becomes angry and then the cloud of disaster hovers over the village. The "sal" tree is the tallest; hence the village god resides on the sal tree. In several villages, branches of sal trees which have broken and fallen on the ground, cannot be touched by anyone except the pahan (priest). After getting information, the pahan purifies himself completely, and accompanied by some villagers comes to the place, and after worshipping and sacrificing a cock he pleases "hatu bongako" and then with his approval (the sign of which only the pahan knows and understands), he picks up the branch of the sal tree from the ground. In this way, "Sarna" is the holy grove of the Mundas and it is the source of inspiration of the religious philosophy of the Mundas. It is on this basis that the religion of the original Mundas has been called "Sarna religion."[2]

Sarna religion has two elements- Nature (forest boundaries, river, mountain etc.) and Bonga. The entire circumstances of religion are confined to forest life and forest produce. In religious rituals and sacred precepts, mainly those materials are used which grow on the forest trees or are grown on the land cleared of forests. Although with the passage of time, due to Hindu influence or influences related to circumstances, some alternatives to materials used in sacred precepts have been accepted, but in the basic form these materials are obtained from the forests. The other influential element of religion is the role of the "bongako." Bongas are wicked and destructive, bongas are simple and beneficial to people, bongas shoulder the responsibility of protecting their area, meaning thereby that bongas of Mundas are the gods of the area and nature. Which means that river, mountain, pond, village, home, tree, grove, everywhere Munda life is surrounded by the bongas. Amongst these bongas, the supreme is "Singbonga." "Singbonga" is the Supreme Being of the Mundas. In religious and social duties, "Singbonga" is remembered. The selection of a bride, fixing proper direction or on occasions of similar other social and religious decisions, Singbonga indicates His approval or disapproval through various signs sent by Him, the analysis of which is done by the pahan, devra, or by special followers who understand Singbonga's language, and they tell the meaning of the signs to the Mundas. Ever since Singbonga has gone into profound meditation, He sends his messages through signs, hence the direction given by the pahan and devra or the faithful becomes the direction given by Singbonga. No Munda can question this.

The Mundas always pay attention to keep Singbonga pleased. They sacrifice white cocks for Him. They recite prayers to Him. The pahan, devra and the other faithful in one voice offer worship to Him by singing paeans to Him. These religious hymns are related to various legends and religious tales. The legends throw light on Creation, the emergence of the Munda tribe and its development. In these songs such incidents are also mentioned which are related to the birth of various clans and their subdivision, totem and taboos. On occasions, tales related to occasions are related and even sung.

In religious songs, legends and traditional folk-tales, apart from imaginary things, some historical parts are also to be found. Imagination cannot be baseless. Imagination has some basis to it.

This basis may be searched in natural incidents or in various activities of Nature (destruction and creation) or in those signs or remnants of signs which are symbols of memory of certain historic or imaginary incidents which have become extinct in the womb of far-off times. When religious songs came into existence, man did not know how to differentiate between "history" and "imagination," hence in those tales whom we have received in the form of religious songs there are elements of history and traditional tales combined. Both have developed together and with the passage of time, history has separated from stories and stories from history.[3]

Sofia Werne has clear views regarding the aforementioned context that religious songs are tales of appraisal of reasons in which the universe, its birth, annihilation, creation, racial-distinction, commercial-distinction, religious treatment, ancestral songs and similar other mysterious actions and the reasons thereof- their analysis is contained in them.[4] Although these reasons may also be impossible, but those who know those religious songs, they believe in the reasons given. The belief in religious songs/tales is the actual inspirational strength of these religious songs/tales. That is the reason why Taylor feels that the religious songs/tales do not depict the history of the incidents mentioned in them-they depict the history of their believers.[5] The meaning of believers relates to the unshakeable faith of those believers who generation after generation, have absorbed this faith in their souls regarding these religious songs/tales and passed them down accordingly.

Sarna Munda does not accept any interpretation of religious songs/tales. He rejects the probability of any question pertaining to the religious songs/ tales. Questions are raised where there is no faith, and interpretation changes the "actual truth" of the religious song/tale. Religious songs/tales relate to incidents pertaining to values which have always and everytime been true, right from the starting era to all other eras. Behind this is a faith in values which is not influenced by country, time and circumstances. That which was yesterday is today and will become tomorrow "nang nang, jugu jugu, Kal-talare." This truth is eternal because in the view of Mundas, Sarna religion is eternal.

The Munda songs/tales can be divided into two parts from the viewpoint of religious history:

First – Man's creation and the reason for his creation.

Second – The downfall of man and his salvation.

In the first part: the work of Creation, the creation of man, development of race, the first plough (for agriculture), the division of time and discovery of tobacco. In the second part: the downfall of the Munda tribe, destruction, re-development, rain of fire and Asur legends are included. (See annexure: legends and religious songs).

In the Munda race, there are many such religious songs and legends prevalent in which the philosophy of religion and religious life of Sarna Munda are easily expressed. Hadam, Singbonga, the birth of Munda tribe from lutkums, protection and expansion: the emanation of clans, totem, the downfall of the Asurs, the emergence of regional gods (bongas), the birth of time, the creation of sun, moon, the division of day and night, etc., are such subjects to which Munda religion is tied. In addition, Munda life is controlled by various religious duties and ceremonies as also customs and practices in which sasan (graveyard), ading (that place in Munda homes where the soul of the dead person is established), akhra (circular place in the middle of the village where various functions are held), ceremonies from birth to death, marriage, ancestor-worship etc. are included. In Munda religion, signs have an importance because through them Singbonga sends His directions. Most of the religious activities of Mundas are related to obtain the grace of Singbonga and to please the bongas and the souls of the dead otherwise they will have to face natural calamities and many domestic troubles. In this way, the faith of the Mundas is based on fear and superstition in which there is minimum possibility of knowledge and love. As such, Kabir, the concepts of Chaitanya Mahaprabhu, the living habits of Hindu kings and landlords, festivals and worship and the influence of recitation of the Ramayana and Mahabharata on different occasions by their preachers, various religious movements and also due to Christian missionaries, the signs of change in the "thinking" of the Mundas and their living habits have been seen, but most pahans and their mankis consider it to be superficial change. According to them, since the religious social institutions, customs and practices, ceremonies and pantheon are confined to religious songs, legends and cultural traditions in their development the religious history of Munda tribe is fully intact.

Modern Times and Munda Religion

We have already seen that after the death of Alivardi Khan on 10 April 1756, the victory of the British in the Battle of Plassey in 1757 and the downfall of Buxar, on 12 August 1765 the Diwani of Bengal, Bihar, Orissa was transferred to the British and alongwith that the whole of Eastern India including Chhotanagpur came within the grip of the British. Till that time although the Mughals collected land rent from the Kings and protectors of the passes (but) they did not interfere in the internal administration of Chhotanagpur and neither did they try to break up the tribal life, their traditional culture or their religious beliefs. But the policy of the British was absolutely different from that of the Mughals. The aim of British entry into Chhotanagpur was to capture it completely, to bring the king and the public to its side by hook or by crook, and to make them go against the Marathas of Orissa. The Marathas had become a terror for the East India Company and the Presidency of Calcutta. Good relations had developed between some kings of Chhotanagpur alongwith the primitive tribes spread all over the forest ranges and the Marathas of Orissa. The Marathas used to raid Bengal and Calcutta after passing through the forest and hilly paths of Chhotanagur and after plundering would return to Orissa by the same route. The public of Chhotanagpur cooperated with the Marathas. Hence, against the Marathas, mainly the primitive tribes had to be essentially won over to their side. If security against the Marathas could be ensured then East India Company and its connected traders could get a safe passage through Chhotanagpur for trading in Central India and the south. Knowledge regarding this aim of the British can be obtained, from the "minute" of the meeting held in April 1832.[6]

In order to fulfil this aim, the British made a lot of effort. The preaching of Christian religion by padres and conversion of tribes to Christianity was one such effort which went in favour of the British. The brotherhood of religion was such a connecting thread through which the British Government could join these sons of the soil who were in favour of the Marathas. Which meant that increasing the number of Christians through conversion of religion, some portion of the original public could be won over to their side. The British officers were of the opinion that even if the missionaries partly succeeded, and mingling with the primitive tribes they became familiar with their customs and practices, then they would succeed in breaking the Marathas and strengthening their administrative hold over Chhotanagpur. The missionaries shouldered this responsibility to a certain extent. During their preaching, they tried to raise the standard of living of the Mundas, they tried to end their superstitious belief in ghosts and spirits and witchcraft, and they tried to inculcate the habit of shunning "hadiya." Although there had been serious pulling each other up between the government and the missionaries regarding the question of "Captaincy fight," and many converted Mundas had started leaving the Christian religion and calling the padres cheats which had badly influenced the preaching of Christian religion, and in the freedom movement of 1857 and the First World War,[7] the enmity between the British and the Germans badly affected the missionaries of Chhotanagpur, still then, the seeds of Christianity sown in this soil by the missionaries ran so deep that from the second decade of the twentieth country, they started getting unprecedented success. In reply to the Christians, the "purification movement" started by the Arya Samajis and the emergence of "Birsa dharm" (religion) had successfully influenced the then Sarna Mundas in their religious activities.

The structure of Munda religion alongwith its development (revolution or change which is called "development" by sociologists) and its direction is the backbone of the history of Munda religion in modern times. The main factors in the structuring of Munda religion as also deciding its form, may be mentioned as religious songs, legends and traditional tales as also customs and practices, ceremonies, institutions, clan, totem, festivals and pantheon etc. but even within the narrow confines of Chhotanagpur, similarity cannot be found in the forms related to these songs/tales and customs and practices. If every subject is independently investigated in detail in Chhotanagpur, especially in the villages of east-south Ranchi inhabited by Mundas and the villages of Mundas in the south-eastern region, then there can be found a clear difference in the religious rules and regulations of worship although the basic religious current remains the same. For example, in the area of Nagri Dishum which extends from Khunti's western area to Doaesa, Palkot, Basiya etc. police stations, when a dead body is kept on the floor, it is taken into consideration that the head should be towards the north and the feet towards the south, whereas in Hasda which is to the east of Khunti, and in which

Murhu and a large part of Khunti police station are included, just opposite to the practice of the Mundas of Nagri Dishum the head of the dead body rests in the south and the feet lie in the north direction, but the traditional basic institution of "sasan diri" is followed in the same manner in both areas. Nearly similar situation prevails regarding some religious institutions and folk-tales. Due to difference in areas differences in certain rules can be seen in the performance of marriage, and in various folk tales differences in description can be seen regarding creation, horse, human doll and the creation of dog or cheetah (leopard) for protection of human-doll and creatures, and the birth of Munda tribe, although religious faith which is at the root is the same. In this way, there is a big difficulty in recording the history of Munda religion because the form of Munda religion is not the same everywhere.

The historical elements available in legends and religious songs have already been discussed and to what extent they may be accepted as history or not has been analysed in detail. When examined on the touchstone of scientific mode of current recording of history, these semi-historical tales are not found genuine yet righteousness, morality, God and His powers of creation and destruction, its expansion, racial expansion etc. inherent in them which are values of faith, they are the apparent "truth" and they are to be found fully in Munda life and confirmation of which is from data available on the basis of first information among the Mundas. Since just like the Hindu codes of law there was no text of Munda religion, apart from some collections by Christian missionaries of certain articles which were mostly prejudiced, hence this effort in writing about the religious history of the Mundas, though the opinions of former writers have been presented in the attempt, is prima facie based on source, hence it is near the current mode of historical recording.

The Deities of Mundas

The history of Munda religion is connected to the history of the emergence of Munda deities along with the character of these gods, the history of their religious importance and according to intervals of time the fall in their importance and their gradual rise to a higher level. The establishing of oneness of Hadam and Singbonga, the condition of fixing levels of the sectoral bongas, the religious condition of the home deity or ading bongako and the limits of the importance of evil spirits, etc., it is essential to not only discuss in brief but also to discuss the fall in the religious importance of some Munda gods during the early British period. With the advent of missionaries, the character and power of Munda deities have suffered grievious hurt. So much so that the missionaries refused to accept the bongas as gods because according to them there is no such thing as "godliness" in the character of the bongas. In this manner, according to these investigators, Munda religion is monotheist. Most of those who favour the opinion of "Monotheist" are Christian missionaries, chief of who are Hoffmann, P. Ponnet, A. Van Exam etc. In the Encyclopaedia

Mundarica, in Khutkutti and Bongako, Hoffmann has tried to prove that Singbonga is the only God of the Mundas. The character of the other bongas is not god-like, hence Munda religion is monotheist. In order to support his argument, Hoffmann has presented examples from "Creation" religious song/tale and "Asur avdan" (legend). According to Hoffman, once upon a time when social life was at its primary stage and individual small families used to live in groups, then the total responsibility of protection of the family and its rearing was on the father who was the master of the family. He used to save the family from outside dangers and due to his close connections with the other members, he used to think about their happiness and facilities and made available to them protection and materials useful for livelihood.

Hence, being influenced by the position of the father in the family and his importance, it was natural that Munda life would instil the qualities of a father in the Creator (Singbonga or Hadam) in the primary stages of religion. In this stage of religion there was no intervenor between man (Munda) and Supreme Power (Singbonga). This position was patriarchal monotheistic religious position[8] in which God was equal to father.

Hoffman has also mentioned about the second position of religion in Munda life which is being presented in support of his monotheistic opinion. According to Hoffmann, in the second position, the king had emerged who was the benefactor of men and who used to protect them from outside dangers. His power was spread all over and for the proper management of his power, the king had distributed responsibilities to some important and faithful subordinates. Some portions of the king's "power" and "qualities" would come over these subordinates. According to Hoffman, in Munda life, in this developed condition of religion can be seen the king and his sharing 'subordinates' like arrangement. Hoffman has termed this condition of religion as monarchical monotheistic condition in which the monarch is compared to God.[9]

In order to confirm his findings, Hoffmann has taken the support of religious song/tale related to Creation and the coming of man, as also Asur legend. We know that in "Asur legend," which is the foundation stone of Munda religion, except for Singbonga, the story related to the birth of the other bongas has been narrated. After destroying the Asurs, when Singbonga started moving towards the sky, then the widows of the Asurs clung to Him. Since Singbonga (king) "baro vidiya ked, tero chhayan ked" (gave rise to twelve learnings and revealed thirteen wonderful performances) had destroyed the Asur husbands, hence the Asur widows pleaded with Him, "How are we going to live now and exist ? Tell us the way out.[10] And Singbonga assured them that in the centre of every village there would be a Munda man of justice who would be offering sacrifices to them beneath a tree from which food would be available to them. But they would have to obey His orders and do His work in the form of protectors of nature. And Singbonga shook them off, and they fell in rivers, streams, ditches, ponds, mountains, forests, marshes.

Whoever fell on a mountain became Burubonga, whoever fell in water became Ikir Bonga, whoever fell in a pond became Nageaera, whoever fell in a Sarna became Chandi Bonga, etc.[11] It has been further sung in legends that in order to worship and serve them (bongas) the pahan came into existence in the village and the junior pahan in a hamlet.[12] Hoffmann and other padres holding similar views think that the other bongas are not deities but souls of the dead whom they commonly call "nature ghosts" and "sectoral ghosts." In every Munda home there is a corner which is called ading and where the bones of the ancestors of the home are placed. In Munda religion, the dead ancestors are also worshipped and in order to satisfy their hunger, food and hadiya are offered. They are called "ading bongako." It is believed in Munda religion that the ading bongako, just like the home deity of the Hindus, protect the home and members of the family from various calamities. Hoffmann and thinkers of his school claim these bongako to be spirits.

But Hoffmann does not appear to be very firm in his thinking. In his Encyclopaedia Mundarica, under the title "khutkatti" he has used the terms god and kampajaladh [13] (deity)). In this book, under the title "Bonga"[14] and especially under the title "Ading Bongako" expressing his opinion, he has said, "we find no trace of anything like a real deification in the Mundari forms of ancestor worship."[15] In this way, apart from Singbonga, he has refused to accept any other bonga as deity in Munda religion. The question arises that when under the title "khutkatti" Hoffmann had then addressed the bongako as deity, then by the time he came to the definition of bonga and ading bongako within that interval why was there a change in his understanding? Had Hoffmann not fully understood the form and character of bongako during the time "khutkatti" was written or the impartiality of his first understanding, with the passage of time, changed from the objective approach to subjective approach when he wrote about bonga and ading bongako? Even in this writing it is apparent that he is not completely clear in his views otherwise he would not have used the adjective "real" in the term "real deification." It is reflected from this that Hoffmann finds "deification" qualities in the bongas but he finds lack of that standard of "deification" which as per his understanding is essential for becoming "actual deity." Nearly every Christian padre has broken and twisted Munda religion and tried to give it a structure as per his understanding of Christian religion. Even P. Ponnet says that Singbonga is the only God of Mundas and in this way they are monotheist.[16] P. Ponnet has mentioned about the views of Hoffmann[17] but he definitely believes that Munda religion is monotheist.[18] The belief of S. C. Roy and followers of his opinion that there are innumerable gods and goddesses in Munda religion has been stated to be erroneous by P. Ponnet.[19]

In the context of Munda religion, the circumstances of "patriarchal monotheistic religion" and "monarchical monotheistic religion" mentioned by Hoffmann can be found in nearly every primitive religion in the primary stages of the development of human life. In primeval society, the father was supposed to be the head of the family, and he used to be the protector of the family. Hence the form of father was seen in God because he is the Creator, Extensor and Protector of humans and human kind, and He is called Supreme Father. In this way, during the development process of society when the monarch and monarchical powers emerged, then God was believed to be king and the common public became His subjects. In the protection of the almighty king his subjects lived a life of security and happiness in the same manner that by the grace and protection of God man lived a happy life and called God "Godly king." Which religion is there which does not find the qualities of "father" and "king" in God. It is not that this belief is found only in Munda religion-it is to be found in other religions as well. Hoffmann has opined that the other bongas are subordinate to Singbonga and referring to "Asur Avdan" (legend) has written that Singbonga had deputed these bongas to do their work so that they could efficiently run the Creation without harming it. According to Hoffmann, this situation is nearly akin to that when a king gives the responsibilities of running the kingdom to his subordinate workers and in this manner some qualities of kingship and portions of power come automatically on these workers, but these workers who get their authority and orders from the king are not called "king." Similarly, the bongas who have derived godly powers but have to carry out the orders of "Singbonga king"[20] do not become God. There is only one God and He is Singbonga, hence Munda religion is monotheistic.

In this context, it is desirable to clarify that it is not necessary for deities to be almighty or that to be almighty is a necessary condition to become deities. We know that in Hindu religion after the importance of Vishnu was established, Ram and Krishna came to be accepted as the reincarnation of Vishnu and they possessed some parts of Vishnu. They did not have the complete Vishnu-element in them. The same was the case with the other gods. There is not one but many deities-god of nature, regional god, home god etc. All these deities assist in management, protection and governance of the creation made by Brahma. Just like the regional bongas, the other bongas also have the responsibilities of protection and management of the Creation made by Singbonga and for this the Mundas will give them offerings of cock-sacrifice-this had been decreed by Singbonga for the other bongas.[21] Later on we will see that in this decree what hand the religion regulatory priests or the creators of "Asur Avdan" had, but the appointees of Singbonga namely, Buru bonga of the mountain, Ikir bonga of water, Nagebonga of the valley, Desauli bonga of the village limits adjoining the forest, Chondor Ikir Bonga of the groves near ponds, and Chandi bonga of Sarna, as also Marang Buru Bonga of the high hills etc. all these bongas were originally feminine but after their birth as bongas they were accepted as masculine and in this form they came to be described and venerated in Munda folk literature. They were called regional gods. Oda bongako are the residing spirits of the ancestors found in the holy place of ading which is found in every Munda home. The main work of Oda bongako is to protect the members of the home from various mishaps, and to try to increase them so that they may be happy and prosperous. In addition to them, there are some "manauti bongas" (bongas who fulfil vows) who are destructive and they are worshipped to please them. According to Munda religion, all bongas can be divided in the following categories:-

(1) God of the First Class

Singbonga : supreme and Almighty God. There is no separate day or special mode of worship fixed for Him. In religious or special social occasions, hymns in praise of Singbonga are sung at the beginning. In order to overcome difficult troubles and disasters, Mundas often call for the help of His powers and offer sacrifice of white cocks. Connected to Him is Misi Singbonga meaning sister of Singbonga or Nagi-Aera-this name is also taken. Some scholars[22] regard her to be of the fourth class because she is a goddess connected with Nature.

(2) God of the Second Class

Regional gods like Hatu Bongako or Desauli Bonga, Jaher Burhi, Chandi Bonga, etc. These gods are helpful in protecting agriculture and growth of the Mundas. They give protection to the Mundas when they hunt in the jungles or in fixing direction of paths. These gods guide the Mundas in nearly every sphere of life. The various incidents which happen in human life are as per their orders. Their worship is done by the village pahan or priest on fixed occasions or festivals or as per vows in the holy Sarna grove according to laid down procedure. These deities are the benefactors of Mundas.

(3) Third Class of God

The home deities are counted in the third class. They are called Oda-Bongako. They are the souls of the family's dead ancestors. The master of the family worships these home deities. There is no need for pahan or priest in their worship. In every Munda family, a corner of the house is kept protected and pure- this is called "ading." In every social work, the blessing of the ancestors is invoked. Even on occasions of religious festivals, the master of the house worships the ancestors with great respect and offers food to them.

The deities coming in the second and third class, namely the village-gods and home-deities are also called "manauti devta" because they are appeased through offerings of worship for getting benefits from them. But these gods hardly ever harm the Mundas. Actually, the nature of village gods is connected to the protection and prosperity of the village and in the same manner the home-deities overcome the troubles befalling the home and family and think about the happiness of the members of the family. Hence the Mundas think it their religious duty to express respect and regard for them through worship and offering of oblations. The gods of both classes are never destructive-they are liberal and welfare oriented towards the Mundas. The offering of worship or oblations is symbolic of the devotion and respect the Mundas have for these gods.

Some scholars, instead of considering the nature of the aforementioned gods, have opined that the offering of worship and oblations to these gods is just to appease them and they have confused them with "banita" bonga who are unsatisfied destructive souls and to satisfy or appease whom they are worshipped and "sacrifice" is offered to them. Be it known that banita bonga do not come in the category of god and the Mundas never worship or offer sacrifice to them thinking them to be gods. As per the belief of Mundas, they are evil spirits who bring many kinds of diseases and troubles. The aim of worshipping them is just to appease them, not to show any regard, whereas Mundas have feelings of devotion towards the village-gods and home-deity and they worship them with regard and offer food. Along with them, the nature of the other gods is to protect the village and homes of the Mundas and is connected to their benevolence. Hence it is a great mistake to confuse "manita bongas" with "banita bongas." The manita bongas are liberal and well-wishers and the feelings of Mundas towards them are of devotion and respect hence they come in the category of gods whereas banita-bongas are destructive, and the Mundas do not have feelings of devotion or respect towards them-they have feelings of fear and escape, hence these bongas do not come in the category of gods.

Banita bongas include churail, muas, apsan, hankar bonga, nasan bonga which are souls of the dead which due to unnatural death (due to accident etc.) of human beings hover in the world as unsatisfied souls. The work of appeasing these wicked souls is not done by pahan or the village priest, and neither are these souls regarded as part of the religious functions of the Mundas, but for worshipping them a special class has emerged which is called najos, mati or ojha. They are mostly not Mundas but belong to other races. Hit by unnatural death, these souls terrorise the people of their area, the members of the family and those people responsible for their death (this fear is a psychological condition and their appeasement through some offerings is also, from a psychological point of view, a solution for the trouble) and ask for sacrifice which the najos, mati or ojha as per their regulations, call upon them and appease them by offering sacrifice. But these souls do not come within the regular worship of the Mundas and no cooperation is taken in their worship from the pahan or village priest. Hence they cannot be counted as gods from any viewpoint, they are not worshipped by the pahan.

(4) Fourth Class of God

In this class are included some gods connected with nature, namely, Buru bonga, Ikir bonga etc. They are positioned in between Manita bonga and

Banita bonga, which means that these bongas are liberal and beneficial and sometimes they also become rigid and harmful. Generally, these bongas are beneficial for Mundas and they protect them in their areas and help in their progress but when some Munda or Munda family or the people of the village neglect and show disrespect to these bongas and in this way they hurt them, then they become committed to harm such Munda families or villages. Under these circumstances, in order to appease and venerate them, najos, devra and at times the village pahan are engaged for offering worship and sacrifice. This is the reason why although the fourth classes of bongas are kept in the category of god and the pahan worships them, it is believed that in special circumstances they become angry and like the harmful banita bongas, they at times harm the Munda tribe.

(5) Fifth Class of God

The bonga called "achhrail bonga" shoulders the responsibility of protecting a prominent family or race. The bonga's work is to stop the tendency of a married woman to steal something from her father's house and to keep it in her in-law's house or at another place or house. Achhrail bonga who shoulders the responsibility of protecting the house and considers such theft to be a crime, visits that house with sickness and troubles wherever the stolen goods have been kept. In this way, this bonga is benevolent and controls the tendency of women to steal. It is only to control that the bonga sends troubles and sicknesses to the house of the thief for torturing her.

Apart from the aforesaid bongas, certain other bongas are found in Munda religion who are worshipped in particular areas, namely, only in the khunti police station area of Ranchi "pangua bonga" is worshipped, and "marang buru bonga" is worshipped in Ranchi district on hills near certain villages and where there are no hills, they are worshipped on some upland; both these bongas are considered to be local gods.

In Munda religion, two notable qualities are mainly found in the nature of supreme God Singbonga- (i) He is always attached to welfare work for the Mundas, and (ii) He always works for the expansion and development of the Creation made by Him. The gods who at their own levels help in the protection and nourishment of His Creation accomplish their responsibility of advancing the work of Singbonga. In this way they acquire "godliness" and they get respect and devotion from the Mundas. They are benevolent bongas. Those bongas who do not get respect and devotion from the Mundas are kept outside the category of god just like the banita bongas. The pahan does not worship them.

It is clear from the aforesaid classification of bongas that-apart from Singbonga, there are other gods too in Munda religion, hence Munda religion is polytheist. The opinion of Hoffmann and his colleagues that the Mundas have Singbonga as their only God appears to be based on this fallacy that they have accepted the other bongas as destructive unsatisfied souls meaning of "banita bonga" category who are worshipped and appeased by people outside the Munda race, by mati, ojha and najoses. Be it known that the pahan of the village does not worship the banita bongas whereas the other bongas are worshipped by the pahan and Priest of the village and for these bongas the Mundas have heartfelt devotion and respect. Hence, according to Munda religion, the bongas for whom Mundas have devotion and faith in their hearts and the right to worship whom is limited to the pahan and village priest, they are gods, and for those for whom there is no feeling of devotion and they are not worshipped by the village pahan or priest, such bongas are considered to be outside the category of god. Since the aforementioned five classes of bongas are revered by the Mundas and their worship is the responsibility of the village pahan or priest only, hence these bongas are undoubtedly worshipped as Munda gods in Munda religion.

It is apparently not logical for the Christian missionaries to limit the other bongas (except Singbonga), call them regional bongas and opine that they are bereft of godly qualities. There are many religions in the world in which the area gods and goddesses have been given much importance.

In the ancient ritualistic book "Indigita menta" of Rome, prayers of Roman priests for various religious occasions have been collected in which gods related to nearly every field of the lives of the Romans can be found. For example, in the field of agriculture, the god related to sowing of seeds is "Saturnus," the goddess related to the increase in yield of crops is "Searish" and the goddess of flowers is "Flora".[23] Similarly among the Lithuanians, the god who protects animals is "Sutvaras," the goddess of the increase of animals is "Gotha," and the nurturer of horses is believed to be "Ratemikja."[24] In the Rigveda and Atharvaveda," "Vastoshpati" and "Kshetrapati" have been described as protector of home and fields respectively. Hence, deriving powers from the Chief God, the emerging sectoral benevolent powers are combined with godliness. It is because of this that deriving powers and responsibilities from Singbonga and carrying them out in their sectors, these benevolent bongas are gods and in this way Munda religion is polytheist. Most of the sociologists (anthropologists) of the nineteenth century who are supporters of the "evolutionary" theory are of the view that the primitive forest races can never be monotheists[25] to which Hoffmann has expressed serious reaction. Yet, Hoffmann seems to agree with the evolutionary interpretation of gods done by German anthropologist Peter Schmidt. According to Schmidt, among the primitive forest races, the gods have developed through worship of each other, also passing through the worship of ghosts and spirits, onward to expansion by worship of many gods.[26]

(A) Some Chief Gods of Munda Religion

Singbonga

In Munda religion, Singbonga is Almighty and Supreme God. He has made Creation and created "mankind." Due to His grace, the Munda race has expanded. He has created many devices for the protection of "mankind" and "race" as also increase in their prosperity. He is the basis of the life of all. There are other gods, but in front of Singbonga the existence of all other gods is of little value. If Singbonga is pleased then the other gods cannot perpetrate any harm.

Singbonga- Sungod is the Master of all. The word "Singbonga" has been defined like Burubonga (Buru=hill, bonga=dweller, meaning god of the hill) or Ikir bonga (Ikir= deepwater, bonga=dweller, meaning watergod). Keeping in mind the aforementioned similarity in defining, Hoffmann has said that in the first instance Singbonga can be described as the sungod (god who dwells in the sun).[27] But the Mundas never accept this definition by Hoffmann. Singbonga is neither the sun nor does He dwell in the sun. Actually He lives in the empty sky. Throwing light on the reasons why the "sun" held sway over Munda religion, Hoffmann's statement is that earlier a different original religion of the Mundas had been prevalent which gradually came under the influence of sun-worshippers.[28] But Hoffmann does not produce any proof to confirm this statement. He ignores this truth that to influence primeval life there is no other celestial body in Creation except the hot sun.

If we study the religious stories of most of the races of the world, then two elements are normally found to be approximately similar. One is the belief that the sun is the biggest god and second that in the beginning only water existed from which the earth was born. In the common view of primeval man, the "sun" must undoubtedly have been seen as the greatest and most powerful, active ingredient of this Creation. There is no other natural power the importance of which can be seen to be equal to that of the sun. In the creation of India, Japan, Egypt etc. the sun has been accepted as a principal god. The sun is the god of the serpents. Most scholars are of the opinion that in Rigveda, Vishnu represents one form of the sun.[29] In this way many religions have accepted the greatness of the sun. Hence in primeval life, that the creation is run through the powers of the sun is apparently a very easy belief. That is why Singbonga (sun god) of the Mundas is the creator and controller of the world. The lesser gods derive powers from him and in obedience to His commands they are engaged in the protection and progress of the world.

Similar to many primitive races of the world, the Munda-religious songs tell us about the birth of the earth from water. This water is not the common water of rivers and streams. This water is of the expansive limitless ocean, an ocean apart from which there was nothing else in Creation. The earth is born out of this water in which there is cooperation from acquatic creatures.

During the wandering of the primitive races on sea-shores, it is possible that in various stages it might have appeared that the earth has risen from the ocean and then it may have been imagined that the earth has come out of the ocean. It may be kept in mind that with the development of imagination, it became the basis of many ancient tales of successive civilisation which are so serially connected that philosophers seek symbols in them and evolutionary thinkers try to find out the thread of evolution in the chain. In the Indian Puranas, the stories regarding the protection of the earth by the incarnations of Matsya, Kachhap, Varaha, Narsingha, Vaman, etc. reflect the elements of evolution.

But in the religious songs of primitive races, there is no spiritual or symbolic meaning. It is the result of just a simple perception. On the seashore, they must have seen many worms and acquatic creatures coming with every wave and drowning likewise, so they must have imagined that the Creator Singbonga must have ordered the turtle, the crab, leech, earthworm to dive into the ocean water and bring mud, and He created this dry earth with the mud brought by the earthworm.[30]

The Munda religious songs and legends are full of descriptions of "godliness" of Singbonga. Apart from these, during the occasions of worship and "sacrifice" and at the start of other religious duties, the hymns which are sung describe the glory of Singbonga which throws light on this fact that Singbonga is the supreme God of the Mundas. In the early religious stories, in which – (1) the making of Creation (2) the birth of man (3) expansion of race (4) the first plough, and (5) division of time are told of, in several Munda-sectors the name of "Hadam" as the Creator has come up. In the religious stories collected by Christian padres "Agnivarsha" (rain of fire) and in later religious stories Singbonga is mentioned but in the earlier religious stories there is mention of "Hadam." Actually due to difference in places, there are two names of Hadam and Singbonga. With the passage of time, the name of "Singbonga" became prevalent in worship and other religious activities.

The Divine Form of Singbonga in Religious Stories

(1) The creation of earth and man: When everywhere there had been nothingness and below the ocean of water, Singbonga had created only aquatic creatures. Now Singbonga thought of creating the earth and He sent the crab to bring mud from the water. When the crab was unsuccessful, Singbonga sent the turtle, fish and the earthworm respectively. Ultimately the earthworm was successful in bringing mud out of which earth was made. Singbonga made "otey-dishum" (beautiful country) in which He grew vegetation, trees, plants, and created animals. In this way if prior to Creation and time there had been the existence of some one, that was the Supreme Singbonga. The pahan sings in praise of Singbonga that, "you were there before Creation and you will remain till the end of Creation, you are without beginning and without end,

you are from time immemorial and till eternity. You have made the earth, grown vegetation, and created all kinds of animals." From the aforesaid the Mundas mean that by arranging for new creatures, Singbonga has tried to make the Creation more balanced. Singbonga made a human figure of clay and put life into it, but the horse came and broke that figure. Singbonga again made a human figure. He put life into it and to safeguard it He positioned a cheetah (leopard) in front of it which made the horse run away due to fright. In this way the creature could be safeguarded. Elsewhere in this story, in place of the cheetah, two dogs "Chowra- Bhowra" can be seen who guard the figure of man.

The story does not tell us what happened after man was created and what Singbonga did with that man. There is no revelation regarding this in the story. Amongst the Santhals, who are the same race as the Mundas, this story is prevalent but in it the horse is called "Pankhraj". The horse being the destroyer of man is the symbol of evil. Singbonga takes recourse to many devices to protect man from evils and disasters. He is the Almighty. We see that earlier to creation, "eternal darkness" and "eternal chaos" had not been able to disturb Him. He was completely victorious over them because He was God.

The Birth of Man and Expansion of Race

Another religious story throws light on the birth of man. At first after creating "beautiful country" Singbonga filled it up with all kinds of small and big animals and birds. Then an important creation took place. The "Hur" bird laid an egg and a boy and a girl were born from it. They were the first humans to be born on this earth.

This story has been differently extracted by the Christian missionary A. Van Exam based on sources available to him.[31] According to him, a huge stork (Indian stork) laid two eggs and it hatched them. A boy was born from one and a girl from the other. The bird reared them to their youth.

Most of the Mundas confirm the incident of "Hur" bird laying one egg. S. C. Roy has also confirmed it based upon the information he derived from his sources.[32] Mundas believe that the "Hur" bird (Swan) lays egg only once in its life time. It is only from this egg that the "ancestors" of the Mundas were born. It seems that in order to make it more logical and practical, the padre has portrayed "Hur" to be the stork and instead of one, two eggs have been talked of from which the boy and the girl were born respectively. He has given no basis of source of information available to him. Whereas "Hur" (swan) in its whole life time lays only one egg from which the "ancestral couple" is born is proved to be more meaningful.[33]

The Expansion of Race

For any race to survive, it is necessary for procreation to continue. The man-woman couple born out of the egg of "Hur" bird were told by Singbonga to sleep in a room and in between them He placed a bundle of hay as a divider. Before they went to sleep, Singbonga told them about the process of making ili (rice wine). They made ili and drank it. According to custom, Singbonga sent them to sleep. When they were sleeping, Singbonga removed the bundle of hay kept between them. Now they behaved like a husband and wife. Next morning they stood like criminals in front of Singbonga and asked for forgiveness for their wrongdoing. But Singbonga told them that whatever they had done was good, it was as per His desire, order and blessing.

Actually it was necessary for Creator Singbonga to try to expand and protect mankind in which was placed the meaning of Creation. Telling the "brother-sister" born out of an egg to go and sleep in a room, instructing them to drink wine, removing the bundle of hay (kept between them) while they were asleep and to encourage their conjugal relationship, were the various stages of the plan of Singbonga. These first ancestors were called "tota hadam" (naked male ancestor) and "tota burhi" (naked female ancestor) and their offsprings were called "horo hoko" in Munda religion.

Munda religion believes that Singbonga's complete plan works behind the expansion of Munda race. He made "otey dishum" (beautiful country), then made the "Hur" bird, produced the ancestors from its egg and after making them drink wine, expanded the race. It is their duty to expand their race because it is the desire of Singbonga. Marriage is the root of expansion of the race, hence in Munda religion it is a very sacred religious action which fulfils the desire and plan of Singbonga.

From this religious story, direct connection of Singbonga with Munda race is established that Singbonga made all efforts for the Munda race to be born and now it is the duty of the Mundas in obligation to worship Singbonga with devotion and faith, and also try to maintain and improve the Creation made by Him. Whoever does anything against it, that is, indulges in the destruction of Creation, will face the wrath of Singbonga (later we will see the Asuras being punished accordingly). Singbonga is now everything for the Munda race.

In this religious story, alongwith Singbonga the religious importance of egg has also emerged. Nearly every Munda holds the egg to be sacred and takes an oath by keeping an egg in his hand which signifies the truthfulness of the oath.[34]

In this religious song, the godliness of Singbonga emerges more clearly when the Mundas say that whatever Singbonga does, it is right. The question is that a brother-sister born out of one egg got related as husband-wife by Singbonga. The Munda mind is clear that being born out of one womb they were brother and sister. The Mundas would not have tolerated forbidden sexual relationships, hence how would they have accepted as virtuous the plan of Singbonga to make the brother-sister as husband-wife. But if Singbonga does not do it then today there would have been no existence of Munda race. Hence, whatever Singbonga did, He did it for the good of the Mundas. He does not commit any mistake. He is the ultimate God.

The story of expansion of race through the relationship of brother-sister is also found among other primitive races. The expansion of the Oraon race was also due to the union of a brother and sister who were hiding in the hole of a crab. During the time of annihilation of Creation, this brother-sister hid themselves in the hole of a crab and they were protected as the form of seed for human race. In the religious song of the 'Ho' race, the brother and sister take shelter not in the hole of a crab but in a drum, and with the passage of time the 'Ho' race expands. This means that in many primitive races, religious songs pertaining to expansion of the Creation through the union of brother-sister are prevalent. Modern man may perhaps think it to be improper and vulgar, but this comment is not so easy as it appears. This imagination is connected to that era when man had at first learnt about procreation through sexual relations of male-female. In that era, relationships had not been made. Man was man, woman was woman. Now we see that due to taking birth from one womb they are "brother-sister" because today our view has already created "relationships." Actually, that brother-sister were the symbol of male-female. And in this way, there was nothing immoral, but in today's viewpoint if there is anything immoral then under the cover of Singbonga it easily receives the approval of religion and society because on the design of Singbonga there is nobody to put a question mark.

The First Plough

In this religious song Singbonga has been shown as married and accompanied by a wife. The Munda race is not ready to accept that Singbonga was married. After creating man, Singbonga had advised him to take up agriculture for livelihood and He started making a plough for him. With great difficulty, He found a tree appropriate for making a plough. He cut it, peeled off its bark and tried to make a full plough out of it which took a lot of time. Seeing the delay, His wife sent mosquitoes which buzzed near Singbonga's ears but His concentration was not broken. Again, she sent a leopard but it, too, could not break the concentration of Singbonga in preparing the plough. As a result, His wife had to come herself. She said that it was impractical to make a whole plough out of one tree, and she declared the plough constructed by Him to be meaningless and weak. She herself made another plough whose parts were all made earlier and separately, and then drilling holes in the plough she fitted all these parts by beating them in those holes. This plough was more strong and convenient. Singbonga was pleased with such skill of His wife and gave orders that from that day no woman would touch the plough and would be freed from the labour of ploughing.

This religious song of the Mundas appears to have developed probably after coming in contact with the Oraons. It was only after the coming of the Oraons in Chhotanagpur that the Mundas adopted agricultural work. In the religious song of the Oraons, Sita is said to be the wife of their Chief God Dharmes. Parallel to this the religious song of the Mundas developed. It is said by the Mundas that in The First Plough the wife who has been mentioned is the manifestation of the intellectual power of Singbonga which appeared in the form of wife. Actually Singbonga is unmarried.

In the current history of Munda religion, the change in the form of Singbonga in the first phase is due to the influence of religious song of the Oraons, and in the second phase, due to the belief that Singbonga is unmarried, the imagination has accordingly developed that His wife is the personification of His intellect. In this religious song the worry of Singbonga is clear that He wanted to see His Munda children prosper through agricultural work. Along with this, Singbonga fixes the duties of men and women that men will work for earning and women will look after the home. It became prohibited for women to touch the plough.

Division of Time

By creating day and night, Singbonga had arranged for man to work and to rest. At first there used to be only the sun in the sky and everywhere there was light. Munda always engaged himself in cultivation. One day Singbonga asked him-when did you prepare this field ? Reply received was "now." Again, when did you prepare the second, third, and far off fourth field? Reply received was "now". Nearby there lay a used leaf-plate and a little further away lay another used, dry, old leaf-plate. Upon asking, the reply was that food of this leaf-plate and food of the other leaf-plate was partaken "now." Upon seeing this, Singbonga thought that it was necessary to give order to the sun to rise half the time and set half the time so that due to lack of light man could rest otherwise in this way through continuous work he will kill himself.

Singbonga ordered the sun to rise half the time and set half the time, and made the moon which would, in the absence of the sun, help the Mundas, through its light, to find out their path ways amidst the forests and mountains.

In this way Singbonga has made the Creation for the benefit of mankind. He has told the sun and the moon to rise and set, keeping in mind the welfare of man. He conducts and controls every natural phenomenon keeping the aim of human welfare in front. He makes rain on time and asks the sun to warm up on time. In order to maintain the balance in Creation, man should always cooperate with Singbonga because He had made the whole Creation for man.

In the religious songs upto now, which mainly deal with Creation and expansion of race, man has always obtained the affection of Singbonga because man not only carried out the orders of Singbonga but also helped with devotion and duty to make His Creation more beautiful. But with the passage of time, alongwith the expansion of mankind there is appearance of vices in man, he turns toward wicked deeds, and the feeling of pride becomes so strong in him that he starts feeling mightier and more capable than Singbonga. He associates himself with the destruction of Creation. His wicked deeds start unbalancing the whole Creation. As a result it becomes necessary that Singbonga punishes them. In the form of punishment two songs come up-(1) Rain of fire (2) Asur Avdan (legend of destruction).

Rain of Fire

In addition to Munda religious song, in the religious songs of the Oraon and Santhal races or similarly in the religious songs of many races can be seen that the Creator has once caused rain of fire or flood for the destruction of whole mankind and has protected a man and a woman couple from annihilation. According to religious song of the Oraons, when Dharmes came to this earth for hunting, He could not get any land which was clear and pure. Everywhere the earth was covered with human faeces, meaning that everywhere sin was ruling and all human beings had become irreligious. For the protection of Creation it was necessary to annihilate them. In the Santhal religious song also it has been described that all creatures had started fighting each other like buffaloes and nobody was ready to listen to the word of Thakurji (God). Hence, for seven days and seven nights there was rainfall and everybody died except "Pilchu hadam" and "Pilchu burhi" who were on Harata Mountain and were saved from this destruction. It is from them that the offspring of Santhals increased.

According to Munda religious song, Singbonga destroyed the whole Creation through rain of fire. Nage Aera, who lives in deep waters, had hid a pair of brother and sister in a crab-hole due to which they remained protected from the rain of fire. After an interval of time, they were the ones to become the root of expansion of the Munda race. After the pageant of annihilation, Singbonga took away this pair of brother and sister from Nage Aera, and having made them imbibe wine He encouraged them to sleep like husband and wife due to which they had a child. Singbonga sent an illness and made the child ill. In that first era, they told Singbonga, "Grand father, see the child is ill." Thereupon they were ordered to offer sacrifice of white cock which would cure the child. Next day, the husband-wife invited the "Supreme Father" and offered sacrifice. They ate and drank and returned home but on the way they remembered that the sacrificial knife had been left behind there. The husband returned to take the knife when he saw the Supreme Father Singbonga licking the blood from a leaf. The husband said- "when I invited you then you did not come and now you are licking the leaves; why is it so Grandfather?" there was no reply and at that moment Singbonga disappeared from view. It is said that after that nobody has seen Singbonga.

The first ancestor had seen Singbonga in the form of Grandfather and known Him and had always addressed him as "Aja" (paternal grandfather). Before He disappeared, till that time Singbonga had been "Aja" for him, not God, because Singbonga had not given him any sign that He was not human but was Singbonga, and was guiding him by appearing as "Aja." From this religious song light is thrown on the following regarding Singbonga's appearance:-

(1) Singbonga does not tolerate sinful human beings and devises means to destroy them.

(2) Singbonga worries about the "Horo" and the expansion of the race given birth to by them. Hence he asked for the brother-sister pair from Nage Aera and encouraged them to live as husband and wife.

(3) The relationship between Singbonga and "Horo," that is mankind, is of Grandfather and grandson. Singbonga is the "Aja" of Mundas.

(4) Singbonga had sent illness in Creation. Prior to this there had been no illness in Creation.

(5) The regulation of sacrifice of white cock has been made to free human beings from disease and for their prevention. Prior to this, there had been no provision of sacrifice.

(6) For the first time a sectoral goddess named Nage Aera has been discussed. She has been accepted in the female form because she reared the pair of brother and sister, a work which is more suitable to the character of women than men. Additionally she has godliness because she protected the ancestors (brother-sister pair) of the Mundas race from the heat of horrendous fire and saved the Munda race from being totally annihilated.

(7) After this religious story, Singbonga disappears for ever.

The divine form of Singbonga appears with greater clarity after this religious story. After the Rain of fire, all human beings have undergone a strange change and every person, even if he be a holy soul, has become unable to see Singbonga. This "blindness" of the Mundas is the result of their downfall because if there had been no downfall of man, then what was the necessity of destroying His own Creation by Singbonga through rain of fire. During the period after the rain of fire, man had to face two main punishments. The first was that his divine sight was taken away and the second was that Singbonga gave him disease and illness from which man had been free earlier.

Asur Avdan

Some scholars think "Asur Avdan" to be exaggerated historical incident. Before the Mundas entered Chhotanagpur, the Asur race used to live in Ranchi and nearby areas. They used to smelt iron. After being defeated by the Mundas, the Asur people went and hid in the hills to the north-west of Ranchi and they settled there in a scattered manner. In this legend of destruction, the misconduct and pride of the Asurs have been shown that they used to think themselves to be greater and mightier than Singbonga, due to which they had to face dire consequences. In Munda religion this tale is all important. The incidents of "Asur Avdan" reveal the natural and supernatural character of Singbonga and also throw light on the emergence of other bongas and their duties.

Singbonga is the Almighty God of the Mundas. He has made this Creation, and created vegetation, trees-plants, creatures-animals. He could not have withstood the pageant of destruction of Creation under any circumstances. The Asurs had started smelting iron day and night in their furnaces as a result of which, due to fire, ashes and heat, the vegetation started getting scorched, creatures-animals started dying, the whole Creation started getting unbalanced. Singbonga sent "Dhichua" and "Kerketa" as messengers to suggest to the Asurs that if they blow their furnaces at night then they should shut them during the day, and if they blow them during the day then they should shut them at night, but the Asurs did not listen. With the return of these unsuccessful messengers, Singbonga sent "Lokonal-pakshi" and "Kajru bocho pakshi" respectively as messengers for making the Asurs understand. When they were unsuccessful then again "Soney ka geedh, Rupa ka kauwa" took the message of God to them, but getting insulted they returned lamenting and weeping.[35] Then Singbonga was left with no other alternative. Hence He prepared Himself for the annihilation of the Asurs. Instead of direct war, Singbonga intelligently prepared for the destruction of Asurs in various phases–

(1) Singbonga sent eczema and afflicted a servant with it who was working in "eighty one plain, eighty three upland."[36] Again He pulled off his whole skin and wore it Himself in the form of a boy and He was called "Khasra Balak" (eczema boy).

(2) Lutkum burha and lutkum burhiya used to stay in a house of the bordering village of "Ekasi maidan, terasi tarh" (eighty one plain, eighty three upland). Singbonga became a servant in their house.

(3) By breaking the iron marbles of Asur boys with hen's eggs and filling up the granary of the lutkums Singbonga astonished them and indicated his Divine power to the lutkums.

(4) When the production of iron decreased, the dewra, the sokha suggested to the Asurs the device of sacrificing white cock as an offering to Singbonga. After doing this, the production of iron increased for a few days and the Asurs were pleased, but after two days the iron in the furnace did not melt again. The Asurs ran to the dewra and sokha with "akshat" (unbroken ceremonial rice). They again told them of device, and in the end told them to give human sacrifice in the furnace. The Asurs were unsuccessful in finding a "person" who would sacrifice himself to become the cause of

increase in production of iron. In this effort they went to Deous Nagar but they were thrashed and thrown out from there.

(5) After becoming hopeless from all four sides, the eyes of the Asurs fell on Khasra Balak. The Asurs took away Khasra Balak by force from the lutkums.[37] Thereupon Singbonga in the form of Khasra Balak started preparing for playing the ultimate game. He told the Asurs to prepare new bellows for the furnace by using skin of white goat. He further instructed that after His entry into the furnace, fasting virgin must blow with the bellows for seven days and seven nights. After seven days, the fire of the furnace should be put out by using pure water of a new pitcher, and thereafter the furnace should be opened. With these conditions the Khasra Balak became ready to sacrifice Himself.

(6) The conditions were fulfilled. After seven days the Khasra Balak came out from the drain of the furnace and –

Khasra boy, your boy, from the path of the drain, from the way of the enclosure came out running, came outside speedily

Holding in His Hand

Plate and pot, bowl

Of gold, of diamond,

Came out, emerged

Shining and glittering

He can be seen, can be noticed.

(from Asur Avdan).

This was a divine miracle of Khasra Balak that even from the tremendous fire of the furnace which melts the iron, He could come out safely, but the Asur people, whose vision was covered by the screen of pride and who thought themselves to be more mighty and virtuous than Singbonga that they could smelt iron, did not come to their senses even after this Divine miracle of Khasra Balak. On the contrary, their greed, their avaricious nature started seeing diamonds and gold treasure in their furnace. Singbonga took advantage of this and crammed the whole Asur race inside the furnace. Pride and greed are such two sins which are definitely punished by Singbonga.

(7) With the destruction of the Asur race in the furnace, the work of Singbonga ended on this earth, so He started going up in the sky. But some Asur widows caught hold of Him and started asking him about their means of livelihood (some pregnant widows remained below and their offsprings became the reason of the existence of the Asur race), but Singbonga shook them off and they fell on various places, and according to the places they became bonga and began getting worship and sacrifice from the Mundas.[38]

On this occasion Singbonga had given the ruling that "all of you in your own sectors help to protect that Creation and maintain the balance of Nature which I have structured. For your maintenance, the Munda race will arrange for worship and sacrifice." (see Annexure : Asur Avdan).

Singbonga, the Supreme God of the Munda religion, sits on His throne in the sky and manages the whole Creation and for helping Him in His work, He keeps on giving commands to the other bongas to fulfil their sectoral responsibilities. Whoever destroys his Creation, meaning, tries to disarrange the balance of Nature, Singbonga destroys his whole race. This He did once through rain of fire, and the second time He destroyed the Asur race which had in its pride tried to upset the balance of Nature by firing their furnace day and night.

Singbonga's Intelligence Personified Wife

The question arises whether Singbonga has a wife or not ? In the Asur Avdan, it has been sung, "Singbonga king, goddess Kumari." When Singbonga readies Himself to destroy the Asurs, then the goddess Kumari alerts Him that the Asur people are large in number and very strong hence He should devise the means of their destruction cunningly- He should display twelve types of learning and thirteen types of sport then only it would be possible to vanquish the Asurs. In the religious song "The first plough," too, there is the appearance of Singbonga's wife. According to the religious belief of the Mundas, Singbonga is unmarried and He does not have a wife. That wife who has been mentioned is actually the power of intelligence of Singbonga which separates from him and argues with Him and correctly guides Singbonga. This subject has been discussed in detail within the influence of various religions over Munda religion in modern times. In this context question has also been raised as to what is the human form/ appearance of Singbonga. The Munda pahans have imagined Him having white hair and a huge beard just like an "Aja" (paternal grandfather)- this appearance has been described by the padres but he wears white dress and sits on a white horse.

According to Mennas Odiya, only four persons have seen Singbonga- the first man-woman (tota hadam, tota burhi) and lutkum burha-burhi as described in Asur Avdan.[39] According to Munda people, the reason for the disappearance of Singbonga is man's lack of reverence toward Singbonga. In the earlier era, people used to venerate Singbonga, thus He used to live amidst them and fulfil their requirements. That was the era of religious songs. The man of today is different from the Mundas of the era of religious songs, which is why Singbonga has concealed Himself from their vision. Invisibility is a necessary sign of being God but along with it God has to exhibit His influence through various signs. In this way, even remaining invisible, Singbonga gives His orders in such a manner that if man wants to remain blind to His orders, then he can never see Divine Light. Man can now neither directly hear or see

His orders. In order to understand them, man has to analyse and understand the various indications, signs, dreams, and good-bad omens coming in the way. He has to talk in the same language in which Singbonga talks to him. Singbonga is the God of Munda race. He loves the Mundas and blesses them. He lives all the time amidst the Mundas. He is omnipresent and sees everything and hears everything and hears everything. He is "soneybana leljan- a- umtani." Dewra sings hymns in His praise "for Him night and day are same. There is nothing hidden from Him."[40]

During religious performances, the pahan invites Singbonga. He sings about His vastness, His greatness and His purity; he sings that His chest is as solid as stone. He sings "dirileka kudumtame" meaning that Singbonga is the solid basis of the complete structure of Creation in which there can be no derangement. "You have given an arrangement for the empty sky and ocean of water. You have crafted animate and inanimate things. It is as per Your desire that change is possible in this Creation because there is unlimited strength in Your arms. You have scattered your beauty in whole Nature." The pahan sings in a high sounding note, "Your teeth are like chameli flowers and your chin is like the lotus flower. You are the first dawn, first sunrise. Your whiteness is like the rising of pure milk and the setting of white curd. You are the controller of the world. O Supreme Singbonga. Divine king. You are the friend of Munda race and its well-wisher. You are "netlang" "Singbonga."

Nage Aera

Nage Aera is supposed to be the goddess of swamps. She is also known as the sister of Singbonga. We come to know of her powers and character through the religious song "Agnivarsha." Singbonga destroyed the whole human race through Rain of Fire but she began to worry of how to rejuvenate human kind and expand it. In this belief that may be in some nook and corner a man-woman couple may have been saved, she sent her faithful birds Kauwa Bhandari and Lipi susari to go and find out. These birds very patiently flew about in their search till Kauwa Bhandari found a leaf-bowl in a swampy land.

Clearly, there would be some human being living nearby. When Kauwa Bhandari could not search out the man, it picked up the leafbowl in its beak and brought it to Singbonga and told Him every thing. Singbonga Himself came in search of the "man" near the swampy land (jiwi) where He met Nage Aera. She accepted that she had hidden a man-woman couple safely from the heat of the Rain of Fire. Since the extension of the "jiwi" (swamp) was twelve "kos" (one kos = two miles) long and twelve "kos" wide this man-woman couple was safe from the effects of fire.

Nage Aera handed over the man-woman couple to Singbonga on condition that He would not again try to destroy mankind. Singbonga accepted the condition and He further said, "from now on you will get the benefit of two parts of the descendants of the human race and I will get only one part."[41] This is a special honour which, except for Nage Aera goddess, Singbonga has not given to any other bonga. There are two main reasons which come to the fore as to why Nage Aera is believed to be a goddess. The first reason is that she looked after the only remaining man-woman couple of Creation, a responsibility which normally a mother carries out. The second reason is that Nage Aera is called "Misi Singbonga" meaning sister of Singbonga. Saving mankind from total annihilation and taking the promise from Singbonga that He would not again destroy mankind reveals the benevolent nature of Nage Aera which is the main quality of gods and goddesses. Again, in important religious functions of marriage and funeral, Nage Aera is offered new pot of water. "Pot of water" is the symbol of a creature. The pahan and the dewra performing religious rites sing hymns on these occasions that the pot filled with water signifies "an egg". This "egg" is offered to those ancestors who spread the human race again in this world, and also to the patroness who with great difficulty and devotion protected and reared the first "couple". That patroness was Nage Aera.

In this way, Nage Aera, Misi Singbonga, is such a venerable goddess that the Munda race worships her with devotion. But Hoffmann and his colleagues have tried to confuse Nage Aera with Ikir Bonga. According to them, there is not much difference between "jiwi" (swamp) and a water pond. Hence, Nage Aera living in a swamp/marsh, and Ikir Bonga living in a water pond are the same. A. Von Exam has said that in "Asur Avdan," when Singbonga became invisible, Nage Aera became Ikir Bonga spirit/ ghost.[42] In this context, the padres should consider that the religious song pertaining to "Agni Varsha" is of a much earlier time period than "Asur Avdan." After the Mundas came to Chhotanagpur, they fought a war with the Asurs, and the Asurs after getting defeated went and hid themselves in the hills to the north-west of Ranchi. "Agnivarsha" religious song is also prevalent among the Santhals when during the annihilation of mankind, Thakurji (God) had directed Pilchu Hadam and Pilchu Burhi to hide themselves in a cave of Harata Hill and after the destruction of mankind the Santhal race expanded due to Hadam and Burhi. Santhals and Mundas are the descendants of the same ancestors. These descendants left Rohtasgarh together and later on split into two groups. Hence, from the point of view of time, this religious song/ story is more ancient than the Asur Avdan, and in this religious story the description of Misi Singbonga or Nage Aera cannot be that of Ikir Bonga at all. The emergence of Ikir Bonga is connected to Asur Avdan which is an incident that took place later than Agnivarsha.

In Munda religion, during worship and various religious rituals, Nage Aera is worshipped and a new water-filled pot is offered to her, whereas no such thing is done for Ikir Bonga. There is a feeling of benevolence in

Nage Aera. She has got kindness toward mankind and Mundas have great regard for her. All these virtues express the divine qualities of Nage Aera. Opposite to this, in certain religious tales, Ikir Bonga has been described as a wicked spirit, and to stop his wicked tendencies Singbonga had to come to the earth.[43] Hence, Nage Aera and Ikir Bonga are two separate personalities. Ikir Bonga carries out the orders of Singbonga, whereas Nage Aera is Misi Singbonga. Singbonga has to come to Nage-Aera as a suppliant. Again, Nage Aera is worshipped in religious performances.

After Nage Aera, the following are some of the bongas who influence Munda religion:–

Hatu Bongako: In some administrative subdivisions, they are also called "desauli bonga." They protect the village. They are sentries of the village limits and stop the entry of harmful maladies and disasters in the village. The Munda farmers worship them so that they would be pleased and would increase their harvests.

They are benevolent gods and are seldom angry.

Chandi Bonga: Chandi Bonga is also called Sarna Devi (goddess). They reside in the Sarna grove of the village and protect the Mundas from sudden misfortunes. The Munda people cross rugged forest pathways without any obstacle due to the grace of Chandi Bonga. During hunting or when trapped in the forest, Chandi Bonga protects the Mundas from wild animals. Chandi Bonga resides atop the huge sal tree in the Sarna grove. The smallest branch fallen from the sal tree is picked up from the ground with great respect and worshipped. The pahan conducts the worship of Chandi Bonga with great devotion in the shade of the sal tree and in the presence of other Mundas. The Mundas do not fear any harm from Chandi Bonga- they expect benevolence from Chandi Bonga.

Buru Bonga: The word meaning of "buru" is god. In the primeval stage of life of the Mundas, apparently to denote Singbonga, "Marang Buru" (meaning supreme God) term was first used. "Marang" is the adjective (supreme) of Buru. With the passage of time, when the influence of the followers of sun-cult fell upon Munda religion, then "Marang Buru" gradually came to be worshipped as Singbonga. But at present the term "Buru Bonga" is used for that god who resides on the high hills. His responsibility is to keep watch over the forest, agricultural fields, village, everything. For Mundas, he is normally benevolent but if he becomes angry, then he troubles the Mundas with various kinds of ailments and disturbances. In such a situation, his position becomes the same as that of evil spirits and he shows traits of banita bongas. As such, desaul, buru, Chandi and Ikir bongas carry out their responsibility of protecting and looking after the welfare of Mundas living within their jurisdictions.

When addressing them, the pahan says, "O Buru, Ikir, Chandi and Desauli Bonga, many kinds of diseases and maladies enter your region from other places. Is our worship meaningless? Please drive them out of the village limits."

Ading Bongako: In some Munda areas, Ading Bongako is also called "Oda Bongako." They are the souls of dead ancestors. According to Munda religion, in this world and after death in the next world it is a kind of sequence without any break. Our dead soul lives in that world which we cannot see. It is the same soul which lives in a living human being. In this way it is the same soul of this world and the next world. During death the restrictions of the body end, but the continuity of the soul remains.

Oda Bonga reside in the ading which is a sacred part of the house. It is here that they are worshipped. There the entry of a non-Munda is banned. Since Oda Bonga (ading bongako) are the dead souls of the family's ancestors, hence according to the belief of the living members of the family, they also have devotion and worshipful attitude towards Singbonga, and remain desirous of His beneficence. They come out of the ading and sit on the same mat which is the sitting mat of "desauli bonga." Here the meaning of "desauli" is all sectoral bongas. In Munda religion, the form of ading bongako has come up in such a manner that they form a connecting thread between the family members on one hand and all bongas and Singbonga on the other hand, and they try that the compassion of all sectoral bongas and Singbonga remains on the concerned family members. This belief has been stretched to such an extent that in whichever region the ading bongako go, they derive the powers of the concerned regional bongas and devise means for the increase of property and for protection of their family members.

In this way, the character of ading bongako has been pictured in such a manner that for the welfare of their family members, from time to time, they mix with the bongas of all sectors or from their side they obtain their powers and try to protect their family from illnesses, misfortunes and natural disasters. They keep vigilance over agriculture. Whenever an elder or an old member of the family crosses the difficult forest paths, then the ading bongako go along with him in an invisible manner, because that person during trouble, out of fear of animals, calls upon his ancestor by name and re-assures himself, increases his courage by saying, "You are also with me walking on my right." In the hymn it has been said that, "since you are aware of my troubles, hence pick up your axe or get ready with your bow and arrow and kill the animal."

A religious rite observed for the ancestors to fill the home with agricultural-wealth, domesticated animal-wealth, is an astonishing feature of the religious life of the Mundas. When it is fully night, some senior members of the house go outside, and three persons remain inside the house in darkness and sit within bolted doors. Everywhere there is darkness with not a single shaft of light. These three persons do not open the door till the persons who had gone out do not return home. The members, who go outside, visit the forest, hill,

Sarna, nearly all those places where the regional bongas are believed to be residing. The Mundas firmly believe that the ancestors accompany the family members who go outside and visit all the places with them and return with them and knock at the door. Before the door opens, some fixed question-answers take place which are as follows–[32]

Question – With what have you returned ? Sorrow or happiness ?

Answer – We have left the sorrows afar and we have come with happiness.

Question – What do you want at our doorstep ?

Answer – We want some place to rest. We are all very tired.

Question – Probably you have brought illnesses with you ?

Answer – We have thrown the illnesses in the flood so that it can take them away in its flow. We have returned only with happiness.

Question – What else have you brought with you ?

Answer – We have brought happiness and many cattle. We have brought paddy and rice and many other similar good things.

Conclusion: "Then all of you come inside, we will give you place to stay." After saying this, the three persons sitting inside open the door and light a lamp and the persons from outside enter the house by saying, "duk-duk," thereby imagining that they are entering the house driving in many cattle with them.

In order to keep the ancestors appeased, the Mundas, before they partake their meal, take out some portion and offer it to them or before imfibing hadiya some drops are dropped in their name. If the Munda likewise does not offer food and hadiya to them, then they become angry and challenge their right to food and drink like this- "what are you eating? what are you drinking?" and this sounds and echoes in the mind of the Mundas. The ancestors do this to remind their living descendants about their duties. But they do not punish them in their anger. Upon getting angry, they do not, like the regional bongas, send animals to destroy or loot their crops ("dingo" their crops) or in greed pester ("hatir") them. Whatever it may be, they are their own offspring, hence they should be brought back to the right path but no harm should be done to them. When the Munda brings home a newly purchased bullock, then after besmearing its horns, the bullock is introduced to the ancestors and thereafter it becomes worthy of working for the house. If this is not done, then the bullock starts having a stomach ache (kuli-laichi-hasu"). But ading bonga veritably becomes very angry when during "mag parv" he is neglected. This festival is mainly celebrated for the worship of ancestors. This is the day of full moon of the month of Paush. During the month of Paush (tenth month of the Hindu calendar) the Munda is very well off with a rich harvest because at this time his harvest starts coming home. The worship of ancestors is very important in the life of the Munda because they enthuse Singbonga and the other bongas to work for the benefit of the family. Ading bongako are the patron gods of the family.

In Munda religion, Singbonga pays the most attention toward the protection and expansion of the Munda race. After Him, the second place goes to Misi Singbonga (sister of Singbonga) which is the famous name of Nage Aera goddess who during the destructive circumstances of Rain of Fire, had saved a Munda brother-sister duo in her marsh of twelve "kos" length and twelve "kos" width, and from whom the Munda race increased, otherwise the Munda race would have been totally wiped off forever. Therefore, Singbonga and Nage Aera are chiefly worshipped as the God and Goddess of the entire Munda race. Apart from them, for the welfare and protection of the family, ading bongako are the ancestral gods from whom the Munda people never expect any probability of harm. The Asur-wives who became regional bongas due to the kindness of Singbonga, they cannot be accepted as totally benevolent gods because by nature they had been Asur-wives. Even then, these bongas get respect and worship from the Mundas and pahans because after having finished off the Asurs, Singbonga had given this ruling. Bongas (Asur-wives) have now joined the invisible world of Singbonga where instead of ignorance and destruction, knowledge and the lesson of Creation reign. Hence, when called upon by the pahan or devra, they now tell them the reasons for sicknesses or their secrets. It is their duty that whatever responsibility had been given to them by Singbonga they should carry them out. Singbonga had told them that pahan and devra will arrange for the food of bongas and will offer sacrifice to them but in return they would have to serve the offsprings of the lutkums meaning the entire Munda race. This is the reason why the Sarna Munda, keeping in mind that the whole Creation is the gift of Singbonga, worships the regional bongas. Singbonga and His helping bongas according to Munda religion, play an active helpful role in the protection and increase of the Munda race and Munda family.

In Munda life, mention is made of certain such bongas whose worship or appeasement is not concerned with the pahan or devra but with ojhas and sokhas. These are wicked and unsatisfied souls which torture the Mundas and for whom the Munda people always have their doors closed. Meaning that their entry into the house is prevented under all circumstances. These destructive bongas are called banita bonga.

Banita Bonga

Most of the work regulations and thinking process of Munda religion are influenced by the souls of the dead. Except for Singbonga and to a certain extent Misi Singbonga or Nage Aera, nearly all the bongas connected to natural places are souls, and Singbonga has given the ruling that in every village there should be arrangement of pahan and devra or priest to appease them by offering "bali" (sacrifice). Ancestor worship is also a device to please the souls of the dead ancestors and through them to gain benevolence of Singbonga and other bongas for the family. This is because the souls of the dead ancestors have the capability of roaming in that invisible world which is of Singbonga and the other bongas. In this way in Munda religion, the expressin of the influence of souls of the dead can be seen in nearly all religious rituals.

Munda religion, which is influenced by souls of the dead, also takes into consideration the souls of those persons who have died an untimely death. Untimely death means that despite duration of life remaining, death occurs. It is believed in the religious philosophy of the Mundas that the body is a leaf-plate and the food kept on it is his duration of life or age. Gradually the food is exhausted meaning thereby that the duration of life ends, hence like a used leaf-plate the body becomes meaningless and falls. At the time of death while expressing condolence amid the gathered people, the pahan or the chief person in the assembly says that Singbonga had been kind enough to have given one "jome sakam." The departing person has departed after having eaten his "Jome sakam" (which means that he has lived his determined age and left). Singbonga has called him back. But the person who does not fully experience his "Jomesakam" what happens to the "rowa" (soul) of that dead person? In Munda religion, such a "rowa" (soul) is thought to be unsatisfied. After death, such souls become restless to quench their unsatisfied thirst. The Munda people do not allow such "rowas" to come to their homes. They are supposed to be outcaste, they live in the forest, they are "mua masanko" or destructive ghosts.

Many a time due to drowning, being killed by wild animals, dying through suicide, pregnant women dying during labour or after child birth, or similarly dying before "jome sakam" is over, all such deaths are called untimely deaths. The "rowa" (soul) which leaves the body remains unsatisfied. The Mundas believe that the "mua masanko of a drowning victim tries to kill other persons by drowning them too. Similarly, a person who has hanged himself, his "mua masanko" tries to misguide others and enthuses them to commit suicide. They are wicked souls. The bodies of such dead persons are not buried in the graveyard of the ancestors- they are buried where the accident happened or near an ant-hill far away from the village or else they are buried among thorny bushes.

This is not done due to malice. According to Munda belief, it is thought that the "rowa" of such dead persons roam near the body and they harm those who go by that way or by frightening them they make them ill. Due to this excuse, the ojha and sokha offer them worship and sacrifice to appease them. In order to get sacrifices, these bongas trouble the people and make them ill although their family members offer enough quantity of rice and rice-wine with their bodies as final oblation and try to quieten them by the following invocation: "You stay in this place. From today this will be your home. What more can we do for you? It has so happened that you have left us. You have left everything-home, race, clan, and have separated. You have adopted another race, you have become virjanam."

Even though the dead person may have been very much loved by the family during his life-time, after untimely death he has to be kept away from home.

When women die during labour pain or pass away before the sixth day of child birth, they become "churail." Those pregnant women who have a living embryo in their womb are called "barjiakan," meaning women having two souls in one body. If such women die in this condition then they too become "churail." Such a woman at times takes on the appearance of a beautiful woman or an animal, etc. Her back is hollow and her ankles are turned the opposite way. She becomes very desirous to be in the company of men. She appears in the nightmares of sick women. She becomes jealous of women, hence any man can pass a churail's place of stay without any harm if he is accompanied by a woman because a churail views with disdain any man accompanied by a woman and she does not go near him. A churail sends sicknesses and the affected person is afflicted with madness of continuous laughter, weeping, etc. and dies. She pulls his tongue out.

The current analysts of Munda religion say that accidents are life's unavoidable flaws. These cannot be stopped, but there is no factual basis in the belief that mua-masanko (wicked ghosts) cause these accidents. An accident should be viewed as an accident, and it should not be connected to the invisible world. But the ancient sectarians of Munda religion say that Singbonga has encircled the whole Munda tribe in a protective circle, and whoever goes out of the protective line he is destroyed and whoever remains within the protective line, that is race and clan, Singbonga is always ready to protect him. The "rowa" of the person going out of the protective circle is therefore not taken back within the race and neither is it given any place in the ading.

The old pahans are unable to clearly define "protective circle." According to them, whoever does any work which goes against the race or with whom Singbonga is displeased, he goes out of the protective circle. Upon being asked that many innocent boys become accident victims so is it that Singbonga is displeased with them also, then often the reply is-this matter cannot be understood by everybody. This can be explained only by the priest and pahan who understand the language and signs of Singbonga. But it is undoubted that due to the displeasure of Singbonga, a person becomes insecure and the "Muamasanko" (evil spirits) easily trap them in accidents and kill them. Hence, the "rowa" (soul) of this person cannot be given any place with our ancestors. As such, Singbonga is the controller of this world. He can shorten the life He has given, can decrease the "Jome sakam." Then, in these circumstances death is natural. Those accident victims are also included in the race whose life does not end in the accident site but after the accident while being looked after, their death occurs. In such a circumstance, the "rowa" of the deceased does not come under the influence of mua-masanko but stays within the racial zone and gets a place in the ading.

A final definition regarding fatal accidents is prevalent in Munda religion- "ranu-dakentaikanai" and after that nothing remains to be said. Ranu means medicine or poison, da means water or verbal form of "rainfall," which means Ranuda=rain of poison. "Ranu da" can be viewed in the context of "sengel da." "Sengel da" meaning "Rain of fire"- its reason was the all pervasive sinfulness of the world due to which Creation was becoming unbalanced and mankind had refused to recognise the Creator Singbonga and to carry out His orders, hence being compelled Singbonga had caused Rain of Fire and annihilated every thing. In the same way, "Rain of Poison" (Ranu-da) also embodies displeasure of Singbonga. Singbonga, Supreme God, Devi-Raja is benevolent and He always looks after the prosperity and protection of the Munda race. The reason for Poison Rain is also to protect Munda race and to maintain its purity. Whoever works against the race has to face "Poison Rain" which means that in the eyes of Singbonga, he does not remain fit to continue in the race. Resultantly, Singbonga puts him out of the protective line, and the insecure person falls prey to the muamasanko." So long as Singbonga's kindness continues, no power on earth can do any harm to any Munda, and Singbonga becomes angry on those who work against the race. This is the reason why the term "ranu daken taikanai" ("this person was affected by poison rain") is used to denote a person who dies in an accident.

The ordinary Mundas believe that "ranu-da" (poison rain) can be sent upon anyperson by Singbonga or any other bonga or any occultist. But this thought is erroneous, and most of the pahans think that in order to establish the supremacy of their professions, the sokhas, ojhas, and matiyas have spread such a mistaken notion among the poor, lower-level Mundas. How can the occultists encourage the other bongas or mua-masankos to destroy the person who is blessed by Singbonga. Hence the only reason for "ranu-da" (poison rain) is the anger of Singbonga, and Singbonga becomes angry when somebody works against the rules and regulations of the race and Creation (which was created by Singbonga). It is difficult to fix as to who and when he worked against the regulations of the race and the Creation. It is only Singbonga's decision because He is omnipresent and He sees and hears everything and He has given this ruling that the soul which worked against the race (and which is cursed by Singbonga) should not be given a place in the ading. In this way, there is a separate invisible world of the banita bongas where those unsatisfied ghosts roam who could not complete their "jome sakam" hence were thrown out of the race.

Occult Practices

The centre of Munda religion is not the person but the arrangement of welfare of the entire race. Singbonga has crafted this Creation and created the

Munda race in it and He always sees to its increase and protection. He has given directions to the bongas for the successful implementation of His work, and has arranged for worship and oblations to the bongas by the pahan and sokha (devra) of every village.[33] Whosoever works for the destruction of the race or against the race, he becomes a victim of the wrath of Singbonga, or he is expelled from the protective line created by Singbonga and in this way he is excluded from the kindness of Singbonga. Which means that Singbonga does not go for his support and he becomes easy prey to accidents being done and unprotected in this world. The souls of such deceased persons are not given place even in the ading because now they are not counted as member of the race. In this manner, the whole arrangement of Munda religion has been made by Singbonga keeping the race as target.

The bongas to whom Singbonga has given various sectoral responsibilities for implementing His goal, are basically of Asur nature.[34] By nature they are conceited and greedy. Although the destruction of Asurs has been due to their conceited and greedy nature, and Singbonga, taking pity on the hapless lives of the Asur widows, has given them responsibility and power after obtaining their promise that they would only do good, but greed and pride surface in the behaviour of the bongas on various occasions. They keep warning the Mundas by sending them diseases and calamities, and keep on receiving oblations (sacrifices) from them. The Mundas cannot guess the number of these bongas roaming around in the invisible world. The Munda residents of various regions cannot guess the number of various bongas. The Mundas of various regions keep worshipping various bongas. The souls of the dead also roam in the invisible world among the bongas. Amongst them, unsatisfied souls of some of the deceased hover around-these are victims of untimely death and have not been able to complete their "Jome sakam." Some bongas from among them take on a wild appearance (they become violent and scare the Mundas and make them ill). The souls of the ancestors of the Mundas sometimes leave their place in the ading and go over to the invisible world for the well-being of the family, and discuss with various bongas and Singbonga regarding the welfare of the members of the family. In Munda religion there is a live supposition of the invisible world. The Munda believes that the rowa (soul) comes out of the body and becomes an inhabitant of the invisible world. The Mundas believe that the invisible world is approximately a parallel world of the visible one, and in it all types of bongas, good or bad, are found. The only difference is that they are not visible, but the expression of their activities can be clearly seen in the visible world which the capable pahan, devra, sokha, etc. read and understand and explain their meaning to the ordinary Mundas.

The belief in Munda religion about the invisible world and the power of the bongas and their character has developed to such an extent that it has become an unbreakable faith in the Munda psyche. As a result, occult practices emerge over a period of time in the form of a new arrangement. It is not a fact that only after coming to Chhotanagpur the Munda race came under the influence of sorcery and witchcraft but we know that the system of occult practices was prevalent in the whole continents of Europe and Asia, and prior to the advent of Aryans in India, for hundreds of years, the Mundas had been under the influence of occult practices. In most of the races of Europe and in India, too, the attribute of witchcraft was normally to be found more among women than men, and even now it is the same.

In Munda religion, too, the religious songs connected with witchcraft express devotion to Nage Aera, their goddess-form. Although Singbonga has given the rank of bonga to the Asur widows, yet after becoming bonga, their female-form has ended and these mentioned bongas are believed to be males and worshipped accordingly. "Nage Aera" is a goddess coming prior to "Asur Avdan"- she had saved a male-female (brother-sister) duo for protection of the race which had been annihilated in the Rain of Fire. After entering Chhotanagpur and coming in contact with Hindu religion a goddess called Parvati gradually came to be prevalent among the Mundas. In the sector of witchcraft, Parvati is the eldest of the seven sisters named in it. In Munda tradition, a religious song connected to witchcraft has gained currency in which it is said that between the two wives of Singbonga, Parvati was the elder one who was an expert in witchcraft. We will see how "Mahadev" and "Parvati" appear in witchcraft or as its remedy, or as Singbonga and His wife in Munda religion.

Before the coming of the British to Chhotanagpur, the whole Munda society was badly besieged with the fear of occult practices and witchcraft. Upon suspicion of being a witch or sorcerer, innocent women and men would be caught and they would either be beaten to death or driven away from the village or upon being given protection by the family their homes would be burnt down. Such descriptions have also been received that the witches would be caught, hung upside down from a tree and fire would be lit below till they writhed in pain and died.[35] With the publicity of Christian religion, the strict attitude of the British and the education of some Mundas some awareness has come against the superstition inherent in occult practices[36] but even now witchcraft and many professionals connected with it are working against Munda religion in Munda society and they have developed such an anti-system which has deeply affected the minds of the ordinary Mundas and it has taken the form of an institution.

Occult Practices : An Anti-Religious System[37]

The influence of witchcraft, occult practices and destructive forces has deeply embedded itself in Munda life and has so extensively overshadowed their day-to-day life that sociologists see this entire arrangement in Munda life as a powerful heretical structure against Munda religion. The pahans have a peculiar argument that Sarna religion itself is not so powerful that it can protect from anti-religious system. According to them, Munda or Sarna religion which is connected to the entire race, meaning that it pertains to the race whereas occult practices which pertain to individuals and in which Mundas have developed unshakeable faith- how can Sarna religion confront this anti-religious system? In order to vanquish witches or sorcerors, a parallel and effective individual-based system would be needed. Unfortunately the bongas, souls of the dead or other invisible powers on which occult practices are based, they are the same invisible powers which are completely connected to Munda religion. "Asur Avdan" confirms this truth. But in Munda religion it has been directed that these bongas will be utilised for the welfare of the entire Munda race. When they become dissatisfied and send diseases and maladies to Mundas to warn them, then the devra finds out the particular bonga and thereafter satisfies him by offering sacrifice or oblation to him. In this way, the patient gets freed from his malady. This religious ritual is performed openly in a gathering of the society. It is believed that this ritual is inherently the implementation of Singbonga's order because Singbonga has ordered the Munda race that they should offer oblations to the bongas. If the Mundas do not do this, then to remind them of their duties the bonga takes recourse to send them diseases and maladies or even other destructive measures just to warn them.

It is inherent in Munda religion to offer sacrifice to the bongas; also, that the bongas become angry and again are appeased are believed by the Mundas. Which means that the powers of the invisible world can be appeased and that they do have the power through which they can positively harm human beings of the visible world. These tenets prescribed by Munda religion form the basis of the growth of a new learning which tries to subdue these invisible powers. By worshipping them, offering sacrifice or other oblations, these bongas are appeased and come under the subjugation of the worshipper and the worshipper gets his work done by them as per his desire. Often, the worshipper and the witch subjugate a particular bonga or spirit through their learning, worship and devotion, and get their desired work done in the invisible world through him. It is said that these witches and sorcerers establish their identification with the worshipped bonga or spirit. Thereafter, gaining control over the powers of the invisible world through magic, devices are set in motion to destroy any enemy, jealous neighbour, the crop or family of an undesirable person etc. or even to kill him, so the complete system of magic becomes anti-religious.[38]

Occult Practices and Initiation of Witches

Information regarding occult practices is mostly obtained from secondary sources. Since this system is strongly shrouded in secrecy, hence it becomes very difficult to know about it from primary sources. No witch declares herself to be a witch and neither does she describe in a simple way the magic and spells done by her. Generally, some information may be through personal viewing and some from others, especially hearing from the devras. The Mundas believe that the devras have knowledge about all the mysteries and mechanisms used by witches for killing. Based on this knowledge, the devras can take steps to checkmate the witches.

The jet black new moon night of Sohrai festival is of significant importance in the world of witches. On this night they sharpen their learning and accept initiation from their guru (preceptor). During the dark night of Sohrai, far away from the village, they assemble in a clearing. They bring along with them a frog, a big, brown locust (kali-sonsorod), a small axe, sickle and a small earthen cup filled with oil. Along with these items they also bring a bound broom and an earthen lamp. All these things are kept on the edge of the cleared space.

In the darkness of the night, shedding all their clothes (they bind the spread out broom at the waist), they stand in a circle. They lift their left knee straight and balance on it an oil-filled earthen lamp in which a single wick floats. The wick is lit. On that jet black night, no body has the courage to see the hideous glittering forms of the witches in the faint light of the lamps burning in the still air slightly above the ground. They keep dancing in that circular form. The lamp balanced on the knee does not fall and its flame is not extinguished despite the time taken for dancing. Even the breeze cannot put out the flame. It is said that their preceptor Mahadev comes and sits near them in the form of a cheetah.

Mahadev is the supreme preceptor of the learning of occult-practices. In addition to Him, every group of witches has its own preceptor. It is from this preceptor that the other witches learn about occult practices and sharpen their knowledge. This preceptor takes a lamp and puts it inside the head of the cheetah due to which the cheetah's eyes, nostrils and ears start emitting light. Thereafter she goes to the centre of the circle. She is accompanied by another witch who comes to the centre of the circle with a small drum.[39] The small drum starts sounding on a low key and thereafter the preceptor administers the oath of secrecy to the initiated witches. The oath is often in Sadani language:

- "When women will hit you with spades and the men with hatchets, will you tell them about all the activities here, reveal the secret, or endure it ?
- "When they will beat you with sticks or burn you by digging into you with flaming firebrands, you will endure it or reveal all the secrets?"

All the disciples say in unison: "We will endure it. We will endure it!" (low sound produced on the small drum due to light beating).

In this way, the dance goes on the whole night. The preceptor in between gives orders to each disciple one by one that–"go and cut the cheetah."

That disciple witch picks up the axe and poses as if she is going to kill the frog. Again the preceptor orders- "go and cut the snake." The disciple witch takes the sickle and poses to attack the locust. Every disciple witch has to repeat this type of action accordingly.

The belief is entrenched among the Mundas that if any man or woman has tried to see the activity pertaining to perfecting the learning of occult practices on the night of Sohrai, and he or she has been espied by the witches in the light of the flame emanating from the head of Mahadev, then after a few weeks, his or her death would be certain. It is possible that while coming through the forest in the darkness of the night, somebody's sight may have moved towards that scene for a few moments after which he may have quickly run away. Because, nobody dares to see this activity on the night of Sohrai.

There is no doubt that some women know about the learning pertaining to magic and spells, and on the night of Sohrai they secretly achieve perfection in it from their preceptor. The dark new moon night of Sohrai is thought to be naturally more suitable for such evil activities. It is generally believed that if an arrow, hatchet and other weapons are honed on Sohrai night, then they acquire killing powers, and if they are kept by one's side then even the wickedest bonga does not dare to touch that person. Medicinal herbs and plants acquire more power on Sohrai night, hence those who deal with them, gather them in the darkness of the night after fully shedding their clothes. The medicinal herbs and plants which are gathered on Sohrai night are more effective than those which are gathered on other days.

The night of Sohrai is full of terror for normal citizens. On the night of Sohrai, the witches acquire so much power that they can steal anybody's "im udurg" (heart) or afflict animals with dysentery. As a means of protection, they besmear the belly, chest and shoulders with an unguent over which a spell has been cast, which the witches cannot cross. Similar unguent is besmeared on the animals on Sohrai night for their protection. On this night, the witches completely subjugate Najom Chandi (bonga) and they scold and torture him and they make Najom Chandi work as per their desire. Najom Chandi dances to their tune just like a subjugated slave. In this way, the new moon night of Sohrai is supposed to be the most appropriate for gaining knowledge about occult practices and achieving perfection in it. That is why, most witches on this day try to get initiated secretly for learning occult practices so that they can get more power in their perfection.

Magic Spells

The witches subjugate the bongas and get them to do hideous and murderous acts. In Munda religion sacrifice is offered to bongas by the devra in order to benefit a tortured or sick person. In this, the role of the devra is to reach the bonga through the medium of the tortured person. At first, the devra connects with the tortured person and thereafter keeping that person in front, he offers sacrifice to the bonga for his wellbeing and prays for his kindness. But in the sacrifice offered by witches, there is no talk of curing a person and neither is the tortured victim made the medium of this activity. On the contrary, the whole activity and sacrifice is done to target a person upon whom a ghost has to be sent. The main ghostly activities are as follows:

(a) Black Cat

Due to attainment of perfection, connection is established between the bonga and the witches. The bonga becomes one soul with the witches and then the witches take on the appearance of a rat or a cat or similar domestic animals and keep watch over the targeted person whom they will make their prey. It is widely believed in the villages that witches take on the form of black cats and hover in the house, or on the parapet of the house or in the neighbourhood of the house, and bring troubles to that house. Some people also believe that in this condition there is no difference to be found between Najom Chandi or the witch because both are believed to be of one soul and one form. In Munda villages, if a black cat is seen, then the villagers pursue it and either kill it or else drive it away very far from the village.

In sorcery, cats are also used in another way. The person who is the target of the entire magic or who has to be afflicted by illness, or who has to be killed, he is made one soul with a cat, meaning, that with the power of magic, his soul is planted in a black cat and thereafter, through incantations and various rituals, that cat is killed (that is, that person dies in an invisible manner), and stuffing its mouth with rice extracted from unboiled paddy, it is burried in that person's field or at the back of his house. This affects the person straightaway and quickly. It is believed that his death is certain within a few days.

(b) Shooting of Arrows

Shooting of arrows from an invisible place to harm an enemy is prevalent in the world of sorcery and is widely believed by the Mundas. Since the witch subjugates Najom Chandi through magic, hence both become one. They take on one appearance. In the faraway forest-mountain or some invisible place, an arrow and a bow is made of grass and after energizing the arrow with incantations it is shot towards its target. This shot never goes in vain. If the targeted person is ploughing his field then the arrow might hit him, he might fall and become ill; if the arrow falls in the field then the whole crop is destroyed and if it falls on the plough, then the plough scatters in pieces. At times, the targeted person if he is himself empowered, then the arrow just touches him (because the arrow never falters from its target) and without doing any harm it returns and falls on its shooter. The "arrow" never goes in vain.

(c) Piercing of Doll

In the world of occult practices, the action of the piercing of doll is the most prevalent. In this activity a small clay doll is prepared in the name of the targeted person. Through various incantations and rituals it is seeded with life to activate it as if the targeted person has come inside the doll (this is a supposition). Thereafter it is prepared for sacrifice by making a mark on it with vermillion, and through other rituals. Najom Bonga is invoked and after piercing the doll with a big needle or knife, it is offered to Najom Bonga. The dead doll is buried near an ant hill and the rice (obtained from unboiled paddy) which had been used during the sacrifice is also buried along with it which signifies the fact that a sacrifice had been offered and it has been cremated. It is accepted that whatever has happened to the doll has happened with the targeted person and in this way that person is presumed to have lost his existence and becomes the prey of Najom Bonga. The Mundas believe that a person killed through a doll has few days to live in this visible world.

(d) Striking through any Part of the Body

In the piercing of doll, sorcery is used for the whole body, but in occult practices another system is also prevalent in which the person, animal or thing that is to be targeted, his cut nail or hair or dust from his feet or old shed clothes, any such item has to be collected. Similarly, if an animal is to be targeted then the hair from its tail or its broken tooth work as a medium. For destroying any crop, a handful of grains from that field is supposed to be enough. According to the learning of occult practices, by catching hold of any part of the target the whole body can be affected. The Munda people remain vigilant that no such item of theirs falls in the hands of their enemies due to which they might become a victim of sorcery. Cut nails, hair or clothes they hide in such a manner that they do not fall into anybody's hands or even if they fall they cannot be identified as to whom they belonged to or were part of.

(e) Installing of Bonga or Evil Spirit

Through the power of occult practices, bonga or evil spirit is made to enter that house which has to be destroyed and then the house becomes an easy target of illnesses and ghostly disturbances. The witch or the sorcerer at first installs Najom Bonga in a lump of stone or in such a thing which can easily be entered in the targeted house, and thereafter places it inside the house. In this work the jealous person who takes the help of sorcery to destroy his enemy has to carefully thrust that lump of stone or thing (in which Najom Bonga has been installed) in the house of the person whose destruction is desired. This responsibility is his. Those who indulge in occult practices never come forward openly. Alongwith the lump or thing the installed bonga also enters the house and wherever the lump goes the installed bonga also goes there. The fundamental difference between the bongas invoked by the witches and the Asur bongas is that Asur bongas are connected to their regions and they do not abandon them to go to other places like for example if the sal tree on which an Asur bonga stays is cut and is taken away to another place, the

Asur bonga does not go along with that tree-instead, it takes its position on another tree in the same region. Contrary to this, the bonga invoked through sorcery goes along with that lump in which it has been installed.

(f) Rowa-Akiding

The bonga subjugated by the witches spreads diseases in the house as per their desire, and causes destruction of the whole house, its domestic animals and agriculture and vegetable gardening. The most mortal blow of Najom Bonga on any person is supposed to be when he takes out his soul and sells it. Actually he does not sell anybody's soul, but he takes out the soul from the body. When the person's soul comes out, then only the shadow of the person remains. And if the soul does not return to the body in a short while, then the person dies. Any person afflicted with "rowa-akiding" suddenly starts appearing as crippled and lifeless, his voice becomes indistinct and he loses vision.

(g) The Use of Poison

The expertise to kill through the use of poison also comes within the learning of sorcery. The witches or the learners of sorcery use two kinds of poison: (i) bisi (ii) maur Bisi is the name of that poison which is found in its basic form and straightaway mixes with the blood of the body through the veins. Being bitten by a snake is "bisi" because the snake's poison directly enters the blood-stream. Sometimes the poisonous head of the gehuan snake (a venomous brown coloured snake) is cut and mixed in food and through this the poison goes directly to the blood and immediately starts showing its effect.

Maur is poison derived from trees and plants and this is mixed with food, and during the process of digestion it enters the blood stream. Hoffmann in his Encyclopaedia has listed 46 kinds of plants from which poison is extracted.[40] Witches are very skilful in preparing "maur," and the "maur" prepared by them is called by the name of "najom" in Munda society. It is deeply entrenched in the Munda mind that "najom" is more fatal and effective than "maur." The reason is clear. In the way that medicinal plants, gathered by herbal doctors, become more effective due to the grace of Singbonga, similarly due to the influence of bongas, maur which becomes "najom" acquires greater efficacy.

The Relationship between Witches and Bongas

Sorcery is that learning which prepares the foundation of inter se relationship between the bongas and the witches, and in this process the witch gets very close to a bonga and subjugates it. It becomes the duty of the witches to regularly worship the bonga and offer him his desired things. The witch cannot show any laxity in performing her duties otherwise the bonga subjugated by her himself takes control over her. Since the witch keeps the bonga appeased through oblations, she is able to take work from him as per her desire. If any special work is taken from a bonga, then accordingly special oblations have to be offered by the witches. Sometimes the witches promise the bongas that if their work is done properly, then the bongas will be offered additional sacrifices. The portion of offerings to the bongas is never neglected, not even in those circumstances when at times the magic released by the witch-enthused bongas is cut by the devras and made powerless and ineffective. It is said that the victim (against whom the magic spell was sent and who was saved from the magical strike by the devra's superior knowledge) is made by the devra to appease that bonga by offering the same amount of oblation as had been promised by the witch to be offered upon completion of the work. In this way, the share of oblation to the bonga is never lost. The bonga cannot tolerate any kind of laxity or neglect, and in such a circumstance expresses his anger through various signs and mediums. Hence, witches and devras keeping contact with the bongas take recourse to all possible devices to keep them appeased.

The influence of occult practices is deeply entrenched in Munda life. This is the result of widespread hold of bongas in Munda religion. In Munda religion, various types of bongas keep on troubling the Mundas due to their greedy and proud behaviour, and obtain "sacrifice" and offerings from them. The witches, keeping in mind the troublesome and harmful nature of the bongas, worship them through the knowledge of sorcery and subjugate them. Thereafter, to fulfil the jealous and envious desires of their clients, the witches target their enemies and through various processes send the bongas to them and harm them, even to the extent that the witches become the reason for their death. The question arises, from whom have the witches gained their power in Munda religion? Is it from Singbonga the Almighty and well wisher of the Munda race? Despite His protective armour, how can the witches trouble the Mundas? Do the witches have any close connection with Singbonga? The existence of the world of sorcery is virtually accepted, and it is also believed that Singbonga's first wife was a witch who was an expert in occult practices.

The First Witch of Creation – Singbonga's Wife

In the religious song prevalent in Munda tradition, we can see the background of the development of the system of sorcery which goes against Munda religion and can be termed anti-religious system. In this song there is mention of "seven mountains" witch sisters and their powers. There is also mention of the development of another system which cuts the anti-religious system and provides for saving the Mundas from magical strikes. This system includes the institution of sokha, devra, mati, etc. who have obtained powers from Mahadev and come up in Munda society. This is a parallel system to render the powers of sorcery ineffective and has the blessings of Singbonga because he had taught "Dantari" all types of learning through which he could make ineffective the killing powers of sorcery.

Singbonga had two wives out of which the elder first one was a witch and childless. The younger wife had one son. The witch drew happiness from death and maladies, but the Munda people used to blame and criticise Singbonga and the witches during death and illnesses. Due to this the witch-wife used to be angry. She instigated Singbonga to send Rain of Fire so that the people of the world would be destroyed forever. Singbonga did as she said, but seeing the destroyed world, He regretted it deeply. Singbonga had not wanted the Munda race to be annihilated. If He would act as per the desires of His witch-wife, then the Munda race due to being victimised by diseases and illnesses would become weak and weaker and one day would die away. In order to give protection from disease and maladies, Singbonga imparted knowledge to a person called "Dantari" and gave him the power of devra. Dantari taught this subject to some of his disciples.

"Knowledge" and "power" are supplementary to each other. It is not necessary that the disciple who learns the subject also acquires power. "Power" is obtained through achievement of perfection. The achievement of perfection is through devotion, and then only the preceptor becomes happy and gives power to the disciple. In the absence of power, the education cannot be completely effective, and in the absence of learning there can be no place for establishing power because whoever has learning only he can obtain power. Singbonga had imparted both "learning" and "power" to Dantari, hence He had made him qualified to teach others and become a preceptor. In this way, Dantari was a preceptor created by Singbonga. Dantari taught his disciples knowledge of devra but he did not give them "perfection."

Due to anger the witch-wife of Singbonga visited the son of the younger wife with disease. Then Dantari was called for treatment. He meditated and in the State of meditation said, "Master, your old utensil is circulating." Singbonga understood. He banished his witch-wife from home.[42] Leaving home, the witch-wife taught the knowledge of sorcery to six sisters living on the mountain. In this way there became total seven witch sisters who are known as "saat parbatiya" or "seven sisters in the Munda world. In this manner, the anti-religious system of black magic and spells gradually developed in Munda life."

In the folk song "Saat Parbatiya," the witch is shown to be related to Singbonga. In order to protect the Munda race from becoming very weak and gradually dying out, Singbonga put a leash on the killing knowledge and destructive tendency of the witches, hence He imparted the learning of a devra to "Dantari" and also gave him the power of perfection or "siddhi." Armed with this "knowledge" and "power," Dantari imparted the knowledge of devra, of various roots, the good properties of barks and birds, medicines, to some of his disciples, but the disciples had not become very capable or devoted to attain perfection. The name and fame of Dantari was spreading through out due to the learning and perfection obtained from Singbonga, and he used to treat successfully the people afflicted by the influence of sorcery or other maladies. But as is evident from the Munda religious songs, Singbonga cannot tolerate anyone's pride; He did not tolerate Dantari's vanity arising out of his fame. One day when Dantari was having a bath and he was rubbing his back with a thin long stick, then Singbonga's witch wife Pratham Parbatiya, threw a magic dart at him. The stick became a snake and bit him on his neck.

In this manner, a war ensued between the witches and the devras based upon their respective fields of knowledge. Dantari took recourse to many devices but the witches through their sorcery and power of becoming invisible nullified all his attempts. At the time of death, Dantari advised his disciples to cut his body into pieces and to eat his flesh after cooking it so that they would gain perfection, but the witches showed their cunningness and ate up his flesh. Thus, the foolish disciples remained bereft of the power of perfection. Among the disciples there was one called Tura. He understood that the witches had tricked them. He searched and on a leaf he found a drop of blood of Dantari- he licked it, and in this way he attained perfection.

On a Sohrai night, Tura hid himself and tried to catch the witches in the midst of honing their magical powers. When it was late in the dark night and the witches were dancing naked, Tura started playing on a magical flute from behind a hillock. The witches kept dancing under the magical spell of the flute. They had forgotten that apart from the spread out brooms covering their bodies they were without clothes and the earthen lamps were burning in low flames. They had neither sense of time nor about themselves. They kept on dancing to the tune of the flute, kept on dancing.

In the morning, a farmer who was going to his field saw this scene and was astounded. He ran to the village and called the villagers to the place. The villagers became highly embarrassed to see their wives dancing as naked witches. They heard their children crying in their homes so, in order to find out the mystery behind it, they ran towards the village. In the meantime, Tura lessened his hypnotic power but did not fully release the witches from its grip. Then the witches realised how tired they had become and how helpless they were under the hypnotic spell. Tura took three promises from the witches and it was only after that he freed them from his magic spell. The three promises of the witches were :

(1) We will never work against the desire of Singbonga.
(2) We will never oppose the power of the devra and
(3) If we have willfully or through jealousy cast magic spell or thrown magic dart against anybody, then the devra can return it to us.

Devra : A Parallel Religious Institution against Sorcery

The religious story of "Saat Parbatiya" is against Munda religion. It advocates the theory of the destruction of the Munda race. Destructive powers are present in Parvati who is the witch-wife of Singbonga. According to Sarna religion, Singbonga is the sole Creator-God of this Creation. As per this religious story, Singbonga appears to be surrounded by wives and various powers, so much so that the services of a devra are required for the treatment of his child.

But Munda religious experts analyse this religious story as being a helper of Munda religion. Singbonga is Almighty, and in order to maintain balance in the Munda race and the Creation, He has delegated some powers to the witches, and has created diseases and maladies. Additionally He has created "Devras" who can protect the Munda race from maladies. As per the rule of Singbonga, death of human beings and "thinning" of population is necessary for the protection of the race. In order to implement His work, He uses the bongas. At times He directly uses the bongas or else works through the magical machinations of the witches. These are all as per His desire and according to His design. He never allows the witches to have an upper hand over the devras otherwise the speed of thinning out the race will gain advantage over the protection of the race. Hence, the destructive power of the bongas and witches, and the protective power of the devras, both are derived from the same God, Singbonga. The mystery of Creation lies in destruction. The witch and devra-both are agents to fulfil the design of Singbonga, hence both are part of Munda religion. Even then, Singbonga does not like the witch because right from birth her soul is full of jealousy, sin and pride. Singbonga has always punished such characters. That is why He drove out His witch-wife from home.

From this religious story it is clear that Singbonga had wanted to create and develop a strong race of devras through the medium of "Dantari" who would mollify the blows of magic and spells. We see the appearance of a strong institution of devotees working against sorcery, and the extension of their powers which gave some relief to the Munda society from the terror of witches and black magic, although the Sadans and Hindu religion had an important role to play in their development.

Actually, the question was not of religion but of that power which would protect the lives of the Mundas from witches and bongas. If the devotee takes the help of any god or religion and acquires the capability, then the Mundas take shelter in him and with his help save themselves from the blows of the witches. The main aim of the devotee is to find out the reasons of a disease, to find out the witch and the bonga who are connected with the disease and thereafter to advise about the remedy or cure. The Munda after understanding it, offers worship in his own way and as per his rituals, or offers sacrifice.

There are many categories of devotees who offer worship and it is according to this that their reputation spreads in Munda society. The best among them is called sokha, whereas hatadevra is a devotee or worshipper of a lower category. Bhagat, marang, Devra, etc. are other categories of devotees. The number of Hindu devotees or Hinduised Mundas is comparatively more.

Sokha: Sokha is a believable worshipper and devotee. Mostly Hindus or Hinduised Mundas become sokhas. Their total behaviour is like Hindu priests. Their household deities are Mahadev-Parvati. The sokha pleases Mahadev and obtains power from Him after undergoing harsh vows, strict control and difficult meditation and devotion. He is totally devoted to his faith. He sets up a round object representing Mahadev on open quadrangle near his hut. In this quadrangle a thick basil shrub is also kept. A trident is embedded near the round object, and a small triangular red flag is tied to a thin bamboo of average height. He regularly worships Mahadev with milk and flowers. He consecrates the round object with clarified butter and puts a vermillion mark on it. He burns incense in clarified butter in front of the round object, and joss-sticks are kept burning near it.

The sokha does not go anywhere on call. He stays in his hut or near his worshipping place. Whoever needs him, goes to him and places his problem before him and asks for remedy.

The sokha listens attentively to the people who are being tortured by witches or bongas. He speaks very little and from time to time does some unfathomable rituals. How far these rituals are meaningful cannot be said but they do have psychological effect on the complainant and his companions. After some time, he touches the round object of Mahadev. He burns incense and aromatic materials due to which the atmosphere becomes fearful. Sokha then rings a bell and blows with all his might on a conchshell or a small horn as if he is inviting Mahadev to come to him. The assembled people stare at the sokha. The whole atmosphere seems to be under the influence of the sokha. Thereafter the sokha gradually starts shaking his head and again goes on to jerk it violently. Mahadev comes upon him. He starts babbling in an unclear language as if he is talking to bongas or invisible powers. His own "persona" becomes numbed. Whatever he says or does is not his-it is Mahadev who speaks through him.

Spiritually roaming in this trance like condition,[43] the sokha sees the witch. He also sees the environment and the people who are near the witch. He hears the name of the bonga who had inclined her to do black magic. He obtains full knowledge about the bonga as also what kind of sacrifice will appease him.

After returning to consciousness, the sokha narrates to the assembled people about what he had seen and heard during his meditation. The audience listens to every word of the sokha with great reverence. The assembled people have full faith in the power of the sokha. Whatever the sokha has said is cent per cent true. The sokha has found out about the witch. He cannot be mistaken.

In the Munda panchayat (village assembly), it is decided what kind of and how much punishment should be meted out to the "witch" identified by the sokha. The "witch" so identified by the sokha cannot deny that she has indulged in the vice of black magic. The sokha has declared her name in front of many people who had been present before him. It is taken for granted that in order to save herself, she will deny it, hence nobody pays heed to the arguments put forth by her or her family members.

What has the sokha got to do with the witch ? He is believed to be an unconnected and neutral person. In order to find out the witch, his various activities, expressions and behaviour, the jerking of his head, babbling in an unclear language, give clear indications that Mahadev has come upon him and whatever he has seen or heard in his trance, every thing is divine, godly. The assembly accepts the Statement of the sokha as final and decides accordingly.

In Munda society, the continuance of the honour of sokhas is due to: (a) the sokha does not go at the call of anybody-whoever requires his services has to knock at the door of his hut and temple, (b) whichever bonga is to be appeased as per his orders, the bonga is from within the fold of Munda religion, the bonga is not any god of the Hindus or others, (c) the sokha respects the tradition and religion of the Mundas and he does not interfere at all in their rules and customs. His work is to find out about the witch, tell the name of the bonga, and to name the animal to be offered as sacrifice to the bonga. All these informations the sokha passes on to the Mundas and the rest of the work is done by the Mundas themselves as per their tradition, their religion, and their rules and customs, (d) sokha is not greedy like the Devra who exploits the Mundas financially by asking them to give lots of offerings and to follow many rituals of sacrifice, (e) The victimised family has to give a fat fee to the sokha. This enhances the prestige of the sokha. The prowess and reputation of the sokha is measured in ratio with the fatness of the fee. There is no bargaining or debate regarding the fee. Whatever the Munda spends he gets it back as fine from the "witch."

It has become a firm belief among the Mundas that the Hindu God Mahadev is more influential and powerful than their bongas. In the following pages we will see that due to intermingling of Munda and Hindu religions, within a period of time how Singbonga and His wife have gained currency as Mahadev-Parvati in many religious stories (although the Munda does not believe in Singbonga being married or having a wife).

Bhagat: The bhagats find second position after the sokhas in the hierarchy of the religious institution which has developed as a parallel to the anti-religious system of magic and spells. The Bhagats, just like the sokhas, are faithful to Mahadev. They pour milk over the rounded stone representing Mahadev, smear it with clarified butter and put a vermillion mark on it. Just like the sokhas, a red flag is hung on a small bamboo pole in their place of worship. Joss sticks and fire are lit which is fuelled by sweet smelling incense. Nearly every thing is like the sokhas, but the Bhagats cannot earn the respect given to sokhas. There is less of quickness in their demeanour and a shortcoming of steadiness. The sokha believes that his work is completed when he as per his reputation, tells his clients about the witch and bonga and the sacrifice, but the Bhagat goes a step further and like the devra, he takes part in the ceremony of driving away the bongas. This work which the sokha hands over to the Mundas who do it as per their system, the Bhagat himself offers to do it. In this way, not only is his standard lowered, he is also believed to be greedy by the Mundas. The Bhagat may be Hindu or a Hinduised primitive tribal.

Marang: The marang copies the Devra and

Devra: Bhagat, and increases his expertise and power as compared to other devras. He is considered to be the best, the greatest. The meaning of "marang" is great. The meaning of marang-devra is greatest among the devras. Since he is the greatest in the category of devras, he is called marang-devra and his position lies between Bhagat and Hata Devra.

The Devra also worships Hindu gods just like the Bhagat. He calls Mahadev or Shiv-Shankar "Joto mahar" (one with the matted hair) in Munda language. In Munda religion, "joto mahar" is the description of "bir Chandi bonga." The marang-devra keeps the ambience of his place of worship just like that of the Bhagat. Any ordinary Munda will confuse the marang-devra with some bhagat or sokha if he sees his red flag and the environment where the marang-devra worships and tells about the witch and the bonga. But when the marang-devra offers sacrifice to appease any bonga, he sings praises of Singbonga in clear Mundari language. In addition to this, the following are the other special characteristics of marang devra:-

(1) Marang devra is a Munda (not a Hindu or Hinduised tribal).
(2) Compared to sokha and Bhagat, he is more easily available.
(3) He is quick in driving away torturous bongas through all the religious devices.
(4) He is available on call at the client's home and offers sacrifice for him which the sokha never does, and the Bhagat also thinks it to be infra dig to go to anybody's place and offer sacrifice.
(5) He primarily uses Mundari language but at times uses Hindi language also. Which means that with respect to language, marang-devra finds a position in between Bhagat and Hata Devra.

Amongst the Mundas, the honour given to marang-devra is more than the other devras, hence he extracts a good fee for identifying witches and diving away ghosts. The flesh of the sacrificed animal is an additional benefit to him. His expensive rituals are indicative of his greed. That is why in Munda society there is a saying, "the stomach of a tiger or that of a devra" (whose stomach is bigger).

Marang devra is the traditional devra of the Munda race, but he is sad that compared to the sokha and Bhagat, the Mundas give him less importance. He is afraid that in this way, as compared to the sokha and Bhagat, his position will gradually fall among the Mundas. Although from the viewpoint of religion and race, he may not weaken but from the point of view of spiritual power and learning his standard is considered to be lower. The confidence with which the sokha and the bhagat declare about identifying witches and bongas and driving them away, the Marang-devra lacks the same self-confidence. He often poses in such a manner, and does some actions, and to drive away evil and stubborn bongas he beats his stick on the floor of the house, beats the walls, and flails it in the air so that the Mundas accept him as equivalent to bhagats, but this does not happen. In Munda society, the position of Marang-devra to be in between the Bhagat and the Hata devra still continues.

Hata Devra: The Hata Devra is Munda by race and uses Mundari language. Amongst all the devras, he is the closest to Munda religion because he does not worship any non-Munda god. He follows all the rules which are traditionally sanctioned by Munda religion. He directly prays to Singbonga. He does not call any god to come upon him. His rules are very simple. The procedure he adopts for worship is called "doreynam."[44]

The Hata devra takes a shovel. Then he takes a stone pestle (used for grinding spices) washes it well with water, kisses it and thereafter puts it on the shovel. The rice extracted from unboiled paddy brought by the ailing person or his man is kept by the Hata devra and he throws it on the pestle. He prays to Singbonga –

"O Singbonga ! sitting on a high throne, O divine king !! you rise like white milk and remain still like curd.[45] Let these rice grains[46] obtain your grace so that they can move the pestle and tell as to who (which bonga) has given these ailments to your child."

After praying to Singbonga, the Hata Devra throws some rice on the pestle, and catching hold of the shovel from both sides with the help of his thumb and finger, he raises it and addressing the pestle he asks- "Is it Buru bonga who has given this ailment ?"

Since the Hata Devra has prayed to Singbonga and has pleaded with Him that the rice grains may obtain His grace so that when the rice grains fall on the pestle then, upon taking the name of the culprit bonga, the pestle may move forward and backward to show its approval, he starts taking the names of all the bongas one by one and keeps on throwing the rice on the pestle. On taking the name of Buru Bonga, there was no movement by the pestle. Which meant that the shovel working under the influence of Singbonga rejected the name of Buru bonga. Again the Hata Devra throws rice on the pestle and picks up the shovel from both sides with the help of thumb and finger. This time he takes the name of another bonga and watches the shovel for any kind of movement. If the pestle does not move forward or backward, then he leaves that bonga and goes ahead. In this way, the Hata devra keeps on putting rice on the pestle and asks about each bonga by turn. When the pestle moves at the name of a bonga, meaning thereby that when the power of Singbonga present in the rice turns the pestle, then the bonga is identified that it is he who has sent the malady to the ailing person.

After obtaining knowledge regarding the bonga, the Hata Devra tries to find out about the desired sacrifice to appease the bonga. The same procedure is followed in this matter also. He takes the names of animals for sacrifice, and throwing rice on the pestle, he lifts the shovel from both sides with finger and thumb. Through this procedure the Hata devra finds out about the desired animal sacrifice for the bonga sent by the witch.

But in spite of all these actions, the Hata Devra is unable to instil confidence among the Mundas regarding his capabilities! There is a general belief in Munda society that the powers of "Hata devra" and "witch" are about the same or the devra's power is more by a hair breadth.[47] In this situation the maximum that he can do is to find out who the witch is but cannot nullify the influence of the black magic of the witch. At times the conclusions of the Hata Devra are challenged by some influential Munda who says that he has not acquired any "power" or ability from any god hence the identification of the witch done by him may not be correct. The Hata devra is unable to justify his conclusions even though he may stress upon or state with full confidence about them.

Actually, the Hata devra is connected to small villages and he is a poor person who often goes upon call to the homes of the Mundas and as per their individual requirement fulfils the action of proffering sacrifice. In exchange he receives some money and the meat offered. The Munda knows that the Hata devra earns his livelihood due to his kindness; hence he has very little faith in the devra's power. This is the reason why, in the hierarchy of devras, the Hata devra, who is connected to common rural Mundas, finds a lower place.

In this manner, to nullify the influence of sorcery and witches belonging to the anti-religious system, the parallel religious system of sokha, Bhagat and Devra has developed. The influence of Hinduism in this parallel system is clearly reflected. Deriving their powers from Mahadev, the sokha and Bhagat have been successful in nullifying the influence of sorcery of the witches and bongas- this success is not matched by the devras who are based on Munda religion. In Munda folk tales, Singbonga is sometimes described as Mahadev and Parvati as His wife.

Mahadev and Parvati : In Black Magic and Parallel Religious Institution

The names of Mahadev and Parvati are used in some way or the other in Munda religion and the institution of black magic. The name of Parvati is specially mentioned as the wife of Singbonga in various folk-tales; she is shown to be equal to Nage Aera, and in the story of black magic she is named as the witch wife of Singbonga who instigated Him to send Rain of Fire.

As per the religious stories of the Mundas, the human beings of this world went on becoming conceited and greedy, and due to them sinful acts increased on this earth. As a result, Singbonga wanted to annihilate them, and to create new human beings and settle them. In such circumstances, the following points are to be noted : (a) Singbonga's wife had suggested small amount of Rain of fire, but Singbonga sent much more Rain of Fire due to which mankind was annihilated. In the religious story, the wife's name is Parvati.

In Munda religious stories, Singbonga's wife has been shown to be kind and welfare oriented.

(b) In the religious story of Rain of Fire, there is mention of one goddess called Nage Aera. This goddess had saved a man-woman duo from the devastation of the Rain of Fire due to which procreation and increase of human kind took place.

Since Nage Aera played the role of a mother, protected the "duo" and brought them up, hence her character is important, kind, and she comes forth as protector of the race.

She has been called "Missi Singbonga" (sister of Singbonga) in the religious stories. In the folk tales, after accepting Singbonga as self-originated, talk about wife and sister seems incongruent. But if there is no female form, then who is the one who protected the duo and reared them up like a mother ? As an alternative, Nage Aera has been accepted as a goddess and over a span of time, when discussion regarding Parvati gained currency in Munda society then in various places Nage Aera came to be confused as Parvati.

In black magic: In the world of black magic too, Parvati has received recognition. But the recognition is as per perception:

- Out of the two wives of Singbonga, Parvati is the senior one.
- Parvati is an expert witch in the knowledge of sorcery.
- Being displeased, Parvati had made the son of the junior wife ill with disease (the witch Parvati had no son). Singbonga drove her out of the house.
- The exiled Parvati taught the skill of sorcery to six sisters and in this way in the tradition of sorcery, at first the seven sisters of the mountain came into existence. Through deceit they ate the flesh of Dantari and thereby attained "perfection" in their learning.
- Amongst witches, Parvati is the first witch and being the first wife of Singbonga, she is therefore connected to the whole Creation.
- In the night of Sohrai, the presence of Mahadev is essential for the function of initiation of witches and the starting of magic. He is the

highest preceptor, and is present in the function in the form of a cheetah. The presence of Parvati and Mahadev is notable.

In the parallel institution: The witch, who, as Parvati, is connected to Singbonga, and having partaken of the flesh of Dantari, had made her power of black magic more deadly, is devising ways to annihilate the race. Since the primordial witch is Parvati and Parvati's husband is Singbonga, therefore in the cycle of time Singbonga became Mahadev. Singbonga, that is Mahadev, Almighty, who can put a leash on the witches or can nullify their deadly efforts. Resultantly, a tradition of such devotees appeared who would worship Mahadev, attain perfection from Him and after identifying witches and bongas would tell about the remedies to get rid of them. Among them, the chief are sokha, Bhagat, Marang Devra, etc.

- The sokha and Bhagat, who are the devotees of Mahadev, are supposed to be more powerful and believable in Munda society than those who pray to Singbonga and try to defeat the witches and bongas through His grace. The Munda panchayat (assembly) treats the declaration of witches by sokha and Bhagat as the final decision and passes judgement accordingly.
- It is clear that in the world of black magic, the devotees of Mahadev are said to be superior and powerful than the devotees of Singbonga because Mahadev is venerated by Parvati.

The pahan is the true server and priest of Munda religion and Munda race. He is directly connected to the race and religion. Some pahans before proffering "sacrifice" take the names of Mahadev and Parvati in their hymns.[48] Obviously these two names have been handed over to the pahans through the devras because the devras are supposed to be more skilled in proffering sacrifice and in the knowledge of nullifying the deadly barbs of black magic. Their religious procedure is different from that of the pahans. Since Parvati and Mahadev hold sway over the world of sorcery, therefore the devras worship them and invoke Mahadev for the benefit of patients. The main aim is to make the patient disease-free, and to nullify the magic of the witches. Whichever god assists in this work, to whatever religion he might belong, makes no difference. In this manner, "Mahadev" reached the pahans. The scholars working in the field of Munda religion have come to the conclusion that due to inter-mingling of Hindu and Munda religions, the Mundas have accepted the mightiest of Hindu gods Shiv as "Mahadev Bonga" and Parvati as "Chandi Bonga".[49] S. C. Roy has spoken about the Hinduised Mundas.

Actually he means the Mundas living in the area of Bundu-Tamar where worship of "Mahadev" is prevalent but they do not follow Hindu religion, they are pure Mundas and give importance to Singbonga. Animal sacrifice is not offered by Hindus to "Shiv" because He is Pashupati, God of animals. Whereas the Mundas offer animal sacrifice to "Mahadev".[50] The Pahan is a pure Sarna Munda. He, too, accepts the authority of Mahadev. But he has his own interpretation of Mahadev. This interpretation is different from that of Mahadev of Hindus as also from that of the Munda world of sorcery. Definitely, the Mahadev of Hindus is a lower category of god in the interpretation defined by Pahans.[51]

As proved by Munda religious philosophy, certain results may be seen in activities which are damaging but the person due to whom such damage is done, he is not aware of the truth and even though he may be innocent, as per Munda religion, he is said to be culpable. At times, some people deliberately try to damage and for this they take recourse to incantatious. We may term this activity to be coming from the anti-religious system, but all these bongas, hags, witches, "Mua masanko," etc. who are perpetrators in the anti-religious system, do not get any place in religion. Apart from the influence of black magic in Munda society, other anti-religious factors are "the evil eye," ill-omens crossing one's path or to coming in front when one is going out for an auspicious work, etc. Blind in one eye, effeminate or even though aged no beard or moustache has cropped up- such persons become the reason for trouble or spoiling one's work. As per scientific opinion of some educated modern-day Mundas, these are all superstitious activities, but Munda religious philosophy finds these activities based on their beliefs to be true and proven.

Other Activities Based on Superstitions: Hambul roa

In Munda religious philosophy, man's "roa" (soul) has been given full importance in trying to understand man. There are two conditions of man's life-one visible and the other of ethereal or invisible world. The human body and whatever is connected to his visible life, they all perish with his death. Man's "soul" is man "himself" which remains even after death. The only difference is that he becomes an inhabitant of the invisible world. It does not mean that while in the invisible world the soul sleeps- the human soul remains fully active. Compared to Christian, Islam, and Hindu religions, the speciality of Munda religion is that it believes in the human soul being fully active. Not only that, the Mundas believe that during dreams, the soul moves out of the body and travels to far off places and after having seen many sights, it returns and re-enters the human body. This is the reason why the Munda does not awaken a sleeping person in haste because it is possible that, the person might be dreaming meaning thereby that his soul might have come out of his body and is roaming. If woken up in haste, it is possible that the person's sleep ends and in this condition his soul might not be able to re-enter his body. Resultantly sudden death of the man might occur, because with the soul being out of the body, the body and life respectively wane away.

The soul's ability to act is expressed in the visible world. It not only can influence the fate of the person, but can also influence the surrounding environment in its own way. The soul is not the slave of anybody's desires.

The soul has some merits or "attributes," and according to them it is active. On the basis of these merits, two forms of the soul are found- (1) heavy soul and (2) light soul. The heavy soul is called "Hambul Roa" in Munda religion.

Whosoever's soul is heavy, meaning thereby that whoever has "Hambul roa," his signs will be indicated through various incidents and actions. When a "Hambul roa" touches an article, it becomes heavy or its speed lessens. Since the "hambul roa" exists in the body of a human being, therefore the touch of the "hambul roa" on any article can only be possible through the medium of that person. When the soul of a person with "hambul roa" falls on anyone or when he leaps over a log of wood lying on the ground, the weight of the log increases and it becomes difficult to remove it. If the shadow of such a person falls on a crawling snake, then the body of the snake becomes heavy so it cannot protect itself by crawling. In this way, during the time of planting of paddy, if the person having "hambul roa" begins the planting, meaning that he plants the first seed, then the development of the paddy plant becomes slow, and the harvest decreases. The person having "hambul roa" gradually acquiries the bad name of being "inauspicious" in society. Often when any person comes out of his home for doing some auspicious work or work related to business, and at that time the sight of a person with "hambul roa" falls on him, then the successful accomplishment of that work becomes doubtful, therefore he goes back home. Again, some time later, when the person with "hambul roa" has gone, then he goes out of his home for doing his job. Persons with one eye, effeminate persons or aged persons who have never experienced beard or moustache on their face, are counted amongst persons with "hambul roa." In Munda life people believe that if such a man's sight falls on a person directly, then that person faces failure or trouble. In Sarna religion, this sight is called "lail doge."[52]

The question arises that what is the fault of such men when they never think of harming or visiting troubles upon others, nor do they have intentions and neither they have any knowledge about it; but Sarna religious philosophy does not free such people from blame, although Sarna religion believes that the soul being heavy or "light" is the gift of God. Human beings have no hand in it. The "roa" (soul) cannot be influenced through worship, profferings or invoking of divine powers. Which means that the heaviness of a soul or lightness of a soul is inborn, it is its attribute, it is the law of the Creator and this law does not brook any interference by human or divine powers. Hence, when the Creator has Himself laid down the rule regarding heavy or light "roa" then why is the person held guilty if due to his influence ominous things happen?

As per the belief in Sarna religious-philosophy, there is a strong answer to this question. According to Sarna religion, the soul of the human being cannot come out of the body of that person to bring troubles to other persons because a living person's "roa," is his soul, his self (not his conscience), it is the "self" of his innermost part. The person influenced by the "roa" is touched by the "roa," is his soul, his self (not his conscience), it is the "self" of his innermost part. The person influenced by the "roa" is touched by the "roa," is felt by the "roa." When a living, alert, moving person's soul lives in his innermost part as "self" then how can its touch reach outside articles-the Sarna pahan defines this touch in reply-(a) the shadow of the person or (b) through the sight of the person the "hambul roa" connects itself to some article. In this way, the innate sight incorporated in the "hambul roa" becomes the medium which falls on the article and influences it.

The Sight of the Evil Eye

In Munda life, "the sight of the evil eye" is a very common happening in every household. There will not be any house in which any child or adult has not suffered due to the evil eye. The sight of the evil eye may fall in various circumstances. In this action two elements are at work. One is the sight and the other is the article which is the target of the sight. The sight of the evil eye is of three kinds:

(1) Lail doge: When the person is completely unaware, and his sight falls on a person going out from home on some business or some auspicious work. Since the person has gained notoriety as being ill-omened, hence to nullify his effect, the other person returns home for some time, and when that ominous person has moved on, he resumes his journey. Such a sight does not affect any non-living thing or tree and animal, but affects another human being. This sight is the awe-inspiring performance of the "hambul roa."

(2) Nazar (sight of the evil eye): The fundamental difference between "lail doge" and "Nazar" is that in "lail doge" the person concerned is unaware,[53] whereas in "nazar" it is essential that jealousy is combined with the sight. There is no meaning to "nazar" if there is no jealousy. The person with the evil eye is aware of his jealousy and desires to destroy his target, but for this he does not put in any effort, nor does he take the help of spells and incantations. This tendency is found more in Munda females than in Munda males.

(3) Nazari baan (dart of the evil eye): When, coupled with jealousy, the help of spells and incantations are taken to harm the target, then this kind of nazar is activated through a special action. The person, who shoots the dart of his evil eye against any person or domesticated animal, looks at him askance while reading the incantation. After invoking the incantation he blows it toward the direction of wherever his target lives. With such blowing the incantation moves like a dart, reaches its target and affects him.[54] The evil eye dart, after it has been blown, comes into an existence of its own and never fails. Whoever is hit by the dart, the influence of the incantation reveals itself in him gradually.

If the target or the person against whom the dart has been sent is aware about the nature of the dart thrower and knows about his connections, and he knows the incantation to nullify the dart, then he becomes alert after having seen the poses of the dart thrower. As soon as the dart comes near him, he ties up the dart of the evil eye through the opposite incantation. This is called "baan dunu." Nullifying the dart sent through incantation with the help of opposite incantation is called tying up the dart which is done through "baan dunu." If this person, against whom the dart of the evil eye has been sent, knows the incantation called "paitchoro," then he sends back that dart with the same speed to the dart thrower.

In this way, according to Sarna religion, "lail doge," "nazar" and "nazari baan"- in the background of these three actions, the soul of the person who shoots the evil eye dart, is at work. In the last two, that is, giving the evil eye and throwing the dart of the evil eye, the person's jealousy is clearly strong, and therefore he thinks that in the evil eye destructive forces come whereas this force remains concealed in the soul which is his innermost self. Since jealousy is the result of greed and is the device to protect pride, both have been held to be the reason of sin in Sarna religion and therefore subject to punishment. The Asur Avdaan is a clear example of how Singbonga destroyed the arrogant and greedy Asurs. Hence, in Sarna religion, greed and pride are not forgivable under any circumstances. Jealousy is the fruit of both, the result of both, hence Sarna religion treats jealousy to be anti-religious, and activities arising out of jealousy to be also anti-religious. Thus, to turn the evil eye or send darts of the evil eye, both activities are anti-religious, although witches and bongas have not been given any place in them. That is why these activities are not kept in the deadly category of sorcery. Apart from this, these activities normally can be seen, more or less, in every village, and in various villages free devices to nullify their effects have been invented.

The person coming within the definition of "lail doge"- although he may be unaware of jealousy, but the ill-effect of his sight falls on the person in front of him and in order to nullify that effect, the person re-enters his house and comes out only when the ominous person has left-Sarna religion does not accept the ominous person being innocent. According to the religious philosophy of Sarna, such a person is also guilty. The whole procedure is analysed by religion thus :

At first the vices of greed and pride had been present in human beings, and out of them jealousy had already been born. It is possible that man's jealousy may not have been targeted against any particular person and had become generalised. The jealousy had become generalised in the sense that it was not for a particular person but for everybody. Such a general kind of jealousy does not have a sharp edge whereas jealousy against a particular person has more sharpness and emotion. Generalised jealousy is kept hidden by the person's nature and which cannot be seen by others through normal eyes. This hidden jealousy settles in the soul. As a result, such a person whom we think to be without jealousy, if he sees another person or comes in front of somebody, then for damaging him or being ominous the person's soul works through his sight and touches the person who has just come out of his home. And in this manner the touched person is affected.

According to the analysis of Sarna religion, the person who is ignorant of overt jealousy is said to be guilty of any ill-effects or damage. Due to him the other brothers of the Munda race have to face damage and the development of the race is obstructed, hence he is a sinner, he is guilty, yet his actions do not come within the anti-religious system.

Aadaat : The Evil Eye of Praise

In Munda life, another system pertaining to the evil eye is to be seen. In this system, the emotion of jealousy is not expressed behind the evil eye. When any woman or man expressing pleasure upon seeing the child of another person says that "O, see how healthy and good looking the child is, how well he jumps up and down, and the sounds of joy he makes. Ah! You have given birth to such a nice baby," etc. such kind of praise is normally expected from close relatives and well-wishers. But the result is that the child falls ill. If a young man is said to be not only good-looking and strong but along with praise of his health he is stated to be very good for purpose of marriage, then it is seen that his marriage does not take place early, and the Mundas say that the evil eye is upon him. Similarly, aborting of a child by a pregnant woman, or the count of grains being very little although the crop has been good, are said to be the ill effects of the evil eye.

The "hambul" does not have any special role to play in the evil eye pertaining to praise, although the "hambulroa" has an effective role to play in the other three kinds of evil eye. Actually the evil effects due to evil eye arising out of praise has been defined in two ways by Sarna religion:

(a) Sarna religion believes that a person's soul comes out of his body when he is asleep and roams around, and whatever it sees, hears and experiences, are dreams of the sleeping person. It is believed that whatever is seen in dreams, just the opposite happens in the visible world. When a person dreams about the death of a sick person, upon awakening he comes to know that he is recovering from the ailment. In this way, dreams are illusions whereas reality is just the opposite. In "Asur Avdaan," Singbonga had impersonated as "Khasra balak" (The boy with the itch or eczema). According to Munda religion, it is a normal procedure that whatever happens in the invisible world (dreams or invisible place), in the visible or real world, things are seen to be just the opposite. Hence whatever kind of praise is offered, within that praise both the heavy and light souls play the same role as they do in a dream, and prima facie, the article which deserves praise because of its goodness, over a period of years the result becomes just the opposite.

(b) According to another analysis, there is a feeling of jealousy behind praise. The laudator may be a kinsman and he may be wishing well from his heart regarding the child, the pregnant woman, the crop, etc., but whosoever he praises, definitely in those circumstances, the desire or greed to obtain the same keeps on working in his inner-most mind. If child, crop or pregnant woman would be his, too, yet even after having everything, his desires will remain unfulfilled and he will say that after so much of toil only this much crop has come up. Meaning thereby that he will believe his own crop to be less, despite the good health and beauty of his child he will remain unsatisfied, and will remain anxious about his wife's health. Whatever is in one's possession, despite having everything, the person is not satisfied with it. Hence, that person praises in whose inner-most mind there is a shortage of that article combined with greed, and an unsatisfied desire to get that same article. As a result, the soul of the man by touching the baby through the sight of the man passes on the evil eye and thereby makes the baby ill.

Hence, the evil eye works behind praise. When a person praises his own article or the qualities of his baby, his ego is working behind it. My child is so healthy and good-looking. Compared to my crop there is no other crop in the village, my young son is the strongest in the nearby surroundings, etc. Munda religion says that man's self-praise is about the same as that of the Asurs. Actually whatever there is, man rejects the grace of Singbonga leading to his punishment just like the Asurs.

When and under what circumstances the evil eye falls, there is no end to it. The evil eye can affect in innumerable circumstances and nobody can guess about it. In order to escape the evil eye, the women of the village settlement devise various means. A parallel system to nullify the effects of the evil eye, along with many procedures is prevalent and used in various villages. In these procedures there are certain ways which are protective in nature. Which means preventive steps are taken to ward off the evil eye. For this, protective procedures like creating effigies in the fields, putting marks on domestic animals, putting black mark on children etc. are adopted. "Soso-tapa" is one such protective method. This is a powerful method which is arranged at home. Mundas believe that with the completion of this method, the house is freed from the ill-effects of all kinds of bongas and black magic or evil eye.

Soso-tapa

There are many devices prevalent in Munda society to escape from the ill effects of the evil eye. For the protection of agriculture, a crooked stick is set up in the field. It is topped by the burnt upper portion of a pot washed with time and hung upside down. Whenever an evil eye is cast upon the crop of that field, prior to that, it falls on the hung pitcher looking like a man and gets blocked there. In this way the evil eye cannot be cast on the crop. Similarly a white, limewashed pot is placed in between the creeper of the bottlegourd which protects it from the evil eye.

After the harvest and "jome nowa" festival, "soso-chhath"[55] must necessarily be celebrated. In this celebration, a soso sapling is planted in the ground. It is split in the middle from the top and its green leaves are fastened on it. It is planted amidst the harvested crop to ward off the evil eye. In order to save themselves from the evil eye, the Mundas use a lot of soso.

Due to many good natural qualities to be found in the soso, the Mundas have a special faith in it that whosoever it protects, it does not allow the evil eye to affect him. Oil is also taken out of it which is used to make marks on clothes, and to strengthen the wheels and axle of the bullockcart. The juice of its bark is poisonous. Nature has given all these qualities to the soso tree which is easily available in the forest. Its black sharp juice makes it immensely useful for nullifying the darts of the evil eye which therefore marks it out as an appropriate symbolic tree in every way.

"Soso-tapa" is the most prevalent religious ceremony among the Mundas for protecting the household, fields and barn from the evil eye. The Mundas often arrange for this ceremony on an individual basis during the time of harvesting of crop. The place for arranging the ceremony is either in the courtyard of the Munda's home or in the barn where the reaped harvest is kept. All the black magic, evil eye and similar ill-effects of nearly the whole year, collectively taken, are targeted for uprooting through this ceremony. The ceremony is also arranged in such a manner that for the coming year the family may be disease-free and there may be prosperity with regard to cattle, agriculture, etc.

The Huring devra, who is a common devra, is believed to be sufficient for conducting soso-tapa ceremony. The programme often begins in the evening and continues till early next morning or at times next after noon.

For conducting "soso-tapa" ceremony, the Huring devra just washes his hands and feet and takes his seat facing the east. The place stands already sanctified by smearing cow-dung on it. For the worship, he at first fills up a square slab with crushed powder of wheat flour, coal dust and red soil of the hearth.

At first the Huring devra draws approximately a one-foot square in which three thick lines forming squares are drawn from inside to outside. The first square is of wheat flour, the middle square is of coal dust, and the outside square is of red soil of the hearth. Actually the meaningfulness of these three squares is connected to the colour and place:-

(a) The lines inside are of white wheat flour. In praises sung of Singbonga it is said that "He is Himself without any blemish and is of bright white colour." Due to being connected with white colour, it is taken for granted that the whole Creation is within the boundary of Singbonga.[56] This means that Singbonga has granted protection to it.

(b) The second boundary is of the black colour of coal dust. The black colour has been inserted to oppose wicked bongas and evil eyes. This means that no sorcery or dart of the evil eye can cross the black colour and come inside.

(c) The outermost square is red in colour having been made of the red soil of the hearth. Since the soil of the hearth has been used, therefore it is clear that this outer square has connection with the home-deities that is the "ading" bongas. In this also the Munda family always expects its protection.

Two diagonals are drawn to divide this square of three colours and three lines. The intersection point of the diagonals is supposed to be the centre of this drawing. Wavy lines are drawn on its four sides denoting the symbol of the sea. In the easternmost side of this inner boundary, two small and slightly below the middle, a cock's legs are drawn. This is not an ordinary cock-it is "agome sim." Meaning thereby the sign of the worshipped cock which will be sacrificed for Singbonga. Slightly south of the eastern direction, "tripund" is made. The way "tripund" mark is made on the forehead, it is nearly the same. Which means, the English letter "U" and in the middle of it another straight line. The form of "U" is drawn parallel to the three lines, nearly touching them, with slight spacing.

In the northern portion of the square, a straight line is drawn to denote agriculture and cultivation. On both sides of it some dashes and dots are made. In the southern portion a sickle is drawn having serrated edge. In the north western portion a dairy farm is drawn with transverse lines having horn-like symbols in between which indicate cows and bullocks. Just below it, in the south, that is in the southwest the granary is made: a circle in which an egg like drawing is made to denote a sack which is coming out. In between the dairy farm and the granary, that means on the western side two cock's feet imprint is drawn to show the movement of cocks on the earthen soil. Nearly at the centre, on the eastern and western sides two figures of "lutkum hadam" and "lutkum burhi" are drawn for which two small circles for the head, straight line for the body, just below the head straight line cutting across denoting hands and below two slanted lines to denote legs. To distinguish "lutkum burhi" two small dashes are drawn just below the two hands to indicate her breasts.

The whole drawing is symbolic of the Creation. The earth, sea, sun, moon etc. in their midst an ordinary Munda household's ambience is shown. The centre-point of this drawing where the diagonals cut each other, there the devra puts rice extracted from unboiled paddy, meant for worshipping rituals and sacrifice. On this rice, the devra puts a fresh egg (the narrow side up) and sets it firmly. Thereafter he takes a thin green branch of the soso tree, which is about a foot long and a centimeter in girth, and splits open the upper portion. In that he inserts a small piece of soso wood in such a fashion that the split part begins to look like the open mouth of a snake. The branch is kept in such a manner that the mouth of the snake falls on the egg. Apart from this, the devra takes five small pieces of the branch of the soso tree, splits them in the middle due to which ten pieces are made. On one side round and on the other side flat (after having been cut). These ten pieces resemble ten snakes. It is taken for granted that all the black magic, the illnesses given by bongas and the disasters which have till date, knowingly or unknowingly, come to the Munda home, are absorbed by these ten snake-like pieces of the split branch of the soso tree.

Now there are two procedures to destroy illnesses. Either the snake-like split pieces of the soso branch which have absorbed the ill-effects of all black magic and evil eye be destroyed, burnt, or they be broken up and thrown outside the village. The Munda does not kill that snake which has bitten somebody. He thinks that the snake takes back its poison, hence by killing it there remains very little chance of neutralising the poison of that person. The "ojha" who exorcises the poison through spells, takes a green grass or a green branch in his hand and starts from the place where the snake had bitten the person. He takes it up and down and along with it chants an incantation to take the poison out. The strength of the ojha's incantation lies in his snake faith. If he will not worship the snake, then his capability to draw out the snake poison will be finished. Hence, the person who worships the snake-how can be kill the snake? If the snake is killed, the effect of its poison is never destroyed. It is only the snake which can draw back its poison. The Mundas give the example of "lur bing." When "lur bing" exhales, then the exhaled poison makes a rainbow in the air. And again when it inhales, then the rainbow enters it along with the inhalation. In this way, the snake takes back its poison.

This is the reason that the small snake-like pieces of the soso branch which have absorbed the ill-effects of black magic and the evil eye, when thrown as dice by the devra, then those pieces which fall on the earth with the rounded side below and the flat side up, that is in a supine manner, then it is believed that freedom has been obtained from the maladies which had been absorbed by them just as a snake becomes supine; and those pieces which fall on the ground with the rounded side up and the flat side down, then it is believed that the absorbed black magic etc. with their ill-effects are still connected to them. The devra throws those pieces like dice on the ground and those pieces which fall supine, that is the flat side up, they are taken out. Those pieces which fell on the ground with the flat side down, they are again thrown as dice on the ground. This activity is done three times. If in the end some pieces remain with the flat side down on the ground then the devra and that household accept that in those pieces the ill-effects of black magic are still present.

Since the ill-effects of black magic or evil eye and their deadly powers are connected to the invisible world, therefore their existence cannot be wiped away. Hence there is no probability of their destruction. They can be returned, and for this, powers contrary to them have to be used. The devra, sokha or ojha do this.

The egg placed on the rice at the centre point has its importance. This is the source of life. The egg can be identified with Singbonga. The snake is trying to take the egg in its mouth. The snake is the symbol of evil, of maladies. In this way, the egg which is the source of life, is in a situation of being swallowed by the snake. This struggle has been going on right from the earliest times.

In "Asur Avdaan," Singbonga as the Khasra Balak (the boy with eczema) had broken the iron marbles of the Asur boys with an egg.[57] In this way, Singbonga had defeated the worst tendencies of the Asurs. Egg is the source of life. There is a possibility of destruction of the Creation if the egg i.e. the source of life is defeated. Hence, to maintain balance in Creation, the toughest iron marbles had to be broken by the egg. The devra is invoking that first phase of the Creation when the movement of water and sky had stopped, so that the good tendencies may defeat the bad tendencies.

The devra takes a bowl made of two or four leaves of "sarjome sal" tree. He fills it with water and offers it to Singbonga. He sings His praises thus- "Netlang Singbonga, Daivi Raja"- and the devra sings the story of how the Creation came into being. In praise of Singbonga, he sings that when the sky was empty, everywhere there was flood, You created creatures which live in water, You created the Earth, You created trees, plants and human beings. Through the songs pertaining to the making of the Creation, the Creator is reminded that "when You had made the Creation, then at that time such kinds of evil had not been there. Again you free this Creation of evils as before. That is why this water is being offered to You."

In Munda religious activities, normally a system has developed that at the onset praises of Singbonga and the making of the Creation be sung through songs. After that "Asur Avdaan" is sung. This is a lengthy song in praise of the life of Singbonga, wherein is described the destruction of the Creation by the Asurs, their pride and greed, and how Singbonga came in disguise and annihilated them. Whenever a scene gets completed in the lengthy saga of "Asur Avdaan," the devra proffers water and rice (extracted from unboiled paddy) to Singbonga and sings hymns like the Creation of Asurs, their deliberate destruction of the Creation and thereafter how the heat of their fire reaches the sky, and the anger of Singbonga, how He sends birds as messengers, His wife's suggestions of defeating the Asurs through the help of "twelve learnings and thirteen deceptions," the coming of Singbonga on this earth, the various sports of the Khasra Balak (the boy with eczema), and ultimately the destruction of Asurs and turning their widows into "bongas".

This story, interspersed with several hymns, goes on for hours. The mystery of singing of the making of Creation and "Asur Avdaan," the significance of both and along with them, in that order, the singing of hymns and praise of Singbonga is clearly spelt out in Munda religious philosophy. The story regarding the making of Creation tells us that in the beginning of Creation, the world was free of all evils namely, black magic, evil-eye darts etc. Again, in "Asur Avdaan" it has been said that when evil increased then You came to the earth and destroyed the evil. In this way, the story of the Creation and "Asur Avdaan" spell out a special aim of focusing on the nature of Singbonga that He destroys all evil and wants to keep the Creation as clean as before.

The first reason to invoke Singbonga in soso-tapa is that the way Singbonga had saved the Creation by destroying the Asurs, in the same way He should rescue the concerned household which has become the target of evil eyes.

In the end, the devra makes a small hole in the egg, and praying to Singbonga says thus- "the whole night I have sat in front of You facing the east and have been praying and have also been offering water and rice to You. I have milk in my mouth just like a new born infant. I am ignorant and innocent. I pray to you. Please ignore my shortcomings."

With the aim to offer sacrifice, he drops some of the white of the egg on the ground. The rest of the egg is cooked and distributed amongst everybody as food partaken by God (blessed food). The shell of the egg is hung on the soso branch near the ceremonial rice. With the help of this sacrifice, victory is gained over the power of the snake. The egg takes away the power of the snake to bite again.

The clear intention of soso-tapa is to find out how the damage done by black magic and evil eye can be compensated although their ability to do further harm has been stopped. In "Asur Avdaan," the Khasra Balak had again filled up the granary of the "lutkums" after the rats and other animals had destroyed it. In the same way the devra prays that whatever damage has been done by the sorcery and evil eyes, that should be compensated.

Whatever has been damaged cannot be seen. It is an incident which has happened at the instance of the invisible world. Nobody knows from where and how many darts of the evil eye and black magic have been shot. This cannot be seen by human eyes. When it comes to fruition, then only man can experience it. Therefore, it is only Singbonga's power which can nullify these evil invisible powers.

The devra assesses the success of his prayer in front of those who have arranged the ceremony. He throws the ten small branches of the split soso, like dice. Those that fall with the split side up, he removes them. Those that fall with the split side down, he again throws them as dice. This action is done thrice. Despite this, if some pieces fall with the flat side down, then that means that still some evil-effects of black magic or evil eye are prevailing in the house and the soso-tapa ceremony has not been fully successful. The devra accepts that all the invisible deadly incantations or magic cannot be removed completely and neither can they be done away with for all times to come. The "snake" cannot be killed, but one can escape from its bite and its effect. Hence, the physical articles symbolizing black magic and evil eye can be thrown afar and a mental condition may be made to escape them.

The devra erases the square completely with his hand. He collects the remaining branches of the soso, takes the eggshell in his hand, and taking some persons along with him, he goes out of the house. He goes towards the east and goes out of the village where he throws the collected items[58] and says that "now I bid you goodbye with these soso branches, this rotten egg, and with wine and rice beer. The people of your race do not live here. Now you go somewhere else and arrange for your boarding and lodging. There they will surely give you good things." After saying this, the devra bids goodbye to the symbols of black magic and evil eye at the end of the village boundary. Thereafter he returns with his companions to the house.

When he returns to the house, he finds that the door of the house has been closed from inside. It is imagined that the companions of the devra are relatives missing for a long time who have returned with wealth and cattle. After some question-answers, the same way as has been earlier described in other religious rituals, the door is opened, and they enter the house making noise as if they are letting in lots of cows-bullocks and goats inside the house.

The bigger branch of the soso made in the form of a snake is thrown towards the east. We have seen that the devra had worshipped facing the east. The figures of sun and moon in the square had been made in the eastern direction. This means that the invisible world is toward the east. The evils which had entered the house due to black magic are absorbed in the branches of the soso. There are many houses which have soso branches thrown to their east. All the calamities, magic-evil spells, darts of the evil eye, evil eye, etc. come with powers from the invisible world, hence they have to go in that direction. They have no connection with the Munda race and they have no right to stay amidst the Munda people. These are "evils" which devise means to destroy the Munda race. Singbonga is the Creator of the Munda race and its Protector. Through the soso-tapa ceremony, Singbonga is involved and these "evils" are banished from the house and the village.

Parv (festivals)

The various festivals observed by the Munda tribe reflect clearly their religious beliefs and social life. Most of the Munda festivals are related to the forest and agriculture. Praying to God for good agriculture and after harvesting the display of gratefulness by arranging festivals in the backdrop of bountiful nature-this goes on nearly the whole year through. The Munda race, which enjoys singing and dancing in the charming environment of nature, is used to living a joyful life which is a part of their character. Throughout the year, the Munda society observes festivals in a never ending cycle. Some of the main festivals are:

(a) Mage, (b) Fagu, (c) Ba or Sarhul, (d) Hone ba, (e) Batauli, (f) Karma, (g) Dasai, (h) Kolome Singbonga, (i) Jomenawa, (j) Sohrai and (k) Soso-bonga.

Mage: Mage festival is very important for Mundas both from religious and economic point of view. This festival is celebrated in the full moon of Paush month[59] (in the Hasda area it is observed in December and in the Naguri area it is observed in January). The Mundas call Paush month by the name of Mage, and Magh month by the name of "Gola mage." By this time harvesting would have been done, and the Munda farmer's house is full of wealth and grains. The Munda believes that this prosperity is due to his dead ancestors; therefore he expresses gratitude by worshipping them.

Actually, Mage festival is the festival related to the worship of "oda Bongako." The head of the household keeps fast on the first day of the worship of the "oda bongako" in the "ading," and on the second day after bathing and purefying himself, he offers rice beer and unleavened rice bread and prays that "your grace may please be upon us, and the children and the elders everybody may remain healthy and happy. When we go to the forest to cut wood, please protect us from cheetahs, wild animals and poisonous thorns. May we, with your grace, get a good harvest so that we ourselves can eat and drink well, can entertain guests and are able to pay land rent."

The Mundas believe that the home-deities "oda bongas," who move around in the invisible world, create positive circumstances through their grace due to which agriculture does not fail and crops are good. Resultantly, during Mage festival, the "oda bongas" are prayed to and worshipped in the "ading" by the Mundas to express their gratitude towards them.

In some places, Mage festival is observed for three days. The young men of the village make a round of the village boundary. During sunset, they go towards the east, dancing to the beats of the mandar (a drum slung from the shoulders) and singing "howwa" (obscene songs), and from there they turn left and circle the whole village. On the last i.e. the third day, the pahan of the village sends a small group of young men to the forest to bring "opononome-opaad", that is, a sapling of sarjome which has sprung up on its own. This sapling is about the height of a man or maybe slightly higher. The men uproot it and bring it. They plant the "opaad" sarjome in the eastern part of the house and that completes a square.

On the third day, the pahan calls for some Mage flowers and "gara-jono" wild grass. He takes out some rice beer through sieving. In this way, he keeps rice beer, cooked rice-bread and other articles meant for fuel for the sacrifice. The pahan offers a white cock to Singbonga, and as per requirement he offers cocks to other regional bongas. The pahan prays to them. The wife of the pahan has with her own hands prepared food for the deities. She offers the food to the "oda bongas" in the "ading" in order to please and propitiate them.

The Re-appointment of Dhangars

Nearly every prosperous head of the household carries out the worship of the "oda-bongas" in the "ading" with great fanfare. After the worship is done, all the members of the household sit and eat a meal with great relish along with their servants and staff. The meal consists specially of bread made out of rice flour. After the meal is over, the annual calculation of the wages of the "dhangars" (servants and staff) is done and paid to them in full. And they go and call upon their relatives or in-laws.

After about a fortnight of festivities, agricultural work starts again, and the "dhangars" are appointed afresh. Dhangars can be new or old (meaning that they had worked for the household before), but for all of them a fresh agreement regarding work and wages for the coming year is negotiated. A simple procedure is followed to negotiate the agreement. The dhangar who is desirous of work stands in front of the master or mistress of the household in a very humble manner. The master takes a small bowl with some oil in it, and drops some of the oil on the ground. After that, he pours some of it on the dhangar's head and keeps the bowl on the ground.

The dhangar takes the oil from the bowl placed on the ground and rubs it on his body. In that bowl some coins have been kept from before. The dhangar either picks those up, or else two bowls of paddy or two bamboo combs kept near the oil filled bowl-he picks them up. This means that the dhangar has accepted the terms and conditions of the master and now till the next Mage festival, for the whole year he will serve the master of that household.

During Mage festival, the custom of bidding goodbye to the servants and staff with due dignity, and thereafter to appoint them afresh is prevalent even among masters of prosperous households. It appears that the popularity of Mage festival has increased not only due to religious importance, more so due to financial prosperity. As it is, Mage festival is a festival to celebrate prosperity with happiness. In this festival, on one hand gratitude is expressed towards the benefits given by the household deities, and on the other hand, the beautiful atmosphere of the winter season is made lively by the songs of "mage and jarga."

Fagu

The festival "fagu" celebrated by the Mundas is believed to be equivalent to the festival of "Holi" or "Fagua" celebrated by the Hindus. This festival is celebrated in the month of Falgun (March-April). On the day prior to the full-moon of Falgun[61], in the evening, the youths of the Munda village, plant a sapling of "jhera daru" (rehr: castor) on the beginning of a road which goes towards a stream or river. In this way the first day is called "jhara fagu." The next day, the Mundas cut down the "idel tree"[62] (silk tree). Hence, the second day is called "marang fagu" (like a big Holi).

In Munda society, "fagu festival" is celebrated as a "hunting festival." From the afternoon, the youths gather grass and weeds or firewood from various homes[63] and load all of them on the castor sapling. They keep with themselves hunting choppers and singing "japi" (hunting songs) they move around.

The castor sapling along with its load of grass, weeds and firewood is set ablaze. Very soon the flames can be seen. The assembled people sing, dance and make merry. After the fire dies down, the assembled youth attack the castor sapling with their choppers as if that sapling was their hunted prey. They chop it to pieces.

The next day, this group of youths, along with their choppers, beating their "mandars" (drum suspended from the shoulders) and singing "japi (hunting songs) enter the forest in their hunting drive. There they cut a red silk cotton tree, and taking the tree, they ceremonially return to the village, singing "japi" and dancing to the beats of the "mandar." They move towards the village singing thus:

Japi[64]

"O god, ruling over madkam Sarna,
Come along with us in pursuit of the hunted,
Papra Chandi, god of the grove, increasing the honour of the hunting party,
He moves along with the village hunters.
For us, Madkam god is the best,
In the sport of hunting, may his arrows fly over and fall on the hunted animals.
Papra Chandi sends us the gift of rain
Due to which our paddy crops are good,
And see the madkam jayar, he kills the agile rabbit,
And takes away his trophy with enthusiasm,
And there in the forest, Papra Chandi shoots an arrow at a peacock
And enjoys the sport of hunting."

Their village friends keep ready to welcome them. From here they take them to that place where the previous day the castor sapling had been burnt down. There the red silk cotton tree is planted and on it are heaped grass, dry leaves and fuel. The villagers assemble on all sides. The pahan of the village comes and offers worship. He worships all the bongas and the regional gods who live in the forest, mountains, streams, plains and the groves, namely

Jayar burhiya, Papra Chandi, Burubonga, Ikir bonga, Marang buru bonga, Desauli bonga, Nage aera, Bindi aera, etc. – he worships and invokes them all, invites them. The pahan offers three unleavened bread made out of rice flour, wine made out of one pot of rice, and one black cock in a collective manner so that the Mundas may have successful hunting in appropriate quantity and without any impediments.

The combustibles loaded on the planted red silk cotton tree are thereafter set on fire. The flames gradually rise high up in the sky. Then the pahan throws the black cock in the midst of the flames. One Munda youth goes forward, takes some straw in his mouth in such a manner that one end sticks far out of his mouth. He ignites this end with the help of the flames. Thereafter, carrying the ignited straw in his mouth, he circumambulates the pahan. During this circumambulation, he and his associates make cawing sounds of crows. Thereafter he throws that burning straw back into the flames.

The pahan lifts the hunting chopper and makes a deep cut on the burning red silk cotton tree. The assembled youth take their hunting choppers and chop up the red silk cotton tree as if their prey is in front of them. They make cuts on the knots from the root upwards at short lengths but let the upper part remain as it was. The pieces cut from near the knots have small branches cracked on both ends. They look like chopped off heads of deer with their antlers on top.[85]

The Munda youths throw these cut pieces toward the neighbouring village, taking the name of the village, and say. "You, too, get the happiness of hunting, and play the sport of hunting the same way we have hunted the deer." The next morning the pahan throws a burnt piece of wood in that direction where the stream flows. That day the stream is supposed to be polluted and nobody uses it.

After the victory merriment of a successful hunt, the assembled people visit the pahan's house singing and dancing, where they are fully welcomed with rice beer. Here there is a good party. After some time, celebrating their happiness in the pahan's house, the householders return to their own homes, and offer unleavened bread made of rice flour, and rice beer to the house-deities in the "ading." The festival of Fagu is concluded here.

The religious rituals and rules of Fagu festival are fully supported by Munda religious stories and Asur Avdaan. The grass-straw and combustibles collected from each home when they are lit, the heat of their flames troubles the pahan in the same way that the furnace flames of the Asurs had angered the Supreme Singbonga. He had sent His messenger "kowwa bhandari" (the crow) to explain matters to the Asurs. Since the crow did not have hands, it had taken Singbonga's message in its beak to the Asurs. The Munda youth by taking the burning straw in his mouth and circumambulating the pahan has given the message to the pahan to destroy the evils which are entwined on the red silk cotton tree. And the pahan picked up the hunting axe and firstly attacked the stem of that tree. The hunting of deer is approved by Munda religion.

All these religious rituals, in which a glimpse can be had of the world during the time of Singbonga, are connected to a sacrosanct procedure. Nowhere should there be anything impure. It is forbidden to take straw from a pregnant woman's house because in that house a child is being reared who has not been included in the Munda race through the sixth day ceremony. Similarly, the pahan throws the burnt piece of wood toward the village stream indicating thereby that all the evils will go away along with that burntpiece of wood into the stream and drown. That is why that day nobody touches the water of the stream because that day its water remains impure.

Although Fagu festival has been adopted by the Munda society on the basis of the Hindu festival of "Fagua," yet all the activities and rituals that are followed are as per Munda religion and tradition. The master of the household worships all the bongas and after appeasing them he appeases the "oda bongas" i.e. the home deities, and he prays to all for a good crop and many other benefits. He prays to all the gods that they accompany him on hunts and help him. The meaning of hunt is "benefit."[65] After Fagu festival, for many weeks one can hear the joyful songs and dances of "jaapi." In this season no marriages are held.

Ba or Sarhul

"Ba-naeg" or Sarhul festival is supposed to be an important festival of Munda religion. The forest region of Chhotanagpur is full of sal trees. In Sarhul festival, the Munda race expresses its gratitude to the sal tree because this tree has deeply influenced the religious, economic and social life of the Mundas. It is on the sal tree that the "hatu bongako" resides.

The influence of Hindu religious saga over the "Ba-naeg" festival can also be seen. Behind the joy and happiness of the festival is the reason of the elderly king Dashrath of Ayodhya obtaining four sons.[66] But all the religious rituals of Sarhul are done as per Munda religion, tradition and belief in which the village pahan plays the chief role.

"Ba-naeg" or Sarhul festival is celebrated in the month of Chaitra (the first month of the Hindu calendar, between February-March). At this time the sal trees are laden with blossoms and the forest appears to be emanating happiness. On the fifth day of the bright moon of Chaitra, the sal tree of the holi Sarna place is worshipped with sal flowers. This sal tree is called "jaher Sarna." Many sal blossoms are collected and the village Mundas assemble at the Sarna place for worship. The village pahan who conducts the worship, fasts the previous day. He offers sal flowers to the "jaher Sarna" and taking the names of all bongas of Munda religion, invokes them and proffers sal flowers to them. On this occasion Chandi bonga is especially worshipped and a cock is sacrificed to him. In the Sarna place, food is cooked on new earthen utensils.

After the worship is completed in the Sarna place, the Munda people return home joyfully dancing, beating the "mandar" (drum slung from the shoulders) and "dholak" (big drum) and carrying branches of sal trees laden with fruit. The garland of sal blossom is hung on the doorway of the house, and the house is decorated with sal leaves and flowers. Every Munda ties a garland of sal flowers on his head or sticks the flowers in his hair. On this day all food and liquids are served in plates and cups made of sal leaves, and people even sit on sal leaves. On this day, pulses of "urad" (a kind of cereal called horse bean) are specially cooked in enough quantity, along with sufficient rice and rice beer. Steeped in the ambience of the sal tree (being decorated and surrounded with flowers, branches, leaves etc.), the Mundas spend this day joyfully celebrating it with singing and dancing.

The master of the household, as he does in every festival, this day, too, offers rice beer and cooked food to the "oda bongako" (home deities) during their worship. He remembers his dead ancestors, worships them and prays that "this home, all the members of this home, we are all yours, hence your grace should always be there with us. Please take care of our health, our cattle, our cultivation and farming always." In this way the master of the household prays to his ancestors living in the invisible world for prosperity of his home, cattle and agriculture.

The next day, in the morning, the pahan collects some branches and flowers from the Sarna place and visits each house in the village. He sticks a branch on the door sill or the thatched roof of every house and moves ahead. Every household as per its capacity, offers some money as remuneration to the pahan. In this way, after purifying every home with the worshipped flowers, he returns to his own home. In the evening a woman from every home takes a pot of water and a small quantity of oil and visits the pahan's home. There she washes the pahan's feet, massages oil on them and again washes them. This devotion towards the pahan is actually an expression of faith of the villagers in him. The pahan gifts every woman two pots of rice beer as blessing.

Sarhul is the celebration of the festival of spring. On this occasion, Munda youth (men and women) decked with sal flowers sing "jadur" songs and in this way express gratitude to the forest deity. At this time, the whole atmosphere becomes festive. This festival with various activities is celebrated for three days. For this period all farming is stopped, there is complete holiday and total happiness.

Hone-ba

"Hone-ba" is such a religious activity which is connected to the starting of planting of seeds and for good cultivation. This festival is not able to take the form of a public fair. There is no fixed date for this festival. When the

Mundas of the village plan to plant the seeds on a particular day, the master of the household offers worship to his ancestors in the ading of his home just the previous day. In this context he also worships the other gods. The aim of the worship is to obtain good harvest of rice crop. The gods are requested through prayers for timely rains, protection from disasters and maximum paddy yield. This festival is observed in Baisakh (mid-April to mid-May) or in Jyesth (mid-May to mid-June).

Sometimes when the paddy sprouts, the pahan of the village goes to his field and offers sacrifice called "goli sing" to Singbonga. Returning from the field, the pahan offers sacrifice to all the ancestors of the village. All the dead ancestors are offered food by him on separate plates made of sal leaf so that the harvest may be good.

Batauli

This festival is also connected to agriculture just like "Hone Ba." But all the arrangements are made group-wise in which the role of the pahan is important. Before planting paddy in the fields, in a different place paddy seedlings are raised on tiny ridges. These paddy seedlings are dug up from these tiny ridges and thereafter planted/ transplanted in the fields. Batauli is celebrated just prior to transplantation. Since the work of transplantation in nearly every village is done by all the Mundas together on the same day, therefore its worship is done before transplantation groupwise. Since the village pahan has to shoulder the responsibility of conducting the worship, he keeps a fast right from the morning. Everybody assembles at the Sarna place. The pahan keeps "akshat" (rice extracted from unboiled paddy), "hadiya" (rice beer) and a sacrificial cock beneath "jaher Sarna" (the sacred sal tree of the village). That day, the leaves of the madua and gandhari plants are also used in the worship.

In some places the pahan plants a branch of soso or bhelwa trees brought by the master of a household, or a branch of the tiril tree brought by somebody on the mound of rice. This rice is meant for "akshat" or to be used in the worship. The branch of the bhelwa tree is poisonous hence it indicates that the paddy will not be attacked by insects, and the tiril tree had been able to withstand the extreme heat of the rain of fire. Hence the attribute of the tiril branch would be passed on to the paddy plants so they would not burn away in the sunshine. After planting the branches, the pahan worships Singbonga. Thereafter he worships all the gods in front of the sal/Sarna tree and then be sacrifices the cock and offers it along with the leaves of the madua (a kind of millet). In the Sarna place itself, chicken and rice along with madua and gandhari leaves are cooked. All the Mundas of the village fill themselves with this blessed food and spend the occasion joyfully. With the onset of evening, the Mundas transport the pahan with due respect to his residence. They carry him on their shoulders to his home so that his feet may not touch the ground.

When they reach the pahan's house, the Mundas are again welcomed with rice beer. This festival is symbolic. Due to difference in places, there are certain deviations in the celebration of this festival, but basically it is celebrated to wish for successful cultivation.

Karam

Karam festival is celebrated on the eleventh day of the bright moon in the month of Bhado (August-September). On this day, the master of the household brings two branches broken from a karam tree and at dusk plants them in his courtyard. The ground near these planted branches is smeared with cow dung and made spic and span, clean and pure. Then the master of the household takes "ghee" (clarified butter), milk and an unleavened bread made of rice flour and applies a mark on the branches with them, and worships the branches. During the time of worship, he invites the regional gods also and worships them. At the doorway of the house, dancing, singing, and the sound of "mandar" and "dholak" (big drum) make the whole atmosphere reverberate.

The next day, in the morning, the worshipped branches of the "karam" tree are respectfully taken in a procession and immersed in the nearby pond or stream. The young men and women of the village sing and dance to the beats of the mandar and lead the procession, being desirous of the kindness of karam god. Some people coming behind them carry the karam branches in which the deity has been invoked. This is a grand procession. The immersion scene at the pond or stream is worth seeing. The karam songs sung at a high pitch give a devotional ambience to the whole atmosphere. The innocent children or the elderly, all are desirous of the kindness of the karam deity. It is a general belief among Mundas that whosoever insults the karam deity and the karam tree, even if he be the king, gradually he will become a destitute, and whosoever obtains his blessings, his position will improve within a few days and he will become financially sound.

Most of the pahans believe that Karam festival is not a festival sanctioned by the Munda religion. It is due to copying the Hindus that this festival spread in Munda society and became famous. Their argument is that in this festival, the pahan cannot be seen anywhere. Then, again, this festival is not celebrated by all Mundas. In Munda religion, it is essential to appease the bongas or Singbonga or "oda bongako" for which a cock is sacrificed. But in Karam festival, there is no place for cock sacrifice, but on the contrary, the Karam tree is worshipped with clarified butter or milk. In this way, the Karam festival does not appear to be as per the nature of Munda religion. Trigunayat also says that "Karma" is not a major festival of the Mundas, but something they have learned from others.[67]

Actually, from the point of view of the Sadans, the Mundas have only two festivals which have received fame and the Mundas celebrate them with great fervour- these are Sarhul and Karam festivals. It is definite that in Karam.

the traditional system has been abandoned in which the "pahan," and sacrifice of cock to the bongas have not been provided for in Karam festival, but the Munda society has adopted this festival in its entirety. Among the Mundas, the Karma songs with their melodious tunes and trilling are the most popular and front runners in acceptance. There are many Karma songs which the Munda young men and women sing in the "akharas" (cultural centres) and become charged with emotion. In this festival these "akharas" are tastefully decorated with flowers and leaves and buntings.

The name and fame of Karam festival amongst the Mundas can be gauged from that folktale which the elderly people narrate to the Munda people. In the story of Karma, before the making of the earth as per description in Munda religious tale, the situation has been described when Hadam (Singbonga) created the Earth with the soil brought by the earthworm. The Karam story repeats these facts. This portion of the Karma story in not at all different from the Munda religious story.

In the "Pupa" country created by Singbonga, there were two brothers named Karma and Dharma. The elder brother Karma went abroad to earn money while Dharma the younger brother remained in his country and tilled the land. He was poor. Karma returned a rich man. Karma called Dharma to welcome him, but Dharma did not go. Karma remarked as to what is there in these trees and plants that Dharma remains close to them. He uprooted all the trees and threw them beyond seven mountains and seven seas, and started living comfortably. A few days later, his wealth dwindled away and becoming poor, he along with his wife became a labourer in the house of Dharma. On one hand, for not getting wages, he started destroying the cultivated fields and field-dividers of Dharma, but on the other hand, the more he cut the field dividers, those dividers all the more sprang up and became dividers as before. Karma, became surprised. Then an unknown person came and told him that since he had uprooted the karam tree that was why he was being punished.

Thirsty and hungry, after passing through many tribulations, he remembered Karam god. Karam god told him, "on the eleventh day of the bright moon of Bhado you return home and plant a branch of the karam tree-all your troubles will be over." He planted a branch of the karam tree on the eleventh day of the bright moon of Bhado and worshipped, Karam god. Thereafter prosperity and wealth came to him. From that day the people plant the karam branch on the eleventh day of the bright moon of Bhado.[68]

In this way, by worshipping "karam bonga" and planting the karam branch, Karma again became very prosperous. Hence, whoever will plant a karam branch on the eleventh day of the bright moon of Bhado and will worship "karam bonga" in this manner, will become wealthy and prosperous. Although in Munda religion, Singbonga does not make anybody a special person with regard to riches or religion, because in Munda race nobody is above the race, yet the prevalence of cultivation and the required labour behind it has the target of prosperity. We know that the Munda people often pray to Singbonga, other bongas and the "oda bongako" that their crops may be good and their granaries may be full of paddy. Hence, Karma, worship is not a deviation from the beaten path of Munda religion despite the fact that in this worship there is no requirement at all of the pahan.

Then again, nobody says clearly as to which puran of the Hindu religion contains the story of Karma and Dharma. If this festival had been adopted by the Mundas after having come in close contact with the Hindus, then undoubtedly this festival should have been prevalent among the Hindus but no such festival which has virtually become very famous and influenced, thereby, other societies, can be seen amongst the Hindus. If in the folk tales of the Hindus, the tale of Karma and Dharma does occur, then to connect that story to the Karma festival of the Mundas would be a forcible effort. The question is of the fame of this story that by copying the Hindus, the Mundas adopted it, and in Hindu religion there is no such festival of so much fame. In this way, S. C. Roy[69] and Jagdish Trigunayat[70] or other analysts of Munda religion-their comments that the Mundas have adopted Karam festival from Hindus have no solid, proven basis.

Dasai

The Mundas celebrate Dasai festival in the month of Ashwin or Kartik. It is the imitation of the Hindu festival of Dashahara. This festival is observed by most Mundas, but sacrificing a he-goat in the name of the Goddess Durga is done only by a few rich householders. The worship is not public-it is individual or of the family. In this festival, there is no need of the pahan, but the Munda young men and women sing and dance in groups. The atmosphere is joyful. The master of the household worships the "oda bongako" (home deities) in this festival, and also invokes the other gods and offers food to them.

Kolom Singbonga

Kolom = granary; Singbonga, meaning the worship of the granary. This festival is observed in the month of Agahan (November) when the ripe paddy crop is to be harvested and brought to the granary. This festival is observed by the pahan in which the other Mundas of the village also participate. First of all, the pahan cleans his own granary or barn. For the worship in the barn, some rice, some plants with ripe paddy, some rice straw and grass [71] are kept. The pahan worships the bongas and sacrifices the cocks (brought by the householders) and proffers them along with rice beer. All the assembled Mundas drink rice beer with the pahan and partake of the food offered to the bongas. Till late in the night songs echo to the beats of the "mandar." It is only after the worship in the barn of the pahan, that is after "kolom Singbonga" that the other Mundas put the harvested paddy in their barns and separate the grain from the chaff with the help of bullocks.

To keep the straw and the grass near the akshat rice (rice meant for worship) symbolises that grace of Singbonga to be obtained when as Khasra Balak, Singbonga had multiplied one grain in the straw and grass hut of the Lutkums and thereby filled up their granary. The desire of the pahan and the assembled Mundas of the village is that through the grace of Singbonga their granaries should have so much of rice that their stores are completely full.

Jome – Nava

The meaning of "Jome-nava" is the "eating of new rice." Actually, this is not a religious festival. This is a function which is connected with the security of agriculture and together with it, is the first joyful use of the new rice through which there is a hope for the future that in the days to come, they should also pass with so much of joy and happiness.

The theft of ripened paddy from the field, the fear of tigers and elephants while protecting the paddy, and during harvesting the danger of snake bites, all of these are often to be seen in Munda life. In order to be protected from them, the pahan plants an arrow made of an iron ploughshare in his field when the paddy crop has ripened and it remains to harvest the crop, take it to the barn and separate the grain from the chaff with the help of bullocks.

While planting the arrow in his field, the pahan invokes Singbonga and prays that- "O supreme Singbonga. I have planted an arrow in this field. Whosoever dares to take away this arrow (meaning cutting the paddy and taking away) may be eaten by a tiger. But when we start cutting the paddy, and picking them up start taking them home, then save and protect us from the attacks of the tiger and bites of the snakes."

Again the pahan addresses the regional and village bongas and offers sacrifice of a red cock to them and speaks about appeasing them. The pahan expects from them that they will protect the crops of the Mundas so that the harvested paddy may safely reach the barn and the paddy spikes may be full of rice grains.

By placing the arrow made of iron plough-share, the pahan wants to remind the bongas of those days when they had to face destruction at the hands of Singbonga when they had been smelting the iron. Since these bongas had been the wives of the Asurs, and they had seen with their own eyes the annihilation of the Asurs, and they had received kindness from Singbonga who had turned them into bongas and had given them responsibility that they would work for the welfare of the Creation and the Munda race, hence the pahan expects that they will shoulder the responsibility of safeguarding the crops of the Mundas. The pahan has fulfilled his part of the duty by offering sacrifice of red cock to them.

But if wild animals come and destroy the crop or attack the farmer, then as per belief of the Mundas definitely the bongas have sent them. Sometimes the bonga comes himself and stealing the rice from the paddy, that is taking the "rowa" (soul) of the paddy, he goes away. The result of which is that when the harvest is done in a field full of paddy plants and after that it is taken to the farm where the paddy is repeatedly beaten, then only slight paddy and rice grains, that too sickly, come out. Seeing the net result of the paddy, any Munda very easily understands that the bonga has stolen the "rowa" of the paddy. Undoubtedly, such bad deeds are done by the wicked banita bongas.

During the paddy harvest, the pahan takes out the arrow planted in his field, but before doing so, he again offers thanks giving worship to Singbonga and the other bongas and gives sacrifice.

Some people think [71] that "jome nova" is actually a Hindu custom adopted by Mundas. Amongst Hindus, the new paddy is turned into flattened rice which is at first eaten with curd and jaggery or milk and jaggery. But the Mundas do not do only this. On this day they drink a lot of rice beer and with happiness offer worship to their ancestors in their own "adings," and offer cock-sacrifice to their "oda bongako."

Ind Festival

Ind festival is celebrated only in some villages by the Mundas, especially in those villages where the landlord is the descendant of Nagvanshi king. In this festival, at first two thin logs of the sal tree are planted in the ground at a distance of fifteen to twenty feet. In the upper portion of these logs (at about the height of fifteen feet) holes are made in which a third log is fixed. In the centre of this third log (at about fifteen feet from the ground it has been inserted in the holes of the other two logs), there is a hole which is called "Ind." There is another log, about 20-25 feet high planted in the ground, the upper portion of which passes through the "Ind" and on it is hung a cage like structure. The landlord of the village, who has given this structure, imagines that it has been done so in memory of the Nagvanshi king Phanimukut Rai, and on the last day he offers rice wine to the gods and distributes it among the assembled people as consecrated food. This festival is celebrated by the Nagvanshi landlords in memory, respect and expression of gratitude towards their king.

Sohrai

This festival is dedicated to the welfare of cattle. In the Munda religious tradition, the new moon night of Kartik month is supposed to be very appropriate for learning or attaining perfection in black magic, evil eye or other deadly incantations and powers. The whole economic life of the Munda farmer is based on agriculture and cattle wealth. Hence he wants assurance of protection of his cattle throughout the year. He knows that cattle are sensitive to the deadly powers and fall ill without any reason and die. Hence Sohrai festival is celebrated to devise means of taking precaution.

The master of the household keeps fast right from the morning of the new moon day, and in the evening he collects all his cattle in one place. Those who have a cattle house, they collect all their cattle there in the evening. A lamp is lit in their midst. Thereafter the mistress of the household brings rice obtained from unboiled paddy on a platter and throws fistful of that rice on all the cattle. This is called the ritual of rice-kissing, meaning kissing them for their welfare. The touch of the rice on the cattle is supposed to be the medium of kissing the cattle. In front of the cattle house a black cock and rice beer is offered to "gauda-goriya" (the patron of the cattle house). "Gauda-goriya" is supposed to be the patron of the cattle house and "birr-Mara" is supposed to be the shepherd of the forest. "Birr-Mara" (the shepherd of the forest) not only protects the cattle in the forest from wild animals and snake bites, but also looks after cattle that have strayed from the track. On this day, the sacrifice of a black cock and proffering of rice beer is done in front of the neat house or the place where the cattle have been collected, to appease them. The lamp burns throughout the night.

The next day, early in the morning, the mistress of the household cleans the horns of the cows, buffaloes, and calves with water and sprinkles holy rice wine on them. Then the master of the household comes and offers sacrifice of the red cock in the name of the bongas and appeases them. After having offered sacrifice, clarified butter is applied on the horns of the buffaloes, and oil is applied on the horns of the cows, bullocks, and calves and they are all offered to eat boiled rice and pulses of horse-bean in adequate quantity. Before they are sent out for grazing, they are decorated with yellow marigold flowers.

Some padres[72] who are scholars of Munda religion are of the opinion that this festival has come from the Hindus to the Mundas because in this festival there is no need of the pahan anywhere and the householder himself does all the sacrifices and worship. Again, all Mundas do not observe this festival. Only those Mundas observe this festival who have cattle-wealth. Padre Exam in support of his opinion has not given any proof, but this much is true that before the Aryans came to India, the Munda people had fully organised themselves as cattle-rearers, and it was not unnatural that the cattle which gave them so much of benefit in their livelihood, they would pray to God for their protection.

Soso-Bonga

Some writers of Munda religion have described "soso-bonga" or "soso-tapa" as a festival. "The darts of the evil eye" and "evil eye" have been discussed when this function was mentioned in detail. This function every Munda does not do; only those Mundas arrange for it when there is fear of influence of black magic and other troubles in their house. They do this for freeing the house from these troubles and to purify it. In this the soso or the bhelwa tree-branch is used. The black, poisonous juice of the bhelwa tree is supposed to have the attribute of having preventive power against magic and spells, darts of the evil eye, etc. The house holder plants two branches of the bhelwa tree in his crop-field so that his cultivation may remain protected from the deadly powers of the invisible evil ones.

According to religious tradition in Munda society, the right to worship Singbonga lies with the pahan, and under any circumstances with the devra. Ojha, mati, or sokha are frequently Hindu or Hinduised Munda who offer worship to give relief to the Mundas from black magic, witches or evil bongas. The master of the household himself worships the home-deities that is the oda bongako.

As per Munda religion, worship and offer of sacrifice is in the law of the making of Creation by Singbonga. Singbonga Himself does not accept any oblation and neither does He eat it. He distributes the oblations of rice and wine to His servants. That is why when the pahan offers oblation to Singbonga, he says. "O, supreme Singbonga, You have no desire for sacrifice or oblations, still then we offer You sacrifice of a white cock and pray that You may accept it and distribute it amongst Your servants."

But Singbonga has ruled that the other bongas will take oblations and be appeased. Singbonga has given this order to the Munda race that they should offer sacrifice and rice beer to the bongas. For that, Singbonga has arranged for pahan and devra in every village.[73]

Before offering sacrifice, the pahan praises Singbonga. In the midst of this praise, he also mentions about other religious stories in which the supernatural divinity of Singbonga can be glimpsed.

The pahan sings in a high pitch songs relating to the making of Creation as well as the Asur Avdaan, making each supplement the other which the Mundas call "darang." The making of Creation, the Rain of Fire and Asur Avdaan are mentioned in between. This is the reason that in Munda religion, it is essential to sacrifice cocks and offer "hadiya" (rice beer) in the worship of Singbonga and the other bongas because in Asur Avdaan Singbonga has given this combined order. He has created pahan and devra to implement this order. They do community/ group worship. Singbonga is not greedy and He does not want any offering. In order to punish the guilty, He sends "gara." (divine punishment):–

> "Singbonga has sent divine punishment to the "horos" (Mundas, human beings)"

Hence as a curative measure, the punished person has to individually worship and offer sacrifice which the Mundas describe as "gara katao" (removal of divine punishment).

According to Munda religion, Asur Avdaan and the story related to the making of the Creation are related and sung along with praises of Singbonga in various religious functions. In many festivals also the excellence of Singbonga is remembered in detail in festivals. Offerings are made to nearly all bongas and the "oda bongako" of the ading and in some festivals, along with worship fairs are also held. The fairs held during festivals or on celebratory occasions are called "jatra" or "buru." In Munda language, the meaning of "buru" is mountain. These fairs are often held on the mountains. Just like the "Jatra" or "buru," the festivals are also connected to songs. The songs can be mainly distinguished as (a) jadur (b) gena (c) or- Jadur (d) karma (e) jarga or mage (f) japi.

The first three, namely jadur, gena and or-jadur are songs of spring. They are sung during the festival of Sarhul. Often, after two jadur songs, one gena song is sung. After the season of jadu, Karma is sung. Karma festival is celebrated on the eleventh day of the bright moon of Bhado, hence Karma songs are sung till the month of Ashwin. Karma is followed by "mage" or "jarga" season "Japi" is song of hunting which is connected to Fagu festival. In this way, the festivals celebrated by the Munda tribe and the related worship rituals and various arrangements have a joyful link in the form of connected songs.

Kili or Gotra and Totem

Kili[74] is the synonym of gotra. The way that a member of a gotra is supposed to be the descendant of a particular "rishi" (sage), similarly the Munda of a kili is supposed to be the descendant of a particular ancestor. In Munda society, marriage between two members of the same kili is forbidden. Often in a village (hatu) all the families living there belong to the same kili. With the increase in the number of families, the area of the kili also expands. Due to the reason of paucity of space in the same village, some families go and settle in nearby places, but the place or village does not make any difference in the kili and the family unity is maintained.

Apart from forbidding of marriage, the kili has another identity in the form of "Sasaan diri." "Sasaan diri" is like a graveyard which is a place just beside the village where the bones of the dead members of a particular kili are interred. This action is due to the belief that in the next world, the soul of the dead Munda is able to meet and be in the midst of his ancestors. In Munda religion, this religious ritual followed after death not only gives a strong basis to the organisational unity of the kili but also assists in finding legal remedies for any dispute regarding ancestral property.

The entire Munda society of Chhotanagpur is divided into various small kilis. The emergence of the custom of kili can be viewed both historically as well as from the point of view of religion. There are many such "kilis" which are connected to some incident or story for its emergence, where they have adopted a particular "totem."[75] The stories relating to kili have religious importance because their certain religious rituals are carried out keeping their "totem" in mind, although from the historical point of view they cannot be said to be backed by facts.

Actually "kili" or "gotra" have emerged as the fruit of the developed condition of human society. In this situation, human beings had taken to agriculture from a nomadic life and settled down at a particular place. The woman, instead of belonging to the whole tribe, began to be the wife of one husband. The mother and father both figure in the offspring but the identity of the offspring began to be with that of the father. The sexual relations between a man and a woman were limited to the circle of husband and wife by bonding them in the sacred binding of marriage with distinct duties. The forbidding of marriage between partners of the same blood gave rise to the custom of "kili." Marriage was accepted as a sacred bonding. In Munda religion it is a divine law, and Singbonga has fixed for every man a wife, and for every woman a husband. If one goes outside this arrangement, then the man-woman violate the desire of Singbonga and become victims of His ire. Sex is meant for creation of offspring. It may be remembered that when the first ancestors felt pangs of guilt after having sex, Singbonga had calmed them by saying that, "You have done well" (see annexure Rain of Fire). The arrangement of "Kili" is to maintain purity of offspring (purity of blood).

It is the Divine law in Creation that the race must multiply; hence reproduction is a religious act. In all the religions of the world, "reproduction" has been said to be God's blessing and connected to religious virtue. That is why marriage is said to be a sacred religious act in which man-woman relationship and duty have been determined in religion and society. The aim of marriage is reproduction. When it is questioned of Munda religion that the first ancestors came from the same womb hence they were brother and sister. Therefore, Singbonga made them drink rice beer and made them behave as husband and wife ? Then a reply comes that to keep the race alive, reproduction has religious sanctity. Again, the first ancestors were originally man-woman. The relationship of a brother and sister is the result of a developed society. Over a period of time, the relationship between a brother and sister were determined by the sanctity of religious acts. The marriage between brother and sister came to be looked down upon. The brother-sister circle expanded, resulting in the expansion of the circle of the clan, and in the same kili the girls and boys of marriageable age came to be equivalent to brother and sister.

In Munda society, a traditional story is prevalent about the social necessity of "kili" and its emergence. According to this story, the original place of the Mundas was "Central Asia." Their first ancestors were Lutkum Hadam and Lutkum Burhi. They had a son called Hembo. Hembo's son was Kus, and Kus's son was Morih. From Morih, many subtribes called Korku, Marko, Santhal, Ho, Bhumij, Larka, Korwa, Pinji etc. came into existence.

Morih took his extended family towards the south and came to Tibet. Again from Tibet through the east-south passes via Nepal to Eastern India and in that order Bihar, Bundelkhand, Jabbalpur and to the south till the banks of the Narmada, northwest India's Punjab and Sindh area, they spread all over. After the death of Morih, Seto Munda was chosen as the leader. He defeated and drove away king Sisirom of Missour (Egypt) when he tried to invade from the northwest border.[76] Centuries later, the Aryas, Gond, Oraons defeated the Mundas. After their defeat the Mundas fled toward the east and south-east and reached Rohtasgarh. Risa Munda was their leader in the battle with Madhodas in Rohtasgarh. After getting defeated, he fled to the Vindhya mountains where he was instructed by Singbonga in a dream to search for "the golden country." He came to Chhotanagpur area with twentyone thousand followers and for permanently settling down crossed the Sahar ghatiya pass and entered Chhotanagpur. After reaching Chhotanagpur, Risa Munda appointed Sutiya Munda for the management of the whole country.

Sutiya divided the whole country into seven forts[78] based on seven supplies, and keeping in mind the huge population of twenty one thousand followers, he divided them into twenty one parganas (each pargana having several villages). These parganas were called "parha." Sutiya made his residence the Sutiyambe fort as the administrative centre of the whole country.

Twenty-one Parha : Twenty-one Kili

With the passage of time, the need arose for a bride for Sutiya's son, but apart from his own family, the rest of the people were not of any other gotra from where he could have brought a bride for his son. He did not think it right to have marital connection between descendants of the same ancestor. Hence, to resolve this problem, he planned to divide the twenty-one parhas into twenty-one kilis so that in future for every kili there would be twenty other kilis to choose a bride or groom from. Sutiya invited to Sutiyambe fort all the twenty-one parha chiefs. He kept some plants and trees, animals and birds in a place in Sutiyambe fort and asked the parha chiefs who had come there to select a plant, an animal or bird as sign of their kili. In this way, the names of the chiefs of the parhas would be joined to that kili whose identity/ symbol (totem) would be the plant, animal or bird chosen. In this way, the following parha chiefs chose their "Kili". They were accepted as the "founder" of their "kili." The details of the "kili" are as follows:

Parha	*Founder*	*Name of Kili*
No. 1.	Sutiya Pahan	Barah
2.	Duka Munda	Horo
3.	Kura Munda	Kerketta
4.	Bela Munda	Kowwa

(Contd...)

5.	Dukhna Munda	Howwa
6.	Gangu Munda	Techua
7.	Lakho Munda	Baba
8.	Lambo Munda	Dung-dung
9.	Jeet Rai Munda	Jojobar
10.	Birsa Munda	Barwa
11.	Champa Munda	Sanga
12.	Karma Munda	Tiru
13.	Gomia Munda	Lugun
14.	Soma Munda	Buddhu
15.	Leda Munda	Herange
16.	Udai Munda	Nag
17.	Mangta Munda	Odi-Kandir
18.	Raiyya Munda	Tuti
19.	Samu Munda	Bag-Suriya
20.	Porha Munda	Hemrai
21.	Sarika Munda	Dahang

In this way with the founding of "Kili", it was decided that no Munda would fix marriage within his own kili. Gradually, with the passage of time, due to extension of the family and change of residence as also adopting new places of habitation, the aforementioned "kilis underwent many sub-divisions. The present day Munda society is divided into more than hundred "kilis." There are many such "kilis" which came into existence after some time due to special incidents. Such "kilis" have come up being influenced by their totems because due to the totem they or their clan have been protected.

Chief Kilis and their Emergence

The reason for the emergence of various "Kilis" in Munda tribe can be derived from the various stories preserved till date and known to the pahans of the concerned "kili." The knowledge regarding the coming into existence of the "kili" can primarily be known from the elders and pahan of that "Kili." This knowledge is accepted to be true if it is confirmed by the elders living nearby or the pahan of another "kili" or a branch of the people which has gone and settled somewhere else. The confirmation can also be had from the respect and reverence shown to a totem by members of the kili. Nearly the same kind of narration can be found in certain essays here and there and in the descriptions given by padres. Hence the facts regarding the emergence of "Kili" are held to be true from the traditional point of view. From the historical point of view, too, the viability of the emergence of "kili" is confirmed to a certain extent especially when members of the "kili" settled at far off places confirm this incident.

The correct description of the geographical place can be seen to historically authenticate the emergence of "kili." The description of many incidents of Chhotanagpur are confirmed by its geography. In addition, the areas growing cotton, tuti and description of various plants is not out of place from the point of view of geography. But no temple, pillar, mound or rounded stone are available which may be connected to some kili or would be historical proof of it. Still then, whatever is apparent cannot be negated. The existence of "kili" is connected in an effective way with the Munda tribe and members of every kili have a worshipful regard for their totem.

From the point of view of influence and sizeable population the following kilis have a lot of importance in the Munda tribe:

Tuti Kili

Due to the number of families being large in Sutiyambe-Korambe, some groups went and settled to the east of Ranchi i.e. Chutia. But due to not being able to settle down properly in Chutia, these people decided to settle in winter season in the eastern direction. In this process they had to cross a river full of water. Some people from this group thought it appropriate to cross the river first. In the winter season they waded in the cold water upto a certain distance and thereafter swam ashore, but after reaching the other bank they started shivering with cold. They had no alternative but to shout across or show through sign language to those who were on the other side to send fire so that they would be able to save their lives. The people on the other side finding no other means, tied a flaming firebrand on the tail of a dog and put the dog in the water for swimming across. They were hopeful that the up swinging tail of the dog would remain above the water and in this way the dog would carry the firebrand across the water to the other side. But this did not happen and the firebrand got extinguished in the water.

In that area, a lot of tuti plants used to grow, the cobs of which people used to eat. The people of this side uprooted a strong tuti plant. They slit open the upper portion and put some burning coals in it. Then they tied that plant to an arrow and with the help of a bow, shot it to the other side. In this way, with the help of the tuti plant the Mundas could save themselves. That day they vowed that they would respect the tuti plant and would not eat it. This family was called "Tuti-kili."

The reverence Mundas hold for their totems is to such an extent that they cannot bear disrespect to tuti in front of their eyes. The excerpt is from S. C. Roy[79] that in Tilma village a Muslim had sown some seeds of tuti in his vegetable garden. When they sprouted, the Mundas who were mostly of tuti kili came to know, so they invaded his house. The Muslim was compelled to uproot the tuti plants and thus satisfy the neighbouring Mundas.

Bodra Kili

The people of Bodra kili and the sub-kilis (a) Tebo bodra kili (b) langbodra kili (c) Aimda or Ramer bodra kili are supposed to be normally greedy by nature because the kili's founder Jirka Pesha and his wife Jirki Nauri were driven out from other kilis because of greed and this is the reason why Bodra kili was founded.

Burha Jirka Pesha and his wife Burhi Jirki Nauri used to stay in Andko village. At one time while partaking of a feast, the Burha due to greed, smeared food on his face. Upon seeing this, the villagers excommunicated him from their kili or gotra. Thereafter he founded a separate kili and named it Bodra.

(a) Tebo-Bodra Kili

The village where Jirka Pesha and his Burhi Jirka Nauri of Bodra Kili used to live, there was a red silk cotton tree in which bees had built a bee-live. The burha-burhi took down the hive and ate up the eggs. The bees again built a bee-live. This time the villagers planned to drink rice beer and to eat the eggs of the hive along with it but prior to this, the burha-burhi took down the hive and ate up the eggs. The villagers drove them away. They went and entered a cave and saved themselves through deceit. At night, they reached the forest of Tebo where a man was roasting the plucked wing of a duck which he had killed. The burha sat down there. The man suspected the intention of the burha, therefore in a fit of anger he threw the dead duck which hit the burha's chest. As soon as the duck fell on the burha it became alive and crying "tebo" it flew away. The burha set up a new village over there and settled down with his family. Thus, the people of that place came to be called "tebo bodra."

(b) Lang-bodra Kili

The people of tebo bodra kili set up another village. One day the people of the village went out for hunting but returned disappointed in the evening. Only one person had hunted a lame bird. At night in the village assembly, their chief, after analysing the whole incident said that it is the order of God that from that day they would not hunt a lame bird nor eat it, and from that day they would be called family of "lang-bodra" kili.

(c) Ramer-boder Kili

People of bodra kili used to live in the village. One day they planned to cook pulses of "urad" (horse bean) and rice and eat it, but some of them due to greed ate up the raw cereals. Since then they began to be called "Ramer boder kili."

Soy Kili

The basis for emergence of soy kili is the soy fish. A farmer had his cotton field near the bank of the river Chilua Ikir. A fish used to come below and destroy the cotton crop. The farmer was very much troubled. One day, in hiding, he saw the soy fish eating and destroying the cotton crop. He killed the fish with an arrow but could not pick it up because it was very big. He called his brothers for help. They cut and distributed the fish among themselves.

(1) The person who had killed the soy fish, his family came to be called "Tuing soy kili."

(2) The person who cut the bones, his family came to be called "jung-sama soy kili."

(3) The person who apportioned the flesh, his family came to be called "til soy kili."

(4) The person who distributed the portions, his family came to be called "soy kili."

(5) The person who placed the leaves for keeping the portions, his family was called "Patra Paira soy kili."

(6) One brother tied the flesh of the fish in a towel of red ochre colour, so his family came to be called "gamchcha soy kili."

Apart from these, there are many other sub-divisions of soy kili, namely, Mandi soy, Tiki soy, Wula soy, Adoy soy, Rura mandi soy, Vranda soy. The various kinds of people belonging to soy kili do not kill soy fish and nor do they eat its flesh. The gamchcha soy kili members do not eat any fish of the colour of red ochre.

Horo or Kachchap Kili

We have seen that the emergence of kili is connected to some special incident in which often divine powers are at work. The ancestors of Horo kili had once been trapped near a swollen river and had wanted to go to the other side. In those days, the animals and birds also used to understand the language of human beings. They cried piteously for help and said that they would be always highly obliged if they and their family members were safely brought ashore by someone. Hearing this, a tortoise came up from the depths of the river, and loading them and their belongings on its huge back brought them safely ashore. According to their promise they kept the name of their kili "horo." Horo is also called "Kachchap kili." Any member of this kili neither kills a tortoise nor eats its meat.

Nag Kili

The ancestors of "nag kili" were grateful for the kindness shown to them by "nag" (serpent). A snake charmer had reared a snake in captivity. One day, after having displayed his sport with snakes, he died a sudden death on the way back home. Upon seeing his condition, the serpent circumambulated him and then tying his body to its coil, it gradually brought him home. His family members, upon seeing this, became highly obliged, and till the snake was alive they fed it with milk and parched rice. The desendants of the snake charmer later on came to be known as of "nag kili." No member of "nag kili" ever harms or injures any snake.

Some Hinduised Mundas of "nag kili" claim to be connected to the clan of Nag Rishi. These people live in adequate numbers in village Manikadih under Sona Hatu police station. Some people also believe that a serpent had protected their ancestors by giving them shelter under its hood hence they come under "nag kili."

There are other stories related to "nag kili" in various places.

Another Story

An old man and an old woman used to live in the forest. A child was born to them. The old man visited his brothers in the village to give this news, while the old woman was left alone. One day, after fetching water she lost her way home. Roaming around, she heard the cries of the child. She came near only to find that a snake was shading the child with its hood.

When the old man returned with his brothers, the old woman narrated the incident to them. After considering it, they decided that it was not a snake but God who had come in the form of a snake to bless the family, hence from that day the family would be known as "nag kili."

Another Story

This is such a story of "nag kili" where the custom is to kill a snake as soon as it is sighted. The story goes like this : A cowherd of the village was grazing his animals; he was playing his flute in the shade of the trunk of a tree. In the meantime, a snake came and bit the cowherd which resulted in his death. His body became blue and contorted. His dead body remained in the same position against the tree with flute in hand for three days. Due to the blowing of the breeze, at times there would be sounds from his flute. The villagers came to know about the incident three days later. They became very angry and decided that wherever a snake would be sighted, it would be killed by them. As a result, the people decided to call them and their descendants "nag kili." This is such an incident which goes against the emergence of a kili. This can be said to be an exception.

The Transformation of Kili

Munda tribe and Munda religion have had maximum contact with the Hindu race and Hindu religion. Those Mundas who have been more prosperous and been upwards in the social ladder, have been connected to Hindu community due to business, politics, religious and social festivals and functions. Due to these inter-connections, the procedure of cultural inter-change was but natural. Such a procedure is development oriented, meaning thereby, it develops individually from below and upwards. Centuries earlier, such Hindu influenced Mundas would copy those characters and implant them within themselves and their families and clan so that compared to other Mundas they would be known to be more civilised, better cultured and honourable. In this process, the transformation of kili may be seen. Since most of the population of panch pargana (to the south-east of Ranchi) is of Hinduised Mundas, hence the sandi kili Mundas gradually transformed to Shandil gotra, and they claimed to be the descendants of Shandil Rishi. This custom did not come into existence just because of similarity of word but to gain higher social level by becoming Hindu- it was a psychological pressure which was the reason. The matter did not rest only with the transformation of gotra- the Mundas of Shandilya gotra established marriage- connections with other Hindus of this gotra. Very soon, most of the Mundas residing in Sonahatu area have changed their kili to Shandilya gotra. Today there is a sizeable population of Shandilya brahmans in Sonahatu area who are by profession farmers and look like Mundas as per their physique and form. Similarly, in village Kota of Tamar Pargana (south of Bundu) the Mundas of Jome Tuti kili believe themselves to be the descendants of Bhoj Raj and call their gotra Bhoj-raj gotra. In Panch Pargana region, mostly Mundas of Nag gotra, Tau (sparrow) gotra, and Sanga kili reside. After revolting against the British and with the gaining of Independence, their racial pride was awakened and now they are very much alert in protecting their religion and cultural heritage.

The prevailing main kili or gotra serial-wise in Munda society : (1) Ode Kandir (2) Odiya (3) Kandir (4) Kamal (gotra) (5) Kula (6) Kerketta (7) Kowwa (8) Gada Kewate (9) Gada Mundu (10) Gomi Buru (11) Champi (12) Jo Jo bara (13) Tuti (14) Topno (15) Dung-dung (16) Techua (17) Totrai (18) Tau (sparrow) (19) Tidu-sankra (20) Tiru (21) Tairog (22) Dahang (23) Dere-Sanga (24) Demta (25) Nag (god and wellwisher) (26) Nag (enemy) (27) Purti Chutu (28) Purti Sandi (29) Purti Sarah (30) Purti Sarkad (31) Purti-Huni (32) Bag-Suriya (33) Badao-Ud (34) Barwa (35) Bando (wild cat) (36) Baba (37) Barla (38) Buddu (39) Bale Machu (40) Bodra (41) Bodra-Tebo (42) Bodra-Lang (43) Bodra-Ramer (44) Bhengra (45) Mundu (46) Mundu (murhu) (47) Mundu (lo) (48) Mudri (49) Runda (50) Langbacherey Badoso (51) Lugun (52) Sankura (53) Sanga (54) Sal (gotra) (55) Surin (56) Soy (57) Adoi soy (58) Ore-soy (59) Gamchha soy (60) Chiki soy (61) Jang-Samsoy (62) Til Soy (63) Turang Soy (64) Tula Soy (65) Patra-soy (69) Soy (Murum) (70) Soy (murum) Ged (71) Soy (murum) Patra-petey (72) Soy (murum)- Atade (73) Sama-soy (murum) (74) Soyen (75) Soso Mundu (76) Hai (77) Hassa (78) Hans (79) Hasda (80) Hemrom (81) Herange (82) Horo (83) Horo and Aind (84) Howwa Kili.

Change in Kili

Just like transformation of kili, incidents of change in kili are few in number. One such incident is of villages Chiur and Chaldandu under police station Karra of Sonepur pargana. Some Mundas of this place had earlier been residents of Ulatu Tendey tola and their kili was "bando" (wild cat). Near today's Bandgaon there was a resident named Patra Mochhiya Parha who wanted to setup a village by clearing a place near Bandgaon but due to the presence of numerous snakes, he remained unsuccessful. He requested a Munda of Chiur and Chaldandu to kill the snakes and brought him along with his family. After ridding the place of snakes, Patra Mochhiya Parha whose kili was "herange" set up the village called Bind hatu and settled the killer of the snakes, too, whose kili was "bando," but now he was assimilated in the kili of "herange." His offspring increased, family expanded and his "sasan-diri" (graveyard) was also built. Some of them, however, returned to Chiur and Chaldandu and started living there. Now the position of the Mundas became such that neither in "bando" Kili, nor in "herange" kili could they arrange for marriage. This circumstance in Munda religious arrangement is called "Kilire-sober." Difference in place and long interval of time give rise to such incidents. About five hundred years ago the Mundas of Bandgaon area, due to pressure of population, went and settled towards the south where the Hos used to stay and gradually became absorbed in Ho tribe. Some families had continued with their original names but most families had adopted name of different kili. The name of this kili was connected to that village which had been left behind when they came to Kolhan region. In this way, there are twentyfour kilis which came from the Mundas and have been assimilated in Ho tribe.[80]

Kili and Parha

We have seen that kili is a surname which came from an ancestor to his descendants or was adopted by a group of families whose members having blood relations, can be identified from the kili. In the beginning, often an ancestor would clear a place and settle down in it and his expanded family would take on the form of a village. In the village itself there would be the Sarna or place of worship and the sasan-diri (graveyard) would be the place just beside the village. If there was any quarrel, dispute or any other problem, then the eldest member of the seniormost family would take a decision which would be binding on all.

Due to the increase in family numbers, the original village would become too small, hence the land nearest to the village would be cleared and in this way the second, third or even fourth village would be set up. The members of the kili who went to the new village, would setup their own Sarna or place of worship as also separate "sasan diri," but they would not be able to resolve their internecine quarrels, disputes or other administrative problems. For resolving social and administrative problems, the kili families of all the villages together would form a joint institution called "parha." This meant that for worship and "sasan diri" all the nearby villages of the same kili had independence but for resolving of social and administrative problems, all those villages would have an organisation called "parha." In this way the "Parha" is the symbol of unity of kili and friendship/kinship of the villages.

"Parha" can be formed of the nearby villages. If families of the kili are too many in number and some of them have gone and settled in far-off places, then they cannot come within the limits of parha. It is not practicable also. In this way, all the villages which are just beside the original village and all the families of the same kili together form a "Parha" for social and administrative arrangement. Fraternity in the kili is the internal strength of the "Parha."

Totem

The ancestors set in motion the custom of kili so that tribes would be separated in groups and there would be no chance of marriage between blood relations. The group of people belonging to one kili are the descendants of same ancestor hence are blood relations, therefore, boys and girls of marriageable age are equivalent to brother and sister, and marriage of brother and sister is forbidden. Due to increase and spread of the family, the totem plays an important role in keeping the identity of kili alive, because every kili has a totem and based on it the surname (title) is added to the name. Also, the members of a kili have a reverential attitude towards the totem, save for certain exceptions. They do not harm the totem in any manner which means that any action which shows disrespect to the totem or becomes the reason for its destruction is forbidden which is called "taboo."

At present, in Munda society, there are more than a hundred small-big kilis in existence. All have one totem or the other. But due to deforestation, most of them have become extinct. There are many whose meaning is not clear and neither incidents are narrated, heard or repeated for clarifying the meaning. If asked, the usual reply is that those elders who knew have all died. Like normal stories, the stories related to totem and the incidents are not known by all people. That is why reverence towards totem, and taboo remain as conventions.

The two sides of the story relating to "nag kili" have been analysed in "kili." In one, the snake acts as a protector and gets reverence due to a god. The people of this kili think it to be a sin to harm any snake. Any kind of harmful behaviour towards a snake is taboo.

There is another side to the story of "nagkili" in which due to snake bite a cowherd loses his life. The members of his family become enemies of the snake and wherever they see a snake they try to kill it. This is also Nag kili but their attitude towards the snake is violent and deadly. Such an attitude towards their totem is an exception in the totemic stories of Munda society. It is possible that there may not be much respect towards the totem, but to have a violent attitude towards it and yet belong to the kili having that totem is definitely rare example.

From a practical point of view, most Mundas, if they have not forgotten their totems, have an easygoing or disinterested attitude towards them. One cannot see reverence running deep for totems. A hauko member of Topno kili (topno meaning the mata or red or ants and their eggs of the trees) will abstain from eating them, but breaking their nests and letting the eggs fall and after collecting them, selling them in the market is not taboo for him. Actually it is today's materialistic practicality which has eroded the former reverence for one's totem. With such incidents the importance of totem is also being forgotten.

The selection of totem is totally divine. To think that in Sutiyambe the Munda chiefs had voluntarily selected their totems is not correct. With every Munda chief there must have been some kind of attachment with some special totem. The truth is that behind every totem there must have been some special incident. Although there are thousands of objects, but only one special object becomes the totem because its selection is not as per one's desire. Its selection is as per divine connection, without effort, in some unknown point of time, some incident connected to some object due to which the relationship to a kili is established. Hence the conjoining of a gotra or kili to any totem is as per a mysterious divine intervention.

The arrangement regarding kili or gotra has been derived from a civilised society. Such kind of an arrangement has been proved to have been there in Munda society even before they entered Chhotanagpur. The war between Risa Munda and Madhodas in Rohtasgarh, in which after getting defeated the Mundas had to leave Rohtasgarh, took place only because Risa Munda could not give his daughter in marriage to Madhodas's son. At that time the Mundas, called kol, also included Santhal, Bhumij, Ho, etc. All of them together fled the place and after entering Chhotanagpur each took its own route. In Santhal, Bhumij and Munda, the same kili of Hemrom, Hasda and Soyen are to be found. It is clear that these kilis were present in Rohtasgarh and when these Mundas, Santhals and Bhumij (who were one tribe in Rohtasgarh) fled Rohtasgarh and went and settled separately, then each one of them kept this legacy intact with them. It is true that in Rohtasgarh, the number of kilis was small.[81] But the Mundas had recognised the religious and social requirement of kili, otherwise a few years after entering Chhotanagpur, why did Sutiya Munda arrange for allotment of twentyone kilis among the twentyone chiefs of twentyone parganas? In the current Munda society, one hundred and thirtythree small or big kilis are to be found.[82]

Kili is a strong religious basis in the social structure of Munda life. No Munda girl or boy can dare to violate its control. From the geographic point of view, family members of one kili stay scattered in nearby villages but they maintain their fraternity and obtain security and protection from the parha administration. The children play together like brothers and sisters, fight each other and grow up. They become young men and women, but the young women are viewed as sisters by the young men. It is the rule of kili that these young women must go as brides outside their own kili. Within the fold of kili, all are brothers and sisters, and this decorum is unbreakable. Thus, the young men and women freely mix with each other and roam around together. There is no suspicion or doubt about them. If perchance some mistake is made and a girl becomes pregnant, then there is no alternative except to abort the foetus even though the girl's life might be in danger; otherwise to face the panchayat (village assembly) and be punished would be very heavy. That is why such mistakes rarely occur. The panchayat keeps everybody in control. The rule of kili exists to maintain the purity of the Munda race.

Sanskar or Purification Ceremonies

Munda life is bound by sanskar or purification ceremonies. From conception to death, there are many ceremonies which connect the Munda race and religion and show correct direction in the journey of life. The rituals pertaining to these sanskars are often extensive or they are not that simple or brief which an outsider often thinks to be. In these ceremonies, not only unshakeable faith and adoration are expressed towards God Singbonga and the different bongas of the Creation made by Him, but the natural, social virtues of the tribes are also expressed when they appear eager to greet and welcome with love and affection the guests who come to their doors. In this way, both religious and social activities are included in these ceremonies.

(1) Birth and its Connected Ceremony

Just like the Hindus, there are certain ceremonies connected to the birth of a child among the Munda tribe. These ceremonies start with the conception of the child. Singbonga has given certain responsibilities to the various bongas in His creation. In these circumstances, the Munda invokes the concerned bonga for some work, and worshipping the bonga expects desired results. But he does not neglect other bongas. He never forgets the bongako of the ading. He also offers oblation to the rest of the sectoral bongas in a group. He knows that Singbonga does not accept oblation. He sings hymns in praise of Singbonga and is desirous of getting His blessings.

(a) Gadasi Bonga

Gadasi bonga is that deity who looks after the child when it comes in the womb and till its birth. As soon as the master of the house sees the signs of difficult time of the child's birth, a red or brown cock, and a pitcher of rice beer prepared separately are kept aside for worshipping Gadasibonga. A day is fixed for the worship and on that day the pregnant woman's father, brother, uncle, etc. come to her house and take part in the worship. Prayers are offered to Gadasi bonga for the good health of the mother and child and for a smooth child birth. After this, the master of the house while completing the worship, sacrifices that cock which had been kept in reserve for this from before.

The master of the house boils the head, heart and tail of the cock together and offers them to his ancestors in the ading, and prays to them that the entry of the new creature (member) in his family be without any obstruction. After the worship is over, the feast of rice beer and meal is started along with the guests.

Gadasi bonga is worshipped for (1) security of the womb (2) birth without any obstruction and (3) the well being of the mother and child. This does not come within the definition of ceremony related to conception. The religious rituals and activities done to mark conception come within the ceremony of conception. These are done after conception. Gadasi bonga is worshipped for the womb and the child and the mother, for their safety and welfare. In Munda religion, Singbonga had presented the device for conception to the first ancestors (lutkums).

The Mundas believe that if Gadasi bonga is not worshipped, then not only there is a fear of miscarriage and death of child and mother at child birth, but the foetus in the womb is also affected. Physical and mental deformities also come upon the child which are not seen at child birth but are revealed when the child grows up. Under these circumstances, it is necessary to worship Gadasi bonga for pregnant women in Munda religion. This worship ensures the child's purification and good upbringing. There is no requirement for pahan or devra for this worship.

(b) Cutting of the Umbilical Card

After the birth of a child, the act of cutting of the umbilical cord takes place. This work is done by the wife of the village iron-smith. She uses a special kind of sickle. Before cutting the cord, she heats the sickle completely. The act of cutting the cord is done very efficiently. If there is no elderly and efficient wife of an iron-smith, then the village iron-smith's wife does the act under the supervision of an efficient elderly woman of the house or of another part of the village.

After the cord is cut, it is accepted that the child is now connected to the visible world, but it is not accepted as a member of the Munda race. By just being born of a Munda father and a Munda mother, a child does not become a Munda but to include him/her in the race, the Chhatti ceremony has to be performed.

(c) Chhatti

For eight days after the birth of a child, the mother is supposed to be impure. None of the fraternity can enter the new mother's home nor can accept anything to eat or drink. After the birth of the child, the mother is given water of boiled kurthhi (a kind of pulse) to drink and instead of stale rice, hot rice is given to eat.

On the ninth day of the birth of the child, the purification rites of mother and child are begun. (Among Hindus who call it Chhatti, this is done on the sixth day after birth). The new infant, mother, and the relatives of the father's side namely, uncle, grandfather, shareholders etc. cut their nails in the morning. Then the mother of the new born, along with women of the house and village goes to the nearest pond or river where she takes her bath and becomes pure. At the time of going to the water body, the mat (which is called "sered pati") on which after birth the baby had been sleeping upto then, and which is considered impure, is burnt. After purifying from the pond or river, upon return to the house, the water kept in a brass pot in which basil leaves and copper coin have also been kept is sprinkled at the doorway and the house to purify it. Rice beer or ranu-da (water in which the root of the plant used to make rice beer is soaked) is sprinkled all over the house. In this way, when the whole house becomes pure all the relatives enter the house along with the master of the household. The master goes straight to the ading where the home deities or ancestors reside and offers them rice (extracted from unboiled paddy) in worship. After the worship of the house-deities, the chhatti programme finishes and everybody starts feasting on hadiya (rice beer) and a meal.

The ceremony of Chhatti is very important in Munda society. Due to this ceremony, the child is given entry into the race and it is counted as a member of the Munda race.[83] This function is called "Chhati hulang."

(2) "Sakha" Function or Name Giving Ceremony

In Munda religious philosophy, it has been accepted that the invisible world and therein roaming invisible powers affect Munda life. According to this supposition, the invisible powers send messages to this material world through signs or other devices due to which decisions are taken whether any work is good or ill-omened. When the invisible powers set up a good combination then the work is supposed to be good and fruitful.

In the naming ceremony of the child, effort is made to obtain approval of the invisible powers to decide about a name. The procedure for name giving which is adopted is as follows. On the second day after "Chhatti hulang," all the close relatives and neighbours are invited to take part in the naming ceremony. The mother of the infant comes in their midst with a round platter full of water. The platter is kept on the ground and nearby some arwa rice (rice extracted from unboiled paddy) is kept. Then the mother puts a grain of rice in the water of the platter. This "first grain" of rice is supposed to be the infant. Whatever name the mother wants to keep of the infant (often the name suggested by the close relatives and family is given preference), she pronounces that name and puts the second grain of rice in the water of the platter. If the second grain of rice touches the first grain (infant) or settles beside it, then it is accepted that the name attached to the second grain is the one, and likewise it is declared amidst them.

If the second grain of rice does not touch or settle beside the grain of the infant then other names are taken and grains put in the water. The rice grain which touches the "infant," the name pronounced with it is accepted to be the name of the infant. The family can keep another desired name for just calling the child, but the name which was kept as per procedure is accepted to be the name having the approval of invisible powers, and the society and panchayat accept that name. After fixing of the name, the "joarni"[84] gives blessings to the infant that his hair be white as the flower of the "hail," and creepers of the "ruta," meaning thereby that the infant may have a long life. After the blessing, the assembled people enjoy the feast.

(3) Sootam-tol Ceremony

This ceremony is also held on the day of the naming ceremony. As per this, some threads are tied around the waist of the infant just like a waistband. These threads protect the infant from the evil eye or darts of the evil eye.

(4) Lutur-tukai or Piercing of the Ears Ceremony

This ceremony is held in the first, second or third year of the child. It is connected to the naming ceremony. In the naming ceremony the person's name which was given to the infant, that person is taken to be the friend or companion of the infant, and he plays an important role in the piercing of the ears ceremony. On the day this ceremony is fixed to be conducted, the friend of the infant brings along with him gifts of sufficient rice, pulses, salt, mustard oil, hadiya, one he-goat, new clothes and necklace of pearl like grains. In the courtyard of the house of the child's father, two parallel four armed squares are drawn with rice flour, the two ears of which cut each other. On this square, interwoven straw is put and on top of it a wooden seat is placed on which the infant's friend sits. After sitting down, the friend takes mustard oil and first applies it on his head and thereafter applies it to the child's head. On this occasion, two persons, often barbers by profession, sit near the square. After getting an indication from the friend, they at first dot the ears of the child with vermillion and thereafter mostly with a silver needle they pierce the ear-lobes. Then everybody stands up away from the square and a black cock is placed in the middle of the square and is sacrificed. The blood of the cock is sprinkled over the whole square. The "joarni" who has been invited to give blessings and sing songs of good wishes invokes the gods for their blessings and says, "O God, protect this child and give it long life." In the evening, after having partaken of a feast and hadiya, all the invitees express happiness and depart for their homes.

(5) Adandi or Marriage Ceremony

In Munda religion and society, the importance of the race has been kept uppermost. An individual is for the race. The race is the centre of the Creation of God Singbonga. Singbonga has always been making efforts for the protection and increase of the race. The traditional religious stories and Avdaan confirm this truth. He has given the responsibility of the protection and well being of the race to the bongas who roam in the invisible world. Marriage is the main duty for the increase of the race. It is necessary to maintain purity of marriage in order to maintain purity of the race. There are two bases of the purity of marriage:

(a) The bride and groom should be of the race but from separate kilis.

(b) The bride and groom duo has been fixed earlier by Singbonga. It is the duty of the family members to bring the bride and groom together through the medium of good and bad omens/signs.

Due to coming into contact, the Hindu rules, regulations and customs have influenced the Munda tribe. We have been able to produce many instances in which due to influence of Hindus there have been changes in Munda tribe, namely, their religious activities, festivals, procedure regarding worship, importance of Mahadev and Parvati, etc. Even the old rules and regulations regarding arrangement of marriage among Mundas have been changed to a great extent due to the contact with Hindus. After India attained independence, the custom of child marriage among the Mundas has waned, otherwise, centuries earlier, hardly any boy or girl would have been found in Munda families[85] whose age would be 8-10 years and he/she was not married. The custom of child marriage among the Mundas was a bad influence of Hindu society, otherwise the old Mundas of Ranchi bring back the memory of those traditional times when a Munda boy was not found suitable for marriage until he could fashion out a ploughshare with his own hands and labour. A similar restriction had been there for the girls also. They had to attain that age when they would be able to make thread from cotton or be able to weave mats with the leaves of the date palm. It is clear that such kind of work girls and boys would not have been able do at a very tender age-they would have been able to do them when their bodies would have developed. It is said that in those times, boys and girls had more independence to choose their life-mates. In various fairs they used to meet girls and boys of other kilis and selected their life mates. It was, of course, that their families would confirm their likings. The marriage used to take place with the approval of the family, but above these approvals and desires, the invisible power of Singbonga would be at work. If through signs and good omens. He gave His approval to the marriage of the boy and girl, then the marriage took place. Gradually, the age of marriage lessened, the choice of the boy and girl held no importance, the family members became the final decision-makers in the fixing of marriage. After everything changed, the question of good or bad signs, however, remained because through these signs Singbonga's approval or disapproval was expressed. Hence, the final decision of the marriage of a girl and boy depends on these good and bad signs which is called "chedey uriko." This is the first stage of a Munda marriage.

Chedey Uri

Within this ritual, the father of the boy or other members of the family, send a messenger to the house of the girl who has been selected by them. He is called "agua" and he takes the proposal of marriage to the girl's house. The "agua" meets the family members of the girl. These family members fix a date when the boy's father along with relatives, and (upon request by the girl's family members) the boy too, go to the village of the girl. On the way whatever good or bad signs are seen are noted by the boy's family. Good signs are- a cow and its calf calling to each other by turn, bundle of paddy being taken, a pot filled with water, clean clothes, a person making a plough and yoke, a fox crossing in front from left to right, meeting a cheetah on the way, a man collecting sand or soil, etc. The bad signs are called "bugin ereko" and these may be :- a man going along with an axe or spade or mattock, a bamboo fishing rod, a cow bellowing without any reason, rice being taken away, the garbage of a house being thrown, a garment/cloth full of soil and ash, a tree falling after being axed, etc.

If the boy's party, on its way to fix the marriage, meets with a very bad sign, then it abandons its effort and goes back, and sends information about it through the "agua" to the girl's house. If by good luck no bad sign is seen, then this party reaches the girl's house. One or two mats are spread in the courtyard of the girl's house on which the boy's party sits down. Thereafter, the boy's "agua" discusses with the girl's "agua" about all the signs seen on the way. If those signs are good signs in the viewpoint of the girl's "agua" or that they are not bad signs, then he orders the girl's party to welcome the guests.

There have been certain developmental changes in the arrangements for the function to be held at the doorstep of the girl. The main intention of these changes is to see and check the complexion and appearance, physique etc. of the girl so that later on there should arise no dispute. This is called "seeing the girl" or "kudi lel." In some areas the boy's father sees the girl and in certain areas the boy and the girl confront each other in the presence of the "agua." This custom is called "daadgu."

Kudi-lel

This custom is prevalent in Hasda area. The guests who have come to the doorstep of the girl stand facing the east. Thereafter the girl along with other girls is brought out. Two near relatives of the girl carry a flaming torch, a pot filled with hadiya and a small metal pot filled with water. The girl is handed over in the arms of her future father-in-law, and he is asked to have a full look at her. Althought this function is held in the day time, the flaming torch is brough close so that during inspection there may not be an allegation of any shortcoming. Then the girl is offered water in a leaf bowl which she gives to her father-in-law. The offering of water by the girl to her father-in-law indicates that the girl agrees to the marriage. Then the father-in-law asks the following questions:

"What kind of water have you given to me?"

"Water of gold."

"Will you give it only for today ?"

"I will give this water to you always."

After the father-in-law, the girl similarly offers water to the other elders who repeat the same questions and answers. After this activity, the girl offers the pot of hadiya to her father-in-law. The father-in-law takes out a leaf bowl full of hadiya from it and gives it to the girl who drinks it. Thereafter the girl returns inside the house with the other girls. The guests begin to enjoy hadiya and a good feast.

The meaning of the father-in-law facing the east and accepting the girl is that he has made Singbonga a witness while accepting her.

"Da-Adgu"

This custom is prevalent in Naguri area. The difference is that instead of the father-in-law, it is the groom who plays the main role. It is clear that these rituals could not have been accomplished in child-marriage- it could be done when the bride and the groom would be adults.

The groom stands along with two of his friends waiting for the girl to arrive. After some time, the girl accompanised by the "agua" and two of her friends comes, carrying a brass pot of water- the pot is covered with leaves. She takes three steps away from the boy and stands still. Then the argua tells the boy and the girl that, "both of you see each other well and if there is any shortcoming, then say so. If you agree, then give and take the brass pot." In certain areas, such types of questions are not asked, and the girl and the boy cannot reply due to extreme shyness. Only the giving and taking of the brass pot is accepted to be their approval. The girl gives the brass pot to the boy and the boy, after holding it, gives it back to the girl. This ritual is done thrice. The agua then takes the brass pot and keeps it in front of the assembled people as proof that the bride and the groom have accepted each other.

The girl's mother brings oil and water and comes out and washes and oils the feet of the guests. This is symbolic of welcoming the guests. Thereafter each guest is given a leaf bowl of water from the brass pot to drink. By drinking it, the assembled guests confirm the marriage arrangement from their side.

Before departing, the groom's party invites the bride's party. On a fixed date, the girl's party starts for the boy's house, and note the good signs on the way. If on the route some ominous sign is seen, then except for the agua, the rest of the party goes back. The agua goes to the boy's home and clarifies the whole matter and not getting Singbonga's approval, the proposal falls through, the matter ends there. And if everything is found to be alright, then the girl's party reaches the boy's home and at the door they are welcomed in the same manner as they had been welcomed in the girl's home. After the washing of feet and in between rounds of hadiya, the "jo arni" from the girl's side takes a leaf bowl of rice beer in his left hand and stands up. He addresses all the assembled people there in the traditional way and saluting them declares by rote "now for this boy and this girl, in the presence of Singbonga in heaven and the assembly on this earth, all the signs have been found to be favourable"- and he ends in this manner- "from the same bundle of straw, the father of the boy and the father of the girl should thatch two houses. May God keep these roofs always protected."

Which means that the family ties of the father of the boy and father of the girl be always strong and remain good. Such a declaration from the girl's side is made to finalise the marriage arrangement. After this declaration, giving expression to their approval, the rest of the people drink rice wine and eat rice, pulses and goat-meat (mutton) and whatever is prepared in their welcome, and wishing each other "johar" they depart.

During departure, the following facts are followed:

(1) The number of people who go to see the girl is an uneven number, namely 5, 7, 11 etc. and often it is seven or eleven. Apart from the boy and his father, some responsible and respectable people are in the group who can identify signs as being good or bad.

(2) The members of the boy's and girl's party go to each other's village on different dates but within one lunar month.

(3) Before departing, at the door, Singbonga who lives in the sky, is saluted through another ritual, and "coughing" and "sneezing" symbolic signs are challenged. While departing, all the members of the group come together and stand at the door. Then, lifting the eyes towards the sky, Singbonga is silently invoked and thereafter with bowed heads and folded hands He is saluted. The leader of the group, taking oil in a sal leaf bowl, says in this traditional manner :

"Singbonga is in heaven and the assembly is on the earth. Today we are going to establish a new connection (the boy's party takes the name of the boy, the girl's party takes the name of the girl)...bride/groom (for which we are going). If Singbonga did not leave our path open, then whoever wants to cough let him cough, whoever wants to sneeze, let him sneeze." (silence for some moments). "Now I am dipping the knuckle of my finger in the oil, whoever wants to cough may cough, whoever wants to sneeze may sneeze" (again silence for some time) "Now I am saying it for the third time, whoever wants to cough may cough, whoever wants to sneeze may sneeze."

When there is no sound of sneezing or coughing, then supposing that all the good signs are favourable, from then on the sacred time starts. For physical purity, the members of the departing group massage oil on their head, face and sometimes the whole body. In this way, at the sacred moment, after having purified themselves, the group departs for the good work to be done. No songs are sung on the way.

(4) Singbonga's approval is conveyed through various signs, the medium being the regional bongas. In the outer limits of every village there is a regional bonga. Hence before entering the village of the boy or girl and deciding upon the road to be taken, complete alertness is maintained. Any village falling in between does not affect in any manner. But if Singbonga does not want this marriage connection to be made, then anywhere He sends clear and serious bad omens, and the members of the party return from there, because then it becomes "hor bagdai jan or the path gets destroyed."

(5) Before the group starts on its journey, responsible young men are sent out in advance in order to do away with the obstacles in the route. This action is a later development of this custom because many good proposals fall through due to absence of good signs. This means that in order to fulfil one's desire, this is a precautionary human device. It should be considered to be wrong. But the pahans have interpreted this human endeavour in a different way. They say that this device is to wake up the bongas or to alert them. It is possible that at that time the bonga may be somewhere else, hence when a person goes in advance, the bonga is alerted and indicates the order of Singbonga through symbols. If no body is sent in advance of the group, then the regional bonga cannot be alerted and Singbonga's approval or disapproval will not be communicated. In the selection of groom and bride, Singbonga's decision is final. For this the boy and girl and family members are helpless. Singbonga's approval is compulsory.

After getting the approval of Singbonga through good signs, and the consent of the bride and the groom, the parties of the bride and groom arrange for a ritual called "varaksha" in which the bride price is decided and which is called "bala". This function confirms the coming together of both families by society.

Bala

Different names as per place and thinking are prevalent for this function. The basis of this ritual is to fix the value of the bride in which the bride's party through different signs demands cattle, clothes, money, etc. and the groom's party accepts some of the demands. Since special people come from both sides in this function and there is give and take in this meeting together, it is called "marang-kupul" or "marang-peda." Since this function is arranged for fixing the price of the bride, it is also called "go-ganang." The meaning of "ganang" means calculation or counting.

The bride's party invite not only close relatives to the function of "bala," they also invite their relations living in other villages. In this way, there gets collected a sizeable group at the door of the bride. Before departing, the girl's father offers hadiya to his ancestors in the ading and obtains blessings from them for the bride and the groom. After conducting worship in the ading, everybody departs for the groom's house, accompanied with musicians playing upon their instruments.

They are welcomed by the groom's party with hadiya-this is called "kata-lagar ili." This means that "your feet must have been cut/injured walking for such a long distance and you all must be very tired, hence please accept this rice wine." After feasting on pulses and rice, they rest for the whole day. "Varaksha" or brideprice fixing function starts the next day.

The next day, both sides sit facing each other but at such a distance that they may not hear or understand each other. The bride's party through different or certain signs sends its demand through the agua to the boy's party.

Signs

(1) They make two balls out of two leaves and tie them to a thin strip of bamboo shaped like a bow to indicate a couple of yoked bullocks. The balls of leaves are the two bullocks and the thin bamboo strip is the yoke.

(2) Rolling the leaves and piercing them by the bamboo strip and tying them to it and to sprinkle slush over them: meaning buffaloes which wade in slush and water.

(3) Open full leaves: As per number of clothes, and as per colour, sari.

(4) Small balls of clay: meaning coins.

In this way, one leaf plate is opened and as per capacity take up some leaves and small balls and the rest are returned. Meaning thereby, that whatever the groom's party has picked up from the plate, they are willing to provide the same, and the rest they are not capable. But why will the bride's party fix a lower value for their bride ? They again send the leaf plate through the agua to the groom's party and the groom's party discusses the matter and picks up something more while returning the rest. On this there is much of laughter and merriment. Everybody enjoys the fun in this game. The agua does not get fed up in running to and fro, rather he feels happy. In the end whatever the groom's party keeps back, it becomes responsible to fulfil it. As per capacity, the main items would be as follows :

(1) Koniya lija : a pair of saris for the bride.

(2) Tenja-Koda duti or sara duti : dhoti, clothes and some money for the younger brother of the bride.

(3) Inga-bage lija : dhoti, clothes, sari, etc. for the bride's mother.

(4) Jiya-ledra : "ledra" means torn and dirty clothes but for the old grandmother it means new clothes.

(5) Pashu-dhan : as per capacity, bullock, buffalo, cow etc. are given.

After "bala" is fixed, the ritual of washing the teeth is held in which the bride's party wash their teeth/clean their teeth and again partake of hadiya which is called "karkad ili." The mother of the groom sends water in a brass pot which the father sends to the father of the girl through the agua. The girl's father takes the brass pot in his hands and again returns it through the agua. The ritual of "udung" i.e. worshipping the he-goat has already been done. Now the agua lifts the brass pot above his head, presents the first he-goat as a gift to the bride's party which is called "bala-merom" ritual. In the same way the second he-goat is offered to the village assembly which is called "pancho merom" ritual.

One relative takes the groom on his back and comes out of the house and presents him for inspection before the bride's party. The intention of taking him on his back is that he may not touch anything impure on the ground. After mutual discussion, the groom is declared "good" and a turban is tied to his head and a bead necklace is put around his neck. In Munda society, tying the turban means that the person has been given new responsibility. We know that whenever a new village is established and a village chief or new Munda has to be appointed, then the Manki officially and as per rules ties a turban on the head of the Munda and in this way the Munda has to carry out the duties and responsibilities of his new post (Manki is the head of a few villages).

The meaning of tying a turban on the head of the groom is that his position has become higher and he has to take on the responsibility of his wife. In this way by tying the turban, the bride's party assimilates him among them. The relationship between these two families is declared by a representative of each village. The groom is once again brought behind the flaming torch before the bride and handed over to the father of the bride. It is examined in detail that all the rituals have been followed as per tradition and that there is no bar to the marriage. Representatives of both parties come forward and after having touched each other's feet, raise one hand and shake hands with the other hand quite vigorously. This ritual of shaking hands symbolises the firmness of the relationship in which it is said that whoever withdraws his hand first, his hand will be cut off.

Lagon-tol or Idi

Through this ritual the date of the marriage is fixed. The groom's father ties rice in a new cloth dipped in turmeric and takes it to the bride's house. The girl's mother comes out of the house and takes the bundle of rice on a leaf plate and puts it down on the ground. Again she bends over and touches the bundle with her fingers, kisses it, and takes it along with the leaf plate inside the house. In the meantime, that place is smeared with cow dung by other women and beside it they make a square with rice flour. On this an empty leaf plate is placed. The mother again brings the bundle of rice along with the leaf plate and places it on its earlier place. The bride comes and sits on the empty leaf plate. The father of the groom places some coins and betel nuts on the square. The rice bundle is opened and the rice is poured out on the leaf plate. The cloth is filled with twice the amount of rice and it is returned to the would-be father-in-law. At that time, the date of the marriage is announced. While fixing the date care is taken that on that day the groom or the bride was not born.

Sanketik Vivah

There is another procedure for fixing the marriage date. In this, the maternal uncle of the girl and the pahan of the boy's village take part. The other rituals are nearly the same. After the date of marriage is fixed, just three or five days prior to the marriage, a canopy is raised in the courtyard of the houses of the groom and bride, and certain symbols which stand for man-woman. Their marriage is carried out. The pahans say that this type of symbolic marriage does away with the present and future omens and troubles of the actual marriage. In this process, the following are arranged :

Mandola-dul

In the homes of the groom and bride, similar rituals are followed. In the courtyard, sal logs are planted on four corners and on them branches and leaves are put to make it into a canopy. In the centre of the mandap or canopy, a different thin and long log of sal alongwith bamboo is erected. Bhelwa branch and seker plant are tied to this thin log, and there a basil plant is planted. Encircling this central sal-log a platform is made of soil brought from a low-lying field at the confluence of two rivers- this platform is called "pindigi." The sal tree is for purity, the bamboo is for the coming generation, its expansion and protection, the bhelwa branch to act as a deterrent to black magic, the seker to act like a sheet anchor and for security, the basil plant for obtaining divine grace.

Kalsa galang

An elderly person of the house stands on the platform of the canopy facing the east. He stands in such a manner that the central log of the canopy comes between him and the house. He takes a utensil (like a pitcher) full of water and takes three branches of paddy and weaves them in such a manner that the ears of paddy on top and the stems below open upand spread out. He ties a woven ear of paddy on the neck of the pitcher and the second he ties to the slender neck of two tiles brought together. The third ear is tied to a small basket. He keeps all three in such a manner that the stems are below and the ears of paddy hang out on the top side. He covers the pitcher and the tiles and makes them go up and down. In this way the tiles and the pitcher get married. In this, the tiles represent the man and the pitcher the woman. The tiles, pitcher, small basket and an utensil of water are tied to the central log with a raw thread "adoa sootam," the tying up being five times or seven times. May it be known that this is the "adoa sootam" which becomes the vehicle of bonga or divine powers normally to come and go. An earthen lamp having four wicks for the four directions is placed on a pot and lit. the pahan offers sacrifice of a red cock and worships "khut-dahda," "desauli," "mua" and the regional bongas. Since the sacrifice is done near the fifth log in the centre of the canopy where the pitcher etc. are kept, and this log, bamboo etc. are thought to be life-trees because the tiles symbolising the husband and the pitcher symbolising the wife are tied, hence it is expected that the bongas who have been worshipped with a sacrifice will keep the future life of the husband and wife free from troubles, and full of happiness.

In this whole symbolic marriage, the mother's role is very important. She comes to the pitcher along with some of her relatives. She sprinkles water mixed with rice flour in three directions which purifies the whole atmosphere. Then she draws three lines with vermillion on the pitcher. In this way, the pitcher symbolising the wife is made to wear vermillion, and the symbolic marriage of the tiles along with the pitcher (boy and girl) is completed. With happiness the mother takes the pitcher on her head, another woman takes the tiles and still another takes the small basket, and dancing and singing they enter the house.

Cho

Before the groom's party leaves for the marriage, a day earlier, the mother and other women kiss the groom. The groom is made to sit beneath the canopy, wearing a dhoti dyed in turmeric. The mother takes rice and "doob" (a kind of green grass-agrostis linearis) and touches the feet, knees, shoulder and cheeks of the boy and thereafter kisses the rice and hands. As per Munda rituals, kissing gives forth a sound "chak" which is heard by everybody. In the same way, the kissing ritual is also observed in the girl's house. This ritual gives good wishes for future life to the bride and the groom.

Uli Adandi

When the groom departs from his house along with his marriage party, then on the route the marriage of mango trees has to be done. All the men in the party go forward on one side, while the mother and other women take the groom to that traditional mango tree near the house where the marriage worship takes place. After this the marriage party moves forward towards the girl's village. Women are also included in the groom's party. At this time musicians play music very loudly.

Daprom or Mangrapi

The agua stations the groom's party at a fixed place near the girl's house, where they have to wait for the bride's people to come and welcome them. This wait may be long also because at that time the programme of "uli adandi" is going on in the bride's house. In the bride's house, the function of "uli-adandi" is observed on the day of marriage.

The bride's party goes to meet the groom's party for "daprom" by holding a sickle on which cloth and oil have been put and made into a flaming torch. The music becomes very loud. Although all these activities are done in the daytime, the torch is lighted as a symbol. The pahans say that through the flaming torch the road leading to the bride's home is shown and in its light all the relations identify each other well. Whatever may be the intention, lighting a torch in the daytime is symbolic. There is another aim of lighting the torch which is that some army is advancing to stop the way of somebody. This is called "chekad." The torch bearer stops the groom and his party from advancing. At that time, the beats of the large drums (nagara) become very loud and a mock battle ensures, which is called "mangrapi, "It is to such an extent that the girls of the bride's party have a shoulder to shoulder battle dance with the girls who have come with the groom. It is possible that this arrangement may be harking back to those days when girls would be abducted and married.

The flaming torch has other usefulness. The sickle is made of iron and has serrated edge. The destructive bongas fear iron. This protects the person from the ill-effects of black-magic and evil eye. Marriage is the most important function because not only are two families connected but the future of the yet-to-come offsprings are also connected. Hence if any kind of destructive element takes the bride and the groom in its grip then the coming generations will also suffer. In these circumstances, all the preventive and protective measures are adopted so that no evil effects of black magic or the bongas may affect the bride and the groom. The flaming sickle (in the torch) is supposed to be most appropriate for meeting such challenges.

Da-hirchi and Chumman

When the groom enters the courtyard of the bride, the women meet him with a brass pot of water in which there is a mango twig, and a pestle in the hand. The women sprinkle water over the groom with the mango twig (its leaves) and showing the pestle to him, scold him jokingly in the traditional manner: "If you are greedy, if you are proved to be a thief, then you will be beaten like this (showing sign) with the pestle."[86] In this way "da-hirchi" ritual is completed and the ritual of kissing the groom is started. In a large metal plate, rice extracted from unboiled paddy (arwa), rice flour, and some small balls of cow dung, and an unleavened bread made of rice flour are kept.

Firstly, the bride's mother and thereafter one by one the other women carry out the kissing ritual. They take rice and "doob" grass in their hands and touch the groom's feet, knees, and finally his cheeks and thereafter they kiss their own knuckles holding the rice. This is repeated with the dung balls and the bread. The meaning of "Chuman" (Kissing) is that the groom is accepted by the women and to bless him and his bride for a happy future life and that they may have children.

Sasang-goso

"Sasang" means turmeric and mustard oil, and "goso" means massage or application. As per this ritual, the groom and bride are applied turmeric-oil. For this, in different places, there are chiefly two types of rules which are followed:

(a) As per the first rule, some women of the groom's party, which has been lodged in the "jalom" or the place where the bride's party has made arrangement for their stay, take turmeric and mustard oil and go to the bride's home and apply the turmeric and mustard oil on her. Before such an application, the bride's nails are clipped, and from the left ring finger a drop of blood is taken out and dropped on a cloth. This is called "sinais". While returning they take the groom along with them to the "jalom." The same ritual is followed with the groom. Women from the bride's party come to the "jalom." They clean the nails of the groom and take a drop of blood from his right ring finger into a cloth. The women apply turmeric and oil on him and then return.

(b) In some villages, there is another rule regarding the observation of the custom of "sasang-goso." The groom does not go back to the "jalom" from the bride's house. Instead, the spinsters of the bride's party, keep a vow on that day and complete "sasang-goso." One of them massages the groom with turmeric and oil and another girl does the same with the bride. This work is done in the shade of the canopy where the bride and the groom have to step on leaf plates or baskets (for every step) to reach the canopy. The "sasang goso" ritual is not repeated in the home of the groom.

Da-au

The marking with vermillion is the most important phase of marriage. With the completion of this ritual, the bride and the groom become wife and husband. The other rituals are not that important. With the application of vermillion, there is another connected religious ritual, which in some places is called "da-au" and in other places it is called "siri-darhi rakab." Meaning, bringing of sacred water and to cut the water "dai-mai." This water is brought in new pots (number of pots may be two or four) filled from the nearby stream mostly by unmarried girls. The water is brought to the house of the bride under the protection of sword and arrow. This water is cut by that sword and arrow, and later the bride and the groom have a bath with it.

Dul-da

The bathing ritual of the bride and the groom is called "dul-da." This is often done prior to the marking with vermillion ritual. But in some places, this is done after the vermillion marking. The pot in which the sacred water was brought and which was cut by the sword and arrow, is covered with a cloth which makes it fit to sit upon. The yoke is the symbol of marriage and the straw that of the thatched house. The saying about the symbol goes like this: "these two houses have been thatched with the same straw" meaning thereby that both families are now tied through the connection of marriage.

The bride and the groom are carried on the shoulders and made to sit on two yokes. The bride sits on the left side of the groom. Both have to go through the ritual of brushing their teeth with a twig and cleaning their tongue while seated. Thereafter they bathe and in the process they rub each other. In this bath, the unmarried girls help them. After taking their bath, the bride and groom embellish each other's hair. They cast off their wet clothes and put on marriage clothes dyed with turmeric which is called "sasang lija." Thereafter they go for the vermillion marking by placing each step on different leaf-plates upto the canopy.

In some places, "dul-da" takes place after the vermillion marking. After marriage, the bride and the groom as per procedure mentioned before, sit on the straw yoke and the girls of the house pour water on them from the four pots. In this way their bath becomes "dul-da" and the soil below becomes slushy. In this slush, the bride and the groom hide separate earthen ware cups which they sportingly search for. After that, they are again given turmeric dyed clothes to wear and they have to mark each other with vermillion.

Sinduri-rakab or sindoori tika

(a) After "dul-da," wearing "sasang lija" (turmeric dyed clothes) placing one-one step together on leaf plates, the bride and the groom reach the fifth log at the centre of the canopy; this fifth log is supposed to be the tree of life. For this marriage, sindur or vermillion is prepared in oil and kept from before. On the platform beneath the canopy, the bride stands facing the east and the groom stands in front of her facing the west. Thereafter the groom presses the big toe of the bride's right foot with the big toe of his left foot, and taking the oily vermillion from the leaf cup makes a straight line in the parting of her hair. On this occasion, in certain places, the younger brother of the bride, stands there with an unsheathed sword and addressing the groom tells him," "you are taking away my sister. Remember that if you ever abandon her I will kill you."

(b) In some places, "sinduri-rakab" is completed before "dul-da". In the centre of the canopy the groom and the bride are made to stand on the platform in the same way as mentioned in (a) above. The person who has to be marked with vermillion, always has to stand facing the east and the person who puts the vermillion, that person has to stand opposite and naturally his face will be towards the west. But in the ritual of marking with vermillion, there are two other rituals which precede it, namely, "sinais" and the second "varmala" or garlanding each other denoting acceptance.

According to "sinais" (that piece of cloth or handkerchief which had taken the drop of blood on it), the groom and the bride when they press each other's big toe then they, prior to that, touch the throat of the partner. This is done three times. After that the bride garlands the groom and the groom garlands the bride. After this the groom puts three lines of vermillion on his head, and then he puts vermillion in the parting of the hair of the bride and thrice he marks her head with vermillion. The bride marks her head thrice with vermillion and then marks the head of the groom thrice with vermillion. The dress of the bride and the groom are tied in a knot. Then the groom, with the bride behind, enters the house from the courtyard. After entering the house, the married couple is made to sit on a clean mattress and given curd, flattened rice and jaggery to eat.

Samdhi-Bhet : Milan

This function is held in the jalom, that is the place where the groom's party had been put up. The father of the groom or the guardian of the groom along with his relatives and influential men of his village remain seated there. The father or guardian of the bride come to meet them along with other relatives and accompanied with a pitcher of rice wine. The groom's party, too, keeps a pitcher of rice wine ready for these guests of the bride's side. A leaf cup of rice wine is taken, and the fathers of the bride and groom drink from the same cup. The same ritual is under gone by the mothers of the bride and groom. The other equivalent relatives also meet in the same way and holding each other's arms, they start dancing. They keep on dancing till they get tired. At the end, the mother of the groom and mother of the bride, and similarly the father of the groom and father of the bride take each other in their arms respectively in a tight embrace. This action is called "hayaroop johar." In this way, "samdhi-bhet" is completed and the girl's party returns.

Kata Anung

Before the bride is bade farewell, the bride and the groom wash the feet of the close relatives. One by one the relatives come and have their feet washed and for this honour they put some money on a nearby brass plate as blessing. When everybody's feet have been washed, then the bride and the groom come back to their place and sit.

Chumavan

In some areas the ritual of "chumavan" (Kissing) is done once again by close relatives and the village women. In this ritual, the newly wed couple is made to sit together in one place. They are encircled by the village women as well as their women relatives. Firstly, the mother brings a brass plate in which there are some rice grains and a lighted lamp. She touches the plate to the feet, knees, head of the bride, then taking it above her head she touches her right shoulder and then from the right shoulder, above the head to the left shoulder of the bride. This is done three times. Then she puts the metal plate down and taking some rice grains from it she repeats the touching ritual on the bride. Finally, she moves the rice above her head and throws them behind her, but these grains are caught by two unmarried girls who have spread a cloth from before to catch the rice grains. This ritual is also done three times. Then she puts her palm over the lighted lamp and thereafter touches the cheek of the bride and after that she kisses her own fingers. This ritual is also done three times.

After this, the aforementioned rituals are similarly conducted by the bride's mother on the groom and finally, after keeping some money on the plate, she steps aside, giving opportunity to other ladies to go through the same ritual. In this way, one by one, all the ladies present complete the chumavan (kissing) ritual and keeping some money on the brass plate they move aside for giving opportunity to others. This ritual is conducted by the bride's party and people of her village.

Baba-hartukam

This is an important part of marriage from the religious point of view. In this ritual, the bride bids farewell to her ancestors and bongas because she is going to leave them to connect herself with her husband's ancestors and bongas in his house. She is not taking away the productivity from her father's home because she is bidding farewell to her "baba-roa." She does not want that her in-laws may allege that she is a "ong-bonga" (bringer of bongas) because then very easily her family members will become victims of black magic.

For this ritual, the mother sits on the doorway of the house, and just in front of her the bride sits facing the same direction as the mother. Then the girl picks up paddy with both her hands from a winnowing fan and throws the paddy behind her head which her mother catches with one end of her sari. Three times the girl and her mother do this ritual. This ritual symbolises disconnecting the married girl from her mother, father, home, and home-deity and the bongas of the village.

Jimma

Now a social ritual of importance remains. This is called "Jimma-dena." In this ritual, the pahan or Munda of the girl's village hands over the married girl to her father-in-law in front of everybody, meaning thereby, that he hands over her responsibility saying that "from now onwards, the girl of this village has become your daughter-in-law. The responsibility of providing security, happiness and nourishment is now of the groom's party."

There are some activities in a marriage which are carried out by the friends of the bride and groom. At the time of bidding farewell, boys of the same age as that of the bride, catch hold of the bride and let her go only when some money is given to them. The groom gets the bride released in this way and makes her sit in the palanquin, and departs for his village.

The vehicle arrangement is as per financial position of the home, otherwise the bride's party reaches them on their shoulders till the periphery of the bride's village, and the groom's party reaches them from the boundary of the groom's village till the groom's home on their shoulders.

The Rituals Conducted in the Groom's Home after Marriage

The married couple is welcomed at the door of the groom's house by showing them a pestle. Then they are taken to the canopy where the kissing ritual (chumavan) is gone through. After that, the couple goes round the tree of life in the centre of the canopy. Again the ritual of vermillion marking is repeated.

The next day "dul da" (bathing with the water of the pitcher) ritual is undergone, and they plant a banana plant in the courtyard. According to Munda custom, the banana plant gives lots of fruit-it is very productive. This is done with the desire to have many children. A feast is arranged for the village people in which the pahan is also invited. The father, brother etc. of the bride also partake of this feast. They are entertained very well.

The groom, along with his bride, visits his in-laws within the marriage week or two weeks or at times one month later and uproots the sal, bhelwa, tulsi (basil) and bamboo etc. from the canopy. He also breaks up the platform which had been set up for the marriage. In this way, after cleaning up the marriage canopy, a feast is arranged in which the son-in-law who has come for the first time after marriage, is specially entertained.

According to Munda religion, Singbonga had motivated the first ancestors to behave like husband and wife due to which the Munda race could increase. In this way, from the point of view of religion, the aim of marriage is procreation because Singbonga is pleased with this. According to Munda religion, the following are the specialities of marriage:

(1) The couple comprising of husband-wife is fixed by Singbonga from before.

(2) The marriage should be in one's race but outside the "Kili."

(3) The marriage is fixed by the parties of the bride and groom after seeing signs of good and evil on their way. Singbonga's approval is contained in this.

(4) Marriage is not only the binding of two persons- it is the bonding of two families. The thatching of the two roofs from one bundle of straw is an indication of this.

(5) Marriage is not only of the individual and the family, it is the bonding of the villages of both sides. It is said that Singbonga and the council of the villagers are the witnesses to marriage.

(6) When the bride bids farewell to her father's home, she takes farewell of her ancestors and bongas of the village in a final manner because now her existence in her mother's home is over and she is connected to her husband's home.

(7) The purity of character has to be compulsorily maintained (a) physically and (b) in relationship. The warning against violating physical purity has been given in the marriage ritual of "da-ma" in which cutting the water with sword and arrow was done, and to maintain morality of relationship with other older men and women (1) calling elders by name (2) sitting with them on the same mat or cot (3) using the same comb for combing the hair (4) touching the clothes of elders etc. are prohibited. In this manner the honour of relationship and keeping a distance will negate the possibility of any immoral act.

(8) In the process of marriage, the ancestors, village, regional bongas, Singbonga, trees, river, streams, ponds, mountains, the whole of nature of the two parties are worshipped so that the future life of the couple would be without impediments, and happy.

In this way, in Munda religion, marriage and the aim of marriage is completely as per norms fixed by Singbonga. Singbonga has created human race for using the Creation and for the protection and nourishment of the race, He has made husband and wife. The central point of Munda religion is race, and marriage is a religious institution for the nourishment of the race.

Shav-sanskar or Dah Sanskar

"Ading" is the identity of a Munda home. "Ading" is that sacred place in a Munda's home where the ancestors live. "Shav-sanskar" or "ritual of the dead" has the aim of bringing the soul of the dead to the "ading" and handing it over to the ancestors so that the soul of the dead can meet the ancestors in the invisible world and be included in their clan. For this process, the following rituals are executed:

Raya

The dead body is wrapped in new cloth and put on a charpoy. Sometimes some coins are placed in the mouth of the body. Thereafter the charpoy along with the dead body is lifted and people start taking it to the cremation ground. The charpoy is put down on the ground at the outer limit of the village, then again it is taken up for proceeding towards the cremation ground, but before they proceed, some rice and mustard grains are put on the ground where the four legs of the charpoy had rested.

In the cremation ground, the funeral pyre has been kept ready. Along with the charpoy, three circumambulations of the pyre is made and thereafter the body is placed on the pyre with the feet towards the south. Then some logs of wood are placed on the body. A flaming torch of bael wood or bael branch is made in the form of scissors and placed on the mouth of the body. After the pyre has burnt out, some female relations of the dead pour water on the pyre. The pyre stands extinguished and the remnants of the dead are picked up and put in a clean cloth.

One person, who is a relation of the dead person, fashions a doll with "doob" grass. On the ground a symbolic figure is made with rice flour or parched rice on which this grass doll is placed facing the south. It is called "bo-kandru." On two peepal leaves, khichri (a preparation of rice and pulses boiled together) is placed and then the leaves along with the khichri are thrice moved from head to toe and back of the grass doll. At the end in a small pot the remnants of the body, the grass doll and the parched rice are put and the mouth of the pot is covered and tied with a cloth. This mud-pot is taken by the people who had come for the cremation and hung on a tree near the home of the dead person. Every body thereafter has a bath in the nearby pond, river or stream, and one person sprinkles water made holy by basil leaves on himself and the rest to purefy them.

Umbul-ader

Umbul is the shadow of the soul in Munda religion. Although Munda religion does not believe in an after-life of this physical body, but the soul is believed to be a body and it is also believed that it has a shadow. This shadow of the soul is called "umbul." Since, in Munda religion, the soul is supposed to have a body, therefore it needs food and water. A body also requires a place to live in. Through the ritual of "umbul ader" the shadow of the soul is given place in the "ading."

"Umbul-ader" is observed on the third, fifth, seventh or ninth day after cremation. If in the meantime some festival falls, then that very day or if the burial of the body took place on the first day of the bright moon, then on that very day the ritual of "umbul-ader" is completed. On the fixed date, the male members/ relations of the dead person assemble, shave their beards, clip their nails and bathe in the nearest pond and become pure. After bathing, the relations take tiril plants and reach that place where at the outer limits of the village the charpoy had been kept while proceeding towards the cremation ground. There three tiril plants are planted in such a manner that two of them bend and meeting each other they cut across and on that point the third tiril plant is planted which comes up. At the place of intersection, a thorn is tied, and on top of it a small earthen utensil called "divi" is hung upside down. The whole thing is covered by rice straw in such a manner that it looks like a house whose door opens towards the north. This small hut like structure is called "Kumba" in Munda language.

The male relatives who have come, sit near the door facing the south and in the worship, rice dyed in turmeric is offered to the "umbul." Thereafter the "kumba" is set on fire. When the "kumba" starts burning, then the dead person is called by name three times over and told, "Come and see your house is burning."

In some areas, a cock is killed on this occasion and its leg is thrown in the burning "Kumba" with the intention that a leg has to be given to the "umbul" so that it can come out of the blazing "Kumba." In some areas, both legs are tied with string and kept dangling. When they near the dead person's home, then the two dangling legs are put on the ground in such a manner that as if a man is walking on his feet. In the meantime, the women of the house prepare rice, pulses, chicken and vegetables and keep them in small leaf cups. They are arranged neatly and they are covered by a winnowing fan. On the floor ashes are sprinkled.

As soon as the sound of the ploughshare is heard in the house, the women of the house close the door from inside and become silent. It seems as if there is nobody in the house. Gradually, by degrees the sound of the ploughshare comes nearer, and coming close a man from the group knocks on the door. From inside upon questioning by the women, the men outside say in one voice "we have taken away sorrow from here and have brought happiness."

Then the door is opened. The brethren come inside. A person carrying a machiya (a small stool) goes and places it in the "ading." Gradually he comes out. He has faith that the soul of the dead person must have come and must have partaken of some of the food covered by the winnowing fan. The proof of his coming can be seen in the mark made in the ash and some part of the food, which is covered by the winnowing fan, being disturbed i.e. some of it going below and some of it coming above, or some food fallen on the ground. The person coming out of the ading inspects in great detail. If no such indication is there, then "umbul-ader" ritual is repeated. Finally an elder of the house enters the "ading" and worshipping the ancestors with rice wine, requests them thus, "The dead person can now come in your race," "Kili" and paternity of the ancestors. Since he is of your clan, therefore, keep him in your race."

After feasting, the ritual of "umbul-ader" ends. Which means, it is supposed that the soul of the dead person has been included in the company of the ancestors.

Jung-Topa

"Jung-topa" is the ritual of burying the bones in the village graveyard. Often, in a particular village the members of the same "Kili" or clan of the family live, and they have their own graveyard in the village." "Sasan" is that place where as per Munda religious custom, the dead persons belonging to the same clan have their bones interred. The meaning of clan is "kili" and people living in a village often belong to the same kili.

The ritual of "jung topa" in every village where for the past twelve months somebody has died, is completed in the midst of invited relatives. The date is fixed after the rabi crop in the month of Paush or magh (Paush= mid-December to mid-January, Magh=mid-January to mid-February). Every village fixes its own date as per convenience.

On the fixed date, the invited relatives bring rice, pulses, salt, tobacco and rice beer in profuse quantity to be given as gifts. Two to four relatives go to a nearby hillock where stone slabs are available and bring boulders of appropriate size. These boulders are brought in two tumbrels which are tied at the side and the boulders are reached to the graveyard. A pit is dug up in the graveyard wherein a funeral urn is kept. Along with the bones, rice, oil mixed with turmeric and some "kiske" are kept in the urn. After filling up the pit with soil, a large piece of flat stone is kept on top of it. The flat stone is buttressed by square pieces of stone on the four corners.

If the dead person was poor, or a small child, and if from before the flat stone had been erected in the graveyard due to death of the father or any other member of the family, then the funeral urn containing the dead person's or child's bones are interred below the flat stone. Otherwise, a new flat stone is set up for the dead person. On the new stone "baba-holong" or rice flour is sprinkled. The closest relative of the dead person, for example, if the husband has died then his widow, offers a few pieces of unleavened bread to the stone. In this way, she throws pieces of unleavened bread on the other flat stones in the graveyard. These stones are also smeared with oil. On the new stone, along with the besmearing with oil, three or five or seven lines are marked with vermillion. The old stones, after being smeared with oil, are marked thrice with vermillion.

After interring the bones in the graveyard, all the assembled people go and have a bath in the nearby pond, river or stream, and on their return, they participate in the programme of having a rice meal.

Roa

In the religious philosophy of the Mundas, the belief of "roa" is very important. According to religion, man is an assemblage of the following elements:

Man = body + roa (soul).

In Munda religion we have seen that when a Munda dreams, then he is alive but his soul goes out of the body and whatever the "roa" sees, hears, experiences, the dreaming Munda experiences the same way. Upon waking up, he narrates whatever his "roa" had seen. Among the Mundas questions have been asked on this score:-

Question: During dreaming when the "roa" goes out of the body and roams around, if immediately the dreamer is woken up, then what will be the position of the "roa."?

Answer: The speed of the "roa" is very fast. If immediately woken up, the "roa" rushes inside the body. But at times it happens that the person wakes up and the "roa" is unable to enter the body.

Question: After waking up, can the "roa" not enter the body again, or during sleeping hours at night?

Answer: When the "roa" goes out of the body of a person, then after awakening it cannot enter the body again. It keeps on hovering. Its power to enter the body is destroyed.

Question: What happens to the person? Without the "roa" he must be dying?

Answer: The person remains alive even without the "roa" because his "jee" (life) has not abandoned the body. The death of a body is connected with "jee" and not with the "roa". But a soul-less person cannot live for long.

In this way, the supposition about "roa" in Munda religion is special. Not only this, whosoever's "roa" it is, after death, it gets a place in the "ading" of the dead person's family, and, for the welfare of the family, it puts in all its efforts in the invisible world where Singbonga and other bongas have their existence. The Mundas believe that the "roa" is a link in the chain connecting the family to Singbonga and other bongas. Sometimes the nature of the "roa" is wicked and he brings trouble. This depends upon the circumstances of death. If a woman dies at child birth or before the ceremony of "chhatti" has been observed for the child, then her "roa" (soul) becomes a "chudail." If a person dies in an accident then the "roa" becomes "muamasanko." In this way, the unsatisfied "roa" hurts others. Actually, so long as it remains in the body, the "roa" is called "roa," and after death the "roa" becomes an inhabitant of the invisible world, and gets assimilated in the race of bongas. The race inhabiting the invisible world is that of the bongas. Hence the "roa," in the middle of its condition, after getting assimilated in the race, becomes a bonga. The bonga cannot again become a "roa" and neither can it get a body. Hence, the bonga does not have a rebirth. The bongas never die, and even though they do not have body, they require material goods. They feel hungry. Singbonga has laid down the rule regarding their appeasement.

The total hypothesis of Munda religion is race centric. The individual is for the family, the family is for the village or "parha," and the "parha" is for the race. Singbonga has made the Creation for the consumption of the Munda race. When the Asurs disbalanced the Creation's environment by smelting iron day and night in their furnaces, then for their destruction "Singbonga Raja baro vidiyan jan" "tero chhaymane jan" took action and in this way made the Creation and protected the Munda race. He made the Asur widows bongas, and gave them the responsibility of protecting the Creation. In this way, the bongas came into existence in Munda religion. After death, the soul of the person called "roa" in Munda language, becomes one with the ancestors in the invisible world and in this manner they come to be worshipped as bongako. Although the bongas are not physically visible to human beings, but according to Munda religion, they have physical needs, they feel hungry and thirsty, and the Mundas have to fulfil their needs through various offerings to these bongas. This is the order of Singbonga and for this He has arranged for pahan and devra in every village or parha. The pahan understands the signs sent by Singbonga and he interprets them for the understanding of the Mundas. He is a link in the chain between Munda race on one hand and the bongas and Singbonga on the other, and works as such.

The total arrangement pertaining to the race moves as per signs received from Singbonga. The husband-wife couple is predetermined by Singbonga. Nobody can break this bond or commit the crime of trying to break the bond. It is necessary to give birth to offsprings and for the offsprings to offer worship to their ancestors ("oda bongako") in the "ading." The regional bongas are connected to river, hill, tree, spring, boundary of a village, etc. all places. It is a part of daily life of Mundas to carry out their responsibilities pertaining to them. Singbonga has encircled the Munda race with a safety armour from all sides. The person who obeys the rules of the race, he stands protected by the protective armour, but whoever neglects the rules of the race, he finds himself to be outside the protective ring and becomes prone to accidents. Singbonga through His gigantic and splendid form protects the race, and in the form of "aaja" He gives love to the babies of the Mundas. He is very harsh yet He is also very much sympathetic and soft. The pahan in his prayer to Singbonga says that He is as steadfast as a rock where His plans are concerned. He is the storehouse of shining whiteness in His considerations; He is the virtual epitome of happiness and the figure of beauty. He is the gigant form of Creation and He is the highest father, He is "aaja" who is always alert towards the prosperity and welfare of His children. He is formless. Sometimes one imagines that He is the white haired old grand father, but there is no figure of Him anywhere. Pahan looks up at the sky and addressing Him sings in a loud voice.

References

1. S. C. Roy: "One or more bits of jungles were specifically reserved for village gods (Hatu Bongako) and called the Sarnas"- Mundas and their country, p. 63.
2. A. Van Exem: "The Sarna is the sacred grove of the Mundas. The word Sarna is nowadays often used to designate the ancestral religion of the Mundas." The Religious system of the Munda tribe, p. 23.
3. Dr. Satyendra Braj: Lok sahitya ka Adhhayan, p. 12, opinion quoted.
4. Dr. Satyendra Braj: "Lok Sahitya Ka Adhhayan, p. 07- the quoted opinion of Sofia Verna."
5. Dr. Wairear Alwynn: "Tribal Myths of Orissa, p. 15 (the opinion of Adbhut Teller in the introduction)."
6. Ranchi Gazetteer: "Captain Camac represented to the Provincial Council at Patna the importance of securing in our interest, the Raja of Chhotanagpur, whose country would form an effectual barrier to the incursions of the Marhatas, thus covering Behar and Beerbhoom, and the same time, giving us the command of the passes into Deccan, through which he stated that Mr. Law had retreated after defeat in Behar," p. 45.
7. The German padre Hoffmanne had been sent back to Germany, since he was a German, in 1914.
8. Hoffmanne : "under Khuntkati" Encyclopaedia Mundarica, p. 2392 under "Bonga" p. 614.
9. Father J. B. Hoffmanne; E.M. p. 247.
10. "How are we to live now ? How will we maintain ourselves? Tell us the means, tell us the means ? They are speaking in this manner, they are stating in this manner." – Excerpt taken from "Asur Avdaan."
11. "God the king, divine virgin are saying, are stating, we had sent messenger, we had sent message, you people did not accept, you people did not hear, you started saying, you people Stated "we are God, we are the big God." God the king, divine virgin, is pulling and throwing, is dislodging them and throwing them in rivers, brooks, ditches, in lakes, in Sarna, on hills, in the forest, in the meadows, they all fell down, they all sank. Those who fell on the hills became Burubonga, those who sank in the water, they became Ikir bonga (Spirit of the water), those who sank in marshes became Nage Aera, those who fell on the Sarna became Chandi-bonga." – Excerpt from "Asur Avdaan."

    (Note: The word "bonga" has been used in masculine gender. According to Munda religion, the soul is sexless, and since Singbonga has been imagined to be a male, therefore the other bongas are also believed to be male.)
12. For their worship, for their service, the pahan was appointed in the village and the sokha was appointed in the "dishum." – Excerpt taken from "Asur Avdaan."
13. Hoffmanne, E. M. Khuntkatti, p. 2392.
14. *Ibid.* Bonga, p. 614.

15. *Ibid*, "Ading Bongako"- "We find no trace of any thing like a real deification in the Mundari forms of ancestor worship." p. 38.
16. P. Ponet in his article "The Ethics of Mundas" Published in the Munda World, p. 121.
17. *Ibid*. "Hoffmanne too used the word "deity" though he firmly holds that the Mundas are monotheists." p. 121.
18. *Ibid.*
19. "Singbonga Raja" (King) word has been used many times in "Asur Avdaan."
20. See Asur Avdaan (in annexure).
21. S. C. Roy, Mu. Country, p. 268.
22. Schroedar, Encyclopaedia of Religion and Ethics, Part 7, pp. 217-18.
23. *Ibid*, p. 30 (a+b).
24. Keith, Religion and Philosophy of the Vedas and Upanishads, Part-I, p. 63.
25. Kumar Suesh, "Birsa Munda aur unka Andolan," p. 21.
26. P. Schmidt, quoted by A. Van Exem in his book, "The Religious System of the Munda tribe," p. 243.
27. E. M., p. 423.
28. E. M......"The victory of the sun cult over a religious system previously prevalent," p. 243.
29. (a) Macdonell: Vedic Mythology, p. 3.
    (b) Grierson : E. A. (1908) p. 253.
    (c) Keith : Religion and philosophy of the Vedas and Upanishads, p. 108
    (d) D. C. Sarkar, A. E. U. p. 431.
30. See Annexure II. Even now the Munda people avoid crushing or cutting the earthworm because in obedience to Singbonga's order, the earthworm had brought soil from below the ocean for creating the earth; it had given the soil to Singbonga who created the earth from it.
31. A. Van Exem, RSMT, p. 30 (Exem names the bird as "Giant Indian stork").
32. S. C. Roy, M. C. p. 328 (Ed. 1912) (names the bird as Swan).
33. The opinion expressed by S. C. Roy is expressed nearly same to same by the various Munda religious philosophers and pahans of Bundu, Tamar, Sonepur, Khunti, and Bargaon. They commented on the missionaries that in order to belittle the Munda race and purity they mentioned the stork (not the swan) which lays more than one egg.
34. E. M. p. 1861.
35. The Asurs had tortured the messenger birds very much. They had tortured them with hot ash, tongs, they had singed them with fire and made them ugly so much so that their white colour became black, brown-different colours and their tails became long, their heads flat etc. The messenger birds deformed in this manner became different from their own species of birds. God Singbonga, upon seeing the anguish of the messenger birds, made some more birds of the same appearance so that they might not be seen as outside their own species of birds. The Mundas believe that prior to rain of fire, all birds were of white colour.

36. "Singbonga Raja......atar tad gay doe"- from Asur Avdaan. (In traditional tales of the Mundas, "ekasi piri tirasi badi" has been mentioned which is believed to be the residence of the "lutkums." Since lutkums are the first parents of Mundas, hence their residential place is the place of origin of the Mundas. This place is connected with the destruction pageant of the Asurs, hence it should be located in Chhotanagpur, but in the geography of Chhotanagpur this place cannot be found. "Ekasi" and "tirasi" words are Hindi words. In Mundari the word "ekasi" is = upunhisi mid, and "tirasi is = upun his api. It is probably due to coming in contact with Hindus that the words "ekasi piri tirasi badi" have crept in.
37. The padres have collected "Asur Avdaan" in which they have said that the Asurs asked for advice from the Khasra Balak regarding the production of iron, and in accordance with his advice, they offered sacrifice to Singbonga, and thereafter they started hunting for a human being to give human sacrifice. Since they could not get a human being, the Khasra Balak offered himself for the sacrifice. "Then, here I am, sacrifice me, he told them- A. Van Exem, RSMT Pg.55 (followed on the next page.).
38. Contrary to this, from the songs related to "Sacrifice" and worship in the Asur Avdaan it is clear that the Asurs crossed brooks and rivers and went to devra, to sokha for finding out a device and they advised them to worship Singbonga and in the end told them to offer human sacrifice. Since they could not get a human being to offer as sacrifice, the Asurs eyed the Khasra Balak and they forcibly took away the Khasra Balak from the "lutkums." In the Asur Avdaan there is no indication that Khasra Balak volunteered himself for the human sacrifice.

    The following lines may be seen:

    > The boys of the Asurs, the children of the Asurs,
    > Did not accept anything, did not hear anything,
    > The Khasra Balak, your boy,
    > They dragged him away, snatched him away,
    > Twelve houses, twelve furnaces (where they were)
    > Asking him, discussing with him
    > How to worship this ? How to sacrifice this (boy).
    >
    > Asur Avdaan.

39. Menhas Odiya, Singbonga, p. 24.
40. Odiya: Mathura Ki Pustika, p. 231.
41. S. C. Roy, "Mundas and their country," p. 33.
42. A Van Exem, "In this myth, she appears as an anachronism; we shall see in the Asur legend that she only became a spirit when Singbonga withdrew from the world," R.S.M.T. p. 44.
43. Jagdish Trigunayak, "Munda Lok Kathayein," No: 10, "Butle Hatu," p. 35.
44. Menhas Odiya has made nearly a similar mention regarding taking away a dead body and burying it. See "Funeral Rites" pp. 726 and 727. Menhas Odiya has collected many religious narratives, religious duties and hymns connected with the Mundas in his manuscript titled "Mathura Kahani." This has been edited and typed by M. Topno in 1963.

45. Menhas Odiya's Manuscript mentions in "Funeral Rites."
46. "It is for their worship, it is for their service, the pahan was appointed in the village, the sokha was appointed in the tola (part of a village).- from "Asur Avadaan."
47. Described in "Asur Avdaan."
48. A. Van Exem, "One wonders there was ever such a time; before arrival of the British, convicted witches and wizards were beaten to death or hanged head down at a tree branch well above the ground, and a slow fire was lit below: they died a horrible death." R.S.M.P. p. 191.
49. S. C. Roy, "In times within living memory, people accused of witchcraft, but denying the charges have sometimes been beaten to death. Since establishment of the British Govt., however, matters have improved immensely and instances of such violence have become much less frequent." – M. C. p. 278.
50. Witch craft; an anti-system in Munda religion.
51. A. Van Exem, "Magic stands as the anti-system of religion" – R.S.T.M., p. 176.
52. This is a special kind of small drum in which one side is covered with the skin of a cow and on the other side it is covered with the skin of a he-goat.
53. E. M., p. 581.
54. As per Badangda (Singbonga's elder brother) religious story, the younger wife is a witch. She is caught by two sokhas Devgaon guru and Madhav Mantri and they try to make her understand that she should abandon this bad habit of hers. As a result, these sokhas imprison her in a cave. Thereafter Badangda captures the witch wife, who had turned into a black cat, in a basket and releases her in the water fall of the Karo river (this place is just below the now under construction Koel-Karo dam). There she becomes the bonga of "pairwa Ghag." The bongas of water are called Ikir bonga. "Pairwa Ghag" is an extremely wicked ikir bonga.

    According to a traditional folk tale, "Pairwa Ghag" Kills any girl who steps into its water or comes near its zone of influence and makes her his wife. This is an indication of the unsatisfaction of the witch. After acquiring the form of bonga, the witch's appearance changes from that of a woman to that of a man. The pairwa Ghag bonga asks for girls in the dreams of the people. The pahan of that place puts a vermillion mark on the girl right after their birth. The bonga thinking that the girl is already married, lets her go. – Jagdish Trigunayak, Munda Folk Tales, p. 24.
55. Room = Deep meditation or a condition of unconsciousness.
56. Dodeynam- worship by swaying. As per this procedure, if the stone pestle moves forward and backward, it is indicative of "yes," and if it does not move, then it is indicative of "no."
57. "Netlang Singbonga, Daivi Raja, Tolekam Turtan, Dailekam Hasurtan"- from hymn to Singbonga.
58. "Ne chauli-jang-Kudi-Jang, hid- Nam- doure-namok" chauli jang= grain of rice, kudi-jang= broken grain (when paddy is reaped, some rice grains break), doure swaying, moving.
59. Mode= dandimente= equal to thickness of silk threads.

60. A. Van Exem, "Much may be made of the fact that a pahan uses the names "Mahadeo" and "Parvati" even in his sacrificial prayer." – R. S. M. T. p. 199.

61. Kumar Suresh Singh, "Birsa Munda aur unka Andolan," p. 14.

62. S. C. Roy, ".... Animal sacrifices are offered by these Hinduised Mundas to the "Lord of Asiatics" (Mahadeo) M.C. p. 169.

63. A. Van Exem, "Thus, if the Pahan accepts these Hindu names, he gives them a content which is not found among the Hindus, nor even in the witch craft myths." R.S.M.T. p. 199.

64. Hoffmanne- E. M. p. 3061.

65. The Pahans of Khunti Area believe that the ignorance of the person and the bad effect happening due to that person have no connection. It is clear that due to that person the bad effect happened. The person whose look or confrontation results in bad effect, that person must be having jealousy in a hidden way in him (otherwise the bad effect would not have come about). This jealousy is actually hidden in the soul. It is not necessary that this jealousy will be found only in "hambul roa," the light "roa" may also have jealousy. In a practical way, if effortlessly the bad effect falls, there is harm, or some trouble comes, then it is definite that there is jealousy. It is not important whether the "roa" (soul) is heavy or light- the inherent jealousy is the decisive factor although being unaware of it, the person's look releases bad effect on the target.

66. (a) This procedure in the Munda world means that he shot the other person with magic.

    (b) and the person who is shot with magic meaning the dart of the evil eye, meaning the person who is made the target, it is called "bane tokan."

67. In some areas it is also famous as "Soso-para."

68. In a different functional procedure of sosotapa, within the white boundary, the whole house and its environment is imagined, and since white is the colour of Singbonga, hence the devra says that Singbonga has encircled the whole house from all four directions and hereafter no evil eye will have any effect on this house. Due to different locations there are certain differences to be seen in the ritual of soso- tapa.

    (1) He shot with a hen's egg
    Which was shining and resplendent
    He shot, and he shot with light
    The shot hit the target, the light went
    And settled on the iron marble,
    The iron marble broke, the light broke,
    The boys of the Asurs, the Asur Children
    They are crying, they are wailing. –from Asur Avdaan.

55. This is called "inda-gidi" ritual. After a religious duty is performed, the throwing away of the remnants in the form of signs/ symbols, is called "inda-gidi" ritual.

56. Paush month is the English month of January. The people of Hasda village observe this festival in the month of December, and the inhabitants of Naguri area observe it in January.

57. "Howwa" songs are full of obsecenities.
58. Since the Mundas count their months and fortnights with the new moon, and not the full moon, therefore the Phalgun month of Mundas is over by the time only half has been crossed of that month in the Hindu calendar. In this way, the Mundas as per their calculation celebrate Phagu festival on the first day of Chaitra. In Bundu and Tamar areas, the Mundas observe Holi as per Hindu calculation.
59. "Idale Vrikash"- The silk tree.
60. No firewood or "Sauri" is taken from that house wherein lives a pregnant woman. Such houses are believed to be impure because in that house there is a living creature which is outside the Munda race. That creature is the child growing in the womb. So long as the ceremony of chhatti is not observed after birth, the child is supposed to be outside the Munda race.
61. The deity presiding over the sacred Sarna,
Come with us to follow the hunt,
Papra Chandi, the deity of the grove,
Increasing the honour of the hunting group,
They roam around with the village huntsmen.
For us, the deity of "madkam" (Sarna) is superior
His arrow must fall on the animals (hunted)
In this sport of hunting.
Papra Chandi sends us the gift of rain
Due to which we have good paddy crops.
And now see the "Madkam jaier"
He kills the nimble rabbit
And takes away his trophy with pleasure,
And in the forest, Papra Chandi
Shoots an arrow at the peacock
And enjoys the sport of hunting.
62. (a) The Mundas keep separate axes for hunting and for felling trees. Religion forbids the felling of trees with the hunting axe, but in this ceremony, the knots of the red silk cotton tree are supposed to be heads of deer, hence to use the hunting axe for this purpose is as per religion.
(b) Since the red silk cotton tree remains moist, therefore it does not totally burn with grass, leaves, straw etc. Like the castor plant, efforts are not made to burn it.
63. It is believed that with more hunting, a Munda's luck would be good that year.
64. Jagdish Trigunayat, Munda Lok Kathayein, p. 98.
65. Munda Lok Kathayein, p. 54.
66. ....Munda Lok Kathayein, p. 106.
67. S. C. Roy, Munda Country, p. 273.
68. Jagdish Trigunayat, Munda Lok Kathayein, p. 54.
69. This grass is called "Sauri" with which the Mundas thatch their roofs.

70. S. C. Roy, 'Mundas and their country," p. 274.
71. Van Exem, R.S.M.T. p. 158.
72. "It is for their worship, for their service,
    The village appointed a pahan,
    The tola (part of a village) appointed a sokha."- from Asur Avdaan
73. The word "Kili" is nearly akin to the Sanskrit word "Kul." Compared to "gotra," Kul is limited to certain families whose place of habitation is limited. In Munda society, kili is akin to gotra.

    Totem – sign/symbol does not completely express totem. Totem is a sign, symbol and in some places it is used as a title.
74. (a) See the book of P.N.J. Purti- "Kursina odo kiliko"- Publishers Adivasi Sahitya Prachar Samiti, Jamshedpur, 1972.

    (b) See Jagdish Trigunayat "Munda Lok Kathayein" for race- gotra, pp. 44-97.
75. S. C. Roy, "Mundas and their Country," p. 332.
76. Ranchi Gazetteer (1970), p. 41.

    S. C. Roy, Mundas- Country, p. 334-there were seven forts :

    (i) Lohar Garh (ii) Hazarigarh (iii) Palamau garh (iv) Manu garh (v) Singha Garh (vi) Kesal garh, and (vii) Surgus garh.
77. The 21 parganas were : (1) Omedanda (2)Doesa (3) Khukhra (4) Sarguja (5) Jaspur (6) Ganguapur (7) Porhat (8) Jiranga (9) Visua (10) Lachra (11) Virua (12) Sonepur (13) Baelkhanr (14) Baelsing (15) Tamar (16) Sohardih (17) Kharsang (18) Udaipur (19) Bonai (20) Kauriya and (21) Chang Bhankar.
78. M. C. p. 232.
79. J. Deeney, S. J. Comparison of the Munda and Ho Language in the Munda world.
80. Jagdish Trigunayat: "It comes in that story of Rohtasgarh when Risa Munda divided them into seven groups for earning separate livelihoods. It appears that in the beginning there were seven or similarly less number of gotras."- Munda Lok Kathayein, p. 73.
81. See- P. N. J. Purti's book "Kursinama Odo Kiliki in horo honkowa."
82. If the infant dies prior to the ceremony of chhati, then it does not get a place with the ancestors in the ading because till that time the infant had not been included in the Munda race- M. Topno, Anthropos, Part 50 (1955) p. 729.
83. The custom of "Joarni" is prevalent in Munda society. This person is a Munda of certain position who carries out his responsibility of giving blessings and good wishes in front of everybody. In marriage ceremonies or other sacred occasions the role of the "joarni" can be seen.
84. There is a folk tale prevalent in Munda tribe about Perwa Ghagrein Bonga (see Munda Lok Kathayein p. 23). As per this tale, the Pairwa Ghag spirit whisks away unmarried girls and marries them. Hence the Mundas put vermillion mark on girls as soon as they are born so that the spirit leaves those girls alone, thinking them to be married. The question arises as to what kind of spirit this is that it cannot understand the cleverness of the Mundas. It appears that this custom and child marriage had started during the time of Greek (Yavan) invasion for the

protection of the girl child.

85. The Munda women are forbidden to thatch the tiles overhead. Although they may touch the semicylindrical tiles but to stand on the roof those tiles might be touched by their feet. Probably keeping this view in mind, the Munda women have been forbidden to go up on the roof for thatching purposes because in the symbolic marriage the semi cylindrical tile has been given the status of husband.
86. If you become greedy, if you are proved to be a thief then you will be crushed/ beaten like this (with sign) with the pestle.

Chapter - 4

Oraon Religion: Sarna Religion

The Oraon tribe is the other important tribe permanently settled in the forested and plateau region of Chhotanagpur. Prior to them, the Munda tribe, also known as Kol, after being defeated in Rohtasgarh, roamed around in search of "sona lakum disum" and crossed the Saharghatiya pass of Lohardagga.[1] They reached that region where the Asur tribe used to stay; the Asur tribe used to smelt iron. The Mundas defeated the Asurs and pushed them towards the north-west hills of Ranchi, while they themselves cleared the forest and settled down. When the Mundas had settled in the west of Chhotanagpur, about 2-3 centuries later, another tribe called Oraon left Rohtasgarh after their defeat, and began searching for a safe and secure place in the same circumstances as Mundas had faced. They crossed the River Sone and entered Chhotanagpur in the west in similar circumstances as the Mundas had entered Chhotanagpur. The Oraons had to confront the Mundas. Compared to the Oraons, the Mundas were much too backward in technical knowledge, implements and cultivation. Resultantly, the Mundas had to flee to the east and south-east direction. The Oraons settled in the place vacated by the Mundas, and they expanded sufficiently both in terms of population and settling down after clearing the forests.

They call themselves "Kurukh" but this tribe is officially recognised in Govt. records/ work as "Oraon." In the word "Kurukh" is interwoven the proud history of the Oraon tribe. The descendants of Raja Kurukh (Karash) and the blood relations of the Kannada speaking people of the ancient kingdom of Pandya of Korkai, this Kurukh tribe when it entered Chhotanagpur area, then they started using metal utensils, implements and ploughshare due to coming in contact with the Aryans. From the banks of the River Narmada to Rohtasgarh-it was a long travel taking centuries, and during this time, this tribe had passed the stage of existing on tubers, fruits, flowers and hunting life, and had started giving more importance to animal husbandry and cattle wealth. This condition prevailed during their travel towards Rohtasgarh because it was not in their social nature to stick to one place and adopt agriculture. In the traditional folk tales of the Oraons, there has been mention of a king who, upon being pleased with the honesty of an Oraon woman, wanted to give her five villages as a reward, but she, instead of taking villages, gave more importance to cattle wealth because at that time the social condition had not reached the stage of agricultural life. Very cunningly she took a promise from the king that on the new moon night of "Sohrai," lamp would be lit only in her cattle-pen. That happened. After the cattle worship in Sohrai, as soon as dusk came and every where darkness started falling, all the nearby cattle entered her cattle-pen because it was the only place where there was light, and her cattle pen became full of cows, buffaloes, and goats. Since the cattle had come voluntarily in the pen belonging to that woman, therefore the woman became their owner and she became rich.[2] This folk tale throws light on the "pastoral" existence of the Oraon tribe which was prevailing after they left the banks of the River Narmada. By the time they came to Rohtasgarh the Oraon tribe had become expert agriculturists.[3]

During the hundreds of years of travel from the banks of the Narmada to Rohtasgarh, the Oraons not only learnt progressive procedure of cultivation, they also adopted in their lives the dietary habits, customs and beliefs which were influenced by Aryan contact. The incidents of Rohtasgarh[4] prove the fact that the Oraons used to celebrate "Sarhul" festival and in a rollicking lifestyle used to heavily drink hadiya, sing and dance. The women too were not behind the men- if occasion demanded, they would face their enemies with vigour. They would don men's clothes and knew how to shoot arrows.

After being defeated at Rohtasgarh, the Oraons in the process reached Chhotanagpur and they confronted the Mundas there. The life style of the Oraons had been affected by the prevalent customs, beliefs and social arrangement of Munda society, and the Oraons had also affected to a great extent the Munda life-style. Cultural exchange, religious faith, believing the "sun" to be supreme god in the form of Singbonga or Dharmes, hypothesis regarding the regional gods being nearly the same and public life being affected by superstition and black magic and many other similarities-due to these reasons, the Hindus who came from outside to settle there, found it difficult to differentiate the two races, so the Hindus believed the Oraons to be "kol" just like the Mundas. Similar to the Munda race, the Oraon people worship "Chala Pachcho" or "Sarna burhi" in the holy Sarna place beneath the shade of a sal tree. On every religious occasion, festival and custom, they give religious importance to the sal tree and its branches. Clearly, the religious duties of the Oraons are connected with the Sarna place, hence this tribe known by the name of "Kurukh"- its religion is notified as "Sarna religion" although there are many basic and structural differences in the "Sarna" religion of the Mundas and in the "Sarna" religion of the Oraons.

Sarna Religion : Kurukh Religion

After defining religion and analysing it, we come to the conclusion that every religion has certain specialities which express the character of that particular religion and on the basis of which the religion gets an identity. In the process of clearing the forests of Chhotanagpur to make a place for settlement and to make cultivable land, the Oraons had left some trees undisturbed and protected because the goddess "Chala-pachcho" prevalent among the Oraon folk, lives on them and protects the village. Since sal trees are found in abundance in Chhotanagpur, and the sal tree is connected deeply with the economic, social and religious life of the primitive tribal society living in that area, therefore, sal trees are said to be the residing place of "Chala Pachcho"- it is a very simple faith-related development, and the place connected with it is the holy place of worship. "Chala pachcho" who resides on the sal trees is mainly worshipped as "Sarna-burhi" by the Oraons and along with the sal tree that place known as "Sarna place"[5] is believed to be sacred, and is the centre of many religious arrangements and religious duties. In this way, the faith, belief and religious customs and duties connected with Sarna place come within "Sarna" religion. The religion of the Kurukhs is "Sarna religion."

The centuries old Sarna religion, to whichever sacred Sarna place it is connected to in every village, there at present may not be the sal trees and neither their signs, but the sacredness of the place and the faith of the Oraons towards that place still remains along with its own inherent sanctity. On special festivals or occasions, the worship of Dharmes and the sacrificial offering of a white cock, are offered at the Sarna place amid the Oraons of the village. On these occasions, the village pahan takes the lead role in performance of all religious rituals. The same place has played a very important role in strengthening the racial unity and community life of the Oraons. Kurukh religion which is definitely racial or limited to tribal feelings, has been very useful in threading Oraon society together. The social responsibility of the Oraons and their being dutiful are totally connected to their religious sincerity. Religion prevents a person to act against his race or to indulge in anti-social work. In the Oraon tribe, religion acts as a powerful controller. What is correct, what is wrong, the decision is completely based on tribal tradition. They have their own social values. It is not necessary that their social values would be equivalent to the values of other developed and conscious societies. Their conscience is the capitalised strength of tribal beliefs. This is the reason that while some progressive societies term superstition to be totally unscientific, as per tribal parameters, they are not only believable, true and socially proved, but that outside them one cannot imagine tribal life. The mentality of Oraons has developed in its own way.

The supreme God of the Oraons is Dharmes. He is also called "Biri-Belas" or sun-god. In Oraon religion there are some superior and some inferior category of gods, the influence of benevolent ancestors is there, destructive souls are there and in addition there are evil spirits bringing pain, misery etc. which influence Oraon life. The gods and goddesses are imagined to be formless. But sometimes a figure is imagined of certain gods and goddesses who have made a deep ingress in Oraon life. For example, the chief village goddess "Chala Pachcho" or "Sarna Burhiya" has been imagined to be of an old woman whose hair is knotted and white as jute. But this imagination of the Oraons cannot be found in such a form. This form is to be found only in the minds of the Oraons and is passed on from generation to generation. Some gods and goddesses are able to change their forms, and, if need be, as per their desire, they can take on the form of an animal. Chandi, the goddess of hunting and war, very often can be seen in the form of animals. In Oraon religion, the numbers of gods- goddesses and souls of the dead are so much that their qualities and knowledge of character are identified with that group whose members they are. Every such group has a special kind of character for which it is famous or notorious. It is according to their character that in the minds of the Oraons a form is imagined. In this way, as per the qualities of the gods and goddesses, imagination, regarding their character and, according to that imagination regarding their form come into the minds of the Oraons. But nowhere can be found any form in the physical sense.

Although Oraon life is influenced by gods and goddesses, natural, pain giving powers of evil spirits, ancestors, souls of the dead and other mysterious powers, but like the Mundas, the Oraons do not think any natural incident and happiness and sorrow of life to be completely given by God or these powers or done by these powers. They also believe in human disposition to act. The Oraon race mainly famous by the name of "Dhangar" has through its labour and activeness carved a prominent place for itself among the tribals.[6] Successful agriculture and for a good crop the favourable grace of divine powers, timely rains by Sarna burhi and invoking the invisible powers for the protection of agriculture and their worship and also to get the desired fruits, the Oraons depend upon their labour also.[7] The activeness of the Oraons and their initiative have influenced their religious beliefs to a certain extent. In this context the influence of the contact with the Aryans cannot be denied. In the nascent stage, the role of the invisible powers specially ghosts, the role of spirits was always frightening and destructive, and their character gradually began to be seen as benevolent. (This fact has also been confirmed by S. C. Roy).[8] Actually, worship and sacrifice of cock or he-goat and offering it have made some spirits to acquire a "benevolent character" which had been notorious for their destructive nature. This was the psychological influence of worship which had overshadowed the Oraon mind and head. But despite being influenced by invisible powers, the initiative, the ability to do labour and industrious nature of the Oraons were maintained even during troubles and disasters.

The Oraon tribe had successfully preserved an immense store-house of knowledge and wisdom based on centuries of experience which they passed on from generation to generation. The knowledge about ferocious beasts of the forest and their behaviour, the usefulness of big trees, the properties of various roots and herbs, leaves and bark and their usefulness in human life, general knowledge regarding the speed of celestial bodies and their relationship with change of seasons, the kinds of soil, fertility of the soil and balancing agriculture according to seasons etc., and in various seasons the relationship/ connection to be established with river, hill, pond, small and big animals, hunting, food and drink, the Oraons had gradually learnt them all through generations. It was their experience which used to tell them in what kind of soil, in which season, what kind of cultivation would be useful and successful. And in this way they would try to have good agriculture and other accomplishments successfully through their industrious nature and knowledge gathered from generations. This knowledge can be called fundamental scientific knowledge. But in this expected effort whenever any unexpected incident happened, the answer to which was not available to their knowledge gathered from generations, then their mind would try to search the reason for such unexpected incidents in the mysterious powers which are to be found in the worlds of religion and magic and spells. The Oraons had to find out a way as per the reason, and according to the way out they had to devise means which meant worship, incantations, the offering of sacrifice etc., so that those invisible powers which brought on the disasters and troubles could be appeased.

In this way, when the actually acquired knowledge of the Oraon became helpless, then the Oraon had to take recourse to various ways of magic and spells, or religious rituals, or both. In special circumstances, the probability of unexpected disasters also forced the mind of the Oraon to adopt caution. Before going out for a hunt, before starting for a far-off forest road, before any such effort in which sudden mortal incidents might occur, the Oraon while starting would appease the gods and goddesses of that area and the world, and the souls of the dead, and he would pray to them for his protection and their grace. This is a cautious way of saving oneself which the Oraon now gets in religious rituals and devices of magic and spells.

The main element in the religion of the Oraon tribe, which is also found in other primitive tribes is a fearful respect of mysterious invisible powers, faith and trust in them, proffering them sacrificial worship, prayers and surrender. In order to escape the unkindness, wrath and misbehaviour of these invisible powers, the Oraon at first worships and prays to them and satisfies them, then again on different occasions also he worships them so that they would be kind enough to give him good crops, increase his cattle wealth, and keep him and his family in good health.

In Oraon religion, the rooting of invisible powers in immovable, inert matter is a pointer to the idea of inert matter having life, prevalent among primitive religions. The idea of immovable, inert matter having a self is that part of the nascent religious philosophy according to which a person thinks an inert matter to be having life and believes that it is the residing place of a living soul. But Oraon religion's form appears to be more special. Actually, the belief of the Oraons in invisible powers is so strong that Oraon religion viewed from the primitive, unclear feeling regarding inert matter having life and its background, it would be appropriate to view it as effect of the divine. Because as per belief of the Oraon, the existence of the soul or life or spirit is separate from the body or matter where it dwells. The Oraon believes in such an invisible life power which in addition to a living person also lives in things or matter, and exhibits its influence in the form of nature's power. Not only the sal tree, hillock, swamp, pond, clump of bamboos, a huge stone boulder lying inert on the ground, but similar many inert matters are there in which Oraons believe that powers reside. They have their own living force due to which they influence the nearby atmosphere easily and at times the sport of invisible powers can also be seen in them.

The prevailing "black magic" in Oraon society is to a great extent based on the thought of the Oraons that inert matter has a soul, so much so that even in a small piece of matter or stone, with the strength of black magic, a destructive soul is made to sit and, in the house targeted for torture, that matter in which the destructive soul is sitting is made to enter that house any how. Thereafter, the evil spirit sitting in that matter starts troubling the members of that family as soon as an opportune moment arises. This black magic is an anti-religious system, and an equivalent parallel or more powerful god or goddess or invisible powers are invited to nullify the bad effects of this black magic. This work is mostly done by ojha, sokha, mati etc. who have been initiated and trained completely in their own tradition.

The form of Oraon religion is open whereas the rule of procedure of black magic is very secretive. The worship and prayer is conducted in the Sarna place of the village or near the cultural centre or some other public place. The rules of procedure of worship and prayer are totally shouldered by the village pahan. The Oraons of the village assemble at the place of worship in the village. Worship and prayer are mostly done publicly and in front of the community.

According to the religious belief of the Oraons, a large number[9] of gods, goddesses, and souls of the dead affect the lives of the Oraons. The pahan of the village worships and offers sacrifice to the main gods and goddesses, Chala-Pachcho, Darha, Desauli etc. along with all the souls of the dead. The gods and goddesses of the village and the souls residing in the "Khunt" are worshipped generally as a preventive measure to protect the villagers, agriculture, cattle etc. from probable disasters although in this effort the welfare of the village, good crop and prayer for other prosperity are inherent in it. Hence, in Oraon religion, from the viewpoint of worship, offerings and benevolent feeling, many gods, goddesses and certain souls of the dead are included.

Actually, from prior to birth till after death, Oraon life is tied to many religious beliefs, religious influences, religious duties and rules and customs. They are all factors of Oraon religion. Apart from gods and goddesses, the various ceremonies observed by the Oraons, the arrangement of kili, festivals, and the arrangement of traditional worship and prayer on different occasions etc. are the main subjects of Oraon religion. The ingress of black magic in tribal life is very deep. In order to make sorcery effective, certain gods and goddesses and souls are invoked and meditated upon, and the witch or the practitioners of black magic please them through their worship and make them do their work as per their desire. In order to nullify the destructive and deadly effects of black magic, in the village society the institution of ojha, sokha, mati, etc. has developed. These practitioners meditate upon and worship the prevalent gods and goddesses of Oraon religion in which there has been an easy admixture of Hindu deities, and at some places worship the power of Mahadeo in form and nullify the effects of black magic. Study has been made within Munda religion regarding the anti-religious system to nullify it. In Oraon religion this study is desirable. Although in these activities there is no role of the village pahan, but in other religious duties the presence of the pahan is not only necessary, without his directions no religious function can be held. The pahan is virtually the centre point of all the activities of Oraon religion.

Pahan and his Assistant

In the rural organisation of the Oraons, the pahan and mahto are two important post holders or functionaries. The pahan is the head of religious activities while the mahto is more like the village mukhiya who looks after judicial and social arrangements.The post of mahto was developed later on by the society. In the primary stage of development of society, all the responsibilities of the village used to be shouldered by the pahan. He used to devise means to maintain racial arrangement, and peace and happiness in the village. Along with religion, he was also the head of 'judiciary'. With the increase in population and the expansion of the village, except for the religious duties, all other responsibilities of the pahan got gradually transferred to the mahto. The pahan and the mahto both have a special place as "Bhuinhars" as well as respect in Oraon society, "Bhuinhar" is the name of that clan which had originally cleared the forest and created land fit for agriculture. In this way, the whole land which some family or people of "khut" had cleared is called Bhuinhari land and those who cleared that land, they have ownership of that land. Since, according to Oraon belief, it is necessary to appease the soul which used to stay in that portion of the forest and due to its clearing has become angry and shelterless, the people of the khut who had cleared the forest, offer special worship to that soul and give offerings to it. This regional "nad" or soul is known as the "khut-nad" of that khut. In this way, the khut nad comes in the category of ancestors. The village pahan is a member of that khut.

From the point of view of racial levels, Bhuinhar[10] or khutkattidar are placed at the highest level of the ladder of Oraon society. It is only a bhuinhar who can be appointed as pahan or his assistant. The Oraons of the other levels do not get this respect. There is another reason-the position of pahan being equivalent to the divine. The Oraons place the pahan on the same worshipful pedestal as Dharmes or sungod. On many occasions, the pahan's feet are washed and blessings are obtained from him. The most important festival of the Oraons is Sarhul. During the completion of Sarhul festival, on that occasion, a marriage between the "Pahan" and "Pahnain" (wife of Pahan) is organised in an Oraon village. This is a symbolic marriage of the sun with the Earth. The Oraons are mainly cultivators and for a good crop they are always putting in efforts. The marriage of the sun with the Earth is done for increasing the fertility of the Earth. In this way, the post of pahan becomes equivalent to the divine on many occasions in Oraon religion.

Assistant

The chief assistant of the pahan is called "Pujar". He makes full arrangements for worship. It is his responsibility to supply pure water for various kinds of work, hence he is also called "Panbhara." In some villages the pahan's assistant is also called "tahloo." Apart from this assistant, in some villages there is another assistant of the pahan who is called "susari." After the conduct of worship and proffering of sacrifice, the food is cooked in the form of blessed food and the responsibility to maintain purity and efficiency while cooking is given to the "susari." There are a few villages in which there is an assistant of the pahan called "Murgi pakowa" (the cook of cocks) or "Murgi jholwa." Due to different places the assistant of the pahan is called by various names, but normally pujar, panbhara, tahloo, Susari or Murgi pakowa are the various names of the same post. His duty is to help the pahan during worship and other similar occasions.

The social prestige and religious importance of the assistant is in ratio to that of the pahan. From the view point of clan and class, these assistants are equivalent to the pahan. They are also connected to such a khut which is "bhuinhar" and they also get all the land related facilities just like the pahan. The rent-free land given to them are called pujar or panbhara khet[11] (field) the same way the "pahnai" field is given to the Pahan. In some villages the post of pahan is hereditary whereas in some villages the term of this post is for three years after which another pahan is selected. The divine directed procedure adopted for selection of pahan, is also adopted for the selection of pujar or panbhara etc. for three years. In this manner, despite being an assistant to the pahan the pujar, panbhara, tahloo etc. in ratio to the pahan get nearly all the importance and facilities which a pahan gets in Oraon religion and society.

The Selection of Pahan and Assistant

The pahan is the centre-point of the Oraon religious organisation. Many important functions and activities of Oraon life are completed on his direction and with his cooperation. Since he is knowledgeable regarding the rules of religion, and, compared to the other Oraons, he is supposed to be nearer to the gods and goddesses, he has more power inherent in him than the common people although he may not be having full divine powers. In some villages the post of the pahan[12] is paternal or hereditary, and the tradition of pahan is going on from the elevated khut of the Bhuinhars.[13] But in some villages, the post of pahan is a term post, normally for three years, and after the term is completed, a new pahan is installed. The procedure for selecting the pahan makes it clear that the desire of the Oraons does not count, it is a divine directed procedure. The pahan is chosen on the full moon day of Magh Month or in some villages of Bero on the full moon day of Aghan. In this process, the role of the winnowing fan is the most important which as perbelief of the Oraons is the seat-mat of Sarnadevi (goddess) or Chala Pachcho and which is called "Sarna soop." This winnowing fan is the symbol of the post and power of the pahan. It is hung from a beam or joist of a sacred and special place in the house of the pahan. This place is called "Chala Kutti." During the occasions of special worship, this winnowing fan is taken with great respect by the villagers to the Sarna place or some other place of worship and set up there; after the completion of the worship, with the same respect and devotion it is brought back to the chala kutti and hung up.

In order to hang the winnowing fan while taking it, a thin branch of a sal tree is taken and one end of it is split into two equal parts. On the day of sselection, the outgoing pahan takes a new winnowing fan, puts some arwa rice (rice extracted from unboiled paddy) on it and brings it towards the Sarna place. The old winnowing fan is handed over to a young boy whose eyes are covered with a band, and he is called "paicha labana." "Paicha labana" is believed to be more sensitive to divine powers and their influence because of his purity and intense feelings. All the assembled people pick up some grains of arwa rice from the new winnowing fan and throw them on the old winnowing fan while saying, "O, Chala Pachcho goddess, be pleased to enter that house where your dear and trustworthy devotee resides." Which means that "you indicate that person who is meritorious enough to become the pahan of this village."

After invoking Chala Pachcho goddess on the old winnowing fan, the outgoing pahan and two-three other senior villagers with bands tied over their eyes, follow the "Paicha labana" boy who leads them towards the village. The boy holds the sal branch in one hand- the old winnowing fan is tied to the split end of the sal branch. The outgoing pahan has the new winnowing fan in one hand and he takes out rice grains in small quantities and, stopping frequently, he throws them down on the way along with water. As per belief in the Oraon religion, Sarna goddess has been installed in the old winnowing fan which had been worshipped at the Sarna place and on which all the assembled villagers had offered rice grains and she is inspiring the "paicha labana" boy to go towards that house where the dear devotee of the goddess, the new pahan lives.

The boy having a band covering his eyes, goes to the door of whosoever's house and leaves the old winnowing fan at its edge, it is taken for granted that Chala Pachcho being a goddess has selected a new pahan for the village. The new pahan takes the new winnowing fan from the outgoing pahan, and along with the people present moves towards the Sarna place. Preceding him, the "paicha-labana" boy carries the old winnowing fan. At the Sarna place, the Oraons of the village await the coming of the new pahan. They feel happy to see the crowd coming and they welcome the new pahan.

In those villages where the post of pahan is paternal, in special circumstances when the lineage becomes extinct or gets converted to another religion, then it becomes necessary to select a new pahan. In such villages the selection process of a new pahan is the same as in other villages.

Amongst Oraons, there is a post called Mahadania pahan. It is said that a long time ago, the custom of "human sacrifice" in order to please the mother goddess was prevalent among the Hindu landlords. It was believed that by offering such sacrifice, the landlords would have victory in all sectors. This sacrifice was helpful even in increasing the clan. The responsibility of this great sacrifice could be shouldered by a special pahan. Such a pahan was called "mahadaniya pahan." This post is paternal. Although the offering of human sacrifice has gradually disappeared, in Chhotanagpur even now "Mahadaniya Pahans" are to be found. For their maintenance, the landlords had given them rent free lands which are entered as "mahadaniya land" in the Bhuinhar register.

Selection of Assistant

The selection of assistant to Pahan, who is also called pujar, panbhara, susari etc., is done in the same aforementioned procedure. This process is called "soop-chalan vidhi" (process of movement of the winnowing fan). From the religious point of view, the pahan's assistant does not have less importance. He also comes from Bhuinhar Khunt and does his duty under the supervision of the pahan. He, too, gets the facility of rent free land. At first the pahan and thereafter the pujar or susari or other assistant, if any selection has to be done, then he is selected as per aforementioned process and thereafter all of them assemble at the Sarna place and immediately from there they go to the village along with the "paicha labana." The whole process of selection is done at the divine direction and control of "Chala Pachcho" goddess through the "paicha labana" boy whose eyes are covered with a band, hence the pahan and his assistant pujar are believed to be the representative or spokesmen of the gods and goddesses, and the decisions of the pahan regarding religious duties and customs are taken to be final and binding on all.

The Gods of the Oraons

Dharmes is the supreme God amongst all the gods and goddesses who influence Oraon life and religious beliefs. Dharmes is known by the name of "Biri Belas" or "Sun God." He lives in the world of the sky, and keeps an eye on all creatures, the activities of all moving and inert things, and He controls and directs them. All the goddesses and the invisible powers work day and night to manage the Creation according to His plan. The chief among them is "Chala Pachcho" or Sarna mai (mother) who resides on the sal tree of the Sarna place, and wishes for the welfare of the village. She also gets installed in the pahan's Sarna winnowing fan and the pahan, who gives religious rulings in the village, obtains direction and inspiration from her. Similarly, "pat-raja" stops disease and disasters from entering the village. According to Oraons, "Pat-raja" resides in hillocks or in some villages he resides in the thorny bushes growing on the boundary of the village. He is the king of all the souls of the village, and the Oraons offer worship and oblations to him as per laid down procedure. This worship is also called "Parta Puja" or "Pahar Puja." In the "darha" upland the "darha desauli," "Mahadev" in the phallus- like stone rock (mandar sala), the goddess of hunting Chandi who resides on the hill slopes or the rounded piece of rock on Chandi upland, the souls residing in the stumps of wood in the soil, and in this way in the special circular roots of bamboos, in the holes of the trees, in the ponds- these are all residing places of the village gods and goddesses or the souls. The belief regarding the characters of these gods, goddesses and souls, and their naming have developed on the basis of those things with which they are connected or in which they live. This condition of religion, which is called "animism", is normally found in most primitive tribes.

Animism is that part of religious thinking process according to which in every inanimate thing an animate soul or power is believed to be residing. This particular power controls and moves that inanimate object. In the religious world of the Oraons, there are many divine powers and souls which are connected to some inanimate object and shoulder their responsibilities. The work areas of these powers are allotted, and they look after their areas, while the "Pat raja" stays on the hill and protects the village from maladies and diseases. Separate arrangement for worship (for the protection of agricultural fields) of various gods and goddesses and souls, is in vogue. As per religious story of the Oraons, Dharmes has given these sectoral gods and goddesses various responsibilities, and their worship and offering of oblations and sacrifice to them has become the responsibility of the ordinary Oraon. Such is the direction of Dharmes.[14]

According to Oraon religious story, after destroying the Asurs, their widows were given various responsibilities by Dharmes to maintain the balance of Creation. The souls of the dead reside in villages, uplands, hills, forests and nearly all the places connected with Oraon life in the form of "naad". The number of "naads" is countless but some responsibilities and character are determined, and there are certain unsatisfied souls of the dead which terrorise the Oraons with fear and destructive influence. But those which are good souls and some who have obtained name and character, they are included in the pantheon of gods and goddesses in Oraon religion. The development of such gods and goddesses in Oraons religion took place in the land of Chhotanagpur. Since prior to the coming of the Oraons, the form of Munda religion and the form of its divinities were stabilising after developing, therefore their influence touched the gods and goddesses of Oraons in their development. Due to the belief in animism, the regional deities increased a lot and developed. Although at first the hypothesis regarding certain deities had been terrifying but they gradually acquired more benevolent characteristics. The qualities of Dharmes began appearing in them. They became the well wishers of the Oraons and the faith of Oraon society on these regional invisible powers developed gradually. In this development process, the role of Hindu gods and goddesses was very influential. In the religion of the Oraons, the gods and goddesses and souls can be categorised as per their good character and ordinary or destructive character. The classification is as follows:

(a) Above any category, the Almighty Dharmes

(b) Gods of Nature: (i) Superior- Benevolent

(ii) Inferior- Destructive/benevolent having both traits.

(c) Naad (souls of the dead):

(i) Ancestor- Benevolent

(ii) Other- Destructive/Benevolent having both traits.

The chief gods and goddesses and "naad" who influence Oraon life deeply, may be classified as under as per their divinity and importance:

(1) Dharmes

(2) The ancestor god or Pach Baler

(3) Village god/ goddess :

(a) Chala Pachcho (b) Pat raja (hill god) (c) Darha-desauli (d) Mahadaniya (e) Mahadev (f) Devi Mai (g) Chhappar Burhiya (h) Chandi Pahar (i) Baranda Peeper (j) Ban Shakti or Garha-Dhorha Chaturseeman (k) Toosa Burha

(4) Gods and Naad :
   (a) Chandi/Chanri
   (b) Aachchrel/ Achrain
   (c) Joda
   (d) Khunt/ Naad
   (e) Baranda- Pachcho
   (f) Chigri Naad, Goensali naad, surjahi (danr raja)

Dharmes

Dharmes is the supreme and Almighty God of the Oraons. The superiority and power of Dharmes is equivalent to the word "Bhagwan" of the Hindus. In the early stages of development of Oraon religion, the sun had great importance, and believing the sun to be almighty, worship was offered to it. Over a period of time the sun came to be recognised as Dharmes and with the interval of time the appearance of Dharmes took on the embellishment of "Bhagwan" of the Hindus, and Dharmes who had been connected to the sun, He took on a separate godliness. In this He left behind the sun in character, knowledge, wisdom, power and sovereignty. Normally all Oraons use the word "Dharmes" for Bhagwan, but in some places, the old name of Dharmes i.e. "Biri Belas" is also prevalent. The Maler and Sauriya Pahariya tribe, whose roots are in Oraon tribe, and whose population is to a great extent in the hills of Rajmahal, and in Santhal Parganas, use the word "Bedu" or "Bero" for the sun god, and call their sovereign God or Bhagwan "Ajo Gosai." From this it is clear that in the religious thinking of the Malers, apart from the Sun god, another God also developed who was more superior and strong than the sun god. They are ignorant of "Dharmes" or Dharmes's importance.

Even in the religious structure of the Oraons, the hold of Dharmes developed separately from that of the sun. This opinion is also held by the famous theocrat and padre Reverend P. Dehan.[15] Definitely this thinking is equivalent to the word "Bhagwan" and its sentiment prevalent among Hindus because the Oraon people not only use the word Bhagwan for their sovereign God, but also in their traditional religious tales when the story of beginning of Oraon race and its protection is told and heard, then mention at time is made of Parwati and sometimes of Sita as the wife of Dharmes. The attachment of the name of Parwati or Sita to that of Dharmes can be said to be the result of the influence of coming into contact with Hindus for centuries. But the question is not of Hindu influence- it is that of the magnificent appearance of Dharmes in which all the powers of the sun are assimilated and gradually Dharmes has been established as the sovereign God of Oraon religion.

Reverend P. Dehan has, based upon his study, come to the conclusion that when the Oraons use the word "Bhagwan", then just like the Kols they mean the sun.[16] But Dehan has not paid attention to the use of the words "Biri" or "Suruj Bhagwan" used by the Oraons. But adding the word "Bhagwan" to "Suruj," the sun's divinity and importance has surely been accepted but it is a simple guess that the sun is not Bhagwan, but like Bhagwan. Whereas Dharmes has been worshipped as the Creator, and in special religious functions and festivals, the prayers to Dharmes, the mode of worship and importance[17] clearly point out that Dharmes is the most superior among the gods. On auspicious occasions and worshipping rituals the Oraons offer prayers facing the east and complete religious duties. In "agnivarsha" (rain of fire) there is reference to the power of Dharmes through which He destroyed proud and greedy mankind. It is clear from this that in Dharmes's power there is heat of blazing fire i.e. the heat of the sun and since His seat is in the eastern sky therefore there is a link between the sun and Dharmes.

The assimilation of all the qualities of the sun in Dharmes and together with it His worship as the Creator and the father of the Oraon tribe (after the rain of fire the brother-sister duo had been protected and reared as per desire of Dharmes) and protector of the tribe, is actually the merging of the sun in Dharmes or unifying the sun with Dharmes. Colonel Dalton has also in his analysis of Oraon religion found the appearance of Dharmes approximately in the same way.[18] But Dalton has failed to properly assess the devotion of the Oraons towards Dharmes, and the faith in the mind of the Oraons in the powers and majesty of Dharmes. Dalton states that the Oraons think that when they are tortured by sorcery or evil spirits, or are afflicted with diseases, then "Dharmes" does not come amidst them to save them. In this way, when the Oraon tribe finds Dharmes to be indifferent towards their protection or welfare, then it is but natural that they should think of offering worship and oblation in appeasement to that god or evil spirit who has sent afflections to them. Hence the Oraons think it to be meaningless to offer worship or sacrifice to Dharmes.[19] According to Colonel Dalton, either the Oraons doubt the power of Dharmes, or are indifferent to Him because of His inactiveness. The basis of Colonel Dalton's conclusions was that compared to Dharmes, the Oraons worship the regional gods/goddesses and the souls more.

Actually it is the result of shallow study of a particular area of Oraon religion that the power and majesty of Dharmes has been projected as inferior to that of the regional gods and evil spirits. This shallow study and its result cannot normally be attributed to the Oraon religion. It is true that the primitive Oraon tribe used to think that the various maladies were caused by the influence of magic, evil spells, wicked and angry spirits and they got the treatment done by experts in this branch of learning, namely, the ojha, mati, etc. Since the ojha, mati, devra, sokha, and other experts of protecting against the evil effects of sorcery or evil spirits used to call upon their gods/ goddesses who were perfect protectors, these experts used to keep themselves separate from the worship of Dharmes. Hence Dalton, who was a biased thinker, came to the conclusion that in the eyes of the Oraons, Dharmes was either unable to or inactive in freeing them from maladies.

In Oraon religion, the pahan has an important role in the rules of worship of Dharmes. In the Oraon religious structure, the pahan is a link between Dharmes and Oraon tribe. The pahan and his assistant pujar or panbhara carry out the religious duties as per approved tradition of the Oraons. They memorize by heart the invocation to Dharmes. They narrate various miraculous stories during occasions of worship in which the Oraons assemble; they not only narrate but also interpret the stories such as Dharmes slaying giants, destroying the Asurs, saving human kind from annihilation and other such main stories. During festivals, auspicious occasions, and other occasions of fulfillment of vows, the worship of Dharmes is conducted under the supervision of the pahan. Without invocation to Dharmes and He being a witness, all religious activities are supposed to be incomplete. While fixing marriage, it is necessary to have Dharmes's desire and approval because then only the couple of husband and wife can be religious and auspicious. In this manner Dharmes is directly connected to the religious life of the Oraon tribe. The pahan who analyses various signs and thereupon defines the desire of Dharmes, forms an important link between Dharmes and the Oraon tribe.

As regards the treatment of diseases and maladies, there are two situations which can be seen in Oraon society. Since the Oraons think that the evil souls, churails and sorcerors are at the root of their troubles, hence in order to be freed from them, it is necessary to appease those who cause them. The learning which developed to appease such evil spirits or to torture them so that the diseased person may get rid of his disease, this is implemented and sustained by the ojha, mati. The institutions of ojha-mati and pahan-pujara roughly appear to be the same, but they are absolutely different. Both worship their tutelary deities. In the worship of the pahans, Dharmes is mentioned. His stories are told and His praises are sung, but ojha-mati do not mention Dharmes. Since black magic and its influence have deeply touched Oraon life and in order to get rid of its influence and make a disease-ridden person free from disease, in that process, instead of Dharmes, people prefer to worship those invisible powers through whom the maladies may be driven away. The conclusion of Dalton is totally superficial and his opinion that the Oraon tribe neglects Dharmes or thinks His powers to be comparatively weak is completely erroneous.

If a fine analysis is made of the religious side of the life of Oraon tribals, then it will be found through the various activities of their life that Dharmes occupies the most superior place and importance in their life. In nearly all main festivals, along with the regional gods, Dharmes is also worshipped keeping in mind His superiority. In the most sacred festival of Sarhul which is celebrated by the Oraons at the main religious place called Sarna place, Dharmes is offered sacrifice of white cock while any other cock would do for the rest as per their choice. From the occasion of chhatti to death, in nearly all ceremonies, the stories of Dharmes are sung and heard and His unlimited powers are expressed as lying scattered everywhere in nature. He is the Creator and the Creation-Controller. In order to nullify the powers of black magic and deadly power of illness and maladies, in Oraon society, the protective procedure of "danda-katta" or "bhelwa-phari" worship is organised. In this function, only Dharmes is worshipped and His eulogies are sung and by appeasing Him protective kindness is obtained. As per Oraon belief, in whichever family "bhelwa-fari" worship is organised, the family remains under the protection of Dharmes and no black magic, nor the evil spirits can do any harm despite all efforts by the ill-wishers to goad them to action. Hence the conclusion of Colonel Dalton [20] that compared to the evil spirits the Oraons neglect Dharmes in their worship, is absolutely wrong. The Oraon people not only worship Dharmes to get rid of sorcery and darts of deadly maladies and after getting rid of them as per vow they give offerings to Him for His grace, they also do small or big religious activities and activities related to charms, superstition, in which Dharmes is invoked, and in so doing, the Oraons protect themselves from the destructive actions and ire of the evil spirits. "Danda-Katta" or "Bhelwa-fari" ceremony is a visible example of this. If Dalton had collected information regarding such religious activities and studied them in which after obtaining the kindness of Dharmes, the Oraons free themselves from the bad effects of black magic or the influence of evil spirits, then Dalton in his current of thoughts would not have opined that the evil spirits connected to black magic were more important as compared to Dharmes.

The sovereignty of Dharmes is also proved from "Asur Avdaan," when He spent a week in the flaming furnace of the Asurs and came out like a divine king embellished with gold jewellery and astonished the assembled Asurs.[21] After having spent seven days in the burning furnace yet remaining alive, and there after the eczema boy (Khasra balak) coming out fully adorned with gold jewellery and looking like a king, undoubtedly speaks of invisible divine powers adorning Him, and this fact the Asurs and their womenfolk realised later on.

In black magic, those invisible powers which the worshipper controls and sends against an enemy or uses them to produce maladies and disasters, those powers are inferior to that of the regional gods and goddesses and souls of the dead whom Dharmes has created. Dharmes has given this much of power to the widows of the Asurs that they may keep control over their areas and if they are neglected then they can punish the Oraons and get their due offerings. These gods and goddesses are believed to protect the Oraons from the deadly powers of black magic. Since the Oraons, afflicted with black magic, often search out remedies to free themselves of illnesses from ojhas and matis, and the tutelary deities of the ojhas and matis are often Hindu gods (especially Mahadev), hence in such cases there is no need of Dharmes. Again, as per traditional prevalence in Oraon religion, Dharmes is connected to pahan and pujar. Whenever in a worship the pahan or pujar is present, it is possible to invoke Dharmes in that worship, but in the worship in which the ojha, mati, etc. are present, Dharmes is not invoked in that worship. In the learning and procedures of the ojha and mati, Dharmes does not come. When the disease becomes incurable, and when ojha and mati also become unsuccessful, then the Oraon has no other option save and except to seek the protection of Dharmes and to free the patient of the disease by offering worship to Dharmes and to obtain His grace. In this way, when all gods fail, then the Oraons take the help of Dharmes. S. C. Roy on the basis of his study has also come to this conclusion.[22]

The supremacy of Dharmes is expressed in the praises sung to Dharmes during worship by the pahan when he says, "You, Dharmes, are our Father. Knowingly or unknowingly if in the worship of any ghost some shortcoming has remained then You stop the anger of that spirit. Your eyes see every thing."[23] Which means that if knowingly or unknowingly, if in the worship of any regional goddess/god or naad some shortcoming has remained, then You, Father Dharmes, stop his anger because our eyes cannot see anything where as Your eyes see everything. Which means that You know everything and You see everything and You can keep control over those naads." According to the belief of the Oraons, nothing is concealed from Dharmes. It is clear from this prayer that Dharmes has got full control over the gods/goddesses, naads and souls of the dead. He is superior to all of them. According to the belief of the Oraons, Dharmes punishes those Oraons who break the yardsticks of approved traditional morality. Hence, to escape this punishment, Dharmes is worshipped with a white cock. His complexion is white and resplendent as the sun, but He is not the form of the sun. The sun has not been personified nor deified in Him. Right from the beginning of Creation, Dharmes has revealed Himself in the form of God because He has made the Creation. The Oraon tribe has accepted Dharmes to be their supreme God.

According to the religious belief of the Oraons, Dharmes is not such a god in which only a vast item of Creation is included or that He is the community social strength of the whole Oraon tribe or that He is the head or controller god of all the souls of dead persons, regional gods and goddesses. The meaning thereby is that Dharmes is not the vast natural thing called the sun, He is not the community social strength and controller of the race of Oraons, and He is not limited to being the head of the invisible forces and gods and goddesses. The Oraons believe that Dharmes is above them all. Dharmes is the Maker, Creator, Controller and Protector of mankind, souls of the dead, gods and goddesses and the whole Creation. His desire is supreme. Whenever and whatever He desires, He can direct and move visible and invisible powers.

The religious stories of Rain of Fire and Asur Avdaan have shown Dharmes to be "the protector of mankind" and this strong characterisation has been deeply ingrained in the psyche of the Oraon race. On various religious occasions, these religious tales are sung by the pahan and explained to the people. Dharmes used to live as the son of a helpless old widow in Belatpur. The king of that place used to send every day a person with rice and eatables to that giant who had been troubling that kingdom. In order to appease the giant, a human being of Belatpur used to be sacrificed every day. Then, one day the turn of Dharmes came. He readied Himself like an ordinary servant and went and slew the giant, thus providing relief to the inhabitants of Belatpur.[24] In order to destroy the foul odour[25] of the dead giant, Dharmes sent Rain of Fire. The pahans say that the foul odour of the dead giant has symbolic meaning. Due to the tremendous increase in sins committed by the wicked, Dharmes sent rain of fire to destroy them and to create a new human race. This thought and work can be done only by the all powerful Bhagwan (God). When the Asur-natured people flood the earth without caring for the prevalent social customs and morality, and "religion gets harmed," the Bhagwan reincarnates Himself and comes and destroys the wicked, and thereafter forms a new creation, develops a new race and establishes the religion of righteousness.

Dharmes did that. Wickedness had increased in the whole country. There was no fear of the religion of righteousness. The bad odour of complete disorder arising out of the inhuman sinful activities of human beings had spread throughout and due to this, Creation started getting unbalanced. At this time it became essential for Dharmes to destroy the sinners through rain of fire. That is why Dharmes had told His "bull" to inform the Belatpur inhabitants to go to "Keonjhar" and protect themselves because the rain of fire was about to start, but the Belatpur inhabitants due to pride and ego, killed the bull.

Dharmes re-developed the race in a new way. He arranged for agriculture, created night and day, created the regional gods and goddesses and gave them responsibilities[26] so that it would be convenient for Dharmes to manage the Creation and maintain its balance. He gave orders to the Oraons to offer food to the gods and goddesses, ancestors and inhabitants of the invisible world, and try to appease them. He also made this arrangement that if the Oraon people selfishly or unknowingly do not carry out their duties, then the invisible powers could send disease and maladies to the Oraons and make them ill as a warning or could send troubles and disasters which would affect the Oraons badly.

That is why, while praying to Dharmes, the Oraons also pray for forgiveness that if knowingly or unknowingly they have not offered food to the regional gods and goddesses or the souls of the dead, then Dharmes should stop the invisible powers from sending calamities because He is Omniscient and the Protector of the Oraon race. On different occasions of worship, the pahan in his prayer to Dharmes eulogises His omnipotence, power, as the Supreme Father of the Oraons having love for them as His children, and describe various other qualities of Dharmes. According to Oraon religion, Dharmes or other gods and goddesses, souls of the dead, but Dharmes also goes unappeased. After the rain of fire, when for some days nothing was offered to Dharmes, then He asked the reason from His wife Parvati and came to know that due to rain of fire, mankind had been annihilated hence who would offer oblations to Him. Dharmes started thinking and found out the brother-sister duo[27] from Sira-Sita and reared them till they could offer worship and food to Him. During the recital of this story, the pahan emphasises on the fact that whatever is ours, that Dharmes has given. Hence at first offering must be made to Him and after that whatever remains, on that only do we have a right.

The Asur-Avdaan regarding Dharmes speaks about the Khasra balak (eczema boy) till the time when the Asur widows were given regional responsibilities, and were to obtain worship and offerings from the Oraons in the form of bongas or gods and goddesses- the whole tale reveals the character of Dharmes on one hand, and on the other, provides evidence of the influence of Munda religion in the development of religious beliefs of the Oraons. As per this Avdaan, all the activities of Dharmes are nearly the same as that of Singbonga. Despite this, there are some basic differences between Dharmes and Singbonga. Compared to the Mundas, the Oraons were closer to the Aryans, and in the development of their gods and goddesses and naads and their character, the influence of the character of Hindu gods and goddesses is clearly reflected. Apart from Asur Avdaan, in the religious tales pertaining to the birth and development of the Oraon race, the story related in the "Agnivarsha" (rain of fire) in which Dharmes had slain the giant, is a copy of that tale in the epic Mahabharat in which during their stay in anonymity the giant is slain by Bhim.

The Forefathers (gods) or Pach Baler

In the religious life of the Oraon tribe, the development of the understanding of "Pach Baler" is very important. According to Oraon belief, the souls of their dead ancestors ("ekh"- soul) live in the nether world which is below the earth.[28] The souls of the newly dead, before the ceremony of the dead, loiter/hover around their home on this earth. But on a fixed time when completing the "Koha-benja-ceremony" (hadbodi)" the village council of five or the eldest person in the home of the dead person prays to the souls of his ancestors living in the nether world that the soul of the newly dead person be included in the "pachbaler." He says this for either man or woman.[29]

The Oraons believe that till the souls are not approved in the "pachbaler" and are not organised, their condition remains abnormal. The souls of the newly dead remain with their old relations and do not want to leave them in a short while. The Oraons believe that these unorganised souls put the family in difficulties and every family wants to be quickly freed from them. Even after arranging for them to stay with the "pachbaler," it cannot be said as to when they will come above the visible world and will torture the family members or the villagers. But the Oraons believe that those souls which cannot get included in the "pachbaler," they are hurtful, yet those which get included in the group of the dead ancestors, they prove to be benevolent for their families. They carry out their duties of being ancestors and oppose the efforts of wicked souls who try to bring disaster to the family. During the time of illness, the soul sits at the head of the bed of the patient, invisibly, and protects him. When members of the family go on a forest road or pathway, the soul walks along as a protector meaning thereby that it carries out the responsibility of a guardian.

The importance of the role of pachbaler in the religious development of the Oraons is equalled by the importance of the those "ekhs" (souls of the dead) in their life. According to religious belief of the Oraons, these souls can be divided in two categories- (1) those which are harmful and wicked and (2) those which are benevolent and well wishers of the Oraons. According to the belief of the Oraons, the aforementioned characters of the souls of the dead depend chiefly upon the circumstances of their death. These circumstances are those of unnatural death, for example, soul of a person killed by a wild animal, soul of a pregnant woman who dies in labour pain, the soul of whom is "nasan" or harmful. It is apparent that the Oraons basically have a tendency to escape from the souls of the dead and to keep a distance from them, and compared to the Munda people the Oraons always try to keep themselves and other living beings at home, from the shadow of the dead ancestors.

In the Munda home, there is an arrangement for ading. Ading is that part of the house where the Munda people establish their ancestors, worship them and arrange for their stay. Meaning that, like the other members of the house, the souls of the dead ancestors are established / installed in the ading and they are treated as part of the family. But there is no such arrangement in Oraon religion. Although Reverend P. Dehan has concluded as per his study that the Oraons through the ritual of "chhain bhitarna" bring the "ekh" into their home just like the Mundas and install them permanently there. Reverend Dehan's conclusion is based on the study of the Oraons of Palamau region- it has not taken into consideration the annual "Kohabenja" ritual. The "chhain bhitarna" ritual or the prevalent correct name among the Oraons "ekh makhna" ritual, is a ritual through which the Oraon people bring the "ekh" (soul) back to the boundary of the house but they keep it only till the annual "koha benja" ritual, and through the "utur-khila" ritual, the soul is made to enter the "pach baler" of the group of dead ancestors.

The hypothesis regarding "ekh" in Oraon religion is parallel to the living shadow of a human being. The "ekh" (soul) and "jiu" (life) are two different elements. The life or "jiu" is the physical strength of a human being and the Oraons believe that at the time of death, life escapes from the body like the wind which nobody knows. But where the soul is concerned, it becomes a member of the "pach baler" and lives amidst them below the earth.

The soul of every Oraon is actually his shadow, which, if required, can come out of the body and go anywhere and can come back speedily to re-enter the body. In Oraon life, dreams are not illusions, they are true and the soul experiences them. The Oraons believe that when a person dreams dreams while sleeping, then actually his soul movesout of the body and sees those scenes and visits those places, and experiences the happiness and sorrow which he finds in the condition of dreaming. By the time the person wakes up, the soul comes back speedily and re-enters his body, that is why the Oraons do not wake up a person suddenly, they wake him up gradually so that his soul may get opportunity to re-enter his body.

In this way, the "ekh" (soul) is the Oraon's living shadow while the life is his bodily or physical strength. With the destruction of the body, the life comes out and merges with the wind, but the existence of the soul remains. The soul is a formless person in which the identity of the dead person remains. He gets place in the nether world amid the family's dead ancestors.

One example will make the matter more clear. The pahan of the Oraons throws light on those circumstances when the soul of an Oraon is outside the body yet the Oraon is alive. The pahan says that when the soul of a sleeping person is roaming far away, then to wake up the sleeping person suddenly would give no time for the soul to come back and re-enter his body. The soul cannot enter the body when it is awake. Hence due to life, the Oraon keeps alive but without the soul he loses his balance and acts like a mad person. He becomes victim of an incurable disease and very soon he dies. Still then, even though the soul has gone out of the body, the Oraon remains alive due to his life-force although his life becomes abnormal.

In this way, it is not necessary to leave the body by the soul, whereas it is essential for the life to come out. There is no opinion in Oraon religion regarding the speed of the life-force. The Oraons are concerned with the soul of the person because the soul gives an identity of the dead Oraon and his "gotra."

In Oraon religion, the soul is divided into two categories based on the sharpness of sensitivity: such a person who is more sensitive to invisible powers, dreams and ghosts/spirits, and comes easily under their influence, and a person who is not easily influenced by them and is traditional or insensitive. The soul of the first category of person is called "nebba ekh" meaning of light shadow, and the second category is called "oththa ekh" or thick shadow. Some Christian missionaries[30] are of the opinion that the Oraons call the "nebba ekh" to their house after death through "chhain bhiterna."

Actually, the categorisation appears to have been done on the basis of the nature of the person. Since "ekh" is the reflected image of a human being hence the sign of his behaviour or nature to be found in his soul is normal. According to Oraon religion the ancestors live below the earth ("khekel kiya") in the same manner as they used to live on the earth, the same kind of house, home, and style of living; after their death on the earth, the soul of the dead goes below the earth and becomes like a family member by being included among the souls or "pach-baler" of the ancestors who live there.

In Oraon religion although there is a fundamental hypothesis of "pach baler," but the nature of the soul of the dead and the form of their behaviour reflect the influence of Munda and Hindu religions. The hypothesis of "nebba ekh" and "oththa-ekh" shows the clear influence of Munda religion. Detailed discussion has been done regarding the heavy and light "roa" of Munda religion. After entering Chhotanagpur, such a hypothesis regarding the souls developed in Oraon religion. Since the Oraons were specially close to the Mundas in Chhotanagpur, and the hypothesis of light and heavy souls had developed already in Munda religion, hence it was natural that the thinking process of the Oraons would accept that direction which had since been accepted by the preceding Mundas earlier.

The Hindu and Munda thinking have also influenced the belief of the Oraons when they used to think that the souls of the dead were troublesome and torturous and they used to try to keep their family away from them. Today the Oraons accept that in rugged forests, in trouble, in various disasters disease, the souls of their ancestors are always ready to help them, but earlier in Oraon religion did the souls of the ancestors have their same nature or it was different? After analysing all the circumstances, it is difficult to say whether in the early stages of Oraon religion according to belief of the Oraons, the souls of the dead were positively fearful or not, but in this thinking of the Oraons, due to Hindu influence, change came after a period of time and the souls of the ancestors gradually came to be recognised as benevolent and adorable and on important occasions oblations started being given to them with faith.

Before the entry into Chhotanagpur, a group of Oraons from Rohtasgarh went towards the hillocks of Rajmahal. The "Khonds" of Orissa and the "Gonds" of Madhya Pradesh belong to the family of Oraons. Apart from them, the "Sauriya Pahariyas" of Santhal Parganas are a part of the Oraon family. As regards the "chhain bhitarna" ritual, the practice of returning the souls of the dead is prevalent among Khond and Gond tribes, and this practice resembles the "Chhainbhitarna" ritual. The Gonds in Orissa stay in contact with the "Sabars," and the Khonds of Madhya Pradesh stay in contact with the "Korkus." Sabar and Korkus are offshoots of Munda tribe amongst whom the practice of installing the "roa" (soul) in the "ading" is prevalent. It is due to the influence of contact that amongst the "Khond" and "Gond," the souls of the dead are taken from the cremation ground and kept at the boundary of the house till "hadbodi" takes place.

Amongst the Sauriya Pahariyas of Santhal Parganas, there is no such custom prevalent of bringing the souls of the dead to the house and installing them. Since the development of the religion of Sauriya Paharias took place without coming in contact with the Munda people, and the influence of some Hindus could take place, hence the custom of "chhaya bhitarna" or "ekh-makhna" or similar rituals pertaining to death ceremony cannot be seen. Oraons and Sauriya Pahariyas are tribes of the same root but "Gond," "Khond" and Oraons adopted the ritual of "chhain-bhitarna" in a limited way and gave place to the souls of the dead for some time, but there is no such ritual amongst Sauriya Pahariyas that the souls of the dead are to be brought back from the cremation ground and installed on the boundary of the house.

With the aforementioned example it is clear that in the religious faith and rituals of the Oraons, the influence of contact with the Mundas can be seen. As regards the matter of residence of ancestors, the Sauriya Pahariyas believe that after death, the souls of the ancestors live below the earth and at times they appear on the earth in the form of "podi." When they reveal themselves on the earth then a peculiar sound emanates. The villagers or their relations feel that it is beneficial to be far away from them, hence through the religious ritual of "pao-tey-kipan edte" sacrifice of cock is done on the boundary of the village and the priest prays thus- "please do not enter the village – and the head of the beheaded cock is left there and the remaining portion of the cock is fried and eaten by the people assembled there as holy food. No part of it is allowed to be brought back to the village. In this way the Sauriya Pahariya tribe tries to remain afar from the souls of the dead because they are destructive and bring sorrow.

In the earlier stages, the aforementioned opinion was prevalent in the Oraon tribe also, because the Sauriya Pahariyas and the Oraons are from the same root and place, and later moved on and settled in different places. Amongst the Oraon tribe "utoor-khila" is such a religious ritual through which device is made either to keep the souls of the dead far away or to save themselves from these souls. During the time of worship the soul of the dead is addressed thus- "Now we are sending you afar. From now on your eyes and your head should not turn towards us."[31] Hence effort is made to remain far away from souls of the dead or to keep them afar. Amongst the Oraons a belief is prevalent that there is "chor deva" which means that the souls of the dead disguise themselves and roam around; they lick the saliva flowing out from the mouth of an Oraon, or peel off the skin from the ankle of a leg or roam around as pygmies of the size of a thumb, touch the hair of somebody to make him ill, etc. which are the acts of wicked souls.

In Hindu religion, worship of the ancestors and thinking them to be gods and protectors, and to obtain blessings from them, definitely gives them a place equal to that of a god. In Munda religion, too, installing the ancestors in the ading as home-deities and to remember them on all auspicious occasions and to give them respect is the same as giving them respect akin to that of a god. In Oraon religion, so much of worshipping tendency for the ancestors has not come about, but still, keeping aloof from the souls of the dead or running away from them-this situation is not there. There are some wicked souls in Oraon religion even now, but due to Munda and Hindu influences, the souls of the dead have now started playing the role of protectors and in times of trouble, sickness and disaster, the dead ancestors protect their children and try to lift them in every way.

"Hadbodi" is the annual worship of the ancestors observed by the Oraon people. Apart from this, during festivals, worship and special auspicious occasions they are remembered, and offerings are made to them. During Sarhul, Karma, and Fagua occasions, the first piece of bread made from rice flour is offered to the ancestors of "pach-baler." During the occasion of "jitiya," balls of rice are offered to them on six leaves, two for the souls of the dead ancestors, two for souls of dead children, one for dead daughter's soul and the remaining one for all the dead of the gotra. Twice when the Oraons observe the festival of "nawa khani"- one in the month of Shrawan when new gondila is eaten after religious worship and prayer, and the other in Bhado or Ashwin when "goda" rice is eaten after religious worship and prayer. In this way, especially on the occasions of "koha benja" and "nawa khani," and in all other normal occasions, the Oraons remember their ancestors and pray to them for giving protection and benevolence and for increase in prosperity. Definitely, the Oraons have developed a belief in the divinity of the souls of the dead, that is the ancestors. The Oraons not only expect increase in their family from the ancestors but also expect protection from diseases and illnesses.

Chala Pachcho

The most popular and most worshipped among the gods and goddesses of Oraon religion is Chala Pachcho Devi. The pahan, on behalf of the village during the occasion of Sarhul festival conducts the worship of Chala Pachcho goddess or Sarna goddess with great fanfare. According to Oraon religion, every village has a Sarna place where the holy sal tree is to be found. Where the sal tree is no longer there, another tree is utilised in the place of the sal tree. Although it is forbidden by religion to cut down any tree of the Sarna place, but who can stop the scourge of seasons for centuries?

At times, Chala pachcho or Sarna goddess appears in the form of a dignified old woman whose matted and bunched up hair is established in the psyche of the Oraons. The Oraons otherwise do not imagine any figure/ idol but with the passage of time, the imagination of an old woman being Sarna goddess is firmly established in the intellect of the Oraons. According to Oraon religion, Sarna goddess sits on the winnowing fan of the pahan as

"Chala Kutti." "Chala Kutti" is that sacred place in the house of the pahan which is reserved for the stay of Sarna goddess. In this place, a pole of either sal tree or bamboo is erected on which the holy winnowing fan is hung up. This winnowing fan is called Sarna "soop." According to Oraon religion, Sarna goddess stays in this winnowing fan.

The door of Chala Kutti is not closed so that Chala Pachcho goddess can come to and fro. In addition to the Sarna winnowing fan, Sarna goddess stays on the sal tree of the Sarna place as per belief, and all the rituals regarding Sarhul are conducted in the Sarna place. In this programme, Sarna goddess also participates. It is said that when Oraon girls dance in an engrossed manner in Sarhul festival, then Sarna goddess enters into one of the girls and thereafter the speed of her dance becomes phenomenal. She jerks her head and makes movement from the waist going up and down as if the body is broken- she dances peculiarly and everybody present comes to believe that Sarna goddess herself is taking part in the dance.

Sarhul festival which is the most famous and popular festival of the Oraon tribe, is related to Sarna place and Sarna goddess. On the occasion of Sarhul festival, the pahan takes the Sarna winnowing fan from the Chala Kutti in a procession to the Sarna place; it is believed that Sarna goddess stays in the Sarna winnowing fan. Beneath the Sarna-tree, a piece of rock is kept which is sanctified by various rituals of worship. It is believed that Sarna goddess has been installed in this piece of rock and many cocks and he-goats are offered to her at this place as sacrifice. The whole programme is conducted by the pahan of the village and the villagers participate enthusiastically in this programme.

Chala Pachcho goddess is not only the first protector goddess of the village, she is also recognised as goddess of prosperity and fertility of agriculture and flora. Her white matted hair becomes the identity of that sal tree which is covered with white blossoms in spring. During the special occasions of festivities and worship, the Oraons remember Sarna goddess and before consuming rice wine, the first helping from every pitcher/pot of rice wine is taken out in a leaf cup and offered to Sarna goddess.

On the basis of the story of Asur Avdaan, the Oraons believe that their gods and goddesses are the widows of the Asurs whom Dharmes showed kindness and placed them amidst the Oraons, giving them responsibilities of certain duties, and has given direction to the Oraons that they should worship them and give offerings to them. Which means that the invisible powers which are tied to the religious life and activities of the Oraons are also the widows of the Asurs.

The story regarding Dharmes as told in the Asur Avdaan is joined also to Singbonga of the Mundas and the whole story is near about the same. The regional bongas related to Munda religion have also come about, as per narration, from the widows of Asurs and Singbonga has fixed certain responsibilities and duties for them and the Mundas. Since the Asurs had fought a war with the Mundas, therefore the Asur Avdaan was directly concerned with the Munda tribe. During the time of war, the Oraon tribe had not entered Chhotanagpur. Hence, the story of Asur Avdaan was forcibly adopted by the followers of Oraon religion which clearly was an imitation of Munda religion.

According to Asur Avdaan, Chala Pachcho goddess is the eldest of the Asur widows.[32] Meaning thereby that she is more superior and respected. But looking at the entire qualities, character and influence of Chala Pachcho goddess, it appears that she is a goddess connected with agriculture and flora, and the emergence of Chala Pachcho goddess in Oraon religion and her development had taken place prior to the entry of Oraons in Chhotanagpur. In this context, the "Chalnad" goddess worshipped in the religion of the Sauriya Paharias of Santhal Parganas can be viewed. Amongst the Sauriya Paharias, the entire character, power and influence of "Chala nad" goddess is nearly the same as "Chala Pachcho" goddess of the Oraons. After getting separated from Rohtasgarh, one group of Oraons which scattered was the Sauriya Paharias. Hence in the past the Oraons and Sauriya Paharias had been uterine relatives. In this way, the "Chal nad" goddess of the Sauriya Paharias and "Chala Pachcho" goddess of the Oraons are originally goddess of agriculture- these goddesses developed as per circumstances of Sauriya Paharia and Oraon tribes and at one place was worshipped as "Chal nad" goddess and at another place came to be worshipped as "Chala Pachcho" goddess, hence "Chala Pachcho" goddess originally is the goddess of nature and her emergence and development had taken place much earlier than the destruction of the Asurs and she had emerged in Oraon religion prior to their entry into Chhotanagpur. Hence to say that "Chala Pachcho" is one of the Asur widows is entirely wrong.

Paat naad or Hill King

Paat-naad or Hill-king is believed to be the master of all naads (souls of the dead). He keeps under his control all the naads of the village. On the boundary of the outskirts of the village is the hill which is the residence of Paat Raja (king). In certain villages where there are no hills, the Paat-Raja's residence is presumed to be in the brushwood on the boundary of the village or a huge tree on the urban limits. The Paat Raja rides on a palfrey and protects the whole village from illness, epidemic and other disasters. Although Paat Raja is invisible (that is why he cannot be seen), but at times his palfrey can be sighted by the Oraons, circumambulating the village boundary.

There was a time when Paat Raja had been worshipped as the most powerful god by the Oraons but with the passage of time, his importance especially among the Oraons settled in the middle of Chhotanagpur, lessened considerably, and Chala-Pachcho goddess acquired a higher position than him. But even today the Oraons believe that Paat Raja protects them and their village and controls all the "naads" of the village. This is the reason why Paat-Raja is also called Desauli-Paat. In Ranchi and central Chhotanagpur Plateau areas, Paat Raja has been associated with "Khunt-naad" and in this region he is known as "Khunt-Paat."

The worship of Paat-naad or Hill God is conducted by the pahan on behalf of the village and he offers sacrifice to him. In the month of Sravan, on the second day of Kadlota festival, the village pahan offers cock sacrifice to the Hill-God and worships him. In the central part of Chhotanagur, in some Oraon villages "dadha" or "dadha-desauli" naad's worship is being given more importance than that of Paat-god. As per the belief of the villages, "dadha-desauli" keeps all the souls of the dead of the village completely under his control. In this process, "dadha-desauli" is replacing Paat Raja and gradually Paat Raja is getting neglected and his influence is slowly ebbing.

Dadha-Desauli

The residence of Dadha-desauli is supposed to be some high land or upland situated on the boundary of the village. That land is called "dadha-tonka" or "dadha-tanr." On this land, one portion is left uncultivated and it is left as a preserve for "dadha-desauli." If this prohibition is broken, then that person or his cattle face death. Just like the Paat Raja, the "dadha-desauli" also protects the village but he is believed to be an ill-tempered and terrible naad or god whose negligence in any way may prove to be ruinous.

In certain villages, there is a belief of the residence of another "naad-desauli." For her, a separate grove or brushwood is earmarked where she stays. In some Oraon villages, it is believed that "desauli" is the wife of "dadha" and in these areas, joint worship of "dadha-desauli" can be seen. There are some areas in central Chhotanagpur plateau where no difference has been made between "dadha-desauli." It is the united name of one "naad." In Palamau region, the wife of "dadha" is called "dheri."

The villagers worship "dadha-desauli" in fixed time intervals following all rituals. The person in whose upland "dadha-desauli" stays, he proffers all the wealth received from that upland in the worship of "dadha-desauli." Although the rules of worship and offerings are different in different places, yet after a long gap of time, a he-buffalo is sacrificed. This gap is of four to five years. In the years coming in between, "dadha-desauli" is appeased with sacrifice of cock or he-goat. The worship generally is conducted by the village pahan but in his absence the owner of the upland can also conduct the worship.

In the upland, a wooden log is set up. In the middle of the log, an iron nail is inserted on which the holy food of meat is hung. For identifying and its protection a mud pot is hung and plastered with mud. Several years later, a new log replaces the old log. At that time a special function is held and a he-buffalo is sacrificed as an offering. Just like other "naads" the witches and sorcerors worship "dadhadesauli" and through him get their desired work done. Since he is supposed to be superior to all the "naads," hence the ojha or mati do not easily find any antidote to his deadly powers. When he becomes angry, he proves to be the most dangerous. Otherwise, obtaining the worship of the villagers at the village boundary, he remains busy day and night for the protection of the village. In this way, this benevolent "naad" has been accepted as equivalent to the gods. The Oraons are careful that there should be no shortcomings in his worship.

Mahadaniya

In certain villages worship is offered to the "Mahadaniya naad." According to the villagers, "mahadaniya" is more dangerous and powerful "naad" than the "dadha-desauli." In some villages people call him "daha-pachcho." It is said that a Mahadaniya can be appeased only with human sacrifice because animal sacrifice is of lower level and "Mahadaniya naad" does not accept it. In Oraon religion the entry of "Mahadaniya" was after coming into contact with Hindu kings and landlords. These kings and big landlords, in order to obtain kingdom, victory and fulfillment of similar ambitious desires, used to worship Mahadaniya and appease him. In the process they used to offer human sacrifice. The Oraons call this "odeka." The identification of "Mahadaniya" is also a log of wood erected in a particular place with an iron nail inserted on the head of the log. It was due to Hindu influence that in some places, a little away from the erected log of wood, a brick enclosure is made and the conditions of the worship indicate that it is a place for "Mahadaniya." The pahan does not conduct the worship of the "Mahadaniya" but there is a separate institution of "Mahadaniya pahan." These pahans used to get rent free lands from the landlords and kings and eke out their livelihood. These lands are recorded even in government documents by the name of "Mahadaniya" lands.

The worship of "Mahadaniya" is gradually decreasing and there are only a few villages which are under the influence of landlords, and during "dassera" efforts are made to appease "Mahadaniya" through sacrifice. Human sacrifice to Mahadaniya has become extinct.

Mahadev

Mahadev is such a God whose connection with the general Oraon is a little less, and more with the ojha, mati, or those worshippers who want to have knowledge regarding the treatment of Oraons who are being troubled by witches and sorcerors, and therefore to gain this powerful knowledge, worship Mahadev. Mahadev is often worshipped in Oraon villages. In the village there is a place called Mahadev-manda or Mahadev-place. Here there is an egg-like stone piece which is thought to be Mahadev and worshipped. Touching the egg-shaped stone piece there is an iron trident which is erected from the ground below. As per belief of the Oraons, the egg-like rock by itself comes up from below the ground. And then the pahan or some person of the village gets an order in a dream that Mahadev has appeared in a particular place after breaking the ground from below and quickly His worship should begin. The word regarding the dream spreads throughout the village, and thereafter "bhui-fore" Mahadev's (coming from below the ground by breaking its surface) worship begins as a public function.

Apart from worshipping Mahadev to release them from the grip of black magic and other maladies, often women of the village who have no children worship Him for getting children. Although the Oraons believe that Mahadev protects their village and protects them from the influence of witches and sorcerers, hence He is their village God, but the worship of Mahadev, its rituals and the prayers clearly spell out that Mahadev is a God of the Hindus which Oraons have accepted.

Devi Mai

Devi Mai worshipped by the Oraons has actually been taken from the Hindus. On the boundary of Oraon villages, there is often a palash tree "devi-sthan" (place of goddess) where "Devi Mai" is worshipped. Often the "devi sthan" is built of four logs of wood with a roof on top. In the centre of the "devi sthan," three, five or seven conical breast-like mud pieces are kept which symbolise "devi mai" and these pieces are worshipped here. In some Oraon "dhumkuriyas" (public places of culture) these breast-like pictures are also to be found. They are the symbols of "devi-ma" (goddess-mother). "Devi mai" and "devi-sthan" are to be found in nearly all Oraon villages and in the Oraon psyche a special faith in "Devi-mai" can be found. Worship of the phallus of Mahadev and breast of the mother is not a new thing for the Oraons- it is an ancient thinking which can be identified with the Oraon thinking about strength and increasing one's offsprings. "Devi ma" looks after the health, prosperity and welfare of the villagers and keeping them hale and hearty helps them in the increase of their family and property.

Chappar Budhiya

There are some "naads" among the community of Oraon gods and goddesses and "naads" who are not recognised among all Oraons- they are prevalent in certain villages and regions and obtain worship from the inhabitants of those villages and regions. The interval of time for worship may be one year to 12 years. "Chhappar budhiya" is just such a "naad" who is worshipped in Bandi Village of Bero police station. On every twelfth year "Chhappar Budhiya" is offered sacrifice of a he-buffalo. The worship of chapper Budhiya and the story of her fear is prevalent among the people of Bandi village. The villagers say that centuries ago, an old woman used to live on the edge of the village and she was getting her roof tiled by Oraon labourers. She told her daughter to cut the pumpkin and prepare a broth of that vegetable so that after the labourers finished their work, they could be given something to eat. The labourers mistook the word "kaddu" (pumpkin) as human sacrifice or meat, and the various activities of the old woman made them feel that she was a witch. The frightened workers returned to the village, and when the villagers came to know everything, then they left that village and went and settled in some other village.

Time passed. Again some Oraons came to stay in that village and started to cultivate. Among them was one Jado Oraon. He was a "mati" and knew how to hypnotise witches and also to counteract their darts. One day he was ploughing his field when the witch appeared before him as his wife and gave him a cup of water to drink. Jado recognised her as a witch hence making an excuse of drinking the water, he spilt it. The next day, the witch came again. Jado was alert, and he had got some iron grams prepared by the iron smith and had brought them with him. He asked the witch to open her mouth and immediately he stuffed her mouth with the iron grams. The witch understood that she had been caught and that escape was difficult so she entered into a compromise with Jado that she would not trouble the villagers but she should get something to eat. According to this compromise, after every 12 years, sheep and buffalo sacrifice are offered to the "Chhappar Budhiya." It is said that the earlier residents came back to the village to stay.

Chandi Pahar

In some villages, the special formation of hills or in similar special natural condition some "naad" or the other is connected to it, and thereafter the custom of worship and sacrifice is begun and the name of the "naad" is kept on the basis of the name of that special place. Within the limits of Lohardagga police station there is a village called Jamgai on the outer limits of which there is a very high hilly portion. Near that there is a cave in which rain water collects in the rainy season. The villagers have accepted the residence of Chandi on the top of this high hill, and they worship her. The village pahan along with the villagers go to that hill, and winding a cloth made of untwisted thread on a bamboo, vermillion is plastered on it, and with that the pinnacle of the hill is marked with vermillion. The specialty of the hill is that the villagers see the footprints of elephants on the slope near the cave.

The worship of Chandi hill is done in month of Sravan. The pahan sacrifices two cocks at the place on the slope near the cave where the elephants supposedly leave their footprints. After that, the pahan's assistant called the pujar goes near the cave and pours milk over the water. It is seen whether the water in the cave turns milky white after the pouring of milk on it. If this does not happen, then it is not accepted to be a good sign. According to the belief of the villagers, the milky water of the cave must rise as milk on the footprints of the elephants. While returning the villagers examine this attentively. If the footprints do not show less dried up milk or wet signs are not seen, then the pujar drops one or two drops of milk as he goes down the slope. The villagers say that according to their ancestors, the milk poured in the cave clearly rises on the footprints of the elephants, but since the past one or two generations, neither the footprints of the elephants are clearly seen nor the specks of milk on them. Despite this, Chandi hill protects the wavering villagers from trouble and sends them rain water on time for their agriculture.

Badanda Peeper

The worship of "badanda peeper" (long pepper tree) is done mainly for rain water. In nearly every Oraon village of western Chhotanagpur, the worship of "badanda peeper" is prevalent. There is a tree named "mui chitkha," a variety of which is also called "haji peeper," which is to be found in every Oraon village. According to Oraon belief, this tree has a direct connection with the clouds and if it is properly and as per procedure worshipped, then on the day of worship or one or two days later, there is bound to be rain. The village women take a clay pitcher full of water and go in a group to the "badanda peeper." Prior to that, the women have smeared with cow dung the nearby soil and sanctified it. Sometimes the pahan also goes along with the women of the village. He offers special prayers and fixes joss sticks on the tree after having lighted them. In some villages, the pahan winds untwisted thread around the tree and thereafter offers the lighted joss-sticks. The women pour the water of their pitchers on the root of this tree.

If that day or within one or two days it does not rain, then the pahan declares that there has been some fault in the procedure of worship, hence all the rituals are again repeated. The "badanda peeper" is supposed to be the "naad" to bring rains.

Vanshakti Garha-dhora-chatur-Seeman

Apart from the aforementioned important village "naads," there are some small "naads" which lie scattered in various places of the village but which do not have any specific name nor are special worships conducted for them, yet they do not forget to influence Oraon life. Among these "naads," the river flowing near the forest-ditch, rivulet, "dhora," the clever ones here and there within the four boundaries, etc. are "naads" which reside in these places and as soon as opportunity arises they trouble the villagers. Sometimes the "garhadhora" pulls a bather by the feet and takes him to the depth and after killing his body, assimilates his soul within itself. In the Oraon villages, these four naads are given a group name, and according to the pahan when need arises then these "naads" are worshipped together with offerings.

Toosa Burha

In the plateau of Chhotanagpur, small-big rivulets are many in number and nearly every village is situated beside one or two such rivulets.

These rivulets are known by the name of "toosi." According to the belief of the Oraons, the "naads" reside in these "toosas." In every "toosa" it is essential to have at least one naad. Sometimes the Oraon people worship the naads of the toosas separately and give offerings, but sometimes all the "toosa naads," are worshipped along with the other gods and goddesses in which worship is offered to them by name. But in some villages, these "toosa naads" are not worshipped they are marked and bound due to which their purity remains.

The village women, on the occasion of the birth of a child, or on the occasion of somebody's death, bathe themselves in a group in these rivulets and believe that after their bath the water of the rivulet has become impure and not fit to be drunk. Hence, for purifying it, they erect a stone piece at the place from where the rivulet emerges and on it they mark with vermillion and sprinkle some water on it and that is how the women purify it after which the water becomes fit to be drunk.

Classified Gods-goddesses and Naad

The meaning of classified gods and goddesses is such gods and goddesses who are worshipped specially by a special class, and this special class achieves success in a special sector by such worship. Chandi is the first name among such gods and goddesses.

Chandi

Chandi is the goddess of the unmarried youth and her jurisdiction is limited to giving success in hunting. Married men are prohibited to worship Chandi. Just like Mahadev, Chandi is worshipped in the form of an egg-like rock piece in which she is installed. The Oraons believe that just like "bhuifoot" Mahadev, the egg-like rock piece denoting Chandi automatically breaks the ground from below and appears on the surface. Chandi sends a dream to some villager that she has emerged at a particular place, hence they should worship her and make all arrangements in this regard.

Below the main rock piece of Chandi similar kind of small egg-like rock pieces lie strewn about. The Oraons believe that these small rock pieces are actually pieces of the big Chandi. They also have the same power. The installed egg-like piece in the main Chandi place becomes large within a few years.

The main worship of Chandi is conducted in the full moon of the month of Magh. About eight days earlier, all the Oraons of the village assemble in the "akhra" and fix the coming full moon day as the day of "aira mokhot."[33] This means the day for eating the he-goat, meaning thereby that on the day of Chandi worship, the flesh of the he-goat is obtained as holy food, hence instead of clearly saying the day of Chandi worship, the Oraons use such a term. The young men go from door to door reminding the householders to prepare enough rice wine for that day. They say, "We will eat the meat of the he-goat on the full moon day of the month of Magh. Rice wine should be prepared quickly otherwise it will not be fit to be used."

On the full moon day, the unmarried youth of the village either stand in two rows or sit down with an aisle between the two rows. That place is sanctified earlier by the wife of the pahan by wiping and smearing it with cow dung. Among those young men, one of them, who is more sensitive to invisible forces, plays the role of "paichalwa," meaning that divine powers come over him and with these divine powers he selects the pahan for Chandi.

Selection of Chandi-pahan : Pestle Movement Procedure

The way that the village has a pahan, the same way a pahan is selected from amongst the assembled youths for conduct of Chandi worship. The Sarna winnowing fan is brought from the pahan's house and on it some "arwa" rice (rice extracted from unboiled paddy) is put. The paichalwa takes a stone pestle and with his palm rolls it over the ground. By that time everybody believes that the goddess has come over the paichalwa and due to her divine power the pestle, moves on its own towards the men standing in line. Whosoever's foot is touched by the pestle that young man is taken to be the pahan of Chandi. Thereafter either everybody assembled there or at least one representative washes the feet of the selected Chandi pahan.

Worship

At about 10 O'clock, the new Chandi pahan reaches the Chandi upland after having taken a bath where the youth of his group have assembled from before. The Chandi pahan puts three vermillion marks on the Chandi stone and offers "arwa" rice. The other young men from the assembly of youth repeat this ritual saying, "Listen to us attentively so that you may make us fit to hunt well." Thereafter, the sacrificial goat is given arwa rice to eat and when it is in the process of eating, the Chandi pahan decapitates the goat in one go with his axe. The head of the goat is put on the Chandi stone for some time so that Chandi's thirst for blood may be quenched. After that the young men skin the head and body of the goat, cut the flesh into pieces and cook it. In a separate vessel, rice is cooked. Accompanied with rice wine, the unmarried youth feast on the rice and meat to their heart's content. This whole programme goes on atop the Chandi upland till after sunset. The conclusion of the worship on Chandi upland is with the "jatra" flag being taken to the "dhumkuriya" (cultural centre) and joining in the function there. All the young men reach the "dhumkuriya" with musical instruments where the village girls meet them and till late night dancing goes on.

There is one ritual related to Chandi worship which remains to be done in which the newly selected young Chandi pahan in the concluding days of the month of Magh, along with one or two companions after midnight, having shaved his head, purified himself by taking a bath, completely naked, fills a pot of dried gourd and reaches Chandi upland, and bathes the Chandi stone with that water and thereafter marks the stone with oil and vermillion. While worshipping he says, "I am worshipping you completely. I am returning home after having offered oil and vermillion to you. My prey which is 12-13 "kose" (one kose is equal to two miles) away may come on horse back i.e. come quickly, and fall in my village."[34]

It is said that Chandi appears in various forms. Sometimes Chandi appears in the form of a tiger, or at times in the form of elephant or snake. If on that occasion the young pahan becomes frightened then definitely he will be punished, in one move he will get fever or stomach ache or he will be afflicted by some other malady. The Oraons believe that when pleased, Chandi appears in various forms.

In the religious belief of the Oraons, it is a normal accepted procedure for "naads" or gods and goddesses to appear in different forms.

Achhrayal/Achhrain

The way Chandi is the adored god of the unmarried Oraon young men, the same way Achchrayal and her companion Jonda is the adored goddess of the Oraon women. Every "khunt" at least once in a life time worships Achchrayal so that every married and unmarried or old women are protected in every way by the kindness of Achchrayal. Achhrayal is not installed in any stone piece or "khunt" or article-she is thought to be formless and worshipped accordingly.

In order to participate in the worship of Achhrayal, all the married female relatives namely, daughter, niece, grand-daughter, sister, etc. are invited along with their husbands. They come over one day prior to the fixed day of worship, and on the day of worship they have to keep a fast till the worship lasts. They bathe and wear new or clean clothes and sit in a row. If due to any reason any girl of the "khunt" is absent, then in her place a rounded mud piece is made to sit in the row to register her presence. Similarly the unmarried girls have a round mud piece sitting beside them to denote their future husbands. In this way, the worship of Achhrayal begins with the presence of all the married and unmarried girls of the "khunt" along with their husbands or future husbands, as the case may be.

A male member of the "khunt" or family, as per his financial condition, offers sacrifice of a pig or a sheep or a he-goat, when offering worship to Achhrayal. While offering the sacrifice, he prays to Achhrayal thus, "O Achhrayal! Please keep the women, the elderly women and the girls of our "khunt" away from suffering and disease. Please do not give them any kind of malady and sorrow."

After the sacrifice, the man who has offered the sacrifice sprinkles the blood of the sacrifice on the assembled women and their husbands and frees them of possible illnesses and suffering through Achhrayal.

The next morning, the girls compulsorily go away with their husband to their in-law's house even though they might come back the very next day.

Such a worship of Achhrayal takes place in every "khunt" at least once for preventing diseases. After child birth, in order to remedy the situation of mother's milk being not enough or the infant falling sick all the time, there is provision for worship of Achhrayal and to offer her sacrifice.

The worship of Achhrayal is related mainly to women. There is a belief that if Achhrayal is worshipped well, then the "naad" of the girl's father's house cannot come with the girl which makes the husband-wife couple happy.

Joda

Just like Achhrayal, Joda is a "naad" benevolent towards women, but Achhrayal is worshipped in all khunts of all Oraon villages whereas Joda is worshipped in some selected Oraon villages. In some areas, the Oraons have no knowledge regarding Joda. The Joda is formless and cannot be indicated through any article or rounded stone.

The Joda is worshipped the next day of the worship of Achhrayal. The rituals and procedure for the worship of Joda is nearly the same as of Achhrayal. In the worship of Joda, the women of the "khunt' along with their husbands or future husbands in the form of rounded mun figure participate in rows, and sacrifice of sheep is offered. The next day after the worship, the girls go with their husbands to their in-law's house.

Khunt Naad

Every "khunt" has a "naad" who has to be appeased by the offering of worship which is the responsibility of that "khunt." It is said that the "khunt" "naad" is the well wisher of the "khunt" and is benevolent but sometimes some "khunt naads" forcibly weigh on the "khunt" and torture the members of that "khunt."

The worship of "khunt naad" had begun in Oraon society in that period when Oraons had come over to Chhotanagpur, and, after clearing the forests, had recovered land for cultivation and building houses. At that time it was believed that the "khunt" after clearing the forest had prepared land for itself, it had disturbed the "naad" settled in that forest area and made it homeless. Hence, where would the "naad" of that place go ? Resultantly, it was decided that the members of the "khunt" would worship their area "naad" and by offering sacrifice would always appease them. Since these "naads" are connected to every "khunt," hence it is natural that the "khunt naad" of a particular "khunt" would compulsorily think benevolently about that "khunt." Some portion of land is reserved for the worship of the "naad"-such a field is called "naad kheta."

There has been a different kind of addition to the "khunt naad" which is undoubtedly a later on development. If any member of the "khunt" has killed a person, then the dead person becomes the "khunt" ghost of that family and overshadows it. It then receives sufficient offerings. Probably it takes its revenge on the family by obtaining such offerings.

The original "khunt naad" is formless and often it is the well wisher of the family.

Badanda Pachcho

Those Oraons who are not Bhuihars and they do not have "khunt-naad," worship "Badanda Pachcho" which makes up for the shortage that the Bhuihars gain in worshipping "khunt naad." "Badanda pachcho" or "bar-pahari" and some other "naads" namely "chingri naad," "goysali naad" etc. are worshipped by the ordinary/ general Oraons because they are not Bhuihars and neither is any "khunt naad" attached to them.

According to the prevalent Asur tales among the Oraons, "Badanda" was the widow of an Asur who had died by being trapped in the furnace by Dharmes.[35] It is said that she had seven daughters among whom the chief were Hankar Bai, Pos Bai, Kiro Bai, etc. In Oraon religion all these daughters receive offerings of worship as per circumstances. "Badanda" is worshipped by particular homes or clan and she looks after the welfare of the clan members.

The worship of "Badanda" is beneficial. The date for worship is normally fixed on the full moon day of Magh month and all the members of the fraternity or the elders of the family are informed through invitation the date of the worship. On the date fixed, the family while keeping a fast, goes to an open field or near a hillock with materials for worship and sacrifice. The place is sanctified by smearing it smoothly with cow-dung, and rounded mud figures of Badanda "naad" are made and set up for three to five days. The mud figures are marked with oil and vermillion. The animal which has been brought for sacrifice is bathed in water and mark of vermillion is also made on it and while offering it to Badanda, the eldest in the family prays thus – "O Dangra naad accept it. Forget about my hands and feet. I have bought this sacrificial bullock and am offering it to you. From today do not give us bad dreams and fever. Be quiet. You are the soul of Asur man/ woman. From today till within a fortnight we will erect "Chingri," or bamboo (meaning thereby that sacrifice will also be offered to Chingri) and will offer sacrifice and worship to "dhaha goysali also."

In the process of worship, it is prayed, "Dangri naad, udd Badanda, neha Badanda, please remain quiet for five/seven/twelve years. This means that after this time period, the family members will again remember you." In the place of "khunt naad" those Oraons who are not Bhuihars, a certain part of their family clan shifts into a different house or due to some other reason starts living separately, and this part of the family will compulsorily have to worship Badanda Pachcho at least once within 3 years to 12 years. The person who is separated due to this worship can be counted as of the same clan as per family tree.

Chingri Naad

Fifteen days after the worship of Badanda Pachcho, two bamboo poles touching each other are erected at the door of the house. By afternoon the invited fraternity assembles and an elder of the family acting as an intermediary arranges for the worship of "danda-katta" for the inspection of which a "mati" is appointed. The story about Dharmes is recounted among the assembled people, and prayer is offered thus- "Today, twelve Asur brothers and thirteen Lodhar brothers have been thrust into the iron smelting furnace with the help of bamboo pole which is twelve feet long and thirteen feet wide. Their foul language speaking faces have now changed to Uhu Badanda, Hankar Bai, Pol Bai, Chigur Gari Daha and Goensali. I appease all of them through this worship. Now there should not be from your side any illness, fever, bad dreams or terrifying acts."

Goensali Naad

Goensali naad is worshipped to keep the cattle healthy and free from any illness. The day Chingri naad is worshipped, on that very day a cock is made to enter the cattle pen and it starts eating the rice lying scattered on the ground of the pen. The elder member of the family enters the cattle pen and observes "tukko othorna" which means that he lets out the cock to fly away. Outside, a person catches the cock and sacrifices it as an offering to Gosoeli Naad or Gohar god or Goriya. After offering the sacrifice of the cock, the following prayer is uttered- "Now we have offered worship to you. Now you take away all our sins and illnesses and go. Please do not trouble us with any sickness or other disasters."

Surjahi Worship

After the worship of Chingri naad, "Surjahi" worship is done. Surjahi god is also called "danr" ṛaja or king, and worship or sacrifice is conducted on a high mound near a river, pond or brook. All the men and women of the family and relatives keep a fast during this worship and participate in it. A white he-goat has to be sacrificed. It is sanctified and vermillion mark is put on it. Arwa rice is scattered on the floor and while the he-goat is busy eating the rice, it is beheaded with an axe and offered as sacrifice. Then a prayer is offered- "O Surjahi god, we are offering sacrifice to you. Please do not give us suffering from today, rather give us good health and prosperity."

Surjahi god is none else but the Sun-god or Dharmes. The name of the god and sacrifice of white he-goat or white cock determines that the worship of Dharmes is being conducted. Amongst all the aforementioned gods and goddesses, the worship of Dharmes is considered to be necessary. After conduct of this worship, that part of the family which has separated to form a new family, their religious responsibilities are nearly complete. After Surjahi worship, it is said that the home is complete.

Magic and Spells

The religious and social life of Oraon tribe have been deeply influenced by prevalent beliefs in magic and spells or superstitions. The gods and goddesses, special invisible powers all worshipped by the Oraons, and which are said to be in the form of sectoral gods and goddesses are worshipped in agriculture, hills, forest, upland; or the souls of the dead which are unsatisfied souls, of whom the Oraons are always terrified; or the "naads" residing in ponds, rivers and bamboo groves which warn the Oraons by sending them maladies regarding the offerings due to them; all of them are worshipped by the Oraons on fixed time and sometimes as per requirement. The aim of worship and proffering sacrifice to the gods and "naads" is mostly to please them and get some benefits from them, but sometimes it is done to appease them so that they might not send any sickness or calamity to the Oraons and afflict them.

It has been the specialty of the religion of the primitive tribes to worship gods and goddesses and the "naads" out of sheer fear. In Munda and Oraon religion, most of the bongas or naads who have over a period of time gained respect and place as gods and goddesses are actually the widows of the Asurs who had been killed by Singbonga or Dharmes through intelligence. Since the Asurs were by nature conceited, greedy, wicked and destructive, hence it was natural that their wives would be having the same family traits. Keeping in mind the background of the Asurs, there could be no expectation of goodness or welfare from the Asur-wives. Resultantly, due to the aforementioned psychological feeling, Oraon general life has been always tortured by these "naads" and invisible powers, and their worship is with the aim to appease and pacify them, although the Oraon also believes that Dharmes by accepting the Asur widows has given them divine form.

Maximum benefit has been derived by the practitioners of black magic from the desire of the "naads" or the destructive nature of invisible divine forces to be appeased through sacrifices. These practitioners through various incantations and worship obtain power over certain "naads" and make them do their desired work or through the subjugated "naads", thrust deadly illnesses on enemies who they want to destroy. Such kind of black magic is so prevalent in Oraon life that an institution has developed of magicians or practitioners of spells and incantations and witches who are connected with such activities. The Oraons secretly utilise the services of such witches and magicians to take revenge on their neighbours or others, or else to ensure their downfall due to jealousy or enmity and they use the subjugated "naads" of such practitioners for the destruction of their enemies.

If there is a disease, then its solution is also found out. In order to nullify the evil effects of the troubles sent by the witches or practitioners of black magic through their subjugated "naads," the institution of sokha and bhagats has developed in Oraon religion. These sokhas and bhagats have acquired such knowledge and learning that they not only find out about the "naads" but at times they offer good offerings to the aroused "naads," win their confidence and bring them over to their side, or else using the power of their gods and goddesses they nullify the effects of the dart of black magic.

In this way, two types of systems have developed in Oraon religion-one is to devise means to destroy an enemy through black magic utilizing the services of "naads" or invisible powers, and second is the opposite of these destructive devices of sorcery wherein other gods and goddesses are turned in one's favour and sorcery is opposed and the effects of sorcery are rendered harmless. The source of power of both systems are those invisible forces equivalent to the same "naads" or bonga or gods and goddesses who are in normal conditions worshipped by all Oraons as per their religion and, on fixed time, offered sacrifices also.

Witch

According to the belief of the Oraons, certain people are to be found in this world whose vision and speech automatically give rise to destructive influence. This trait of a person is often from birth. The meaning of person is both male and female but after study it was found that this characteristic is mostly found in females. If the sight of such a woman falls on an infant then it will immediately fall ill. Or if from the mouth of such a woman some destructive words come out, then immediately its result starts. The soul of such a woman or man is supposed to be wicked.

Although in Oraon society such women are supposed to be having an evil eye and everybody tries to hide her child from such a woman, but she does not have to endure the detestation meted out to a witch. There is a difference between women with wicked souls and witches. Actually the witch has to learn the skill of black magic from a teacher and has to train for it after which she acquires the capability to practice black magic so that she can subjugate "naads" and compel them to do her bidding.

Witch-Initiation

The initiation of witches is done only once in a year. The entire work of initiation is done on the new moon night of Kartik month, far away from habitation in a lonely spot and conducted very secretly. All the witches from the nearby villages come to the fixed place and after midnight, taking off their clothes, they wear at the waist a broom of grass spread out like a thin skirt and the witches start dancing. The skull of a cheetah is kept nearby on which an earthen lamp is lit, giving out faint light. All the rituals regarding black magic are taught in between the dancing. Incantation, throwing magical darts or intercepting them, and the other technicalities of the knowledge of black magic are told in detail by the teacher/preceptor who also makes them practice. These witches who have learned this skill before act as assistants in this training workshop. According to the religion of the witches, the new trainees have to take a solemn vow that even if they lose their lives they will not break the secrecy of this skill. This oath-taking is a necessary part of the training activity. The preceptor along with the other witches together ask the newly trained witches thus- "will you like to be punished with the handle of the axe or the head of the spade or will you reveal the secret?" In reply, the new witches state that they will endure all kinds of punishment but will not divulge the secret of their religion, that is, religion of witches. In one voice they reply, "O master preceptor, we will endure, endure, endure."

The Oraon villagers believe that if the dance of the witches is seen by a man and if a witch's sight falls on him, then very soon he dies. Often these witches take out the heart of such a man through their magic and wrapping it in a peepal leaf, place it on the peepal tree. The man does not experience anything. Thereafter on a fixed day the witches through some incantation destroy the heart. On that day at that very moment the man dies. Hence the villagers always try to avoid being seen by the witches.

Witches-work Procedure

In order to kill, trouble or sicken their targets, the witches take recourse to the following procedures :

(a) Masan Procedure

According to this procedure, the witch takes an old torn cloth and makes it into a bundle or some witches take a small earthen pot and put the following ingredients in it and cover it-fried arwa rice, leg of a cock, cock's head, some pieces of flesh and, blood, horn and bones of some animal. Such kind of a bundle or earthen pot is buried in that village or within the boundary of that house very secretly which is the target for sending trouble. These items which are under a spell invite the subjugated naad because the naad knows that after fulfilling the work given to him by the witch it will get the offering of cock and animal sacrifice. Hence, according to the witches, this blow of magic definitely succeeds and the affected village or house is surrounded with disasters. It is only a skilled ojha or such who can treat this blow of magic. He takes out the bundle or earthen pot from its hiding place and assures the naad of giving better sacrifice.

(b) Magic-dart or Dart of the Evil Eye

This arrow of magic incantation has got a long range of hitting. The witch takes a small arrow of grass and casts a spell on it through incantation and aiming it at the target she shoots it. Its aim never fails and on whosoever or whichever animal this arrow falls, he/it starts getting pain on the face or the joints of the body without any reason. According to the belief of the Oraons it is clear from such kind of sudden pain that a magic arrow has hit the target and immediately an ojha or bhagat is called for its treatment.

(c) Heart-Removal

It is an experienced and skilful witch who has knowledge of taking out somebody's heart through magic. This practice is chiefly carried out on the new moon night of Sohrai. From the viewpoint of black magic, the new moon night of the month of Kartik is an extremely sensitive night and the magic or incantation practised on that day never goes in vain. Whosoever has to be killed, on this night the witch takes out his heart through incantation and wraps it in a peepal leaf and puts it on the peepal tree. She fixes a day for his death. It has been seen that such a person dies without any reason.

(d) Chor Deva or Black Cat

The witch is an expert in changing form, especially black cat or at times she becomes a human being of thumb size and like a thief enters the targeted house quietly. She licks the saliva oozing out of the mouths of sleeping persons and makes them ill or she puts her shadow on them and gives them night mares so much so that after awaking they become mentally abnormal. If the Oraons see a black cat inside the house or near the house, they immediately catch it and kill it. According to their belief, as the cat's body is broken up at the same time the witch's body inside it is also broken up and with the death of the cat, the witch also dies.

At times the naad which is worshipped by the witch becomes angry and hits out at the witch and her family. Hence the witch is very careful in using the naads, in their worship and according to their entitlement the offering of sacrifice.

Just like the witches, "Bis-ha" is also skilful in sending diseases and death through black magic. Bis-ha is male. He has not received so much of notoriety in his act as the witches have received, yet some Oraons take his help to kill or defeat their enemies and devise means for the same. Bis-ha can be seen here and there in the villages but their numbers are few. It is said that Bis-has have good knowledge of poisonous substances. The Bis-ha, along with black magic, devises such poisonous means that his target cannot escape him. Along with witch craft, the Bis-ha knows about black magic and use of poison. Bis-ha is the later on development of the black magic sector.

Mati

Although the mati finds out the naads and delivers the Oraons from the troubles and disasters brought by them, but upon demand, just like the witches and bis-has, he can send ghosts for bringing trouble or indulge in the wicked deed of doing away with somebody's life, therefore, he is not kept in the same category as bhagat and such who think only of freeing the victims from illnesses and get a position of respect from people of society. The mati is supposed to be expert in both black and white magic. In Oraon, matis are enough in number and can be found in nearly every village.

The mati acquires his knowledge of black magic and its solutions from a well known preceptor whose shelter he takes and does hard duty for him. The preceptor sits cross-legged on the floor of the training room, and in front of him forming a half-moon his students/disciples sit in the same cross-legged fashion on the floor. On his knees is a winnowing fan with some arwa rice in it. On the palm of his right hand he takes some of the arwa rice and rubs them against each other. This he does while maintaining a rhythmic balance so much so that the whole room, which is closed, develops a divine atmosphere. Gradually, one of the disciples who is more sensitive, starts jerking his head and body. These are those signs from which one can conclude that the naad has come upon him. At this juncture the preceptor lights joss sticks, and welcomes the naad by ringing a bell, sounding a gong and blowing on a conch shell. When the sounds abate somewhat, naadsong is sung in which description is given of various kinds of sacrifice. The matis believe that this song satisfies the naad. Thereafter "utarna" song is sung to bring down the naad.

The Desired Goddess of Mati : Kali Mai (mother)

The naads invoked by matis are of ordinary category or naads which have gone astray, but the desired and adored goddess of Matis is Kali Mai or Burhi Mai. It is said that Kali Mai has two attendants- Ranth and Dank- who if required, can catch hold of any naad or divine power and present them before Kali Mai.

The mati pays full attention to the installation of Kali Mai and her worship and offering of sacrifice. On the day of Rath Yatra in the month of Ashar, often the mati makes a platform of a plank or of mud, and on it installs three rounded figures of mud. Near these figures he plants an iron trident from which emanates a feeling of the local Kali Mai. Thereafter he scatters some copper coins near the mud figures, and marks the figure of Mai with oil and vermillion.

In this way, after the ceremony of imparting life to the figure of Kali Mai on the plank is completed, a red cock and a black he-goat are sacrificed, and offered to the Goddess along with oblation of rice wine. There are some disciples of the mati who look after the place of worship and assist in all the duties pertaining to conduct of worship of Kali Mai. The "paat-chela" is that disciple who every morning brings white mud or plaster mud and applies to the whole place of worship and purifies it. The "phool-chela" is that disciple who arranges for "gulachi" flowers with which worship of Kali Mai is conducted. On the new moon night of Kartik month or the ninth day of Sohrai, the mati worships Kali Mai with great fanfare and offers sacrifice of black he-goat and proffers rice wine.

Treatment by Matis

The porch of the house of the patient or any other outer room is purified by smearing with cow dung and the patient is made to lie down on a cot. Near the Mati is placed a winnowing fan with "arwa" rice, oil and clarified butter in mud vessels, a new earthenware lamp in which there should be oil and wick, some articles meant for the sacrificial fire. The mati ignites the fire and starts chanting prayers in which all gods and goddesses, ghosts and spirits, preceptor and well known deceased matis are invoked and prayed that the mati, who is conducting this worship to get the patient rid of his illness, may be helped. The mati takes out rice from the winnowing fan and makes a circle and ties it down with prayer. This ritual is called "bhoomi bandhna" ritual (tying the place). The intention is that if any naad, ghost-spirit, witch or mati tries to put an obstacle in the conduct of the worship, then that effort will return after hitting against the line of the circle. Thereafter through "pind-bandhna" Mati ties his body with prayers, so that wicked powers do not influence him. Now the mati lights the lamp and dipping his middle finger in its oil he marks the space all around the four directions of the lamp on the ground. This is called "deepbarna" ritual. The mati tries to install Ranth in the flame of the lamp through chanting of prayers and in this he becomes successful.

Thereafter, the mati breaks a hair from the tuft of hair on his head and burns it in the flame of the lamp and drops some mud on the ground. In this way, by burning his hair, he symbolically conducts human sacrifice and by dropping mud on the ground he says that it has been turned to mud meaning thereby that the funeral rites have been performed.

Finding out the Naad

After having completed all the preparations, the Mati tries to catch hold of or find out the naad for which he starts the ritual. These rituals are of two kinds- some matis catch the naad through the arwa rice while some catch through the flame of the lamp. This depends upon the learning and training/ procedure of the matis.

(a) The procedure to catch a naad by counting the arwa rice is quite long. The mati takes a pinch of arwa rice in his fingers and chants a prayer thus:- O king, if (he names the naad) naad is in this figure then the five time periods of the day wrong things should not be considered, this is the earth and above is God Almighty and in between the god should consider while taking on the form of arbitrator/judge. Just like a god. He should separate milk from water, like the forward flow of milk and the flow of milk behind it, of a cow. The dog eats the flesh of the cow but the cow does not eat the flesh of the dog. Your plate is full, see O Naad, it is full, and you do not have to search for it."

In this manner, after praying in Hindi, the pinch of arwa rice is kept on the floor and duos of two-two rice are separated. If after formation of duos, one rice remains, then this ritual is done five times and it is seen that the conclusion was correct. Hence in the name of whichso ever naad the lone rice is left, declaration of that naad is made in front of everybody that such and such naad has entered the patient.

When all the rice form duos then the Mati interprets that "the ghost is deluding, it is not coming to the forefront." Then the mati through the ritual of "naad rasgiya" finds out the naad and declares in front of the patient.

(b) Through the flame of the lamp: Some matis light another lamp apart from the lamp burning on top of the rice. The second lamp they put on their palm and confront it with the first lamp which is giving a steady light. Then the mati serially pronounces the names of the naads and with every name throws some rice on the first lamp which makes its flame go this way and that way. If the flame moves towards the lighted lamp on the palm of the mati then the naad is caught. In this procedure, since it is taken for granted that Ranth has been installed in the flame of the first lamp hence it knows the murderer, that is the naad which has given the sickness. When the flame moves towards the mati, it is believed that Ranth through its knowledge has accepted the name of the naad. In this way, with the sign of the flame of the lamp, the naad is caught, and declaration is made in front of the patient.

"Bahi-Pakarna"

Thereafter the mati picks up one grain of rice from the collection of rice; with this grain of rice two-three grains also come up. The rice sticking to the rice in the pinch of the mati's fingers is known as the rice of the ghost. The mati catches hold of that rice and takes it outside and states thus, "from today you will not enter this house." In order to satisfy the ghost, the Mati promises to offer sacrifice to it. He breaks turmeric into three pieces and draws three lines which thereafter cannot be crossed by the naad to regain entry into the house.

The Handing over of Naad to Darha Naad

The mati fashions out a trumpet with sal leaves or leaves of other trees, and, winding some cloth makes a brush out of the cloth. He dips the brush in oil and draws the figure of a man on the floor. Now he takes out near the lamp some salt, vermillion and from his bundle some cloth, medicinal plant or some solid article with a spell on it and which is called "banck" in the relevant language and keeps them near the vermillion. He pricks a finger on his left hand and takes out blood. That blood is used to mark the rice through which the naad had been found out. The brush is then ignited like a torch. Then the mati says, "Mercy, nat-natin – the ghost of this figure has fled somewhere and is in hiding, bring it out of hiding." After saying this, the mati stares at the flame of the torch as if "nat-nati" have caught hold of that naad and made it sit in the flame. The mati catches hold of the right hand of the patient and one by one takes the name of all the gods who are in his knowledge- "burhi mai," kali mai, etc. The mati moves the torch around the vermillion and says thus, "I'll give you nine maunds of vermillion, nine maunds of kohl, all things needed for your makeup, thirty two skirts," and so saying he puts out the flame of the torch with his left foot. Sometimes he puts it out by covering it with the winnowing fan.

The torch is relit with a lighted lamp and is taken round the figure of the man drawn on the floor. The mati says, "I am giving you a figure in place of another figure. From today you are being marked. You should not go forward or backward. If you go forward and backward, then you will be born as an animal."

The mati lifts his left foot and puts the trumpet beneath it and quickly inserts the torch in the trumpet and closes the mouth of the trumpet. Thereafter he says, "Mercy, O Darha of Nagapur, I am handing over the responsibility of the naad to you, you take over the responsibility. Eat meat and keep the bones. The day I will search for it, that day you will give it. I ask you for six months time then I will offer worship to mali-mati and install it there where it belongs. And if I will not search then make me like mud."

The mati gives the responsibility of the wicked naad to the powerful naad Darha of Chhotanagpur for atleast six months, and respectfully sends back all the gods who came from the east to the east, and those who came from the west to the west. The whole place is then cleaned up with the besmearing of cow-dung.

When the six months are about to be over, then a member of the house hold contacts the mati and asks him how the next worship is to be conducted. And the mati worships on the fixed date and appeases the banished naad and the darha naad. The aforementioned learning of the mati through which he treats patients, relieves homes from the clutches of wicked naads, and nullifies (through his learning) the naads and troubles sent by witches and bis-has, are for the benefit of society, hence the religious and social positions of mati are not repulsive whereas the whole learning of witches and bis-has is applied for destruction, thus society not only sees them with revulsion but also punishes them if they are caught, and at times they are banished from the village. Actually, witches, bis-has and the use of black magic are anti-religious and their system is anti-religious system. Dharmes had vested capability and powers with the naads not for misuse but had given them the responsibility of doing welfare of the race, but these naads due to greed and wicked nature are not only subjugated by the witches and bis-has but also devise means to destroy the Oraon race.

Since these naads are a part of Oraon religion and their responsibility is to do good to the race, but despite being a part of the religion they work against it, and it is their powers which are utilised to do such irreligious work as black magic, hence the system based on serving the naads can be called anti-religious.

In order to cancel this anti-religious system, the institution of bhagat, sokha, ojha has developed which runs parallel to religion, hence it is a parallel-religious system in which more superior and powerful naads and gods and goddesses are utilised to nullify the effects of projected black magic. These accomplished people mostly worship Mahadev and Devi Mai, and getting the benefit of their powers they cancel the evil effects of the projections of naads. The worship by the mati is connected to Kali mai who is more pleased with the offering of sacrifice, whereas the worship of Mahadev is with fruits-flowers, milk and sweets. In many villages of the Oraons, Mahadev sthan (place) may be found. Most of the time, Mahadev Himself appears in the form of a rounded stone from below the ground and gives information about his appearance in the form of dreams or similar ways to His beloved devotees. He is known as "bhui-phoot" Mahadev (appearing from below by breaking open the surface of the ground).

Bhagat or Sokha

The bhagat or sokha draws all his powers specially from the kindness of God Mahadev, but God's kindness is not to be found easily. The Oraon who is fully dedicated mentally to Mahadev and lives such a life which has the signs of the devotees of Mahadev, he is thought to be the loved one of Mahadev, and Mahadev encourages him. Some days later it is seen that the devotee in his devotion to Mahadev keeps awake for several nights and keeps on murmuring. This fact spreads among the Oraons that the devotee talks to Mahadev throughout the night. Such condition of the bhagat at times becomes a matter of concern for his family members. The bhagat or the sokha do not have any regular training like the mati. His powers come automatically to him due to his devotion, although various activities like naad, exorcism, freedom from disease, various devices of freedom from disease as per kind of disease, etc. their procedures he has to learn. Some bhagats and sokhas declare that they do not learn prayers/incantations but that they automatically are pronounced by them.

In this way, the bhagat and sokha do not receive formal training from any teacher yet despite their devotion, they do have to take training in many things. Either he learns by observation or by acknowledging a preceptor and learning from him the treatment of diseases and relevant rules and regulations and also learning about the articles needed for various processes-he memorises the list thoroughly. The bhagat and sokha as per prevalent situation, do not have formal training like the mati. Their powers are due to the grace of Mahadev.

Getting the Position of Bhagat or Sokha

The ordinary devotee of Mahadev cannot get the position of bhagat or sokha. For this he not only needs devotion bordering on madness but also to arrange himself, there must be a place of worship in the limits of his house or nearby in an appropriate place- this place of worship is called "Mahadev-Kuri" or "Dev-Kuri." Before the Mahadev kuri is set up, the bhagat faces two situations. He gets a dream that by piercing the soil above, at a particular place the rounded stone of Mahadev has come up from below. In this manner, it is God's order to his beloved devotee that he should serve that rounded stone, and the second situation is that in the madness of devotion he goes out of his house and goes to a far and lonely place and there he spends one full day or days in the meditation of God and in this manner word spreads in the village and the house holds that a particular person is talking directly to God and he is the beloved devotee of God.

Even amongst matis, under such circumstances some bhagats come out. It is seen that while taking training from the preceptor, in the process one or two trainee-matis who are more sensitive and of a purer nature, by remembering God's name suddenly stand up and like mad persons go away to the forest. After a few days, in the peaceful atmosphere of the forest and undertaking difficult devotion towards Mahadev, they witness His appearance. Thereafter they return to their village. In the meantime word spreads in their village and other neighbouring villages regarding their devotion and the appearance of Mahadev before them. The bhagat or sokha returns peacefully to the village and builds/sets up a "devkuri" at home and in full form starts his profession. By getting an order through a dream or witnessing the appearance of Mahadev in the jungle during meditation, the bhagat or sokha gathers widespread reknown and this becomes the basis of acknowledging his position as also his behaviour with the patients showing psychological skill, and his body-language play an important role in getting him the acceptance of far off villages.

Mahadev-Kuri and Worship of God

The name and fame of a bhagat or a sokha not only depends upon his skill but also the grandeur of arrangement in the "dev sthan." The bhagat dreams that the rounded stone of Mahadev has come from below the ground and, piercing the soil above, it has appeared above ground. Often this rounded stone is seen in the outer corner of the bhagat's house and then he spreads the word regarding his dream to his neighbours and arrives at that place where he gets the rounded stone of Mahadev. The Oraons call that stone "bhui-phoot" Mahadev. The place is then used to raise a mud platform and in the centre the rounded stone of Mahadev is planted and life is installed into it. Near the rounded stone an iron trident is planted. The rounded stone is then bounded on four sides in such a manner that the proffered water, milk, fruits etc. i.e. the holy food, can come out via a definite outlet and can be collected together. On the platform a bamboo pole 10-12 feet high with a red flag is planted so that from afar it can proclaim that it is a Mahadev-sthan. The whole platform at times on all four corners has bamboo poles or logs of wood with a thatched roof.

The worship of Mahadev is conducted wholly with milk, fruits, flowers, honey and sweets or jaggery. Joss sticks, clarified butter and things needed for the sacrificial fire are utilised. For arrangement of the worship, there are some disciples who have their work allotted to them. Before sunrise, one disciple besmears the place of worship with cow dung and makes it clean and pure while another disciple collects flowers and brings all the ingredients needed for worship. Every day in the morning the bhagat has his bath and without having taken any food or drink he prays to Mahadev and worships him. He bathes the rounded stone with milk. He sprinkles flowers, arwa rice, burns joss sticks and also uses the metal bell, gong, and conch shell. The whole "devkuri" smells of the fragrance of the joss sticks and resonates with the loudly uttered prayers and the sound of the bell and gong. Such kind of worship normally induces deep impact in the minds of the Oraons.

The Social Life of the Bhagat

The social life of the bhagat is guided by the sanctity of his profession. From morning to night his programme is fixed. Regular bath, worship, meditation, attending to the incoming patients and their well-wishers and deriving information from them and giving them advice. If called, with great difficulty he visits a home (a bhagat does not want to go to anybody's house because this reduces his respect and seriousness). While talking to people he uses guarded language. He speaks very little, and not by language but by expression he communicates.

The bhagat strictly maintains purity of diet. The bhagat can lead a married life and can bring a girl from another house to his home. If he is married, and has a son, then he can bring a girl from another house for his son. Meat and wine are completely prohibited in a bhagat's house. Everybody has to live on pure vegetarian food. The girl who comes as his wife or daughter-in-law has to rigorously follow this rule. The parents of the girl might be "Mahua Oraon" meaning thereby that they might be Oraon drinking wine and eating meat, but after marriage, the girl has to follow the rules of the bhagat's household. When she returns to her parents' home, she is supposed to avoid wine and meat and should not touch those vessels which have been used for wine and meat. She cooks her own food separately in a pure manner and keeps utensils separately for herself.

Even though he may be devotee of Mahadev, the bhagat does not neglect the procedures of traditional worship followed by the pahan and neither does he look down upon them because they are procedures tied to and approved by society. He worships the ancestors with arwa rice and rice wine. He contributes to the worship of Chala-pachcho and also participates in it, but does not participate in giving animal sacrifice and neither partakes of the holy meat. In this way he remains connected to the society in other festivals and worship but he remembers his own limitations and does not break the sanctity of his life at any cost. Actually the purity of his life has a direct relationship with the effective capability of his knowledge\learning as well as with his name and fame and respect in life.

The Cure and Treatment of Disease

Depending upon the name and fame of the bhagat, people from far and near come for their own treatment or the treatment of their children. For this the bhagat has fixed timings. The time starts after the sun is a bit high in the sky. Those who come to him bring offerings of a basket full of fruits, flowers, honey, milk, jossticks, turmeric, vermillion, materials for the sacrificial fire, incense, twelve kinds of cereals etc. The disciple offers the basket to Mahadev and thereafter keeps it with him but when the patient is leaving then some of it is given to him as holy food.

A belief has firmed up among the Oraons that due to the grace of Mahadev the bhagat has another supernatural power. Normally the bhagat does not take the responsibility of exorcising a " naad" but due to his supernatural power he can see those naads which have become the reason for disease or trouble He picks up a flower or leaf in front of the patient or in his name and reciting some prayers he starts staring at the petals of the flower or the leaf. After some moments, it appears as if the naad has clearly appeared on the petals or the leaf which the bhagat sees and declares its name.

In order to destroy the effects of the black magic or the ghosts and rid the patient of disease, the bhagat sits in front of the patient. If the patient can sit, then he is made to sit otherwise he is made to lie down on a cot. The bhagat takes a piece of turmeric, twelve kinds of cereal, coal-dust, the burnt red soil of the mud oven, mixes them and powders them and closeby he ignites cow dung cakes. He takes the powders in his right fist and circulates it around the patient. In the process he touches the patient once with his fist. While doing this, he invokes and prays to Mahadev and "dharti mai" (mother earth) that they assist him to drive away the naad. After having encircled the patient with his fist and touching him, the powdered ingredients in the fist are poured over the fire burning nearby. Some bhagats do not use fire- they throw the powdered ingredients outside. This ritual is done at least five times. The intention is that when the fist holding the powder touches the body of the patient, then the naad in the patient's body is sucked out by the powder. Thereafter the powder is poured on the fire where it burns out and the naad goes out of the house in the form of smoke. After this ritual, the bhagat blows with his mouth on the patient and addressing the naad, he says "You accept all the ingredients mixed with turmeric and go back to the place from where you have come. If you look back at the patient, then your leg will be broken." In this way, the language the bhagat resembles rulers of authority whose influence falls on the patient. It is said that the bhagat gives some medicine also to the patient who becomes free of the disease.

Some bhagats acquire a lot of fame about their learning and powers in some villages and they get a sizeable crowd of patients. All these patients as they come serially with their baskets of offerings, are checked up in that serial. Wealth, status, social respectability, any kind of influence- nothing can break this serialised check up. If it is broken then it will be breaking the rules of Mahadev.

After the death of a bhagat, his following a pure life has a deep effect on the neighbouring Oraons. Some disciple of the bhagat or his son, whoever is qualified, carries on with the responsibilities and work of the bhagat. Later on, from among them a bhagat initiated by a Brahmin or gosai (saint), who is called "nemha bhagat," started getting perfection after offering sacrifice of black goat to Mahadev and Devi Mai. The "nemha bhagat" does not accept that mutton and fish are prohibited. In the month of Ashar, regular worship as per rules is offered along with sacrifice of a black goat to Mahadev and Devi Maa once a year. But the bhagat who is in the tradition of Vaishnav Gosai preceptor is against the killing of any creature and partakes of very limited food minus meat and wine and lives a disciplined life.

The faith and devotion of the bhagat towards God Mahadev and his pure life not only became a matter of respect and following among the Oraons of the area but due to this, Mahadev's superiority over most of the gods mentioned in Oraon religion became established. The gods of Oraon religion are in a practical way chiefly connected to the widows of Asurs, and the naads of paat, daha, hill, upland and other places. It is said that in the forest as many leaves there are, the naads are present in equal measure in every step of Oraon society. Whenever, wherever, howsoever any naad came to the forefront regarding some incident, he was worshipped, regular worship was started and gradually in that area the naad settled down and became influential. Due to so many naads, superstition increased in Oraon life and along with it the living style, food habit, eating and drinking of meat and wine brought about a down slide in their living standard. Due to the prevalence of bhagat community there has been expected improvement in Oraon society and due to the influence of Mahadev, there has been a decrease in the powers and terror of the naads, due to which Oraon religion is gradually turning more towards God. Instead of worship through fear, Dharmes is now being worshipped with faith and devotion.

Gotra and Totem

In Oraon society, "gotra" has developed into a social institution. Gotra has a direct connection with the institution of marriage and the desire of Dharmes. The meaning of gotra is the entire expanded family of a clan which has spread out like a family tree out of one ancestor. Since this family has come into being from the blood of one mother and father and has expanded, hence the Oraons believe that a young man and woman of one gotra are brother and sister thus there cannot be any marriage between the two. In order to maintain the purity of blood through marriage, the institution of gotra came into being and developed.

In Oraon religion, marriage ceremony is given a lot of importance because without the desire and approval of Dharmes, marriage cannot be held. As per belief of the Oraons, Dharmes has right from the beginning fixed the marriage partners. The Oraons living on the earth have the duty to find out these couples and tie them in marriage. For this work, Dharmes helps the Oraons by guiding them through various symbols and signs. Although Dharmes had encouraged the first man and woman (brother-sister) to act like husband-wife for the increase of Oraon race, yet at that time the first couple was just man and woman, and feeling of brother and sister had not developed at that time. With the coming of that feeling, the problem of one clan, same blood surfaced and it was determined that marriage in the same gotras was against religion and against the desire of Dharmes.

For identifying gotra, a "totem" was affixed to every name. In Hindu religion, gotra is identified through the name of a "rishi" (sage) who would be the first father of that gotra, but in Oraon society some moveable or immovable object or creature which was accepted as a totem by the original family, it is through that name that wherever members of that family may be staying, in a village or in the country, they can be identified. If a family being in trouble asked for the help of some creature and that creature helped the family to come out of the trouble, then the family members respectfully accepted that creature as totem for the clan. Eating of its meat is prohibited for the members of that clan / family and instead of harming it they serve it out of gratitude.

There are many stories of any one family adopting a special totem in Oraon society. As per Kachchap gotra, their ancestors had been helped by a tortoise to cross a river when the family had been in trouble, therefore, in order to show gratitude and respect, the ancestors declared that they should be identified by "Kachchap" (tortoise) gotra, and from then on the name "kachchap" is adjoined to the names of all the members of the expanded family and they have a lot of respect for the tortoise.

The same situation prevails with "Kujur" gotra. As per a legend, one Oraon went to sleep beneath a kujur tree in the forest. Upon seeing this, the kujur tree spread a creeper over the sleeping Oraon which wound itself in such a manner that the Oraon was protected from wild animals eating him up or snake to bite him. When the Oraon awoke, then he felt very much obliged so much so that he named his clan "Kujur." In this way, any Oraon adding the name of Kujur to his name, belongs to the Kujur gotra. He never harms the kujur plant.

In Oraon society, every totem of the society has some incident or the other connected to it. Some incidents due to repeated descriptions vary from the basic situation, or people of that gotra, when they settle somewhere else, then they add different details to the story. This is the reason why there are two-three stories connected with certain totems prevalent in Oraon society. The following main totems are common in Oraon society :

(1) addo (bullock), (2) alla (dog), (3) angal toppo (a kind of grove), (4) amri (liquid of rice), (5) aind (a snake like fish), (6) ekka (tortoise), (7) ergo (rat), (8) orgora (bird), (9) oruga (field rat), (10) Kanda (squill), (11) kinda (coconut), (12) kinduar (a kind of fish), (13) kis (pig), (14) kispotta (intestines of the pig), (15) kujur (a kind of fruit), (16) kundri (a juicy vegetable used to make curries), (17) kusua (a kind of fish), (18) kayond (a kind of fruit), (19) kane (a type of fish), (20) kendi (a kind of tree), (21) kerketta (sparrow living in the bushes), (22) kaithi (a kind of vegetable), (23) Kokro (hen), (24) kosuar (a species of fish), (25) khalko (a kind of fish), (26) khakha (shining black crow), (27) kheksa (a kind of vegetable), (28) khess (paddy), (29) khoiya (wild dog), (30) garwa (crane), (31) gari (common monkey), (32) gidhi (vulture), (33) gislih (a kind of bird), (34) gayday (duck), (35) godo (crocodile), (36) gondrari (a kind of tree), (37) chiglow (jackal), (38) chidra (squirrel), (39) Jabbi (marshy land having a source of water), (40) toppo (a kind of bird having a long tail), (41) tirkey (baby rat), (42) tigga (a species of monkey), (43) tirkuar (a species of bird), (44) tiru (a species of fish), (45) dheyhua (a small black-coloured bird having a long tail), (46) panna (iron), (47) pusra (the fruit of the kusum tree), (48) putri (a kind of tree), (49) barwa (wild dog), (50) bakula (a bird which feeds on paddy), (51) bakhla (a kind of tree), (52) bandh (a place where water has been dammed), (53) bando (wild cat), (54) bara (55) wasa (a kind of tree), (56) Viah (a big fish which has spikes on its back), (57) bekh (salt), (58) madgi (the mahua tree), (59) minj (a species of fish), (60) gunjniyar (a kind of creeper), (61) sanda (fox), (62) rori (a kind of tree), (63) lita (a species of fish), (64) Lakra (cheetah), (65) Linda ((a species of snake like fish), (66) sal (a kind of fish), (67) halman (hanuman- species of big monkey).

Gotra and Totem

Study of the aforementioned totems makes it clear that the Oraons living in the forests are such a tribe that they have close connections with rivers, ponds, and ditches. Various kinds of fish occur as totems and they are in good number. Apart from them, various kinds of birds and trees can also be counted.

No clan of the Oraons has adopted any totem easily or without any reason. Some or the other grateful incident is connected with the totems which is told or heard traditionally in the concerned clan.

The custom of adopting a totem by a clan was for the main reason of identifying the descendants of that clan. From one home to many homes, villages settled, and again spread to far off places but by adding the totem to their names, their identification with one clan continued and they were members of the same gotra for whom marriage in the same gotra was forbidden. The young men and women of the same gotra move around freely in the village or upland, take part in various activities, dance and sing, and there are plenty of probabilities for love to blossom and physical contacts to be made, but the emotion regarding gotra deeply influences them so that they look upon each other as brother and sister. Although there are some examples (their numbers are few) when not knowing about gotra, physical relationship has developed between young men and women of the same gotra. Such husband-wife have to give a feast to all members of the parha as a punishment.

Gotra and totem are fully connected to each other. From totem one can recognise the gotra. In Oraon society adding the name of the totem to one's own name is the prevalent rule, thus when any man or woman's father's name comes up, then the title with the name makes known the gotra.

Totem: Division and Change

Regarding totem, one can find a mixed behaviour of respect and prohibition among the Oraon tribe. The Oraons are grateful to their totems and maintain a feeling of respect. Prohibition is the result of this feeling of respect. The meaning of prohibition is that some acts are forbidden like for example, they cannot harm the totem in any manner; killing it, eating its flesh, cutting of branches or leaves of the tree or burning the tree as firewood, etc., are forbidden. Amongst the Oraons of tirkey gotra (baby rat) the prohibitions are such that killing a rat, eating its flesh or harming it in any manner is prohibited and along with that it is prohibited to see a puppy, kitten etc. which has not opened its eyes, because if they do then the memory of a new born rat comes alive. Such a kind of prohibition is already prevalent in tirkey gotra.

Gradually, over a period of time, the appearance of a totem and its nature inclines some over ambitious people to have an inferiority complex about them, so they add good totems to their names. Although such examples are few in number, but the inclination to add or adopt a new totem can be found among some Oraons.

The meaning of "kispotta" is intestines of a pig, and the anthropologists have tried to name the Oraons as the race eating pig's meat, but due to gratitude in special circumstances one clan adopted the "Kispotta" totem and they came to be declared as "Kispotta" gotra. Over a period of time, in some village within the jurisdiction of Lohardagga police station, some people of Kispotta gotra adopted "Kasai" totem. "Kasai" is a species of tree. Now they have adopted the prohibitions of kispotta for the kasai tree and although they still follow the prohibitions for kispotta, they prefer to be called kasai which they think is more respectful.

Such kind of transfer from one totem to the other is actually due to the encouragement of being connected to a superior totem, although while adopting the new totem, their nearness to it, their respectful attitude etc., become the cause for it. Similar other conditions have been seen when a clan of a particular totem has adopted a special part of the totem and formed a separate totem.[36] Dr. Frazer has named it a divided totem. The example of kispotta may again be seen. Kispotta totem has broken from the "kis" totem and become a new totem. The meaning of "kis" is pig and the meaning of "potta" is intestines. In Oraon society "kis" totem is fully prevalent. Some Oraons of "kis" totem adopted one organ of the pig i.e. intestines (potta) and made a new totem and came to be declared by the name of the new totem.[37]

The Religious Side of Totem

The Oraon tribe normally has an attitude of respect, friendliness or at times routine towards the totem. But some totems are so powerful that the Oraons have regard and devotion in them just like they have towards their gods. In the cultural get together (called "Jatra") of the Oraons, often it can be seen that young Oraon men from different villages have a wooden plank on their shoulders on which tiger (lakra totem), pig (kis totem), bullock (addo totem), bird or trees etc. different totem figures of clay or wood are displayed. Sometimes some gotra prepares its totem with a sheet of brass and respectfully participates in the jatra.

Before proceeding on the journey to the jatra, the totem is worshipped in every parha. The village pahan marks the totem figure with vermillion after having conducted certain rituals prescribed by Oraon religion; he offers cock sacrifice to it and offers rice wine also. It is after religiously worshipping and offering oblation that the villagers proceed towards the jatra upland.

According to the belief of the Oraons, their totems have strange powers which are awakened through worship and offering of oblations. During the time of jatra every gotra has its flag on which often the picture of the totem is depicted. The flag bearing the picture of the totem is worshipped. The aim of this worship is to awaken the inherent powers of the totem. In the jatra when a competition takes place between two groups, then due to the grace of the totem its side wins.

If the journey to the jatra upland is long, then the Oraon youths put down the totem from their shoulders in the "akhra" (cultural centre) of the village and rest for some time. The people of that village worship the totem figures and offer cocks. The cocks which are offered are not sacrificed, instead they are tied to the wooden plank and after returning to the village they are given away to somebody.

The flag bearing the picture of the totem often becomes the symbol[38] of the village, but the respect and devotion shown to it by the villagers and the worship done religiously by the pahan, they become the reason for the totem not to remain an ordinary creature but for that particular village it becomes a divine figure having divine powers. Apart from jatra, when the Oraon goes to the forest for hunting or for any other work, he remembers his totem before leaving. He believes that if the totem had helped his ancestors, then surely it will help him. The people of the gotra give a superior position to the totem compared to ordinary creatures.

Although totem is not related to Dharmes but the worshipping rituals are adopted in the same manner. The use of the totem is for the gotra, and the use of the gotra is to prevent marital relations between brother and sister. The gotra plays a praiseworthy role in the selection of groom and bride, and in arranging marriages outside the gotra. Nowadays, the prevalence of gotra (totem) is gradually decreasing and its usefulness is limited only to marriage. The youth of today do not even know the gotra of their mother or their near relatives. No Oraon can marry in the gotra of his father but he can marry a girl from the gotra of his mother.

Festivals

The actual expression of the life of Oraon tribals is through the festivals, dances and songs throughout the year. The festivals cannot be held without dances and songs being organised. The songs and various arrangements focus on religion as the central point and are accordingly related to the festivals. There are three main substances at the root of religion:

(a) Dharmes and / or ancestors and / or regional gods (naad)- prayers to them that they foil all troubles in the personal life, family life and village life, in domestic cattle and agriculture, and that they protect them and make them prosper.

(b) Pleasing all the related gods or naads through various festivals otherwise there would be a fear of being victimised through disasters should they become angry, and

(c) Festivals celebrated to obtain favours and express obligation.

The religious life of Oraons is bound by these festivals throughout the year because from the month of February-March (Chaitra) these festivals start and in nearly every month, in some season or the other, they are associated with the well being of the forest, success of hunting, good agriculture and animal husbandry, etc. This is the reason that when these noble hearted and simple Oraons participate in the religious functions of these festivals after undergoing hard physical toil, then it seems that the gods mingle with them in their song and dance in various ways and start dancing with them.

The main festivals of the religious life of the Oraons are as follows:

Festival	**month when celebrated**
Phagu	February-March
Sarhul	March-April
Hariyari	June-July
Kadlota	August (Bhado, tenth day of the moon)
Karma	August (the next day after the festival of kadlota)
Jitiya	August-September (the tenth day after karma)
Sohrai	October-November (Kartik)
Kharra Puja	November

Although the Oraons are supposedly cultivator tribe, but even now the Oraon women go in groups to the forest to collect edible seeds and flowers and bring back such useful minor forest produce like mahua, prunes, edible roots or tubers etc. The main festival of Khaddi or Sarhul of the Oraons is connected to forest edibles and flowers. Hunting is also included in forest produce. Phagusendra is related to the hunting drive of the Oraon youth. Similarly, Phagu and Sarhul both are connected to forest life and in Oraon songs it is sung that both these festivals must be celebrated:

"Hai re, Khaddi manaot!......Hai re, phagu manaot!"

(come, let us celebrate khaddi)......(come, let us celebrate phagu)

Phagu

Phagu festival is celebrated to ring out the old year and ring in the new year in the English month of February-March and thereafter the month of Chaitra starts.

A day earlier to the festival, the Oraon youth bring castor plant and branches of the red silk cotton tree and plant them in an open field near the village. They put grass, straw and wood on it and pile it up very high the same way Hindus prepare Holika. If there be any Hindu landlord in the village, then incense etc. is offered by him or on his behalf to the pile of wood otherwise the village pahan offers incense sticks and rice bread to the pile. In some villages, no such worship is done, and the assembled villagers shouting with glee light the bonfire and start jumping and showing their happiness with the rise of the flames.

The Oraons view it as a mere pile of wood. There is no importance of the ash of this fire. The ash is neither scattered over the fields to increase its fertility and nor is it rubbed by any Oraon on his forehead or body. The dirt of the mustard unguent of the house is not burnt in this bonfire like the Hindus and there is no thought in the minds of the Oraons regarding the story of the burning of Holika. At best, this bonfire is dedicated to prosperity for the coming new year.

But the important part of this festival is the observance of Phagu-Sendra on the next day. On the day of Phagu-Sendra, the Oraon youth go out on a hunt. This festival is totally connected to the success of the hunt and the worship of Chandi, the goddess of hunting. The Dhangar Pahan[39] right from the first day of the bright moon to the full moon day, visits the place of the goddess Chandi alone at night without wearing any clothes. He takes with him a pot of water, and goat-milk collected from a few villages, and bathes the rounded stone of Chandi with water or milk, places a mark of vermillion mixed with oil on the goddess and worships her. At times two-three youths accompany the Dhangar-pahan at night during his visit to the goddess's place but all the religious rituals are personally carried out by the Dhangar-pahan himself.

On the next day of Phagu, the village youth observe the traditional religious rituals related to hunting-this is called "lodho-sendra." In some villages the religious rituals pertaining to "jarjari shikar" are celebrated which mark the final phase of Phagu-Sendra. During "jarjari-shikar," the gathering of fruits-flowers or other edibles from the forest has been an inseparable part of Oraon life. The collected material is firstly offered to Chalapachcho goddess established in the pahan's home, and thereafter the offerings are partaken of by the Oraons.

Although due to the gradual denudation of the forests hunting has become the ritual of a custom, yet the Oraon youth after obtaining the blessings of goddess Chandi go out on a hunt. In Oraon society, the hunting of deer is more appreciated, but rarely does a deer become the target of the arrow of an Oraon youth, yet a sister has great expectation that her brother would return successfully with a hunted deer. Who can ignore reality ? In the Oraon phagu songs, the sister also jokes about this matter.[40]

In this way, the festival of Phagu celebrated by Oraon tribals is fully connected to collection of edibles from the forest; this includes the worship of goddess Chandi for going out on traditional hunting, its success and personal protection.

Most of those who have studied Oraon religion and life accept that Oraons have adopted Phagu festival from the Hindus. The same thing is said about the Mundas also. If the Phagu festival celebrated by Munda and Oraon tribals is deeply analysed, then the name "Phagu," the castor plant and the bunches of the red-silk cotton tree laden with grass and straw copying the wood pile of Holika of the Hindus and burning it are two points which apparently are similar to the Holi of the Hindus. The burning of Holika in the wood pile, its religions facts or spirit of the festival of Holi is not to be found in the wood pile of the Oraons. It is neither worshipped nor is its ash thought to be sacred. There is also no such feeling that all the sins of the year are burned in the wood pile. It is just an action of merry making for the Oraon youths, and its organisation has no connection with religion in any way.

Phagu festival of the Oraons is celebrated about a fortnight prior to the festival of Holi of the Hindus and basically it is a prelude to the great festival of Sarhul. The way Oraon life is related to forest produce, similarly, Phagu and Sarhul are also related to forest produce. That is why the celebration of Sarhul and Phagu features in the traditional songs of the Oraons. Many theologians[41] of Oraon and Munda religion accept that Phagu festival has been taken from the Hindus by the Oraons, but this is not rational. None of the religious or social implications of the Hindu festival of Holi or Phagua can be seen in the Phagu festival of the Oraons. Hence, apparently this festival celebrating the festival of Sarhul of the Mundas and Oraons has been named "Phagu festival" which is celebrated in the month of Falgun. With this festival, that is the last date of Falgun, preparations start for celebrating Sarhul festival. Hence in all probability this festival may have been the primary phase of Sarhul, but it had no name. With the passage of time, after coming in contact with the Hindus, this festival may have been named "Phagu." Later on, the name "Phagu" became seemingly attached to the first phase of Sarhul. Earlier the festival celebrations used to last for a month and would be finally closed with a lot of fanfare. The position of Sarhul has also been the same. In this way, only the name of Phagu festival has been adopted but there are no religious or social similarities of rituals or activities followed by the Hindus. Hence to say that the Oraon and Munda tribes have adopted Phagu festival from the Hindus is not proved and is completely irrational. The naming of phagu for this festival is a later on development.

Phagu festival is fully connected with Oraon life and religion. Without detailed analysis, the scholars have accepted that the festival has been influenced by the Hindus. They say that the burning of Holika in Phagu festival has been copied from the Hindus because in Oraon tradition there is no such incident which can be an equivalent of Holika. The lighting of fire by the Oraons in Phagu festival is a symbol of the new Creation. The Oraons have nothing to do with "Holika." We know that when the Creation became overburdened with sin and it was difficult for good simple folks to live, then Dharmes had planned to destroy the sinful Creation and create a new Creation, and for this the "Rain of fire" was sent. In Phagu festival, the Oraons burn the pile of sins which symbolises the "Rain of fire," after which the new Creation was made. We know that after the month of Falgun the new year starts in the month of Chaitra. Thus, Phagu festival is celebrated completely in memory of tribal religious legend in which last year's sins, meaning the sins of jealousy, ill feeling, hatred, etc. which they had harboured among themselves, are burnt by the Oraons who then begin the new year with renewed vigour and life. Whatever analysis may be done out of ignorance regarding Phagu festival, the Oraons celebrate this festival in memory of "Rain of Fire". The tribal festival has nothing to do with the Phagu festival of Hindus.

Sarhul/Khaddi/Khekhel Benja

Sarhul, or Khaddi or Khekhel Benja as described in Kurukh language is a festival celebrated in the month of Chaitra (March-April). This is the most popular festival of the Oraon race. Both the Munda and Oraon tribes give utmost importance to Sarhul. The preparation for Sarhul starts from the Phagu festival itself. The pahan declares the dates of observance of fast, worship and other activities of Sarhul festival. Until Sarhul festival is celebrated in the village, no Oraon (male or female) may collect fruits, seeds, flowers, roots and other edibles from the forest nor can partake of them. Actually, Sarhul is the festival of new fruits and flowers of Nature which dedicates its entire prosperity to these tribals, and these tribals accept them with immense pleasure after observing much worship and religious rituals as if accepting the first blessing of Nature.

The Oraons call Sarhul festival by the name of khaddi or Khekhel Benja. The meaning of Khekhel Benja is the marriage of the Earth. The Earth means one who contains the entire wealth of Nature. The Earth is married to the Sun during Sarhul festival. The heat of the Sun and the fertility of the Earth have direct connection. In the religions of many races, this geographical mystery of Nature has been variously described as the marriage of the Earth and the Sun. In Sarna religion, on this occasion the village priest (pahan) is taken to be the Sun and his wife (pahnain) is taken to be the Earth and their marriage is celebrated. This marriage is conducted in the presence of all the villagers by the village head and his wife in great style. As per the belief of the Oraons, the effect of this marriage directly influences their agricultural produce.

The Oraon tribe has to complete many religious activities in several phases before it arrives at the main function of Sarhul festival. These activities are :

Declaration of Sarhul Festival and Preparations

Nowadays in nearly the whole of Chhotanagpur, Sarhul is celebrated on a fixed date, but centuries earlier when there was hardly any contact or exchange of information among the tribes settled in far and distant places, there could not be any fixed date, hence the village mahto and the pahan after consulting each other would fix the date of Sarhul festival. This used to be normally celebrated 15-20 days after the Phagu festival. Hence Sarhul was not celebrated on a fixed date in the whole of Chhotanagpur like it is done now. In those days, the village pahan and the Mahto had to publicly announce the date of the festival and accordingly start preparations for it. Preparations meant the provision of required materials for the festival.

The responsibility to collect materials for the festival lay on the pahan and the pujar. The pahan used to collect one "paila" (a measure) of paddy or mahua from each family of the village in the name of "Chilgi Maiya"; the collected material would then be changed into currency with which the potter would be paid for pitcher and other necessary clay utensils. The iron-smith used to prepare a knife for the pahan which would be used for the first time during sacrifice. Apart from this, in some villages the iron smith had to make "baithi" (a cutter used while squatting on it) and ladle for the pahan because the villagers follow the tradition of using new utensils to distribute sanctified food. Nowadays, after collecting monetary donations, the pahan easily assembles all these materials.

Along with other preparations, the preparation of "hadiya" has an important place. The pahan boils three-four seers (one seer is nearly a kilo) of rice in the clay pitcher, cooks it, and after that he mixes "bitchchi" ranu in it to make it into wine, and thus preparing "hadiya" it is kept pure for the festival of Sarhul. In some villages, even the pujar prepares wine of three-four seers of rice and keeps it reserved for Sarhul festival.

Dari-chhitna

The aim of this religious activity is to clean that source of water which is used by the village throughout the year. Nearly every Oraon village is settled on the bank of a river or near a stream. In the absence of these, there will be a lake or a pond which works as a "Sarna-dari." In a village where there is no such facility, a ditch is dug and filled with water to carry out the ritual of "dari chhitna." The pahan, pujar and mahto along with some Oraons of the village go to the "Sarna-dari." They take with them a flat plate made of clay or a "nahula" or "jogi" (utensils) of bamboo for swishing the water. It is also necessary that they carry materials for worship, namely vermillion and oil.

After swishing the waters of the Sarna-dari, the pujar rubs oil on a piece of stone which has been traditionally worshipped, marks it with vermillion and performs regular worship. After worshipping Sarna-dari, the entire group along with the pahan goes and bathes in another river, stream or pond. After the purification bath, the group goes to the home of the pahan where home-made hadiya is offered to them to drink. This holy hadiya made from rice is called "dari-chhisua hadi."

The Chandi flags which are the holy property of the village, are kept safely by the pahan in a bamboo box at home, and on special occasions with great devotion and prayers he takes them out while saying, "Maghi maghi parwa doe nayango." These Chandi flags are tied to two small pieces of wood, and thereafter they are tied to the two bamboo poles fixed to the ground at the door of the pahan's house; they are tied about two-three feet below the top of the poles in such a manner that both flags face the same direction.

After hoisting the Chandi flags at the door of the pahan's residence, all the rituals to establish Chala-Pachcho Devi in the Sarna winnowing fan are completed. The Chandi flags are not brought down till Chala Pachcho Devi is not established in the winnowing fan. After Chala Pachcho Devi is established, the Chandi flags are brought down and with great devotion the pahan returns them to the bamboo box. The hoisting of the Chandi flags atop the bamboo poles marks the official start of Sarhul festival, and bringing them down after the establishing of Sarna Devi in the Sarna winnowing fan for the whole year marks the close of this festival.

Nega-Amm

This religious ritual, marking the close of Sarhul, is carried out to give a fore-knowledge of the position of the coming rainy season and also the direction from where the monsoon will come. The life of the Oraons which has moved on from forest edibles to being dependent on agriculture is greatly influenced by rains. Favourable rains mean good agriculture.

A little after midnight, the pujar along with the pahan/mahto or other one or two Oraon villagers go to the Sarna-dari with a pole having two pitchers hanging on each side. They make an effort that no human being comes in their path and even if anybody comes, they ignore him and go towards the Sarna-dari. The pujar fills the four pitchers with the holy water of the Sarna-dari. There is a special way to fill these pitchers. The pitcher is kept straight and is dipped in the water with its mouth up. There should not be any tilting of the pitcher. When the pitchers are accordingly filled up with the holy water of the Sarna-dari, then again they are hung two on each side of the pole which the pujar takes to the Sarna place. In the Sarna place with the help of the sharp edge of the bamboo pole four pits are dug in four directions which are joined by deep lines forming grooves, thus forming an oblong shape. The four pitchers of holy water from the Sarna-dari are placed on the four corners. The whole ritual is conducted in silence in a quiet atmosphere so that the attention of Chala-pachcho, the goddess of agriculture, is not diverted from the pitchers. The invocation to the goddess is inherent in the silence.

The next day at sunrise, the pahan, pujar, mahto and other elders of the village come to the Sarna place together. One by one, the pahan lifts the cover of each pitcher and sees the level of the water. If the pitchers are found to be full, then everybody becomes happy that there would be enough rain that year. If in one or two pitchers the level of water comes down, then accordingly decision is taken as to from which direction the coming of the monsoon would be minimal and from which direction its coming would be more. Since Chala Pachcho is the goddess of agriculture for the village, and all these symbolic conclusions have been drawn under her aegis, hence the Oraons have full faith on these conclusions so they plan out their agricultural operations based on these predictions.

The Collecting of Cocks, Fishes and Crabs for Worship

After obtaining knowledge regarding the good and bad of the monsoon from the water of the pitchers, all the people assembled at the Sarna-place come to the home of the pahan where they partake with relish the rice-wine made at home. It is during this time that some villagers are directed to collect animals for worship. Some people visit every home to collect cocks while some people go to the nearby pond or river to catch fish. A broth called "dubki tiyan" is prepared during Sarhul in which fish, sun-dried lumps of horse-bean pulse, and pulses must be present. For a good harvest of pulses, the crab is required for worship rituals, hence some youth gather crabs with the help of spades. Although ploughing the fields, digging them or similar activities are prohibited before Sarhul, the digging up of crabs for worship by the pahan is permitted. In some villages, goats are also sacrificed to Chala-Pachcho Devi.

The Religious Bath of Sarhul

The pujar, mahto and other Oraon elders of the village assemble at the home of the pahan for the religious bath of Sarhul. The musician remains in readiness from before at the pahan's home along with his "nagara" (kettledrum), bugle and flute etc. instruments. Thereafter the musician leads everybody to the identified pond or river, all the while beating the drum and playing on his musical instruments. He leaves them to bathe and moves back towards the village, all the while playing on his musical instruments. Half way on the route he stops.

The pahan is the first to bathe in the water body before everybody else lined up at the banks. The bathing ritual is specific. The pahan raises his hands towards the sky and dips into the water. During bathing, if any portion of the hands touches any part of the body, then in the coming year the whole village will suffer from a plenitude of spiders. Hence all the bathers take care that their hands are kept straight up while bathing. After bathing, everybody returns to the village under the leadership of the pahan.

When the village women hear the music of the musician coming from half way to the village, they understand that the men are returning after taking bath and now it is their turn. The wife of the pujar positions herself on the left of the wife of the pahan and leads all the village women for bathing, towards the river or pond. The pahan's and pujar's wife keep a clay bowl on their heads in which water soaked horse-bean pulse is kept. This group of women covers the half distance and thereafter moves forward to take their bath.

At the half-way distance, the musician breaks small branches of the "toong" tree or if this tree is not available, then of any tree, and spreads them on the path. The pahan and those accompanying him tread on these while returning home. The musician reaches all of them to the pahan's home, all the while making music. He then returns to the point of half-distance and stops there where all the women in wet clothes reach under the leadership of the pahan's wife after having taken their bath. The musician reaches this group, too, to the house of the pahan with constant music.

The pahan and members of his group while returning home sing loudly, and when they sing the refrain "hiya hi dal dal…." They stamp their feet on the ground as they reach home.

Song

O God of the keond tree!
O God of the sal tree, Phagu god! Sarhul god!
O this is now Sarhul! o this is Phagu'
Phagu god ! Sarhul god!
Come let us all play, let us all play.[43]

The women sing while returning:

God of new rice wine! The level of wine in the pitcher!
O, this is Sarhul! O, that is Phagu,
Phagu god! Sarhul god!
Come let us all play, let us all play.[44]

Water Sport

The men have all assembled from before at the home of the pahan. Many pitchers filled with water have been kept there. The sound of music begins to be heard which means that the women were returning from their bath. All the men take position in the courtyard of the pahan with the pitchers of water, and as soon as the women enter the courtyard, they start pouring water on them with gusto. The women jump around here and there and the men chase them to pour water till they are fully soaked. The surface of the courtyard becomes thoroughly wet. The drenched women abuse the men by singing songs which are traditionally sung during the occasion of water sport and which are full of abusive words and innuendos. They also otherwise utter filthy abuses which the men happily accept, and for sometime a riotous and merry situation prevails in the pahan's courtyard. Thereafter the pahan orders his wife to prepare holy wine for the worship. The pahan's wife goes inside the house and the pujar's wife goes outside the courtyard to the open field to prepare "hadiya" for "Madna bharna." The rest of the villagers depart for their homes.

Isoom Sindri or the Marriage of Pahan-Pahnain

In the religious activities of Sarhul festival, the marriage of pahan and pahnain (wife of the pahan) occupies a significant place. It is a symbolic expression of marriage of the sun and earth with the aim of having a good harvest. Marriage is made for reproduction and this is the living religion of Creation.

After the event of water sports, the villagers bring rice, pulses or whatever possible in baskets for the purpose of worship; they especially bring rice, and hand over these materials to the pujar. The pujar accepts them with his blessings and keeps the baskets piled up, one on top of the other. There is a special rule to keep these baskets. The population of the village is divided in some clan boundaries or "khunts," namely pahan's khunt, mahto khunt, Munda -khunt, etc. Some villagers are not landholders or "bhuinhars" but have come and settled from different villages- they are called "gairo". The pujar keeps the baskets one on top of the other according to khunt or clan boundary; in this way the baskets are placed vertically as per khunt. Those who are "gairo" and do not figure in any clan or khunt, their baskets are kept with the baskets of that khunt in whose upland they stay or with whom they are closely related.

Thereafter the mahto keeps a big slab of stone (used for grinding condiments etc. with a muller) in the courtyard of the pahan. He puts three bundles of straw on it and on top of that he puts a yoke. He splits the ends of three-four mango leaves, stitches them with straw in the form of cups and keps them near the slab of stone. Then from the courtyard he respectfully calls, "O pahan-pahanain. The gifts of villagers have come. Please get ready to come."

The pahan, along with the pahnain, comes out of the house. He sprinkles the freshly prepared hadiya on the Sarna-winnowing fan. The Sarna winnowing fan or "ketar" hangs on the hook of the holy Sarna room. After sprinkling rice wine, he keeps the winnowing fan on the ground and sits cross-legged on the ground. He keeps the Sarna winnowing fan pressed by his side. Then the pujar brings water in a pot and sits cross-legged down on the eastern side of the pahan. The wife of the pahan puts "arwa" rice (rice of unboiled paddy) on the winnowing fan of the pahan, and the pujar's wife pours water from the new pot in the pot of the pujar. Then the pahan stands up with his winnowing fan, and the pujar stands up with his pot. The wife of the pujar pours the remaining water on the heads of the pahan-pahnain. The pahan-pahnain gradually move towards the slab of stone. The pujar goes in front dropping water all the way from his pot and behind him the pahan comes dropping small quantities of rice. Upon reaching the slab of stone, the pahan sits down on the yoke kept on the slab along with his winnowing fan. The pujar sits cross-legged on the ground on his right. The pujar's wife and the pahan's wife go there in wet clothes. The pahnain sits on the left of the pahan and the pujar's wife sits on the left side of the pahnain. The old knife, which had been inserted in the left corner of the Sarna winnowing fan, is taken out and the pahan gives it to the person standing in front. A new knife is formally inserted in the same place of the Sarna-winnowing fan.

The village mahto takes a cotton sheet called "Chadar" and with that he covers the heads of the pahan and pahanain as well as their faces. The wife of the mahto takes mustard oil in a small earthen cup, some vermillion and a comb of bamboo or wood, and first of all goes to the pahan. She applies oil on his head and combs his hair, and using the tip of the little finger of the right hand she puts mark of vermillion on both eyebrows and ear-lobes of the pahan.

Again, she applies oil on the head of the pahnain and taking a pinch of vermillion with the right hand, she applies it with a comb in the parting of the hair of the pahnain. In this way, amidst the presence of all, the mahto and his wife conduct the marriage of the pahan-pahnain. The same procedure is adopted for the pujar-pujarin.

Invocation of Pach-Balar

After the marriage of pahan-pahnain, the mahto invokes his ancestors living in the nether world. He pours freshly made hadiya in the mango leaf cups kept beside the stone slab. Then stating that "you must be tired and thirsty," he touches the lips of the pahan and pahnain with the hadiya filled cup; again, he touches the cup to the lips of the pujar-pujarin and thereafter with enthusiasm he calls out loudly "uloo, uloo" and throws the leaf cup on the thatched roof of the house. This ritual is carried out three times.

Again the mahto prepares three cups of sal leaves and fills them with hadiya. Two of the cups are given to those standing in front and the third cup is kept on his left palm. He dips his right hand fingers in the cup and sprinkles the hadiya on the ground, all the while invoking his ancestors. We know that as per belief in Oraon religion, the bodiless spirits of his dead ancestors live below the ground in the same manner that the living bodied Oraons live on the earth. The ancestors are also divided by "khunts" or boundaries of clan the same way that living families above the ground are recognised by their "khunts." The mahto calls out to his ancestors that "today is Sarhul festival, we inhabitants of this earth are celebrating this festival, you also be satisfied[45]," and sprinkles the hadiya of the sal-leaf cup on the ground. The members of every "khunt" similarly satisfy their ancestors living in the nether world. But those people face problem who are not original landholders of the village but come as relatives or those who live beyond the river Koel in foreign lands. One representative of all such people offers hadiya of rice to the ancestors on everybody's behalf. This means that people of all clans or khunts living in the village invoke the dead ancestors of their clan, or those who do not have any clan invoke their ancestors and sprinkle hadiya on the ground as an offering. They bend and touch the ground with their heads. In this way, after this salutation to the ancestors, they bid farewell to them.

Distribution of Blessed Rice

The baskets of the pahan-khunt are kept separate from the other khunt rice baskets. Any one person takes two handfuls of rice three times from the rice baskets/ winnowing fans of the pahan khunt, puts them in the winnowing fan of the pahan which is kept for worship and bends low in obeisance to the pahan. The pahan picks up a pinch of rice from that and puts it in the winnowing fan of his khunt. This rice is called "blessed rice" for the khunt people, During agricultural operations this rice is mixed with the seed along with some cow dung and copper coins. As per religious belief of the Oraons, the mixing of the worshipped and blessed rice with all the rice seeds makes them pure and protects them from the wicked "naads" so that the harvest is good.

Every khunt has separate blessed rice. The blessed rice of mahto khunt is accordingly separated and sown along with the seeds. Those who are not "bhuihar" or original landholders, they obtain the blessed rice of the nearby khunt or clan and complete the work of mixing them with rice seeds and sowing them.

Chalam Gucha or going to the Sarna Place in a Procession

The pahan starts from his home for the main worship and proceeds to the Sarna place of the village in a group along with musicians playing music. The pahan holds the Sarna winnowing fan full of "arwa" rice (extracted from unboiled paddy) while the pujar goes along with a pot of water. The others carry the other materials for the worship-somebody slings the rice on both sides of a bamboo pole and carries it on his shoulders while another carries cocks and hens in a net. Ladle, utensils, cups of sal leaves, raw thread, vermillion etc., essential items of worship, reach the Sarna place in a procession. The pujar circumambulates the main Sarna tree in such a manner that ultimately the Sarna tree is on his left. The pujar keeps on dropping drops of water from his pot as he comes. The pahan sits down on a stone, facing the east, and the pujar stands on his left with his pot of water.

The Preparation for the Worship

After a few minutes, the pahan gets up and goes to that place where the previous year the fire-place had been made with pieces of stone. He separates those pieces which he thinks are alright. Some of the villagers come forward and picking up the stones of the old fireplace build a new fire-place. In the meantime the pahan ties the trunk of the main Sarna tree, three or in some places five times with the raw coarse thread after likewise circumambulating it. The pujar clears a place of its grass which is one and a half feet broad and eighteen feet long-this place is called "akhra" and it is used for offering sacrifice. Arwa rice is placed at short distances in small quantities which the sacrificial cocks feed upon. This rice is called akhra's sacrificial "kuri." On the southern boundary of this oblong, about four-five feet away from the last "Kuri," one handful of rice is specially kept which the white cock feeds on and which is offered in sacrifice to Dharmes. The pahan, pujar and other helpers sit down facing the east. In some villages, goats or pigs are also offered in sacrifice- if this be so, then a plot of ground one and a half feet wide and four-five feet long is cleared of its grass for preparing the sacrificial place otherwise all other preparations are the same.

The Offering of Sacrifice

The pahan asks for water from the pujar. The pujar gives water from his pot with which the pahan washes his hands-face-feet, and sprinkles water on his head and other parts of the body to purify himself. Then he takes rice in the hollow of joint palms of his hands, moves a bit away from the kuri and forms three lines of rice on the ground as if sowing rice seeds in the paddy field. In the meantime the pujar separates the cocks as per their colour for offering to different gods-goddesses or spirits (naads). Red cocks (in some villages black and white mixed cocks) are for "dadha-deswali," brown hens for Chala Pachcho, black hens for Chandi, white cock for Dharmes. Cocks and hens of the remaining colours are offered to all regional gods and goddesses by addressing them as "Garha-dorha-chatur-seeman." All naads of the four directions are included in this address.

The pujar takes out the knife from the Sarna-winnowing fan and gives it to the pahan. Then the pujar catches hold of a red cock and washes its head, feet and tail with water from the pot, and gives it to the pahan. The pahan gives arwa rice to the cock to feed. When the cock is in the process of feeding, the pahan cuts its head with the knife and says, "O Dadha-deswali or village gods, we all offer this sacrifice to you."

Similarly, one after the other, brown coloured hen to Chala-Pachcho or Sarna-budhiya, black hen to Chandi and the rest to "Chatur seeman," "khunt," "dant" etc. regional gods and spirits are offered. But their heads are not totally cut off from their bodies-they hang a bit. The pahan says, "O naad, mua, churail and your whole group which may be in the directions of east, west, north, south, in whichever "parhas" (groups of villages) your are, this sacrifice and the meat there of is for all of you; take your fill and divide it amongst yourselves, and see to it that the young and old men and women of our village dance and sing a lot in Sarhul and obtain maximum prosperity and property."

At the end sacrifice to Dharmes is offered in a special way. The pahan cleans the knife thoroughly with water so that even a speck of blood does not remain on it. Then he cleans his hands. He goes to the southernmost point of the kuri line for offering sacrifice to Dharmes. A white cock is offered as sacrifice to Dharmes, and if white cock is not available then a white egg is sacrificed in its stead. While offering sacrifice to Dharmes, the pahan prays:-

"O Dharme, our father! Whatever deficiencies have been committed by us knowingly or unknowingly, you complete them. Our eyes cannot see the spirits (naads). Your eyes can see them. You are our father. You keep all of them under control those who we see or know and those naads who we do not know."[46]

The offering of sacrifice to Dharmes in the end and from the southern end indicates that he controls the ghosts and spirits, benevolent and malevolent souls and regional naads from the south. The southern edge of the kuri land which goes from the eastern side of the Sarna tree to the north is drawn in such a manner that people can be easily controlled from that portion. This teaches the importance of place and direction.

The pujar takes the knife from the pahan and after cleaning it, inserts it in its fixed place in the Sarna winnowing fan.

The pahan offers milk and water brought by the milk-men of the village to the kuri rice then the legs of five sacrificed cocks are held by him. He flaunts them in the air in the four directions and after that throws them among the gathered clan-less non-bhuihar villagers by saying. "We are giving this to you. Cook them." The sacrificed chicken are dressed and cleaned and cut into some pieces. The first four cleaned chicken are cooked with about a kilo of rice taken from the winnowing fan. Later on, rice and the remaining cleaned chicken are cooked separately.

The cock offered to Dharmes is kept separate from the rest. It is cleaned, mixed with some rice and put in between four sal leaves. These sal leaves are joined by a skewer which turns it into a bundle and this is gradually fried in the flame of the fire-place.

When all the cooking activity is under way, if the villagers have brought pigs and goats for sacrifice (a practice which is gradually being discontinued), then for them a separate plot of land is cleared for use. The front and rear legs of the pig are bound together and it is made to lie down at the place of sacrifice. The pahan throws a handful of arwa rice on the mouth of the pig. Thereafter two-three villagers come with an axe and hit the head of the pig with its reverse side. This is how a pig is sacrificed but this sacrifice is not offered to any deity or regional naad-it is offered to those nameless ghosts whose number is not known to any body conversant with religious practices. The pahan does not take part in this sacrifice.

The cleaning of the pig and cooking of its meat is done separately by some people or in some family home. The same situation prevails in the sacrifice of goats. This sacrifice is also offered to nameless invisible powers. The goat is brought at an identified place in the Sarna place and the pahan gives it arwa rice to eat. The pahan performs the sacrifice of the he-goat the same way he sacrifices cocks and hens. For this he uses a "baithi" (an iron blade which is normally used in squatting posture) or if available a sword.

The sacrificed goat is separately cleaned and cooked by the villagers. For this a separate fireplace is set up in the Sarna-place or at times the meat is got cooked in the home of some family.

Kakro Sarjana or the Frying of Crabs

While collecting the ingredients used for worship, it had been seen that some of the village youth had gone out with spades to catch crabs. During Sarhul the way the crabs sputter while being roasted, the same way the bunches of "urad" (horse-bean pulse) and other pulses will spurt forth. This work is given to those women who do not fast during Sarhul.

During evening some people keep on going from the Sarna place to the pahan's home to check whether the feast is ready or not. For final information the pahan, pujar, mahto and other elders of the village along with the village musician playing music start for the pahan's home where the fasting women are busy in preparing the food. As soon as they hear the music, the women who have not kept a fast and are at home start roasting the crabs on their stoves. This activity starts with the entry of the pahan in the village. The crabs are directly roasted in the fire and some crabs are hung above the fire on strings. This activity is conducted to ensure a good harvest of pulses. When the crabs sputter in the fire and make crackling noises, the women say that the pods of the pulses may spurt likewise, and the legs of the hanging crabs become hard and straight as the stems of the pulses would become.

In this way, those women who do not keep a fast during Sarhul festival celebrate kakro sarjana ritual for ensuring a good harvest of pulses.

The Welcoming of the Pahan by the Pahanain

The sound of music indicates that the pahan along with other co-villagers is returning, hence in order to welcome him the pahanain and the wife of the pujar come and stand at the door. The pujar's wife has a pot of water in her hand, and the pahanain has a lighted earthern lamp in one hand and mustard oil in the other. The wife of the pujar rubs oil on the feet of the pahan and thereafter washes them with water. She does the same thing with the pujar.

After being welcomed in this manner, the pahan goes to the place where the holy Sarna winnowing fan is hung. The pahan keeps the winnowing fan below the place where it is hung and sits down cross-legged. The pujar keeps his water pot on the right side of the winnowing fan and sits down cross-legged beside the pahan. The pahan takes a leaf cup, fills it with "tapawan-hadiya" (rice hadiya specially prepared for the occasion) and offers it to the Sarna winnowing fan, and the rest he drinks it himself.

The pahan gets up with the pujar and together they inspect the preparations of the feast. Thereafter he prepares to return to the Sarna place along with the other companions. In the process when he bends to pick up his winnowing fan and water pot, the wife of the pujar fills the water pot with water from a big pitcher and the rest of the water she pours over the pahan and the pujar. In the meantime, the other women start throwing water from pots and other utensils on the pahan, pujar and other men assembled there and besmear them with mud. Accordingly, soaked with water and mud, the pahan and his companions return happily to the Sarna place with music playing all the way.

Cheprai Murga

In the absence of the pahan, some cousin brother whom the pahan had left at the Sarna place, strangulates a cock, dresses it, and after cleaning it hides it in the sludge. This cock is called "Cheprai murga".

Ona Mokhna

By the time the pahan returns to the Sarna place, the mix of rice and chicken has been cooked. This mixed food prepared with the meat of the first sacrificed four cocks and hens and the fried meat of the cock offered to Dharmes which is called "patpur" are offered by the pahan to the gods and goddesses on the four edges of the fire place. They are Dadha, Deswali, Chala-pachcho and Chandi.

In the meantime the assembled Oraons sit down in rows to eat. The pujar puts a sal leaf in front of each person and the pahan ladles out the mixed holy food on these leaves. He keeps the mixed holyfood separately on four leaves which would be for himself, his wife, the pujar and his wife. The pahan and the pujar do not touch the holy food kept for their wives on the leaves. The pahan at first eats one or two mouthfuls from his leaf and thereafter allows the other Oraons to start eating. After eating the holy food, the pahan and pujar get up and wash their mouth and hands.

The pujar again places leaves in front of the assembled villagers on which the pahan lays out the mixed food prepared with the remaining chicken. The pujar and the pahan get up together and washing their hands and feet sit down for taking meal. At this time the person with the "cheprai murga" suddenly gets up and without washing his hands and mouth runs towards the village. He is chased by some with burnt logs who shout "Catch him, beat him," and after some distance they come back. The gorait (musician) and the "ghasi" sit separately from the rows and partake of the food, but milkmen who supply milk and the potter who has supplied utensils get approval of the pahan to cook and eat their food separately. The mixed food containing chicken is the chief holy food of the entire arrangement. The holy food prepared at the Sarna place is prohibited for women.

The Feast of the Women

By the time the women finish eating, it becomes late night. In the meantime, after cleaning all the articles and utensils, the villagers take them to the village. The whole night they sing and dance and drink "hadiya". The songs and dances continue throughout the night.

Dhangar Pahan or Mutri – Chandi's Pahan

After the dancing at night, everybody goes home. In the evening, the "dhangar pahan" is chosen. Dhangar pahan is chosen by the unmarried youth from among themselves. This selection is done in the "akhra" in the evening. The pahanain sanctifies the site of the "akhra" by besmearing it with cow dung. In the evening all the bachelor youths of the village congregate at the "akhra". They bring along a pestle with them and also a winnowing fan full of "arwa" rice. The winnowing fan is kept on the floor in an east-west direction. As per the belief of the Oraons, an invisible power called "Lugu" (a power or a spirit) lives in the pestle. One youth presses the winnowing fan with his left hand while the other youths pick up a handful of rice each and stand in two parallel lines through which anybody can come and go.

The youth who is considered most sensitive, whose soul is thought to be light and on whom divine powers can easily manifest themselves, is told to grasp the pestle. Very soon the pestle is activated by spiritual powers and whichever youth's foot is touched by it, that youth is chosen as the "dhangar pahan" of that village. It is the "dhangar pahan" who is authorised to worship Mutri-Chandi, the goddess of hunting; hence he is also called "mutri pahan".

Poomp Kherna or Phul Khusi

This is an important part of the celebration of Sarhul which is observed before the pujar hands over his "batari" or water pot and the pahan establishes the winnowing fan. The village musician goes to the house of the pahan playing music while his wife follows him with a basket of sal blossoms and leaves. She gives the basket to the pujar. The pujar places the buds, flowers and leaves of the sal separately in a winnowing fan. It is to be remembered that the Sarna winnowing fan along with its sacrificial knife is kept by the pahan prior to this in the fixed Sarna Kyri otherwise if the Sarna winnowing fan comes in contact with anything evil or restless then the villages might have to bear the wrath of Chala Pachcho devi.

The village mahto and other people gradually come to the pahan. The pujar fixes sal blossoms on the ears of the men and hair of the women assembled there, and another person welcomes the people with hadiya. After the conclusion of "poomp kherna" ceremony in the house of the pahan, the pahan along with the pujar goes to the Sarna room and sits down cross-legged just below the hanging Sarna winnowing fan. The pujar sits on the left side of the pahan in cross-legged fashion. The pahan and pujar are given hadiya on sal leaves. Out of these sal leaf cups, the pujar and pahan offer some hadiya to the earth and sing:-

> "take ! take ! take ! God of wine made of new rice.
> Take hadiya for relatives
> This is Sarhul God.
> O celebrate this Sarhul, celebrate this Phagu."[47]
> The women also sing with the pahnain –
> "Taste the rahar pulse God,
> Taste the Jhurunga pulse God,
> Taste the baroi pulse God,
> Taste the khesari pulse God,
> Let us celebrate Sarhul, let us celebrate Phagu,
> O all you gods."[48]

Then the pujarin brings a pitcher of water and after filling the pujar's pot with water, the remaining water she pours over the pahan and pujar. Wetted in this way with water, the pahan picks up the flower filled winnowing fan and the pujar picks up his water filled pot, and accompanied by the musician and senior villagers they start moving from house to house of the village. When they reach the doorstep of an Oraon, then the pujar drops some water and makes a circle at the door. Thereafter the pahan and pujar go to that part of the house where the agricultural store house is located-it may be the granary also. In this place, the pujar makes a big circle with his water and within that circle both of them sit down cross-legged facing the east. The pujar sits on the right side of the pahan. The lady of the house brings a brass salver, water and mustard oil and goes to the pahan. She places his feet on the salver and applies oil on them. Thereafter she washes his feet. The same procedure is followed for the pujar also. The remaining oil is applied on their chest and hair, and the other elder-visiting Oraons have also their feet applied with oil and thereafter washed with water.

In this way the lady of the house welcomes everybody. After that she spreads one end of her sari before the pahan who takes flowers in his cupped hands and puts them on the spread sari. The lady of the house touches the sari end full of flowers to her head and expresses gratitude to the pahan. This activity is repeated three times. The pujar affixes flowers on the ears of the other assembled men and in the hair of the women. He wets the floor with water from his pot and taking the wet mud marks the foreheads of the assembled people and blesses them.

As soon as the group of the pahan and pujar departs from one house for another, then the pahanain, pujarin along with a group of women enter that house and going near the "mora" (the mound of dry bunches of paddy) where the pahan and pujar had worshipped within the circle of water, start dancing. They keep on dancing till the rice wine is not prepared and brought. They drink a leaf cup each of rice wine and after putting sludge on the "mora" and crumpling it they leave for the next house, dancing and singing songs of "rahar chakhna." Effort is made that this ritual is completed in all the houses coming within the limits of the pahan at least once and that everybody receives flowers from the pahan. By evening, the pahnain and pujarin along with their women companions return home and await the arrival of the pahan. The pahan returns home accompanied with music, the pujar and other companions after having distributed the sal flowers.

Two brass tureens are placed to welcome the pahan and pujar who step on to them. At first the pahnain and the pujarin rub oil on the feet of their husbands, thereafter the pujarin rubs oil on the feet of the pahan and the pahnain rubs oil on the feet of the pujar. Thereafter their feet are washed with water which the pahnain and the pujarin do consecutively. From this place the pahan and pujar straightaway enter the Sarna kuri made in the house and sit down cross-legged beneath the hanging Sarna winnowing fan. The pahan keeps his winnowing fan on the floor and the pujar keeps his water pot beside this fan. Nobody can enter this room without the permission of the pujar, so much so that the pahan's household members may not touch the Sarna winnowing fan till hadiya is not offered to Sarna Devi residing in the winnowing fan.

After the worship in the Sarna place, this is the most important religious and social act of Sarhul festival. It is compulsory for the pahan to visit every home in the village and bless it with Sarna flowers.

If some houses remain uncovered, then the next day the very same procedure is followed and the pahan, pujar and the village elders move around accompanied with music. If the village is big then this programme continues for three days or till all the houses are touched.

The Handing over of the Batari (water pot)

The handing over of the batari and the keeping of the Sarna winnowing fan in the house are the concluding items of Sarhul festival The "batari" is related to the pujar while the Sarna winnowing fan is connected with the pahan. "Sarna-Kuri" is that room where, after having completed "poomp kherna" (distribution of sal flowers) in all the houses of the village, the pahan and pujar sit beneath the Sarna winnowing fan in a cross-legged way. The pujar's wife brings a pitcher of water and fills the "batari" of the pujar and picks up the batari and gives it to the pujar who keeps it pressed with his left arm. In some villages, the pahnain or another elderly woman respectfully gives a lighted "hukka" (hubble-bubble) to the pujar. The pujar is reached home in style. He rides on the shoulders of young men, the batari pressed by his left arm and the right hand smoking the "hukka." The pahan, pahnain and all the people present in the pahan's house join the procession to reach the pujar from the pahan's home to his own home. Upon seeing the pujar's procession coming the Oraon people assembled at the pujar's house bring an earthern pitcher full of water in the courtyard and pour out the water of all the pitchers in the courtyard. When the procession comes to the house, everybody starts dancing due to which the whole courtyard becomes slushy.

As per the belief of the Oraons, the more the courtyard becomes wet and slushy, the more rainy will be that year and the land will be more fit to be ploughed and harvest will be good. The function is concluded with hadiya and food. The hadiya is poured in the batari and distributed.

The Seating in the Winnowing Fan

The pahan makes Sarna goddess sit in the winnowing fan for the whole year and this is the final ritual of Sarhul festival. While seating the goddess he prays to her to remain peacefully seated in that winnowing fan.

The Sarna winnowing fan is the place of Chala Pachcho Devi or Sarna Budhiya.

Next morning a pitcher of rice wine, which is called "hadiya of the seating in the winnowing fan" is brought to the Sarna kuri. The pahan enters the Sarna-kuri, takes a leaf cup full of hadiya and sprinkles some of it over the Sarna winnowing fan, pouring the rest of it on the fan. He prays that now Sarna Devi may remain seated in the winnowing fan for one year.

The Oraons believe that if there is any movement or disturbance in the Sarna winnowing fan, then the Sarna budhiya comes out of the fan and is angry. Hence when hanging the Sarna fan on the peg it is taken care of that, under any circumstances, even during storms, this fan does not move. The fan is tied to the peg and affixed firmly against the wall.

After having completed the arrangement regarding the Sarna winnowing fan, the seating in the fan, offering of hadiya to Sarna devi, satisfying Sarna budhiya or Chala Pachcho for the whole year, and praying that till the next Sarhul festival she should quietly sit in the winnowing fan, when the pahan comes out of the Sarna kuri, then the flags hoisted a day earlier to the festival at the door of the pahan (the Chandi flags) are brought down formally by the Oraons. The bringing down of the Chandi flags marks the closing of the Sarhul festival and is considered the religious declaration of it.

Hariari Festival

Hariari festival is celebrated in the month of Asadh (mid-June to mid-July) when the seeds of paddy, "gondli" (a kind of cereal), "madua" (a kind of millet) and cotton are sown and every where the earth looks fully green: Hariari worship is community worship although at times the worship may be done individually. It is after this worship that the Oraons transplant the paddy seedlings. In Hariari worship in addition to the regional gods, the worshippers offer sacrifice to their ancestors and the dead ancestors of the clan or "khunt." But more often than not, this whoship is conducted by the villagers as a community.

There is no fixed date for Hariari worship. As per convenience, the mahto of every village in consultation with the pahan, fixes the date for this worship. In order to meet the requirement of cocks for sacrifice, either the villagers give donations or else every year one household after another consecutively has to arrange for the cocks. The mahto gives order to the "gorait" (musician) as to from which household he has to bring cocks for the current year.

On the fixed day, when the sun goes higher in the sky, the pahan along with his assistant pujar and the "panbhara" reaches that special upland of the village where every year "Hariari Puja" (worship) is conducted. This place is besmeared with cowdung from before to purify it. The winnowing fan of the pahan along with the sacrificial knife is kept on the ground. The cocks and hens brought for sacrifice are given handfuls of rice to peck upon. The rice is put at certain distances and in whichever deity's name it is offered, it is called the "Kuri" of that deity. If on this occasion some he-goat has to be sacrificed, then the pahan or pujar sanctifies it and marks it with vermillion. Now the pahan takes each cock and hen by turn in his hand and addressing each deity he says, "I am offering hariari. You see that no disease or disaster enters the village. You are the lord of the village. If any disaster or disease enters, then you divert it. Please see that every inhabitant of this village lives a life of peace and happiness. You give good rains so that our village may prosper and be well off with good harvest."

The pahan picks up every cock and hen which has pecked at the kuri rice and prays in this fashion to all the gods and ancestors and the pujar keeps on giving them to him. This action is repeated when the pujar again gives the cocks and hens one by one to the pahan for sacrifice. The pahan offers the cock or hen in the name of the deity with his knife and sprinkles the blood of the fowl on the half eaten rice of the kuri. Every god is offered a fowl of that colour which is traditionally thought to be liked by the deity. Dharmes is offered white, Dadha is offered red, Sarna Budhiya is offered brown, Desauli is offered brown cock/hen as sacrifice. The speckled fowls are offered to the ancestors and dead ancestors of other clans.

The heart of the sacrificed fowl is taken out, closed in a sal leaf and boiled, and the rest of the flesh is mixed with rice to prepare a hotchpotch. The pahan takes out some portion of the heart and offers it to invisible powers and keeps it on the ground. He drops hadiya on it and thereafter gives permission to the assembled people to drink hadiya. After this everybody partakes of the hotch potch meal which is holy food. Only men are allowed to partake of this feast-women are prohibited.

After the feasting, the stones of the fireplace, the earthenware utensils, the leaf plates etc., whatever had been used there, are buried in the ground. Thereafter everybody returns to the village and from the next day they are authorised by religion to start paddy transplantation work.

Kadlota

The Oraons observe kadlota festival for the safety and security of the rising crop. Kadlota festival is a safety measure against black magic, evil words, evil eye and their ill-effects. In kadlota festival, the village deity called "dadha-desauli" is chiefly worshipped so that he may protect the agricultural harvests from evil eye and such practices of people. On the second day of kadlota, worship called "dandakatta" is conducted in which there is a procedural arrangement to ward off black magic, evil eye and its practices, evil spells or similar destructive efforts.

Kadlota is observed on the tenth day of the moon in the month of Bhado in nearly every Oraon village. The way cocks and hens are collected for the Hariari festival, in the same way for this festival also by turn the materials for worship are collected. The sacrifice of the cocks and hens and prayer rites are the same but in the prayer it is further added that the deity of the village, the naads of various places to whom the offerings are being made, "please see that nobody destroys our verdant crops through the evil eye, evil practices or black magic." Whenever in a visibly good crop the harvest is comparatively less and weak, then the Oraon farmer believes that somebody has attacked the crop inwardly and destroyed it.

In order to escape the evil effects of black magic or evil eye and evil practices, the Oraons often use "Bhelwa" branches. Even in danda-katta worship, the bhelwa branches are chiefly used. On the day of kadlota festival the village youth go to the forest and from there they bring bundles of bhelwa, kand and sinduar branches. The branches of these trees are poisonous. A pinch of arwa rice of the worship is tied to a branch which is planted in the crop field. The Oraons have full belief that such a safety measure will ward off any kind of evil eye/evil practice or black magic and their influence on their agriculture.

Karam Festival

Karam is a very famous and a very much followed festival of the tribals of Chhotanagpur. The aim of this festival is to please God Karam through his worship because of which the worshipper's home remains full of wealth and property and he does not have to face bad days. Amongst the Oraons, karam worship is mainly observed by women. It is clear from the karam songs that the sister worships karam for the prosperity and good health of her brother. [49]

The Growing of Jawa Flowers

The preparations for karam festival start nine days ahead by the village young men and women. On the first day, the young women assemble after having their bath, and dancing and singing they go to the nearest river for getting sand. At the river they fill sal leaf plates with sand and keeping them in their baskets, they return to their respective homes singing and dancing. The basket is kept in some sanctified place in which barley and wheat are sown. Everyday these young women worship them with incense and joss sticks, and after watering them with turmeric water, they accept any food. This ritual goes on till the day of karam-puja (worship). On the ninth day, the seeds sown inside sprout-these sprouts are called "jawa flowers."

The Cutting of Karam Branch

On the day of karam puja, all men and women fast and create a circular place of worship. During evening, some unmarried young men assemble at a particular place for cutting the karam branch. These young men start for the karam tree, dancing and singing on the way, carrying with them axe, arwa rice, coarse/unrefined thread, vermillion, incense and joss sticks, ghee (clarified butter) and fire. They purify the roots of the Karam tree by smearing it all round with cow dung. One youth gets up with the raw thread and binds the tree seven times by going around it seven times, puts a vermillion mark on the tree, and offering fire, incense, joss sticks, ghee, beseeches Karam god for his grace and blessing, and requests him to come to the place of worship.

"O karam king ! O Righteous king ! All these days you have remained in the upland of the forest, on the border-today we have come to take you. Today you will be in the "akhra" (place of worship), stand in the "akhra." O karam king, righteous king ! See we are raining flowers so that your grace may come on our agricultural-wealth, village-country, children, on all."

After this prayer, the youth climbs up the tree and cut down three branches of four to five feet length, and preventing them from touching the ground, they go back to the place of worship, dancing and singing on the way. At the outer limits of the village, the waiting men and women ritualistically welcome them and with great fanfare take them towards the village.

Planting of the Karam Branches

A fasting youth or the pahan upon reaching the village akhra, digs three pits at short distances. These pits are dug in the ground which has been daubed with cow-dung. A small pot of water, milk, raw thread, vermillion, incense, ghee and fire is already kept from before. The karam branches are firmly planted in the pits which are then filled with mud. The water from the pot is poured on these three pits to give strength to the firmness. Every such planted branch is thereafter bound seven times with the raw thread by going round them. After binding with the thread, incense and ghee are burnt in fire whose sanctified smoke is moved before the branches. Thereafter, milk and arwa rice are offered following which, after three salutations, the worshipper gets up. In this way, the phase of planting the karam branches is completed and then the sermon/story of karam is begun.

There are two legends related to karam worship prevalent in Oraon society. The story of Karma and Dharma, two brothers, is prevalent in Ranchi, Lohardagga and nearby areas of Gumla. The story of seven brothers and one sister is very much prevalent in Chhattisgarh and Madhya Pradesh. But the purport, sequence of incidents and in the end the advice and moral of the stories is the same. In brief, the gist of both is the same.

The song of the seven brothers is sung in all the folk songs. Although this story is not a matter of history, yet the entire Oraon society is completely influenced by it and the concerned convention connected to it are developed in their society.

Synopsis of a Prevalent legend[50]

There were seven brothers and one sister of a family in a village. All the brothers were married. Their wives used to be jealous of the sister but all the brothers used to love their sister. The eldest brother loved her very much.

One day, all the brothers went out to trade. The eldest brother was Karma and the second brother was Dharma. The sister also wanted to go along with them because she was afraid that in the absence of the brothers their wives would torture her. But the brothers were not ready to listen to her. The sister had to stay behind with their wives. From this one can guage her sense of sacrifice and love towards her brothers.

After the brothers left, their wives starting planning to get rid of her. The plans were as follows:

(1) Milk of the tigress:-In order to get rid of her......The sisters-in-law told her to go to the forest and bring milk of a tigress. This was such a chore that, let alone bringing the milk, the tigress would have eaten her up. Weeping and lamenting, the girl picked up the pitcher and went towards the forest. There she met tiger cubs playing among themselves. Seeing them she started weeping. When the cubs asked her, she told them the truth. The cubs told her, "You put the pitcher down and run to hide yourself." After a short while the tigress came back to suckle the cubs. The tigress said, "The smell of human being is coming," but the cubs said that it is not so, and started drinking her milk. After suckling them when the tigress was about to leave, then the cubs said, "we feel hungry when you are not here, so pour some milk in this pitcher." The tigress put her milk in the pitcher and went out hunting in the forest. Then the girl came out and, taking the pitcher with the tigress's milk, happily returned home. The sisters-in-law did not believe that whosoever is protected by karam god, no harm can come upon him.

(2) Water in a leaky pot:-This time the sisters-in-law thought of a new plan. They made seven holes in a pot and told her to go and fetch water from the river other wise she would be driven out of the house. The girl picked up the pot and went to the bank of the river but the water would come out of the pot. She started crying. On hearing her weeping, a she-frog of the river felt sympathy for her. Seven tadpoles entered the pot and stuck themselves in the holes. The girl returned happily with the water.

(3) Help from a snake:-Now the sisters-in-law became more jealous of the girl. This time they thought of a new ploy. They told her to go to the forest to bring a bunch of wood but if she used rope to tie the bunch then she would not be allowed to enter the house. The girl went to the forest and collected the bundle of wood and started crying. Upon hearing her crying, a snake came in front of her and asked her the reason for her crying. The girl told the snake the full truth. The snake wound itself around the bundle like a rope and the girl returned happily. She kept the wood, the snake went away, but the sisters-in-law were very surprised. They began thinking of a new plan.

(4) Gathering the rye mustard seeds:-This time the sisters-in-law took a seer (about a kilo) of rye mustard seeds and scattered them in a field. The girl was told to gather all the rye mustard seeds failing which she would be turned out of the house. But this was an impossible task. The girl started crying sitting among the scattered mustard seeds. Some birds came near her and asked her the reason of her crying. Thereafter they got busy in collecting the mustard seeds. After some time the scattered seeds got collected in the basket. The girl returned home with the basket of mustard seeds. Due to this, her sisters-in-law became very angry. Thereafter, they made a final plan to take the girl in the thick forest and to abandon her there. They took the girl to a very thick forest. They made her climb a wild fig tree and told her to pluck wild figs. The girl climbed up the tree and started plucking the figs and giving them to her sisters-in-law. When their stomachs were full, they left the girl on the tree and went back home. They thought that the girl would survive on the figs and thereafter she would die of starvation. The girl started living there.

After some time, the family gradually started becoming impoverished. There was shortage of cereals, there were diseases, and quarrels which started destroying the home. All the women together started thinking of how to overcome this distress. They remembered Dharma that he was an expert in religious matters and could conduct any religious worship. Ultimately, the women decided that since "Karma" is the eldest brother in the family, hence worshipping him would get rid of their poverty. They went to the forest and from there they brought three branches of the karam tree and after planting them in their courtyard, they started worshipping them. These three branches were (a) in the name of "parne davar" (b) in the name of the village and (c) in the name of the family and planted accordingly. In the meantime, all the brothers returned home after completing their trade. Since they were exhausted in their long walk, they halted at a short distance from the village. The anxiety about home started troubling them, hence in order to get up-to-date information, the youngest brother went home. When he reached home, he found his wife and other sisters-in-law immersed in karam dances and songs. The brother also joined them and forgot that he had come to gather news. When the youngest brother did not return, then the eldest brother asked the brother just elder to the smallest to go and get news, but he too joined the dancing and singing. One by one all the brothers were sent but all of them became very much involved in the singing and dancing. Now only the eldest Karma remained. Being angry with the neglect of his younger siblings, the eldest brother Karma got up and went towards the village. After walking for some time he came across a wild fig tree. He sat down beneath it and started taking rest. This was the same fig tree on which the sister had been abandoned by the sisters-in-law. When she saw her eldest brother, her love overwhelmed her and tears kept falling from her eyes. When the tears fell on the brother then he saw his sister crying. He got her down from the fig tree and upon hearing the cruelty meted out to her during his absence, he went home with his sister in a fit of rage. He saw that all the members of the family, without bothering for his arrival, were absorbed in singing and dancing. In a fit of rage, he overturned the milk kept for offering, and uprooted the karam branches and threw them. Karam god became angry with such behaviour of Karma, and the days of destruction of Karma's family began. It started with his loss, quarrels with the brothers and unrest at home. Karma's wife explained to him that this is the result of showing disrespect to Karam god. Karma understood what she said. He brought three branches of the Karam tree in a sanctified manner, planted them and duly worshipped Karam god. Due to the grace of Karam god, he became more prosperous than before and his home was filled with grains and wealth. There are some other stories pertaining to Karam-Dharam which are known. The centre point of all these stories is that due to insulting karam god by uprooting the planted branches they were reduced to penury and after correcting their mistakes they again became prosperous.

Brief Summary of the Second Popular Story[51]

Karma and Dharma were two brothers. Due to natural disaster, they were going through great financial crisis. Hence, they went out into the world to earn money. In the outside world, luck favoured them and they earned a good amount of wealth. Many days passed. When they remembered their home, then both started for their home \ village. After crossing forests, hills and mountains, they reached the outer limits of their village in the evening of the eleventh day of the moon of Bhado month. The whole village was echoing with the sound of drums, cymbals, singing and dancing. There was happiness all around. As per tribal belief, a person should not enter the limits of the jurisdiction of the village deity without observing certain ritual. Hence both brothers stopped at the limits, and requested the passersby to inform their house for performing the rituals for welcoming them. But nobody enquired about them on this happy occasion. Being compelled, Karma sent his younger brother Karma but he too became immersed in Karma worship and forgot to tell anybody about Karma. Feeling insulted, Karma himself came to the village. When he saw the scene in the village, he become very angry. He destroyed the place of worship, uprooted and threw away the Karam branches and punished his family. Time passed. Karma's misfortune began. The wealth he had amassed was quickly used up and he reached the point of starvation due to which he and his wife started working as labourers in the household of Dharma. Day by day, Dharma began to prosper. One day, during the feast of paddy transplantation, Karma had to face some mismanagement which he took as an insult. Resultantly, he went to the field of Dharma and uprooted the paddy seedlings and cut the field divider, but everything became alright again. Karma stood stupefied upon seeing this. Then an oracle happened which told him that since he had uprooted the planted Karam branches of karam worship, he was being punished for that sin, and that was the reason for all the troubles in his life. He was asked to do penance for his sins before Karma king and if he worshipped Karam, then all his good days would come back to him.

Karma had a change of heart. With due respect he went out in search of Karam god. In the process he came across a pond. He picked up some water by cupping his hands, but saw that there were insects in the water. The owner of the pond told him to get the answer from Karam god. In the process, he came across..... an orchard in which the mangoes were infested with pests; he came across a cow but blood was coming in her milk; he came across a woman preparing flattened rice but the rice was breaking up; ultimately he came across a crocodile which was in great pain. All of them asked him to find out their remedies from Karam god. The crocodile took Karma on its back and crossed the seven seas. In front there was a huge luminescent karam tree. Karma bound the tree seven times with raw thread, showing great respect. He offered arwa rice, oil, vermillion, incense and joss sticks and prayed with deep regard. He asked for forgiveness of his sins, and prayed for his blessings and kindness. Thereafter, he cut three tender branches of the karam tree, put them on his shoulders and praying to karam god started back for his village. On the return journey, he told the crocodile that he always used to sell flattened rice in greed during karam worship; after the cow gave birth to a calf, the owner of the cow never offered the first milk in worship and neither did he distribute it; the owner of orchard never gave any mango to a hungry traveller without extracting money, and when the mahto\ pahan asked for mangoes for karam worship, he used to scold them; the owner of the pond never gave permission to anybody to use his pond so much so that it used to be out of bounds even for karam worship. After knowing the reasons, all of them worshipped Karam god and chanted his name in complete surrender. Karma reached his village, and following all rules and rituals, he planted the karam branches and worshipped them.

While narrating this story, the fasting worshipper gives arwa rice to the assembled people from time to time and tells them to offer them to the branches by scattering them. After the story ends, the Karam branches are worshipped by going around them seven times, and a lighted lamp, incense and joss sticks are shown to them, and they are marked with vermillion and oil. After that, singing and dancing start which continue through out the night. Early next morning, the karam branches are uprooted and taken from door to door of the village. The people mark them with vermillion and pour milk on them. Ultimately, the karam branches are immersed in the nearby pond, water source or river. Thereafter, after having a bath at home, "danda katta" or "bhelwa farhi" is done and the bhelwa branch (branch of the cashew nut tree) is planted in the rice field.

Karam Darshan[52] (philosophy)

Karam worship is equally famous as Sarhul in Jharkhand. The religious philosophy of Karam is not different from Sarhul and basically it is grounded in agriculture and expresses deep love between brother and sister. In tribal lore it has been said that Karma and Dharma were two brothers. In the story, any other tribal name would have sufficed but no scholar has tried to reveal the innate religious philosophy behind it. Actually life is the result of duty and religion. The farmer cannot run away from his duty. He has to labour but life is incomplete based only on doing one's duty. Hence, he requires the grace of Dharmes (God)[53]. The karam tree is born by itself hence it is godly. It is clear from the story of karam that originally "Karam" gets diverted from the true path therefore becomes the reason for grief. Just opposite is Dharam which shows the correct path and accordingly treading the path as desired by Nature, earns happiness.

Actually, the whole Creation is managed by matter and energy which in Vedic literature have been named inanimate and animate. When the animate enters the inert, meaning thereby that when there is correct coordination between the inanimate and animate, then Creation undergoes balanced management. "Karam" and "Dharam" symbolise the inert and the animate. Inert by itself is death while animate by itself is not useful. When the inert and animate coordinate and balance each other then Creation awakens, is activated, and everywhere life's illumination spreads. This philosophical analysis marking the highest achievement of civilisation, indicates the height of mental thinking of the tribe.

In Oraon society, often married women visit their parents during karam festival where they dance in the akhra with their old friends. Since the sister worships karam Raja (king) for the welfare of her brother, it becomes necessary for her to visit her parent's home. On this occasion, the "mati" takes his disciples in an open place away from the forest and village, and uses his chants on them due to which some of them get influenced and start behaving as if gods and goddesses have come upon them. They swirl and swirl till their heads touch the ground. The disciples who are unable to do this, they are whipped with a grass whip. In this way, the "matis" profitably use the day of karam for sharpening their professional skills.

In this festival, importance has been given to wishing for the welfare of the village and its homes, prosperity and to sisters. Karam festival is celebrated in various places with slight changes, in different ways and their own aims. In this way, the celebration of Karam festival differs as per the god, and as per rules and aim, the brief worships can be identified in the following manner:-

(a) ghuriya or budhiya karam (b) asari karam (c) baroya karam (d) thhapdi karam (e) thariya karam (f) lahsooya karam (g) lujhki karam (h) dasai karam.

Jitiya Festival

The jitiya festival is celebrated on the twelfth day of Karam festival. The aim of this festival is to secure the protection of one's offspring and wishing a good future for them. This festival is mainly observed by mothers after undergoing strict fast and worship. This festival is not celebrated as a community festival. In an individual way, those Oraon families which have been traditionally observing jitiya festival for the protection of their sons, they take special interest in this festival. But this observance has caught on, and in nearly every Oraon home jitiya festival is observed and in some way or the other, this festival is observed by all Oraon families. This festival has received a good response among the Oraon race and the pahan also participates in it.

Although jitiya is not observed in a public place, even then the women of every home in the village assemble at a particular home and listen to its connected story and celebrate it in a group. In order to celebrate jitiya festival, every year a particular village home is earmarked for it. The women observe a waterless fast one day prior to jitiya festival. In the evening, they take a bath and on the doorway of every room they hang a cucumber leaf, a cucumber, flowers of the pumpkin and ridge gourd, and a piece of bread all threaded in one thread. The cucumber symbolises the male child. After this, in the courtyard of the pahan's house three branches of the tree called "jitiya-peeper" are planted and he worships them with incense. The women of the house also do the same. They light earthen lamps of ghee (clarified butter) beneath these branches. At night, a knot of string \ thread is hung from the jitiya peeper branches and tied to it. In some village this knotted string is tied to the arms of the children.

The next morning, before sunrise, collecting the jitiya peeper etc., the senior married woman (whose husband is alive) of the house in silence proceeds outside the village and going far to some pond or lonely place, puts all these materials there and returns home. This fast and observance is of about 24 hours. When she returns, then as holy food she partakes of cucumber and its pieces are also distributed.

Although jitiya festival has entered Oraon tribe some centuries ago due to contact with Hindus, it has now become a very prevalent festival of the tribe. According to Oraon pahans, the cause for the popularity of the festival is the connection it has for the well being of children. Along with it the fast kept by the mother is very difficult which has aroused the respect of other women towards this festival. As per Oraon nature, on the night of the festival every family partakes of hadiya and feast but prior to this, the share of the ancestors is respectfully offered to them.

Sohrai

Sohrai festival, which is related to protection and increase of cattle wealth, is individually observed in nearly every Oraon religion on the new moon night of Kartik month. Just like the Deepawali festival of Hindus, earthen lamps are lit in karanj oil and placed in cattle shed, cow dung pit, kitchen, trees in the courtyard, in front of and behind the house, in every room, shelf and doorstep right from the beginning of new moon night of Kartik month.

Efforts are made that the lamps remain lighted throughout the night. In the cattle shed incense and joss sticks are burnt, and at night horse beans, mahua and beans are specially cooked for the cattle which is given to them to eat the next morning.

The next day, the cattle are taken to a nearby water source, river or pond and given a thorough bath. In the meantime, the women at home clean the cattle shed well. When the cattle return home after being washed, then the lady of the house sprinkles hadiya over them, and the cattle are offered "ol" (a tuber) along with salt. Their houses are marked with oil and vermillion, and vermillion mark is also made on their forehead.

As per tradition, cocks are sacrificed to appease "Godaiya" or "Gohar", god of the cattle shed. Rich Oraons who possess good cattle wealth, duly offer pig sacrifice to "Godaiya". In some village, often collecting donation, a pig is bought and publicly duly offered in sacrifice to "Godaiya" for the well being of the village cattle.

After having duly offered sacrifice to "Godaiya", the horse bean pulse which had been cooked the previous night is given to the cattle to eat. Thereafter, a male member of the house takes the cattle to the forest and upland for grazing. Some wealthy Oraons appoint "ahirs" (milk men- a sub-caste of Hindus) to look after their cattle and take them out for grazing. This appointment is done on the event of Sohrai. These "ahirs" are mostly Hindus and settle down in Oraon village.

The next day, "daasa-maasa" is observed. It is a burlesque which is performed by bachelors. They dress up like men and women with the help of straw and grass and collect donations from every house. They pretend to drive away mosquitoes and flies, and noisily and happily go round the village. These boys are called "dundu" in Oraon society.

The Oraons show full respect to the Ahirs on the day of Sohrai. After offering sacrifice to "Godaiya", the Ahir reaches the home of the pahan dancing to the beats of the "nagara" (big kettle drum) and drum where the wife of the pahan ("pahnain") makes him stand on a brass salver and washes his feet with a bottle of water. After that, the Ahir sits on a palm leaf and he is offered rice beer (hadiya) to drink. In the meantime, the pahnain marks the stick of the Ahir (stick with which he controls the cattle) with vermillion and oil. The Ahir goes straight to his home from the pahan's home, and taking his wife ("ashirin") along with him, follows the musician's kettle drum and drum, dancing and singing. He visits all those homes the cattle of which he takes out for grazing. In every home, the ahir is welcomed the way he was welcomed in the pahan's home-he moves round the whole village dancing and singing. All Oraons place some food grains at the side of the brass salver which the ahirin collects. After throwing the water from the brass salver, some money and hadiya is poured onto the salver which the ahir sips, bending just like an animal, and, picking up the money, proceeds to the next home.

Although the Oraon tribe is chiefly agriculturist, still they depend upon pastoral life to a great extent. They often take the help of one or two ahir homes of their village for the protection of their cattle. The Oraon tribe honours labour, hence during Sohrai, they not only worship the cattle and offer sacrifice to the deity of the cattle shed, but the pahnain and lady of the household wash the feet of the ahirs and give them due respect after having appointed them for one year to look after the cattle and take them out for grazing.

Kharra Puja (worship) or Kharihani

Kharra puja is the last festival of the year. This festival is celebrated when the harvested crop has been brought to the barn and the work of separating the grains from the chaff through bullocks is yet to begin. Any farmer of the village completes the kharra puja before beginning work in the barn.

Kharra puja is celebrated as a community festival in the village but some wealthy Oraons individually conduct the worship of their fields and barn. For the community worship, the village pahan fixes a date for it. On that day, the villagers under the leadership of the pahan have an early bath and gather in the upland of the village. This place is a plain rocky place hence there is no inconvenience regarding the site. The pahan gets cocks and hens collected by the villagers, and on a place which has already been cleaned by smearing it with cow dung, the pahan places kuri of arwa rice. The cock and hens peck the rice from every kuri. On the southern edge, a separate kuri is kept in a very sanctified manner from which the white cock, meant for Dharmes, pecks the arwa rice.

The pahan lets the poultry peck the rice and offers them in sacrifice in the name of every deity and spirit. Finally, after cleaning the knife well, the white cock is offered in sacrifice to Dharmes. The blood of the cock and rice beer is offered to every kuri. After kharra puja, the pahan returns home in a group and work starts in the barn. Thereafter the other villagers can also start the work in their barns.

Some Oraons individually perform kharra puja. Along with other spirits, they also worship the ancestors of their clan and after satisfying them they start work in the granary. The way Sohrai is connected to cattle-wealth, kharra puja is connected to agriculture.

Sanskar

As per the religious belief of the Oraon tribe, the various categories of deity and spirit of their religion influence the movement of their lives at different levels. In the Oraon tribe, right from conception to death, and even after death to include the soul of the dead amongst the family of the formless souls of the clan and ancestors living in the nether world through religious rituals is believed to be a level of life which comes within "sanskar." Actually, Oraon life is divided in many levels, and to enter each level certain religious rituals have to be followed prior to that so that the concerned level of life may pass in happiness without any obstruction for the Oraon. Every level of life is really a preparation for the entire life and works as a background for the upcoming level. This is the reason why there is a chain of "sanskar" and Oraon life crosses every step of "sanskar" to go ahead. The "sanskar" at every level is fixed as per the age of the person. In this way, "sanskar" helps to propel Oraon life at every turn of life to achieve the fixed target. Oraon life is bound by the following chief "sanskars":

(a) fifth day or purification ritual
(b) naming ceremony
(c) "judo-eda" or tying of hair ceremony
(d) "Jokh edpa" or ceremony of granting entry into "dhumkuriya"
(e) Marriage ceremony
(f) Death ritual

Fifth Day or Purification Ritual

On the fifth day of the birth of a baby, the "Chhatti" or purification ritual is conducted. From the day of birth till the fifth day, the mother, all her clothes and goods, her room, etc. are supposed to be impure. During this impure condition, the mother and the child are completely segregated from the outside world. The Oraons believe that during this time the mother and child are in a very vulnerable condition therefore they fall victim very easily to black magic, evil eye, evil spells, touch of ghosts and spirits or shadows or any magical dart aimed at them. Hence they are kept completely protected from the outside world. In addition an iron weapon or piece of iron is kept at the head side which will ward off any touch of the evil ghosts and spirits.

Actually, preparation for protection from evil spirits and ghosts starts from the time of conception. The Oraons believe that when a girl of any village comes over after marriage to the home of her in-laws, then the spirit of the village of the girl's father as also the "naad" of the clan comes along with her. In order to get rid of such "naads," puja or worship is conducted as per "joda-kamna" procedure. This is done only during the first conception.

Joda-Kamna

When the signs of conception are evident, then the pregnant girl's father is invited by the son-in-law or the father of the son-in-law to come over. He reaches the daughter's in-laws' house along with some close relatives. As usual, they are welcomed with washing of feet and made to sit out in the open on a mat.

A pig is brought for sacrifice. In front of the people who have come from a different village, the pig is given "arwa" rice to eat and "arwa" rice is also sprinkled over it so that it may become fit for sacrifice. Thereafter its head is severed with the blow of an axe. The sacrifice is offered by saying the following words, "from today, you deity, naad or dead ancestor of the pregnant mother, accept this offering and free this woman."

It is taken for granted from this sacrifice that the deity, naad of the clan, and other naads belonging to the pregnant girl's father's village, become satisfied and leaving the girl return to their own places. Thus, the girl is purified from the influence of the naads of her paternal home and starts belonging to her husband's home.

"Joda-Kamna" ritual is completed as per convenience within the first three months of conception otherwise the evil influence of the deities and naads of the pregnant girl's paternal village may fall on the unborn child. When the child is born and the ritual of cutting the umbilical cord is completed, then nearly every baby is thrown in the "gandoor gaddha" (a pit to collect cowdung). Some women of the house take the newborn infant to the pit. The woman carrying the baby pretends that the baby is meaningless and puts it on the cowdung. At the same moment another woman picks it up and all the women return. This ritual is followed to cheat ghosts and spirits and regional naads or to confuse them so that they might not be interested in the baby thinking it to be neglected. The umbilical cord of the baby is put in an old basket along with on old broom and some arwa rice, and it is buried deep near the house at the place where utensils are washed or rubbish is thrown.

When the navel of the baby dries and the root of the umbilical cord comes off, then it is immediately and quietly buried in a secret place. As per the belief among barren women and those women who are unable to produce children among the Oraons, if they eat up the root of the umbilical cord then they develop the capacity to produce children and the woman, whose baby's cord root is eaten up, becomes barren. Such kind of protective measures adopted by the Oraons living amidst religion, black magic and superstition, have become part of their religion.

Paisari

In every Oraon household, on the day a child is born or within two three days of its birth, paisari puja (worship) is conducted to ward off any disaster over the child. The village pahan conducts this worship and pleases the village deity.

The village pahan takes some arwa rice and money and touching the head of the infant with them circles them over it and places them on the floor. The same way he takes a cock, makes it peck at arwa rice and thereafter circling the cock above the head of the baby, puts it on the floor. This is the sacrificial cock which the pahan as per his own desire will take home and offer in sacrifice. In this way through paisari, the pahan takes away......all the troubles or disasters from the head of the baby and incorporates them in the arwa rice and the cock which are offered to the village deity. In this manner, the infant is blessed with long life, free from all disasters.

After paisari, shashti or day of purification comes. This day comes generally on the fifth or sixth day after the child is born. The woman who has given birth to the baby, and other women of the house go to some nearby water source, river or pond for bathing. The nails of the mother are cleaned, and turmeric and oil are applied. After having her bath, the mother has to wear clean clothes. In the meantime, the whole house is besmeared with cow dung to clean and purify it. The mother and the other women return home after having had their bath.

The "chhatti" bath is forbidden in any water source, pond or river of the village because there is a fear that they will be polluted with the mother's impurity and dirt. That is why the bath takes place in a water body outside the village so that the outside water body may absorb the impurity and dirt of the mother and thus the water bodies of the village will be saved from becoming impure.

After the "chhatti" ceremony, the new mother and child can touch everybody and come in contact with them. This is a very important ceremony in Oraon religion because it is only after this that the child is accepted in Oraon race, meaning thereby that leaving the last impure life it steps on the staircase of a new life.

Naming Ceremony or "Name Pinjna"

In the Oraon tribe, there is a special procedure prevalent for naming the child. The child's name is determined with the help of ancestors and invisible powers. When the child becomes about six months (or even more) old, then its parents arrange for its naming ceremony. The naming ceremony is often conducted within six months to one year. Prior to this, the child's name follows the day it was born. The son born on a Monday is called "Semra" and the daughter is called "Somari." Similarly, mangra-mangri (for Tuesday), Budhwa-Budhini (for Wednesday), Birsa-Birsi (for Thursday), Sukra-Sukri (for Friday) (even Sukkar for Friday)...Shanicharwa-Sanichari (for Saturday), and Aitwa-Aitwariya (for Sunday). If a child is born on the day of a festival, then the child is called after the festival and not the day, namely, Karma-Karmi, Fagua-Faguni, Jitna-Jitni (for those born on Jitiya festival) and so on.

Through the formal religious ceremony of "name pinjna" the naming of the child becomes its real name, which is used during marriage or other occasions. This name is often kept after the name of a dead ancestor. In the morning of "name pinjna," the village barber-cum-musician ("gorait") shaves the head of the boy leaving the top knot on the head. The shaved off hair is immersed in a nearby river.

According to the belief of the Oraons, this immersed hair ultimately comes in contact with the shaved off hair of another boy or girl in the sea or a big river. Whichever girl or boy's hair merges like this with that of another boy or girl, he or she becomes the future spouse in married life of that girl or boy. This coming together occurs as per Divine law.

After shaving off the hair, the barber brings a big leaf cup of water before the child. Three arwa rice grains are dropped into the water in front of the pahan and other village elders. These grains are often dropped in the water by the village "panch" (councillor) or the eldest person. When the three grains of arwa rice are being dropped in the water, another person present there takes the name of a dead ancestor from the child's paternal or maternal side.

If the rice grains floating in the water touch each other through the corner which had earlier joined them to the paddy husk, then it is taken for granted that the invisible powers have indicated approval of the name of the dead ancestor to be given to the child. And the panch accordingly declares the name of the child. But if the rice grains do not touch each other and a little later sink in the water, then it is taken for granted that the invisible powers have not indicated approval of the name being suggested for the child.

If there is no success, then the procedure is repeated with three different grains of arwa rice and the name of a different dead ancestor. After waiting, if there is no success, then again the ritual is repeated till the invisible powers connect the rice to the name of a dead ancestor, and thereafter the panch declares the name of the child.

As soon as the real name of the child is declared, the barber's wife applies oil and turmeric on the child, bathes it in cold water and makes it wear new clothes. The barber is given some cereals or money for this job.

Although the divinely fixed name is given to the child after the naming ceremony, the family members and other well-wishers try to keep this name confidential. As per rules, after having got an actual name, the name of the child based on day or festival should be dropped because in the same village many girls and boys can be found to have the same names, but the parents and other family members of the child do not normally spread its actual name. The Oraons think that those who indulge in black magic if they become ill, then it is easier for them to hurt the name with the help of spirits because the name has been approved by spirits of the nether or invisible world. Hence, taking precaution against enemies, efforts are made to keep the real name of the child confidential. This effort is possible only in the early days. As and when the child grows, he begins to be identified by the name given to him during "name pinjna" or the naming ceremony.

Joodo-Eda or Tying of Hair

The joodo-Eda ceremony is observed to mark the end of childhood and beginning of adolescence among Oraon boys and girls. All the men and women of the village, boys and girls, assemble on the next day of full moon of Magh in the home of the mahto or the panch. They bring along with them one "morha" of paddy. The "morha" of paddy places the boys in one row and in front of them the girls in a separate row. The boys and girls of every family sit face to face on the "morha." Thereafter, a woman of the village pours oil on the head of every boy and girl from one end to the other. This ritual is also done by the other assembled women due to which the oil becomes excess. Every girl's hair is rubbed with oil and a parting is made after spreading out the hair fully. Thereafter a knot is tied in the hair and a wooden comb is inserted in it. In this way, wooden comb is affixed in the knot of hair of every girl.

The same procedure is followed for the boys but it is done by a man. He rubs oil in the hair of every boy and parting the hair in two parts, ties a knot and puts a comb in it. In this way when knots are tied in the hair of every boy, then with the evening feast the religious ceremony of "joodo-eda" is considered to be over.

Prior to "joodo-eda," no embellishment of hair of any boy or girl is permitted. This ceremony marks the entry of a boy or girl in the stage of adolescence. Without having undergone the ceremony of "joodo-eda" no girl is considered eligible for marriage. Similarly, for gaining entry into a "dhumkuriya," it is essential for an Oraon boy to have undergone "joodo-eda." But, for the past hundred years, the "joodo-eda" ceremony is slowly dying out in the villages and it is being replaced by "jokh-edpa."

Jokh Edpa or Entry into Dhumkuriya

Dhumkuriya is an institution peculiar to the Oraon tribe in which the Oraon youth are imparted education and they acquire work skills. After joodo-eda the boy becomes eligible to enter "Jokh-edpa" but it is not necessary that all Oraon youths gain admittance to Dhumkuriya. Seeing the number of candidates, it is often that in every village new adolescents are given entry after every three years. On the first day of the bright fortnight of the month of Magh, the dhumkuriya youth go out for hunting in the afternoon. When evening descends, these boys gather in an open space at the edge of the village along with their hunted prey. The candidates who want entry into the dhumkuriya, clean that space, and flaying the skin of the hunted prey, they cut them into pieces making them fit for cooking. In the meantime, the older boys of the dhumkuriya discuss among themselves about whom to select for giving entry into the dhumkuriya. When they take a decision, they prepare packets of sal leaves put some of the meat inside them, seal them and send them to the homes of selected candidates. After eating the meat from the packet, the new adolescent candidate becomes a member of the dhumkuriya.

Accordingly, the parents of the selected candidates donate karanj oil, paddy, wood, or some such necessary goods for the conduct of the Dhumkuriya which is recognised as fees. The practical and intellectual education of Oraon youth are completed while staying in the Dhumkuriya. This institution inspires culture among the Oraon boys and girls from religious and social viewpoint.

Marriage Ceremony

Marriage is supposed to be a necessary religious ceremony among the Oraon tribals. Even in 8-10 villages, after much effort, one may still not find an unmarried Oraon. In Oraon religion, the arrangement of marriage in nature, agriculture, festivals and development of the whole creation has been made. Wells, ponds, fruit bearing trees are duly got married. Prior to paddy plantation, its marriage is necessary for giving bumper crop. The chief festival of Oraons, that is Sarhul (Khaddi Benja) is celebrated as symbolic of marriage between earth and sun, and the village religious priest, that is, the pahan along with his wife are made to undergo duly a marriage ceremony on this occasion in front of the villagers every year. The Oraons believe that this is essential for good agriculture, good harvest, enough water and every kind of prosperity. If the wells and ponds are not married, then there will be a shortage of water, and whatever water will be available it will be infested with insects making the water undrinkable. The fruit trees will not have much fruit and whatever fruits will come forth will be infested with insects. The paddy crop will not come to fruition and will be attacked by pests. Similar kinds of bad results are connected to unmarried human life. Hence, the fear of becoming mad or undergoing unnatural ailments ensures that in Oraon society there is hardly any unmarried man or woman to be found.

Marriage is the order of Dharmes. He has fixed the husband and the wife. One does not have to depend on the boy or girl or their parents as to who their life partner will be. If one goes against the law laid down by Dharmes, then Dharmes will express His disapproval and anger in the form of many calamities. Often Oraon boys and girls, taking into consideration their "gotra," select their life partners and inform their guardians. The guardians study the matter after discussion, and thereafter in the midst of fixing the marriage, they also study the signs and messages sent by Dharmes. If everything is found to be proper, then the marriage is held.

In the Oraon tribe, the religious rituals pertaining to marriage can be divided in two parts:

(a) religious rituals to fix the marriage
(b) religious rituals pertaining to marriage procedure
(c) In Oraon religion, the procedure to fix marriage is comparatively more

Apprehensive than the marriage itself, and the elders and matchmakers observe a lot of caution in this. The boy's father after eliciting the desire of the boy, or himself making the move, sends the match-maker to the parents of the girl. The match-maker is called "agua" and in some places "agiya".

He obtains information regarding the parents of the girl, their ancestors, their gotra, number of brothers and sisters, etc. and tells about the eligibility of the girl to the boy's parents. After both sides express basic approval, the "agua" visits the girl's house in the month of Bhado after Karam festival, and places the marriage proposal on behalf of the boy's side. The guardians of the girl, in order to know about the justification of the proposal, send one or two trustworthy and clever friends or relations to the house of the boy so that they may know about the condition of that side. They visit the home with the excuse to get some tobacco.

When both sides agree to the marriage, then the bride's side invites the groom's side for the ritual of "khednorhna" or "washing the feet." On that day, three or five relations of the groom's side reach the bride's house. They start early in the morning at cock's crow for the village of the girl. The intention to start early is to find out devices for protection from bad signs. When they reach the girl's home, there, too, the women of the house come forward to welcome them with an earthenware container containing oil and one or more than one (as per capability) brass salver. They apply oil on their feet and wash them on the brass salver.

Decision Regarding Signs and Bad Signs

After welcoming them and seating the guests in the courtyard, verandah or some room by placing mats on the floor, one person from the bride's side comes to the "agua" and asks him if on the way they had come across bad signs. If there is denial, then everybody feels satisfied and further programme is decided.

According to Oraons, good signs include filled pitchers, lighted lamp, people carrying a bier. Bad signs include raucous cawing of the raven, a fox crossing one's path from left to right, sight of an empty pitcher, coming across a person taking cow dung in a basket either in a pit, field or anywhere, etc.

According to the belief of the Oraons, if the efforts of the "agua" are as per desire of Dharmes, then he sends good signs on the way, while leaving the village and on other occasions. In this way, through the various signs, experienced Oraons assess the approval of Dharmes. But in contrast, if the Oraons try to bring together a wrong couple, then Dharmes through various signs indicates his disapproval to the Oraons. Despite this if a wrong couple ties the knot and due to selfish reasons the marriage takes place, then as per the belief of the Oraons, it will result in the death of one of the sides.

The signs or bad signs are repeatedly studied lest any error be made. The persons who have come to the bride's house from the groom's side are asked about the signs and bad signs they faced on the way, and they are seriously considered after which they are given dinner. At the time of dinner, a new lamp is lighted with the help of a thick wick and mustard or karanj oil. If the lamp remains lighted till the dinner served to the guests is over, then it is presumed that there is complete approval of Dharmes for the wedding. If certain insignificant bad signs had been come across during the journey, their evil effects are mollified by the steady flame of the lamp lit during dinner time. But if the flame gets extinguished, or due to some reason falls down or breaks, then despite all the good signs on the way, all the efforts regarding this marriage are stopped and the people from the groom's side stop their dinner. The extinguishing of the flame indicates definite death of one party.

In addition to the extinguishing of the lamp if, till the guests remain in the bride's village, any earthen pitcher breaks or a branch falls off a tree without the reason of rain or storm, or an utensil of oil turns turtle and the oil spills over the ground, then the marriage proposal is abandoned there and then. These are bad omens indicative of death of one of the sides. Hence these signs are given more importance than all the signs seen on the way and the Oraons believe that Dharmes has given final warning because in his design there is no place for this couple. But if inspite of this the marriage takes place and the warning of Dharmes is ignored then definitely one or the other side is punished.

Muhi-Era

Prior to the commencement of dinner, a pitcher of rice beer is brought which as per the occasion is called "kheta bina borey" or "neg borey." Hadiya is made by putting water in the pitcher. Thereafter, the hadiya is poured out into another earthen pitcher out of which three "sarkhi" (an earthenware utensil) filled with hadiya are taken out Two sarkhis are given to the members of the bride's side and one sarkhi is given to the panch of the village. The "Sagua" or a senior Oraon member of the groom's side takes the beer in a sal leaf cup and offers the beer to the ancestors by thrice dropping it on the ground and prays to them thus, "so and so (the groom) and so and so (the bride) have had their marriage fixed. You kindly ensure that both of them live their life happily. Please ensure that both may live to a ripe old age."[54] After that an experienced person from the groom's side stands up and as per tradition gives a small speech which is replied in similar vein by a member of the bride's side Thereafter, the bride comes, and the father of the groom has alook at the face of the girl or carries out the work of observation of the girl. At the end, as a reward for having seen her face, as per capability, the father of the groom gives a good gift to the bride-to-be. This is called "muhi era."

This ritual is known by various names, but when it is gone through before the meal then it is called "muhiera," or in certain places giving importance to the wine which has been served, this is called "negbody."

After the ritual of "muhi era" is completed, both sides partake of a joint feast. During the feast, a person from the groom's side exchanges his leaf rice plate with the rice plate of a person of the bride's side. Similarly the bride's side also does this once. In this manner, rice is exchanged between the people of the groom's side and bride's side, particularly those who sit alongside or opposite.

After the meal is over, another important work called "bai - nodna" remains to be done. The meaning of "bai - nodna" is "rinsing the mouth". A woman from the bride's side brings water, and some water mixed with turmeric and takes on the responsibility of washing the hands and mouth of groom's side. As they wash their hands and mouth, the woman applies the turmeric water on a corner of the "dhoti" of each guest. That very night or early next morning, the groom's party departs for its own village.

A similar ritual is conducted by the groom's side at the time of kharihani or when the harvested crop is brought to the barn and separating the grain from the chaff has been done. Five or seven invited members of the bride's side reach the house of the groom, and the women of the house welcome them by washing their feet. Thereafter, with due respect they are seated within the house on the outer verandah and welcomed with hadiya or rice wine. When the warmth of the hadiya takes away their tiredness, then the bride's party becomes enthusiastic, and thereafter the groom is asked to appear. The groom comes with his two friends and salutes by bending before all the members of the bride's party. During this time the members of the bride's party critically observe the groom-to-be. After being satisfied, as a token of their approval, all of them give him some gift or the other. The groom-to-be is made to sit on the lap of bride's father or some senior member of the bride's party. This is done to facilitate observation at close quarters. The satisfied father-in-law lets the groom go after giving him a good gift. After the feast, the bride's party often returns the same day to its village. At the time of their return, some straw is collected and burned at the entrance of the house of the groom as if any supposedly ill effects of bad signs or black magic have been destroyed outside the door.

Lagan Bandhi

After proper observation of the bride and groom from both sides, the next step in the whole process is to fix the date of marriage which is called "lagan bandhi". After a week or two subsequent to the return of the bride's party from the groom's house, two-three Oraons from the groom's side visit the bride's house to fix the marriage date, and fix it accordingly. Thursdays and Saturdays are not considered good for carrying out auspicious work. The birth day of the bride or groom is also not fixed for marriage. Although there is no specific procedure amongst the Oraons to record birthdays, yet the naming of the child as per birthday makes nearly every family aware of the birthday of the groom and bride. The third, fifth, seventh, ninth, eleventh and thirteenth day of the bright side of the moon is considered to be auspicious. Consequent to the finalisation of the marriage date, the guests are welcomed with rice and hadiya.

Koha–pahi

"Koha - pahi" is celebrated once in the groom's house and once in the bride's house. A few days prior to the marriage date, the "agua" along with one or two elders of the village of the bride visit the groom's house. As per traditional custom, their feet are washed and they are served rice beer (hadiya), and food is prepared for them. After a few days, a pig or goat is slaughtered and both sides together flay and cut it into pieces.

By the time it is afternoon, 18-20 Oraons from the bride's side along with the barber-cum-musician and his musical instruments, kettle drums and long trumpets reach the groom's house. These guests are also welcomed by rubbing oil on their feet and washing them on brass salver. When everything has been taken care of, then any male or female Oraon (except widower/widow) of the groom's side takes a mat in his hands, goes outside and shakes it up and down rigorously thrice in the air. There after he returns with the mat. Another person brings a pitcher of hadiya prepared specially for this occasion called "khetaun - bode" and mellows it by mixing water in it. This hadiya is then poured into new earthen pitchers, one of which is given to the "panch" of the girl's village and one is given to the "panch" of the boy's village.

The panch of the groom's side, along with some colleagues, takes the hadiya to the "akhra" while the people of the girl's side, along with the panch, go to a neaby open space. Here they freely partake of the wine but before this, the village pahan takes a cup of sal leaf, fills it with hadiya and thrice offers it to the earth. The first offering is in the name of the "khunt" or clan ancestors of the opposite side i.e. the groom's side offers to the clan ancestors. The second offering is in the name of the ancestors of the bride and vice versa. The third offering is in the name of their own village deities. In this way, partaking of the holy offering i.e. khetauna- bodey, both parties return to the house of the boy and take their seats.

At this time the groom enters along with two companions, one ahead of him and the other behind him. The groom has a sword or a flat iron rod in his hand. Thereupon three Oraons from the bride's side get up, pick up the boys in their arms and sit down with the boys sitting atop their knees. The people from the bride's side getup one by one, present the groom with gifts and thereafter return to their seats. When the gifts are being given, then all three boys touch the feet of the guests and thereafter touch their own heads. This ritual is called "gore lagi" meaning touching the feet ritual. So long as this ritual goes on, somebody from the bride's side burns a wet cloth on a sickle like a torch. Although it is still daylight, this lighting of the torch is done to facilitate complete observation of the groom by the bride's side.

Poomp-Mejhna

The ancient ritual of gifting flowers to guests is undergone prior to the wedding. Three youths from the groom's side appear with flower baskets to welcome the guests. At first they give a flower each to every present member of the bride's side and undergo the "gore-lagi" ritual by touching their feet and thereafter touching their own heads. If a person has long hair, then the flower is stuck in the hair or placed behind the ear. After offering flowers to the people of the bride's party, the same ritual is undergone for people of the groom's side and the "gore lagi" ritual is undergone. In this way, one can see "Poomp-mejhna" in the way flowers are offered in modern civilised society with respect and affection.[55] On this occasion, the panches fix the "bride price." After some initial disagreements, the panches fix an amount as bride price. After that, the bride's side lays claim to clothes. On this point, the decision of the panches does not matter. Whatever the bride's side demands that is accepted as correct. At least, clothes for the bride's mother, the bride's paternal grandmother (if she is alive) and the bride's younger brother are considered essential.

Milanee

After this, the panches of both sides along with some village elders sit in opposite rows on a mat which has been spread in an east-west direction. In front of them a pitcher of hadiya and some utensils are kept. Among these utensils are two brass jugs which symbolise the groom and the bride. Both jugs are filled with rice hadiya prepared specially for this occasion. In some villages these jugs are filled with water only. The jug symbolising the bride is kept on a comparatively higher level than that of the groom's. The jug is kept in such a manner that whenever hadiya is poured in the bride's jug, the groom's jug gets automatically filled with the same. As per capability a silver coin is put in the jug. Both jugs are placed in such a manner that they touch each other.

Both sides joke with each other. Although the panches have already fixed the bride price, the people from the bride's side send more "baris" (a bari is a lump of pounded pulse) to the people of the groom's side compared to the number of "baris" which had been placed at the time of fixing of bride price. But the groom's party returns that much of "baris" due to which the already fixed bride price is re-fixed. Thereupon everybody becomes happy and each takes the other in his arms and starts singing and dancing. The offered hadiya is drunk. Again, hadiya is brought from the groom's house and offered to the people of the bride's side. They sit in a different place and eat fried goat's leg and drink hadiya. This goes on till the night feast is served.

Koha-pahi

Similar to the groom's, the ritual of Koha-pahi is completed in the bride's home. On the second or third morning, at least two persons called "jurab khitu," reach the bride's place from the groom's house. Nearly all the rituals are conducted similarly as were done in the groom's house. The difference is that the bride along with two companions comes specially dressed for the occasion. One companion has a water pot on her head and the other has a pot of hadiya. After the bride completes the "gore lagi" ritual, the bride price fixed by the panches and the clothes are handed over by the groom's party to the bride's father or guardian. After receiving the bride price, preparations for the wedding start.

Preparations for the Wedding

The day the ritual of "koha pahi" is completed in the bride's home, that very night, rice balls or "laddus" are prepared for distribution in the bride's and groom's house. Additionally, the following ingredients are assembled for the wedding preparations:

One new winnowing fan, a new big basket, new small basket, new earthenware water pot, an earthenware lamp which can accommodate four wicks on four sides, "doob" grass (a kind of fine grass), vermillion, rice dried in the sun, "arwa" rice dried in the sun, salt, mustard, turmeric stick, a bundle of paddy, straw, horse-bean pulse, mustard oil (which has been pressed from mustard seeds by a woman whose husband is alive, and who has kept a fast the whole day) two pitchers of hadiya (one of rice, the other of mahua).

All the aforementioned ingredients are kept beyond the touch of widows. Full precaution is taken when making the paddy bundle. A young man, after having undergone his morning ablutions, with full concentration selects the paddy stalks before they are divided and assembles them. In the meantime, he cannot indulge in any work or act considered unholy; no saliva should come out of his mouth and he should not spit.

On the day of the wedding, right in the morning, the courtyard, the outer portion of the house or the verandah, and the other open spaces are cleaned and cow dung is smeared on them. All the ingredients of the wedding are thereafter kept in the inner courtyard. Arwa rice, turmeric, "doob" grass, mustard seeds are put in the water pot. The paddy straws are selected and placed in such a manner in the water pot that the ears of paddy are on top and the leaves are spread in such a manner that they completely cover the mouth of the pot like a proper cover. A big lamp is kept on it; two wicks come out on two corners. Mustard oil and horse bean pulse are put in the lamp which is then lighted. In the small basket, a sari for the bride's mother, small amount of rice, vermillion and oil are placed for the "isungsindri" ritual, and the basket is covered with sal leaves and bound by a rope fashioned out of paddy stalks. The basket and the pot are kept side by side in the courtyard.

The pahan comes. He applies three marks of wet arwa rice and vermillion on the pot and basket. He brings a little bit of rice wine in a sal leaf cup, and sprinkling it on the pot and basket calls upon the village deity. He prays, "You are the presiding deity of all the spirits of the village, hence please ensure that the entire marriage ceremony is conducted without any obstacle and the newly wedded couple lives happily." The same routine is completed in the houses of both bride and groom.

If the groom belongs to a prosperous family, then, if he does not come on a pony, he comes walking with other members of the groom's party to the village of the bride. He is given some iron implement to hold, like, for example, a sword, an iron rod or stick etc. This is given for protecting against obstacles and difficulties on the way. If on the way, the groom comes across a mango tree, then he halts for some time in its shade. He goes round it thrice with raw thread and marks it thrice with wet arwa rice and vermillion. Since the groom's party consists of both men and women, some experienced married woman (whose husband is alive) guides and helps the groom in such rituals). The groom's party brings along with it eatables and hadiya because until the marriage is completed, they cannot accept any food that day from the bride's home. The groom and the bride keep a fast till the ceremony of marriage is completed.

As soon as the groom's party reaches the limits of the village, all the men, women, and the youth of the girl's party, go there to welcome them. The youth take along with them sticks, rods, maces and such common weapons as if the people who have come from outside want to loot them so it is their duty to oppose them. Nowadays it is just a formality and is a mime of war although various legends abound and are repeated in the villages when two such sides had actually fought, people had been injured and they had to be carried back.

On this occasion, abuses are hurled by both sides at each other, and songs with filthy abuses are sung. This indicates kinship. In the meantime a married woman (not a widow) comes forward from the bride's side with a small water pot on her head which (the pot) is covered with mango leaves. She takes out water from the pot with the mango leaves, sprinkles it first on the groom and there after sprinkles it on the other people. This is a benedictory welcome.

After this, two or three men from the bride's side lift the groom on their shoulders and take him from the village limits to the bride's home without the groom having to touch the ground. One or two persons of the groom's side follow him till the bride's home, but the rest of the groom's party move towards the pre-appointed rest houses and busy themselves in arranging food.

Gurkhi-nikharna

This is an important ritual which is observed by nearly every Oraon within the country or outside, that is, everywhere. After reaching the home of the bride, the feet of the groom and bride are washed. They are made to stand atop a yoke which is placed on five bundles of paddy straw which in turn are placed on top of a pot. The bride stands in front of the groom in such a manner that the groom grips the right ankle of the bride in a pincer like manner with the big toe and the next toe of his left foot. This ritual is conducted behind a curtain. Inside, one or two women remain present to help them. Outside the curtain, some youths brandish swords in an effort to ward off evil effects of black magic and evil eye. Outside the "gorait" plays on his flute and beats the kettle-drum while inside the house women sing wedding songs.

After some time, the curtain is removed and the bride and the groom are taken to a different place for having their bath. Here they are bathed by pouring water from head to toe-this water has been collected in two pitchers by village maidens from the nearest water source, be it a river, or stream or any other source. The boy is bathed by a woman of the bride's side who vigorously rubs his head and body. The same is done by the woman of the groom's party while bathing the bride. After the bath is over, the groom marks the head of the bride with vermillion mixed with oil. In the process women pick up the grinding stone, the stone pestle, a water pot, and a bundle of paddy straws etc. and putting them on their heads start singing and dancing. As long as this singing and dancing goes on, the wet groom and bride are made to put on new clothes. Thereafter the groom departs for some time and joins his party at the "janwasa" (the place where they have been put up).

Isung Sindri[56]

Isung sindri meaning applying vermillion is the basic act of marriage. After some time when the groom returns to the bride's house from the "janwasa," then as soon as he comes, a mat is tossed with a jerk up and down in the air three times and placed on the floor in a south-north direction. Then the bride and the groom sit on the mat facing the east. The bride sits on the left of the groom. The women of the bride's house come forward with a "kiya kindri" (a small vermillion container made of wood). The women of the groom's party are ready from before with their "kiya kindri." Both sides exchange their "kiya kindri." In the meantime the elder sister of the bride (or the wife of her brother) combs the hair of the bride and groom.

She parts the hair of the bride and after combing ties a bun on her head. The groom takes vermillion soaked in oil and fills the parting and head of the bride. The bride applies vermillion on the head and ear lobes of the groom. In some places, as per custom, completion of the application of vermillion is done by the bride's elder sister or "bhabhi" (brother's wife). During the application of vermillion, flutes are played and marriage songs are sung with gusto. After the ritual of "isung sindri, "the girl becomes a daughter-in-law and immediately she has to bring about a change in her behaviour that from henceforth she does not belong to the land of her parents- she now belongs to the land of her father-in-law. Many Oraon folk tales speak of the importance of applying vermillion.

After "isung sindri" the ritual of "isum sindri" takes place in which the women of the groom's party offer one pitcher of rice wine in sal leaf cups to the women of the bride's party, and similarly the women of the bride's party offer hadiya made of rice to the women of the groom's side. Before they partake of the rice wine, those women of the bride's side who had bathed the groom with turmeric water and assisted in the applying of vermillion offer three sal leaf cups of hadiya to the groom to drink. When he partakes of the hadiya then the women start sipping the hadiya from their sal leaf cups. In some villages, the pahan comes on this occasion. Before the act of drinking hadiya begins, he takes three sal leaf cups of hadiya and pours it on the ground while offering it to the village deity. Thereafter the clan ancestors of the bride are offered hadiya.

When everybody starts drinking hadiya then the bride and groom after greeting everybody present leave the place. The bride goes back to her room in the house and the groom returns to the "janwasa" to his party.

Khiri Tengna

In this marriage ritual the groom and bride are offered rice wine five times in sal leaf cups. The cups are touched to their lips and thereafter accompanied with ululation they are thrown on the tiled roof of the house or shack. This ritual has a joking twist to it, hence the elder sister of the bride or her brother's wife are the main users of this rice wine. But the rice wine touched to the lips is not drunk. This is a kind of spell due to which if there is any illness or obstacle, then the same will be absorbed by the hadiya and being thrown on the tiled roof will banish it from the house. Similarly hadiya cups are touched to the lips of the bride five times and thrown on the tiled roof.

Thereafter, the groom and bride are addressed and given some advice regarding their future life. This advice is often given by an elderly man to the new couple. A capable woman may also give the advice. The main points of advice are as follows[57]:

(a) Your man goes for hunting. He gets injured by an arrow and he becomes lame. O mother, do not call him a cripple. Do you hear me?

(b) O mother, if he defecates on the stove or urinates on the mortar in which paddy is dehusked by pounding, then do not say that he has dirtied the stove or urinated on the mortar. O mother, are you listening to my words or not ?

(c) If he goes to cut the body of a dead animal and brings its flesh, will you cook it ? Both of you eat fifty-fifty of the meat. O gentleman, if she partakes of more meat than you, then do not say that "you have eaten more." Are you listening or not ?

(d) And if she goes to pluck "bhootang" from the "pakar" tree (the citron leaved Indian fig tree) and in the process she falls down and breaks her leg, breaks her hand, then O gentleman do not tell her that she is lame in the leg or maimed in the hand. Are you listening to me or not, gentleman ?

(e) Do your work well, drink well. Gentleman listen and you too, O mother, listen. From today work together and eat together.

Now both of you make obeisance to everybody and go inside.[57]

Sabha Sindri

After "khiri tengna" the bride and the groom are taken to complete the ritual of "Sabha sindri." On a mat the bride is made to sit on the left of the groom, facing the east. The women of the bride's side and groom's side mark the bride and groom with vermillion soaked in oil. The newly wedded couple makes a round of all the elderly people, pays obeisance to them and obtains their blessings. The bride thereafter returns to her house and the groom goes back to his companions.

Mandi ona

The groom is again brought from the janwasa and along with the bride is offered a meal of rice and curry made of lumps of horse bean pulse. After they finish their meal, the people of both sides of the marriage take their meal. After the feast, the groom's party takes leave and the bride goes with them. She is given an arrow or an iron implement to ward off evil eye, black magic or other obstacles. Her family members accompany her till the limits of her father's village.

Welcoming of the Bride in the Groom's House

As soon as they reach the home of the groom, a woman from the groom's house washes the bride's feet on a brass salver. Thereafter two baskets are brought. The boy and the girl have to step on these baskets to enter the house. The girl is in the front and the boy at the back. The boy clamps the ankle of the girl with his big toe and the next toe, and every step is taken together one by one on the baskets. Both move their feet simultaneously, and go forward accordingly. When they reach the door, the younger sister of the groom does not allow them to enter unless and until she is given some compensation. When the bride enters her room, then the whole procedure of "danda-katta" is undergone- it is only after that the bride can go out anywhere. She is made to bathe with the water brought from nearby river, stream or pond, and a woman of the household or the wife of the "gorait" combs her hair and applies vermillion in the parting of her hair.

The newly arrived bride has to see the water source of the village- this is considered essential. Hence, the next morning the couple visits the stream or river of the village, and the wife after bathing marks the stone of the water source with oil and vermillion. The vermillion she has brought is immersed in the water there. When they return, they take back with them two pots of water. The husband carries these pots on a bamboo rod slung on his shoulder. When they reach home the water pots are taken over by the brother of the husband.

He tries to pour the water on the husband and the bride, but the bride escapes it and enters the house. This act between the elder brother of the husband and the bride symbolises the prohibition of any kind of touch between the two. In this manner the bride settles down in the house of her in-laws.

Death Ceremony

According to the religious philosophy of the Oraons the human body has two different powers within it- life and soul. Life is concerned with the materialistic body and the soul is the basic and free element. The soul can leave one body and roam around wherever it wants to and thereafter return to the body. This often happens when the human being is sleeping or is in a condition of losing consciousness due to excessive illness. The body and life of a sleeping individual do remain but the soul may not be there. Whatever a person sees in a dream, he experiences and sees through the roaming soul. As soon as the individual wakes up, the soul immediately enters the body. The Oraons believe that a soul-less body may remain alive but only for a few days in a state of illness and loss of consciousness. For example, if a dreaming individual is suddenly woken up and his roaming soul is unable to enter his body, then as a result after waking up the person becomes mad and ill and after a few days, his body and life are also destroyed, that is, he dies.

The Oraon religion believes that in death, a person's material/ physical body, and his life (which is the energy of that body) are destroyed but his "ache" or soul is immortal and indestructible. The Oraon religion describes the soul as a bodyless person meaning thereby that the soul or "ache" feels hunger, thirst, happiness, anger, affection-hatred just like a person with body feels. The soul can make out who is his own and who is an outsider. Since the soul moves about in the invisible world in which god and goddess, regional "naad," ghost, spirit roam around, it can see the troubles about to befall the members of its family and it tries to protect them also.

The Oraon religion believes that after a person dies, his soul goes and meets the ancestors living in the nether world. In this manner, the way the tradition of lineage/ posterity, clan or "gotra" is carried on amongst living Oraons, the same way after death the soul or "ache" settles down among the souls of his clan in the nether world. Lineage and family are also considered amongst the souls. The most important ritual of death ceremony is the proper placement of the dead person's soul amongst the family souls in the family of the ancestors, and to pray to the ancestors that "this soul which is going to you is the son or grandson of so-and-so of your lineage, hence accept him."

"Arwa" rice is prohibited for use in death ceremony-parboiled rice is used. After death, before taking the body to the cremation ground, it is bathed, and parboiled rice and coins are placed in its mouth. This work is often carried out by women of the household. They say, "Take, eat. Why have you left us now. You have seen your way now. Go and take with you all our illnesses and sins."[58]

Oraon convention gives highest importance to death ceremony. Through this ceremony, the soul of the dead person is made to be included in the family of the ancestors living in the nether world in a similar fashion that a newly wed leaves her father's home and joins her husband's new home forever. The group of ancestors in the nether world is such a family in which the soul, departing from the mortal world, is assimilated/ included as a member. The religious ritual pertaining to this inclusion is completed when the bones of the dead person are buried beneath the ancestral stone slab standing upright in some river or water hole. As per religious philosophy of the Oraons, this forms the entrance path for the soul to reach the ancestors in the nether world. In this way, "har-bori" or immersion/ burial of the bones are a religious activity which is called "koha-benja" in Oraon convention. The meaning of "Koha-benja" is "great marriage" in which immersion/burial of the bones or "har bori" is the central act.

Before "koha benja", in order to prepare for this ritual, the death ceremony has to go through several phases which come in between death and the travel of the soul for "koha benja." In this process, as per Oraon convention, an extraordinary but special phase comes within the death ceremony which is seldom to be found in any race or tribe of the world. In this phase, the body is buried for some time, and after the time period is over, it is exhumed and cremated. Burial and cremation rituals are carried out with the same body, which is approved by Oraon religion. This procedure is adopted for those dead persons whose death takes place between the festival of Sarhul and "koha-benja."

The aforementioned extraordinary phase of death ceremony although difficult yet it is rational. The religion, customs and conventions are influenced also by the natural environment in which the race has been living for centuries. In the forests and plateau part of Chhotanagpur, the Oraons living there have to face heavy rainfall from about the month of April to October-November. At times it rains cats and dogs continuously for a week without any break. In those circumstances, it became impossible to take the dead body to the cremation ground and to cremate and then to conduct the rituals for the death ceremony. Hence, the custom developed that till the rainy season was on, the body would be buried in the earth- this was for protection of the body. Since the rainy season marks its presence from Sarhul festival (April month) to kharra puja (October-November) hence this extraordinary ritual crept in the death ceremony of Oraons that in the period between Sarhul and kharra puja, the dead body of a person will not be taken straightaway for cremation in the cremation ground- it will be buried in the ground, and a few-days prior to kharra puja it will be taken out and cremated on a pyre. Those who do not die within the aforementioned period, they are straightway taken to the cremation ground and burned on a pyre.

The ritual of koha benja is conducted in a community manner for the whole village and "gotra." For this ritual, the pahan and mahto fix an appropriate date. This date is often the sixth day of Kartik purnima (purnima is full moon). In some villages koha benja is fixed on the sixth day of Aghan purnima. As per the "har-bori" activity of "Koha benja," the bones of the dead are immersed in the water source where the ancestral stone slab stands. Hence, all those families keep the bones of the dead in a pot as per procedure for the annual ceremony of koha benja- these are the dead who had been straightaway cremated on the funeral pyre of the cremation ground. Those bodies which had been buried, later taken out and burned in the cremation ground, their bones are collected in a pot, and on the day of koha benja, these bones are immersed in the water. In this manner, on the day of koha benja, the pots containing the bones of all those who had died in the past one year, within or outside the country, are collected and ceremonially, group-wise, immersed in the water as per gotra in the water hole of the gotra.

Ache Makha or Chhai Bhitarna

The ritual of "ache makha" or "chhai-bhitarna" is as per religious philosophy of the Oraons, an extremely important part of death ceremony. In Oraon religious philosophy, the "ache" or soul has been described as a body-less person, meaning thereby that even after the destruction of the body, the person does not die- he exists in the context of his connections. This connection is related to above the earth and below the earth in the nether world of the ancestors settled there. On a single day in a year, which is often the sixth day of Kartik purnima or sixth day of Aghan purnima, the souls of all those who have died within that year are connected to the ancestors living in the nether world- this is through koha benja ritual. Now the question arises that after death and till the immersing of the bones in water during koha benja, what is the position of the soul ? Does it roam around freely or the family members establish the soul somewhere till koha benja ? If the soul is allowed to roam around freely, then there would be a possibility of a chaotic situation arising in the world. In this situation, it would be difficult to get hold of the soul for "koha benja" on fixed date. Hence after death, the first step taken is to settle the soul in a fixed place so that it need not roam around, and be available on koha benja day. Establishing the soul at home after death till the day of koha benja- this action is called "ache makha" or "chhai bhitarna" ritual. This ritual is completed on the day of death itself, that is (a) after burying the body if death has taken place in the period between Sarhul and "koha benja," or (b) after the body has been burned on the funeral pyre if death has taken place between "koha benja" and Sarhul.

The Ritual of Chai Bhitarna

This activity is carried out to examine whether the shadow of the dead person has returned home. In the room where the person had breathed his last, a small red cock is brought and left to peck on parboiled rice given from a winnowing fan. One person stays in the room which is kept closed from inside. Within the room, a lamp with oil and wick is placed atop a brass pot filled with water and having leaves on top. The lamp is lit.

In the mean while women of the household proceed towards the cremation "ghat" (place near a water source, like river, stream). They take along with them three firm twigs, some straw, a piece of burning coal, ploughshare and a sickle. After having covered half the distance to the cremation ground, they stop on the way. There they plant the twigs on the ground, spread the straw atop them making the structure look like a cottage and then set it on fire. Indicating this symbolic cottage on fire, they address thrice in a raised voice thus, "O so and so (the name of the dead person)," "your cottage is burning."

The intention behind burning the "cottage" and calling out the name of the deceased is to call the "ache" or soul of the dead person near the "cottage." With this ritual, it is accepted that the soul has come near the "cottage." Then clanging the ploughshare with the sickle, they return home. They maintain silence on the way back, reach home and find the door closed. There is quietude everywhere. Standing in front of the door they say. "Open the door." The person sitting within the house asks, "Who are you, kinsmen or unknown ?" The reply comes, "Kinsmen". The person from within asks, "have you brought sorrow or happiness?" The women reply, "Happiness."

Upon coming to know that the women have driven away sorrow and brought happiness, the person inside opens the door. At that time everybody's gaze is fixed on the flame of the lighted lamp. If the flame is found to be steady, then it is believed that the soul of the deceased has not entered the house. If the flame starts flickering then it becomes clear that the soul of the deceased has entered the house. But to be doubly sure, ash is strewn on the floor because the shadow or soul of the dead person may enter taking the form of a small animal or snake. If this happens, then the strewn ash will reflect its footprint or any imprint. This is observed/ looked at with great care. In this way, the soul of the deceased is not left in a chaotic state to roam around- through the ritual of "chhaya bhitarna" the soul is brought back home and established till the time of "koha-benja".

Formal Burial

In the rituals pertaining to the death ceremony of Oraons, a particular period occurs within which if there is a death then the body is not consigned to the flames but is buried in the ground to await the time period to be over so that thereafter it can be taken out and duly cremated on the funeral pyre in the cremation ground. This period falls within April-May to October-November. Heavy rains start from May and the paddy seedlings become ready for transplantation. Hence from the coming out of the paddy seedlings till the harvesting of the crop that is till the month of October-November the people dying within this time period are temporarily buried in the ground. After harvesting is over, the dead are taken out of the ground and burned in the cremation "ghat." This activity is completed within the annual ritual of "koha benja".

According to the custom of burial, a north-south pit is dug five-six feet deep. Three long branches of the "Karanj" tree are cut, bent like tongs, and placed firmly on the surface below-they must touch the eastern and western walls of the pit. Similarly, keeping the dead body on the right hand side of the pit, the body is taken around the pit thrice and thereafter kept in the pit. In the mouth of the body, and in some places, in a piece of cloth to be tied and kept beneath the head, as per capability, copper, brass or silver coins are kept. A close relative is the first to put a handful of mud in the pit and thereafter gradually the pit is filled up with mud. An earthenware pot full of water and having three small holes below is kept near the head above the pit level so that slowly the water may come out and spread over the pit. Three "datuns" (twigs for brushing teeth) and called "masna-dantan" are also placed there.

After this ritual, everybody goes and has a bath in some river or pond. When they return to the house of the dead person, then the inner courtyard is cleaned by smearing cow dung. In one corner of it husk is kept. A burning piece of wood is kept in front of every individual. The husk is brought from the corner and put on the wood. Oil is also poured. With the burning of the husk and oil, smoke arises which touches everyone and purifies him. Nearby every religion has acknowledged the purification value of the smoke arising out of sacrificial fuel. After being purified by the smoke, the person scatters the burning wood with his feet. In this way, after being purified by smoke, every person takes some turmeric water kept there and sprinkles on himself to further purify himself. After having purified themselves from the impurity of dead body ceremony, all of them leave for their respective homes.

The Rule and Method of Death Ceremony

After the special ceremony regarding burial of the dead body in the ground if death takes place within the period of Sarhul and kharrapuja, the cremation of the body and all activities related to death ceremony are completed within five days. These activities cover removal of the dead body from home, burning, "harbori" and "paddakamna." On the first day of the activities, taking out the dead body from the pit and consigning it to the flames are included. Since as per tradition, koha benja is observed as a community function on the sixth day of Kartik purnima or in some villages on the sixth day of Aghan Purnima, hence four days prior to this, the other rituals pertaining to death ceremony are taken up for completion. In this way, in Oraon death ceremony (Shraddh-karm) till purification, it takes total five days.

The First Day

The process of death ceremony entails first of all that the dead body is dug up and consigned to the flames on the funeral pyre. Men have to come forward in the village to do this work. They cut wood from mango trees and prepare funeral pyre in the "masna" or cremation ground. Wood may be obtained from any tree in the village for which there is no prohibition. After preparing the funeral pyre, the men start digging the grave with spades and when the dead body is sighted, they stop, and send information to the household of the dead person. As soon as information is received, all the family members and guests come in groups to the "masna" place, lamenting all the while. When they reach, the dead body, which had been kept on a mat or logs of wood, is lifted along with the mat or logs of wood and placed alongside the grave. The sorrowful family members offer teeth cleaning twigs to the dead body, lamenting all the while. They also bathe the body after which it is marked thrice with turmeric and vermillion. Thereafter some rice, coins and shells (small) are put in its mouth.

After digging out the body and bathing it, the body is placed atop the funeral pyre. Water is again offered to the body on the pyre and three marks of turmeric and vermillion are put on it, and thereafter it is covered with a shroud. In the meantime women scatter grains of parboiled rice on the whole cremation ground. The head of the dead body is kept in the south direction and the feet are towards the north direction. The son or close relative of the dead person touches the flame to his mouth.

There is no rule to bury those who die in the period between kharra puja and Sarhul- they are straightaway taken to the cremation ground and consigned to the flames on the pyre. As soon as a person dies in the house, women start wailing loudly. The other women of the village upon hearing the wails, reach that household with a winnowing fan or small basket (nachua) of paddy. By that time the dead body is taken out of the room and placed in the inner courtyard. An empty basket is kept near the dead body in which the paddy brought by the women of the village is poured.

The dead body is taken out of the main door of the house. Ash is sprinkled in the room in which death had taken place and the door is kept closed till the people return after having gone through all the rituals in the "masna" place. The dead body is bathed in cold water. If the body is of a married woman (not a widow) then mark is applied on her head with vermillion mixed with oil and vermillion is put in the parting of her hair.

In the meantime, some men of the village prepare a wooden bier. The dead body is kept on this bier with the head in the southern direction and the feet in the northern direction[59] and the body is covered with a shroud of new cloth. Formerly, it had been the practice that irrespective of the dead person having been a man or woman, the bier used to be carried by women on their shoulders till the "masna" place[60] but gradually this custom was discontinued and now the bier is carried by men to the cremation ground where the dead body is placed on the funeral pyre prepared from before. The rest of the activities are the same as mentioned before, that is, before touching the fire to the lips of the body, all the close women relations pour oil on the head, place parboiled rice and coin in the mouth of the body, etc. even the "mota" kept near the pyre is burned.

When the pyre becomes completely engulfed in flames, then the women leave for the water front for taking bath. On the way, they pluck a special kind of grass called "foot-chiri" till they reach the waterfront. This water front is separate from the water body near the cremation ground. After taking their bath (sick women only wash their face, hands, feet etc) they sprinkle water on themselves with the help of "foot-chiri" grass to purify; they also sprinkle turmeric water or turmeric on themselves. After having purified themselves in this manner, the women depart for home.

Thereafter comes the turn of the men to have a bath. In the cremation ground (which is also called "masna"), two-three men stay behind to the take care of the burning pyre while the rest go to the water front to bathe. All activities are repeated as mentioned above. After having a bath, and thereafter sprinkling themselves with turmeric, they too depart for home.

At night, all the people assemble at the Sarna place. Prior to that, the pahan completes the formality of purifying the cremation ground by sprinkling turmeric and water. Hadiya is offered to the "pach-balar" (ancestral family) in the Sarna-place. The assembled people also partake of "hadiya." This goes on till late in the night. From that day, the whole village is acknowledged to be impure because mourning has begun. Henceforth no guest visiting the village can be offered meals cooked at home. The guest is given food prepared outside the home in pure utensils- this food is served on leaf plates. The mourning period ends with the rituals of purifying the village after the ceremony of "koha benja."

Second Day

On the second day of cremation, the activity of "naal oda tirikhna" ("done chiri khundna") is completed. Early in the morning, a group of naked men moves towards a water source in which there is minimum water and more of weeds and bushes. In such a condition, birds build their nests in these bushes. The pahan is also with the men. The young men catch a special kind of bird and hand it over to the pahan who ties it on the top of a bamboo umbrella and teases it. The young men wear their clothes and cover a fixed distance, all the while plucking paddy from a paddy sheaf and collecting it in a cloth. Thereafter they all reach the Sarna place where the "gotra" stone deity is worshipped and a water pot is established. The water pot is established in the same manner as when the water pot was established during the marriage ceremony. The paddy sheaf is placed on top of the water pot in such a way that the paddy is outside the pot and the stalks are inside the pot. A cover is placed on the mouth of the water pot, and on top of that cover, a three point lamp is placed. Three pots filled with mustard oil are kept at the place of the pahan and mahto. The earthenware pots are readied by the man who fills water in water pots. The programme goes on in the Sarna place till eight to nine in the night after which the people return home.

On this day there is another special programme. At night, the gorait makes a round of the village, beating his nagara (big kettle drum). By constantly beating the nagara, he re-establishes the souls of the dead at their fixed places if they have come out of them- the echo of the beats ensures that this is done. The gorait completes this job thrice, once at 9 p.m., then at midnight and finally at 2 a.m. The aim of thrice making a round of the village beating the nagara is to ensure that if the souls have been unable to reach their fixed places after the first round at 9 p.m. and second round at midnight, then in the third round at 2 a.m. they will surely go back to their established places. The gorait beats his drum continuously without any break. He starts from his house beating the drum, and beating it without stopping, he goes round the village till he re-enters his house.

Third Day

Early in the morning of the third day, some well-known people of the village along with the pahan assemble near the barn where kharra puja takes place. The place is cleaned by smearing it with cow dung. Some rice is scattered on it and a cock is tied. Everybody takes a bath and reaches the kharra place. A stone fireplace is built, it is purified with water, turmeric is sprinkled, and three marks are made with vermillion on the stone of the fireplace. The cock is sacrificed and its blood is offered to the stone fireplace.

The stone fireplace is purified duly, and thereafter fire is lit. Parboiled rice pounded in a "dheki" (an appliance for pounding paddy) along with the flesh of the cock are cooked together. In this concoction, only salt is added. This food along with hadiya are offered to the earth and proffered to the ancestral family (pach baaler). All the assembled people partake of hadiya and the proffered food, and return home via the Sarna place. After this the ritual of "utur khila" is started.

Utur Khila

A pit having a circumference of one foot and six-seven inch deep is dug in the courtyard or outer verandah of the dead person. Fried cotton seeds, horse bean, "totni", iron dust, parched rice, jitiya put in peepal leaf cups are placed at the edge of the pit. In one leaf cup, turmeric mixed with water is also kept. After these things are prepared, an elderly person of the village sits on the western edge of the pit, facing the east. He is given a red cock which he sacrifices by taking apart its head and beak with bare hands. The blood coming out and its beak are put in the pit. After this, the other assembled people take with their left hand the fried cotton seeds, horse bean etc. placed from before and pour them in the pit. Thereafter they touch the turmeric mixture and purify themselves. When they pour the grains in the pit, they pray to the ancestors living in the nether world that they may include the soul of the dead person of their clan within the ancestral family.

Along with this ritual, danda-katta or "bhelwa-phari" religious ritual is also observed so that any act of semi-divine omission/ commission and disasters may be prevented, and there may be protection against black magic or ghostly influence.

Hochole-poomp Pesa

The women of the household go to the cremation ground and collect the remnants of the dead person with their left hand. They wash them and smear them with turmeric. Thereafter they keep them in a small pot of clay. The relatives put some coins also in this earthenware pot. This small pot is kept on a straw-holder. A small lump made of "kush grass" and symbolising the dead person is prepared and kept with the remnants in the small pot. A woman smears cow dung where the funeral pyre had been to clean it, and another woman taking a branch of the sinduar tree brooms the place which has been cleaned with cow dung. Half-boiled rice is also put in the pot along with the remnants.

Harbodi or Immersing of Bones in Water

Harbodi or immersion of bones in water is the central activity of koha benja which is observed in order to establish the soul of the dead person amidst the souls of his ancestors. According to the religious arrangement of the Oraons, it is essential to reach the soul of the dead to the nether world, (where his dead ancestors live) through various religious rituals and, to whichever "khunt" or clan the dead belongs, pray that his ancestors may accept him, so that there may be peace in the village, hill, earth, all directions and at home. The series of prayer taken recourse to after death is often to be clearly seen in all the due observances, but "harbodi" is a community function of the prescribed ritual of the ceremony in the observance of which the soul is bid good-bye from this world and got settled down and accepted by the ancestral family of the clan in the nether world. On this day, the small pots containing the duly collected bones of the dead are taken by women on their left palms who go towards the "kundi" in a group accompanied by music. "Kundi" is the place of stones planted upright in any river, pond or flowing stream where the bones of the "bhuihars" (first settlers) and elder peasants are immersed in water. Normally, the "bhuihars" of a village have one "kundi." On the edge of this kundi big or small stones are planted upright. (These are rock stones or large and flat stones). These rock stones are called "pulkhi." The bones of all the dead persons of the village belonging to different "gotras" (clans) are immersed beneath the "pulkhi" marked for each particular clan, according to religious procedure. It is this door through which the soul of the dead makes its way to be assimilated with its ancestors in the nether world.

Sometimes Oraons leave their village and settle in some other village. Under such circumstances, on the day of "harbodi", they have to go to their original village along with the bones of the dead and immerse the bones beneath the traditional "pulkhi" stone of their "gotra." If there is an increase in the number of inhabitants of the same "khunt" in the village and they set up their own proprietorship of land parallel to the original settlers of the village, then gradually they have their own separate kundi slightly at a distance from the original one. In this manner, every settlement of the village or the original settlers have one kundi and at the edge of the kundi there are rock stone pulkhis which are fixed gotra-wise. On the day of harbodi, right from the village to the kundi amidst playing of music it becomes a scene of marriage ceremony.

The village women move in a group towards the kundi, taking the small pots containing the bones on their left palms, while the gorait or village musician leads in front playing music and the men follow the women. When they reach the kundi[61] then the women stand near the pulkhi as per gotra. Thereafter the men of their family snatch the pot and quickly turn it upside down for the bones to fall out and smash the pot against the pulkhi stone. Then the women wash the pulkhi stone of their gotra and put "khichri" (a dish prepared by boiling rice and pulses together) on it as an offering. The pahan sprinkles turmeric water in all directions to purify the place. After this the men move upward from the kundi and go and bathe in a naad-pond or "ghat" (bathing place on the bank of a river). The women also go and bathe in a naad pond or ghat made for women. When everybody leaves the "kundi," then the village storekeeper rubs some tobacco and lime on his palm, places it on the ground, and calls out, "ancestors, we dedicate this tobacco and lime to you, please accept it; we are now departing. All obsequies have been done, we are going." After bathing in the naad-pond or ghat, the men and women move towards home, plucking one or two "phootchiri" grass on the way. When they reach home, turmeric water is sprinkled on them with the help of the "phootchiri" grass, and turmeric water is poured on their palms. Thereafter oil is offered to them. They rub this oil on their head and sprinkle and rub it on their body- this is a purification process. Again, everybody assembles in the "akhra" near the "dhumkuria." A burning wood piece is placed before every person. Husk is taken from a corner and placed on the burning wood. Oil is also poured on it. The smoke arising due to the burning of the husk and oil touches and thereby purifies every assembled person. After having been purified by smoke, the person kicks the burning wood and scatters it.

Thereafter, the water pot akin to the water pot used for adornment during marriage, and prepared one day earlier, is brought to the "akhra" and its lamp is lighted. The wooden elephant and horse kept in the "dhumkuriya" are rubbed with oil. Three marks of vermillion are put on them and after following all observances, a coloured cock is sacrificed. After this the elephant/ horse are placed in the "akhra." The village pahan, pujar, mahto or a respectable person sits on the elephant/ horse, and with blaring music and singing the whole village moves towards the "jatra tanr" (upland). When they reach the "jatra tanr" this journey turns into a festive function. The people circumambulate the "jatra tanr" speedily (three times) with the elephant/ horse and water pot, and thereafter in the end put the elephant/horse and water pot on a pre-determined spot. Some people guard them while the rest participate/ take interest in the entertainment programme and singing and dancing. This programme goes on till late in the night, and this is how the activities of the third day end.

Fourth Day

According to Oraon religion, the programme of "naig bainja" is extremely important among all the activities related to death ceremony. This is organised on the fourth day. The word "naig" pertains to pahan or pujar, and "bainja" means marriage arrangement of pahan-pahnain or pujar-pujarin. This function starts in the home of the pahan where the villagers assemble. In this place all the rituals related to marriage are observed and the pahan-pahnain and pujar-pujarin are duly got married. After completing the marriage programme in the house of the pahan, the people assemble at the "akhra." The young men and women who have received three years training in the "dhumkuria" and are betrothed for marriage, come to the "akhra." The young men bring pumpkin with them and the young women bring nine "paillas" ("pailla is the earthen cover of a pot and serves as a measure") of dry fried rice or puffed rice. The pumpkin is kept in a special place, and the youth who has brought it is expected to break it with one blow of his fist. If he is unsuccessful then he has to pay a fine, the amount of which is used for a feast or other activities.

The pahan and pujar cook the pumpkin. The young men and women who have taken part in the ritual, along with members of their families partake of this community meal. In the meantime, the three water pots set up a day earlier in the homes of the pahan and mahto are brought to the "akhra." Dancing and singing goes on till late in the night and in the end the water pots are again taken back to the houses of the pahan and mahto where they are once more set up. And with this, the activities and rituals of the fourth day are taken to be completed.

The programme of the fourth day of the death ceremony is entirely related to marriage. Not only the marriage of the pahan-pahnain and pujar-pujarin are solemnised in "naig bainja," but also those betrothed couples who would be married in the future are included in the feast of the fourth day; this is thought to be essential and auspicious. In this activity, the mystical idea of "union" is included. There are two extreme ends of death. According to Oraon religious philosophy, one end is eternal separation and the other end is eternal union. Marriage is the symbol of union. In most of the religious philosophies of the world, the idea of union of Nature (female element) and procreator (male element) can be found at the root. The mystics accept this union to be the merger of the soul with the Supreme Spirit and all the rituals related to death to be marriage, meaning "the departure of the bride to the husband's home." The "husband's home" is the master's home where the soul or, after being repeatedly marked by vermillion mixed in oil, the soul is bade farewell from this physical world.

The ritual of "koha benja" which is the main activity of the third day, is the point of union which can be called eternal meeting. This means that after being marked by vermillion, the mystical philosophy of the union of the bride with her most beloved husband is innate in this thought. Hence, from a normal viewpoint, the philosophy of koha benja is understood by scholars who are not aware of religious philosophy of the Oraons. The justification of the fourth day's activity called "naig-benja" may be viewed from this angle. According to Oraon religion, although the marriage rituals conducted in the home of the bride are considered main, but after the bride is bade farewell, the marriage rituals are repeated in the home of the bride-groom. The ceremony of marriage is considered to be complete after the carrying out of the marriage programme in the home of the bride-groom. In this way, koha benja is concluded with naig benja, and the "ache" (soul) merges eternally with the "pachbaler" (family of ancestors). It is to be noted that this union is permanent, and this is the reason that in Oraon religion there is no concept of re-birth.

The religious importance of naig benja of the fourth day is connected to future marital relationships. The period between Karam festival and naig benja is prohibited for marriages. So long as koha benja, meaning the great marriage, does not take place, as per religion, there can be no marriage of girls and boys in the village. It is after naig benja that marriages can be solemnised in the village. Naig benja is the last activity of death ceremony yet even then the village is considered to be in mourning. The fifth day's activity of "padda kamna" is carried out to end the period of mourning in the village. Since mourning takes place due to death, hence the activity of the fifth day called "padda kamna" comes within the death ceremony.

Fifth Day

On the fifth day, i.e. the last day, all the villagers gather at the akhra.

A water pot from all the homes in which death had taken place that year, is sent to the place of the small pots. In addition, water is filled in empty pumpkin/ gourd shells or in two new water pots which do not have any black spots or deformity. The pahan puts a copper coin in one and a silver coin in the other. In this way, the water becomes purified. Thereafter, under the leadership of the pahan, all the people move out of the akhra in a procession and enter the village from one end, and sprinkle all the small and big places and houses on the way with water from the gourd shells or water pots to purify them. In the process, on his way, he addresses the "pachbaler" thus:-

"I purify the kundi of so and so gotra, may the village remain happy and prosperous."

In the final phase of circumambulation of the village, a white cock is offered as sacrifice to Dharmes and it is prayed thus, "O Sun God ! now we are purifying the village. Henceforth our work may be done satisfactorily. If we go anywhere, let no thorns prick us."

Thereafter, the flesh of the sacrificed cock and the rice brought from the houses of the dead are cooked together. This dish is called "soori." When cooking "soori," only salt is added-no spices or oil/ clarified butter are added. All the people present in the "akhra" partake of "soori" and are purified. Despite being cooked without any spices, "soori" has an extraordinary taste." "Soori" is the holy food of Dharmes and is cooked in a sanctified manner- the soul, body and mind become purified after eating it. After the meal, the people happily return home.

The activity of "padda kamna" is carried out in order to quieten the village and free it from mourning of the dead. In this manner, on the fifth day, the death ceremony is concluded.

In special circumstances, the extension of death ceremony is reduced from five days to four or even lesser number of days, but all the phases of death ceremony have to be completed. A difficult situation arises when in the midst of death ceremony activities, some one in the village dies. If the "ache" of this dead person is not included in the activities of death ceremony, then for the whole year the soul will be in a position of indecision. Resultantly, as soon as news of the death is received, that very moment and in that condition the dead person's soul is included in the death ceremony.

In Oraon religion, the death ceremony is given the utmost religious and social importance. This is the reason why it is called "Koha benja." There is more than one activity in any ceremony. Among these activities, the most important or central activity lends its name to the whole gamut of activities. Actually the activity within which the bones of the dead are surrendered in the "Kundi" of the "gotra," that is called "koha benja." This activity is the central activity of death ceremony. As per religion, the ancestors or "pach baler" of every "gotra" or clan reside in the ground beneath the earth. Through the activity of the surrender of bones, the soul of the dead is merged with the ancestors, and he leaves the world to enter into a permanent union with his ancestors- this is koha benja or great marriage. All the preparations pricr to it, i.e. all activities are preparations for koha benja, and after this all activities are concluding activities of koha benja which are confirmed through "naig benja." Thereafter through the activity of "padda kamna" the mourning phase is ended, and the village, body and soul are quietened and purified.

It is desirable to assess the importance of "khekhel benja" in the context of "koha benja." We have seen that khekhel benja or Sarhul is, as per religion, the marriage of the earth with the sun. Symbolically, marriage takes place between the pahnain and pahan, and pujarin and pujar, and its imitation takes place on the fourth day of death ceremony which is called "naiga benja." This is the basic speciality of Oraon religion. "khekhel benja" and "koha benja" are two extremities in the midst of which the farmer Oraon maintains a sense of proportion with nature. If "khekhel benja" i.e. the marriage of Earth is symbolic of seeding for fertility, then koha benja is its end or completion. It is only after koha benja that the phase of mourning ends and the cereals of the granary become fit for eating. The journey from "khekhel benja" to "koha benja" is the journey from sprouting of seeds to its end or closure just like "khekhel benja" and "koha benja" are the two ends of life's journey- one is of sprouting and the other is its conclusion.

The observance of mourning or defilement after death has entered deeply in the life of the Oraons, so much so that it has received religious and social approbation. If a member of the family (inclusive of pastoral animals like cow-bullock etc.) dies on the day of any festival or ceremony, then that festival or ceremony is not observed until the birth of a creature takes place on the day of that festival or ceremony in that house. In this way there are several beliefs pertaining to death which are prevalent in Oraon religion and entire tribal society. Similarly there is a belief that if in a difficult, desolate or frightful place, any person lies down motionless (with his head towards the south) just like a corpse, or thus goes to sleep, then he is protected from wild animals, naads and other dangers. The village elders even go to this extent to claim that hunting animals do not eat the flesh of that prey which falls on the ground with its head towards the south or which lies accordingly or dies in this manner. This feeling among hunting animals, doubtless, must have entered centuries earlier when the animals had a strong community life. The elders state this on the basis of their experiences. Actually it is another matter to consider the justification or nonjustification of such beliefs but the custom which has passed through centuries and after having faced many tests, has acquired firm form, its basis cannot be imaginary or weak.

Here it is very much desirable to remark that entire Oraon life is controlled and comes within the chronological order of khekhel benja and koha benja. All the activities of Oraons, whether they be festivals and festivities, ceremonies or social arrangement, move according to these time periods throughout the year. Along with this, there is a strange confluence of collectiveness, community feeling and cooperation. All festivals and ceremonies, barring a few exceptions, are celebrated with the community and not celebrated individually. But the exceptions ultimately end in community participation. For example, if Sohrai festival is for the prosperity of granary, cattle sheds, home, cattle wealth or personal prosperity, even then on the next day it is concluded by participating in the Sohrai "jatra" along with the community. Similarly, in the village, there is only one wedding on a day. The whole village is responsible to welcome the bride – groom's party in a proper manner. The invitees from the bride's side and the village guests contribute vegetables, oil and cereals to the house where the marriage is being held as community help. They also gift items to the newly wed couple to enable them to start their married life, but these gifts are more or less returned to the givers on similar occasions. All the festivals and ceremonies of the Oraons are celebrated in the cooperative process of give and take. No discrimination is made in welcoming and offering meals. The prevailing Oraon axiom is that "even if the caste is torn asunder, let it be so, but the community should not be torn."

Similarly, in death ceremony, after burying or burning the body of the dead and completing the rituals, the people assembled for the same take a bath, purify themselves with the smoke of husk and oil, as also smearing of turmeric, and proceed for home. If the body is cremated, then the leftover bones are collected in a pot by people of the dead person's household, and this pot is kept in a special place in the house or hung safely from the branch of a tree in the courtyard. This action can be taken anywhere within and outside the country. Again, during koha benja time, the complete process of "sraddh" (concluding function of funeral rites in which water, food, etc. are offered to Brahmins in honour of manes) are completed in the village/ cremation ground of the gotra/kundi with the participation of the community. Koha benja or sraddh ritual is not of any special family, or special village-it is of a "parha" region/ area in which several villages numbering 5-7 up to 21 or 27 villages are included. In some places, koha benja is observed in several parhas together on the same day in their own cremation ground/ kundi. It is worth seeing "koha benja" (great marriage) with its vast and grand activities when the whole village is totally engrossed in this ritual.

References

1. Ranchi District Gazetteer (1970), p. 41.
2. Han-Oraon folklore number 4, pp. 29-30.
3. S. C. Roy : The Oraon of Chhotanagpur, p. 27.
4. The "mlechchas" (barbarians) taking advantage of the occasion of Sarhul festival, suddenly attacked the Oraons at night and defeated them (see details, along with proof, of the incident, on p. 43.

5. The meaning and definition of the word "Sarna" has been given in Kudukh Kosh (lexicon):-
   (a) in verb form – move forward, prosper, be simple.
   (b) in noun form- sacred forest grove, kudukh place of worship (Kudukh Kosh, Nagaland Bhasha Parishad, Kohima).
6. "Dhangar" is a Hindi word used galore for Oraon young man or labourer. Since these "dhangars" while working in various regions of the country came in contact with the then British writers, as a result the word "dhangar" used for them came to basically denote the whole race. See:-
   (i) Walter Hamilton, in Description of Hindoostan, Vol.1, p. 288.
   (ii) East India Gazetteer, Second Edition, Vol. I, pp. 415-16.
   (iii) The Kurukh or Oraons of Chhotanagpur are the people best known in many parts of India as "Dangers" Col. Dalton in Ethnology of Bengal, p. 245.
   (iv) Grierson, Linguistic survey iv, p. 410- "Dhangari" is the language of Dhangars.
7. S. C. Roy : "He (Oraon)" recognises that natural causes and conditions as well as human effort and human industry may ordinarily produce definite desired result" – O.R.C., p. 3.
8. S. C. Roy : "Although it appears that originally by none of the Oraon spirits was regarded as beneficent, contact with higher culture has since helped in investing a few of them with a beneficent or rather potentially beneficent nature."– Oraon Religion and Custom, p. 2.
9. S. C. Roy : "......the Earth is full of spirits as a tree is full of leaves." O.R.C., p. 66.
10. The word "bhuihar" is a slightly changed form of a Hindi root word which was adopted by the Oraons during their sojourn in Bihar. The Mundas call it "khunt kattidar." The Oraons found the word "bhuihar" to be more acceptable than the word "khuntkattidar." It appears that in this context the word "bhuiya," over a period of time, became "bhowmick" in Bengal and was thus used. In this context the historic incident of barah bhuinya can be viewed when in the seventeenth century, twelve prominent chiefs had divided the whole of Bengal among themselves. "Bhuinya" or "bhuihar" are people of the highest and influential class.
11. In the beginning, there was no arrangement regarding land rent. Bhuinhars were just expected to worship those "naads" and kept them pleased from whose area the jungle had been cleared to get land. It was just this much. But due to the prevalence of custom of land lords and land settlement, all the lands of bhuihars were roped in for land rent. Yet, lands belonging to pahans and the assistants to pahans were kept outside the purview of land rent. Under the land settlement introduced by the British, "khunt-bhootkheta," "gairahi bhoot-kheta," pahnai and pujar lands are rent free. The pahan or pujar may benefit from their fields but cannot sell or gift them because the fields are connected to their position, and the position is transferable.

    - Bengal Act- two, 1969 (Chhotanagpur Tenure Act.)- within this Act, based on pahnai land in bhuihari register.

12. The pahan is called "baiga" and in some villagers he is also called "naig." This is a kudukh name.
13. They are called "adya" meaning "original inhabitants" or "exalted tenants."
14. Then he (Dharmes) said,

    "you become Chala Pachcho,

    You lesser ones become desauri, khunt,

    Chiro, and human beings

    Will offer you holy food and sacrifice.

    (meaning that they will arrange for your victuals)- Oraon religious story (see Annexure)."
15. Rev. P. Dehon : When they use Dharmes, the idea of God is entirely separated from the sun.
16. Rev. P. Dehon : when they use Bhagwan, they naturally look to the sun as kols do.

    - Memoirs of the Asiatic Society of Bengal (1906), Vol. 1, p. 125.
17. (a) S. C. Roy : O.RC. p. 16

    During the time of Sarhul, moving away from the other gods- goddesses, Dharmes is offered sacrifice of white cock.
18. Dalton, "......like the Mundas, they acknowledge a supreme God, adored as Dharma or Dharmes, the Holy One, who is manifest in the Sun."- Descriptive Ethnology of Bengal, p. 256.
19. Dalton, "Dharmes cannot and does not interfere when the spirit of evil once fastens upon us......it is therefore, of no use to pray to Dharmes or to offer sacrifices to him." D. E. B. p. 256.
20. Col. Dalton, "......though acknowledged, recognised and revered, he (Dharmes) is neglected whilst the malignant spirits are adored."

    - Descriptive Ethnology of Bengal, p. 256.
21. "Then covered with gold and silver He came forth."
22. S. C. Roy, "Finally, in extreme distress, when other deities or spirits fail him, the Oraon offers prayers and sacrifices to Dharmes as a last resource." O.R.C., p. 16.
23. Hindi translation : "you Dharmes are our father. If due to ignorance or knowingly there has been any mistake in the worship of any spirit, you stop the anger of that spirit. Your eyes see everything."
24. "The boy threw a spear and brandished a sword. Then the ogre died."

    - Extract from "Agnivarsha" (Rain of Fire).
25. "Dharmes thought that the corpse of the ogre would spread bad odour. Since the human beings would not enjoy their food, therefore He sent rain of fire."

    - Extract from "Agnivarsha" (Rain of Fire).
26. ".........Then he said –

    The eldest among you become Chala Pachcho,

    All the juniors become desauri,

Khunt, chiro, mankharin,

The human beings will arrange for food to be offered to you."

- from "Asur Avdaan."

Note: The meaning of Chiro, mankharin, khokra pertains to the wild thorny creepers called chiro, Aslago and RamBhawan. These creepers tie the feet of the Oraons in the forest paths and thereafter their feet start bleeding. According to the belief of the Oraons, blood thirsty naads live in these thorny wild creepers.

27. In the Sira-Sita plain
    The brother and sister used to
    stay in the cave of the crab,
    Sira-Sitas,
    there chiru grass had sprung up
    there the pair of brother-sister stayed.
28. There is a general saying among the Oraons that the souls of the dead stay beneath the Earth-the souls of the ancestors live in the nether world while Dharmes lives in the sky.
29. If the dead person is a male, then the words "Isin Ha, and if the person is a female, then the words "Idin Hu" are used."
30. Rev. Dehon and thinkers of his school.
31. Now I am sending you afar. From henceforth, your eyes and head should not be turned towards me.
32. The seniormost become Chala Pachcho.

    -............
33. The day for eating mutton. Meaning, on the day of Chandi puja (worship) holy food of mutton is received, hence instead of openly saying "the day of Chandi Puja," the Oraons use the aforementioned language.
34. "I am worshipping you in every manner. After having offered oil and vermillion to you, I am going home. (My hunted prey) after having speedily covered 12-13 "kos" on horseback, it should fall in my village."
35. According to Rev. P. Dehon, Baranda is a male naad who was born from the womb of an Asur widow.

    - See "Memoirs of the Asiatic Society of Bengal" Vol. 1 No. 9 p. 132.
36. Dr. Frazer : Split Totems- Totemism and Exogamy, Vol.1, p. 10.
37. Ibid: ".........the segmentation of single original clan which had a whole animal for its totem into a number of totems, either of which took the name either of a part of the original animal or of a sub-species of it." p. 54.
38. The symbol on the flag, and the totem-normally researchers can not find the difference. But the symbol on the flag has not been given the importance like the totem. The respect with which the bhuinhar or original settler views the totem, that awe is not to be seen after a period of time due to intermixing. Difference has also cropped up between totem and symbol on the flag.

    For example:

    In village Jamgayi, P. S. Lohardagga, the Lakra (cheetah) totem of the bhuinhar is taken to the jatra in the form of a wooden cheetah.

But in village Chitar kota, Ranchi, the bhuinhar minz (a kind of fish) take to the jatra the statue of a bullock as a symbol.

In village Kudarko, although the gotra of the bhuinhar is Tirkey (small rat) but in the jatra they take the figure of a horse.

In village Dighiya, the gotra of the bhuinhar is khess (paddy) but in the jatra they take the symbol of elephant.

In village Weenweesa, the gotra of the bhuinhar is toppo (a bird) but in the jatra they take a stake as a symbol.

39. Dhangar-Pahan : Just like the pahan of a village, as per desire of Sarna Devi, young bachelors are selected. The religious duty of the Dhangar pahan is to worship goddess Chandi.

40. Where are the five brothers,
Where have they shot their arrows,
The deer has gone,
Where did they shoot their arrows.

41. The Munda and Oraon tribes have adopted Phagu festival from the Hindus-this thought is held by most of the theologians, the chief among them have been delineated below. But they have not given any argument or proof to confirm such a thinking :

(a) S. C. Roy – O.R.C., p. 140.

(b) A. Van Exem- RSMT, p. 153.

(c) Hofmann E. M. – p. 3200, and many others.

42. Dry lumps of horse bean pulse.

43. O God of Keyond tree! O God of Sal tree
Phagu God! Sarhul God!
O now it is Sarhul! O that is Phagu
Phagu God! Sarhul God!
Come let us all play, let us all play.

44. God of new rice wine! Level of the pot of wine!
O this is Sarhul! O that is Phagu
Phagu God! Sarhul God
Come let us all play, let us all play.

45. While offering hadiya to the ancestors, the mahto says thus- "O the ancestors of our gotra ! Today Sarhul festival is being celebrated. O ancestor-soul, you have eaten and drunk. And ancestor-soul, do not be saddened by our "bua" (Paternal aunt) and "Masiyon" (Maternal aunts), by our maternal uncles, by enemies and friends, staying within and outside the country."

46. "O Dharmes, our father ! you complete all the short comings that remain because of our ignorance or even knowledge. Our eyes cannot see the naads. Your eyes see them. You are our father. You control all those whom we see or know, and also the naads whom we do not know."

47. Take ! take ! take ! God of new rice wine !
Take hadiya for relatives

This is Sarhul God.

O celebrate this Sarhul, celebrate this Phagu.

48. Rahar, Murung= Bodi, barai, khesari are the names of various pulses which are used as savouries and appetizers along with hadiya. In this Sarhul song sung by the women, pulses are mentioned as connected to the act of "Kakro Sarjana" meaning the act of frying of crabs. The women find the sound and act of cracking of the crabs similar to the sprouting of the pulses.

49. The karam branch will be planted on the

    Eleventh day of the bright moon in Bhado,

    Parwati comes fasting,

    She has pushed "nawa" flowers in her hair,

    The admirer comes beating the "mandar" (a small drum).

50. Based on facts decided in the Pahan Conference of 26/ 06/ 98, Sisai, Gumla.

51. Based on facts decided in the Pahan Conferences of 4/10/98, Bero, Ranchi, and of 5/11/98 Mudma, Ranchi.

52. Based on facts decided in the Pahan Conferences dated 4/10/98 Bero, and 5/11/ 98 Mudma, Ranchi.

53. *Ibid.*

54. "Marriage is fixed between so-and-so groom and so-and-so bride. You kindly ensure that both of them may live happily. Also ensure that both of them live to a ripe old age."

55. Since when "poomp-mejhna" ritual became a part of marriage rituals of Oraons is not known, it is shrouded in time. Is this ritual symbolic of the forest life of the Oraons (hence their own ritual) or is it the result of some external influence? Prior to Rohtasgarh, the Oraons had been in contact with the Aryans, and after coming to Chhotanagpur, they came in contact with the Mundas and the local Hindu settlers. As regards the Mundas, there is no such ritual apparently visible in their marriage rituals. As regards the Hindus, it was much later when prosperous families during "Puja" adopted the custom of garlanding the bridegroom's party as a token of welcome. But this custom is only a few centuries old. Hence it is apparent that the ritual of "poomp-mejhna" is peculiar to the Oraons and is a traditional, centuries old ritual in which the act of touching the feet and the offering of flowers symbolise respect and affection. Now, in nearly every religion and society of the world, guests are welcomed with flowers and garlands. Can this custom, prevailing at present in civilised societies, of offering flowers and garlands be traced to the ritual of "poomp-mejhna" among Oraons? It may be mentioned that the use of flowers in deity-worship or any worship is a contribution of Dravid-culture. (See first chapter).

56. See annexure: Isung Sindri.

57. (a) Your man goes for hunting. He gets injured by an arrow and he becomes lame. O mother, do not call him a cripple. Do you hear me?

    (b) O mother, if he defecates on the stove or urinates on the mortar in which paddy is dehusked by pounding, then do not say that he has dirtied the stove or urinated on the mortar. O mother, are you listening to my words or not?

(c) If he goes to cut the body of a dead animal and brings its flesh, will you cook it ? Both of you eat fifty-fifty of the meat. O gentleman, if she partakes of more meat than you, then do not say that "you have eaten more." Are you listening or not?

(d) And if she goes to pluck "bhootang" from the "Pakar" tree (the citron leaved Indian fig tree) and in the process she falls down and breaks her leg, breaks her hand, then O gentleman do not tell her that she is lame in the leg or maimed in the hand. Are you listening to me or not, gentleman?

(e) Do your work well, drink well. Gentleman, listen, and you too, O mother, listen. From today work together and eat together.

Now both of you make obeisance to everybody and go inside.

58. "Take, eat. Why have you left us now ? Now you have seen your path. Go, and take with you all our diseases and sins."

59. In some villages, in Oraon society, the dead body is placed in such a way that the head is towards the north and the feet are towards the south.

60. S. C. Roy, O. R. C. p. 126.

61. The word "Kundi" appears to have been taken from the Sanskrit word "Kund." In the rivers, "jalkund" are those places which are used for religious activities. Apparently, the ritual of immersing the bones of the dead has been taken by the Oraons from the Aryans. The Oraons had been in touch with the Aryans during their journeys from the banks of the river Narmada to western India and Eastern India.

62. Although the religious legend of destruction of the world through water can be found in many religious texts, but the escape of Manu from the total annihilation of the world and again the increase in the human race from him-this legend has clearly been taken by the Mundas from the Hindus. In this legend, the Munda element occurs in the eight children of Manu, four males and four females. Munda, Roda, Manka, and Sodto are Mundari names whereas the hero of the legend, Manu, remains the great personage of the Hindu legend.

Chapter - 5

Conclusion

It was the Christian missionaries who first started serious study of the religions of the Munda and Oraon tribes in 1850. Although their efforts were self-centred and with a particular aim in mind, yet their collected and published material can be called praiseworthy achievement upto now. In addition to the missionaries, a few efforts have been made by various institutions and individuals, but all these efforts have been limited to anthropological or sociological study. Till date, effort has not been made to consecutively connect the religious development of these tribes of Chhotanagpur.

In this consecutive connect, (a) the religious life of the Mundas and Oraons in Rohtasgarh prior to their entry into Chhotanagpur and from their place of origin to Rohtasgarh covering hundreds of years of roaming, (b) after entry into Chhotanagpur, their fight with the Asurs, and the advent of bongas and naads in Sarna religion, (c) the development of parallel religious institutions of devra, ojha, mati and sokha against the anti-religious black magic and spells, (d) the influence of Vaishnav faithful and followers of the Kabir sect in the 15th and 16th centuries, and in modern times the drifting in of reformist tendencies, are mentionable phases.

Munda Religion

The place of origin of the Munda tribe, also called "kol", and the traditional proofs of its migration to India, William Schmidt's proofs regarding language, Hogson, Hutton, etc.'s proofs regarding race and historic proofs of Dani – after analysing them the conclusion was reached that this tribe travelled in groups from the Yunan province of south-west China to southern Mongolia, Tibet, came through the various Himalayan passes to Himachal Pradesh and to the north-west till Sindh province, and spread in the south to the banks of the river Narmada. The Mundas had to move east-south after fighting the

Oraons, Gonds and Aryans and being defeated by them. They had traditional enmity with the Vrishnis. The Mundas sided with the Kauravas in the Kurukshetra war against Krishna. With the downfall of the Kauravas, the Mundas fled in various groups, hiding in the jungles and mountains, to the plains of the rivers Ganga–Yamuna and crossing many districts of Uttar Pradesh, they ultimately reached the safe area of Rohtasgarh. During the period of centuries of living and roaming, some of these groups in their effort to protect themselves became extinct in the forests and mountains or else they are still living a forest life. Some groups became Hinduised after coming in contact with and being influenced by the Hindus. They have lost their racial characteristics as well as identity related to language, culture and religion. Among these groups are Shabar, Kharwar and Chero races.

Keeping their language, tradition and religion intact and facing many odds and tribulations, the Mundas reached Rohtasgarh. There they had settled down for a few centuries when the Kharwars attacked them. According to traditional and historical proofs, the Kharwar chieftain Madho Das had requested Risa Munda, the Munda chieftain, for his daughter's hand in marriage for his son, and the Mundas thought it derogatory to give their daughter in marriage to the Kharwars who had lost their religion. As a result, there was war, the Mundas were defeated and again they had to move on. After some time, the Mundas crossed the River Sone and moved towards the east. One group reached Shikharbhum and over a period of time began to be called Santals, and the other group, as directed by Singbonga to Risa Munda in a dream, crossed the Saharghatiya pass on the northwest of Lohardagga and in their quest for settling down permanently they reached "sona lakum dishum" (golden area) of Chhotanagpur.

It is clear from these incidents that the Munda tribe which entered Chhotanagpur had, to the best of their ability, tried to maintain their culture, their religion, their tradition and their tribal pride. Although the then Mundas had been found to be on the lower rungs of the ladder of civilisation due to their dietary habits and life style based on forest living, but because of their rigid, fundamental, narrow behaviour, easy change in their traditional customs-rituals, their culture and in their religion could not be expected. The illusive powers, sports of spirits, and sacrifice oriented worship believed by brother Asurs and adopted by them accordingly as family deities, influenced the Munda tribe (also called Kol) in Chhotanagpur when the Mundas entered this area and also even after fighting the Asurs.

Rev. F. Hoffman says that during the migration and roaming period of the Mundas, some "sun cult" influenced them. Hoffman's thought arose aiming at the all-mighty God Singbonga of the Mundas. Singbonga i.e. Sun God. It has been seen that in the early stages of most of the religions of this world, utmost importance has been given to the Sun star which gives energy to the whole creation, has tremendous heat and fire, and is resplendent. Hence, for the Mundas to think the Sun to be All Mighty God was but a natural development of their religion. In the religious narratives of the Mundas:-

(a) the coming into existence of the earth from amidst the water-flooding, the birth of flora, fauna and humans, extension of the human race, the first plough, division of time, etc. religious narratives are related to the primordeal time period of human beings.

(b) Rain of Fire: Due to increase of sin among human beings, there is a provision of once annihilating human kind in order to set up Creation afresh.

(c) Asur-Avdaan: This is related to the downfall of the Asurs. In the Munda religious narratives, mention has been made of Azeemgarh (the district Azamgarh of Uttar Pradesh) in the story related to the Earth, man and birth of human race. After the creation of the Earth and the coming into existence of flora and fauna, a duo of brother and sister was born from the egg of the Hur bird. This was the first human pair. In this manner, according to the religious narrative of the Mundas, the place of origin of the Mundas has been Azamgarh, and from here their race has extended.

Actually, Azamgarh has had great importance during the migratory period of the Mundas. In this area, archaeological evidence have been found regarding the stay and influence of the Mundas. This is the reason why Azamgarh has been given more importance in the religious narratives. It has come to be known from local traditions that when Dashrathi Ram, scion of the thirty seventh generation of the Ikshavaku Clan had passed through Azamgarh, then by that time the Shabars and Asurs had left Azamgarh, and the Rajbhars were prominent there. If the time period of Ram be thought to be 2000-1500 B.C. then the Mundas had left Azamgarh in 3000-2500 B.C. Since the Mundas had to leave Rohtasgarh in about the 6th century B.C., hence all religious narratives upto "Rain of Fire" are definitely connected to their religious life prior to their entry into Chhotanagpur.

The following throw light on the religious condition of the Mundas prior to their entry into Chotanagpur :-

(1) The relationship between Singbonga and "Horo" (man) was that of paternal grandfather and grandson.

(2) Singbonga used to come physically to the first human-duo and give directions to them.

(3) Singbonga sent maladies to this Creation. Prior to this, there had been no maladies.

(4) "Sacrifice of white cock" was the remedy for freedom from disease and for its prevention, as told by Singbonga. The tradition of sacrifice for the prevention of disease started accordingly.

(5) Singbonga himself does not partake of the holy food i.e. the sacrificial meat- he distributes it among his servers.

(6) When the first human duo asked him as to why he only licked a few drops of blood, Singbonga became invisible for all times to come. Even now he moves amongst the Mundas, but the Munda people cannot see him because their supernatural power has been destroyed.

(7) Singbonga is self-begotten.

(8) An imaginary appearance of Singbonga as paternal grandfather had been hypothesised, but there had been no idol or temple of him.

(9) There had been a rule of sacrifice as a form of worship, but no place of worship or arrangement of priest had been developed.

(10) Singbonga had no wife. He was unmarried.

Rain of Fire and Singbonga

(1) Rain of fire is a part of the solar strength of Singbonga.

(2) Singbonga cannot tolerate sinners, so he devises means to destroy them.

(3) Singbonga is anxious for the extension of "Horo" (Man) and his race, hence he asked for the return of the "brother-sister" duo from Misi-Singbonga or Nage Era who had protected the brother-sister duo by hiding them during the Rain of Fire, and thereafter he encouraged them to live as man and wife.

(4) Till that stage, a regional goddess called Misi-Singbonga, meaning Singbonga's sister, had appeared in Munda religion. This goddess can withstand extreme fire, and is the goddess of swampy or marshy land or watery area. She had saved the brother-sister duo from the extreme fire of Singbonga through her own valour. She had returned the duo to Singbonga on the condition that he would not send Rain of Fire again. After the downfall of the Asurs, Misi-Singbonga developed as Nage Era, and signs of demoniac behaviour entered in her character.

In the religious story of Rain of Fire, apart from Misi-Singbonga, mention is made of another female form called Parvati who is supposed to be a wife of Singbonga. She had requested that Rain of Fire may be limited, otherwise the whole Creation would be destroyed. Most of the Munda pahans are not ready to accept that Singbonga was married and that he had a wife. According to Munda religious philosophy the wisdom of Singbonga used to argue with him on any problem. The mention of wife is the personified appearance of the wisdom of Singbonga. In Munda religion there are three main ceremonies- Chhati, Marriage, and Death Ceremony.

Prior to entry into Chhotanagpur, marriage ceremony had been given importance in Munda religion but the institution of gotra had not developed till then. Yet the Mundas were not in favour of fixing marriage with any race. "Chhati" ceremony (celebration of sixth day after birth) began to be given importance in Chhotanagpur. According to Munda religion, it is only after the Chhati ceremony that a child is assimilated within the race. But this ceremony had no importance prior to coming to Chhotanagpur.

In Munda religion, "death ceremony" is a necessary and important religious activity. It is through this ceremony that the soul of the dead is assimilated in the "soul-family" of the ancestors. Before coming to Chhotanagpur, "sasaandiri" in death ceremony had not developed among the Mundas. This is a later development.

Organised form of ancestor worship had not developed. Centuries after coming to Chhotanagpur, gradually the rules and regulations of worship of "ading" and "odabongako" developed, which are evident in the important place of ancestors in Munda religion.

The Appearance of Sarna Religion

When the Mundas, with the aforementioned background of religion, entered Chhotanagpur, they came face to face with the Asurs who had been living there from before. In the fight for supremacy, the Asurs were defeated, and they were driven off by the Mundas to the western side. It is evident from "Asur Avdaan" that the Mundas did not remain untouched by certain religious and cultural arrangements of the Asurs.

After entering Chhotanagpur, the Munda clans had cut trees and cleared the forest to reclaim land for themselves and in the process they had bounded off a portion of the jungle and left it alone. This place was called the Sarna place. According to the belief of the Mundas, the "hatu-bongaku" lived on the trees of this bounded area- they protected the whole village from various disasters. After the downfall of the Asurs, when Singbonga transformed the Asur-widows in the form of bongas and gave them responsibility of various regions/ sectors, then there was an increase in the number of deities in the form of bongas in Munda religion. According to this arrangement, the responsibility of Sarna place was given to Chandi-bonga. Chandi bonga not only protects the village, but also protects them from animals when they go out for agriculture or hunting. In this manner, Chandi bonga is the most useful, worshipped, and close to the Mundas compared to other bongas. Over a period of time, Chandi bonga came to be known as Sarna burhi, and the Sarna place came to be connected with most worships and religious activities, and in this way Munda religion appeared as Sarna religion.

After victory over the Asurs, the following developments took place in the Sarna religion of the Mundas:

(1) The acceptance in Sarna religion of Asur widows transformed by Singbonga as bongas. The increase in the number of bongas in Sarna religion.

(2) The development of the new institution of pahan and pujar. The full control of pahan over religious activities. The selection of pahan as per the desire of Sarna Devi, and in this way a link between pahan, Munda and deities.

(3) The development of a fixed place for major religious and community activities, and that place is the Sarna place. Prior to this, the Mundas did not have any special place, and used to carry out their religious activities individually.

(4) The development of Ading bongako, and the arrangement of a place for the souls of the ancestors inside the house of every Munda family, and their worship on most occasions.

(5) Religious importance of both Sarna place and Sarna tree.

(6) The rule regarding the sacrifice of cocks of a particular colour for a particular bonga, and absolutely separate from the rest-the sacrifice of white cock for Singbonga.

The Development of Sanskar (ceremonies) and Festivals

(1) Gradual increase in the number of ceremonies and festivals. Influence of Hindu contact.

  (a) Importance of "Chhati" "sanskar." Prior to this ceremony, the child in the womb or just born is supposed to be impure. After purification through the ceremony of "Chhati", the child becomes a member of the Munda race.

  (b) If the child dies before Chhati ceremony, then no ceremony is observed for the child, but if death occurs even one day after the Chhati ceremony, then all the rules pertaining to death ceremony are followed because by that time the child has become a member of the Munda race.

(2) (a) Marriage ceremony : Singbonga fixes the marriage pair of boys and girls right at birth. After considering the good and bad omens on the way, decision is taken on determining the groom and bride. If Singbonga does not desire, then he sends ill-omens on the way to inform the guardians, and the effort to form the relationship is there and then ended. The groom and bride parties do not neglect the bad omens.

  (b) Marriage is a divine bonding.

(3) (a) Increase in the rituals of death ceremony. The beginning of the tradition of "sasaan diri" and its development. The burial of bones of the dead as per clan.

  (b) The activity of settling the soul of the dead in the family "ading."

(4) Increase in the number of festivals: In Chhotanagpur, due to increase in agricultural work, the festivals got connected to agriculture, namely- "batauli, jomnawa, hariari," etc.

(5) (a) celebrating the festival of Sarhul or Ba. In Chhotanagpur, the beginning and development of the festivals of Phagu, Dasai, Karma, Soso Bonga, etc.

(b) Consideration of Hindu influence on the festivals of Phagu, Dasai, Karam, etc.

(6) (a) Sohrai festival is an old festival celebrated in the night of the new moon of Kartik month for the protection of domestic animals. There is no need for the pahan. This festival had developed prior to the appearance of the pahan.

(b) The night of the new moon of the month of Kartik provides important opportunity to the "Vaidyas" (indigenous physicians/ medicine men) to collect medicinal plants and roots. It also provides opportunity to witches to be initiated in witchcraft. It is believed that the new moon night of Kartik develops accomplishment sharply and successfully. It is also the custom among Hindus to hone their "Mantras" on Diwali night.

(7) Alongwith and according to the festivals, the combination of songs, dance and community celebration in a special place.

(8) Provision of worship through pahan in certain festivals, particularly those which are observed community-wise. In some festivals, the householder himself or the mistress of the house conducts the act of worship.

(9) The process of reform in ceremonies and festivals is going on continuously. There is more inclination to give priority to cultural programmes and enjoyment/ entertainment in festivals.

The Development of Necromancy, Witch and Devra etc. Institutions

Although prior to entry into Chhotanagpur, Munda life was influenced by necromancy and illusive powers, yet after the downfall of the Asurs there was sufficient increase in this direction. With the transformation of Asur widows into bongas by Singbonga, and establishing them in Sarna religion, the number of bongas started increasing automatically. Several bongas got connected to small frightful places and local arrangement began to be made for their worship and placing of offerings. There was no dearth of frightful scenes and places for the Mundas who lived amongst forests and mountains. Again if at a special bathing place of a river or in a pond, there was an incident of a Munda boy drowning, then the presence of a bonga there was imagined. and with the repetition of incidents gradually the bonga became famous and began getting regular offerings. There is a saying among the Mundas-which is more, the leaves in a forest or the number of bongas ?

Along with the increase in the number of bongas, necromancy deeply influenced Munda life. Theologians and pahans objected that necromancy or witches are not related to Singbonga, and neither they are related to those bongas whose worship is conducted by pahans authorised by Singbonga. Actually, with the increase in the number of bongas, they came to be divided into two categories- one, those bongas which were worshipped by pahans, and two, those bongas who were not considered traditional and sanctioned by religion according to the pahans and whose worship was considered an insult to themselves by the pahans. Those bongas who were not worshipped by the pahans, were not considered sanctioned by religion and those were the bongas worshipped by the witches.

We have seen that in the Middle Ages, the influence of necromancy and witches had deeply affected Munda life and often started controlling many religious activities and occupations of Munda life, and their belief in them.

The bongas worshipped by witches and necromancers were believed to be denizens of the invisible world just like the other bongas. In order to break the monopoly of the pahans, the witches had connected themselves to Singbonga, and amongst Mundas, the first wife of Singbonga, called Parvati, got good publicity as the "first witch." Thus, the sect of "Saat Parbatiya" had started. In this way, witches deeply and extensively influenced the Munda tribe. But most of the religious activities of the witches used to be secret and destructive hence they came to be called "heretical current." After a period of time, it came to be circulated in Munda folk tales that due to the malpractices of Parvati, Singbonga threw her out of the house. In this way, the activities of witches and necromancy did not get approval of Singbonga due to which they came to be believed as irreligious.

In Chhotangapur, the parallel religious institution of devra, Ojha, sokha developed to nullify the killing powers of the heretical current of necromancy. For this, Hindu gods and goddesses, and the mantras (incantations) in Sadani language were used. It was a common belief that the Hindus are more progressive and powerful than the Mundas hence their gods were also more powerful so the destructive powers of the bongas would not be able to assert themselves before them. These institutions got the benefit of such mental condition. Such gods and goddesses are chiefly Mahadeo, Kali, Chandi and Durga.

Although anger had appeared spontaneously in Munda society against necromancy and witches, some religious preachers tried to enlighten this tribe not only against necromancy and witches but also regarding the life style of the Mundas, their diet and food-habits and the evil practice of sacrifice. The conduct of the followers of Kabir Panth influenced the Mundas in two ways. One was directly by the followers of Kabir Panth, and the second was through the closeness with the Swansis. Most of the Swansis were followers of

Kabir Panth and they were weavers by profession. The followers of Kabir Panth stressed on fasting and abstinence from vile food. They criticised the racism of the Mundas. The followers of Kabir Panth tried to publicise among the Mundas the idea of kindness to creatures, sincere affinity and feeling of firm belief in the Almighty.

The life of the Mundas living in the region of Panch Pargana had come under the influence of Vaishnav religion. In the fifteenth century, Chaitanya Mahaprabhu stopped in Panch Pargana area for some time while on his way from Nilanchal to Puri. It was at that time that he had influenced the tribes there through his preachings. A feeling of disgust towards killing of animals and meat eating had arisen among those tribes due to which it had adversely affected worship of bongas through sacrifice. The poet Vinand Das who had been influenced by Vaishnav religion, had added his religious thoughts in his songs related to Karam festival which the Mundas lovingly sang and accepted.

The various temples built in Chhotanagpur area and the images within them, and the way of worshipping them, and the conduct of the Hindus connected with them-after seeing them there has been improvement among the Mundas beyond expectation. The Shiv-Shakti-Surya sect temples built on the style of Orissa temple architecture, and the Vaishnav sect temples which have been built in Buradih, Haradih, Bamla, Panadih remain centres of attraction for the Mundas. The remains of the temples in the valley of the Kanchi and Karkari rivers are of sixth-seventh century and are evidential proof of their deep influence on Munda life. The area of Panch Pargana has been populated mostly by Mundas. The temples of the Vaishnav sect found in Deosanagar, Jaggarnathnagar, Bodeya, Korambe (mostly populated by Mundas) have successfully influenced the lifestyle and religious thinking of the Mundas living there.

Birsa Munda, the founder of Birsa religion, was also influenced by certain virtues of Vaishnav religion. He had given sufficient emphasis on the purity of food habits. Birsa religion was influenced by certain virtues of Sarna religion. Birsa religion was an effort to move parallel to Sarna religion and go ahead with some followers- in this religion Birsa was accepted as "Bhagwan" or God, but most of the Mundas were not willing to accept it. By calling himself God, Birsa has insulted Omnipotent Singbonga and in this way he has insulted Sarna religion of the Mundas. The importance of Birsa lies in his leadership of a fighting movement, not in religion.

Due to Christian missionaries and modern day education, there has been expected improvement in the Sarna religion of the Mundas. This improvement is related to their superstitions, dietary habits and lowly life-style. Most scholars of Munda religion, especially Christian and Hindu scholars of British Government times have openly publicised that the Munda race worships wicked and destructive bongas who get happiness in sending drought and various diseases, epidemics and death to torture the Mundas. The aim of the

Mundas is to worship these wicked supernatural powers, to satisfy them so that they do not become the reason for the destruction of the Mundas. The religion of Munda race has been defined as "belief in ghosts and spirits" which is completely wrong and misleading.

It is true that the bongas created by Singbonga were of Asur origin. After a lapse of time, it would be wrong to involve the Asur-origin bongas with the destructive bongas. The wicked bongas who developed later on have no place in Sarna religion, and the pahan does not worship them. It is not convincing to call Munda religion "animism" based on these bongas and thinking them to be important when actually they have no connection with Munda religion.

In Munda religion there is a provision of punishment by Singbonga of those bongas who fail in their duty. This punishment is sanctioned by religion. Religion provides that the bongas may send maladies or similar pains to the Mundas for cautioning them and bringing them to the right path. On such occasions, the Mundas give offerings to the bongas to satisfy them and ask for forgiveness for not doing their duty. The friendly form of bongas clearly come out in nearly every festival, community religious organisation and other religious activities. Desauli bonga or Hatu bongako or jaher burhi, Chandi bonga, etc. carry out the responsibilities of increase in agriculture and protection of Munda youths from ferocious animals during hunting : Oda bongako or ancestor deity think about the protection of the family and its extension. Similarly other bongas are also in the same position. All these bongas carry out their responsibilities of regional deities the same way as the vedic regional deity Vastoshpati and Kshetrapati, or the Lithuanian regional deity Sutvaras, Bouchis, Jariksious and Gotha, or Roman regional deity Saturnus, Ceres and Flora.

All the bongas approved by Singbonga have a part of him in them, and they carry out the responsibilities given to them by Singbonga. Singbonga is the omnipotent God of the Munda race. We can call Singbonga "Sun God" but not today's Sun god; he is the Omnipotent and supreme Sun of the Rigveda period whose one form is represented by Vishnu. In course of time when the influence of Vishnu increased, then we know that from Him there emanated many incarnations and forms of deities. Singbonga, too, gave rise to various regional bongas and empowered them with some part of his power and gave them some responsibilities- that is how he developed godliness in them. In this way, Munda religion or Sarna religion is far away from "animism" and has developed into a religion of many deities.

Oraon/Kudukh

In the course of studying the history of the religion of Oraon tribe living in Chhotanagpur, it has been seen that in the migration of the Oraon tribe from their place of origin, and from that place to Rohtasgarh, this tribe has been influenced by certain developed races after coming in contact with them.

In the context of their travel from the place of origin to Rohtasgarh, two main hypotheses can be considered- the first hypothesis is of Col. E. Dalton, Rev. P. Dehan and S. C. Roy who believe that south India is the place of origin of the Oraon tribe which is of Dravidian root. They present the map of their travel from Konkan to Gujarat, their going east following the River Narmada, they cross the Vindhya mountain ranges, Amarkantak forest and the River Sone till they come to Shahabad, Rohtasgarh. But these writers are silent on the question as to whether the ancestors of Oraons originated in South India, although S. C. Roy admits that the life of the Dravids is connected with that era of south India the darkness of which has still not been illumined by history. In this context:-

(a) The geologists state that after the gradual receding of the deluge, there was enough scope for the coming into existence of flora and fauna in the Deccan plateau.

(b) R. C. Majumdar mentions in "Ancient India" that some historians are of the opinion that "early man" originated in south India and they migrated to the Punjab in the last phase of the first Ice Age where in the beginning phase of the second Ice Age, that is about five lakh years earlier from now, they have been found which has been confimed by the stone segments and pieces and other archaeological evidences uncovered from the base of the Shivalik hills.

(c) R. K. Choudhary states that man called Homo Sapien was found in south India about 40 thousand years before Christ.

(d) Language- Scholars believe that Dravidian language has developed in south India on its own and it is not connected to any language from outside.

The above facts direct our thoughts to whether south India was the place of birth of primordial man? But the western anthropologists and historians are not ready to accept that primordial man came into existence in India.

The second hypothesis is of western historians. According to them, the Dravidians came into existence with the merger of the Mediterranean Aegean (Proto-Australoid) and the West Asia Minor Armenide races. The Dravidian people had crossed the Arabian region from the Mediterranian and had entered North West India about five thousand years before Christ. M. L. Tirkey, who had been appointed by Government of India for the study of tribal life, has traced the migration of the Oraons from Mohenjodaro and Harappa, gradually crossing the Yamuna-Ganga plain, to Shahabad and Rohtasgarh. According to Tirkey, after having been defeated by the Aryans in 1750 B.C., this tribe reached Shahabad in about eighth-seventh century B.C. In Shahabad, this tribe extended its influence well. After Shahabad, the Oraons got a protected place in Rohtasgarh. By that time the Mundas had fled to Chhotanagur after having been defeated by the Kharwars in Rohtasgarh.

In the migration period and even earlier, the Oraon tribe had come in close contact with the Aryans, and their life-style and thinking had undergone sufficient refinement. The various dissipative references in their traditional tales and Balmiki Ramayan confirm this fact that at the time of Dasrathi Ram's expedition to Lanka, this tribe had been living in the jungles of South India. Being mainly dependent on tubers, roots, fruits and agriculture, this tribe used to maintain purity in its dietary habits. The traditional religious stories regarding the birth and extension of the tribe have conformed to their forest life. Being born out of the bosom-blood (bosom= "ur") of a meditating saint of the forest region of the south, their progeny came to be called "Oraon". The religious story which connects the Oraons to a meditating saint, indicates Aryan influence over them.

The traditional religious story of "Rain of Fire" which describes the downfall of the tribe and re-creation, also indicates Aryan influence over Oraons. This legend is closer to that legend of the Mahabharat when Bhim, during the period of remaining incognito, replaced the only son of a Brahmin (to protect him) and offered himself to the demon whom he slayed later on, thus giving relief to the citizens Dharmes had taken the form of a widow's son and had similarly given relief to the inhabitants of Belatpur by slaying the demon. In order to protect the Creation, Dharmes thought it necessary to do away with the foul smell emanating from the corpse of the demon. In the legend, the bad odour symbolised sin, pride, jealousy and the increase of various vices in human kind, due to which normal life of man had become painful. Hence, in order to destroy the then human race and again to create a new race, Dharmes had caused the Rain of Fire. In this context, the description of Dharmes against the background of his wife Sita and nephew Haluman (Hanuman) appears to be that of Dasrathi Ram.

Prior to entry into Chhotanagpur, till Rohtasgarh, two dialectically opposite invisible powers had developed in Oraon religion- one was benevolent, and the other was malevolent. Benevolent God was in the form of "Dharmes" while "nazar-gujar" and "bai-bhak" powers were malevolent. In the nascent stage of religion, just like the other tribes, the Oraons had also accepted "Surya" (sun) as the highest god. The understanding of the virtues and form of Dharmes, the highest god of the Oraons, has developed from the sun.

Before entry into Chhotanagpur, the "highest God" of the Oraons was known as "Biri-belas," which means "Sun-god." During their flight from Rohtasgarh, the Oraons got divided into two groups. One group reached Chhotanagpur and came to be called "Oraons," and the other group settled down in the hills of Rajmahal in the name of "Maler" tribe. The Maler tribe used to call their highest and omnipotent God by the old name of "Bero."

This name was commonly prevalent till the early decades of the eighteenth century. Bero means Sun. The name of Dharmes is unknown to the Maler tribe, which means that the name of Dharmes, God of the Oraons, has developed in Chhotanagpur. Another tribe of Dravidian origin called Khond call their creator-God "Bedu-Pennu," and this tribe is also unaware of the name of Dharmes.

Actually, it is after the entry into Chhotanagpur that in Oraon religion, the understanding of "Dharmes" has developed like Bhagwan of Hindus. Dharmes who used to be manifest from the Sun, gradually rose above the Sun, meaning that he came to be recognised as the highest power. When the Oraons address the Sun, they use the term "Suraj Bhagwan." Obviously, according to this, Suraj Bhagwan comes below Dharmes and has been placed in a lower category under Dharmes. It is a peculiarity of Oraon religion that the demonic forces also develop godliness when they come under the influence of Dharmes. According to Oraon tradition, "Chala Pachcho" or goddess of agriculture, had earlier been believed to be a destructive ghost; gradually, she got embellished with godly powers and came to be called "Dharti Ma" (mother Earth) whose marriage is celebrated every year with the Sun-god, according to Oraon religion, on the occasion of "Khaddi" or Sarhul festival in which the community participates. The development of Chala Pachcho had taken place in Rohtasgarh, prior to Chhotanagpur. In Oraon religion, there have been other naads who have been placed in the category of deities after they developed benevolent character while coming in contact with Dharmes. This development has taken place in the land of Chhotanagpur. This is a mentionable phase of the history of Oraon religion.

Before entering Chhotanagpur, the Oraon people used to wear the sacred thread, maintain purity in dietary habits; dancing and singing was inherent in them. They used to believe "Biri Belas" or Sun to be omnipotent benevolent God, used to celebrate Khaddi and other festivals as per the season, they believed that death meant the loss of body and the "aikh" meaning the soul to be a bodiless person who, after leaving the body, maintained contact with relatives. There was provision of ancestor worship but "gotra had not been classified. They believed in the malevolent invisible powers of time, assisted in the development of necromancy in Chhotanagpur. Similarly, the influence of "naads" continued in Oraon religion till about the eighteenth century.

After entering Chhotanagpur, the Oraons confronted the Mundas. By that time, the Mundas had settled down completely in the western area of Chhotanagpur, and Sarna place and the importance of pahans had been established. Some historians like S. C. Roy, Hoffmann, N. Kumar, etc. believe that after entering Chhotanagpur, the Oraons had taken shelter of the Mundas and had accepted their dietary habits and religion, and the Munda people had vacated their hearth and home for them and re-settled in the eastern direction. This matter has been discussed before in detail. Actually, when the Oraons entered Chhotanagpur after crossing the passes in the northwest part of Chhotanagpur, then due to their pressure the Mundas had been forced to flee, leaving behind hearth and home, towards the east and east-south direction. Since in this area a religious arrangement of the Mundas had already been established and the Oraons at that time were in a transitional phase, hence they had no objection to connect with the readymade Sarna place. Compared to the Mundas, the Oraons are more cheerful, social and liberal. Orthodoxy or conservatism cannot be seen in their racial characteristics. The Oraons taught improved agricultural technology to the Mundas and turned their lives towards agriculture instead of eking a livelihood through hunting. For centuries those tribes pursued their livelihood living in the same geographical and financial conditions, as a result of which there was enough intermixing of culture, religion and blood. Since till that time Oraon religion had not developed in the background of Chhotanagpur, therefore most of the rules, regulations and worshipping rituals of the Oraons came to be influenced by the Mundas. In Munda religion, due to contact with the Asurs, the influence of bongas had been easily established, the effect of which could be seen in the original religion of the Oraons wherein najar-gujar and bai-bhak developed into naads. In this way, except for Dharmes and Chala Pachcho, the other deities have been completely accepted from Munda religion in Chhotanagpur. Gradually, the entry of Hindu deities can also be seen in Oraon tribe but most of these deities have apparently been given Oraon identity.

"Naad" means one who harasses; over a period of time, its meaning as ghost which harasses became traditional. This thinking of the Oraons was a result of the bad tendency to put the blame on the activities of "naads" for any common incident. If a thorn pricked the foot of a person walking on a path, then definitely there was a blood-thirsty naad in that area which hid in a thorn and pricked so that it could drink blood. Hence, for the Oraons, it became essential to satisfy the naad of that area by offering it a cock as sacrifice. In Oraon religion, the number of naads was not less than the number of leaves in the forest. There were two categories of naads – wicked naad would be the souls of those dead persons who had faced unnatural death, and normal naad would be the souls of those dead persons who had faced natural death. In Oraon religion there is no place for wicked naads and pahans do not worship them.

In Oraon religion, "pach-baler" have great importance. "Pach-baler" is the ancestral group which always thinks about the well being of the concerned family. Pach baler find a high place in the pantheon- they come after Dharmes and Chala pachcho.

"Pat raja" controls all the naads of the village. In this manner, he protects the village from disease and other disasters. Pat raja's habitation is often on a mountain located on the border of a village. Pat raja had more importance than "Chala Pachcho", but gradually there was a decrease in his power and worship, and he got connected to "desauli" as "desauli pat" or got connected to "khunt naad" as "khunt-pat" and came lower down the hierarchy. Chala pachcho continued to be more worshipful because of her connection to Dharmes. The entry into Oraon religion of "Devi mai" and "Mahadeo" is thought to be the influence of Hindu religion. Temples or idol-worship is not prevalent among the Oraons, but on the border of the village, three-five or seven earthen breast- like lumps are fixed with a trident erected near it, and worship of "Devi mai" is done with flowers, cereals, milk etc for the welfare of the village. Special worship of "Devi mai" is conducted in the month of Sravan. There is no provision to offer sacrifice, but when epidemics spread in the village, then sheep are sacrificed. This place is known as "Devi sthan" (Devi's place) or "Devi manda" (mandap = pavilion). Often "Mahadeo manda" can be found near Devi sthan – Mahadeo is worshipped here and the responsibility for this is mostly on mati, ojha and bhagats.

The entry of Devi mai and Mahadeo in Oraon religion was a strong effort to counter the increasing terror of the naads. Due to contact with the Mundas, the influence of necromancy and witches had started spreading fast, and by the time the Middle Ages came, the institution of ojha and mati which had developed to destroy this terror, gradually started giving more importance to the worship of the power of Hindu God Mahadeo and Devi Mai. The higher level of life style of the Hindu and the magnificent worshipping rituals of Hindu gods and goddesses gave rise to an impression in the Oraon mind that compared to the naads the Hindu gods and goddesses were more powerful. Along with that, the religious legends pertaining to these gods and goddesses successfully imprinted in the Oraon mind the mark of their higher divine power. In this manner, in order to fulfill the requirement of nullifying the increasing anti-religious current of necromancy and witches, the parallel religious current of ojha, mati and bhagats, who dealt with Hindu gods and incantations, developed automatically. The pure food habits and life-style of the bhagats and the sanctity of their worshipping process as also their pious spirit could enable them to form the background of the "Bhagat Andolan" (movement) in Oraon religion.

The influence and extension of naads in Oraon religion are the result of contact with Mundas in Chhotanagpur. Prior to Chhotanagpur, there was an understanding in Oraon religion of destructive invisible powers in the form of "najar-gujar" and "bai-bhak," but their extension took place in Chhotanagpur itself. The Oraons believe that after the body is destroyed due to death, the soul or "ache" of the dead person maintains all relationships as before. According to the religious philosophy of the Oraons, the ancestors of every gotra have their abode in the nether world. After death and the ceremony of "Koha benja," the soul of the dead person is sent to stay among his ancestors in the nether world. The soul of the dead person keeps on roaming in the world till the aforementioned death ceremony is not performed. As per religious rules of the Oraons, the death ceremony is not performed for all dead persons, especially for those whose death is unnatural. Resultantly, the souls of such dead persons keep on roaming as unquenched souls and come to be called wicked naad. In ordinary/common language, such naads are called "ghosts." This understanding is the later on development of Oraon religion.

Among the various ceremonies prevalent in the Oraon race, the three ceremonies of "chhati," marriage and death have special importance. The chhati ceremony enables an infant to be included in the race, marriage ceremony helps the plan of Dharmes for race-extension, and death ceremony sees to the inclusion of the soul among the ancestors living in the nether world. In "koha benja," the "Pulkhi" stone and the "kundi" are used according to gotra or clan. The bones of the dead of one gotra are buried beneath one "pulkhi." "Koha benja" is that death ceremony which means "the great marriage." This is celebrated every year in the month of January-February. It is only after this activity that the soul of the dead can be included within the "Pachbaler."

In Oraon marriages, the bride and groom are selected from outside the gotra. According to Oraon belief, Dharmes has fixed from before the bride and groom couple. Dharmes helps the parents in the search of bride or groom through various good and bad portents. In this manner, marriage is a religious relationship which is fixed as per the desire of Dharmes. It is not a social contract which can be broken at will. Despite this, the Oraons accept as legal, divorce and re-marriage in various circumstances. But due to Hindu influence and various movements, the institution of marriage has speedily developed, and divorce and pre-marital sexual relationship is viewed with disgust by the Oraons.

Dancing, music and tension free life is the racial speciality of Oraons. This characteristic is manifested with full force in the festivals celebrated by them. Dancing and singing are connected to the religious feelings inherent in the root of the festivals. There are chiefly three quintessential points at the root of the festivals:-

(a) Festival in the form of prayer and worship of Dharmes, ancestors, regional gods for requital against oncoming disasters- personal, family and the entire village, domestic animals, agriculture.

(b) Festival and worship of gods and naads to prevent their displeasure.

(c) Festival displaying ingratiation and obligation. These main festivals are Phagu (February-March), Sarhul (March-April), Hariari (June-July), Kadlota (August), Karam (August), Jitiya (August-September), Sohrai (October-November), Kharra Puja (November-December).

The influence of Hindus and Mundas has been seen in the gradual development of these festivals. Most of the festivals of Mundas and Oraons are similar- they originated and developed during their stay in Chhotanagpur.

Hindu influence is apparent on Phagu, Karam and Jitiya, but the religious philosophy of the Oraons is more powerfully entrenched in their basic thought. Hunting and worshipping Chandi, the goddess of hunting, are traditional religious activities of the Oraons. The basis of Phagu festival is "Phagu-sendra" in which Oraon youths go out hunting, but in the Hindu festival of Phagu the basis is burning of Holika. This is a basic difference. The legends of Karma and Jitiya are influenced by Hindu religion and the concerned rituals have mostly been adopted accordingly. We have already discussed this matter. Sohrai festival is celebrated on the new moon night of Kartik. The householder, through established rituals, celebrates this festival for the protection of domestic cattle. In Oraon folk-tale, mention of Oraon woman observing Sohrai festival during their Shahabad migration has been made. It appears that at that time the social condition of the Oraons had not risen above animal husbandry. Although Sohrai festival is related to the cattle rearing life of the Oraons, but apart from animals, Kartik new moon night holds other importance among the Oraons. The new moon night is considered best for initiation and training for witches, necromancers and vaidyas (Ayurved medicine system practitioners). The medicinal herbs and roots collected during the night of the new moon have special power. Hindus believe that the night of Deepawali is the best for learning of necromancy. In Oraon religion, even now the process of development of festivals and fairs is continuing which gradually get connected to various cultural programmes. The development of "Jatra" is one such example.

The two basic tendencies in Oraon religion pertaining to "najar-gujar" and "bai-bhak" were very much encouraged due to contact with the Mundas. Due to unlimited increase in the number of ghost-spirits and wicked naads, the extension of the influence of necromancy and witches got a fillip. On the basis of the strength and high living of the Hindus, a thinking emanated easily in the Oraon mind that compared to their various deities whom they worshipped, the Hindu gods were much more powerful. The character of the Hindu God Mahadeo finds favour with Oraon nature, plus, amongst Hindus, Mahadeo is the God available to everybody; one can find that He is worshipped in all places- village, mountain, highland, cave etc. The Oraons started adopting Mahadeo in order to crush wicked tendencies and to nullify their destructive powers. Prior to the Bhagat movement, the worship of Mahadeo played the main role in the development of the institution of matis, sokhas and ojhas. During the course of training given by matis and ojhas in the role of preceptor to many disciples, especially in a closed meditation chamber where initiation, incantation and singing of religious hymns took place, due to the encouragement received, a disciple having a sensitive soul would get up in a manical condition and run into the forest. As per the belief of the Oraons, during his lonely stay in the jungle, the disciple would receive the beneficence of Mahadeo, and when he returned, he would be credited of having become a "sidh bhagat" (a pious devotee who has obtained supernatural powers) in the village and nearby villages. Since, as per belief of the Oraons, naads were responsible for diseases, therefore they would come from far off places to that bhagat to get themselves cured of those diseases. The bhagat maintained purity in lifestyle and food habits. In this manner, there was an increase of another kind of bhagat who used to be worshippers of "bhui phoot Mahadeo." The bhagat used to have a dream that in a particular place, Mahadeo was present in the land or even above it and that he should worship Him. After spreading word regarding the dream, the bhagat would recover the rounded stone lump of Mahadeo from that place and re-establish it in his own courtyard by constructing a platform. The worshippers of Bhui-phoot Mahadeo also led lives of purity, and instead of joining ordinary Oraons for meals, they would obtain uncooked cereals. Apparently the development of Mahadeo bhagats started in the ninth-tenth century A. D. In mid fifteenth-sixteenth century, the Krishna Bhakti of Chaitanya Mahaprabhu could not influence the Oraons to that extent as it influenced the Mundas of Panch Pargana, but the influence of the Kabir Panthi sect was impressive on the lifestyle of the Oraons of Western Ranchi.

In the sixteenth century, after the return of Chhotanagpur king Durjanshal from his incarceration at Gwalior, the whole area was swept by a revolutionary wave in social, economic and religious life. After having seen the magnificence and other activities of various kings of India, Durjanshal increased the presence of religious Brahmins and Kshatriyas in his court and Chhotanagpur, and also organised various festivals and religious functions. Such organisation successfully brought about revolutionary change in the religious thinking of the Mundas and Oraons. This directional change became valuble in the religious movement of the coming centuries.

The followers of Kabir entered the western part of Ranchi in the early decades of the nineteenth century. They had come to the districts of Raipur and Bilaspur of Madhya Pradesh and had influenced the Oraons with their preachings. The Kabir panthis had advised the Oraons to refrain from killing creatures, and to abstain from meat and intoxicating liquor. They had opposed idol worship and had stressed upon the worship of Param Brahma – God. They dispelled the superstitions of ghosts, spirits and necromancy. They preached about the greatness of the guru preceptor, and explained to the Oraons that having faith in the guru and conducting oneself according to his preaching would result in man's well being. Their guru used to come from Chaknoori Math of Patna town, and would initiate the Oraons by making them wear necklets of tulsi beads. The Oraon Kabir Panthis are in good number in western Simdega of Ranchi, Gumla and Ghagra. Their living and food habits are pure and pious.

The rise of the Tana bhagats in the second decade of the twentieth century is a mentionable chapter in the history of Oraon religion. The Tana bhagats have played an important role in improving the religious, social and economic condition of the Oraons. They have spread word in their society that the ghosts, spirits, naads and other gods whom they have been worshipping for centuries, have not helped them to improve their lot. As against this, they who had been people of a developed race, have been fully deva stated having come under the influence of those exploitative gods and ghosts- they have become lowly from the social point of view, and economically weak. Actually, those gods are not gods of the Oraons- they are bongas of the Mundas whom the Oraons have allowed entry in their religion. According to the Tana Bhagats, the original religion of the Oraons is "Kudukh religion" from which the Oraons have diverted. The Tana Bhagats exhorted the Oraons to return to their Kudukh religion. The main points of the movement of the Tana Bhagats are as follows:-

(1) Banishment of all the ghosts, spirits, bongas and naads, all gods imported from Munda religion.
(2) Leading a normal and pious life by distancing oneself from hadiya, meat-eating, sacrifice, worship at Sarna place, pre-marital sex, jewellery, etc.
(3) Discarding the ancient marriage process, and worshipping one God Mahadeo in whom Dharmes manifests Himself.

Apart from the Bhagat movement, the purification drive of the Arya Samaj, started in 1894, the efforts of Sanskrit Vihar to attract the tribes towards Hindu way of living and religion through various programmes, the efforts of "Divine light mission" of Bal Yogeshwar, especially in Simdega and Gumla areas of preaching to the tribals the principles of self-development through devotion, etc., were some such efforts which aimed at not only stopping the conversion of tribals to other religions and to wean away the converted by re-purifying them and bringing them back to the racial fold, but also for their religious uplift. These movements have directly and indirectly affected the Munda and Oraon tribes in some places, and there has been appreciable improvement in their religious beliefs and life-style. The expansion of education and the extension of industries has increased the speed of reforms.

Comparative Historical Survey of Sarna Religion of the Mundas and Oraons

The Asurs used to live in Chhotanagpur prior to the entry of the Mundas, and they used to smelt mud in order to make iron-that was their main profession. The name of Asurs, along with the Mundas and other tribes, figures as Kol. Hence, the Asurs and Mundas had the same roots, but compared to the Asurs, the Munda race was more refined in food habits and religious thinking. After defeating the Asurs, when the Mundas settled down, then due to more dependence on agriculture than hunting, there arose a requirement of land. They started clearing the forests in order to set up their villages and retrieve farm land. In the process, the Mundas left alone a small portion of forest land just beside the village, which they bounded. This was because as per their religious belief, the "hatu-bongako" living in the bounded area would protect the village from future disasters, diseases and other divine troubles. After a period of time, the place of habitation of hatu-bongako came to be called the Sarna place. The Asur Avdaan indicates that the Mundas had adopted in their religion some powerful regional spirits of Asur origin (later called gods) and called them "bongas." Among these bongas, Chandi bonga became established in the Sarna place and gradually came to be worshipped by the pahans as "Sarna burhi" and "Sarna Devi." Apart from the Sarna place, consecutive arrangement of establishing bongas in mountains, rivers, ponds, valleys etc. was started in Munda religion, and worship of various bongas started for good agriculture, protection of cattle-wealth. Oda bongako in the form of ancestors was established in the "ading" inside the house. All these bongas used to protect the village and family from future disasters and diseases, and used to protect the Mundas from agricultural loss and troubles befalling the family. The Mundas used to regularly worship them and offer cock-sacrifice to them as per law laid down by Singbonga. All these bongas were friendly and contained a portion of the supreme God Singbonga within them. This is the reason that those students who have seriously studied these facts, they believe Munda religion to be multitheistic. Over a span of time, there was an unprecedented increase in the number of bongas. Munda life became tortured with the increase and terror of the wicked bongas from incident to incident, place to place. The friendly bongas got dragged in with these wicked bongas and Munda religion came to be called "animism" which is not the real picture of Munda religion. The bongas created by Singbonga are gods.

When the Munda tribe was nearly getting settled in Chhotanagpur, at that time the Oraon group, after having been defeated in Rohtasgarh and fleeing to a safer place, entered Chhotanagur through the Saharghatiya pass of western Lohardaga. Since the entry of the Oraons had been from the west and the Mundas had also settled in the west, therefore the Oraons had confrontation with the Mundas; the Mundas left their hearth and home, cultivable fields and meadows and the Sarna place, and moved towards the east and south-east in flight. Due to closeness with the Aryans, the Oraons had a more refined and developed life-style, food-habits, and knowledge of agriculture. They used to believe "Biri-Belas" i.e. the Sun, as God or the Supreme Being. They had also protected and brought their memories of "Ram-Ma- Sita-Haluman." The Oraons are very simple in temperament, hard working and of liberal nature. They did not destroy the place of worship of the Mundas- they accepted them as they were, with the difference that in the Sarna place as per their traditional and religious belief they established "Chalapachcho Devi." Similarly, the Oraons established, respectively, pat-Raja on the mountains bordering the village, Darha-tanr or Darha-desauli on tanr (upland), Chandi Devi for good hunting and protection from wild animals, Pach Baler in the form of ancestors for the protection of the family. They are all friendly gods. Gradually, in Oraon religion, just like the bongas there was an excess of naads, and it became very natural for the Oraons to connect some destructive naad or ghost-spirit with every incident or place. The Bhagat-sect believes that the influence of ghosts, spirits was imported from the Mundas, and the original religion of the Oraons is "kudukh religion." But in Chhotanagpur the most popular, most worshipped and chief goddess Chala Pachcho of the Oraons, getting connected to the Sarna place as Sarna Devi, and nearly all community religious activities of Oraon religion being performed at the Sarna place, gradually made Oraon religion famous as "Sarna-Dharam" (religion). As time went by, the Oraons crowded Chhotanagpur and expanded. In the first century A.D., when Chhotanagpur's first king Phani Mukut Rai was coronated, the Oraons had completely settled down in Chhotanagpur. The Oraons had also helped the Mundas in selecting Phani Mukut Rai as king. Over a space of time, when the Mundas started asserting their right over Phani Mukut Rai who was of non-Munda origin, then the Oraons spread a story. According to the story, Phani Mukut Rai was of Oraon origin and his paternal grandfather Lakhan Bhagat used to stay at Sutiyambey.

Since the Mundas and Oraons shared the same environment, and faced the same geographical and economic conditions, there was not only sufficient religious, cultural and social exchange but also inter-mingling of blood. Since the racial quality of the Oraons was of being simple and liberal, and the Mundas were by nature harsh and fundamentalist and had been living in Chhotanagpur prior to the Oraons, hence the influence of Mundas has fallen on religious activities, institutions and procedures of worship of the Oraons. In addition, many festivals and ceremonies of the Mundas have influenced the development of these institutions of the Oraons. Despite this, however, the religious faith and understanding acquired prior to coming to Chhotanagpur have continued to work for the development of all the institutions of the Oraons. This is the reason that the gods, festivals, ceremonies etc. of the Mundas and Oraons which appear to be the same superficially, seem different when explored in depth. Similar confusion related to "Sarna Dharam" prevails among most scholars. Some historians even claim that the Oraons took shelter with the Mundas and adopted their religion and culture, but this is not true. Basically, the difference between the Sarna religion of the Mundas and the Sarna religion of the Oraons is the same as the difference in understanding of Singbonga and Dharmes and their form.

Singbonga versus Dharmes

Singbonga is the Almighty God of the Mundas while Dharmes is of the Oraons. The development of both Gods took place in Chhotanagpur. The historical development of these Gods and other gods has already been discussed. We have seen that before coming to Chhotanagpur, the Munda people had been under the influence of some "sun-cult." The meaning of "sing" is sun and that of "bonga" is residence. Due to the analyses of Christian missionaries, the word "bonga" gradually but firmly came to mean ghosts-spirits. Hence, in "Singbonga" the presence of the word "bonga" takes away that divinity which is present in the word "Dharmes." The Oraon tribe of pre-Dravidian origin had "Biri Belas" as their God-Biri Belas transformed into "Dharmes" in Chhotanagpur. The understanding of Dharmes coincides with "Bhagwan" of the Hindus. In hierarchy, Sun or Sun God comes below them. In many traditional religious stories, Sita and Hanuman have been depicted along with Dharmes due to which flashes of Dasrathi Ram can be seen in Dharmes. As against this, at times the name of Parvati has been mentioned along with Singbonga due to which Singbonga appears to be close to Mahadeo. The name of Parvati has been used to denote "first witch", too. This gives the feeling that in the form and character of Singbonga, the bonga element is more strong compared to that of Dharmes. If the meaning of "bonga" had not been twisted then Singbonga would have been equivalent to the Indian vedic sun from whom Vishnu etc. Gods have emanated.

Other Gods

In Munda religion, all the other gods developed in Chhotanagpur as regional gods on the orders of Singbonga. The "bonga" element is to be found in the names and nature of all these gods. Some examples, Burubonga or the god living on the hill, Ikir bonga or the god living in deep waters, Chandi bonga or the god living in the Sarna place (gradually developed as Sarna Devi), Oda bongako or ancestor god, etc. In Oraon religion, Chala Pachcho had developed prior to entry into Chhotanagpur. The background of "pach baler" had been prepared till Rohtasgarh, but it developed in Chhotanagpur. Pat Raja, Darha Desauli, Chandi Pahar, Chhappar Burhiya, Baranda Pachcho, Garha-Dhorha or Chatur seeman the development of such gods took place in Chhotanagpur. Due to Hindu influence, such gods and goddesses as Mahadaniya, Mahadeo, Devi Mai, Chandi etc. have entered Oraon religion.

In Mundari language, "bonga" is supposed to be masculine. Although Singbonga had made the Asur widows bongas, they however are supposed to be masculine after becoming bonga. Among Oraons, both gods and goddesses are prevalent. The entry of Hindu gods and goddesses among Oraons has been more than among Mundas.

Festivals

Living in the past millennia within the same environment, there has been sufficient religious and cultural exchange between the Mundas and Oraons. As a result, most of their festivals and community and religious activities are observed in a similar manner. Yet, some festivals have developed on the basis of the religious beliefs of these tribes.

The Main Festivals of Mundas

Mage - Phagu - Ba or Sarhul - Hone Ba – Batauli – Karma - Dasai.

Kolom – Singbonga – Jomnawa – Sohrai – Sosobonga.

The Main Festivals of Oraons

Phagu – Sarhul or Khaddi or Khekhel Benja - Hariari – Kadlota – Karam.

Jitiya – Sohrai – Kharra Puja.

In Mage festival, the servants appointed for agriculture are given a kind of annual contract that they would work for the whole year and how much cereal and other facilities they would get as wages. Such contract is given a religious basis and confirmed. The development of this festival is to be found among the Mundas because most of the Oraons themselves look after agricultural work.

Most sociologists believe in the influence of Holi of the Hindus on "Phagu," but although this festival has taken the covering of Holi festival of the Hindus, it is basically a tribal festival. The philosophy of Holika Dahan cannot be found in it, instead, "phagu sendra" is celebrated in which Chandi, the goddess of hunting of Mundas and Oraons, is worshipped and the youth go to the forest for hunting. Apart from burning some wood and dried grass, no form of Holika can be seen in it. On the contrary, the "Asur-Avdaan" gets reflected when the young men taken straw in their mouths and cawing like crows move round the burning pile in circles.

Compared to the Mundas, the Oraons celebrate Sarhul with more gusto. It is basically a festival of the Oraons. Sarhul and Sohrai are the two festivals which Oraons used to celebrate even before coming to Chhotanagpur.

The Oraon tribe celebrates "Kadlota" festival for the protection of the standing crop. In this festival, in order to ward off "najar gujar" and "bai bhak" and other probable troubles, the branches of the poisonous "bhelwa" tree (cashew) are planted amidst the crop fields. This festival developed in Chhotanagpur when the destructive influence of the naads or wicked souls had increased.

Karam festival apparently developed due to Hindu influence. Among Oraons, mothers observe "jitiya" festival for protection of their children. It is a complete adoption in Oraon form of "Jiutiya" prevalent in Hindu society. The Mundas do not observe this festival. Most of the festivals are related to agriculture and cattle and their protection, and all have developed in Chhotanagpur.

"Sosobonga" is organised by the Mundas for the protection of family and home from ghosts and spirits. This function is held mostly by those Mundas who have a fear of being hit in the family by necromancy.

Study of the historical development of the festivals of Mundas and Oraons shows that most of them have developed in Chhotanagpur and these are related to protection and promotion of agriculture, cattle, hunting and family in which efforts to protect from najar-gujar and wicked bongas or ghosts have also been a part. In some festivals the Hindu influence can be seen. Compared to the Mundas, various types of dances and songs have been absorbed more in Oraon festivals and these are typical of the nature of the festivals.

Ceremonies

The life of both tribes, Munda and Oraon, is bound from birth to death by various ceremonies of which chhatti, marriage and death ceremonies are most important.

The Main Ceremonies of Mundas

Garasi bonga (for the protection of the child in the womb)- nal chhedan-chhatti-namkaran- sootam toll (tying of the kardhani on the waist)- lutur-tukai (piercing of ears)- arandi (marriage)- shav or dah sanskar.

The Main Ceremonies of Oraons

Chhatti or purification- name pijna- juro era- jokhe- erpa- vivah- mrityu sanskar or koha benja.

In both Munda and Oraon tribes similarity can be found in most ceremonies from the viewpoint of intention and procedure, namely, chhatti ceremony, namkaran or name pinjna (naming ceremony), arandi or vivah sanskar (marriage ceremony) etc. In Oraon tribe, juro-era meaning ceremony of tying the hair in a bun is carried out symbolising the entry of girls into adolescence. Similarly there is also "Jokhe-erpa" ceremony. Dhumkuria is prevalent in Oraon society. In the village, dhumkuria is a building or a cottage where unmarried young girls and boys assemble, and they are given training regarding married and family life. This ceremony is carried out during the entry into dhumkuria.

Differences are to be found in the death ceremony of the Munda and Oraon tribes. According to the religious philosophy of both Munda and Oraon tribes, man is always connected to the soul of the dead i.e. the "rowa" or "ache." But Oraons have the concept of their ancestors being established in "patallok" or nether world, and on this basis they bury the bones of the dead beneath the "pulkhi" stone in the "kundi" (water body), and once a year the community function of "koha benja" is observed in which the souls of the dead are made to be assimilated with the ancestral group. Arranging an annual death ceremony together for all the dead of the year is not only the religious but also the racial speciality of the Oraons. No such annual function is held among the Mundas.

The Mundas house their ancestors in a protected place at home, called "ading." In Munda religion, in order to establish the ancestors and to keep them involved in happiness and sorrow of the family, they have been given place in the "ading" which is within the home.

Gotra or kili

In both Munda and Oraon tribes, gotra or kili is taken into consideration. In Munda tribe, kili started on a special occasion, which can be termed a historical incident, which happened in Sutiyambe with the consent of "ikkis parha." Gradually, with the increase in population, the number of kili and totem is also increasing. There is some story or the other connected to nearly every kili and totem.

In Oraon tribe, the development of gotra is not connected to any historical incident. It has developed naturally by itself. Along with gotra, totem also finds mention in some story or the other. Till date, amongst Mundas and Oraons, in either tribe more than a hundred kili or gotra have developed. During the time of study it was found that in one or two kilis there was change of form and mutation. The people of Pargana Sonpur village Chiur and Chaldano, had been of "bando" (wild cat) kili, but most of them, due to a special incident, had gone and settled in Bingaon and were adopted in the "herenj" "Kili" by the parha of that place. After some time, when they returned to Sonpur, the members of the "bando" kili prevented the family from performing last rites of the dead in the sasandiri of the kili. But this kind of religious problem is an exception in the history of gotra or kili. Example regarding change in form of gotra can be seen among the half-Hinduised Mundas of Panch Pargana. Although in this area Mundas specially belonging to "nag," "tau," "sanga" gotra are to be found but the Mundas of "sandi" (bull/bullock) gotra gradually declare themselves to be of shandilya gotra. Amongst Hindus, this gotra is connected to the saint Shandilya. There is a good number of "shandilyas" in the eastern region of Panch Pargana.

Although one or two examples of change of form and mutation can be found, yet due to increase in population, sub-division and part-division in gotras and kilis have happened.

Annexures

Annexure - 1

Manowa Kob: Dobra Gonom

Once upon a time, Chintamani gave a pot of water to her husband Manu to brush his teeth. Manu saw a small fish in the water which was telling him, "Manu, you save me and I will also save you one day." Manu became quite surprised on hearing the words of the small fish. Manu asked, "How do I save you? O fish, and you will be able to save me from which difficulty?" The fish said, "So long as I do not become big, it is very frightful for me because the fish eat up the small fry, hence you keep me in a pitcher. When I grow a bit then you release me in the pond. And when I become big then you take me to a river. When the flood comes then you make a boat. The whole world will drown in that flood and all human beings will be destroyed-only you will be saved."

After listening to the fish, Manu did as he was told. That very year a terrible flood came. The fish held aloft Manu's boat on its horns. The whole world drowned. The water level rose above the high mountains. For fifty days the Earth remained submerged, all creatures died, only those two remained.

When the flood waters receded, Manu became very anxious as to how flora and fauna would be restored on this earth. He built a platform for the worship of God and offered sacrifice. Thereafter he asked for boon from God.

God became pleased with him and restored flora and fauna on this earth. Manu had eight children of whom four were sons and four daughters. When they grew up, they married each other. All were given separate work to do. The eldest son was called Munda, the second Rora, the third Manka and the youngest son was called Sodto. After Manu, the children of these sons peopled the entire country.

Annexure - 2

The Creation

Prior to Creation, there was water everywhere. Singbonga was in deep thought regarding the Creation. At first He created the turtle, and thereafter He created the crab and the earthworm respectively. He ordered all three to bring mud from the floor of the original sea. Only the turtle was successful in bringing mud from the sea-floor. Singbonga made "ote Disum." (Beautiful country) with this mud. He grew various trees, plants and herbs on it. Thereafter Singbonga created birds and animals of various shapes and sizes which started roaming the Earth and making noise. After that a very memorable incident happened. The "Hur" bird laid an egg. Out of this egg a boy and a girl, first man and woman (tota hadam-tota burhi) emerged. They were the first parents of the Horo Honko (Mundas).

This first couple had no knowledge of sexual relationship. Singbonga taught them how to make Ili (rice wine-hadiya). After drinking ili they both became intoxicated, and from them three sons, named Munda, Nanka and Rora, were born and their offsprings spread in the whole world. This incident happened in Azamgarh.

Special

This is the reason why the Munda people try to save turtles from being killed.

- According to the belief of the Mundas, the Hur bird lays its egg on swampy land, and it lays only one egg in its entire life time.
- The Munda people take oath with an egg in the hand. This custom confirms their belief that their race emerged from an egg.
- Azamgarh is a district in Uttar Pradesh. On the basis of this folk lore, S. C. Roy has tried to prove that the Mundas went from Azamgarh to Rohtasgarh and thereafter to Chhotanagpur, but this is not historically proved.
- Ili or rice wine has so much importance in Munda life and religion that no religious activity can be completed without ili.
- In the religious story of "Maha Pralaya" (great annihilation) there is mention of four sons and four daughters of Manu through whom human kind spread in this world. These four sons are Munda, Rora, Manka and Sodto. In the description of the Creation, three sons have been mentioned.

Annexure - 3

Asur Avdaan

MUNDA DHARMGATHA

Original in Munda Language

Aaho Singbonga Raja Devi kuwari
Amag-aa dishum do, amag-aa gamay do
Bilkan gay do, harub kan gay do
Purbo kona re, pachimi kona re
Utro kona re, dekhino kona re
Amag-aa sirijan amag-aa upojan.

Aaho gomke, aaho chomke
Lel nam taile, chin nam taile
Akasi pidhi re. tirasi badire
Baaro bhai asur ko tero bhai devta ko
Sipud tan gay ko, lebed tan gay ko,
Alang tan gay do, ayur tan gay do
Sirm dudugar oteyo kobansi
Chilang chikai, mere lang rikab.
Date ho sirabiyon, dase hi sira sang
Sone kera ddunti rupe kera taini
Chawnra bownra bandi ja bisiri
Sengail gam hit. bandi jete khiti
Man tiang lekowayi bujhatiang lekow.

Singbonga Raja Devi kuwari
kaji ked gay kiang, bakann ked gay kiang
abain hale tabu, lang chede lokhon
abain hale tabu, bowo-a chede kujru
abu-aa disumre, abua gawam re
aiem betekaw duku aad balay tana
baaro bhai hasur ko, tero bhai devta ko
nid- singi ko sipud tan gay do
singi-satub ko lebed tan gay do
ailang tan gay do, ayur tan gay do
upal ba pukhuri, anjed tan gay do
tadya ba bandel road tan gay do

Mar lang seneya, bharlang virid
Seno jan geya kiang birid jan gay kiang
Hudhiyange durang d-aa marang gay during d-aa
Hudhiyange ranchi buru, marang gay ranchi buru
Teb-aa led gay kiang seter led gay kiang
Nere chiy baabu nere chim do.
Heya dadaa, heya bahiya
Nere gay di rna, nere gay tha kid maa.
Purwo lelemey, pachimo lelemey
Utro lelemey, dakhino lelemey
Soben tai marang maa, soben te pur-aa maa.
Hende ni-aa ko ornama hende ni-aa aath mein
Ar-aa ni-aa ko omama ar-aa aath mein
Kabra ni-aa ko omara kabra ni aath mein
A talang om mein pundit e pundi sim
A talang ched mein pundt te pundi meram.
Marang jo betay, ranchi buru re

Asur ja hon ko, asur ja gan ko
Kako manatiang jan, kako bujhatiang jan
Kasra kodh do toro kodh do
Tar teeray ko sab ki-aa gay do
Lutukum hadham kiang lutukum budhai kiang
Tar teeray ko sab ki-aa gay do
Alopay idiya, alopay oriya
Pati ja ba ba do, sudhtaja koday do
Din- aa gay horo jad ini-aajangi jad
Mente derang kiang kajiya ko tan do
Mente derang kiang kudum ko Tan do
Hasur ja hon ko kaa geko mantiang jan
Hasur ja gan ko ka geko bujhatiang jan
Kasra kodh do taro kodh do
Or ki-aa gay ko, idi ki-aa gay ko
Gail bar kodh hisi bar kudhi
Teba li-aa gay ko, seter li-aa gay ko
Land tan gay ko, rasik tan gay ko
Hasur ja hon ko hasur ja gan ko
Kupuli tan geya ko kapaji tan gay ko
Chilikabu bongai mareybu pawdhaye.

Kasra kcdh do taro kodh do
Kij ked gay do kudum ked gay do
Bonga dope bonga e pawdha dope powdhaye
Nawage ganidaki, nawage bitaal
Pundi merog urte chapuw tabu dabepe.
Dind ma kudhi kiang, jalmay kodh kiang
Sipude kaking lebed kakiang.
Gail bar kodha re hisi bar kudhi re
Kasra kodh do taro kodh do
Bolo jan gay do, sodho jan gay do
Kodha bitrate, kudhi atomaate
Kaji tan gay do, jagar tan gay do
Aema nid, aema singi,
Sipudiang pe ho chapadiang pe ho
Aema nid, aema singi
Howa jan geya do, puravjan gay do
Dinda kudhi kiang jalgay kodh kiang
Nawa chatu da-te, uli sudh sakmate
Hirchi ki-aa gaye ko, tipri ki-aa gay ko
Kasra kodh do toro kodh do
Naari hor te ghera hor te
Nir udhudh lenai, seter udhang lenai
Sonage Samadom hirage bowra
Lota do do, thadi do, chipado dubado
Sab udhang kedai seter udhang lenai
Niti-miki tan do, jak jak tan
Lelki-aa gay ko chin-aa ki-aa geya ko.
Re-aa jai gaye ko chin-aa ki-aa geya ko.
Kasra kodh do toro kodh do
Kaji ked gaye ko, bakang ked gay ko
Alope regi, aalope rachaing
Apedo hag sangi, apedo boy sangi
Gail bail bar kodha, hisi bar kudhi do
Sona te chandi te paray kan gay ko
Heratay rupatey, tunsia kan gay ko
Aau jom geya pe, seter jom gay pe.
Hasur ja hon ko hasur ja gan ko
Gail war kodha re, hisi bar kudhi re
Nil' bolo jan ko, nir' ader ked ko

Kodh bari kodh ko, bolo jan geya ko
Kudhi baar kodh ko, bagge jan geya ko
Kasra kodh do toro kodh do
Kaji ked geya do, toro kodh do
Hey bonga juguni mar telang lei kom
Ukuwan danang kan soben ko leI kom
Baago juguni lei tan gay do
Nele henetey lei tan gay do
Lei nam tae do, chin-aa nam tae do
Hey baabu kasra, hey baabu toro
Naye derang nat-aa re, ni derang nat-aa re
Ukuvukan geyaye, danang kan geyaye.
Kasra kodh do toro kodh do
Sen nam kiyaye, seter nam kiyaye.
Kajiy tanay, kudarnayi tanay.
Am ho hag, am ho boy
Sona samdom, hira bowra
Kako omam, kako chedarn
Amo bolo me, sodho jan geyaye
Bolo jan geyaye, sodho jan geyaye
Kasra kodh do toro kodh do
Sana didi do, rupa kowa do.
Kajiy tana do, bankdhai tana do.
Koter ukuvakan jayta re danang kan
Soben ko daindha korn, joto ko khojar kom
Sona didi do, rupa kowa do.
Dainda tan gay do, khojar tan gaye do
Lel nam tae do, chin-aa nam tae do
Haniy kasra, haniy toro
Jul pidhigiray atiritey-aa haruwa kan.
Sen nam kiyaye, seter nam kiyaye
Bora re-aa sajuki gadh re atu ki-aa
Atu jan goway, buwaal jan gayeya.
Kasra kodh do to ro kodh do
Hasur ja kudhi ko hasur ja budhi ko
Kajiyko tan do, toro kodh do
Marna sipudepe, marna lebede pe
Sipud jad geya ko, lebedh jadh gaye ko.
Kodha bitrate, kudhi atomaate

Aayumo-aa tan do, ateno-aa tan do
Ayang tan geya ko, ab tan gey ko
Ra-aa tan gay ko, iyam tan geya ko
Hasur ja kudhi ko, ayum ked gay ko
Hasur ja kudhi ko, aten ked gay ko
Boro tan gay ko, chiri tan gay ko
Alay kasra alay toro
Alay-aa kodh ko, ley-aa hug ko
Chiko chik tan mere ki rik tan
Ra-aa tan gay ko, rumbule tan gay ko
Alope rasya, alepe rumbule
Hug ko sangiy, boy ko sangiy
Sona gay samdom, hira gay bowra
Repe-aa tan gay ko, racha tan gay ko
Udhdho-aa gay ko, setero-aa gay ko
Mente derang hoy, kajiy ko tan do
Mente derang hoy, kajiy ko tan do
Mente derang hoy, kudum ko tana do
Naari hora te, ghera hora te mayom
Mayorn ge lingi tan
Kirum gay siring tan
Hasur ja khudi ko, hasur ja budhi ko
Ra-aa tana gay ko, iyam tana gay ko
Kasra kodh do toro kodh do
Kaji ked gay do gen ked gay do
Mera gay mayom mera gay kiroom
Sangi hag tekowa, sangi boy tekom
Paan ko jaam tan kasaili ko nabay tan
Be-aajad geya ko, thu jad gay ko
An gay lingi tan, 'ain gay paring tana.
Dobaa chatu da-aa te, hes sakam te
Hirchi keda ko tirpi ked ko
Gail bar kodha, hisi bar kudhi
Ot-aa keda gay ko, ni-aaked gay ko
Jang te jauge, mukute mukugay
Lei ked gay ko, chin-aa ked gay ko
Hasur ja kudhi ko, hasur ja budhi ko.
Ratan gay ko, iyamtan gay ko.
Singbonga raja, devi kuwari

Bari bidiya ked, teri chaya ked.
Tudhi sutamte, badi bayar te
Sirma tey rakab, tan, chetan tea senoa tan.
Hasur ja kudhi ko, hasur ja budhi ko.
Ra- aa tan gay ko, iyam tan gay ko.
Singbonga raja devi kuwari
Baari bidiya ked, teri chayan ked
Tudhi sutarn te, badi bayar te
Sirma taye rakab, tan, chetan te-aa a seno-aa tan.
Hasur ja kudhi ko.hasur ja budhi ko
Ti reko sab ki-aa kat rekho rach-aa ki-aa
Kaji tan gay ko, ajirtan gay ko
Aley-aa apsul, aley-aa jopoton
Udub tukalem, chundul tukalern
Mente derang ko, kijiy tan do
Mente derang ko, baknaye tan do.
Singbonga raja, devi kuwari
Kijiy ko tan do, bakdhanko tana do
Kul dutam ken e, kul darann ken
Kagepe manaati, kagepe bujhaati
Alege singbonga alege marang devta
Mente pe kaji ked, mente pe bakkan ked
Singbonga raja, devi kuwari
Rach-aagidhi jad ko, hudum gidhi jad ko
Gadh re dhora re, doba re, ikir re
Sarana re, buru re, bir re, kandar re
Uyu-aa jan keya ko, bati jan gaye ho.
Buru re uyu-aa jani-aa buru bong jan do
Ikir re uyu-aa jani-aa ikir bong jan do
Dobare uyu-aa jani-aa nage era jan do
Sama re uyu-aa jani-aa chandi bonga jan do.
Inku asul nang, inku jonotan nang
Hatu tal re pandh hone-a a do ki-aa
Disum tal re sokha hone-aa a jogaw ki-aa.
Hasur ja kudhi ko, hasur ja budhi ko.
Kajiy ko tan do, kudum ko tan do
Kaji pe ayum re, bakkan pe aten re
Asulo-aa gay pe joton-aa gay pe
Sinbonga raja, devi kuwari

Tudhi sutam te, badi vayar te
Rakab jan gayay, chetanen jan geyaye
Upalba pukhuri, tadhay ba bandel
Pere-aa jan gaye ko jadhang jan geya do
Gacheyo, nirichastha, sudh, jan geya do.

Tasad ja runag ornaan jana gay do.
Chariyo prithi, chariyo kana
Manawa hon ko, jeev jantu ko
Chene- mipurud, chairya chun-gani
Sobena ko bugin jan, jato ko suku jan
Soben ko uang tan, ko paam tan.
Singbonga raja, devi kuwari
Disum taabu do, bipati tabu do
Wai rudh ke do, sughadh rudh ked do
Duku tabu do bipati tabu do
Seno-aa jan gay do, nir' jan gaye do
Hising chaint soben bu bage-aa ka
Hag ko boya ko niral butain ka
Mente derang ko japgar tan do
Mente derang ko kapaji tan do

Asur Avdaan
From Munda religious tales
Translated in to English from Munda Language

O God, O master.
We have seen, we have identified .
In eighty four plains, in eighty three uplands.
Twelve Asur brothers and thirteen brother gods.
Whiffing, blowing with bellows.
Flames are appearing, the bellows are being applied.
The sky is stormy, the fog is spreading over the earth.
What do we do ? How do we live ?
O bring siraviya, O bring sirasanga,
A "dooti" of gold and a "taindri" of silver
Chowra-Bhowra, Badiya Visiri
Seeds of fire and cultivation of fire
We will go and pacify, we will go to put it out.

O God king, O Divine Virgin
God has said, God has told-
O brother Lokon Lang-Pakshi, O Kajru Wocho Pakshi,
In our country, in our world
We are experiencing great sorrow, we are facing great torture.
In eighty one uplands, in eighty three plains
Twelve brother Asurs and thirteen brother gods,
Day and night are whiffing, day and night are blowing with bellows.
We are feeling the heat of the flames, we are being scorched.
The lotus pond, the tank of water lilies
Are drying up, are being heated,
Let us go, let us get up. They went away, they got up
In smaller Duranda, in bigger Duranda
They went away, they reached
The little mountain of Ranchi, the big mountain of Ranchi
They reached there, they got down there
O gentleman, what will you keep here ?
O grandfather, we will keep it here, O grandfather we will leave it here
Look at the east, look at the west, too
Look also at the north, look at the south, too
We will welcome you
We will complete everything
If black people are given, then bring them along
If red people are given, then also take them
If "Kavra" is given, then take the "kavra"
Give me the white cocks
Give me the white he- goat
He left his elder brother on Ranchi Mountain.
The boys of the Asurs, the children of the Asurs
Do not accept, they do not understand
The eczema boy, your son
They have caught one of his hands, they have clutched his hand
Lutkum burha, lutkum burhiya
Have caught the other hand, have clutched the other hand
Do not take him away, do not snatch him away
The paddy on the reed mat, the "madua" on the stone
This is God, he is the protector
They were saying like this, they were telling like this

The boys of the Asurs, the children of the Asurs,
Did not pay heed at all did not hear anything
The eczema boy, your boy
Was dragged away by them, snatched away by them
Twelve mansions, twenty two furnaces (where they were)
There they took him, there they reached him
They are very happy, they are laughing very much
The boys of the Asurs, the children of the Asurs
Are questioning him, talking to him
How do we worship him ? How do we sacrifice him ?
The eczema boy, your boy
Said to them, told them
Let me say something, Let me tell something
You will give sacrifice ? You will offer worship ?
The blowing with the bellows should be anew, the whiffing should be a new,
The bellows should be covered by white hide
Virgin girl virgin boy
Should do the whiffing, should blow the bellows.
In twelve mansions, in twenty two furnaces
Then he entered, then he merged himself.
From inside the mansion, from inside the furnace
He says, he tells –
Whiff for seven days, blow the bellows for seven nights
The seven days were completed, seven nights were over
The virgin girl, the virgin boy
Took water from a new pitcher, and through new mango leaves
Sprinkled on the mansion, sprinkled on the furnace,
The eczema boy, your boy
Through the passageway of the drain, through the path way of the boundary
Came out running, ran outside
With golden plate, a diamond pot and bowl held
In his hand
Came outside, emerged
Shining and glittering
He is being seen as such, felt as such
People are looting him, they are snatching from him,
The eczema boy, your boy

Started saying, started telling-do not loot, do not snatch
You are so many brothers, you are so many kinsmen
Twelve mansions, twenty two furnaces
Are filled with gold and silver, diamonds and silver
Go and bring them, enter them and take them out.
The Asur boys, the Asur children
In the twelve mansions, in the twenty two furnaces
Did they run into and entered them quickly
All the men entered, all the males went inside
The eczema boy, your boy
Started telling them, started saying
O firefly, go and see
While under cover, look at every one,
The firefly started observing, started looking here and there
She espied one, she identified one
O Eczema gentleman, O gentleman
Look over there, see that side
See how they are hiding, see how they are concealing
Eczema boy, your boy
Went there, reached there
Started saying, telling them
O brother, O friend
Gold and silver, diamonds and silver
They will not give you, they will not distribute to you
You also go and enter, you also find access
They also should enter, they also should go and sit,
Eczema boy, your boy
To the golden vulture, to the silver crow
He is saying, he is telling
See whether any body is hiding, whether anybody is concealing
They are looking, they are searching
They have seen, they have come to know
O eczema boy, look here, see here
Covered with a cover on the rim of the stove
He went near, he reached nearby
Put him in a sack, crammed him in a sack
He poured him in the river, he set him afloat
Then he went, he got drowned.

Eczema boy, your boy
To the young women of the Asurs, to the old women of the Asurs,
Started saying, started telling
Go and blow the bellows, go and whiff
They blowed the bellows, they whiffed
From inside the mansion, from inside the furnace
It can be heard, it is being known
"O mother " they are saying, "O father" they are telling
The Asur wenches are hearing, the Asur women are coming to know.
They are getting frightened, they are getting alarmed
O you Eczema boy
To our men, to our brothers
What have you done, what has happened to them
That they are weeping, that they are lamenting ?
You people do not weep, you people do not grieve,
They are many brothers, they are many kinsmen,
They are looting gold and silver, diamonds and silver,
They are plundering and snatching.
Those people will come out, they will come out from inside
He was speaking thus, he was explaining thus.
Through the route of the drain, through the way of the fencing,
Blood is flowring, blood is coming out
The wives of the Asurs, the old women of the Asurs
All are weeping, are lamenting
Eczema boy, your boy
Is saying, is telling
No, this is not blood, no, this is not blood
These people are many brothers, they are many kinsmen
They are eating betel leaves, they are chewing betel nuts
It is this mixed saliva, it is this spittle
Which is flowing, this is what is coming out
Taking out water from an old pitcher through peepal leaves
He sprinkled it over the mansion, he sprinkled it on the furnace
Twelve mansions, twenty two furnaces
He opened, he broke
There were bones packed in them, there were ashes packed in them
He saw and he came to know
The women of the Asurs, the females of the Asurs
Are weeping, are grieving

King God, divine virgin
Performed twelve learnings, showed thirteen wonders
Started climbing up the sky through thread, through rope kept on going up

The Asur wives, the Asur women
Caught hold of the feet, caught hold of the hand
They were telling him, they were pleading with him
How do we now live ? How do we get nourished ?
Tell us the remedy, tell us the way out.
This is the way they are saying, the way they are telling.
God king, Divine Virgin
Are saying, are telling
We had sent messenger, we had sent message
You people did not accept, you people did not pay heed,
You people started saying, you people started telling
We are God, we are big God.
God king, the Divine Virgin
Are pulling them off and throwing them, are removing them and throwing them
In rivers, in rivulets, in ditches, in lakes,
In Sarna groves, on mountains, in forests, in valleys
They all fell down, they all sank.
Whoever fell on a mountain became Buru bonga,
Whoever fell in water became Ikirbonga (water spirit)
whoever fell in a ditch became Nage Era
whoever fell in the Sarna became Chandi bonga
It is for their worship, it is for serving them
Pahans (priests) came into being in villages, colonies came up in Dhodhar.
To the wives of the Asurs, to the women of the Asurs
They are saying, are telling them
If you accept what is said, if you obey our instructions
Then surely you will be looked after, surely you will live
God king, Divine Virgin,
Through thread, through rope
They climbed up, they went away above.
The pond of lotus flowers, the tank of water lilies
Became full of water, became full to the brim
Tree and plants came up, grass and hay increased,
Throughout all the four directions

Mankind and fauna, birds and winged creatures, insects and moths
Everybody was happy, everybody was happy
Everybody started thinking, everybody started considering.
Singbonga king, Divine Virgin
Recreated our country, our world, made them anew,
All our sorrows, all our har dships
Went away, became things of the past
Everyone should let go of jealousy and envy
All brother kinsmen should live properly
This way they spoke.

Annexure - IV
From Oraon Dharma
Original in Kudhukh Language

Baaro bhair asurar tero bhair
Lodhrar, din-na-rait panna dhuknar-aa
Hans-raj-pankh-raj dharmesh-gahi ghodo
Daana mal mukhi. Antle dichua
Mangru mahto barjaa-kera- ana haro
Bhairo, din-na-rait panna ambaa
Dhuka." Ar aniar" baaro bhai
Asuram tero bhai lodhrarn
Din-na-rait panna chukdam; amimaga
Dharmesh imim belam

Anitale dharmesh panna dhuknaan barajaage
Khasra-khusru manjas, dara tusa-Duhare-nu
Ukkiaas. Anitale baaro bhai asurar
Tero bhai lodhrar-gaahi tang mukk bagar
Amm ho: aa barcham, Khasra khusru
K ukkos aarin aniyas "chi a-ang arnm."

Aaramjhi onta randi paccho
Rahcha aadi-gusan nechas.chi
Ayang amm." "Are beta akatrati
Bharchakaye? Isan baaro bah! asurar
Tero hai Iodhrar gahi name- jagraki
Ra-i, alarin pitnar. "Aad - amm chicha

"Asurar aidnar." "Mal kalon, pitor choir"
Antile taam-taam aniar"kala haro

Aasin dhar-aa ondra-aa" antale aas mainjas
"Aindra manja haaro bahirot aar aniaar
"Panna amhaye bagdara; huhungar-jhungur
Nannar-chi-a a." "Ingan kutinu mankha
Nisgar.Chia, saate ulla saate makha dakhua
Punna bisalinu amm odor-aa tatkha
Dahudha-turu chitakakay. Uthpuri chari-turu
Valin kolke. 'khasra-khusrum ekase
Aniyas Aname nanjar. Antle sona ara
Rupa-turu jhabrakas Urkhaas. Ar aniar
"Ana bhai Aksan, ebadan bidkay?"
"E" ag kuthino biddkan. Nim bagge
Ra'adar, Nim-ga-bagge beddor."Antle
Korom ka?, "ko-ra-aa" Korchar hor mar.

"Dhakua bachaas dhukchar
Kheagey hormar armuraar, Tangmukh-
Bagar manger" "inder mannar bang?"
A kukkos, aniaas "aar aanna- lagnar
Mukka-khad-gay-bagge-ho-om: Aaunge arba
Nakhraa-Iagnar Kecchaar hormar
Sabad mala khakreev. "Tisagaa mokhro
Bisalinu amm ondra-aa" Khokando dahudhan
Odra-aa dara chitka, Balin kola."
Ar kulliyar. Khochol hurhuri. "ana
Bang. ainder nanjykaye?"
Ghodo nu dharmesh argias challraas.
Kerarki mukkar jhekchar."aimagey
Jeena-paani aida. "Antile aas anias
Kohan "nin chala paceho maanke
Sannidin"deswari manke, khunt maanke
Kiro maanke, makhrin khokhrake,
Ar bhog argor nibhage."

From Oraon religious legends
Translated from Kurukh language

Twelve brother Asurs, thirteen brother Lodhars
Day and night smelt iron through bellows
Hansraj, Pankhraj the horses of Dharmes
Do not eat grains. Then the king of crows

Mangru Mahto decided and said
"O brother, do not heat the iron day and night."
He said, "Twelve brother Asurs, thirteen brother Lodhars"
Day and night we will smelt the iron, we ourselves
Are God, we ourselves are king

Then in order to stop the smelting of iron
God became the Eczema boy and sat down on the road leading to the well
Then the wives of twelve brother Asurs and
Thirteen brother Lodhars came to take water.
The Eczema boy said, "my mother, give me water."

There was an old widow amidst them. He addressed
Her also, saying, "mother, give me water."
"O son, from where have you come ? Here the twelve brother Asurs
The thirteen brother Lodhars are wicked
They kill human beings." She gave him water.

"Asurs are calling you," "I will not go, they will kill me."
Then they themselves said, "go and catch hold of him."
Then he asked, "What has happened, O brothers?"
Then they replied, "Our iron is not being smelted. Do some sorcery."
"Put me in the furnace, cover it, blow it for seven days and seven nights"
Bring water in a new pitcher, sprinkle the water with the help of leaves of mango stalk.
Open the door with the whole stalk," Whatever the Eczema boy said
They carried out accordingly.
Then laden with gold and silver he came out of the furnace.
He said, "O brother, from where did you get this." "You are many.
You can get much more". Then, "Should we enter ?"
"Enter." Then they entered the furnace.

"Blow," said the boy. The Asur women blew
While dying their bodies writhed. Their wives asked-
"O son, what are these people doing ?"
That boy said – They are saying
That in order to collect also for their children and wives
They are all fighting. They have all died."
The words cannot be heard. "Open, bring water in a black pitcher
Bring a branch of the sinduar tree.

Bring, sprinkle water, open the door of the furnace."
They opened. The bones tumbled out rapidly. "O son, what did you do?"

Riding astride his horse, God started moving
When the wives stopped him,
"What will happen about our upkeep ?"
Then he said to the eldest, "You become Chala Pachcho"
To the younger ones he said "You become Deswali, You become Khunt."
Become Chiro, Upon being hit, human beings
Will offer sacrifice to you."

Annexure - V
Agni Varsha – Rain of Fire
(From Oraon religious legend)

(This religious legend related to the coming into existence of tribals is sung during various religious functions by pahans, matis, sokhas and pujars, etc. The singing of the songs of this legend and of Asur Avdaan during the occasions of danda-katta or bhelwafari worship has become a tradition).

(Today I am narrating the original story of ancestors, the king of Belatpur and the demon).

The demon used to swallow every human being carrying parboiled rice. One day it was the turn of the son of the old widow. The old woman wept and told him not to go. But he picked up a sword weighing twelve "Maunds" (about thirty seven kilograms per maund) and took a spear weighing thirteen maunds. He filled up his bullock cart with rice and when he started moving, the demon could hear the fearful sound of the bells of the bullock cart from a distance of thirty "kos" (one kos is equivalent to two miles). Then the boy told the frightened demon to open his mouth and eat him too. Then the boy pushed the spear in his mouth and killed the demon with the blow of his sword. Thereafter the boy (Dharmes- God of the Oraons) thought that when the corpse of the demon will rot, then people will not be able to eat or drink. Hence the symbol of sin, that is the dead body of the demon should be destroyed by rain of fire.

Parwati told her husband Dharmes- Pour the fire from a small bowl (Parwati was kind and did not want annihilation of the Creation by excess rain of fire). Then Dharmes told Haluman- "Nephew ! Be with me. When I pour down rain of fire, then beat the drum so that people may become alert and save themselves." Dharmes filled a brass plate with fire and rained it down. Haluman mean while became busy in eating "tela-kand" (a kind of tuber) and forgot to beat the drum. Thereafter a disastrous fire raged. All countries, flora, fauna, were reduced to ashes. But Parwati hid a male and a female (brother-sister) amidst the bushes of gangla which place is now known as "Sira Sita"- she hid them there in a crab hole.

And she gave them half split lentils to eat. They survived on this for seven days and seven nights. Then Dharmes told Parwati- I am dying of hunger (because there was nobody to offer him holy food and this holy food is the meal of the gods). Parwati replied- I had prayed to you to go in for limited amount of rain of fire but you sent a huge amount of this rain. Now where will one get human beings who would offer holy food ? Then Dharmes prayed to Parwati. After that Parwati said- "Two creatures are hiding in gangla bushes." Dharmes took a golden cane and started searching for them, being accompanied by "chill kohi (a bird), dogs" "lily," "bhuli" and "Khairi." Then the dogs through their sniffing started barking near the crab hole amidst the gangla bushes. Dharmes found the male-female couple and gave them a plough, seeds, and made day and night for them. During the cultivation of rice when, on one hand locusts and on the other rats started harming, then Dharmes told the brother-sister duo to protect agriculture by offering danda-katta or bhelwafari worship which prevent the damage. This would also save it from the evil eye. Then Dharmes placed a log of wood between the brother and sister and said, "O my grandson, when you will cross this log and go and sleep on the other side, then mankind will increase."

This is how the Oraon tribe multiplied from the first "brother-sister."

Annexure – VI
Isung-sindri
(Oraon folk tale)

(The most important religious function in a marriage is to put vermillion on the bride. Just through this action the woman becomes the wife of the person putting vermillion on her. In Oraon folk tale the importance of isung-sindri has been described).

Four friends left their home for foreign lands in search of employment. During the journey, they had to spend one night in a deep forest. They slept under a mango tree. Three would sleep while the fourth one had to keep awake to guard. The first friend, who was guarding, was adept in wood Carving. His sight fell on a broken branch of the tree. With the help of a chisel, he carved out the likeness of a beautiful woman. There after it became the turn of the second friend to stand guard. He was a gold smith. When he saw the likeness of a beautiful woman in the carving, he made jewellery and decorated her with the same. Then the turn of the third friend came to stand guard. He was a weaver. When his sight fell on the carving, he dressed her in a sari. The fourth and last friend was a trader of vermillion. When the other friends went to sleep, then at that time his sight fell on the carving. He took some vermillion with which he marked the woman in the carving. As soon as vermillion was applied on her, she became alive. When they saw this, the four friends started claiming the woman so much so that they nearly came to blows.

Right at that moment a sage appeared. The four friends presented their individual cases before him and asked him to do justice. The sage decided thus:–

The person who carved out her likeness is the father of the girl.

The person who dressed her in sari is her brother.

The person who decked her up with jewelry is her maternal uncle.

The person who applied vermillion on the parting of her hair is her husband.

Bibliography

Aquique MD : Social History of Ancient India, Abhinav Pub. Houz Khas, New Delhi (1978)

Bage, Marsallan : Phanamenolic der Munda-Religion. Berlin (1960)

Bhattacharya, S. : Studies in Comparative Munda Linguistics Indian Institute of Advance Studies, Simla (1975)

Bhattacharya, S. : Some Munda Etymologies in N.H. Zide. Studies in Comparative Austro-Asiatic Linguistics Mouton (1966)

Bhattacharya, S. : Some More Munda Etymologies Prestidanam, MOUTON (1969)

Banerjee, G.C. : Introduction to Kharia Language Bengal Secretariate Press, Calcutta (1894)

Boniface Tirkey : The Smiling Uraon Navjyoti Niketan, Patna, 1989.

Burrow, T. : The Sanskrit Language, London (1955)

Bailey, F.G. : Tribe Caste and Nation, Oxford University Press in India (1960)

Bose, N.R. : Cultural Anthropology, Asia Publishing House, Bombay -1961.

Campion, Edmund : My Oraon Culture, Catholic Press, Ranchi

Cassirer : The Philosophy of Symbolic Forms Vol. II Mythical Thought, Yale University Press, London (1965)

Campbell Gorge : Specimens of Language in India Including those of the Aboriginal Tribes of Bengal, Central Provinces and the Eastern Frontier Bengal Secretariate Press, Calcutta (1874)

Cardon, L. : The Kharias and Their Customs Lonvarin, Belgium (1903)

Chatterji, A.N. & T. Das : The Notes of Saraikela, Calcutta (1928)

Dalton, E.T. : Descriptive Ethnology of Bengal Govt. Press, Calcutta (1872)

Dani, A.H. : Pre-History and Proto-History of Eastern India, Calcutta (1960)

Dasgupta, D. : Linguistic Studies in Juang, Kharia. Thar Lodha and Mal-Paharia, Ghatwali Pahariya (1778)

Dhan, Rekha O : These are my Tribesmen,- The Oraons, GEL Church Press, Ranchi,1967

Das, A.K. : Impact of Tea Industry on the Life of the Tribals of West Bengal Central Research Institute, Calcutta-1964

Dalton, E.T. : Tribal History of Eastern India, Cosmos Publications, Delhi-1973

Desa. F. : Crisis in Chotanagpur A Redemptive Publication, Banglore (1975)

Eickstedi, E.Von : Diesore in Anthropologic her Anzeiqer, Stutt-gart -1928.

Elvin Verrier : The Murie and Their Ghotul, Oxford University Press, Calcutta-1943

Exam, A Van (SJ) : The Religions System of the Munda Tribes, Hans Volker and Kulturen, D-5205, ST. Augastin (1982)

Evans Pritcharo : New Religion. Clarendon Press, London,Oxford (1956)

Evans Pritcharo : Theories of Primtive Religion. Clarendon Press, Oxford (1865)

Fuch S (Stephen) : The Origin of Man and his Culture Asia Publishing House, Bombay (1963)

Fuchs Stephen : The Aboriginal Tribes of India, The Royal Asiatic Society of Bengal, Calcutta (1946)

Griffiths W.G. : The Kol Tribes of Central India, The Royal Asiatic Society of Bengal Calcutta (1946)

Guha, B.S. : Racial Elements in Indian Population. Oxford Pamphlets on Indian Affairs, Oxford ,1944

Ghurey G.S. : The Scheduled Tribes. Popular Book Depo. Bombay (1959)

Ghurey G.S. : The Aborigines-"So Called" and Their Future, Gokhale Institute of Pol. & Eco. Poona.

Hahn. F : Oraon Folk-Lore. Govt. Press, Patna (1931)

Gopal Lallanjee : Economic History of Northern India, New Delhi (1969)

Hodgson, B.H. : Essaye Relating to Indian Subjects. Calcutta (1974)

Hoffmann, John S.J. : Encyclopaedia Mundarica 15 Vols. Govt. Press, Bihar, Patna (1950-74)

Hunter W.W. : The Annals of Rural Bengal, New York (1868)

Huton J.H. : Caste in India, Bombay (1957)

Jha, J.C. : The Tribal Revolt of Chotanagpur (1831- 1832) Patna, Reprint, 1987.

Mishra A.K : Economic History of India, Patna (1986)

Mishra P.K : Religion in Puranas, Camec Pub., New Delhi (1989)

MishraY.K : Religion in Bihar, Gaya (1977)

Know, Sten. : On Some Facts connected with the Tibeto-Burman Dialect spoken in Kanawar ZDMG. Vol. 59 Leipzig (1905)

Minz, N. (Ed) : Tribal Awakening Christian Literature Society, Madras (1965)

Mahato, S. : Hundred Years of Christian Missionaries in Chotanagpur, G.E.L. Church Press, Ranchi (1972)

Mazumdar D.N. : Races and Cultures of India, Universal Publishes Ltd. Lucknow (1944)

Mazumdar D.M. : Himalayan Polyandry. Asia Publishing House, Bombay (1962)

Mazumdar R.C. : Ancient India. Motilal Banarsi Das, New Delhi (1982)

Orea Mennas Ram : Singubonga or, O, Eta, Eta Bongako Berlin (1975)

Patnayak J. : Social History of Ancient India, Bhubaneswar (1979)

Prasad Dineshwar : Poetry Hoffmann on Mundari Jyoti, Ranchi-1979.

Prasad N. : Land and People of Tribal Bihar. Bihar Tribal Research Institute, Ranchi (1961)

Przyluski J. : Les Langues de Modde 4 Vols. 2nd Ed., Paris (1953)

Ponette P. Ed : The Munda World. Catholic Press, Ranchi (1978)

Purti P.N.J. : Kursinama oro Kiliko. Adivasi Sahitya Prachar Samiti, Jamshedpur (1972)

Rosner Victor : The Flying Horse of Dharmes Satya Bharti Publications, Ranchi-1982.

Raghavaiah, V. : Tribal Revolts. Andhara Rastra Adimjati Sevak Sangh Netter (A.P. (1971)

Roy Choudhary P.C. : Chhau Dance in Inside Bihar. Bookland Pvt. Ltd ., Calcutta (1962)

Roy S.C. : The Mundas and Their Country Man in India, Ranchi, Reprint, 1995.

Ray S.C. : The Oraon of Chotanagpur Ranchi, Reprint, 1984.

Roy S.C. : Oraon Religion and Customs Calcutta, Reprint, 1972.

Risley, HH. : The Tribes and Castes of Bengal, Secretariate Press, Calcutta (1891)

Risley, H.H. : The People of India, Calcutta (1915)

Sharma P. Dash : The passing Scene in Chotanagpur Maitryee Publications, Ranchi (1980)

Sachchidananda : Profiles to Tribal Culture in Bihar, Calcutta (1965)

Sarjorious J . : Migration in Chotanagpur Centre for International Studies MIT Massachusetts (1972)

Sebeok T.A. : An Examination of The Austro-Asiatic Language Family in Language, Baltimore (1942)

Sarkar S.S. : The Aboriginal Races of India, Calcutta (1915)

Schmidt W. : Dic Man-Khmar Voelker. Ain Bindeglied Zwischen Voelkern Zentral asiens and astrenesians Braunscweig, Calcutta (1906)

Sachchidananda : Birsa : An Adivasi Fighter for Freedom

Sachchidananda : The Tribal Villages of Bihar Munshi Ram Manohar Lal , Delhi (1968)

Srinivas M.N. : Religion and Society Among the Coorgs of South India. Clarendon Press, Oxford (1952)

Srivastava S.C. : The Thorns; A Study in Culture Dynamics. Agra University, Agra (1958)

Singh KS. : Colonial Transformation of The Tribal Society in Middle India. Govt. of India, Ministry of Home Affairs, New Delhi (1978)

Singh Rajeshwar : Buddhism in Ancient Bihar, New Delhi (1979)

Vidyarth L.P. : Cultural Customs of Tribal Bihar. Punthi Pustak, Culcutta (1964)

Sinha & Chattopadhya : Chotanagpur Tenancy Act 1908 Rajpal & Co., New Delhi (1983)

Vidyarth L.P. : Cultural Configuration of Ranchi. Punthi Pustak-Calcutta (1969)

Vidyarth L.P. : Study of an Emerging Industrial City of Tribal India J .N. Basudeo & Co . Calcutta (1960-62)

Vidyarth L.P. & Shay K.N. : The Dynamics of Tribal Leadership in Bihar. Kitab Mahal, Allahabad, Calcutta (1976)

Side, N.H. : Munda and Non-Munda; Austro Asiatic Languages Current Trends in Linguistics 4. Mounton Calcutta (1968)

Tirkey Boniface : The Smiling Oraon, Nar Jyoti Niketan, Patna, 1989.

Tete, P. : A Missionary Social Worker in India, J.B. Hoffmann Sany Bharti, Ranchi 2nd Ed. 1986.

आर्चर, डब्लू, जी. : लील खो–रआ खेखेल
विधापति प्रेस, लहेरिया सराय, बिहार।

अहमद, जे, : बिहार के आदिवासी
मोतीलाल बनारसी दास, दिल्ली (1957)

शर्मा एवं विक्रम : छोटानागपुर का भूगाले, राजेश पब्लिकेशन्स, नई दिल्ली, 1999।

त्रिगुणायत जगदीश : मुण्डा लोक कथाएँ।
बिहार राष्ट्रभाषा परिषद, पटना (1968)

त्रिगुणायत जगदीश : बन–देवता।
शिक्षक सहयोग भण्डार, राँची

मुण्डा, दुलाल, चन्द्र : सुड़ा–सेंगेन
कल्याण विभाग, बिहार सरकार, पटना, 1967

विद्यार्थी ललिता प्रसाद : बिहार के आदिवासी
कॉलेज सेन्टर, पटना (1960)

Index

A

Aachrel bonga/Achrain, 123, 247, 268, 269

Aajo Gosai, 247

Ache (soul), 253-256, 336, 338, 339, 347, 348, 369, 371, 380

Ading, 19, 114, 119, 121, 139, 145, 176, 179, 187, 190, 202, 211, 221-223, 225, 226

Ading Bongako, 119, 139-141, 362

Adowa Sootam, 19, 214

Afghanistan, 77

Agiya (agua), 25, 207, 208, 211, 215, 325, 226, 329

Agnivarsha (Rain of fire), 81, 126, 132, 135-137, 144, 154, 162, 189, 248, 252, 253, 292

Agra, 64

Alivardi Khan, 95, 115

Andaman Islands, 48, 72

Arab/Arabia/Arabian, 48, 61, 70, 75, 76, 78

Aravalli (Vindhya), 61, 65, 67

Arwa/Akshat rice (for blessing), 133, 182, 186, 215, 243, 267, 271, 276-278, 298, 300, 302, 304, 319-222, 331, 336

Arya Samajis, 43, 116, 375

Arya/Aryan, 39, 41, 54, 55, 61, 63, 65, 75, 77, 80, 82, 84, 88, 90, 95, 97, 101, 111, 146, 188, 192, 235, 236, 238, 253, 358, 367, 368, 376

Asoka, 87, 89

Assam, 38, 46, 48, 49, 55-57, 59, 62, 68-69

Asulo, 19

Asur, 19, 35-37, 40, 42, 62, 65-67, 81, 82, 98, 114, 118, 128, 132-135, 141, 145, 151, 167, 169, 173-174, 179, 186, 226, 235, 249-250, 252-253, 259-260, 272, 284, 357-361, 366, 370, 375-376, 378, 391-396, 398-400.

Asur Avdaan, 118, 120, 131-135, 137, 146-147, 167, 168, 173-174, 179, 189, 206, 250, 252-253, 259-260, 270, 359, 361, 376, 379, 400

Asur Widows, 134, 141, 145-146

Austric, 48, 50-52, 56

Azamgarh, 38, 60-63, 359, 384

B

Ba festrival, 22, 176, 180, 363, 379

Baba Hartukam, 219

Bai Bhaak, 29, 368, 370-371, 373, 379

Bal Yogeshwar, 43, 375

Balmiki Ramayan, 82, 368

Baluchistan, 46, 49, 72-3, 77-80

Banita bonga, 122-124, 138, 141, 144, 187

Baranda Pachcho, 247, 265, 270-271, 378

Baranda peeper, 246

Batari, 305, 307

Batauli, 21, 176, 182, 363, 379
Battle of Plassey, 95, 115
Belatpur, 252, 368, 400
Bengal, 46, 49, 68, 69, 73, 95, 115
Benja, 29
Bero Pennu, 369
Bero/Bedu, 243, 247, 263, 368, 369
Bhado Ekadasi (eleventh day of moon of Bhado month), 314
Bhagalpur, 33, 66
Bhagat, 29, 36-37, 156, 158-161, 163, 273, 275-276, 280-284, 371, 373-374, 377
Bhagwan, 247-248, 352, 365, 369, 378
Bhai-bahin (brother-sister), 29
Bhars/Rajbhars, 85, 87-88, 359
Bhelwa branch/tree, 182, 189, 213, 220, 310, 370
Bhelwa Far, 250, 344, 400-401
Bhim, 253, 368
Bhuinhar, 241-244, 270, 298, 300, 344-345
Bhuiphoot Mahadev, 29, 36, 41, 43, 263, 266, 280-281, 374
Bhumij, 65, 191, 201
Bihar, 86, 88, 115, 192
Bilaspur, 43, 374
Biri belaas, 43, 237, 245, 247, 368-369, 376, 369-378, 376, 378
Birsa Munda/Birsa religion, 365
Bishop Caldwell, 73-75, 79
Bonga, 22, 35, 37, 40, 42, 113-114, 117-124, 134-135, 137-142, 144-145, 147, 149-153, 157-161, 172, 178, 180, 183-190, 202, 210, 214, 219, 221, 225-226, 259, 273, 357, 361-366, 375-378
Bongako, 113, 118, 202
Brahwi, 49, 71-5, 78-80
Buru bonga, 119-120, 122, 125, 138-139, 160, 179, 378, 396
Buxar, 95, 115

C

Calcutta, 115
Central Asia, 49, 55, 61, 74-75, 191
Chai Champa, 66
Chain Bhitarna/Ekh makhna, 254-255, 256-257, 338-339
Chala Kuti, 243, 259
Chala Pachcho, 26, 35, 41, 43, 236-238, 240, 243-246, 258-259, 260, 283, 291, 294-296, 301, 304, 307-308, 369-370, 371, 376, 378, 400
Champa puri, 66
Chandi, 26, 41, 96, 178, 180, 238, 245, 247, 264, 266-268, 291, 301, 304, 364, 373, 376, 378
Chandi bonga, 23, 43, 119-120, 138-139, 163, 361, 366, 366, 378, 396
Chandi Jhanda/flag, 294, 308
Chandi Pahan, 267
Chandi pahar, 246, 264-265, 378
Chandi puja, 264, 353
Chandi tanr/Upland, 243, 267-268
Chappar Burhiya, 246, 263-264, 378
Charpangu, 20
Chati jowar, 20
Chatu, 20
Chatur seeman, 41, 246, 365, 301, 378
Cheetah, 117, 127, 148, 176, 274
Chekad, 215
Cheros, 44, 54, 65-67, 85, 87-89, 91, 103, 358
Chhotanagpur, 13, 33-35, 38, 40, 42-43, 50, 61, 65-67, 69, 79, 81-82, 83, 87, 89-97, 101-04, 111-112, 115-116, 130, 132, 146, 180, 190, 192, 194, 201, 235, 237, 256, 260-261, 265, 279, 310, 337, 357-361, 363, 366, 368-369, 370-379, 384
Chilgi Maiya, 294
Chingri Naad, 247, 270
Chondore Ikir bonga, 23, 120
Chor Dewa, 257
Chowra Bhowra, 20, 127, 391

Christian/Christianity/Missionaries, 13, 16, 33-34, 42, 96,112, 115-117, 119, 126, 146, 255, 357, 365, 378
Churail, 122, 143, 225, 301
Col. E. T. Dalton, 34, 39, 68-69, 103, 248-249, 250, 367
Copper Age, 71, 76, 81
Creation, 113-114, 117-119, 123, 125-136, 141, 144, 156, 162, 171, 173, 186, 189, 191, 202, 205, 221, 226, 245-46, 250-251, 292, 297, 316, 359-360, 384, 400

D

Damodar river, 67, 97
Danda Katta, 27, 81, 250, 271, 309-310, 344, 401
Dangra naad, 270
Dantari, 20, 153-154, 155, 162
Darha desauli, 41, 240, 261-262, 301, 304, 309, 376, 378
Darha tanr, 261, 376
Dasai, 176, 185, 363
Dasrathi Ram, 40-1, 43, 63, 82-83, 96-97, 120, 359, 368, 376, 378
Desauli bonga, 23, 41, 120, 138-139, 179, 214, 304, 309, 366, 371, 400
Devi Mai, 36, 41, 43, 96, 263, 280, 284, 371, 378
Devra, 21, 35, 37, 40, 113, 136, 141, 145, 148-149, 153-154, 155-156, 159-161, 172-173, 175, 189, 203, 357, 364
Dhanbad, 33, 44
Dhangar Pahan/Dhangri, 68, 177, 238, 291, 304-305
Dharmes, 7, 27, 40-41, 43, 81-82, 102-103, 130-131, 236-237, 242, 245-253, 259, 270-272, 279, 284-285, 289, 292, 300-302, 309, 316, 319, 325-326, 327, 348, 368-372, 375, 377-378, 398, 400-401
Dhumkuriya, 263, 267, 320, 324, 345-346, 380
Divine Light Mission, 43, 375
Diwani, 95, 115
Dravid/Dravidian, 38-39, 46-47, 49-50, 70-80, 103, 359, 367
Dul da, 217-218, 220
Durga, 36, 41, 185, 364
Durjanshal, 42, 374
Durvaasa, 66

E

E. A. Gait, 67
Earthworm, 126, 384
Egypt (misr), 62-63, 75-77, 125
Encyclopaedia Mundarica, 34, 117-119

F

Father A. Vanghan Exam., 34, 117, 127, 137, 188
Father Han, 34, 68
Father J. Hoffmann, 34, 117-120, 123-125, 137, 358, 369
Father P. Ponnet, 34, 117, 119
Footchiri, 342, 345

G

Gajipur, 63
Ganga, 84, 87-88, 91, 367
Gaura Goriya, 188
Gena, 190
Gharha Dhora, 265
Ghosts and spirits, 42, 66, 366
Giti ora, 20
Godaiya devta, 318
Goensali, 271
Gohar devta, 271
Gomke, 20
Gondwana, 11, 33
Gorait, 304, 308, 322, 333, 335, 343
Gotra, 26, 40, 190-192, 201, 255, 285-289, 325, 336, 338, 348, 350, 360, 369, 371-372, 381
Gujarat, 39, 46, 49, 58, 367
Gumla, 33-34, 43, 311, 374-375

H

Hadam, 24, 39, 60-61, 114, 126
Hadbodi, 30, 253, 257-258, 337, 345
Hadiya, 119, 182, 189, 209, 236, 294, 299, 304, 307-308, 318, 327-334, 342-343, 384
Haji peeper, 265
Hambul roa, 164-166, 168
Hanuman/Haluman, 81-82, 368, 376, 378, 400
Hariari, 290, 308, 363, 372, 379
Harishchandra, 14, 85
Hasda, 24, 116, 176, 198, 201
Hata devra, 159-161
Hatu, 98, 100, 112, 190
Hatu bongako, 40, 138, 180, 366, 376
Hazaribagh, 33, 44, 67, 97
Herbest Risley, 45-47, 77, 86, 88-89, 103
Hindu, 33, 37, 40-43, 61-62, 65-66, 68, 88-89, 96, 100-104, 111, 113, 115, 117, 119-120, 140, 146, 156-159, 161, 163-164, 177, 180, 183, 185, 189, 197-198, 202-203, 206, 236, 244, 246-247, 250, 253, 256-258, 262-263, 285, 290, 291-293, 317-318, 358, 362-365, 369-373, 375, 378-379
Ho, 97, 101, 129, 191, 199, 201
Holika/Holi, 177, 290-292, 373, 379
Homosapien, 70, 367
Horo, 68, 132, 189, 192, 196, 198, 359-360
Huding devra, 170
Hur bird, 60, 127, 359, 384
Hutton, J. H., 47, 55, 57, 59, 357

I

Ice Age, 70, 80
Ikasi pidi te, tirasi badite, 19
Ikirbonga, 23, 119-120, 122, 125, 137-138, 139, 378, 396
Ikshwaku, 14, 63, 359
Ind festival, 187
Indian/Indian's, 33, 38, 45, 47-66, 68, 70, 72-74, 76-81, 89, 104, 111, 125, 146, 188, 192, 206, 357, 378
Indra prastha, 61
Iran/Iranian, 47-8, 61, 80
Iron age, 71
Isursindri, 297, 331, 333, 401

J

Jadur, 181, 190
Jam gai, 264
Japi, 178, 180, 190
Jarasandha, 66
Jarga or magi, 177, 190
Jatra/Jatra tand, 190, 288, 346, 350, 373
Jatra/Jhanda (flag), 190, 267, 288
Jawa flowers, 310
Jayer burhiya, 121, 366
Jee/Jin, 20, 225, 254-255
Jenom jugre, 20
Jharkhand, 33, 96, 315
Jitiya/jitiya peepal, 290, 316-317, 322, 372-373, 379
Jndo Eda, 320, 323-324, 380
Joda kamna, 27, 247, 320-321
Jokh aerpa, 320, 324, 380
Jome nawa, 170, 176, 186-187, 363, 379
Jome sakam, 20, 142, 144-145
Joto mahar, 159
Jung topa, 224
Jungles/forest, 61, 63-5, 67, 82-83

K

Kabir/kabir sect, 35-36, 41-43, 96, 115, 357, 364-365, 374
Kadlota, 261, 290, 309, 372, 379
Kahalgaon, 66
Kaimur (mountain range), 61, 67, 85
Kali, 36, 41, 276-277, 280, 364
Kalyuga, 65
Kaman, 25
Kannada, 72-73, 75, 79, 235
Karma–Dharma, 184-185, 311-316

Karma/Karam festival, 26, 176, 183-185, 190, 258, 290, 310-316, 322, 326, 347, 363, 372-373, 379
Karushas/Karush Country, 64, 66-67, 85
Kaurav, 39, 61, 64, 358
Keonjhar, 252
Khaddi, 26, 290, 293, 325, 369, 379
Khariya, 65
Kharra puja, 290, 319, 337-338, 340-341, 343, 372, 379
Kharwar, 65, 67, 85, 87-89, 97, 358, 368
Khasra Balak/Eczema boy, 133,-134, 168, 173-174, 186, 250, 253, 392-396, 399
Khekhel benja, 293, 349, 379
Khorpos/Maintenance, 20
Khunt, 20, 240-243, 268-280, 298-300, 329, 344-345
Khunt katti/Khunt kattidar – 92, 98-100, 112, 118-119, 242
Khunt naad, 242, 247, 261, 269-270, 371, 400
Khunt Paat, 261, 371
Khunti, 116
Kili, 19, 40, 190-202, 206, 221, 224, 381
King Karash, 67, 235
Kisani Kurukh, 68
Koha Benja, 26, 253-254, 258, 337-338, 340, 342, 347-350, 371-372, 380
Kol – 34, 38-39, 48, 51, 55, 59, 62, 64-67, 88, 101, 235-236, 357-358, 375
Kolhan, 101
Kolom Singbonga, 176, 185, 379
Kompat Munda, 20
Korku, 191, 256
Korwa, 65, 67, 191
Kotil, 78
Kumba, 223
Kundi, 26, 344-345, 348, 350, 372, 380
Kurukh, 26, 34-35, 42, 67-69, 72, 79, 85, 87-88, 101-103, 235, 237, 366, 375, 377, 398
Kurukshetra, 38-39, 64, 66, 85, 358

L

Lail doge, 166-167
Lakhan Bhagat, 95, 377
Lemuri island, 50
Lipi susari, 23, 136
Lohardagga, 33-34, 98, 235, 264, 311, 358, 376
Lugu, 304
Lur bing, 172
Lutkum, 24, 61, 114, 133-134, 135, 141, 174, 186, 191, 203

M

Madagascar, 61
Madho Swarup Vats, 71
Madhya Pradesh, 43, 70, 256, 311, 374
Magadh, 66-7, 87
Magi/Mag Parv, 23, 140, 176-177, 379
Mahabharat, 62, 64-5, 85, 115, 253, 368
Mahadaniya, 244, 246, 362, 378
Mahadeo Manda, 29, 262, 371
Mahadev, 36, 41, 96, 146, 148-149, 153, 157-158, 159, 161-164, 206, 241, 245-246, 250, 262-263, 266, 280-284, 364, 371, 373-374, 375, 378
Mahadev Kuri, 281
Mahaprabhu Chaitanya, 42, 96, 115, 365, 374
Mahto, 241, 293-308, 315, 324, 346
Majhiyas, 23
Malabar, 73
Maler/maley, 85, 90-91, 247, 368-369
Malyalam, 79
Manauti bonga, 121-122
Manbhum, 61, 67-68
Manki, 23, 95, 212
Manu, 60, 67-68, 383-384
Marang buru bonga, 23, 120, 123, 138, 179
Marang Devra, 156, 159, 163
Marang Kanda, 23
Maratha, 115-116

Mati, 29, 36-37, 41, 122, 144, 153, 189, 240, 249-251, 262, 264, 271, 276-281, 316, 357, 371, 373

Maula Kol, 66

Mecca-Medina, 70, 80

Mediterranean sea, 38, 48-89, 58, 70, 77-78, 80, 367

Megasthenes, 90-91

Metal Age, 71

Misi Singbonga, 121, 137, 141, 162, 360

Modi, 68

Mon Khmer, 54-55, 57-59

Mongol/Mongolia/Mongolian/Mongoloid, 38, 46-49, 55-7, 71-77, 357

Monotheist, 16, 117, 124

Morih, 60, 191-192

Mua Masanko, 23, 142-143, 144, 164, 214, 225, 301

Munda, 13, 17, 18

Mundari, 34, 50-55, 61, 78, 92-93, 96, 159

Muslim/Mughals, 33, 86-90, 103-104, 115, 194

Mutri Chandi Pahan, 304-05

N

Naad, 27, 37, 41, 246-247, 251, 253, 261-266, 268-280, 283-284, 289, 300-302, 320, 336, 345, 357, 369-372, 374-375, 377

Nagi Aera, 21, 119, 121, 131-132, 136-138, 141, 146, 162, 179, 360, 396

Nagi bonga, 23, 120

Nagri dishum, 21, 116-17

Nagvanshi king/Nagvanshis, 87-88, 94, 187

Naig, 28, 346-347, 349

Najom Chandi, 149-151

Name pinjna, 28, 322, 380

Narmada, 101, 192, 235-236, 357, 367

Nawa Khani, 258

Nazar gujar/Nazar, 27, 166, 368, 370-371, 373, 379-380

Nazri baan, 166-167

Nebha ache, 255-256

Negrito/Negrid, 47-48, 72

Nemha bhagat, 284

Nepal, 55-57, 61-62, 73-74, 192

New moon night, 148-149

O

Oda bongako, 121, 139, 176, 181, 183, 185, 187, 189-190, 226, 361, 366, 376, 378

Odeka, 262

Ojha, 25, 35-37, 41, 141-142, 172-173, 189, 240, 249-251, 262, 275, 357, 364, 371, 373

Omedanda, 19, 67, 97-98

Oraon, 13, 17, 33-43

Oraon religion, 7, 41, 235, 237, 240-241, 248-249, 251, 255, 258, 260, 374

Orissa, 44, 46, 68, 95, 115, 256, 365

Othya ache, 255-56

P

P. Dehan, 34, 247, 254, 267

Paat raja, 28, 41, 245-246, 260-261, 370, 378

Pachbaaler, 28, 246, 253-256, 299, 342-343, 347-348, 370, 372, 377-378

Padres, 15, 119, 126, 137, 188, 193

Pahan, 98-100, 102, 113, 119, 122-124, 135, 138-139, 141, 144-146, 163, 178-189, 193, 203, 210, 213, 226-227, 237, 241-245, 249, 251, 253, 255, 258-259, 262-265, 267, 283, 288-291, 293-309, 311, 318-319, 321, 331, 334, 342, 345-348, 360, 362, 364, 369-370, 376, 396, 400

Paicha labana, 243-245

Paisari, 321

Palamu, 33, 44, 67, 85, 91, 97, 254

Palash tree, 263

Panbhara, 242-243, 249, 308

Pandya Kingdom, 235

Parbatiya, 40

Parha/parha raja/panch, 102, 192, 199-200, 226, 288, 301, 323-324, 329-331, 350, 381

Parv (festival), 175, 289
Parvati, 40, 82, 96, 146, 157-158, 161-163, 206, 247, 253, 360, 364, 378, 400-401
Phagu, 176-180, 258, 290-293, 297, 322, 363, 372-373, 379
Phanimukut Rai, 87, 94-95, 103, 187, 377
Poomp Mejhna, 329, 330
Pre-Dravidian, 70, 83, 378
Presidency, 115
Primitive tribes/races, 64, 68
Ptolemy, 87
Pujaar, 242-243, 249, 251, 264-265, 293-309, 346-347, 362, 400
Pulind Kingdom, 64-65
Pulkhi, 28, 36, 38, 345, 372, 380
Pupa country, 184

R

Raipur, 43, 374
Rajhas, 23
Rajmahal, 90, 368
Rajput, 87-8, 103
Ramayana, 115
Ranchi, 33, 44, 67-8, 87, 92, 97-8, 101, 111, 116, 123, 132, 194, 198, 206, 235-236, 261, 374
Ravan poot, 69
Reformist movement, 42
Rigveda, 14, 124
Roa/rowa, 23, 142-143, 152, 164-166, 187, 225-226, 256, 380
Rohtasgarh, 34-35, 38-39, 41, 66-67, 85-91, 93, 97, 101, 137, 192, 201, 235, 256, 260, 357, 359, 366-369, 376, 378, 384

S

Saat Parbatiya, 40, 154-155, 364
Sabar, 63-65, 87, 256, 358
Saddan/Sadaani, 96, 148, 156, 183, 236, 364
Sanskrit literature, 82, 85, 88, 112
Santhal, 33, 50, 56, 65, 67, 97, 101, 127, 131, 201, 358
Sarguja, 61
Sarhul, 86, 89, 180-181, 183, 190, 236, 242, 249, 258-259, 290, 292-297, 301-303, 305, 307-08, 315, 325, 337-338, 340-341, 349, 363, 369, 372, 379
Sarjome, 173, 176
Sarna, 24, 35-36, 38, 40, 43, 119-120, 121, 178, 180, 199
Sarna burhi, 40, 236-238, 301, 307-309, 361, 376
Sarna dari, 294-295
Sarna Devi, 40, 138, 243-245, 258-259, 295, 307-308, 362, 376-378
Sarna grove, 138, 396
Sarna Ketar/Chala Ketar, 29, 298
Sarna Kuti/Chala Kuti, 30, 305, 307-308
Sarna religion, 36, 101, 111-114, 146-147, 156-165, 167-168, 235-236, 237, 293, 357, 361, 363, 365, 375, 377
Sarna soop/Sarna winnowing fan, 29, 243, 245, 258-259, 294, 298, 300-301, 303, 305, 307-308
Sarna sthal/place, 40, 42, 181-182, 236-237, 243-245, 249, 258-259, 295-296, 300, 302-304, 307, 342-343, 361-362, 369-370, 375-376, 377-378
Sarna tree, 180, 182, 258-259, 300-301, 362
Sasaan, 24, 64, 114, 224
Sasaan diri, 38, 117, 190, 199, 361-362
Satyaki, 64-65
Seben leltan, 24
Seto Munda, 192
Shah Alam, 95
Shahabad, 35, 39, 66-67, 85, 88, 90, 367, 373
Shandilya, 381
Shikharbhum, 67, 358
Shivalik hills, 70
Sikh, 33
Simdega, 43, 374-375

Sinais, 216, 218
Sindhu (Indus), 25, 46, 58, 63, 70-72, 81
Sindoori rakab, 217-218
Sindoori tika, 217
Singbhum, 33, 44, 85, 96-97, 101
Singbonga, 19-20, 39-40, 60-61, 100, 113-115, 117-121, 123-139, 141-147, 153-156, 158, 160, 162-163, 167-171, 173, 175, 179-180, 182-187, 189-192, 202-203, 205-206, 208-210, 220-221, 225-226, 236, 253, 259-260, 272, 358-266, 376-279, 384, 397
Sira sita, 30, 253, 401
Sirmareni, 24
Sita, 41, 82, 130, 247, 368, 376, 378
Sohrai festival, 96, 148-149, 155, 162, 176, 187-188, 236, 275, 290, 317-318, 319, 350, 363, 372-373, 379
Sokha, 35-37, 40, 141-142, 145, 153, 157-159, 163, 173, 189, 240, 273, 280-281, 357, 364, 373, 400
Somdev, 65
Sone river, 67, 97, 235, 258, 367
Soori, 348
Soso tapa/soso bonga, 24, 169-170, 174-176, 188, 363, 379
Soso vriksh/tree, 172, 175, 182, 189
Stone age, 48, 61, 70-71, 81
Sumer, 71-72, 76-77, 80
Sun cult/Sun, 39, 76, 96, 125, 293, 358, 369, 376, 378
Surjahi puja (worship), 247, 271-272
Surya Bhagwan/Sun god, 40, 42-43, 83, 247-248, 271, 293, 368-369, 376, 378
Susari, 36, 242
Sutiya Munda, 192
Sutiyambey, 40, 95, 192, 194, 201, 377, 381

T

Tahloo, 242-243
Tamil, 73-74, 79
Tamralipti, 73-74
Tana Bhagat, 36, 41, 374-375
Telegu, 73, 79
Tibet, 48-49, 54-57, 59-62, 73, 79, 192, 357
Toosa burha, 246, 265
Tota hadam, tota burhi (Lutkum hadam, lutkum burhi), 60, 128, 133, 135, 184, 392
Totem, 190-194, 200, 285-289
Treta Yug, 65, 85

U

Ula, 25
Umbul, 19, 222-224
Utur Khila, 254, 257, 343

V

Vaishnav religion, 35, 41-42, 44, 96, 284, 357, 365
Varun, 14
Vedas/Vedic tradition/Vedic Culture/ Vedic religion, 59, 62-63, 65, 77-78, 111, 316
Vindhya mountains, 85, 192, 367

W

West Bengal/Bengal, 46, 49, 68-69, 73
Witch initiation/witch craft, 146, 273-274
Witch wife, 40, 153-154, 156

Y

Yaksh, 73
Yamuna, 64, 367